INSIDERS' GUIDE® TO
CHARLESTON

HELP US KEEP THIS GUIDE UP TO DATE

We would love to hear from you concerning your experiences with this guide and how you feel it could be improved and kept up to date. Please send your comments and suggestions to:

editorial@GlobePequot.com

Thanks for your input, and happy travels!

INSIDERS' GUIDE® TO
CHARLESTON

Including Mt. Pleasant, Summerville, Kiawah & Other Islands

THIRTEENTH EDITION

LEE DAVIS PERRY

INSIDERS' GUIDE

GUILFORD, CONNECTICUT
AN IMPRINT OF GLOBE PEQUOT PRESS

All the information in this guidebook is subject to change. We recommend that you call ahead to obtain current information before traveling.

INSIDERS' GUIDE ®

Editor: Kevin Sirois
Project Editor: Heather Santiago
Layout Artist: Kevin Mak
Text Design: Sheryl Kober
Maps: XNR Productions, Inc. © Morris Book Publishing, LLC

ISSN 1546-329X
ISBN 978-0-7627-6468-6

Printed in the United States of America
10 9 8 7 6 5 4 3

CONTENTS

Directory of Maps

ABOUT THE AUTHOR

Lee Davis Perry was raised in Charleston and returned to her beloved city in 1987 after pursuing her education and a 9-year stint away in "the urban fast lane." Lee received a journalism degree from the University of Georgia in 1976 and did graduate work there in public relations. In 1979 she began her career in Atlanta, working for several ad agencies, among them J. Walter Thompson USA, where she was a senior media planner.

The pull of the ocean and the traditions of her childhood proved too strong to abandon for long, though: "Who says you can't go home again? Being away from Charleston only sharpened my focus on the city's enduring appeal." Since returning, Lee has worked as a freelance advertising and marketing consultant on local and regional accounts, creating and implementing many award-winning campaigns.

Lee has also coauthored, with Michael McLaughlin, a short volume of stories relating South Carolina history, Globe Pequot's *It Happened in South Carolina* (2004) and also *South Carolina Curiosities* (2011). Her recent endeavor for a popular Globe series is *More than Petticoats: Remarkable South Carolina Women,* a collection of brief biographies of outstanding women from her native state.

Lee and her husband, Rhett, divide their time between the Lowcountry and the Midlands of South Carolina renovating an old house (ca. 1803) in Charleston's historic district or relaxing on the serene waters of Lake Murray. Both locales provide the perfect settings to contemplate the timeless beauty, vitality, and diversity of the Palmetto State.

ACKNOWLEDGMENTS

For their input, expertise, and assistance in many forms, many thanks go to all who helped with the production of this book, including the research departments at the Charleston Area Convention and Visitors Bureau, the Avery Research Center for African American History and Culture, the Charleston County Public Library, Historic Charleston Foundation, the South Carolina Department of Natural Resources, and the Public Affairs office of the 437th Airlift Wing at Charleston Air Force Base.

Gracious thanks go as well to the various Lowcountry attractions whose staffs provided information enhancing descriptions for this book.

We also thank the Greater Charleston Concierge Association for their support, enthusiasm, and groundwork in gaining access to so many great dining establishments and Lowcountry attractions.

We express our deep appreciation to David Ratts, whose "chronological" introduction to Charleston back in 1979 was the genesis for the approach recommended in this book. His enthusiasm for the "holy city" made learning about its history a delightful and life-enriching experience.

Lee also extends her appreciation to her mother, Rachel Davis, for her diligent archival research and to her husband, Rhett Perry, for his encouragement and support.

Immeasurable thanks go to Mike McLaughlin, coauthor of previous editions, for his beautiful descriptions of the Charleston Lowcountry and his ongoing updates and support for this 13th edition.

Thanks go to Amy Lyons, Kevin Sirois, and Heather Santiago for working with us on a schedule that was career-friendly for all concerned. Finally, thanks to Globe Pequot Press for recognizing the value of the Insiders' Guide series and for opting to bring it to the people in markets all over the country, where the information can be used and appreciated.

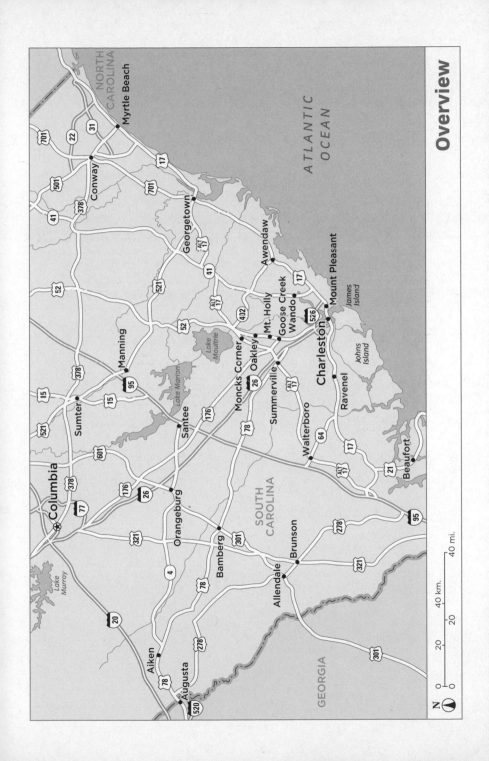

Overview

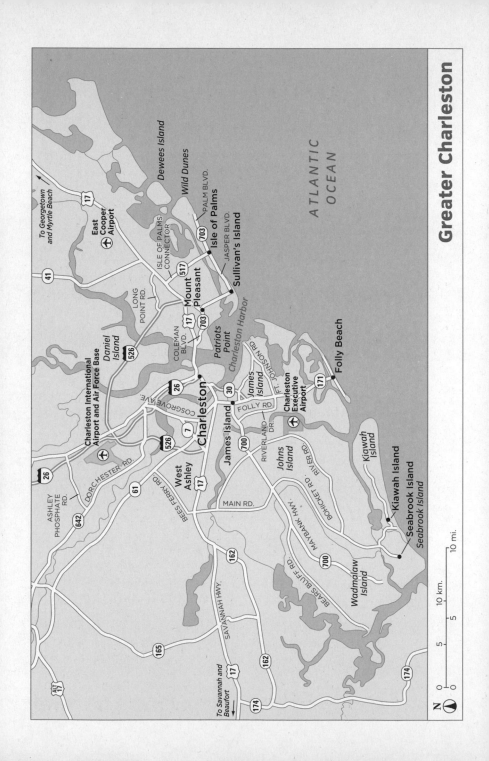

Greater Charleston

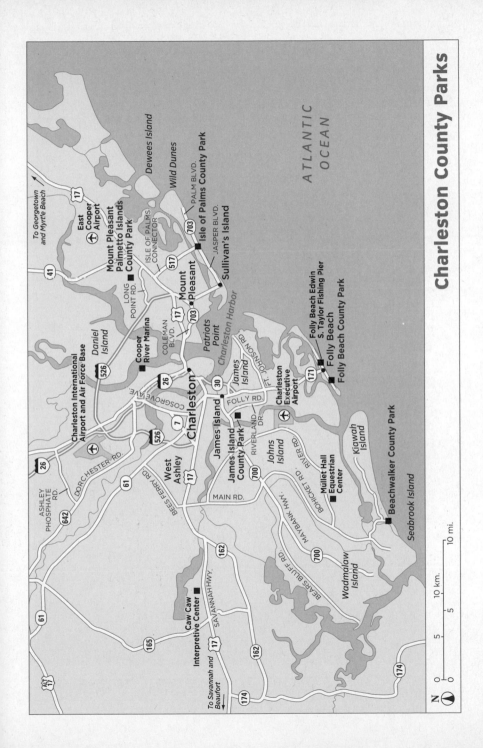

Charleston County Parks

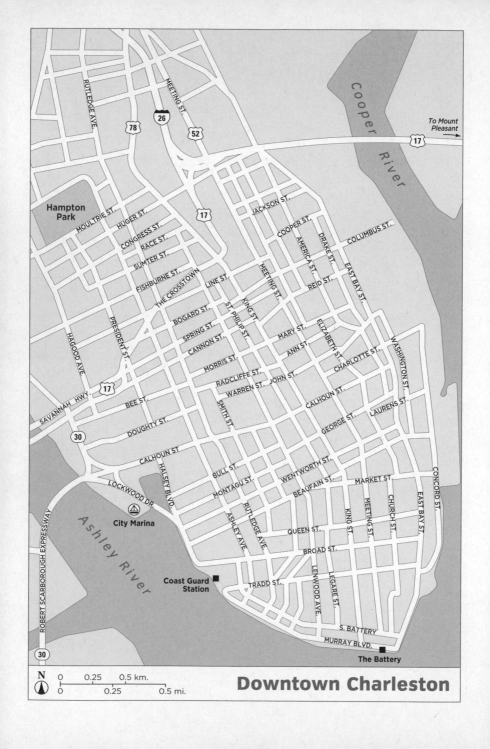

Downtown Charleston

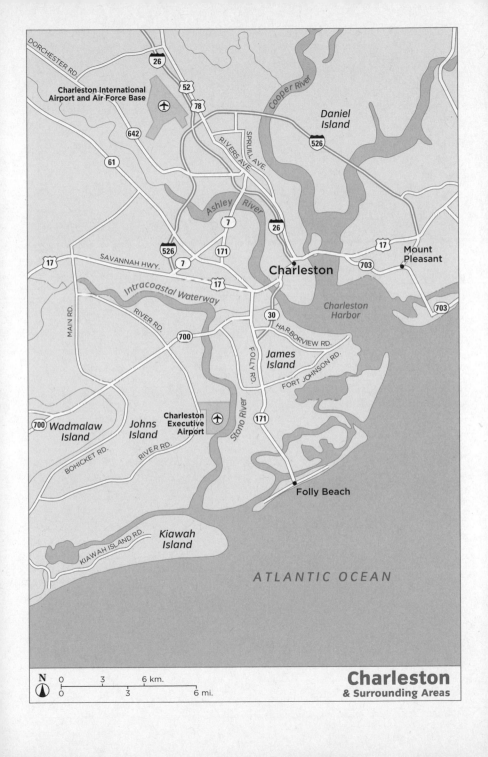

Charleston
& Surrounding Areas

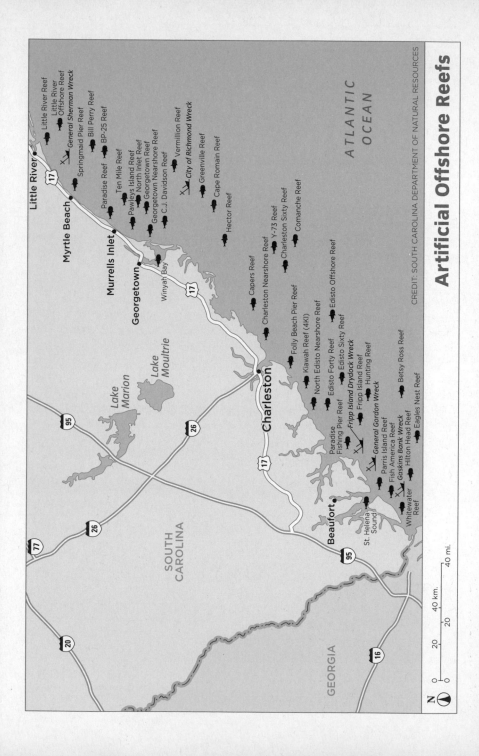

Artificial Offshore Reefs

GEORGIA

SOUTH CAROLINA

ATLANTIC OCEAN

Little River
Myrtle Beach
Murrells Inlet
Georgetown
Winyah Bay
Charleston
Beaufort
St. Helena Sound

Lake Marion
Lake Moultrie

Little River Reef
Little River Offshore Reef
General Sherman Wreck
Springmaid Pier Reef
Bill Perry Reef
BP-25 Reef
Paradise Reef
Ten Mile Reef
Pawleys Island Reef
North Inlet Reef
Georgetown Reef
Georgetown Nearshore Reef
C.J. Davidson Reef
Vermillion Reef
City of Richmond Wreck
Greenville Reef
Cape Romain Reef
Hector Reef
Capers Reef
Charleston Nearshore Reef
Y-73 Reef
Charleston Sixty Reef
Comanche Reef
Folly Beach Pier Reef
Kiawah Reef (4KI)
North Edisto Nearshore Reef
Edisto Forty Reef
Edisto Sixty Reef
Edisto Offshore Reef
Fripp Island Reef
Hunting Reef
Betsy Ross Reef
Paradise Fishing Pier Reef
Fripp Island Drydock Wreck
General Gordon Wreck
Parris Island Reef
Fish America Reef
Gaskins Bank Wreck
Hilton Head Reef
Whitewater Reef
Eagles Nest Reef

N

0   20   40 km.
0   20   40 mi.

INTRODUCTION

Welcome to Greater Charleston, where three South Carolina counties—Charleston, Berkeley, and Dorchester—blend together and create the scenic backdrop for a unique and wonderful lifestyle.

This is a land of history, the home of Revolutionary statesmen. This is a city of gallantry, glory, folly, and pain—where democracy was nurtured and secession proclaimed. This is where, very early on, beauty was deemed as important as survival, whatever the cost. Pride was encouraged. Families were sacrosanct, and God was dutifully acknowledged in mind and matter.

The sociopolitical passions and turbulent economies that made Charleston such a fascinating place 200 years ago are still very much with us today. Only now the canvas is larger, the paintbrush wider, and Charleston's colorful story just gets bolder as the years go by.

One of the reasons Charleston seems so timeless has to do with geography. The historic Peninsula (the heart of Charleston's identity) is bound by two rivers, the Ashley and the Cooper. Despite whatever else those rivers have meant to Charleston and its people over time, the waters effectively impounded the 18th-century city. This watery restraint forced all real growth and change northward—pushing it upward, spilling it over onto neighboring lands. Even today, neighborhoods that were built "east Cooper" or "west Ashley" always carry the unspoken phrase "of the Peninsula" and bear indirect witness to the old city's powerful presence.

The natural containment of the Ashley and Cooper rivers (effectively protecting the Peninsula from change) had an accomplice in the Lowcountry itself. The southeastern third of South Carolina is physically low, close to sea level, prone to swampland, marsh, and innumerable shallow creeks and streams. The land was hostile toward early settlers and planters, and it was costly to railroad builders and almost every other developer. It didn't welcome growth, and it resists change to this day.

In many ways Charleston was isolated and remained something of a cultural island while America pushed westward into its destiny. Charleston and its captive Peninsula effectively stayed behind, surrounded by its many coastal distractions.

As it has for eons, the endless marsh seems to change color every day. Unspoiled beaches can be caught playing tag with a restless (occasionally punishing) sea. Charlestonians know that not far away they can find dark and mysterious swamps that, in certain moonlight, whisper primordial secrets in the native tongue of an ancient higher power.

If this is isolation, then it's splendid isolation. This is the Lowcountry: a place, a people, a unique perspective on the world.

Is it any wonder we love living here?

HOW TO USE THIS BOOK

This guide is made up of data-packed chapters that provide the kind of practical information you need to enjoy the Greater Charleston area. The early chapters of this book are generally focused on tourism, history, and attractions. This information is useful to visitors (and residents alike) who want to know more about the city and the surrounding area. Starting with Relocation, the latter chapters are especially helpful to newcomers who have decided to make the Lowcountry their permanent home.

If you are planning a visit or move to Charleston, surf the chapters to make contacts ahead of time. If you are already here or on your way to the city, flip to the Getting Here, Getting Around chapter to determine the best route to your desired destinations, or flip to one of our Accommodations chapter for information on lodging. And if you have arrived and are carrying the book around as a reference tool, just zip to a particular chapter to find the best or closest restaurants, entertainment, recreation, lodging, kidstuff, and attractions. The index at the back of the book can help you pinpoint a specific subject or place quickly and easily.

We have worked to create chapters that stand alone but are cross-referenced so that you can easily set your own pace and schedule for getting to know Charleston. You decide when to immerse yourself in the history and culture of the community and when to make more immediate decisions about where to eat, where to sleep, what to do at night, and where to shop. Our job is to coordinate the information and organize it clearly so that you can make every minute here count.

Up front, we've provided area maps to help you get your bearings here in the Lowcountry. We give you brief vital statistics, **Insiders' Tips** (indicated by) for quick insights, and more lengthy **Close-ups** with information that is particularly interesting, unusual, and distinctly Charlestonian.

You'll also find listings accompanied by the ✳ symbol—these are our top picks for attractions, restaurants, accommodations, and everything in between that you shouldn't miss while you're in the area. You want the best this region has to offer? Go with our **Insiders' Choice.**

The Day Trips chapter is designed to help you branch out from the immediate area, and the chapter called Kidstuff is offered as a collection of some of our favorite ways to show your children a healthy good time. The former is heavily peppered with historical references (because so much of the Lowcountry is all the more interesting when understood in the context of its past). The latter is a subjective overview of venues and activities that have afforded us hours of fun with children we know.

You will notice that throughout the guide we refer to four main general areas—downtown Charleston, east of the Cooper (River), west of the Ashley (River), and the western islands. **Downtown** includes the Peninsula and the area slightly north; **east of the Cooper** includes Mount Pleasant, Sullivan's Island, and Isle of Palms; **west of the Ashley** refers to the area just across the Ashley River bridges. The **western islands** are James, Johns, Folly, Kiawah, and Seabrook.

Within chapters such as Restaurants, Nightlife, Accommodations, Parks & Recreation, and Neighborhoods, expect to find geographical subcategories for your convenience. Further, Shopping is organized to benefit two broad categories of readers. We start with a rundown for tourists and visitors who want to explore the major shopping venues downtown. We organize the shopping opportunities by merchandise categories. Then we direct newcomers and residents who seek the convenience of shopping in the outlying areas, again, according to merchandise categories.

Moving to the Charleston area or already live here? Be sure to check out the blue-tabbed pages at the back of the book, where you will find the **Living Here** appendix that offers sections on relocation, child care, education, health care, retirement, and much more.

Whether you're a visitor to Charleston or you've chosen to live here, we hope this guide proves helpful in many ways.

AREA OVERVIEW

Year after year, Charleston has been recognized in popular tourist magazines as one of the top 10 domestic travel destinations. It's even been proclaimed by etiquette guru Marjabelle Young Stewart as the "most mannerly" city in America. We hope that will turn out to be your experience as well.

Here's an overview of Charleston and the surrounding area. This chapter is arranged in the geographical order used throughout this book and offers some information that will help provide a peek at what's here now to see and enjoy.

CHARLESTON

Exactly 768 miles from New York City, 590 miles from Miami, and almost 2,500 miles from Los Angeles, Charleston remains an undeniably livable city for those fortunate enough to call it home. It's a city of unhurried grace and distinct Southern charm, blessed with an uncanny number of historic structures, many of which have been transformed into handsome offices, restaurants, stores, and homes.

Charleston is the second-largest city in South Carolina (Greenville takes first place). The city's 2000 Census Bureau count was 96,650. In 2008, that estimate had jumped to 111,978. The city's Standard Metropolitan Statistical Area encompasses three counties: Charleston, Berkeley, and Dorchester. This is sometimes called the "Tri-County Area" or the "Trident Area," and in 2000, the population of this area totaled 549,033. By 2008, the estimated total was 644,506.

Charleston has a warm climate. In January the average temperature is 48 degrees; in July, it's 82. It's prudent to note that summertime temperatures can peak above the 100-degree mark, and the humidity, which is

considerable in the Lowcountry during any season, makes the hot seem hotter and the cold colder. Spring in Charleston, however, more than compensates for any discomfort during the other seasons. Many consider it the best time of year in the area; days are warm, nights barely chilled, and the whole world appears to be dripping in wisteria vines and azalea blossoms.

The Charleston economy continues to be sound and growing. The economic activity is most evident in the vast, newly connected lands of Daniel Island and Cainhoy. Just to the east and north of peninsular Charleston, these areas were annexed in 1991 to the city of Charleston. Daniel Island, which is 4,500 acres, is now being developed as a planned, environmentally sensitive community. (See the Neighborhoods chapter.)

In 2010 the South Carolina State Ports Authority (SPA) handled more than $45 billion in cargo through the Charleston customs facility. As the ninth largest cargo port in the nation (and still the fourth-largest container port on the East Coast), the port directly and indirectly provides over 280,600 jobs paying close to $11.8 billion in wages to South Carolinians.

Throughout its history, Charleston has stood as the cultural capital of the South. The performing arts are well represented here, with a symphony orchestra, community theater groups, and several ballet companies. The Gibbes Museum of Art and a growing number of independent art galleries display the city's impressive appreciation for the visual arts. The abundant examples of architectural preservation, showing the city's long-standing heritage of building excellence and craftsmanship, also bear witness to this aesthetic awareness.

MOUNT PLEASANT

Anyone who crosses the Cooper River via the new Ravenel Bridge into Mount Pleasant will never forget the journey. (See the Close-up "View to Thrill over the Cooper River," in the Getting Here, Getting Around chapter.) Directly across the Cooper River from Charleston, Mount Pleasant dates its founding to 1680. The original heart of Mount Pleasant is the area known as the Old Village. It is designated a National Register Historic District, with its gracious homes from both the colonial and antebellum periods. Today, the city carefully preserves its rich heritage and small-town appeal. The 2000 Census count for Mount Pleasant was 47,609 (a 58.1 percent jump from the 1990 Census figures). Estimates for 2008 were 65,472.

The population numbers for this thriving community certainly qualify it as a "city." But, as the name implies, the "town" of Mount Pleasant is an apt description for the state of mind and the attitude of the businesses you'll find there. Although it serves as a major bedroom community to the Charles-ton Peninsula, it's still a viable community unto itself.

The days when Mount Pleasant residents were dependent on the Peninsula for primary shopping, dining, and entertainment venues are gone. Mount Pleasant's $40 million Towne Centre is clear proof of that, with its 15 separate buildings housing about 65 tenants within 425,000 square feet of upscale shopping space.

Patriots Point, the world's largest naval and maritime museum complex, is Mount Pleasant's biggest attraction. It is dominated by the aircraft carrier *Yorktown*, World War II's famous "Fighting Lady." You can also board tour boats at Patriots Point to visit Fort Sumter National Monument, where the Civil War began. (See the Attractions and Tours chapters.)

Adjacent to Patriots Point is Patriots Point Links, one of the area's most popular public golf courses. The 18-hole, par 72 layout provides spectacular views of Charleston Harbor and the Peninsula's skyline. (See the Golf chapter.) The Mount Pleasant Visitor Center at 99 Harry J. Hallman Jr. Blvd. off Coleman Boulevard is a good place to start when exploring Mount Pleasant.

SULLIVAN'S ISLAND

South of Mount Pleasant and across the Intracoastal Waterway, Sullivan's Island is one of Mount Pleasant's three true barrier islands (Isle of Palms and the private island of Dewees are the other two). Access to the island is via the Ben Sawyer Causeway (SR 703) from Mount Pleasant or via the Isle of Palms Connector (SR 517) through the Isle of Palms.

Largely a quiet, residential island of old and new beach houses, the island's estimated population in 2008 was 1,870. There is also a smattering of charming 19th-century "summer homes" that have somehow managed to survive the hurricanes and changing fashions of vacation architecture. The few restaurants and pubs on the island are crowded along Middle Street and create something of a strip for strollers who might want to "pub hop" during the evening hours.

Sullivan's Island is the site of old Fort Moultrie and its accompanying interpretation center, which is operated by the National Park Service. There you can trace the fort's history from the American Revolution through World War II. (See Forts in the Attractions chapter.)

Another interesting by-product of Sullivan's Island's military days is the fine old row of quarters (not far from the lighthouse) that date back to World War I. Still standing at attention along a quiet side street is a handsome line of large frame houses that once served as "officers' row" for the garrison at Fort Moultrie. Now private homes, these former examples of elite military housing speak eloquently of another time from the island's (and our country's) past.

ISLE OF PALMS

Over the years, the Isle of Palms has grown increasingly popular as a resort and residential island. In 2008, the estimated population was 4,678. But when you add the seasonal renters and the day visitors, the island can host thousands of additional people on any given summer day. Its proximity to Charleston is one of the reasons; its 6 miles of wide, sparkling beach is another attraction.

Those who are here for the short term can enjoy a wide range of accommodations from one end of the island to the other. The island also has a full complement of shops, restaurants, goods, and services to make life very comfortable.

World-famous Wild Dunes Resort, at the northeast end of the island, offers fine restaurants, conference facilities, a fitness center, multiple tennis courts, and two championship Tom Fazio–designed golf courses. Wild Dunes is a busy destination all year long. (See the Neighborhoods and Accommodations chapters.) The Wild Dunes Yacht Harbor is one of the finest marinas on the Eastern Seaboard. Maybe best of all, Wild Dunes is still only 15 miles from downtown Charleston, offering visitors the chance to enjoy the best of both worlds.

NORTH CHARLESTON

North Charleston, incorporated only in 1972, is geographically the third-largest city in South Carolina, with an estimated population of 94,407. Its reputation as the hub of the Lowcountry is justified; it's clearly the business and transportation center for the lower half of the state. The international airport and the Amtrak station are here. Also, I-26 and the Mark Clark Expressway (I-526) make getting anywhere in the Lowcountry a snap. (See the Getting Here, Getting Around chapter.)

Once known as the location of Charleston's huge naval facility, North Charleston has outgrown that economic dependency. One of the city's main attractions is the Charleston Area Convention Center Complex, which includes the 14,000-seat Coliseum and the 2,250-seat Performing Arts Center. These state-of-the-art venues draw crowds from all over the area and host a wide variety of events ranging from Broadway shows to major rock concerts and ice shows. The Coliseum is also the home of the South Carolina

Stingrays, our local ice hockey team. (See the Spectator Sports chapter.)

Not only does the area have more than 6,000 hotel rooms, but the rates are also generally lower than those found elsewhere in the Lowcountry (especially downtown Charleston). This makes North Charleston a favorite haunt for business types and convention travelers. If you're arriving via I-26, you may want to stop at the North Charleston Visitor Center just across from the Coliseum. You'll find plenty of area information there.

BERKELEY COUNTY

In the 1980s, Berkeley County, just north of Charleston County, was the fastest-growing county in all of South Carolina. The boom came when major new industrial concerns invested more than $1.7 billion in the county economy.

The greatest concentration of population and residential and commercial development has been in the southern portion of the county near Moncks Corner. Berkeley's central town, however, remains Goose Creek. Other county towns include Hanahan and St. Stephen. Total population of these towns is more than 60,000, according to recent estimates.

Currently, industrial development is concentrated along US 52 north of Goose Creek and on the island formed by the Cooper River and the Black River and its tributary branches. The major Berkeley County employers are Santee Cooper (electric utility) and Nucor Steel.

Much of the northern portion of Berkeley County is still productive, cultivated farmland. Most of the eastern portion of the county and large areas of the west remain as beautiful pine forests—one of the county's most distinctive features.

DORCHESTER COUNTY

Dorchester's $127 million in economic development in recent years largely came from the expansion of existing industries. The major employers in Dorchester County include the Robert Bosch Corp. (anti-lock braking systems), Industrial Products, Inc. (industrial textiles), Lieber Correctional Institute, and the Dorchester County School District II.

Although St. George, with its estimated 2008 population of 2,121, is the county seat, the part of Dorchester County currently seeing the greatest amount of economic growth is Summerville. With a 2008 estimated population of 45,193, the town's healthy mix of retail, commercial, and tourist-related businesses, along with light manufacturing concerns, seems to be attracting both newcomers and business investors.

(For a historical perspective on Summerville and a brief driving tour of the town's historic homes, see the Day Trips chapter.)

WEST ASHLEY

The City of Charleston annexed its first West Ashley tract in 1960, and the area has been growing ever since. The population figure for this area is more than 60,000 according to recent estimates.

West Ashley is a patchwork of old and new neighborhoods and businesses that line the major traffic arteries (US 17 S. and SR 61). Many of the older neighborhoods have graceful old live oaks and spacious, well-tended lawns. In fact, there's a movement afoot to do some strategic planning aimed at preserving this "village" atmosphere—especially in the area surrounding the foot of the Ashley River Bridge. And please note, the local residents don't live in West Ashley or at West Ashley, they simply "live West Ashley."

West Ashley is home to Charles Towne Landing State Historic Site, a nature/historic theme park on the site of the original English settlement. It also claims the beautiful Ashley River Road, which leads to Drayton Hall, Magnolia Gardens, and Middleton Place (see Historic Plantations in the Attractions chapter). You'll find Charleston's largest shopping center—Citadel Mall, with well over 100 tenants—in West Ashley. The area also has the "Automile," a strip of new and used car dealerships along Savannah Highway (US 17 S.) and one of the major engines of the local economy.

By far, the largest employer West Ashley (you'll get used to saying it that way) is Bon Secours–St. Francis Hospital. (See the Health Care chapter.) This huge, 32-acre medical complex added 875 new jobs to the area economy, and many other spin-off businesses have followed suit.

JAMES ISLAND & JOHNS ISLAND

Geographically, James Island, which lies due west of the Charleston Peninsula, is less rural than Johns Island. It is essentially a bedroom community for Charleston, with many shopping strips scattered along the main roads of Maybank Highway and Folly Road.

What remains of James Island's rural character may be threatened by the easy access now made possible by the James Island Expressway (SR 30). This increasingly busy roadway connecting the island to the Peninsula is fueling rapid development—especially along Folly Road toward Folly

Beach. The remaining tracts of farmland are likely victims of rising land values and are prime targets for real estate developers.

While Johns Island may be still agricultural in appearance, change is in the air. A recent study showed that Johns Island was home to more than half of the nearly 2,000 people employed on the resort islands of Kiawah and Seabrook (plus most of the 400 more who work there during the busy season). After the opening of The Sanctuary, Kiawah's hotel and spa, the number of James and Johns Island employees jumped considerably.

FOLLY BEACH

This eccentric and diverse beach town likes to call itself "the edge of America." Only 10 minutes from historic Charleston, this is a tourist's world—one where there's plenty to see and do.

First of all, there's the beach—Folly's claim to fame. It runs almost 6 miles along the Atlantic side of the island. Folly has had serious erosion problems in the past. Periodically the beach is "renourished" by mechanically pumping millions of cubic yards of sand back onto the shore. But there's always plenty of sand, sun, fun, and (yes) folly to go around.

The island has a year-round estimated population of 2,412. But the population swells enormously on any summer day, when the hoards of beach lovers, young and old, come out to play. Employment opportunities are almost exclusively limited to the tourist trade.

Crabbing, sunning, surfing, swimming, surf fishing, biking, waterskiing, and sailing are going on nearly year-round. You name it, Folly Beach has it. Folly touts its 1,000-foot fishing pier, complete with snack bar, tackle

Charleston Vital Statistics

Charleston mayor: Joseph P. Riley Jr. (D)

South Carolina governor: Nikki Haley (R)

Population:
City of Charleston: 124,593 (in 2009)
Metro Area: 644,506 in 2008
South Carolina: 4,479,800 in 2008

Area (square miles):
City of Charleston: 88.14 square miles
Business district: 7.6 square miles
South Carolina: 31,113 square miles

Nickname/Motto: "The Holy City"

Translation of Latin motto from the city's official seal: Aedes Mora Juraque Curat, "She guards her buildings, her customs, and her laws."

Average temperatures: Jan: 48° F July: 82° F

Average rainfall: 52 inches per year

City/state founded:
First English colony of Carolina founded: 1670
Officially separated as Royal Colony of South Carolina: 1729
Incorporated as City of Charleston: 1783

South Carolina's major cities: Columbia (state capital), Charleston, Florence, Georgetown, Greenville, Hilton Head, Mount Pleasant, Myrtle Beach, North Charleston, Spartanburg, Sumter

Major colleges/universities: Charleston Southern University, College of Charleston/University of Charleston, The Citadel, Trident Technical College, Medical University of South Carolina

Important dates in history:
1670   Founding of Charles Towne colony
1680   Colony moved to safer location on peninsula
1719   Revolt leading to establishment of South Carolina as province of British Crown

shop, and full-service seafood restaurant. The pier is reminiscent of the old days when beach pavilions were all the rage for dance bands and swing music. (For more on area piers, see the Hunting & Fishing chapter.)

Although there are walk-throughs along the beach that lead from Arctic and Ashley Avenues to the surf for day visitors, it's best to go to the west end of the island and visit Folly Beach County Park. Admission is $7 a vehicle, but once you're inside, you've got restrooms, showers, drinking water, limited parking, and probably the best open vistas on the island. (See the Parks & Recreation chapter.)

1783	Newly liberated city changes name to "Charleston"
1822	Denmark Vesey slave uprising
1861	Outbreak of War between the States
1886	The Great Earthquake
1904	Construction of US Navy Yard
1977	Debut of Spoleto Festival USA
1989	Devastation by Hurricane Hugo

Major area employers: Medical University of South Carolina, Charleston Air Force Base, US Navy, Charleston County School District, Roper St. Francis Healthcare, Berkeley County School District, JEM Restaurant Group, Santee Cooper, Robert Bosch Corporation, Piggly Wiggly Carolina Company, Inc.

Famous sons and daughters: Charles C. Pinckney—youngest signer of the US Constitution; John Rutledge—another signer of the US Constitution; John C. Calhoun—statesman, US vice president; Edward Rutledge and Arthur Middleton—signers of the Declaration of Independence; Francis Marion, "The Swamp Fox"—Revolutionary War hero; Eliza Lucas Pinckney—entrepreneur of rice and indigo culture; Dubose Heyward—author of Porgy; Philip Simmons—world-class wrought iron artisan; Septima Clark—educator and civil rights activist

Major airports/interstates: Charleston International Airport; I-26; I-526 Public transportation: CARTA (bus system); DASH (downtown area shuttle)

Military bases: Charleston Air Force Base (437th Airlift Wing) and 315th Airlift Wing (Reserves); United States Coast Guard Group Charleston Station; Naval Weapons Station Charleston

Driving laws: Right turn on red permitted; seatbelts must be worn at all times in moving vehicle; headlights must be on when wipers are used; speed limit on state highways is 55 mph; speed limit on interstates is 70 mph in designated limited access areas.

Alcohol laws: Legal drinking age is 21 years; blood-alcohol content of .08 percent or higher is DUI in South Carolina, but .06 percent to .09 percent can also be designated DUI at arresting officer's discretion.

Daily newspaper: *The Post and Courier*; daily circulation, 88,939; Sunday, 95,289

Sales tax: 8.5 percent city/state sales tax (1 percent sales tax discount for citizens age 85 and over), 12.5 percent city/state accommodations tax

You'll find many reasonable short-term accommodations at Folly Beach. (See the Accommodations chapter.) There are also seasonal rentals and a lot of interesting full-time residents on the island. It is Charleston's truly original beach playground. (See the Accommodations chapter.)

KIAWAH ISLAND

Only 21 miles from Charleston is Kiawah Island, renowned for its natural beauty and environmentally responsible development. The endless acres of marsh, the 10 miles of pristine Atlantic beach, the thick forests, and abundant wildlife are only the beginning.

Among all this are championship golf, first-rate tennis, exclusive shopping, and fine dining. Like the beach itself, the opportunities for enjoyment here go on and on.

Golfers have a selection of courses to play. They can choose from Turtle Point by Jack Nicklaus, Cougar Point by Gary Player, Tom Fazio's Osprey Point, and the famed Ocean Course by Pete Dye (site of the memorable 1991 Ryder Cup). (See the Golf chapter for more details.) In November 1997, the Ocean Course hosted the 43rd World Cup of Golf with teams from 32 nations competing. Televised in more than 80 countries, this was the world's most-watched golf tournament to date. In fall 2003, the World Cup returned with 24 nations participating in this much-heralded international golf championship. More excitement returned with the Senior PGA Championship in 2007. The next major upcoming event is the PGA Championship in 2012. Also on Kiawah, tennis buffs have two complete tennis centers with fully staffed pro shops and extensive instructional facilities.

The island's accommodations are all outstanding. Some guests prefer being pampered at The Sanctuary, the island's hotel and convention facility with luxury spa, which opened in 2004. Others prefer the privacy of furnished villas or cottages conveniently scattered around the island. Bear in mind that Kiawah Island is a private community with access limited to property owners, guests of the resort, or designated rental agencies. Full-time residents number 1,118, according to a recent estimate. But seasonal visitors swell this number to more than 7,000. Public access to the beach is available at Beachwalker County Park at the west end of the island. (See the Neighborhoods, Accommodations, and Parks & Recreation chapters.)

SEABROOK ISLAND

Seabrook Island is on the Atlantic shore just 22 miles south of Charleston. It is unique in that it is totally private and completely owned by its residents. Entry to the island is controlled by a security gate for the privacy of residents and guests. The beauty of the island is striking. Visitors can enjoy 3.5 miles of unspoiled beach along the Atlantic and the banks of the Edisto River, which flows into the ocean at Seabrook.

The Club at Seabrook offers championship golf courses: Crooked Oaks, designed by Robert Trent Jones Sr., and Ocean Winds, designed by Willard Byrd. A beach club, a tennis center, and a beautiful Island House Club with restaurants, bar lounges, and a golf pro shop are here. Also unique to Seabrook is its equestrian center.

The island has more than 450 villas available for rent as well as more than 1,200 permanent residents, whose homes are situated along the beach, marshes, lakes, and golf courses.

Bohicket Marina, just outside the Seabrook Island gate, is a superb marina with dockominiums plus an attractive shopping area. About 60 rental slips are available for all sizes of motor cruisers and sailboats. Boat rentals and charters for deep-sea fishing, crabbing, shrimping, or exploring the miles of ocean creeks are also available. (See the Boating & Water Sports chapter.)

GETTING HERE, GETTING AROUND

Visitors to the Trident area who arrive via different modes of transportation are faced with challenges unique to each form. For instance, if you drive, fly, ride the bus, or take the train, how are you going to negotiate the trip into town or—worse yet—out to the fringes? Say you come in on a yacht, or you are a passenger on a cruise ship. What next?

We've answered these questions individually, and the headings identify each transportation mode. It may seem a little lengthy, but we've tried to take you by the hand to lead you each step of the way in the Lowcountry.

GETTING HERE BY AUTO

We have tried to give very specific directions and many options for travel into and around Charleston. Our reasoning is both practical and designed for those interested in getting more out of their drive than simply moving from point A to point B. With heavy seasonal traffic (in spring, as many as half a million visitors come to Charleston by car), seemingly constant road and bridge work, and a peculiar system of one-way city streets, getting around Charleston is not always simple on first try. A new DASH route serving this area makes a continuous loop from the visitors center around King, Broad, East Bay, Market, and Meeting Streets and, best of all, is free.

Also, parking is always a problem. The city has made strides toward managing the situation to the benefit of both residents and tourists, with restricted parking hours in residential neighborhoods and parking garages for public use. Metered parking spaces are limited but convenient when you find them.

To avoid costly tickets, a parking garage is your safest bet.

While there are ways to maximize speed in travel around the Lowcountry, there are other ways to chart your journey to take advantage of the beautiful setting. Here are our suggestions for both, tailored to arrival from the main highways.

Charleston via US 17 N. (from Savannah, Hilton Head, Beaufort)

To Johns Island, Kiawah, & Seabrook

If you are south of Charleston and driving north on Savannah Highway (US 17) and your destination is Kiawah, Seabrook, or Johns Island, the fastest route is to take a right on Main Road. Look for a major intersection with a green sign indicating Kiawah and Seabrook. When you cross the Limehouse Bridge, you are on Johns Island. To go to Kiawah or Seabrook, continue to the end of Main Road, which turns into Bohicket Road, and follow the signs. Kiawah will be on your left, and Seabrook will be to the right at the traffic circle.

To James Island & Folly Beach

If you want to go to James Island or Folly Beach from US 17, take a right before you reach the Ashley River Bridge at the intersection of Wesley Drive and US 17. Stay on Wesley until it merges with Folly Road. Cross the Wappoo Bridge to James Island and stay on Folly Road to Folly Beach.

To Downtown Charleston

If your destination is the city, you can take either a panoramic approach or the shortest connection.

The Scenic Route: Should you have the extra minutes and the inclination, turn right at Wesley Drive as if heading to James Island or Folly Beach. Stay on Wesley until it merges with Folly Road, cross the Wappoo Bridge, and stay on Folly Road until you see, on your left, the turn for the Robert B. Scarborough Bridge (also called the James Island Expressway or SR 30).

In terms of time from Savannah Highway, this will take about 10 minutes longer than the quickest route to Calhoun Street, a main street traversing the Peninsula from east to west. However, the splendid views can make it a nice option when traffic snarls on the Ashley River Bridge.

The Speedy Route: If you prefer the most direct route downtown, cross the Ashley River Bridge on US 17 and veer right onto Lockwood Drive. You make your next decision at the first stoplight: If you are interested in visiting the medical complexes or the College of Charleston, shops on King Street, or the Charleston Visitor Reception and Transportation Center, go left, and the road will actually curve into and become Calhoun

Street. King Street intersects Calhoun, and you can turn right or left to park and shop. To find the visitor center, follow the green and white signs that will direct you to upper Meeting Street, an intersecting street that is just 1 block past King, off Calhoun, on the left.

If you need to reach the southern portion of the Peninsula, follow the straight arrow at that first stoplight. This will be a continuation of Lockwood Drive. You'll drive past the City Marina and Rice Mill Building, round the corner by the Coast Guard Station, and turn onto Broad Street. Broad eventually dead-ends at East Bay Street. Take a right on any intersecting street to find addresses referred to as "below Broad."

To the Northern Peninsula

To use US 17 N. to reach the northern Peninsula, cross the Ashley River Bridge in the second from the right lane of the bridge that reads "Lockwood Drive N." Continue straight off the bridge to the traffic light, and turn left onto Lockwood Drive North. A Charleston RiverDogs sign pointing left is at this intersection. Continue up Lockwood through the next traffic light, where RiverDogs and Citadel signs direct you around onto Fishburne Street to Riley Park, sports fields, and on over to Hagood Avenue. Turn left onto Hagood Avenue at the stop sign, and The Citadel Bulldogs' Johnson Hagood stadium is on the right. To reach the Citadel campus, follow Hagood Avenue until it dead-ends into one of the Citadel entrance gates.

To North Charleston

There are two ways to get to North Charleston. First, you can take a left onto SR 7 (Sam Rittenberg Boulevard), follow it until it merges with SR 171, then cross the Memorial

Bridge (which locals call the North Bridge) into North Charleston. Another option is to take a right onto the ramp from US 17 onto the Mark Clark Expressway (I-526), which will take you by the Charleston Area Convention Center Complex and the airport or to I-26 and the commercial districts of North Charleston.

To Mount Pleasant, Sullivan's Island, Isle of Palms

To reach Mount Pleasant and other East Cooper areas from US 17 N., take the Mark Clark Expressway (I-526), and stay on it until it intersects (again) and dead-ends at US 17 N. in Mount Pleasant. To go to the Isle of Palms, take a left on US 17 N., and after about 5 miles, look for the Isle of Palms Connector (SR 517) exit on the right.

If your destination is Sullivan's Island, take a right on Georgetown Highway (US 17), and follow it until it intersects with Coleman Boulevard. Take a left at the light, and follow Coleman (also called Ben Sawyer Boulevard at this point) as it crosses the Ben Sawyer Bridge to Sullivan's Island.

Another way to reach Mount Pleasant and other East Cooper areas from US 17 is to cross the Ashley River Bridge and the overpass to the Crosstown. You'll see signs for I-26 to the left, but you'll want to stay in the right lane under the signs to Mount Pleasant. Once on the Arthur Ravenel Jr. Bridge over the Cooper River, negotiate into the right lane. (See the Close-up "View to Thrill over the Cooper River" in this chapter.) Across the bridge, take the lane marked S.C. 703. You will see the Mount Pleasant welcome sign on the left as you drive down Coleman Boulevard (SR 703). Eventually, this road crosses Shem Creek near the historic Old Village residential area. It later becomes Ben Sawyer

Boulevard (still SR 703) before it crosses the Ben Sawyer Bridge to Sullivan's Island.

To reach the Isle of Palms, take a left on Jasper Boulevard (also SR 703) and drive across Sullivan's Island to Breach Inlet. Cross the bridge over the inlet, and you are on the Isle of Palms. To find Wild Dunes, the largest resort development on the island, follow Palm Boulevard (SR 703) across the island and look for the signs to the Wild Dunes Reception Center.

If you intend to head north on US 17 to reach Mount Pleasant destinations such as Hobcaw, Towne Centre, Snee Farm, Boone Hall, or, eventually, McClellanville and Georgetown, stay left on the Arthur Ravenel Jr. Bridge over the Cooper River and follow US 17 N.

Charleston via US 17 S. (from Georgetown, Myrtle Beach)

To Isle of Palms, Sullivan's Island, Mount Pleasant

If you are headed south on US 17 and want to go to the Isle of Palms or Sullivan's Island, take a left onto the Isle of Palms Connector (SR 517), which goes to the Isle of Palms. At the end of the connector, take a right to go to Sullivan's Island and Mount Pleasant or a left to go to Wild Dunes Resort.

To North Charleston

If you want to go to North Charleston, take a right onto the Mark Clark Expressway (I-526) off US 17 S. The airport, the Charleston Area Convention Center Complex, and other destinations are clearly marked along the way.

To Downtown Charleston

If you want to drive into the city, follow US 17 S. to approach the Ravenel Bridge. If you want to go to the southern parts of the

Peninsula, we recommend two options after crossing the bridge. For King Street (its shopping district and the nearby visitor center), stay in the left lane and take the Interstate, I-26 E. exit, heading downtown. Follow I-26 E. and bear to the right on US 17 S. (the Crosstown). Stay right and take the first exit to King Street. Turn right at the stop sign onto King. Another option is to stay in the right lane of US 17 S. and take the Rutledge Avenue exit, then stay on Rutledge Avenue until it intersects with Calhoun Street. Take a left for destinations off the Calhoun route (such as the College of Charleston campus and King Street shopping) or a right to reach the medical complex. You can also stay on King Street or Rutledge Avenue until it dead-ends at Murray Boulevard (the Battery), getting a glimpse of some of the city's more desirable real estate along the way.

If you are looking for The Citadel or points around the school (such as Joseph P. Riley Jr. Park, Hampton Park, and sports fields), stay on the Crosstown until you come to Hagood Avenue, and take a right. You will pass sports fields and can drive straight to the back gate of The Citadel. Hampton Park is just outside the front gates of the school.

To West Ashley

If you're going to West Ashley on US 17 S., there are two options. First, you can take a right on the Mark Clark Expressway (I-526) and stay on it until it intersects with Sam Rittenberg Boulevard (near Citadel Mall) and eventually dead-ends at an intersection with US 17. The second option is to stay on US 17 S. until you cross the Ravenel Bridge, the Peninsula via the Crosstown, and eventually the Ashley River Bridge.

To Other Points West

For James and Johns Islands, Kiawah, Seabrook, and Folly Beach, stay on the Crosstown (US 17 S.), cross the Ashley River Bridge, then take a left at the first stoplight at the intersection of US 17 and Wesley Drive. Stay on Wesley one block until it merges with Folly Road (SR 171). To reach destinations on James Island, Johns Island, Kiawah, or Seabrook, cross the Wappoo Bridge, and take the first right onto Maybank Highway (SR 700). For other destinations on James Island and for Folly Beach, stay on Folly Road (SR 171).

For another route to James, Johns, or the resort islands, while still on the Crosstown take a left at the last light (Lockwood Drive) before crossing the Ashley River Bridge and look for the Folly Beach exit onto the Scarborough Expressway (SR 30). This route will take you on a panoramic ride and deposit you on Folly Road on James Island. Take a left to go to Folly Beach or a right to go back toward West Ashley. If you are headed to Johns Island, Kiawah, or Seabrook, take a right on Folly Road, then turn left at the stoplight at Old Folly Road before the Wappoo Bridge, turning left again on Maybank Highway (SR 700). If you are going to West Ashley or downtown, cross the Wappoo Bridge, and go straight. Then, you may either bear right to access the Ashley River Bridge into town or bear left on Wesley Drive to intersect with US 17.

Charleston via I-26

To North Charleston

For travelers coming in on I-26 from the west, there are several options depending on your desired destination. You will pass

Take a Number

Bombarded by highway designations that seem to be blurring into one another? Confused by well-meaning Lowcountry direction givers who throw out numbers faster than a lottery-ball machine? Take heart! Below is a brief listing of highways and connectors that are often referred to by locals without the state or US prefixes.

For cross-referencing ease and your information, please note these numbers, with a few of their local incarnations:

US 17 N. (the Crosstown, the Bypass, Johnnie Dodds Boulevard, Georgetown Highway)

US 17 S. (Savannah Highway)

US 52 (Rivers Avenue)

US 78 (Summerville Highway)

SR 7 (Sam Rittenberg Boulevard, Cosgrove Avenue)

SR 30 (James Island Expressway)

SR 517 (Isle of Palms Connector)

SR 700 (Maybank Highway)

SR 703 (Coleman, Ben Sawyer, Jasper, and Palm Boulevards)

SR 61 (St. Andrews Boulevard, Ashley River Road)

SR 171 (Folly Road)

I-526 (Mark Clark Expressway)

Remember, don't be afraid to ask for specifics. When true Insiders are pressed for directions, they can almost always find a way to shepherd you from point A to point B.

through North Charleston on I-26, so check exits for specific locations. To go to the airport or Charleston Area Convention Center Complex, take a right on I-526 (Mark Clark Expressway) and look for signs.

To West Ashley, James Island, Folly Beach

If you want to go to West Ashley, exit right at Cosgrove Avenue, which becomes Sam Rittenberg Boulevard (SR 7). Sam Rittenberg forks at the Ashley Landing Shopping Center, and you can either bear to the left on SR 171 toward the Ashley River Bridge, or stay to the right on Sam Rittenberg Boulevard. The boulevard is intersected first by SR 61, then by US 17. Take a right onto SR 61 to go to the many historic gardens and plantations or a left to go to the Charleston Peninsula.

Another option for reaching West Ashley is to stay on the interstate as it ends and winds around to become US 17 S. (the Crosstown), then cross the Ashley River Bridge.

To access James Island and Folly Beach, take the Cosgrove Avenue exit and cross the North Bridge, where Cosgrove becomes Sam Rittenberg Boulevard. Stay left on Sam Rittenberg (SR 7) to SR 171, which leads to SR 61. Follow SR 61 to Wesley Drive (at the In & Out Car Wash), and turn right. Cross US 17 on Wesley until it merges with Folly Road (SR 171). To reach destinations on James Island, cross the Wappoo Bridge, and take the first right onto Maybank Highway (SR 700). For other destinations on James Island and for Folly Beach, stay on Folly Road (SR 171).

Take a Load Off

If you just need to scoot from point A to point B downtown and you're tired of hoofing it, you can summon one of the handy **rickshaws** that orbit the Market area in the evenings. The three-wheeled (bicycle-like) wonders pedal about the streets after 5 p.m. every weeknight, running until midnight. On weekends, they're around until 2 a.m. All are "driven" by strong-winded college kids who know the city and the bicycle rules of safety. You can hail one anywhere you see it, or you can call the dispatch number at (843) 723- 5685, and one will pedal to your location (approximate response time: 5 minutes). Rates are $9 one way (for about a 10-minute ride).

To Johns Island, Kiawah, & Seabrook

To go to these destinations, take a right on I-526 (Mark Clark Expressway), which will eventually end at US 17 S. Continue on US 17 south of town, and turn left onto Main Road at the major intersection with the green sign to Kiawah and Seabrook. Cross the Limehouse Bridge to access Johns Island. To go to Kiawah or Seabrook, continue on Main Road until it becomes Bohicket Road at Maybank Highway (SR 700), and follow the signs. Kiawah will be on your left, and Seabrook to the right at the traffic circle.

To the Northern Peninsula

If you want to go to the Peninsula, here are a couple of options. Take the Meeting Street exit off I-26, turn right on Meeting, and follow the signs to the Charleston Visitor Reception and Transportation Center. Another route is to follow the interstate until it ends at the Crosstown (US 17 S.), then take the Rutledge Avenue exit off the Crosstown. Both streets run south and culminate at the Battery. If you are looking for The Citadel or points around the school, stay on I-26 until it ends at the Crosstown. Look for Hagood Avenue (just before McDonald's), take a right, and drive straight to the back gate of the school.

i Beware! Many Charleston streets and alleys are one way. With so many interesting distractions vying for your attention, it's easy to miss the signs. So keep a lookout and be careful.

To Mount Pleasant, Sullivan's Island, Isle of Palms

If you are heading to East Cooper from the interstate, there are two options. For the first, take I-526 (Mark Clark Expressway) or US 17 N. If you choose to take I-526 to Mount Pleasant, you'll be treated to beautiful scenery, but watch your speedometer. Radar-equipped patrol cars are common. From I-526, you can go to Sullivan's Island by taking Chuck Dawley Boulevard until it intersects with Coleman Boulevard (SR 703) at the light. Turn left on Coleman (which becomes Ben Sawyer Boulevard), and cross the Ben Sawyer Bridge onto Sullivan's Island.

If you want to go to the Isle of Palms, there are again two possibilities. First, you can take a left onto Jasper Boulevard after crossing the Ben Sawyer Bridge. This will lead to a bridge across Breach Inlet and onto the Isle of Palms. For the other route, take a left onto US 17 N. after exiting from I-526 and then a right after Sweetgrass Shopping Center onto the Isle of Palms Connector (SR 517). This route offers direct service and allows you to bypass Sullivan's Island traffic and the inevitable openings of the Ben Sawyer swing bridge. The connector also offers a stupendous view of the island and the sparkling Atlantic Ocean spread before it.

The second East Cooper option from I-26 is to take the Mount Pleasant exit onto the Arthur Ravenel Jr. Bridge (US 17 N.), which takes you to Mount Pleasant and the islands. Exit the bridge following the signs to Coleman Boulevard (SR 703). Eventually, this road crosses Shem Creek at the edge of the historic Old Village residential area. It later becomes Ben Sawyer Boulevard before crossing the Ben Sawyer Bridge to Sullivan's Island. To reach the Isle of Palms, take a left on Jasper Boulevard, and drive across Sullivan's Island to Breach Inlet. Cross the bridge over the inlet, and you are on the Isle of Palms. To find Wild Dunes Resort, follow Palm Boulevard (SR 703) and the signs to the Wild Dunes Reception Center.

However, if you intend to head north on US 17 to reach Mount Pleasant destinations such as Hobcaw, Towne Centre, Snee Farm, Boone Hall, or eventually McClellanville and Georgetown, stay left on the Arthur Ravenel Jr. Bridge continuing on US 17 N. (the Bypass).

Charleston via I-95

If you are heading north on I-95 (from Savannah), the shortest route to Charleston is via exit 33. The signs will direct you to Charleston and Beaufort. See "Charleston via US 17 N. (from Savannah, Hilton Head, Beaufort)," above, for further directions into the city. If you are heading south on I-95 (from Fayetteville, North Carolina), the best idea is to take I-26 just past Santee, South Carolina (exit 86). Travel about 50 miles along I-26 to access all Charleston area destinations. (See "Charleston via I-26" above.)

GETTING HERE BY AIR

Charleston is more accessible than ever by air. The Trident area boasts a full-service international airport with major carriers taking off and touching down throughout the day. Major national rental-car agencies service the airport, limousine and shuttle services are available, and the terminal has a 1,200-space covered parking garage, plus additional surface parking on-site.

There are also four Lowcountry locations serving the needs of private pilots; one location is an auxiliary service of the Charleston International Airport. All are reasonably convenient to the downtown area, and specific amenities are noted below.

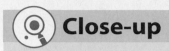

View to Thrill over the Cooper River

The opening of the **Arthur Ravenel Jr. Bridge** over the Cooper River in the summer of 2005 was a major event for Charleston and the entire Lowcountry. Indeed, at a cost of $632 million, it was a major economic event as a construction project—10 years in the planning—affording employment opportunities to thousands. When finished, it provided our growing port with easier transportation to multiple markets throughout the southeastern United States. As an accomplished feat of state-of-the-art engineering, it became the longest cable-stayed span in all of North America.

Great as the opening celebration was, a certain lump remained in the throats of older locals who will always recall the two former spans, the **Grace Memorial Bridge** (1929) and the **Silas Pearman Bridge** (1966). Each in its own time was considered a miracle of engineering. Each brought a vast improvement to the Lowcountry lifestyle.

Grace Memorial, the oldest of the former bridges, replaced a ferry system that (in one form or another) ran back and forth between the Peninsula and Mount Pleasant since Civil War days and even earlier. The old Grace was alarmingly narrow by today's standards, and crossing it was a white-knuckle experience for drivers and passengers alike. In 1946, a ship blown by gale-force winds collided with one of its pillars, causing a 240-foot section to fall into the deadly waters below, taking a car and its passengers down with it.

When the wider Pearman came along with its three lanes to help ease traffic, it was considered state-of-the-art. It offered a reversible lane that changed directions during rush hour. But the explosive growth in Mount Pleasant soon made even this modern bridge obsolete.

Ground was broken for the new Arthur Ravenel Jr. Bridge in July 2001. Construction went well, and the span with its 8 lanes and 15 ramps was finished well ahead of initial estimates for completion. It runs 3.5 miles from Charleston's Crosstown Connector to Johnnie Dodds Boulevard in Mount Pleasant. Its main cable span is 1,546 feet long, with a 12-foot-wide bicycle and pedestrian lane along the ocean side. The two diamond-shaped tower piers include viewing platforms stretching 12 feet out over the water at a breath-taking height of 198 feet in the air. All this is suspended by 128 individual cables—each one capable of carrying over a million pounds, or 500 tons.

During most of the year, tourists marvel at how beautifully lit the Ravenel Bridge is at night. But those lights are considerably dimmed during nesting season of the Lowcountry's endangered loggerhead sea turtles. The fragile young hatchlings are guided by moonlight in their life-or-death scramble from beachside nests to the relative safety of the sea. Wildlife experts fear the massive bridge lights may confuse them.

Major Airport Service

CHARLESTON INTERNATIONAL AIRPORT

5500 International Blvd., North Charleston
(843) 767-1100, (843) 767-7009
www.chs-airport.com

This 280,000-square-foot facility has 10 gates, all served by covered loading bridges. The walking distance from the terminal entrance to the most remote aircraft gate is only about 800 feet. The international area and customs service inspection area have 25,000 square feet of space and process international passengers quickly. If you're interested in business opportunities at Charleston International Airport, contact the Aviation Authority Development Office at (843) 767-7000 or visit www.chs-airport.com.

Flight Information

Major airlines serving the Trident's international flight facility include Continental, (800) 525-0280 (reservations), (800) 335-2247 (baggage); Delta, (800) 221-1212 (reservations), (800) 325-8224 (baggage); Southwest Airlines, (800) 435-9792 (reservations and baggage); and USAirways, (800) 428-4322 (reservations), (800) 371-4771 (baggage).

Commuter airlines serving the Charleston International Airport are American Eagle, (800) 433-7300; and United Express, (800)241-6522.

The number to call if you want to check an arrival time for an incoming flight is (843) 767-7009. Checking before leaving for the airport can save time and frustration. The airport's information desk always has the most updated flight schedule data available.

Rental Cars/Parking

Chances are, your preferred rental car service has an airport outlet in Charleston. The seven national companies that serve the airport are Avis Rent-A-Car, (800) 831-1212 or (843) 767-7031; Budget, (800) 527-0700 or (843) 767-7051; Dollar, (800) 800-4000 or (843) 767-1130; Enterprise, (800) 736-8222 or (843) 767-1109; Hertz Rent-A-Car, (800) 654-3131 or (843) 767-4550; National Car Rental, (800) 227-7368 or (843) 767-3078; and Thrifty, (800) 647-4389 or (843) 552-1400.

The terminal parking facility offers 1,200 covered spaces for a fee of $15 per day. A surface lot slightly farther away from the terminal offers additional parking at $8 per day. A valet parking service is available from 5 a.m. to 1 a.m. (or until the last flight arrives) 7 days a week and can be reached at (843) 552-6060.

i One way to avoid the somewhat pricey long-term parking fees at Charleston International Airport is to use one of the off-site parking facilities nearby that can deliver you to the front door of the airport in time for your flight and safely store your car while you're gone. Upon return, just call their shuttle for a quick ride to the lot, where your car will be ready and waiting for you. One of the best options is Park & Go, located at 3621 West Montague Ave. Call (843) 302-2288 for rates and information.

Getting to the Airport

As a simple rule of thumb, plan on allowing at least a half hour to get to the airport if you're driving from downtown Charleston. Allow even more time during rush hours or on busy holiday travel dates. You may want to call ahead and get time allowances for security procedures.

Take I-26 west (toward Columbia). Exit off I-26 at exit 212-B marked AIRPORT AND I-526 SAVANNAH. Continue approximately a mile on I-526 (toward Savannah), and exit at the Montague Avenue exit. A sign will also read TRIDENT RESEARCH AUTHORITY, COLISEUM, AND AIRPORT. Turn right at the light (at the exit to International Boulevard), and continue approximately 1.5 miles to the terminal.

If you are driving south toward the city on I-26, take the Mark Clark Expressway (I-526) exit. The airport exit off this highway is clearly marked, and you'll again head into the terminal area via International Boulevard.

For local residents and those who need ground transportation to the airport from downtown or other locations, there's a central phone number through the Charleston Aviation Authority that will redirect your call to the next available option. Call (800) 750-1311 or (843) 767-7113 for this airport limousine/taxi pick-up information.

i Start early on your trip to the airport. International Boulevard has gained a reputation as a notorious speed trap, so be sure to keep an eye on your speedometer. Many travelers have missed flights thanks to a heavy foot and the ever-vigilant officers.

Taxi, Limo, & Shuttle Service from the Airport

Several Charleston area hotels, motels, and bed-and-breakfast inns offer shuttle service to and from the airport. Check with your reservation agent, your inn's concierge, or your hotel for specific details. Near the baggage carousel, you'll find a lighted courtesy board showing several of the area's better hotels, motels, and bed-and-breakfast inns. The attached phone offers speed-dial service to those places offering airport pick-up service.

If you're left to your own resources for transportation into the city, you have a couple of options. Outside the baggage claim area, across the pick-up zone, is a small booth offering taxi and limo (van) rides to Lowcountry destinations. Various cab companies, as a service of the Aviation Airport Authority, take turns picking up fares from this booth. Here's the gist: If you are in a great hurry, a taxi will take you immediately at a metered rate of $2.15 a mile for the first two passengers. Additional passengers will pay $12 each. The average ride from the airport to a downtown hotel will be around $27 to $29. If you're willing to wait about 15 minutes, you can catch a shuttle (really a van) with several other passengers at a much-discounted rate of $12 per person.

Passengers heading to the nearby Charleston Air Force Base can catch an immediate taxi for around $12. A trip for one or two to Kiawah or Seabrook by taxi is about $62 or $65, respectively, for the 30-mile journey. Those heading for Wild Dunes can expect to pay about $51. Other approximate fares are available on www.charleston-arrives.com. If you want private limousine service and make reservations in advance, you can choose from a number of limousine companies available in the Lowcountry. (See the "Limousines" listing later in this chapter.)

Private Plane Service

Greater Charleston offers four options for private pilots, all convenient and uncongested.

City & County Parking Facilities

Here's the general rule for most city-owned and county-owned parking facilities: It's $1 for the first half-hour, $1 for the second half-hour, then $1 per hour. The all-day rate is $10 in city garages. The overnight rate (where offered) is $12 with a hotel registration, and the monthly rate (where available) is $110. City garages located near hotel facilities may be slightly higher. In any case, unless your accommodation provides off-street parking or you want to feed a hungry meter, these parking options may turn out to be your only choices:

Aquarium Garage, 24 Calhoun St., (843) 579-7681, 1,093 spaces

Camden Exchange Garage, 34 John, between John and Hutson Streets off Meeting Street, (843) 720-3866, 308 spaces

Charleston Place Garage off Hasell Street, between Meeting and King Streets, (843) 724-7419, 404 spaces

Concord-Cumberland Garage, corner of Concord and Cumberland Streets, (843) 724-7387, 624 spaces

Cumberland-Meeting Garage, 90 Cumberland St., (843) 724-6786, 958 spaces

East Bay–Prioleau Garage, between Mid-Atlantic and South Atlantic Streets, (843) 724-7403, 339 spaces

First Baptist Lot, Market Street between Anson and Pinckney Streets, (843) 579-7565, 85 spaces

Gaillard Municipal Auditorium Garage, off Calhoun Street and Alexander, (843) 973-7207, 596 spaces

George-Society Lot, off King Street, between George and Society Streets, (843) 724-7384, 146 spaces

King-Queen Garage, off Queen Street, corner of King and Queen Streets, (843)724-6786, 427 spaces

Queen Street Garage, 93 Queen St., (843) 965-4981, 323 spaces

34 St. Phillip Street Garage, 34 St. Phillip St., (843)577-8393, 598 spaces

Majestic Square Garage, Market and Archdale Streets, behind Saks Fifth Avenue, (843) 853-1682, 366 spaces

Marion Square Garage, 401-C King St., just north of the Francis Marion Hotel, (843) 965-4104, 308 spaces

Market and Horlbeck Lot in the block between Market and Horlbeck Streets, (843) 724-7385, 118 spaces

Visitor Center Garage, 63 Mary St., (843) 973-7290, 723 spaces

Visitor Center Lot, 375 Meeting St., adjacent to the Charleston Visitor Reception and Transportation Center, (843) 724-7174, 62 spaces

Wentworth-St. Philip Garage, 81 Wentworth St., (843) 853-7559, 235 spaces

ATLANTIC AVIATION (NORTH CHARLESTON)
6060 South Aviation Ave., North Charleston
(843) 746-7600
www.atlanticaviation.com

Just across the runway from the Charleston Air Force Base, off Aviation Avenue at Charleston International Airport, Atlantic Aviation's terminal and service facility offers two runways (7,004 feet and 9,001 feet), nine instrument approaches, and 24-hour all-weather service. This is your best choice if you want to land a private plane in close proximity to downtown. Both jet fuel and AV gas are available. Customers not buying fuel are charged nightly tie-down fees: $10 for single engine and up to $50 for mid-size jets. Larger aircraft should call for rates and facilities.

Atlantic Aviation also offers a wide range of services—from rental cars to limousines to dinner reservations and catering arrangements.

ATLANTIC AVIATION (JOHNS ISLAND) AT CHARLESTON EXECUTIVE AIRPORT
2742 Fort Trenholm Rd.
(843) 559-2401
www.atlanticaviation.com

Private pilots wanting access closest to Kiawah and Seabrook will most likely want to choose Atlantic Aviation's airport on Johns Island, 12 miles south of the city. Charleston County and the Federal Aviation Administration spent $2.3 million on this facility in 2005, upgrading its landing strips, enlarging its jet park area, and planning for future expansion. It presently offers 2 runways, 5,000-by-150-feet and 4,313-by-150-feet long. The facility offers jet fuel and 100 LL gas. For customers not buying gas, handling fees range from $10 all the way up to $650. Rental cars are available on the premises, and limited limousine service to Kiawah and Seabrook is offered. Travelers heading for The Sanctuary on Kiawah may call the hotel for transportation to the island. Operating hours are 6 a.m. to 10 p.m.

MOUNT PLEASANT REGIONAL AIRPORT
700 Airport Rd., Mount Pleasant
(843) 884-8837
www.chs-airport.com

Private pilots have access to the East Cooper area (including Wild Dunes) via the Mount Pleasant Regional Airport in Mount Pleasant. Managed by Atlantic Aviation, this facility offers a 3,700-foot runway, tie-downs, jet fuel, and AV gas service. Rental cars are available on the premises through Enterprise. The office and terminal are open from 7 a.m. to 7 p.m. in the winter, with hours extended to 8 p.m. after Apr 1. Helicopters are accommodated on site.

PELICAN AVIATION
890 Greyback Rd., Summerville
(843) 851-0970

This facility for private pilots flying into the Summerville area and Berkeley County has a 3,700-foot runway. It offers airplane detailing, general maintenance, and flight training, plus jet fuel and AV gas. Tie-downs are $5 per night (with first night waived with purchase of fuel). There's a courtesy car on-site for daytime transportation to area resorts and restaurants. The office and terminal are open from 8 a.m. to 6 p.m. through the winter and 8 a.m. to 7 p.m. after Apr 1.

GETTING HERE BY OTHER METHODS

By Bus or Train

If you are arriving or departing by bus, the Greyhound Terminal, 3610 Dorchester Rd., is in North Charleston and is a routine stop for cabs. Call (800) 231-2222 or (843) 744-4247 or visit www.greyhound.com for rates and schedules.

The Amtrak Train Station, 4565 Gaynor Ave., (843) 744-8263 or (800) 872-7245, www.amtrak.com, is also in the north area. Amtrak runs on the CSX Railroad lines, and there are two northbound and two southbound stops each day. Call for ticket prices and train schedules.

By Boat

There is a growing leisure craft and passenger ship industry in Charleston.

Cruise ships dock at the passenger terminal off Concord Street in the historic district. In the daytime, walking there is fine, if you have the time and the stamina, but we endorse travel by cabs or limousines at night for safety and convenience. (See the listings for taxis and limousines following.)

Private yachts moor (pending availability) at any of several marinas in the Trident area. (See the Boating & Water Sports chapter for more information.) Cabs or rental cars are the best solution for ground transportation unless you are docked at the City Marina, which is centrally located on the Peninsula near popular destinations and on the DASH route. (See more on the DASH system under "Public Transportation," following.) The nearby Ashley Marina has easy access via walkway to the City Marina and connecting DASH routes.

Charleston Water Taxi

It's hard to go far in Charleston without crossing over water, but here's another option—the **Charleston Water Taxi.** This water taxi service runs every hour from 10 a.m. to 7 p.m. (more limited hours during the winter) between the Charleston Maritime Center near Aquarium Wharf downtown and the Charleston Harbor Resort near Patriots Point in Mount Pleasant. Tickets are $5 one-way, or $8 round-trip; children under 5 are free. What a fun way to catch a harbor boat ride and have a spectacular view of the Ravenel Bridge! Call (843) 330-2989, or visit **www.charlestonwatertaxi .com** for more details.

GETTING AROUND THE LOWCOUNTRY

Taxis, Limos, & Rental Cars

Taxis can be scarce here in the Lowcountry, especially at odd hours. Because of that, savvy travelers needing cabs should keep a list of taxi phone numbers in their purse or wallet. The more popular solution is to rent a car from one of the nationally recognized car rental companies, all of which are represented in the area.

Limousines, it seems, are more loosely defined. A limousine can be anything from a stretch Caddy to an airport van. What follows is a list of taxi, limousine services, and rental car options.

Taxis

To get around by taxi, here's some options:

- **Charleston Taxicabs:** (843) 830-7673
- **Green Taxi:** (843) 532-0527
- **Metro Limo-Taxi:** (843) 572-5083
- **North Area Taxi:** (843) 554-7575
- **Yellow Cab:** (843) 577-6565

Limousines

Some limousine services available include:

- **AAA A-1 Airport Shuttle & Limo Service:** (843) 834-1998
- **A Stretch Limousine Taxi Service:** (843) 745-6288
- **Above and Beyond Limousine Service:** (843) 402-0600, (800) 755-8667
- **Carey Limousine:** (843) 744-8900, (800) 336-4646

Rental Cars

Rental car agencies abound. Companies servicing the area include:

- **Avis Rent-A-Car:** (843) 571-3190, (800) 831-2847
- **Budget:** (843) 577-5195, (800) 221-8822
- **Dollar Rental Car:** (843) 767-1130, (800) 800-4000
- **Enterprise Rent-A-Car:** (843) 723-6215, (888) 305-8051
- **Hertz Rent-A-Car:** (843) 573-2147, (800) 654-3131
- **National Car Rental:** (843) 767-3078, (800) 782-4064
- **Thrifty Car Rental:** (843) 552-7531, (866) 331-8178

Public Transportation

Public bus transportation in the area is a great way to circumvent the city's automobile congestion and parking woes altogether. This service is provided in the Lowcountry by the Charleston Area Rural Transportation Authority (CARTA). Under CARTA's auspices is the Downtown Area Shuttle (DASH), a separate system generally dedicated to the transportation needs of tourists in the downtown area and historic district. Together, CARTA and DASH operate more than 20 routes linking downtown, West Ashley, Mount Pleasant, and North Charleston.

While the green DASH trolleys are not considered tour vehicles per se, their turn-of the-20th-century "antique" trolley look is clearly an eye catcher—and it's one way to quickly identify a DASH vehicle from the more modern-looking (yellow and green) CARTA buses that operate in the metro area. DASH trolleys and metro CARTA buses stop at designated shelters, benches, and trolley stop signs located throughout the city. For safety reasons, drivers are not allowed to pick up passengers at locations other than the designated color-coded stops.

One-way and all-day CARTA and DASH passes are available on board the vehicles. You are expected to have exact change. One-way fare is $1.75, although those with a senior-citizen or Medicare card can ride for 85 cents each way seven days a week from 9 a.m. to 3:30 p.m. or after 6 p.m. Disabled riders pay 50 cents. An all-day pass is $6. Transfers are 30 cents. Inside the Visitor Reception and Transportation Center and at area Piggly Wiggly (grocery) stores, you can buy a 10-ride pass for $14 or 40 rides for $49. A 31-day pass is sold for $50. A student pass is $70. Children under 6 can ride for free when accompanied by a paying adult. Police, guide, signal, and service dogs are the only pets allowed on board.

Call (843) 747-0922, or visit www.ride carta.com for more information.

Bicycling

If you plan on spending time on the Peninsula or out on the beaches, why not park the car and consider renting a bicycle by the hour or day? Now you can even put your bike on a CARTA bus (with their new front-loading bike racks) and enjoy the convenience of public transportation. For in-town and Mount Pleasant service, we recommend **The Bicycle and Outdoor Shoppe,** www .thebicycleshoppecharleston.com, which offers two locations: 280 Meeting St., (843) 722-8168, and 1539 Johnnie Dodds Blvd., Mount Pleasant, (843) 884-7433. These folks rent single-speed adult cruisers and hybrids. Also serving Kiawah and Seabrook Islands is **Island Bike and Surf Shop,** www .kiawahislandbikerental.com, 3665 Bohicket Rd., Kiawah Island, (843) 768-1158. Another option is **Mike's Bikes,** www.mikesbikes charleston.com, 709 Coleman Blvd., Mount Pleasant, (843) 884-5884, or on James Island at 808 Folly Rd., (843) 795-3322. For delivery and three-day or weekly rental to many of the islands, try **Carolina Bike and Beach,** www.carolinabikeandbeach.com, (843) 747-BIKE.

HISTORY

With cultural roots as deep and colorful as the surrounding blue-green waters, Charleston is a rich mixture of early English, Scottish, Irish, French, Spanish, German, Swiss, Santo Domingan, African, Native American, and Caribbean influences.

While each of these cultures left its mark on the city in a unique way, no influence was stronger than that of the British. Archaeologists tell us countless generations of Native Americans lived on and around the land now called Charleston before the first permanent English settlers arrived, but little remains of their occupation outside of the archaeological record in the ground itself. The first English settlers, arriving in the spring of 1670, were adventurers coming to lands granted by King Charles II to eight lords proprietors, who claimed ownership of the "Carolinas"—presumably extending from the Atlantic to the shores of the Pacific.

EARLY HISTORY

As the settlers navigated into what is now Charleston Harbor, they passed enormous mounds of bleached, white oyster shells at the tip of a peninsula where two rivers met and named the area Oyster Point. Seeking higher ground, the colonists sailed farther up one river to a high bank they called Albemarle Point and established the first crude encampment there. They dutifully named the new settlement Charles Towne for King Charles II. The two rivers, called the Kiawah and Etiwan by local tribes, were renamed the Ashley and Cooper, respectively, in honor of one of the lords proprietors, Anthony Ashley Cooper, Lord Shaftesbury. The original settlement area is now a South Carolina state park called Charles Towne Landing State Historic Site. (See the Attractions, Kidstuff, and Parks & Recreation chapters.) A decade later, because of their need for protection, the Charles Towne colonists were drawn back to the Oyster Point peninsula between the

two rivers—clearly a more defensible location. Here, the foundations of what is now Charleston were first laid.

By 1719, the colonists were tired of being exploited by the proprietary government, and friction ensued. This resulted in the colonists coming under even more discipline from the English crown, which meant forced allegiance to a series of appointed royal governors. This troublesome governmental entity stayed in place for the colonists until the American Revolution.

In 1725 the British sent over a plan for the new settlement called the "Grand Modell," intending to guide the development of 600 prime acres on the peninsula into a proper town. Amazingly, traces of that early English plan are still evident in the plat of today's Charleston Peninsula.

Owing to the great success of this busy English port and its merchant-planter aristocracy, the town soon became a small

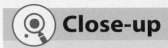 **Close-up**

Meet You at "The Four Corners of Law"

The intersection of Meeting and Broad Streets is affectionately known in Charleston as **"The Four Corners of Law."** The old line (mostly used these days by carriage drivers and guides for walking tours) is meant to imply that you can do literally everything legally required in life right here at this one important Charleston intersection. On the first corner you can get your mail (at the oldest operating post office building in South Carolina). On the second corner you can get married (at St. Michael's Episcopal Church, built in 1761 and the place where the visiting George Washington once worshiped). On the third corner you can pay your taxes (at the Charleston County Courthouse). And on the fourth corner—if necessary—you can get divorced (at Charleston's City Hall, built in 1801). This attitude thinly disguises the notorious Charlestonian belief that, indeed, this intersection is the center of the universe. The tongue-in-cheek attitude ranks right up there next to the other one-liner that graciously allows, "The Ashley and Cooper rivers come together at Charleston to form the Atlantic Ocean."

city. To many, the 18th century will always be Charleston's golden age. Early travelers to this thriving colonial port took back to Europe impressive stories about Charles Towne's elegant architecture, wealthy citizenry, and sophisticated lifestyle. Indeed, during these heady, pre-Revolutionary years, rice and indigo from the plantations were sent out to eager markets all over the world. In exchange, hundreds of boatloads of enslaved Africans were brought to Charleston to ensure a cheap labor force to work the land. In stark contrast to this grim exchange, the arts flourished, and Charles Towne was considered the brightest jewel in England's colonial crown.

Many of the seeds of the American Revolution found fertile ground here in the Carolina Lowcountry. Political passions ran high, and once war broke out, there were many high-profile Charlestonians deeply involved on both sides of the issue. Actually, the first decisive American victory during

the Revolution occurred at the Battle of Fort Sullivan just outside the city. However, at first the war didn't go well. For a while, Charleston fell to the British, and during this time, the city suffered the first of its two unseemly "enemy occupations."

i Insiders tend to find an even kinder welcome if they show an interest in Lowcountry history. Feel free to ask questions and learn more. Most Lowcountry residents are historians at heart—they grew up with it!

Newly liberated after the war, the city became incorporated in 1783 and adopted a new, shortened name: Charleston. As the 19th century dawned, the young city of Charleston experienced an incredible building boom. Today you can still see an extraordinary number of Adam-style buildings from this remarkable period. Among them are the Joseph Manigault House at 350 Meeting

St., built in 1803, and the Nathaniel Russell House at 51 Meeting St., built in 1808. (See the House Museums section of the Attractions chapter.)

As cotton and tobacco were added to the plantation products earning handsome profits in the international marketplace, and even more money flowed into its thriving port, Charleston continued to grow. By the early-19th century, Charleston's flourishing middle class of merchant-tradesmen offered services and locally-manufactured goods from small, street-front shops. Many of these shops were clustered along what is now King Street.

Some traders sold simple things such as household necessities and fresh produce brought in on wagons from outlying gardens. Others were true artisans in their own right and produced work such as early Charleston-made silver pieces and locally-crafted furniture that are highly prized on the antiques market today. This flourishing "wagon trade" on upper King Street preceded the retail stores that make up the present shopping district.

THE CIVIL WAR & SUBSEQUENT STRUGGLES

Disputes over economics and slavery left unresolved by the young country's founding fathers had festered into a battle between the federal government and individual states by the mid-19th century. In April 1861, Confederate soldiers fired on Fort Sumter in Charleston Harbor, thus signaling the start of the devastating War between the States. After the city's second "enemy occupation," this time by Union troops, Charleston was at its lowest ebb. Years of relentless bombardment, sweeping fires, and economic starvation had taken a terrible toll on the once grand city.

Because Charleston was widely known as the "seat of secession," it is probably true that Charlestonians received especially severe punishment during the Reconstruction years. Recovery was slow to come and sometimes halfhearted. Some say Charleston never did recuperate from the Civil War until the arrival of the Navy Yard in 1904 and the subsequent economic booms of the two World Wars.

i Charleston has been the scene of numerous historical firsts. The first regularly scheduled passenger train service in America was established here in 1830.

Fires, earthquakes, hurricanes, yellow fever epidemics, and even the boll weevil threatened Charlestonians' health and wealth during the late-19th and early-20th centuries.

After the arrival of the Navy Yard, things started looking better. Phosphate, an organic fertilizer, was mined along the Ashley River and processed in several local factories. This proved to be a significant new source of income for many old plantation families who still owned phosphate-rich lands. Other landowners converted to timber farming as the South slowly rebuilt a working economy.

It has been observed that in the most difficult of times Charleston citizens were "too poor to paint," but they were also "too proud to whitewash." This inability to modernize maintained an almost timeless feeling throughout the city and actually worked to preserve Charleston's now-legendary cache of historic homes and public buildings.

CULTURAL RENAISSANCE
& AN ECONOMIC BOOM

In the 1920s, a kind of artistic renaissance occurred in Charleston. The city's now-quaint architectural backdrop inspired a new generation of artists, writers, poets, and musicians who captured regional and national acclaim. (See The Arts chapter for more about this fascinating period in Charleston's history.)

i Another Charleston first: In 1786 the nation's first golf course, played on an open field called Harleston Green, established America's earliest golf club, called the South Carolina Golf Club. The course has long since been absorbed into the urban landscape, but a proliferation of newer courses has kept the Lowcountry in the swing of things.

At the same time, the aesthetic and economic value of Charleston's architectural legacy started to be realized. This was when the city's early preservation ethic was first formulated, and it was kept alive through the especially difficult Depression years of the 1930s.

World War II brought another boom to Charleston, with the Navy Yard expanding to produce war materials and more job opportunities than Charleston had seen in

decades. After the war ended, many workers drawn here by the Navy decided to stay on and settle down. The sea, the mild weather, and a growing business climate kept pulling newcomers to the Lowcountry through the 1950s and 1960s.

In the 1970s, Charleston's chamber of commerce launched a national advertising campaign based on the simple slogan, "Charleston: America's Best Kept Secret." This, of course, was intended to let this cat out of the bag, and it worked splendidly. With high-profile events such as Spoleto Festival USA and the (almost always sold-out) public house tours every spring and fall (see the Annual Events chapter), the message was getting out—Charleston was a beautiful, historic, and highly desirable place to visit. Many visitors decided to move here and make the Charlestonian lifestyle their own.

CHARLESTON TODAY

Today Charleston's collection of historically significant architecture attracts visitors from around the world, and the city's remarkable preservation ethic is now a model for historic cities all over the industrialized world.

In 1996, an estimated three million tourists visited Charleston, each spending about $124 per day here. By 2011, that figure is estimated to grow to be more than 4 million visitors, each infusing Charleston County with about $170 per day.

ACCOMMODATIONS

If the Lowcountry knows a thing or two about putting up guests, it's because millions of them visit the Trident each year, and no one sees an end to this upward trend in sight. To accommodate these visitors, developers are poised to build new and better tourist accommodations both downtown and in the burgeoning North Charleston and Mount Pleasant areas to reap the benefits of this incoming tide of dollars. Through the years, Southerners have established a reputation for hospitality, and they often compete to maintain the highest standards. Research and experience tell us that Charleston area visitors arrive with varying expectations, and a diverse accommodations industry has evolved to meet those needs.

We have included in this chapter what we consider to be good choices for people who may be looking for vastly different accommodations. We start with Trident area hotels and motels—some for the bargain-minded, some that are large and grand— then discuss the more intimate bed-and-breakfasts and atmospheric inns and vacation and beach rentals. Like friends in an eclectic gathering, each accommodations category has something different to offer. Prices vary greatly as well.

Downtown Charleston has the greatest number and the widest variety. We start our listings with downtown properties, then extend our coverage using the geographical order detailed in the How to Use This Book chapter. We end with information specifically helpful to the Lowcountry visitors who arrive by air and those among them seeking accommodations convenient to the airport. Unless we tell you otherwise, expect that these lodgings offer smoking and non-smoking rooms and access for wheelchairs and that they do not allow pets.

OVERVIEW

There are several viable lodging options in the East Cooper and West Ashley areas. The resort islands of Kiawah and Seabrook feature an array of cottages, villas, condominiums, and private homes. For the most part, rental companies for the resorts and other traditional vacation spots (Isle of Palms, Sullivan's Island, and Folly Beach) prefer to deal with stays of one week or longer. See the Vacation & Beach Rentals section for a list of companies that handle resort and vacation properties.

A friendly word of advice: Charleston attracts droves of visitors year-round (there are major events scheduled nearly every month; see the Annual Events chapter), and we strongly recommend that you make reservations well in advance. For major events like Spoleto Festival USA and holiday weekends, it's advisable to plan up to six months in advance.

Price Code

Although rates are subject to change, we use the following pricing code to indicate the average rate for a one-night stay, in season, for two adults. Note that these rates do not include taxes (12 percent accommodations tax), gratuities, or add-on services such as room service or premium TV channels.

Offseason rates are, of course, lower. Mar through July and Oct through Dec are usually considered peak seasons.

$................. Less than $65
$$ .... $65 to $95
$$$ ....$95 to$150
$$$$ .... $150 to $200
$$$$$ .... More than $200

Middleton Inn, Charleston, 56

The Thomas Lamboll House, Charleston, 50

$$$-$$$$

Ansonborough Inn, Charleston, 52

Barksdale House Inn, Charleston, 45

Best Western King Charles Inn, Downtown Charleston, 32

Charleston Harbor Resort & Marina, East Cooper, 37

Days Inn Historic District, Downtown Charleston, 34

Doubletree Guest Suites/ Historic Charleston, Downtown Charleston, 34

1837 Bed & Breakfast and Tea Room, Charleston, 47

Embassy Suites Airport– Convention Center, North Charleston, 43

Fantasia Bed & Breakfast, Charleston, 47

King George IV Inn, Charleston, 48

Lowndes Grove Plantation Bed-and-Breakfast, Charleston, 48

Marriott Charleston Hotel, Downtown Charleston, 36

Old Village Post House, Charleston, 49

Shem Creek Inn, East Cooper, 38

Thirty-Six Meeting Street Bed & Breakfast, Charleston, 50

Vendue Suites, Charleston, 51

$$$

Hampton Inn at Patriots Point, East Cooper, 37

Hampton Inn Historic District, Downtown Charleston, 35

Hilton Garden Inn Charleston Airport, North Charleston, 44

Holiday Inn Express, North Charleston, Mount Pleasant, 40

Holiday Inn/Mount Pleasant, East Cooper, 38

Holiday Inn Riverview, West Ashley, 40

MainStay Suites, East Cooper, 38

SpringHill Suites, West Ashley, 40

$$-$$$

Best Western Sweetgrass Inn, West Ashley, 40

Comfort Inn Riverview, Downtown Charleston, 33

Days Inn Patriots Point, East Cooper, 37

La Quinta Inn & Suites Charleston Riverview, West Ashley, 40

Merhaven Bed, No Breakfast, Charleston, 49

Ramada Charleston Airport, North Charleston, 44

Sheraton North Charleston, North Charleston, 44

Town & Country Inn & Conference Center, West Ashley, 41

$$

Comfort Inn Coliseum, North Charleston, 43

North Charleston Inn, North Charleston, 44

$-$$

Days Inn Airport/Coliseum, North Charleston, 43

Masters Inn, East Cooper, 38

HOTELS & MOTELS

Downtown Charleston

BEST WESTERN KING
  CHARLES INN   **$$$-$$$$**
237 Meeting St.
(843) 723-7451, (866) 546-4700
www.kingcharlesinn.com

The King Charles Inn, another in the Best Western chain, completed a major renovation of its facade and common areas a few years back. The location is ideal for those wanting to explore King Street shopping and the Market area on foot. (See the Shopping chapter.) Those of us who drive past on sweltering Charleston afternoons envy the guests we see frolicking in the second-level outdoor swimming pool. The nearby fountain makes a sparkling show for guests in the dining room. The decor is traditional Charleston, with mahogany reproductions and Lowcountry art. Rooms feature 19th-century–style furniture, and some have adjoining guest rooms or balconies. The parking garage is underground and free for guests. The north area location is referred to as the Best Western Airport Inn & Suites and is an atrium-styled hotel with many of these same amenities and the Best Western Charleston Downtown is near the hospital complexes. Two more locations are at 146 Lockwood Dr. (843-722-4000, 888-377-2121) and 2470 Prospect Dr., North Charleston (843-574-0186, 800-780-7234), www.charleston bestwestern.com.

CHARLESTON PLACE $$$$$
205 Meeting St.
(843) 722-4900, (800) 701-1559
www.charlestonplace.com

In terms of size, Charleston Place Hotel is the granddaddy of Charleston accommodations, with 490 luxury suites and superbly appointed rooms in the massive complex in the city's downtown shopping district. The hotel, with its impressive lobby and reception area, opens into the walkway of a mini-mall that includes such famous stores as Gucci, St. John, and Godiva. (See the Shopping chapter.)

The full-service European spa with its on-staff masseur and masseuse has an indoor-outdoor swimming pool among the luxury amenities. Under the auspices of Orient-Express Hotels, the rooms at Charleston Place have taken on the aura of Europe in the 1930s.

Expect to find marble bathtubs and gold fixtures in the roomy baths, and notice the little touches in the rooms, such as art deco lighting and the subdued use of color. They add just that much more romance to your lodging experience. Several superb dining options are available right under the Charleston Place roof. Foremost among them is the **Charleston Grill** on the main floor tucked away among the shops and boutiques. (See the Restaurants chapter for more on the Charleston Grill.)

COMFORT INN RIVERVIEW $$–$$$
144 Bee St.
(843) 577-2224, (800) 228-5150
www.choicehotels.com

As part of the Comfort Inn chain, the Riverview's 129-room version offers a string of discounts and other standard features plus its most desirable asset, views of the Ashley River. It is just outside the historic district (but still on the Peninsula), and tours are available from the hotel. A fitness room appeals to many travelers, and the outdoor pool with its river view is a big hit with all ages. Continental breakfast is included in the price of the room, and there is no charge for parking. This location makes it a popular option for visitors to The Citadel, area hospitals, and the College of Charleston. Comfort Suites in North Charleston is the north area's option that can be reached at (843) 725-5400, and Comfort Suites West of the Ashley on Savannah Highway is at (843) 769-9850.

COURTYARD BY MARRIOTT
HISTORIC DISTRICT $$$$
125 Calhoun St.
(843) 805-7900, (877) 805-7900
www.marriott.com

For almost 40 years, the corner of Calhoun and Meeting Streets was known by frequent Charleston visitors as the location of a convenient and affordable 1960s-style high-rise.

It went by a number of names over the years and is now a Courtyard by Marriott. There are 176 guest rooms and suites, a full-service restaurant and lounge, conciege service, a fitness center, valet laundry, an outdoor heated pool, and courtyard. Best of all, it's still just steps away from King Street shopping, Marion Square, the visitor center, and Gaillard Auditorium. Business travelers have 3 phones with 2 lines, voice mail, and dataports in-room.

COURTYARD BY MARRIOTT
WATERFRONT $$$$
35 Lockwood Dr.
(843) 722-7229, (800) 449-0320
www.marriott.com/chscy
Overlooking the Ashley River at the base of the Peninsula, Courtyard by Marriott Waterfront offers 178 spacious guest rooms, all with 2 analog dataport phones, wireless Internet, voice mail messaging, and a work desk. In-room coffeemakers and movies on demand via cable are some of the other amenities. A waterfront swimming pool, an indoor whirlpool spa, and a fitness center are available, as well as a daily breakfast buffet in the **Courtyard Cafe.** Golf packages are available for 19 Lowcountry courses. There's ample on-site parking. This Courtyard by Marriott, which is near the Calhoun Street medical complex, cuts a high profile for those entering Charleston via SR 61, US 17, and SR 30. For a list of additional locations, visit the website.

DAYS INN HISTORIC
DISTRICT $$$–$$$$
155 Meeting St.
(843) 722-8411, (866) 683-8411
www.daysinn.com
The newly renovated 124 units of this Days Inn are air-conditioned and fairly typical of the rooms in this chain—clean and comfortable, with few frills. Enjoy a swimming pool and being only 1 block away from the Market, fine restaurants, plus shops and galleries. Limited free parking on-site is available. You can't beat this option for its ideal location and standard reliability. (See the East Cooper and I-26 Corridor sections below for other Days Inn locations.)

DOUBLETREE GUEST SUITES/
HISTORIC CHARLESTON $$$–$$$$
181 Church St.
(843) 577-2644, (877) 408-8733
www.charlestondoubletree.com
A relative newcomer to the Market area, and formerly known as the Hawthorn Suites, this comfortable courtyard hotel consists of oversized suites. Units have "the Charleston look" and include complete kitchens, separate bedrooms, and living rooms. Life is made easy with a breakfast buffet, and you can unwind with on-the-house refreshments at the afternoon reception. For those who enjoy burning the calories they consume, there's a fitness center and a heated whirlpool spa in the courtyard that seats at least 12 comfortably (great for relaxing while gazing at the stars). When energy levels diminish, the hotel's movie library is available to complement your cable television service. There are 5 suites that are completely wheelchair accessible. The hotel provides valet covered parking for an additional fee.

*EMBASSY SUITES HISTORIC
CHARLESTON $$$$–$$$$$
337 Meeting St.
(843) 723-6900, (800) 362-2779
www.historiccharleston.embassy suites.com

This all-suite luxury hotel is located in the historic district in what was originally The Citadel's first home (ca. 1820). Unmistakably a military building, the echoes of young cadets marching off to the Civil War still seem to bounce off these old walls. Enjoy 153 handsomely furnished 2-room suites with private bedrooms and living rooms. The decor recalls the grandeur of the colonial West Indies. All guest suites open onto a stone-floored atrium with giant palms and a 3-tiered fountain. Amenities include in-room wet bars, telephones with voice mail and dataports, complimentary Wi-Fi, free, cooked-to-order breakfast, and complimentary beverages each evening. This is an ideal location, a stroll from the visitor center, the Charleston Museum, and special events in Marion Square. (See the I-26 Corridor section, which follows for the north area location.)

✳FRANCIS MARION HOTEL $$$$$
387 King St.
(843) 722-0600, (877) 756-2121
www.francismarioncharleston.com
Built in 1924 and beautifully renovated, the Francis Marion is now one of the city's most popular hotels. Named for Revolutionary War General Francis Marion, also known as "The Swamp Fox," the hotel offers all the traditional services of a grand hotel—valet parking, concierge, doorman, bell service, and room service. In all, there are 232 guest accommodations ranging from rooms with 2 double beds to 2-room king suites. All have been handsomely re-appointed with custom detailing. At 12 stories tall, the hotel affords visitors a bird's-eye view. It's near upper King Street's fast-developing shopping district, the Charleston Museum, the College of Charleston, and the visitor center.

The hotel's signature restaurant, the **Swamp Fox Restaurant & Bar,** offers a very pleasant atmosphere on the first-floor King Street side. A complete day spa and Starbucks are on-site too. Ample parking is just next door in a city-owned garage.

HAMPTON INN HISTORIC
  DISTRICT $$$
345 Meeting St.
(843) 723-4000, (800) 426-7866
www.hamptoninn.com
There are 171 rooms in the downtown Hampton Inn Historic District, conveniently located across from the visitor center, trolley transportation, and the Charleston Museum. One of downtown Charleston's newer inns, the Hampton offers the attractive features of an older, restored building mellowed with time but beautifully decked out in crisp, new furnishings. The courtyard is probably the largest on the Peninsula, and the large pool is a welcome oasis for travelers. Double rooms have 2 queen beds, and an impressive continental breakfast is part of the deal— muffins, bagels, other breads, cereal, and coffee cake. The Hampton Inn Airport/Coliseum location—just off Ashley Phosphate on Northside Drive—is handy for airport travelers and convention visitors. Visit the website for additional locations.

MARKET PAVILION
  HOTEL $$$$–$$$$$
225 East Bay St.
(843) 723-0500, (877) 440-2250
www.marketpavilion.com
This boutique hotel at the corner of South Market and East Bay Streets features guest rooms and suites for tourists and business travelers. For the latter, there are meeting rooms and banquet facilities, and an

ACCOMMODATIONS

executive boardroom on tap. Guests have access to a rooftop pavilion with a pool and an open-air bar providing spectacular views from this popular reception area. An upscale restaurant, **Grill 225,** completes the picture (see the Restaurants chapter). Valet parking is available, and the location couldn't be more convenient to the Market's shopping adventures and its after-hours nightlife.

MARRIOTT CHARLESTON HOTEL $$$–$$$$
170 Lockwood Dr.
(843) 723-3000, (800) 228-9290
www.marriott.com

If you are crossing the Ashley River Bridge into Charleston, look to your left to see the towering 14-story Marriott Charleston Hotel behind riverside Brittlebank Park. There are 340 rooms and suites in this option, many with views of the river, and this venue is a popular one for conventions and meetings. A swimming pool and fitness center are part of the facility; and the rooms have premium channels and movie rentals. Abundant parking is available at no charge. An on-site restaurant called **Saffire** with American fusion cuisine and a rooftop lounge are part of the sophisticated offerings here.

i Low-cost accommodations on Charleston's historic Peninsula are few and far between. A hostel-style inn *has* opened recently at 156 Spring St. that offers a no-frills, economy-minded alternative. Visit www.notso hostel.com to learn more.

✳MILLS HOUSE HOTEL $$$$–$$$$$
115 Meeting St.
(843) 577-2400, (800) 874-9600
www.millshouse.com

Of the city's grand hotels in the historic district, the Mills probably enjoys the oldest, grandest reputation. It is located on the corner of Meeting and Queen Streets, next door to the imposing white-columned Hibernian Hall (site of many a debutante ball and home of the Hibernian Society). Modern in its comforts and antebellum in its decor, the Mills House has always been a favorite with affluent travelers. The original Mills Hotel (ca. 1853) standing on that site was deemed unworthy of restoration in the early 1960s, so it was razed and replaced with a new, fire-safe structure taller by a couple of floors but with lobby areas and public rooms copied from the original hotel. So exacting are the reproduced details and antebellum appointments that frequently the Mills is used as a backdrop for movies and TV shows needing a period hotel setting. The beautiful courtyard, outdoor pool, and deck add a casual side to the Mills experience. The in-house restaurant and bar, called the **Barbados Room,** draws local patrons as well as the international set. You'll find live entertainment somewhere on the premises each night, and turndown service is part of the pampering. It's hard to beat the Mills for location, as it is only a stone's throw from the Four Corners of Law, the King Street antiques district, several museums and galleries, plus the bustling Market area.

RENAISSANCE CHARLESTON HOTEL $$$$–$$$$$
68 Wentworth St.
(843) 534-0300, (800) 468-3571
www.renaissancecharlestonhotel.com

Opened in early 2001 in the heart of the city's downtown business district, The Renaissance is steps away from King Street shopping and area restaurants. The location is ideal for visitors to the College of Charleston campus just a short stroll away. The 166 elegantly appointed rooms are decorated in a Charleston decor with bonnet beds and other charming details. Some rooms open onto the pool deck; others have balconies with city views. The on-site restaurant, **The Wentworth Grill,** serves a continental cuisine with a Charleston flair. There's a fitness center, a heated outdoor pool, and ample meeting space for business travelers and conventioneers. Hotel valet and self-parking is just across Wentworth Street.

East Cooper

*CHARLESTON HARBOR RESORT & MARINA $$$-$$$$
20 Patriots Point Rd.
(843) 856-0028, (888) 856-0028
www.charlestonharborresort.com
The 130 room Charleston Harbor Resort was a long time coming to this breathtaking waterfront spot at the very tip of Mount Pleasant overlooking the Holy City. After 13 years, 2 different developers, and a major hurricane, this prime real estate resisted successful completion of a planned resort until Hilton arrived to save the day. Now under new management, the hotel and marina complex is one of Charleston's best destinations for fun, sun, sea, and golf. The resort's decor is maritime—teak-trimmed and nautical. The state-record blue marlin catch is triumphantly displayed in the main foyer.

Indoor facilities include meeting rooms, the **Indigo Grille** restaurant, a cocktail lounge called the **Reel Bar,** and a ballroom. Suites and rooms are available with king-size or 2 queen beds. Room phones have voice mail. Outdoors there's a swimming pool as well as a man-made, private sandy beach. The USS *Yorktown* and Patriots Point

Maritime Museum are just next door. Golfers have discounted greens fees at the Patriots Point course just outside the gate (see the Golf chapter). Guests can take advantage of the 459-slip marina with water taxi service to downtown. (See the Boating & Water Sports chapter.)

DAYS INN PATRIOTS POINT $$-$$$
261 Johnnie Dodds Blvd. (US 17 Bypass)
(843) 881-1800, (866) 637-8781
www.daysinn.com
One of the most popular amenities at this Days Inn is the pool area—sheltered for privacy by mature shrubbery. All rooms are air-conditioned, and the 24-hour on-site restaurant is a plus in our book for early risers who like to be close to that first cup of coffee. The rooms are in the standard Days Inn tradition. They're clean, comfortable, economical, and kid-friendly. High-speed wireless Internet is complimentary.

HAMPTON INN AT PATRIOTS POINT $$$
255 Sessions Way
(843) 881-3300, (800) 426-7866
www.charlestonpatriotspoint
.hamptoninn.com
This is a 121-room Mount Pleasant hotel with inside hallways rather than the outside breezeways that characterize many motels. There is no charge for local calls and high-speed wireless Internet. There is a business center for work and a fitness center for working out. The rooms here are a little grander than in most off-highway accommodations. The service says hotel, but the price says motel. A deluxe continental breakfast is on the house. The Hampton Inn on the Isle of Palms connector features deluxe suites, which are popular with traveling families. It

is located at 1104 Isle of Palms Connector (843-856-3900 or 800-426-7866).

HOLIDAY INN/MOUNT PLEASANT $$$
250 Johnnie Dodds Blvd. (US 17 Bypass)
(843) 884-6000, (800) 290-4004
www.himtpleasant.com

This elegant, full-service hotel has views of Charleston Harbor and the Cooper River and is only minutes away from the city as well as Patriots Point. Rooms are furnished with period reproductions, and a concierge level provides additional service and convenience. Visitors can enjoy a fitness center with a sauna, an outdoor pool, on-site restaurant, and bar. Plenty of free parking is available.

i The average daily rate for a room in Charleston peaks in April. In 2010 that average was $125 per night (according to the city's Convention and Visitor's Bureau). The occupancy rate for the city's hotel and motel accommodations in prime season is a healthy 77 percent.

MAINSTAY SUITES $$$
400 McGrath Darby Blvd.
(843) 881-1722, (877) 424-6423
www.mainstaysuites.com

This 71-unit, 3-floor, all-suite hotel offers unique accommodations to business travelers and vacationers who enjoy traveling as families. Half of the units at MainStay have 2 bedrooms and 2 baths, with doors that separate the kitchen, living area, and bathrooms from the sleeping rooms. The other half are roomy efficiencies, with full kitchens equipped with all the necessities

for preparing meals. You'll also find a heated pool, an exercise room, and guest laundry services. There's even a barbecue area for outdoor cooking. The check-in desk is manned only from 6 a.m. to 9 p.m. Mon through Fri. On weekends, it's open until 6 p.m. If you arrive outside of that envelope, follow the check-in instructions in the lobby.

MASTERS INN $-$$
300 Wingo Way
(843) 884-2814, (800) 633-3434
www.mastersinn.com

This 120-room option is a bargain and offers great proximity to the city (3 miles) and the Isle of Palms (7 miles). There are some extras as well, such as a pool, cable television, and free local phone calls and wireless Internet access. A lounge and restaurant are on-site, and free continental breakfast is served each morning. Efficiencies with kitchenettes are also available. The inn is also pet friendly. Children younger than 18 stay free with parents. The North Charleston location is convenient to the airport and the Air Force Base at 6100 Rivers Ave. (843-744-3530 or 800-633-3434).

SHEM CREEK INN $$$-$$$$
1401 Shrimp Boat Lane
(843) 881-1000, (800) 523-4951
www.shemcreekinn.com

With views of the shrimp boats moving in and out of their docks and the sun sparkling off miles of marsh, Shem Creek Inn is fun for both children and adults. A large waterfront pool is perfect for relaxing or watching all the creek action. Each of the 50 rooms has a private balcony, and king-size rooms have garden tubs. All guest rooms have microwaves and refrigerators. There is convenient parking under the building, and complimentary continental breakfast is served each morning. All the Shem Creek nightlife goes on close to the inn, and boat dockage is available.

Sullivan's Island & Isle of Palms

These two islands are popular vacation destinations and abound with rental property. With no hotel, motel, condominium, or resort development, Sullivan's Island has less to offer in terms of overnight rental but has an assortment of old and new island homes for rent in weekly or monthly increments.

On the Isle of Palms, in addition to weekly house rentals, Wild Dunes, a major resort, offers flexibility in length of stay (see subsequent listing). Please note: Summer reservations on both islands are often booked by late winter, so start making plans with a rental agency or other entity at least six months ahead. Most do not allow pets, but it is always worth asking.

THE BOARDWALK INN AT
WILD DUNES $$$$–$$$$$
5757 Palm Blvd., Isle of Palms
(843) 886-6000, (888) 778-1876
www.wilddunes.com
Opened early in 1998, the Boardwalk Inn at Wild Dunes is a $12 million luxury hotel with 93 rooms or suites near Wild Dunes' 2 famous golf courses and 20-court tennis center. All this is situated along 2.5 miles of unspoiled white sand beach. The Boardwalk Inn has an on-site gourmet Lowcountry-style seafood restaurant and lounge plus a tropical pool complex. Even locals enjoy the attractive bed-and-breakfast packages for special occasions.

✳WILD DUNES RESORT $$$$–$$$$$
5757 Palm Blvd., Isle of Palms
(843) 886-6000, (888) 778-1860
www.wilddunes.com
Rental possibilities at Wild Dunes are widely varied. This 1,600-acre oceanfront golf resort is 20 minutes north of Charleston. Accommodations include 1- to 4-bedroom villas next to the ocean, golf courses, tennis courts, or lagoon. You can rent 3- to 6-bedroom homes with ocean, fairway, and Intracoastal Waterway views. Guests choose their location based on proximity to the beach, pool, tennis courts, marina, or fairways and, of course, on price. The accommodations provide linens, dinnerware, televisions, and washers and dryers, plus a cleaning staff takes care of the messy parts of vacationing. You just focus on the fun. Golf is a big attraction, with 2 excellent courses: The Links, designed by Tom Fazio and ranked as a top course by *Golf* magazine, and the Harbor Course, with holes along the Intracoastal Waterway. (See the Golf chapter.) There are Har-Tru tennis courts for day and night play, and tennis clinics and lessons are available. Of course, the sandy beach is beautiful, and there are many activities for families. Wild Dunes does not allow pets but will recommend local kennels. (For more about Wild Dunes see our Neighborhoods, Golf, and Parks & Recreation chapters.)

West Ashley

The following West Ashley options provide good value with proximity to the Peninsula. At most, you'll be about 20 minutes from the hustle and bustle of the historic district. Note that most properties are on or near US 17, which is called Savannah Highway throughout this area.

BEST WESTERN
SWEETGRASS INN $$–$$$
1540 Savannah Hwy.
(843) 571-6100, (877) 798-4727
www.thesweetgrassinn.com

This Best Western is only 3 miles from the Peninsula and is a very tasteful, affordable option. Continental breakfast is complimentary, and everyone loves the large outdoor pool. All 87 guest rooms have a microwave and refrigerator plus wireless Internet access is offered throughout the inn. We think this is one of the area's real values. It is convenient to the gardens and historic plantations along SR 61.

HOLIDAY INN EXPRESS $$$
1943 Savannah Hwy.
(843) 402-8300, (888) 465-4329
www.hiexpress.com

This hotel is a moderately priced option for traveling families. The rooms and suites are comfortable without the extras. There's still little more to be desired with a pool, fitness center, laundry facilities, sundeck, computer access ports, wireless Internet, micro-fridges, and free off-site parking. It's located near I-526, making travel to most destinations in Charleston quite convenient. Other locations are at 7670 Northwoods Blvd. in North Charleston (843-553-1600 or 800-465-4329) and at 350 Johnnie Dodds Blvd. in Mount Pleasant (843-375-2600 or 877-227-9927).

HOLIDAY INN RIVERVIEW $$$
301 Savannah Hwy.
(843) 556-7100, (800) 972-2513
www.holiday-inn.com

For obvious reasons, locals refer to this circular hotel just across the Ashley River Bridge as the Round Holiday Inn. Many of the 180 units

and 4 suites have spectacular water views unmatched by any other accommodation in the city. Up top, a restaurant and bar offer panoramic vistas of peninsular Charleston and the meandering Ashley River. The pool area is an outside appendage to the hotel, unusual because of its elevated height and the view it provides. Guests enjoy the 24-hour business center, newly renovated fitness center, complimentary shuttle service to downtown, and free on-site parking.

LA QUINTA INN & SUITES
CHARLESTON RIVERVIEW $$–$$$
11 Ashley Pointe Dr.
(843) 556-5200, (800) 753-3757
www.lq.com

Out of the mainstream, this La Quinta is on a road called Ashley Pointe Drive, off Albemarle Road west of the Ashley. Other nearby landmarks are Ripley Light Marina and California Dreaming restaurant at the end of the street (see the Restaurants chapter). Ideal for visitors to the Lowcountry arriving by boat, this motel is a modern, multi-story facility with great views of the Ashley River and the adjoining marina. There are 175 rooms in all. Some have 1 double bed, others have 2 doubles, and there are business king rooms with king beds, enhanced workspace, cordless phone, and a 32-inch TV. Continental breakfast is complimentary.

SPRINGHILL SUITES $$$
98 Ripley Point Dr.
(843) 571-1711, (888) 287-9400
www.marriott.com/chssh

Across the Ashley just past the round Holiday Inn you'll find this all-suite Marriott hotel, which is popular with boaters tying up at Ripley Light Marina. Close to downtown and SR 61 (out to the plantations), this hotel also offers many luxury amenities. Each suite has a mini-kitchen, a sitting area, cable TV, 2-line telephones with dataports, wireless Internet, voice mail messaging, and a spacious work area. Guests also enjoy a free continental breakfast, outdoor pool and whirlpool spa, exercise room, and same-day valet service. Next door is the slightly more upscale Marriott Residence Inn offering 1 or 2 bedrooms, fully equipped kitchens, some suites with fireplaces, and other luxuries. Call (843) 571-7979 or (800) 331-3131 for reservations or more information.

TOWN & COUNTRY INN & CONFERENCE CENTER $$-$$$
2008 Savannah Hwy.
(843) 571-1000, (800) 334-6660
www.thetownandcountryinn.com
What will strike you first about this West Ashley establishment is the electronic billboard out front that gives a running message about the services within. Next, you are likely to be amazed by the fact that this is as much a fitness center as it is a motel. Guests have access to facilities, and locals can buy memberships. With an indoor pool, racquetball courts, exercise equipment, sauna, and more, a stay here can qualify as a fitness vacation.

The regular rooms feature 2 queen beds or 1 king-size bed, and built-in hair dryers. The phones offer voice mail service, and the 37-inch flat screen TVs all have 56 cable channels, including HBO. Laundry service is an option and, if you are traveling light, efficiencies are available. The restaurant, **Trotters,** is popular as well (especially with the after-church crowd on Sundays) and runs unusual specials—just check the sign! (See the Restaurants chapter.)

Folly Beach

Visitors interested in staying on Folly Beach will find a range of accommodations, including an oceanfront high-rise hotel (see listing) and old-style beach houses available for rent. Again, to rent a beach home, see the list of agents in the Vacation & Beach Rentals section of this chapter.

TIDES FOLLY BEACH $$$$-$$$$$
1 Center St.
(843) 588-6464, (800) 972-2513
www.follybeachhotel.net
This is the only oceanfront hotel, restaurant, and bar in this part of the Lowcountry. All rooms overlook the ocean at Folly Beach, and private "Juliet" balconies make wave watching all the nicer. Standard rooms have either 1 king-size or 2 double beds. Microwaves and refrigerators, voicemail, data ports and complimentary Wi-Fi are some of the many room conveniences. There is an oceanfront pool for those who do not dip in the salt water, and **Blu Restaurant and Bar** has terrific coastal cuisine and flowing spirits at its bar.

Kiawah & Seabrook

These world-class resort destinations offer some extraordinary rental options that might be just what you are looking for: everything from a private villa to luxury homes to an upscale hotel. Look for descriptions of Kiawah and Seabrook in the Neighborhoods, History, Area Overview, Golf, and Parks & Recreation chapters.

KIAWAH ISLAND RESORT $$$$-$$$$$
12 Kiawah Beach Dr., Kiawah Island
(843) 768-2121, (800) 654-2924
www.kiawahresort.com

Called "South Carolina's joy of a resort isle" by *Vogue* magazine, Kiawah Island is a 10,000 acre, semitropical island with rental options galore. Choose from villas, cottages, and private homes. Kiawah's newest premier spot is The Sanctuary, a $126 million hotel, spa, and convention complex with 255 rooms. (See following listing.)

There are actually three resort areas, or villages, within walking or biking distance of island shopping and dining. Villas and cottages are fully equipped and have as many as 4 bedrooms, while luxury homes for rent in adjacent residential areas have as many as 7 bedrooms and elaborate extras.

Other accommodations are basically clustered in the West Beach Village, the East Beach Village, and the Vanderhorst Plantation. In the West Beach Village, villas have views of the forest, ocean, lagoon, tennis courts, or golf courses. East Beach villas are parkside, linkside, courtside, or oceanside and offer some very appealing options. There are 2 pools for guest usage, one of which is an Olympic-size option in the 21-acre Night Heron Park, where guests will also find a covered pavilion, arcade, soccer field, and lake for fishing. The Vanderhorst Plantation is an exclusive gated community with very large homes and ample privacy.

Plan to swim, bike, shell hunt, boat, and fish, and explore the many nature trails that encircle the island. Oh, and expect to break out the clubs too. According to *Golf* magazine, Kiawah is one of the best golf resorts in America (see the Golf chapter). It was home of the 1991 Ryder Cup Matches, the 1997 World Cup of Golf, the 2003 WGC World Cup, and the 2007 Senior PGA Tournament. The next exciting PGA event coming to Kiawah is the 2012 PGA Tournament.

Kiawah's tennis program, with state-of-the art facilities at two centers, also ranks high nationally. Kiawah's kids' programs are a hit with young families.

✳ THE SANCTUARY AT KIAWAH ISLAND $$$$$
1 Sanctuary Beach Dr., Kiawah Island
(843) 768-6000, (800) 576-1570
www.thesanctuary.com

The Sanctuary at Kiawah Island opened in 2004 with much hoopla and anticipation among locals and regular visitors to the Lowcountry. The opening of this 255-room hotel and spa built right on Kiawah's legendary 10 mile, pristine beach came after a decade of planning and construction—marking a new era in luxury accommodations for coastal South Carolina.

Guests of The Sanctuary may think of it as a destination unto itself, although the island's world-class golf and tennis programs are major draws. Nearly all the unusually large rooms and suites offer sweeping ocean views, and the hotel's decor harks back to the gilded age of beachfront mansions built by America's 19th-century aristocracy.

Two dining rooms vie for hungry guests' attention; the **Jasmine Porch** (with its Lowcountry cuisine) and the **Ocean Room** (a fine-dining option serving dinner only with a New American menu—see the Restaurants chapter). An on-site full-service spa tempts guests with an ample selection of relaxing and healthful pamperings available to both men and women. Along with every imaginable beach amenity (including indoor and outdoor pools plus an outdoor bar and grill), The Sanctuary offers guests an arcade of smart shopping boutiques, and an on-site staff of wildlife experts is available to lead guests on a variety of nature adventures—all Kiawah style.

SEABROOK RESORT $$$$–$$$$$
1002 Landfall Way, Seabrook Island
(843) 768-2300, (800) 554-8222
www.seabrook.com

This resort offers family vacations in a residential, island setting. Here you'll find 1-, 2-, and 3-bedroom villas—some in the maritime forest, others overlooking the marsh or the sea. These properties come equipped with spacious kitchens, sundecks or screened porches, cable hookups, and everything from linens to dinnerware. All are in proximity to one of Seabrook's two golf courses, Ocean Winds and Crooked Oaks.

Along with these championship courses (see the Golf chapter), Seabrook has a tennis complex and the area's only resort equestrian center. Swimmers choose between glistening pools and a beautiful stretch of beach along the Atlantic Ocean. Children can enjoy supervised, old-fashioned fun such as puppet shows, finger painting, and ice-cream making while their parents relish precious private time. Seabrook recently completed a 5-year $31 million renovation, so all facilities are top-notch.

I-26 Corridor
(Charleston International Airport)

For business travelers, commuters to Charleston Area Convention Center meetings (in North Charleston), and vacationers who need accommodations convenient to the airport, a number of options await them along the I-26 corridor and the I-526 loop around the heart of the Lowcountry.

We've listed many of these options in the entries for well-known chain hotels and

motels above. Here are a few more choices offering a variety of amenities and prices.

COMFORT INN COLISEUM $$
5055 North Arco Lane, North Charleston
(843) 554-6485, (877) 424-6423
www.choicehotels.com

This Comfort Inn has more extras than you might imagine and is a good value. Complimentary continental breakfast and a daily paper start the day off right. There is free cable TV with premium channels and free wireless Internet access as well as laundry facilities and an outdoor pool. Business guests will find phones with voice mail and dataports. The Comfort Inn Coliseum, where pets are welcome, is just a mile from Charleston International Airport, Tanger Outlet Mall, and the North Charleston Coliseum.

DAYS INN AIRPORT/COLISEUM $–$$
2998 West Montague Ave., North Charleston
(843) 747-4101, (800) 329-7466
www.daysinn.com

The familiar name in affordable comfort has 149 rooms with cable TV, pay-for-view movies, free high-speed Internet, and refrigerators and microwaves. Like most others in the chain, this has an on-site family restaurant, an outdoor pool, and playground. This location is ideal for sports fans attending events at the Coliseum, only 3 blocks away. There's also free airport transportation for guests.

EMBASSY SUITES AIRPORT–
CONVENTION CENTER $$$–$$$$
5055 International Blvd., North Charleston
(843) 747-1882, (800) 362-2779
www.embassysuitescharleston.com

ACCOMMODATIONS

One of the first full-service hotels built to serve (and literally connected to via a climate-controlled skyway) the north area's convention center complex, this 255-suite high-rise hotel is very impressive. Surrounding the 9-story garden atrium, the 2-room suites feature a wet bar with refrigerator and microwave, and two cable TVs. Facilities include ample meeting space, a pool, fitness center, and a state-of-the-art business center for conventioneers. Services at the Embassy Suites include a complimentary breakfast as well as an evening reception and an airport and historic district shuttle to make doing business here as pleasant and convenient as possible.

HILTON GARDEN INN
** CHARLESTON AIRPORT $$$**
5265 International Blvd., North
Charleston
(843) 308-9330, (877) STAY-HGI
www.charlestonairport.stayhgi.com
Hilton's bid for the business travelers' attention is minutes from Charleston International Airport. The Garden Inn boasts a full array of amenities. A complimentary airport shuttle is another plus. The 168 rooms feature refrigerators, microwaves, and coffeemakers, plus work desks, adjustable lighting, and ergonomic chairs for comfort and on-task productivity. When work is done, the **Great American Grill** offers cocktails and dinner service, and a hearty breakfast, too. The indoor pool and fitness center add another option for relaxation. There's evening room service for those who wish to stay in. All this convenience is 2 blocks from the North Charleston Convention Center and Coliseum, yet downtown Charleston's many attractions are only a short drive away.

NORTH CHARLESTON INN $$
2934 West Montague, North Charleston
(843) 744-8281, (877) 464-2700
www.northcharlestoninn.com
A slightly more affordable alternative to the Convention Center hotel choices is this independent hotel just off I-26. The 80-room facility has an outdoor courtyard pool, in-room voice mail, free wireless Internet, and video entertainment, plus some rooms have limited kitchen facilities and laundry service for long-term stays. The on-site restaurant, **Arena Bar and Grill,** always has a game on the big-screen TV. The North Charleston Inn is pet-friendly.

RAMADA CHARLESTON
** AIRPORT $$-$$$**
7401 Northwoods Blvd., North
Charleston
(843) 572-2200, (800) 252-7466
www.ramada.com
Conveniently located just off I-26 at Ashley Phosphate Road, this 197-room tropical atrium hotel has an indoor/outdoor swimming pool with separate whirlpool and sauna. A full buffet breakfast and afternoon social comes with the room, and there's free shuttle service to and from the airport. Rooms have premium channel cable TV, microwaves, refrigerators, and complimentary high-speed wireless Internet. Guest laundry service is available, too. Ample free parking accommodates cars, RVs, buses, or trucks.

SHERATON NORTH
** CHARLESTON $$-$$$**
4770 Goer Dr., North Charleston
(843) 747-1900, (888) 747-1900
www.sheraton.com

This recently renovated, 289-room hotel is right off I-26 at Montague Avenue, 5 minutes from Charleston International Airport. Its refreshing indoor–outdoor pool and fitness center are a boon to the busy convention business. **Monikers** is its on-site restaurant, and the nearby lounge is a favorite with guests and locals alike. Parking is free, and so is the hotel's shuttle to the airport.

BED-AND-BREAKFASTS

ASHLEY INN BED & BREAKFAST $$$$
201 Ashley Ave.
(843) 723-1848, (800) 581-6658
www.charleston-sc-inns.com

A real taste of Charleston, this home was built around 1832 and is a mansion even by today's standards—6 bedrooms and a suite, with fireplaces throughout the house and a lovely garden. All rooms have private baths and are tastefully furnished with antique, four-poster pencil-post, or canopy rice beds. Breakfast is served on the piazza and features such gourmet delights as savory sausage turnovers with cream cheese and chive scrambled eggs or baked cheese blintzes with triple berry sauce. Afternoon wine with homemade treats are part of the hospitality. The inn has bicycles for guests to use and provides off-street parking. This may be the best option for guests wishing access to MUSC facilities. They are literally across the street.

BARKSDALE HOUSE INN $$$–$$$$
27 George St.
(843) 577-4800, (888) 577-4980
www.barksdalehouse.com

This bed-and-breakfast inn is in proximity to King Street shopping and the College of Charleston. In fact, the facility was once a fraternity house. No one would guess that fact

Historic Bed-and-Breakfasts

Historic Charleston Bed & Breakfast, (843) 722-6606 or (800) 743-3583 (www.historiccharleston bedandbreakfast.com), is a local business that has been matching guests with in-home accommodations since 1981. The reservation service books more than 50 different private homes and carriage houses within the historic district. With very few exceptions, these accommodations date from 1860 or earlier. Agents for Historic Charleston Bed & Breakfast know each property intimately. They know which ones are appropriate for children and which are not, they know which ones are accessible to persons with disabilities and the elderly and which are not, and they can arrange for late arrivals and special transportation. Historic Charleston Bed & Breakfast also sends out excellent pre-arrival materials, including maps and shopping and dining recommendations.

Accommodations booked through Historic Charleston Bed & Breakfast can range from $95 to $295 for 2 adults in a 1-bedroom setting, an average of $275 for a 2-bedroom accommodation, and as high as $500 to $600 for luxury 3-bedroom offerings during high season. Rates can be slightly higher for special events and peak weekends like Cooper River Bridge Run, Spoleto Festival USA, and New Year's. Off-season rates are, of course, lower. March through July and October through December are usually considered peak season.

today, as the Barksdale House Inn includes 14 beautifully appointed rooms, each one different from the others. All have cable TV, free wireless Internet, and private telephones. Five rooms are equipped with fireplaces and whirlpool baths (oh, what the frat brothers would have given . . .). Continental breakfast is served in your room or in the rear garden, and a nightly turndown service and afternoon tea or sherry are included. Free parking is available.

BATTERY CARRIAGE HOUSE INN $$$$–$$$$$
20 South Battery
(843) 727-3100, (800) 775-5575
www.batterycarriagehouse.com

The Battery Carriage House (ca. 1843) is located right on the Battery, Charleston's very best address for a couple of hundred years. You couldn't be closer to the picturesque, historic park and beautiful views of Charleston Harbor. The 11 guest rooms to the rear and under the piazza are small, but completely charming—most with queen-size canopy beds and interesting furnishings. Three rooms are available with king-size beds. All rooms have cable TV with HBO, and wireless Internet access, and you'll find individual controls for heating and air-conditioning. Some rooms have large steam showers; others have whirlpool tubs. Fluffy terry cloth robes and down pillows add to the pampering. Silver-service continental breakfast is served in the room or in the garden under the loggia, your choice. Happy hour wine is served in the lobby. The service here is very cordial, the ambience very European—a bit like an Italian pensione. There's usually plenty of parking just across the street.

CANNONBORO INN BED & BREAKFAST $$$$
184 Ashley Ave.
(843) 723-8572, (800) 235-8039
www.charleston-sc-inns.com

This historic 1853 home has 8 beautifully decorated rooms for guests—all of which offer antique four-poster or canopy beds. The all no-smoking rooms are done in a handsome palette of pastels that complement the original hardwood floors. The house is furnished with an assortment of period antiques, and all rooms have air-conditioning and private baths. Guests have cable TV, wireless Internet, and private telephones, too. Complimentary wine is served each afternoon along with an assortment of home-baked goods. Awake to the aroma of sizzling sausage and freshly baked biscuits. A full gourmet breakfast is served each morning on the columned piazza overlooking a Lowcountry garden and fountain. Off-street parking is provided, and complimentary touring bicycles—an especially nice option in this part of town—are available for guests.

CHARLOTTE STREET COTTAGE $$$$$
32 Charlotte St.
(843) 577-3944
www.charlestoncottage.com

Ever wish for your own, private separate house when visiting downtown Charleston? Here is a great choice. The Charlotte Street Cottage is an elegant, historic guest home available by the day, week, or month. This beautifully restored brick cottage is an original kitchen house built in 1820. It is centrally located in the historic district just off East Bay Street and near the Gaillard Auditorium and other Spoleto venues, the Charleston Museum, the Aquarium, and attractions at Liberty Square. Bicycles are provided for easy access to other historic district destinations. A kitchen (with the original fireplace), breakfast nook, living room, and half bath are downstairs, and two bedrooms, full bath, and washer/dryer are upstairs. Just step out of the kitchen door onto your private patio and garden. Cable TV, telephone, fax, and high speed and wireless Internet access are all a part of the complete package. There is complimentary gated parking.

1837 BED & BREAKFAST
AND TEA ROOM $$$–$$$$
126 Wentworth St.
(843) 723-7166, (877) 723-1837
www.1837bb.com

Two artists have restored this historic (ca. 1837) house near the College of Charleston and King Street shopping. All nine rooms and the brick carriage house have air-conditioning and are beautifully decorated. Guests are treated to a sumptuous gourmet breakfast and have access to off-street parking. Afternoon tea for registered guests is complimentary. Rooms have private entrances and baths, refrigerators, and televisions. To quote *The New York Times,* it is "a perfect place to unwind."

FANTASIA BED &
BREAKFAST $$$–$$$$
11 George St.
(843) 853-0201, (800) 852-4466
www.fantasiabb.com

Here in this 1813 classic Charleston Single House, you'll find a charming bed-and-breakfast in Charleston's tradition of hospitality. The main house's two bedroom suites are upstairs over a pair of first-floor drawing rooms that give visitors the feel and flavor of Charleston life before the Civil War. The piazza with its lazy hammock overlooks a

handsomely landscaped garden accented with fountains and a cobblestone drive. A carriage and kitchen house with another bedroom actually sleeps four with a pull-out couch. A full southern breakfast is served in the main house, and a continental breakfast is available for carriage house guests. Wine and soft drinks await visitors after a busy day of shopping and touring the city's sites. Off-street parking is available, and short-term lease agreements are offered for the carriage and kitchen house facilities.

✳15 CHURCH STREET: THE PHILLIPS-
YATES-SNOWDEN HOUSE BED AND
BREAKFAST $$$$–$$$$$
15 Church St.
(843) 722-7602
www.bedandbreakfast.com

Some say that lower Church Street is the quintessential Charleston address. Its picturesque bend at Water Street and narrow brick-paved pathway have been the subject of countless photographs depicting the charm and beauty of this location just off the High Battery and White Point Gardens. An opportunity to stay within one of the historic homes here is a special treat for the discerning traveler. Homeowners Jack and Annelise Simmons welcome guests to a truly Charleston experience in their lovely 1840 home. A full breakfast is served either in the dining room or on the piazza (side porch) or in the garden. The fluffy Virginia pancakes or crustless sausage quiche are signature items, but special dietary restrictions can be accommodated as well. After a day of sightseeing the piazza is once again a welcome spot to relax with wine and cheese and share your adventures with your hosts who, by the way, speak both English and French. When it's time to retire there is a choice of king or queen bedrooms on the third floor of the main house with beautiful views of the harbor or antebellum rooftops. A king bedroom (convertible to two twins) on the ground floor has a private entrance. Each room has a private bath, telephone, fireplace, and Wi-Fi. The carriage house (parts of which date to 1759) is perfect for families with two bedrooms, one-and-a-half baths, living room, dining room, full kitchen and washer/dryer. Off-street parking is another plus here. As you enter the property note the two cannonballs mounted on the gateposts which were two of the four that struck the house during the Civil War.

4 UNITY ALLEY—A B&B $$$$
4 Unity Alley
(843) 577-6660
www.unitybb.com

Unity Alley is steeped in history; according to legend, George Washington quartered his horse here on his visit to Charleston back in 1791. Today, this quiet alley in the bustling French Quarter boasts a renovated warehouse beautifully transformed into a grand home with charming guest accommodations. Furnished with antique and reproduction furniture, the building surrounds a restful atrium garden perfect for entertaining and dining. Opened in 1998, 4 Unity Alley offers three suites, each with a private bath. A full breakfast is served each morning, and rarest of all, there's indoor parking available for guests.

KING GEORGE IV INN $$$–$$$$
32 George St.
(843) 723-9339, (888) 723-1667
www.kinggeorgeiv.com

At this 4-story, Federal-style house with decorative fireplaces, wide-planked hardwood floors, and 3 porches, you're just off King Street with its many antiques shops and fashion boutiques. And Charleston's colorful City Market is only a 5-minute walk away. This was originally the 1790s home of Charleston writer and early newspaper publisher Peter Freneau. Freneau was of Huguenot descent, and his brother Philip was called the "poet of the Revolution." All 10 rooms are furnished with antiques, cable TVs, and telephones, and have air-conditioning and Wi-Fi. Eight of the rooms have private baths. Each morning, a full Southern breakfast is served until 10:30 a.m. in the Breakfast Room or you may choose to eat on the porch. There is free off-street parking for guests.

LOWNDES GROVE PLANTATION
BED-AND-BREAKFAST $$$–$$$$
266 Margaret St.
(843) 853-1810
www.lowndesgrove.com

Now listed on the National Register of Historic Places, Lowndes Grove (ca. 1786) is the only plantation on the Ashley River actually within today's city limits. The house and grounds, with spectacular views of the water, make a lush setting for wedding receptions and other festivities. There are three air-conditioned guest rooms with private baths and a two-bedroom, air-conditioned guest cottage for families (babysitting is available). As elegant as the house is, the spacious grounds, pool, Jacuzzi, and river dock also make it a comfortable, almost rural setting. The house is especially convenient to The Citadel and Hampton Park, once the site of the 1901 West Indies Exhibition, a World's Fair–like extravaganza that attracted dignitaries from all over the world. At the time, Lowndes Grove hosted former President Theodore Roosevelt.

MERHAVEN BED,
NO BREAKFAST $$–$$$
16 Halsey St.
(843) 577-3053

Although this listing doesn't fit the bed-and-breakfast category in the strictest sense, it's a close relation. In fact, this is what *The New York Times* called "the no-frills option" in Charleston. You'll find two large, light-filled, air-conditioned rooms with a private entrance but, sorry, no eggs and grits. Actually, coffee, tea, and a refrigerator are available in each room, which means you can easily prepare your own breakfast. Both rooms are nonsmoking, and there's a shared bath. Guests have their own TV and an in-room extension of the family phone line. There's a delightful courtyard, too, with a hammock that's ideal for an afternoon siesta. Guests appreciate the off-street parking and the fact that the College of Charleston and MUSC and the hospitals are within easy walking distance. No credit cards.

OLD VILLAGE
POST HOUSE $$$–$$$$
101 Pitt St., Mount Pleasant
(843) 388-8935, (800) 549-7678
www.oldvillageposthouse.com

There are 6 bedrooms in the newly reno-vated Post House, formerly the Guilds Inn (ca. 1888), each beautiful and typically "Old Village." Every room has a private bath, and the on-site restaurant offers gourmet meals for dinner. A continental breakfast, cable TV, wireless Internet access, and daily newspapers are complimentary. There's even a full-service tavern, too. Rooms vary in size; there's an executive suite, and honeymooners can request the special bridal suite with over-sized whirlpool tub. Guests enjoy the charm of this quaint neighborhood, where evening walks are a popular pastime. (For more on the Old Village Post House restaurant, see the Restaurants chapter.)

THE PALMER HOME
BED & BREAKFAST $$$$–$$$$$
5 East Battery
(843) 853-1574
www.palmerhomebb.net

This bed-and-breakfast is in one of the most high-profile mansions on the Battery. The huge pink Italianate single house (some-times called the "Pink Palace") offers spec-tacular views. From the piazza, guests can see across all of Charleston Harbor, with Fort Sumter silhouetted on the horizon. There are four guest rooms on the third floor (stair climbing is required) and a swimming pool in the garden for cool refreshment. There's also a more expansive carriage house with two bedrooms that can accommodate up to eight adults. A full Southern breakfast buffet is served in the dining room or on the piazza at your choosing. Afternoon wine and cheese in the drawing room allows opportu-nity to meet the other guests. There's plenty of off-street parking, too.

PHOEBE PEMBER
HOUSE $$$$–$$$$$
26 Society St.
(843) 722-4186
www.phoebepemberhouse.com

This elegant, 200-year-old Federal-style home in Ansonborough was the birthplace of Civil War heroine Phoebe Pember. She was the wealthy daughter of a 19th-century Charleston businessman. As a nurse, she traveled to Confederate hospitals during the war and wrote about her experience in her memoirs, *A True Southern Lady's Story*. The interiors here are remarkably authentic yet very comfortable. The four guest rooms have fireplaces and canopy beds. Business travelers like the fact that rooms have desks, telephones, wireless Internet, and fax machines. There's cable TV to enjoy once the work is done, and a popular day spa is just around the corner. The carriage house, with its gardens, is available for business meetings as well as short- or long-term rental. You're only blocks from the City Market (see the Shopping chapter) and all the nightlife offered there. Special events at Gaillard Auditorium are virtually across the street. The College of Charleston is close by as well. There is off-street parking, and a silver tray continental-plus breakfast (this usually entails fruit, a selection of breads, and coffee, tea, or juice), plus evening wine and cheese is included.

i Travelers interested in the bed-and-breakfast options may want to visit the Charleston Bed & Breakfast Association's website, www.charleston bb.com, for more detailed information and photos of member properties. All must meet certain standards of quality and service and boast innkeepers ready to share their love of Charleston with their guests.

✳THIRTY-SIX MEETING STREET BED & BREAKFAST $$$–$$$$
36 Meeting St.
(843) 722-1034
www.36meetingstreet.com

This handsome (ca. 1740) home is only a little more than a block off the Battery and offers 3 guest suites, each with its own private entrance. One is on the ground floor of the carriage house and another is on the second floor, each with 2 bedrooms and a sitting area and private baths. In the main

house there is an exterior spiral staircase that leads to a 1 bedroom and bath on the second floor. All rooms have four poster mahogany queen beds and kitchenettes, and there's an inviting walled-in garden with tables and chairs for relaxing after a busy day. A continental breakfast is provided in the kitchenette—ready whenever guests rise and wish to partake, and the morning newspaper is left at your doorstep. Off-street parking and bicycles are available.

THE THOMAS LAMBOLL HOUSE $$$$
19 King St.
(843) 723-3212, (888) 874-0793
www.lambollhouse.com

Named in honor of colonial-era judge Thomas Lamboll, this Charleston single house (ca. 1739) is now a private home with 2 lovely third-floor guest rooms offered to bed-and-breakfast guests. Each is elegantly furnished with reproduction and antique furniture, has central air-conditioning, a fireplace, cable TV, and a telephone. French doors lead onto the third-floor piazza with distant views of Charleston Harbor over the treetops. Continental-plus breakfast is offered in the formal dining room every morning. Children are welcome, and off-street parking is available.

21 EAST BATTERY BED & BREAKFAST $$$$$
21 East Battery
(843) 556-0500, (888) 721-7488
www.21eastbattery.com

Within the urban compound of Charleston's historic 1825 Edmundston-Alston House (see House Museums in the Attractions chapter), is this charming bed-and-breakfast created in the property's former stables, carriage house, and slave quarters. The old hayloft is now the master bedroom overlooking a lovely garden. Where carriages were once stored are now a spacious living room and a dining room with hidden kitchen facilities—stocked for a gourmet breakfast. Additional rooms in the museum house's rear dependency can accommodate up to a total of 10 people. This high-end option located right on Charleston's famous High Battery is ideal for multiple couples celebrating a special event or traveling families.

TWO MEETING STREET INN   **$$$$$**
2 Meeting St.
(843) 723-7322, (888) 723-7322
www.twomeetingstreet.com
This elegant 1890 Victorian mansion is at the intersection of Meeting Street and South Battery facing White Point Gardens. Guests stay in one of nine air-conditioned rooms, each with a private bath. The rooms are all different, but each carries out the Victorian theme in every detail. A hot Southern breakfast is served in the garden or the formal dining room, depending on the weather. Or you may decide to lounge in your luxury cotton bathrobe (provided with the room) and have breakfast delivered to your guest room. Afternoon tea and evening sherry is included in the rate. Much of Two Meeting Street's charm comes from the lacy Queen Anne–style veranda stretching across the front of the inn. Its lazy ceiling fans and rocking chairs make the scene an inviting option for afternoon tea. No credit cards.

VENDUE SUITES   **$$$–$$$$$**
30 Vendue Range
(843) 723-2228
www.venduesuites.com
Located close to Charleston's picturesque harbor and near many of the city's best restaurants, Vendue Suites is tucked away just off East Bay Street. This B&B-style inn has three guest suites for short or extended stays. There is a one-bedroom, one-bath with satellite TV, Wi-Fi, air-conditioning, ceiling fans, and a fully stocked refrigerator complete with continental breakfast each morning. The other suites are two-bedroom with one and a half baths with whirlpool tubs in addition to the other amenities. Repeat guests have praised the comfort, cleanliness, and superb location in their reviews. The suites give the feel of having your own apartment mere steps away from Charleston's charms. Native Charlestonians Tradd and Weesie Newton are the proprietors here and have a reputation for quality hospitality offerings with close attention to detail. (Read about their **Fleet Landing Restaurant** in our Restaurants chapter.)

i When negotiating your way through Charleston streets, you may encounter several street names that Charlestonians choose to pronounce in their own inimitable fashion. Here's a quick translation: If somebody mentions "Le-GREE" Street, it's Legare Street. And when directed to Hasell Street, note it is called "Hazel."

✴ZERO WATER STREET   **$$$$$**
31 East Battery
(843) 723-2841
www.zerowaterstreet.com
Zero Water Street is actually a quiet, private entrance to 31 East Battery, one of Charleston's classic mansion houses built on the Battery in 1836. Water Street is in the very heart of the old city's historic district, and 31 East Battery directly overlooks Charleston Harbor and Fort Sumter. Your room (with its private bath) and

the adjoining piazza will offer spectacular views. The guest suite has 12-foot ceilings, air-conditioning, private telephone, cable TV, wireless Internet, and off-street parking. A continental plus breakfast is provided either in your room or in the lovely Victorian garden with its antique play house. Children over age 12 are welcome. A 2-night minimum is required. No credit cards.

INNS

Many inns in Charleston offer some of the same personalized touches that make the bed-and-breakfasts special, but on a larger scale. Most, but not all, operate in modernized facilities either renovated or built specifically for lodging. You can usually expect a great deal of charm along with complimentary continental breakfast, afternoon wine or sherry, and evening turndown service. What distinguishes one from another is location, authenticity of decor, trendy amenities, and management style. Prices per night vary with the seasons, and our price guides reflect the same coding ranges and caveats used for the bed-and-breakfasts. Unless otherwise indicated, all addresses are in Charleston.

ANCHORAGE INN $$$$
26 Vendue Range
(843) 723-8300, (800) 421-2952
www.anchorageinncharleston.com
Close to the Waterfront Park and some of Charleston's best restaurants, this fascinating luxury inn is one of the city's premier accommodations. While so much of Charleston revisits the 18th century, this inn replicates the ambience of a 17th-century English coachman inn. Every detail is delightfully conceived—period antiques and one-of-a-kind handcrafted reproductions, made specifically for the inn. Deluxe Hot Continental Breakfast is

served in the dining room. Afternoon wine and cheese is offered, and guests enjoy evening sherry and turndown service at night. There are 2 suites included in the inn's 19 rooms, and 4 rooms have Jacuzzi tubs. Complimentary high-speed wireless Internet access and concierge services are conveniences here as well. Ample parking is available in the city garage (with guest rates) just to the rear of the inn.

ANDREW PINCKNEY INN $$$$–$$$$$
40 Pinckney St.
(843) 937-8800, (800) 505-8983
www.andrewpinckneyinn.com
The Andrew Pinckney Inn is at the corner of Church and Pinckney Streets on the very edge of Charleston's historic Market. All of the Market's famous diversions—quaint shops, craft stalls, nightclubs, and fine restaurants—are nearby. Even the horse-drawn carriage tours are just a few steps away. The recently remodeled and expanded inn features a rooftop garden terrace for catching Lowcountry sunsets, and the attentive concierge service can arrange special golf and fitness packages on request. A continental breakfast is part of the package, and all rooms feature handsome antique-style furnishings. There's even a fully equipped conference room available for business or group travelers.

✳ANSONBOROUGH INN $$$–$$$$
21 Hasell St.
(843) 723-1655, (800) 522-2073
www.ansonboroughinn.com
The award-winning Ansonborough Inn is at the end of Hasell Street off East Bay. There are 37 suites that have been cleverly fashioned out of a turn-of-the-century warehouse. Heart-of-pine exposed beams (measuring 12 inches by 12 feet) and locally made red brick have been incorporated into the decor to give

the inn a remarkably warm feeling, even with its magnificent 16- and 18-foot ceilings. The facility's 3 floors are wheelchair-accessible and surround an open central atrium. The suites are equipped with full kitchens, and some have lofts. There's an on-site English-style pub and rooftop bar. Guests receive complimentary afternoon wine and a 24-hour monitored parking lot is available. One favorite amenity is the continental breakfast with fresh-baked breads. Choose from banana, apple-raisin, and blueberry muffins delivered each morning from Saffron, a popular bakery just down the street (see the Restaurants chapter). The business traveler is treated to multiple dataports, wireless Internet, and on-site conference facilities.

ELLIOTT HOUSE INN   **$$$$**
78 Queen St.
(843) 723-1855
www.elliotthouseinn.com
Elliott House is next to the popular 82 Queen restaurant (see the Restaurants chapter) and across the street from the Mills House Hotel. This is life as it should be in the refined fast lane—breakfast served on silver service, afternoon champagne in the courtyard, and a heated Jacuzzi at night. Guests stay in one of 24 air-conditioned rooms, complete with Oriental rugs and period furniture. Since 82 Queen draws a big (but respectable) crowd to its bar, the action is just a few strides away for Elliott House guests. Complimentary bicycles are available for exploring the neighborhood, and parking is across the street in a city garage.

FRENCH QUARTER INN   **$$$$**
166 Church St.
(843) 722-1900, (866) 812-1900
www.fqicharleston.com

Located in Charleston's original French Quarter district in the historic Market and Church Streets area, this independent offering opened in Jan 2002.

There are 50 rooms and suites elegantly appointed with an eclectic array of French pieces, Provençal beds, European-style bed dressings, and a pillow menu of seven different comfort choices. Some of the rooms feature working fireplaces, whirlpool tubs, and balconies overlooking the festive Market area. Amenities include silver service breakfast in the room, afternoon wine and cheese, turndown service, and complimentary 24-hour coffee, tea, and snacks. Valet laundry and parking is part of the upscale service.

Last-Minute Reservation

If you arrive in Charleston without reservations, help is available at the **Charleston Visitor Reception and Transportation Center** at 375 Meeting St. Open daily from 8:30 a.m. to 5:30 p.m., the visitor center offers help finding rooms at inns, hotels, and motels in the Greater Charleston area. This is, in effect, a clearinghouse of last-minute accommodations and a real life-saver for those impromptu visitors to the city. Later in the business day, these rooms are often offered at discounted rates. The desk personnel cannot secure reservations for you via phone; you must be there in person. They can, however, make a room reservation using your credit card once you're there.

FULTON LANE INN $$$$–$$$$$
202 King St.
(843) 720-2600, (800) 720-2688
www.fultonlaneinn.com

This cozy inn is a nonsmoking facility nestled just off King Street in the heart of Charleston's fascinating antiques district. Built post–Civil War by Confederate blockade runner John Rugheimer, the inn is a fascinating taste of a time gone by. The 45 rooms are decorated in Southern plantation style, and some feature fireplaces, king-size canopy beds, luxury baths, and whirlpool tubs. Nightly turndown service and a continental breakfast delivered on silver service are part of the hospitality here. Public parking is available just outside the door. This inn is part of the Charming Inns of Charleston group.

THE GOVERNOR'S
HOUSE INN $$$$$
117 Broad St.
(843) 720-2070, (800) 720-9812
www.governorshouse.com

Built in 1760 by John Laurens, this is the oldest house in Charleston currently being used as a bed-and-breakfast. Edward Rutledge, the youngest signer of the Declaration of Independence and once governor of South Carolina (1798–1800), lived here. Today, the house boasts 11 elegantly appointed guest rooms. The Grand rooms feature 12-foot ceilings with fireplaces and private verandas. The Roofscape room provides lovely views over the area's historic architecture. The Kitchen House suite has a separate living room, private porch, wet bar, and an original 1760 fireplace. A Southern gourmet breakfast is served, as are afternoon tea and evening sherry. The location is ideal from several standpoints. You're at the edge of the original Grand Modell city and today's prestigious Below Broad residential area, and you're within easy walking distance of King Street's shopping and antiques district.

HARBOURVIEW INN $$$$
2 Vendue Range
(843) 853-8439, (888) 853-8439
www.harbourviewcharleston.com

This is one of Charleston's best luxury inns right in the heart of the downtown historic district. Its location, directly across from Waterfront Park, is one attraction. The 52 high-end, luxury rooms and suites close to the area's many fine restaurants, shops, galleries, and nightclubs are another. The inn, with its handsome nautical appointments throughout, offers nightly turndown service, elegant in-room continental breakfast, all day snacks, and afternoon refreshments in the atrium. Top-floor rooms have spectacular views over Charleston Harbor—hard to find on the Peninsula. Ask about the "Celebrate Romance" package for a special weekend with your significant other.

INDIGO INN $$$$
1 Maiden Lane
(843) 577-5900, (800) 845-7639
www.indigoinn.com

The Indigo Inn fronts on Meeting Street and is across from a bustling shopping and restaurant district not far from Charleston Place. The 3-story inn has 40 rooms around a private courtyard and fountain, and it prides itself on impeccable service. The traditionally decorated rooms feature massive four-poster beds and evoke a plantation atmosphere. A hunt (continental-plus) breakfast and the morning paper are complimentary, as is the on-site parking, a blessing in the heart of the city. Well-behaved pets are welcomed at an additional charge.

THE JASMINE HOUSE $$$$$
64 Hasell St.
(843) 577-5900, (800) 845-7639
www.jasminehouseinn.com

This classic Greek Revival (1843) mansion sits in the historic Ansonborough neighborhood, between the Market and Gaillard Auditorium. Six guest rooms are in the main house and feature 14-foot ceilings, Italian marble baths, and original architectural details. Four others in the carriage house open onto the private courtyard and Jacuzzi area and have charming brick floors and second-level piazzas. Guests enjoy a hot continental-plus breakfast and complimentary parking. Rooms in the main house are handsomely decorated in themes appropriate to the period of the house and Charleston's pre-Civil War heyday. Check-in is handled at the sister property, Indigo Inn, at the corner of Maiden Lane and Meeting Street.

*JOHN RUTLEDGE HOUSE INN $$$$–$$$$$
116 Broad St.
(843) 723-7999, (800) 476-9741
www.johnrutledgehouseinn.com

Built in 1763 by John Rutledge, a signer of the US Constitution, the house at 116 Broad St. has been completely renovated and transformed (as part of a three-building complex) into a swank inn with 19 rooms in all. The house is a designated National Historic Landmark, and the National Trust for Historic Preservation named it among the top 32 Historic Hotels of America for good reason. George Washington himself had breakfast here and was one of many patriots, statesmen, and presidents who came to call on Mr. Rutledge. The main residence contains elaborate parquet floors, Italian marble mantels, and molded plaster ceilings. Rooms have been modernized to

include private baths, refrigerators, televisions, and individual climate controls. Afternoon tea is served in the ballroom, and evening turndown service includes chocolates at bedside. Continental breakfast and a newspaper are delivered to guests each morning. The Rutledge House is dog friendly for an additional fee. This inn is part of the Charming Inns of Charleston group.

KINGS COURTYARD INN $$$$–$$$$$
198 King St.
(843) 723-7000, (800) 845-6119
www.kingscourtyardinn.com

The Kings Courtyard Inn has an interesting history in that the building has come full circle in its lifetime. The Greek Revival building, dating from 1853, began as an inn catering to 19th-century plantation owners and businessmen. Then it was a private residence; after that, the downstairs housed some of Charleston's most fashionable shops; and now it once again serves guests with luxury accommodations. The inn, with its garden oasis, is nestled among many fine antiques shops on King Street.

Rooms and suites are modernized with air-conditioning and private baths, and no two are exactly alike. Some offer canopy beds; others feature fireplaces, and many offer views of a lovely courtyard below. Wine or sherry is provided upon arrival. You may expect a continental breakfast and a newspaper delivered to you each morning, or you can have breakfast in the courtyards or the breakfast room. Guests may order from a menu if they like. One of our favorite details at the Kings Courtyard is the garden spa, used by guests year-round. Cocktails are available in the courtyard bar, and brandy is provided each evening on the first floor. This inn is part of the Charming Inns of Charleston group.

MEETING STREET INN $$$$–$$$$$
173 Meeting St.
(843) 723-1882, (800) 842-8022
www.meetingstreetinn.com

In the heart of the city on bustling Meeting Street, this is a convenient option for a Charleston inn experience. The front portion of the inn is over 140 years old, while the back section is a recent addition. Four-poster rice beds in every room add to the 19th-century ambience of this elegant accommodation, convenient to many fine restaurants, antiques shops, and the colorful City Market area. Continental breakfast may be taken in your room or out in the courtyard. The courtyard's heated Jacuzzi is popular with guests any time of the day. Afternoons at the Meeting Street Inn include complimentary seasonal refreshments and bar service in the lobby. Evening turndown service means a freshened-up room and bath plus a delicious chocolate on your bedtime pillow.

✳MIDDLETON INN $$$$
4290 Ashley River Rd.
(843) 556-0500, (800) 543-4774
www.theinnatmiddletonplace.com

In our estimation, Middleton Inn is the kind of place you really want to write home about. Situated on the grounds of one of the most beautiful and historic plantations in the South, Middleton Inn overlooks the Ashley River and the nation's oldest landscaped gardens and is just 14 miles from downtown Charleston. Guests have access to the nature trails, gardens, house museum, and stableyards. You'll also find an outdoor pool, horseback riding, bicycling, kayaking, and an on-site cafe for continental breakfast. Middleton Place's famous restaurant is just a stroll away through the woods. The facility itself is of national award-winning

design, contemporary and starkly modern in its simplicity. It has 55 rooms with charming fireplaces and European baths. (See the Attractions chapter for more about Middleton Place.)

PLANTERS INN $$$$–$$$$$
112 North Market St.
(843) 722-2345, (800) 845-7082
www.plantersinn.com

As charming and roomy as an antebellum Charleston home, this inn has a European flavor and an understated elegance that radiates quality. It came as no surprise to us some years back when Planters Inn captured Lodging Hospitality magazine's first-place award in the guest room category. From four-poster beds to mahogany armoires, authentic Charleston reproductions are showcased in spacious rooms with traditional high ceilings. The inn is in the colorful City Market area and is home to the popular **Peninsula Grill** (see the Restaurants and Nightlife chapters). Silver-service breakfast is delivered to your room and a gourmet breakfast is served in the dining room. A nightly turndown service sends you sweet dreams with a chocolate and a weather card to plan tomorrow's activities. Parking is available—a rarity for this busy location.

VENDUE INN $$$$–$$$$$
19 Vendue Range
(843) 577-7970, (800) 845-7900
www.vendueinn.com

Situated between East Bay Street and the famous "walk through" fountain of Waterfront Park is this upscale European-style inn with one of the best reputations going for fine service and attention to detail. There are 65 rooms and suites in all—each one carefully furnished with authentic antiques and 18th-century reproductions. Junior and deluxe suites offer gas fireplaces, marble baths, separate showers, and whirlpool tubs. Deluxe suites even go so far as to include separate living rooms, stocked wet bars, and fresh fruit baskets. A rooftop terrace and bar offer one of the best views in the city (see the Nightlife chapter), and the Vendue's on-site restaurant, the **Library,** is one of Charleston's intimate dining adventures. Guests start the day with a complimentary Southern breakfast buffet or enjoy a continental breakfast in their room. Business travelers will find two-line phones as well as wireless Internet in every room, making computer hook-ups easy. Wine and cheese in the Garden Room is available every afternoon. The Vendue Inn is a pet friendly hotel.

✳WENTWORTH MANSION $$$$$
149 Wentworth St.
(843) 853-1886, (888) INN-1886
www.wentworthmansion.com

This elegantly refurbished inn was built from 1885 to 1887 as one of Charleston's few great Victorian townhomes. Articulated in what is called the Second Empire style of architecture (after a French fashion popularized during the reign of Napoleon), it was originally the private estate of Francis Silas Rodgers. Rodgers was a Charleston cotton merchant who made a fortune in phosphate after the Civil War. His mansion survives today as the city's most opulent ode to the long-lost Gilded Age of Innocence. Remarkably unchanged, the property features 21 rooms and suites individually decorated and furnished with 19th-century antiques. All rooms have king-size beds and baths with oversize whirlpool tubs. Most have working gas fireplaces.

Guests enjoy the mansion's common rooms such as the Rodgers Library, the Harleston Parlor, and the atrium-like Sun Porch—where guests savor leisurely elegant breakfasts, afternoon teas, and evening wine and hors d'oeuvres. Local guides lead guests on tours of the city, and an on-site fine dining restaurant, **Circa 1886,** offers seasonal specialties. (See the Restaurants chapter.) With its private spa, Wentworth Mansion brings a whole new level of service to Charleston's already renowned tradition of unparalleled hospitality.

✳WOODLANDS RESORT & INN $$$$$
125 Parsons Rd., Summerville
(843) 875-2600, (800) 774-9999
www.woodlandsinn.com

Although this upscale option is beyond the geographic boundaries of this listing, it is so extraordinary that it should not be overlooked. Woodlands Resort & Inn is a unique venue in the best tradition of the English country house hotel, only this one has a decidedly Southern flair. The 42-acre estate now called Woodlands was once the winter retreat (ca. 1906) of a wealthy Northern industrialist. Today it is a 19-room luxury inn and conference center with English red-clay tennis courts, a croquet lawn, heated pool, and upscale spa facility. Each room is handsomely appointed and stocked with thoughtful personal amenities ranging from heated towel racks to fresh-cut flowers and soothing glycerine soaps. The inn's on-site spa offers special pamperings such as therapeutic massage, herbal wraps, and facial masks.

Perhaps best of all is the Woodlands dining experience. Their Five Star culinary team has consistently earned rave reviews from local and international food critics alike. They call the cuisine "contemporary regional American," but we call it unforgettable.

Summerville is 30 minutes from downtown Charleston via I-26 (see the Day Trips chapter), and many Charlestonians plan mini-vacations to Woodlands just as their ancestors did a century ago when Summerville offered a pine-cooled retreat from Charleston's muggy humidity.

> **i** Vacationers to Kiawah and Seabrook islands can take advantage of the seasonal fresh fruits and vegetables grown on Johns Island and sold by vendors in roadside stands along Bohicket Road. Rosebank Farms is one of these, and Newton Farms supermarket (at the southern end of Betsy Kerrison Parkway) offers the gourmet version.

VACATION & BEACH RENTALS

Beach rentals, especially those on the barrier islands of Kiawah, Seabrook, Sullivan's Island, Isle of Palms (home of Wild Dunes Resort), and Folly Beach, are considered a real estate specialty here in the Lowcountry.

AVOCET PROPERTIES
38 Center St., Folly Beach
(843) 588-6699, (800) 951-2470
www.avocetproperties.net
This company has a new name but has handled real estate for over 18 years in the West Ashley area. Avocet focuses on vacation rentals, property management, and real estate sales on Folly Beach with friendly, reliable service. Its office is in the first 2-story building you'll see on Center Street as you come off the bridge to the island. It offers a wide variety of accommodations ranging from the casual basics to oceanfront luxury condominiums and homes. The company hopes to be your "key to a lifetime of

memories." Write or call for a brochure of Folly Beach properties.

BEACHWALKER RENTALS
140 Gardener's Circle, Johns Island
(843) 768-1777, (800) 334-6308
www.beachwalker.com
This independent resort-rental company specializes in Kiawah and Seabrook Island vacations. With more than two decades of experience, the company has built a solid reputation for value and friendly service. Many loyal families return to Beachwalker year after year, with these folks handling all the arrangements from bike rentals to golf. Call for the annual catalog of beachfront and nearby properties, and ask about the off-season discounts. Online booking is available on the website.

CARROLL REALTY
103 Palm Blvd., Isle of Palms
(843) 886-9600, (800) 845-7718
www.carrollrealtyinc.com
This firm, which started in 1981, specializes in the sale and rental of resort homes on Isle of Palms, including Wild Dunes, and Sullivan's Island. Its offices are between the islands on Palm Boulevard.

DUNES PROPERTIES OF CHARLESTON
31 Center St., Folly Beach
(843) 588-3800, (800) 476-8734
www.dunesproperties.com
Specializing in coastal real estate and vacation rentals, Dunes Properties of Charleston has been doing business in the Lowcountry since 1989. They handle rentals only on Folly Beach. About half this company's business comes from repeat customers who use its services year after year. Vacation planners can request Dunes Properties' annual

catalog describing rental listings or view them online.

FRED HOLLAND REALTY
50 Center St., Folly Beach
(843) 588-2325
www.fredhollandrealty.com
Experience is the key word for Fred Holland Realty when it comes to Folly Beach real estate and rentals. The company has been finding vacation homes for Folly visitors for more than 30 years. It handles a range of beach rentals from two- and three-bedroom condos to oceanside beach houses and even small apartments. The agents also arrange many long-term (yearly) leases annually. About 65 percent of their business is repeat customers coming back for more. The spring brochure features the year's offerings for summer rentals. Call for more information.

ISLAND REALTY
1304 Palm Blvd., Isle of Palms
(843) 886-8144, (877) 250-7743
www.islandrealty.com
Since 1977, this firm has been a major player in property sales and resort rentals on Isle of Palms (at Wild Dunes), Dewees Island, and Sullivan's Island. It also has a beachfront meeting and convention center with resort amenities available and golf packages at Wild Dunes. Island Realty's large staff prides itself on meeting your vacation needs.

PAM HARRINGTON EXCLUSIVES
4343 Betsy Kerrison Pkwy., Johns Island
(843) 768-0273, (800) 845-6966
www.kiawahexclusives.com
This company, with headquarters just before the traffic circle leading to Kiawah and Seabrook, does a lion's share of business on Kiawah Island. It's been helping visitors secure luxury accommodations and premium real estate on Kiawah, Seabrook, and Johns Island since 1978. For sales information, call (843) 768-3635.

RESORT QUEST
1400 Palm Blvd., Isle of Palms
(843) 886-9704, (800) 870-4078
www.greatbeach.com
This company offers rental homes, cottages, and villas on Wild Dunes, Isle of Palms, Sullivan's Island, Kiawah Island, and Seabrook Island. More than 700 offerings of accommodations are available ranging in size from one to nine bedrooms (depending on the island). Golf packages and kids' programs are available. The yearly catalogue of rental listings is free upon request. A second location is at Two Beachwalker Dr., Kiawah Island (843-768-2300, 800-554-8222), or call (800) 742-2532 (843-821-7101 locally) for Seabrook Island rentals.

RESTAURANTS

Believe it or not, you won't have to go very far to find a Charlestonian who will tell you that as recently as 25 years ago there were only a few white tablecloth restaurants in the entire city. That seems incredible today, when there are easily two dozen truly fine dining options to choose from on any given evening out on the town.

With the revitalization of our downtown area and the draw of people to all places South, there has been an accompanying influx of outstanding new culinary talent and the interest to match. In fact, Charleston has been home to some of the country's most respected culinary institutions. This deepens the talent pool for dining establishments all over the Lowcountry. Now establishments and styles fit almost every whim while making a true effort to share and preserve the traditional cuisine of the Lowcountry. We have included information, typical fare, and opinions in this chapter that may help you with your selections. Menu items are frequently seasonal and subject to change.

OVERVIEW

The list here is not exhaustive but gives, we feel, a fair representation of what is available on the downtown Peninsula, in Mount Pleasant, on the islands east of the Cooper, and in the areas and islands west of the Ashley River. Not included in our descriptions are the familiar national restaurant chains. Eateries are categorized by type of food offered. Bear in mind that many of the downtown restaurants are housed in old and historic buildings that may not be wheelchair accessible. If that's an issue for you or your party, it's always good to call ahead.

Whatever your budget, we feel confident you'll find in the following listings the perfect setting for enjoying Lowcountry meals that will augment your stay in the Trident area.

Price Code

The reference guide should be used to translate the average price ranges of dinner for two persons, minus cocktails, wine, or gratuity. We caution that prices, hours, menus, and means of payment are frequently subject to change, so if you have any doubts about an important issue, call ahead. Since most restaurants will accept cash, traveler's checks, and all major credit cards (but almost never personal checks), we inform you only of those establishments that do not take plastic.

Here are our breakdowns for average entree prices for two and the correlating symbols.

$	Less than $20
$$	$20 to $35
$$$	$35 to $60
$$$$	More than $60

Locklear's Fine Seafood, Mount Pleasant, Seafood, $$, 87

Long Island Cafe, Isle of Palms, Delis & Cafes, $$, 71

Magnolias Uptown/Down South, Charleston, Lowcountry Cuisine, $$$, 78

Marina Variety Store & Restaurant, Charleston, Seafood, $$, 88

McCrady's, Charleston, Nouvelle American, $$$–$$$$, 82

The Med Bistro, West Ashley, Delis & Cafes, $–$$, 71

Mellow Mushroom, Charleston, Pizza, $–$$, 84

Melvin's Southern BBQ & Ribs, Mount Pleasant, Barbecue, $, 68

Mercato, Charleston, Italian, $$, 76

Metto Coffee & Tea, Mount Pleasant, Delis & Cafes, $, 71

Miyabi Japanese Steak House, West Ashley, Asian, $$–$$$, 67

Mustard Seed, Mount Pleasant, American, $$, 64

Noisy Oyster, Charleston, Seafood, $$–$$$, 88

Oak Steakhouse, Charleston, Steakhouses, $$$–$$$$, 90

The Ocean Room, Kiawah Island, Nouvelle American, $$$$, 83

Old Towne Restaurant, Charleston, Greek & Mediterranean, $$, 74

Old Village Post House, Mount Pleasant, Lowcountry Cuisine, $$–$$$, 79

The Palmetto Cafe, Charleston, Delis & Cafes, $$$, 72

Peninsula Grill, Charleston, Nouvelle American, $$$–$$$$, 83

Poogan's Porch, Charleston, Lowcountry Cuisine, $$–$$$, 79

Queen Anne's Revenge, Daniel Island, American, $$–$$$, 64

Red's Ice House, Mount Pleasant, Seafood, $$, 88

Rosebank Farms Cafe, Seabrook Island, Lowcountry Cuisine, $$–$$$, 79

Saffron Cafe & Bakery, Charleston, Delis & Cafes, $–$$, 72

Sea Biscuit Cafe, Isle of Palms, Delis & Cafes, $, 72

Sea Island Grill, Isle of Palms, Nouvelle American, $$–$$$, 83

Sermet's Corner, Charleston, Greek & Mediterranean, $$, 74

Shem Creek Bar & Grill, Mount Pleasant, Seafood, $$, 88

Slightly North of Broad, Charleston, Lowcountry Cuisine, $$–$$$, 80

Starfish Grille, Seabrook Island, American, $$, 64

Station 22, Sullivan's Island, Isle of Palms, West Cooper, Seafood, $$–$$$, 89

Sticky Fingers, Mount Pleasant, Barbecue, $–$$, 68

Sullivan's On the Island, Sullivan's Island, American, $$, 65

Sunfire Grill and Bistro, West Ashley, American, $$–$$$, 65

Sushi Hiro, Charleston, Asian, $–$$, 67

T-Bonz Gill & Grill, West Ashley, American, $–$$, 65

39 Rue de Jean, Charleston, French, $$–$$$, 73

Tommy Condon's Irish Pub and Seafood Restaurant, Charleston, Irish, $–$$, 75

Toast, Charleston, American, $$, 65

Triangle Char & Bar, West Ashley, American, $–$$, 66

Trotters Restaurant, West Ashley, American, $$, 66

Vickery's Bar & Grill, Mount Pleasant, American, $$–$$$, 66

Water's Edge, Mount Pleasant, Seafood, $$$, 89

Wild Wing Cafe, Charleston, Delis & Cafes, $, 72

The Wreck of Richard and Charlene, Mount Pleasant, Seafood, $$, 89

Ye Ole Fashioned Ice Cream and Sandwich Cafe, West Ashley, Delis & Cafes, $, 73

AMERICAN

ALEX'S RESTAURANT $
302 Coleman Blvd., Mount Pleasant
(843) 881-7714
www.alexsrestaurants.com
Open 24 hours a day, this Alex's is a popular spot for breakfast on the way to the beach or a late-night meal on the way home. Recently, the Sunday lunch crowd has been thick too. The restaurant is large and attractive, and draws locals as well as visitors to the area. You can't beat its standard bacon, eggs, and biscuits with plenty of hot joe. Other Alex's Restaurants are scattered throughout Greater Charleston, with a location in North Charleston at 3713 Dorchester Rd. (843-747-9198), and in Summerville at 522 N. Magnolia St. (843-871-3202).

CALIFORNIA DREAMING
RESTAURANT AND BAR $–$$
1 Ashley Pointe Dr.
(843) 766-1644
www.californiadreamings.com
You can go to California Dreaming by car or by boat (yes, you can tie up at a dock), and it's always an adventure. The kids pretend it's an old fort (although it isn't), and the views of the Ashley River are mesmerizing. The restaurant and the bar do an incredible, nonstop business year-round. The interior is colorfully decorated with flags and divided into two dining levels, with seating for 260 (and the place is often full). The little ones are welcome and can order nonalcoholic drinks (such as a blue concoction called a Smurf) and food from a special menu. Patrons really go crazy for the soft, buttery croissants and the house salad (topped with eggs, almonds, ham, and bacon—almost a meal in itself). The twice-baked potato is another big hit. All

fish is fresh and local, and the burgers, ribs, and "Pittsburgh-style" steaks are popular. A decadent dessert list includes the fabulous house special—apple walnut cinnamon pie. Lunch and dinner are served every day, and hours are extended on weekend nights. Reservations are suggested. (See the West Ashley section of the Nightlife chapter.)

EASTERBY'S FAMILY GRILLE $$
2388 Ashley River Rd.
(843) 556-5707
Easterby's on Ashley River Road (SR 61) is a comfortable, affordable place for casual dining and local seafood. It's a popular lunch stop for tourists heading out to the plantations along the highway (see our Attractions chapter). Dinner patrons enjoy the same seafood (fried or not), steaks, and pastas, she-crab soup, catfish stew, shrimp creole, and soft-shell crabs. Spirits are available, and reservations are not necessary unless you're in a large group. Lunch and dinner are served Mon through Sat until 10 p.m.

FISCHER'S SPORTS PUB & GRILL $
1883 Andell Bluff Blvd., Johns Island
(843) 243-0210
If Ernest Hemingway were alive today, you'd find him at Fischer's. This authentic, family-owned pub at the Bohicket Marina is a perfect place to rub shoulders with the locals. Come in flip-flops straight from the beach and enjoy the best fried shrimp/oyster baskets anywhere around; even the french fries are exceptional. Whether you're watching the game on the big-screen TVs, shooting a round of pool, or just throwing back a cold beverage, Fischer's is a hangout you'll enjoy frequenting any day of the week from 11:30 a.m. to 2 a.m.

FONDUELY YOURS $$
853 Coleman Blvd., Mount Pleasant
(843) 849-6859

It is safe to say that Fonduely Yours is a one-of-a-kind dining experience in this area. As the name suggests, this restaurant specializes in fondues. Try cheese, vegetable, seafood, teriyaki, and sirloin fondues, and don't miss the chocolate fondue for dessert. The food is tasty, and the whole concept is lots of fun. With fondue, you're the chef, and you do the cooking right at your table. Dinner is served each evening starting at 5:30 until 9:30 p.m., Fri and Sat until 11 p.m.

*MUSTARD SEED $$
1036 Chuck Dawley Blvd., Mount Pleasant
(843) 849-0050
www.dinewithsal.com

This simple, yet sophisticated, eatery is a big hit with the vegetarian crowd—although the Mustard Seed offers pork and seafood, too. Clearly, not everyone who frequents "the Seed" has abandoned beef; they simply enjoy the varied and creative menu offered here. In addition to a regular menu, there's a blackboard with daily specials that shows why there's sometimes a waiting line out the door. The artichoke, spinach, and Parmesan fritters are one example. The huge and authentic Greek salad is another. Desserts are very special, too. The coconut cream cake and chocolate cream pie are superb. A conservative but adequate wine list keeps customers amused if, in fact, a short wait is necessary. Be patient; it's worth it, and the food is a good value, too. Lunch is Mon through Sat 11 a.m. to 2:30 p.m. Dinner is served from 5 to 9:30 p.m. on weekdays and to 10 p.m. on weekends. Additional locations are at 1970 Maybank Hwy. (843-762-0072)

and 101 North Main St., Summerville (843-821-7101).

QUEEN ANNE'S REVENGE $$–$$$
160-B Fairchild St., Daniel Island
(843) 216-6868
www.qarevenge.com

Beside the Hampton Inn on Daniel Island is this unique steak and seafood restaurant that's a cross between a pirate museum and an upscale eatery. Don't mistake this for a theme restaurant; this is all about fine food. But the setting just happens to be the home of a rare and fascinating collection of art and artifacts reflecting the golden age of piracy—once very much a part of the Charleston scene. Among the armor, rapiers, and blunderbusses handsomely displayed, the food is served fresh with flair and style. The pan-roasted mussels in garlic white wine sauce are as good as any from Chesapeake Bay. The barbecue ribs fall off the bone, and the steaks are equally well prepared. Of course, a full array of fresh seafood entrees is offered nightly. Because the atmosphere is so interesting, this is a good choice for family dining, and a children's menu is available. It's open for lunch and dinner 7 days a week. Grown-ups will enjoy the roomy bar, where life-size pirates Stede Bonnet and Blackbeard sit and plot their next raid on hapless Charlestonians.

STARFISH GRILLE $$
520 Folly Rd.
(843) 762-9252
www.starfishgrille.com

This attractive little bistro is located in the Merchant Village Shopping Center on Folly Road. The restaurant's digs sport a strictly casual feeling. The Grille offers a full gamut of sandwiches, salads, and pasta dishes.

Appetizers include Greek-style shrimp with angel hair pasta and feta and grilled salmon salad. Entrees range from Carolina crab cakes to smoky pulled pork terrine. Of course, there's always a fresh catch of the day. The place is open for lunch and dinner every day of the week. It's a pleasant option for Sunday brunch, too. No reservations are required, but call ahead for parties of 6 or more. There's a full bar with ample varieties of beer and a limited wine list by the glass. Don't forget the appealing array of frozen and dessert drinks.

SULLIVAN'S ON THE ISLAND $$
2019 Middle St., Sullivan's Island
(843) 883-3222
www.sullivansrestaurant.com
A favorite with the islanders and others in the know, Sullivan's is a family restaurant with affordable, good food. Not fancy, Sullivan's is just what the regulars want—a place to order delicious, traditional specials that include steaks, burgers, shrimp and grits, or oysters and scallops with a veggie and dessert for less than $20. Dinner is served every day starting at 5 p.m. There is a children's menu, and Sunday brunch is served from 11 a.m. to 2 p.m.

SUNFIRE GRILL AND BISTRO $$–$$$
1090 Sam Rittenberg Blvd.
(843) 766-0223
www.sunfiregrill.com
The white tablecloth dining options in West Ashley are somewhat limited. That's why it's good to know there's Sunfire Grill and Bistro on Sam Rittenberg Boulevard across from the Park Center office complex. This trendy restaurant and pub is popular with business folk at lunch and locals after work and when the dinner hour comes. The salad

bar is plentiful and fresh. But more ambitious appetites are well-served by entrees like their lowcountry crab cakes with a lemon-caper sauce. Steaks, chops, chicken, and daily specials round out the menu offered Mon through Sun. The after-church crowd enjoys their Sunday brunch.

T-BONZ GILL & GRILL $–$$
1668 Old Towne Rd.
(843) 556-2478
www.tbonz.com
Another vibrant, happening spot with a couple of locations throughout the city, T-Bonz serves a wonderful filet mignon (when you say rare, they take you at your word) as well as fresh gourmet burgers, and even seafood. There's plenty of beer on tap, including T-Bonz' own custom-brewed ales like "Cooper River Red" and "Market Street Wheat." Photographs of regular customers and Western paraphernalia adorn the walls, and you can't miss the enormous painting of the renegade cowboys on horseback. Regular customers order side veggies (sautéed and delicious) and feel comfortable having the kids along. Takeout is another option. They're ropin' 'em in for lunch and dinner 7 days a week. A second location is at 80 North Market St. (843-577-2511).

TOAST $$
155 Meeting St.
(843) 534-0043
www.toastofcharleston.com
Toast has accomplished an alchemy that few Charleston restaurants have been able to achieve. Here's a simple, convenient, friendly place to get an amazingly hearty breakfast, lunch, or dinner that's unpretentious, yet creatively prepared and, best of all, affordable. Toast is that rare find that's become almost

extinct in downtown Charleston. The chalk-board outside the door lists an array of daily specials that are American and Lowcountry favorites. Look for coconut and pineapple to add zest to the fare. Come hungry; portions are generous. Toast is open daily starting at 6:30 a.m. for those who want to get an early jump on the day.

TRIANGLE CHAR & BAR $-$$
828 Savannah Hwy.
(843) 377-1300
www.trianglecharandbar.com

With its 2-story-tall windows, the Triangle Char & Bar is a fun, open place to meet friends for an evening meal or just to enjoy the great desserts, cordials, and specialty coffees at the bar. Situated on a triangular piece of land between Savannah Highway and Magnolia Road, it offers plenty of out-side seating for pleasant summer evenings. From the live charcoal grill, you can order from the daily specials that may include fresh fish, chicken, pork, or steaks. Don't miss the chicken liver appetizer with creamed corn and Tasso gravy over grits. Sandwich favor-ites include the fish tacos and the classic cuban. Sunday brunch is from 11 a.m. to 3 p.m. Dinner is served Mon through Sat start-ing at 4:30 p.m., and lunch runs from 11 a.m. to 2 p.m. (See the Nightlife chapter.)

TROTTERS RESTAURANT $$
2008 Savannah Hwy.
(843) 571-1000
www.thetownandcountryinn.com

Trotters Restaurant, in the Town & Country Inn, is a good find for an all-out buffet—breakfast and lunch as well as weekend seafood spreads. Sunday brunch is popu-lar with the after-church crowd. The buffet table always groans with a wide selection of meats, seafood, vegetables, and desserts. There's no Saturday lunch or Sunday dinner, but Trotters is open for all other meals every day. (See the West Ashley section of the Accommodations chapter.)

VICKERY'S BAR & GRILL $$-$$$
1313 Shrimp Boat Lane (Shem Creek),
Mount Pleasant
(843) 884-4440
www.vickerys.com

Vickery's Bar & Grill is on Shem Creek, and is as talked about for its unusual bar as for its good food. There's always an eclectic bunch of interesting folks to meet—young professionals and rebels with a cause. The fare here is vaguely Cuban, with a Southern twist. The original Vickery's is in Atlanta and has always earned good reviews there. Grab a booth or a table, inside or out, and order a burger (with piping hot, hand-cut fries) or a delicious seafood entree. Vickery's is open for lunch and dinner 7 days a week. (See the Nightlife chapter.)

ASIAN

DRAGON GATE CHINESE
RESTAURANT $
1739 Maybank Hwy., James Island
(843) 795-3398

Dragon Gate, in the James Island Shopping Center, serves authentic Chinese food. It has a full bar and a lunch buffet with all your favorite Chinese dishes, such as sweet-and-sour pork, Szechuan beef, and egg drop soup. The prices are quite reasonable, and takeout and delivery are options here. The restaurant is open Mon through Sun from lunch through late night.

KIM'S KOREAN AND
JAPANESE STEAK HOUSE $$
North Bridge Shopping Center, 1716 Old Towne Rd., SR 171
(843) 571-5100

Kim's Korean and Japanese Steak and Seafood House offers authentic "table show cooking" for dinner 7 days a week. Not only is this a fun experience, but the food is also well prepared and a delight for the palate. Choose either the beef or pork bulgoki with the spicy Korean sauce, a house favorite. Sushi fans will find creative options here too. Takeout is available, and reservations are not required.

MIYABI JAPANESE
STEAK HOUSE $$–$$$
688 Citadel Haven Dr.
(843) 571-6025
www.miyabicharleston.com

This Japanese steak and seafood restaurant rates high on the family entertainment scale because of the hibachi style of tableside preparation and the knife-juggling Japanese chefs. Meals include a light soup, salad, and entree, and the food is consistently good. If you have never experienced this form of dining, be advised you may be sharing grill and dining space with strangers. Try the steak and shrimp for a sample of what the hibachi does for surf and turf. Try the sushi bar if you like yours untouched by the flame. Dinner and drinks are served 7 nights a week, and early-bird specials are common. Call for reservations.

SUSHI HIRO $–$$
298 King St.
(843) 723-3628
www.yadokarisushihiro.com

Sushi Hiro is a small sushi bar nestled between M. Dumas and Ye Old Fashioned Ice Cream & Cafe on King Street. In addition to à la carte sushi, there is a varied appetizer menu including tofu salad, shrimp tempura, and even soft-shell crab. Complete dinners range from chicken or beef teriyaki to a combination sushi plate. If you like your seafood unscathed by the flame, this is the downtown place for Japanese sushi delicacies. In addition to stools around the prep station, there are several freestanding tables for those seeking more privacy. Management does not welcome tank-top-clad patrons. Sushi Hiro is open for lunch and dinner Mon through Sat.

BARBECUE

BESSINGER'S BARBECUE $
1602 Savannah Hwy.
(843) 556-1354
www.bessingersbbq.com

Bessinger's serves tasty Southern meals featuring ribs, chicken, fried catfish, pot roast, and of course their famous barbecue with various sauces. The Southern buffet is a favorite on weekends (Thurs through Sun), as is the next-door sandwich shop, which is open Mon through Sat, late morning to late evening. There's drive-through service when you're on the run. The catering operation, aptly named "When Pigs Fly," can be reached by calling the number above.

FIERY RON'S HOME TEAM BBQ $
1205 Ashley River Rd.
(843) 225-7427
www.hometeambbq.com

Bring up the subject of whose Southern barbecue is best and you can always count on an argument. In fact, we don't even agree on how to spell the subject—but we sure like to eat it. One place getting a lot of business from barbecue lovers is this little gem tucked away West Ashley on SR 61. Fiery Ron's Home Team BBQ, as the name suggests, offers 6 different Fiery Ron's housemade BBQ sauces to fire up your generous plate full of food. Their specialty is Memphis-style dry-rubbed barbecue ribs, chicken, and pork shoulders and all the fixin's that go with them. We're talking Brunswick stew, rib platters (you can order in ½, ¾ or full racks), smoked chicken, collards, squash casserole, mac 'n cheese, poppyseed coleslaw, and cornbread. There are salads, tacos, sandwiches and wraps, and a kid's menu too. This place is nothing fancy, just a BBQ shack/juke joint atmosphere with indoor and outdoor seating and lots of TVs to catch your favorite team in action. Beer, wine, and drink specials help cool down the fire and add to the mix of good food, good music (live bluegrass on Wed or Thurs) and good times. Home Team BBQ is also a caterer, so many folks choose them for parties and family get-togethers where barbecue is a staple. It's open for lunch and dinner Mon through Sat and Sunday brunch. A second location is at 2209 Middle St., Sullivan's Island (843-883-3131).

MELVIN'S SOUTHERN BBQ & RIBS $
925 Houston Northcutt Blvd., Mount Pleasant
(843) 881-0549, (888) 635-8467
www.melvinsbbq.com
The delicious barbecue, cole slaw, onion rings, hamburgers, and vegetables at Melvin's make it a good bet for a quick meal. This has been a Lowcountry outlet for barbecue since 1939. The prices are quite reasonable, too. Melvin's is open Mon through Sat for lunch and dinner. A second location is at 538 Folly Rd. (843-762-0511).

STICKY FINGERS $–$$
341 Johnnie Dodds Blvd., Mount Pleasant
(843) 856-7427, (800) STICKYS (784-2597)
www.stickyfingers.com
If you're a parent, the place to go on Tuesday night is Sticky Fingers. This barbecue restaurant has a special menu and room set up just for kids, so the parents can take advantage of the option of dining alone (or not). Any day (or night, for that matter) is great for ordering Sticky Fingers' famous ribs. They come in about every style possible: Tennessee Whiskey, Carolina Sweet, Memphis, and Texas Style, to name a few. You may even want to take home a bottle of one of their 5 signature barbecue sauces after chowing down here. The eatery also serves chicken, salads, and sandwiches. It offers a full bar and is open 7 days a week for lunch and dinner. Two more locations are at 235 Meeting St. (843-853-7427), and 1200 North Main St., Summerville (843-871-7427).

CAFES & DELIS

BEAR-E-PATCH CAFE $–$$
1980-A Ashley River Rd.
(843) 766-6490
www.bearepatchcafe.com
Every once in a while a simple, affordable, neighborhood restaurant strikes gold with the right combination of good food, generous portions, nice atmosphere, and friendly service. And that's what the Bear-E-Patch has going for it. This relatively small and unpretentious eatery is popular with locals.

The breakfast menu is so hearty and creative with several specials offered daily that it's available until 3 p.m. and makes a dandy lunch. A deli-like lunch menu is offered also, along with grilled burgers and such. But at least one down-home special is right out of Grandma's Lowcountry cookbook. An on-site bakery turns out fresh bread (sourdough is a specialty) and pies, which adds to the allure. Dinner is served Mon through Sat until 9 p.m. The cafe is closed on Sun.

*BLOSSOM CAFE $$–$$$
171 East Bay St.
(843) 722-9200
www.magnolias-blossom-cypress.com
Blossom Cafe is another see-and-be-seen place downtown but offers the bonus of being as affordable or extravagant as your budget allows. The cafe, open every day, has indoor and outdoor dining, an in-house bakery, a cappuccino bar, and an extensive New American menu with Italian and Medi-terranean influences. The menu is the same for lunch, dinner, and late-night dining, fea-turing pastas, seafood entrees, and gourmet pizzas from the oak-burning oven. An added bonus is free parking just next door (after 5 p.m. on weekdays).

CARPENTIER'S WINE AND
DINE DELI $
976 Houston Northcutt Blvd., Mount Pleasant
(843) 884-9386
www.carpentierscatering.com
Insiders know the deli at Carpentier's is a gourmet's delight. Choose from prepared meats, European breads and cheeses, home-made pâté, and daily specials. The distinctive aroma of roasted coffee and fresh-baked cookies and pastries fills the air. A selection of imported beers and fine wines is available, and there are a few small tables for dining in the store. Carpentier's is open for breakfast and lunch Mon through Sat. Gift baskets can be ordered by calling (843) 830-3042.

CHARLESTON'S CAFE $–$$
1039 Johnnie Dodds Blvd., Mount Pleasant
(843) 856-7796
www.charlestonscafe.com
Formerly known as downtown's Bookstore Cafe, Charleston's Cafe serves the same won-derful fare at breakfast and lunch and sells freshly baked goods. Far enough from the madding crowd, this cafe offers some seren-ity along with its daily specials. Menu items include its signature potato casseroles. Spe-cials might be quesadillas, a focaccia sand-wich, roast pork, and fried green tomatoes. Take home some rhubarb-raspberry jam and beer bread. The cafe opens at 8 a.m. Mon through Fri; Sat and Sun hours begin at 8 a.m. Closing time is 2:30 p.m. weekdays and 2 p.m. on Sat and Sun.

CRU CAFE $$
18 Pinckney St.
(843) 534-2434
www.crucafe.com
There's nothing quite like Cru Cafe in Charles-ton. Sure, we have other restaurants in single houses, and you can dine on the porch at those as well. But Cru Cafe is unique. The menu features "upscale comfort food" that's nourishing and desirable to the palate and the eye—but not so exotic as to be intimi-dating. For instance, there's their buttermilk fried oyster salad, salmon and lemon risotto, seared maple leaf duck breast, and double-cut grilled pork chop. Lunch and dinner are served Tues through Sat. Seating is limited, so we recommend that you avoid the peak hours of noon to 1 p.m. Reservations are suggested.

DOE'S PITA PLUS $
334 East Bay St.
(843) 577-3179
www.doespita.com

Doe's offers healthy fast food that's a hit with the lunch crowd. The fresh-baked pita bread for pocket sandwiches and salads is prepared to order (right there in plain view) while you wait. Although there are several tables and chairs in the front and back, most people think takeout when they think of Doe's. For variety on the side, sample Doe's ethnic fare such as baba ghannouj, tabouleh, or Lebanese potato salad. Children love the banana-and-peanut butter pocket and do well in the high chair stationed in the rear dining area. Nonalcoholic beverages are sold. Doe's is open daily from 8 a.m. to 8 p.m. Mon through Fri and until 5 p.m. on Sat and Sun. A second location is in North Charleston at 5134 North Rhett Ave. (843-745-0026).

EAST BAY DELI $
334 East Bay St.
(843) 723-1234
www.eastbaydeli.net

Sometimes, what's called for is a quick bite grabbed en route to somewhere else— when the art of fine dining and fancy dress must wait in the wings for another time. Still, you want that bite to be tasty and prepared with care. You want it served with cleanliness and pride, too, and available from a location easy to find. That's exactly what East Bay Deli has to offer, and it's become a hit with downtown shoppers and business types on the go, as well as students and hungry visitors entering the city via the busy East Bay corridor. Here you'll find traditional deli sandwiches, wraps, salads, giant spuds, chicken wings, hot dogs, plus prepared fin and fowl—good to enjoy on-site or take

with. They open at 8:30 a.m. and stay around until 8:15 p.m. or so Mon through Sat. Look for other area locations of this expanding deli restaurant, including the Mount Pleasant branch at 1120 Oakland Rd. (843-216-5423), 4405 Dorchester Rd. in North Charleston (843-747-1235), and their newest addition at 858 Savannah Hwy., (843-571-2244).

JACK'S CAFE $
41 George St.
(843) 723-5237

The turnaround at Jack's is fast, and the food is as typically American as the no-frills apple or peach cobbler. College of Charleston students, professors, and alumni as well as King Street merchants frequent Jack's for old-fashioned burgers (served in plastic baskets) and milk shakes. The value is definitely part of the draw, but so is the vegetable soup (and, in fact, all of the food). People eat at booths, the counter, or around a few tables. It's all very low-key and functional. Take-out service is available. Jack's is open weekdays only for breakfast and lunch. No credit cards.

KAMINSKY'S MOST
EXCELLENT CAFE $
78 North Market St.
(843) 853-8270
www.kaminskys.com

Kaminsky's is an A-plus addition to the list of indulge-thyself Peninsula eateries. The surprise is its just wonderful desserts and the right coffees and spirits to accompany them here. The handsome brick walls of the Market Street location make a backdrop for a nice showcase of art, and the cafe's intimate size contributes to its appeal. Try an exotic coffee or nonalcoholic drink with a delicious dessert. The milk shakes, for instance, are legendary. Be prepared to face a dilemma: There are 150 other choices. Relax with a martini or hot toddy Kaminsky's is open every day from 4 p.m. until late night Mon through Thurs, and Fri and Sat beginning at noon.

LAURA ALBERTS $$
891 Island Park Dr., Daniel Island
(843) 881-4711
www.lauraalberts.com
A welcoming atmosphere beckons from Laura Alberts on Daniel Island's Island Park Drive. The neighborhood place to stop for a little Lowcountry cuisine with a bit of flair, Laura Alberts fills the bill. This mother/daughter–founded cafe is also a place for fine wine, craft beers, and gifts. They serve lunch Mon through Sat plus a Sat brunch menu from 10 a.m. to 3 p.m. An ample selection of hot and cold sandwiches, pastas, salads with seafood or other toppings, and tasty appetizers are all prepared with fresh local and South Carolina–grown products. Dinner is offered on Wednesday nights only to help you get "over the hump." Wednesday is also host to their "Growler Hour" from 5 to 7 p.m. where you can taste what's on tap from their selection of over 100 craft beers. Their boutique-quality wines are extensive with over 27 varietals and 600 distinct labels. This is a great stop too for picking up boxed lunches for a picnic or boating adventure.

LONG ISLAND CAFE $$
1515 Palm Blvd., Isle of Palms
(843) 886-8809
Long Island Cafe became a local favorite soon after its doors opened way back in 1986, and it still has a loyal following. The changing menu is always interesting. The stuffed shrimp baked with crab, parmesan-crusted salmon, and pork loin with ginger-garlic

sauce are all popular with patrons. A nice selection of soups, salads, and sandwiches is also available. The management is terrific with children and sometimes displays kiddie artwork on a wall. Long Island is open every day for dinner, and lunch Mon through Sat. Its Sunday brunch, where the cheddar-ham-and-apple omelet is a favorite, is from 11 a.m. to 2 p.m.

✳THE MED BISTRO $–$$
90 Folly Rd.
(843) 766-0323
www.themedbistro.com
Talk about your neighborhood magnets. The Med Bistro is a real draw for West Ashley and downtown diners. It has a high-tech look with lots of chrome and glass, and desserts are now the specialty. Not only is the food good and predictable (the menu doesn't change, and favorite specials are repeated), but it's also just 5 minutes from the city, and parking is no trouble. Connoisseurs of spirits will enjoy the great selections of wine and imported beers here. Regulars are partial to the pita pocket sandwich with fried green tomatoes or black bean soup at lunch. For dinner, try the pasta specials; there are plenty of variations on the theme. There is live music on weekend evenings. The Med Bistro is open from late morning to late night every day but Sun when they serve brunch from 10 a.m. to 3 p.m.

METTO COFFEE & TEA $
354 West Coleman Blvd., Mount Pleasant
(843) 216-8832
For a delightful treat, try Metto's salads, paninis, pastries, and bagels, and the like while taking advantage of the large selection of fresh-brewed coffees and teas. One exciting plus is that Metto's has a drive-up window

to make it handy for pick-up lunches or java-to-go. It's open Mon through Sun from early morning until late afternoon. (See Coffehouses in the Nightlife chapter.)

*THE PALMETTO CAFE $$$
130 Market St., Charleston Place
(843) 722-4900
www.charlestonplace.com

This restaurant is inside the large Charleston Place complex and serves breakfast and lunch in a relaxed but upscale cafe atmosphere. The breakfast buffet on Sat and Sun is a very elaborate event with several choices of entree and salad, fresh vegetables and fruits, plus desserts. The garden atmosphere is particularly attractive and convenient to those staying in the hotel or shopping downtown. It falls in the pricier category, but everything is beautifully presented, and it is well worth the price on a special occasion (like your first visit to Charleston). For lunch, there's nothing like the spring rolls with duck confit, glazed mushrooms and goat cheese. Follow that with lump crab and avocado served with grilled chayote squash, bibb lettuce, and mango slaw. This stylish restaurant features optional courtyard dining and is open daily.

SAFFRON CAFE & BAKERY $–$$
333 East Bay St.
(843) 722-5588
www.saffroncafeandbakery.com

This is a light and airy restaurant, contemporary in design and good for solo ventures or joining friends. The pitched-roof, modern building is divided into a gourmet product section with imported pastas and olive oils; a full bakery (you'll be seduced by the scent and leave with a loaf of bread); and a dining room with booths and tables scattered about. Popular menu items include the seafood and spinach salads, pasta dishes, and the classic carrot cake. It's open for breakfast, lunch, and dinner 7 days a week. Saffron does a Sunday brunch from 9:30 a.m. to 2:30 p.m.

SEA BISCUIT CAFE $
21 J. C. Long Blvd., Isle of Palms
(843) 886-4079

This is one petite charmer—complete with a tiny front porch, substantial side porch (for dining), and really good island fare. The Sea Biscuit, tucked away on one of Isle of Palms' less chaotic streets, serves breakfast or brunch with the house specialty: fabulous biscuits. Try shrimp and gravy with grits and eggs, seafood omelets, quiche, and even eggs Benedict. The cafe serves a delicious house tea, and children can order a pancake that's a Mickey Mouse look-alike. Get there early, or expect a wait. Lunch is served after breakfast Tues through Fri; breakfast only is served Sat and Sun. No credit cards.

WILD WING CAFE $
36 North Market St.
(843) 722-9464
www.wildwingcafe.com

Wild Wing Cafe is popular with the younger-than-30 bar crowd, but also has appeal to those of us who have topped out the age group but not our attraction to a good time. Wild Wing serves a wonderful platter of chicken wings (of course), dressed in all kinds of herbs and spices—from the Ginger Wing to the Flying Fajita. There are great dips, sandwiches, and salads as well as buckets of beer for a table packed with thirsty friends. The bar serves a variety of bottled beer and spirits as well as nonalcoholic beverages.

Wild Wing is open for lunch and dinner every day. Visit the website for additional locations.

YE OLE FASHIONED ICE CREAM AND SANDWICH CAFE $
474 Savannah Hwy.
(843) 766-4854
www.yeoldfashioned.com

This is a quick stop but a change from the usual fast food. There are several locations within our coverage area and a few more beyond. This cafe serves triple decker sandwiches, homemade soups, and, of course, lots of ice cream. There are scores of flavors. Their 10-slices-of-bacon BLT and the all-beef hot dog are big hits, too. If you use the drive-through window, you may want to call ahead for soup and sandwich take-out orders. All the food is delicious, and local kids love this place. Hours are midmorning through late night daily. Check their website for more area locations.

FRENCH

*39 RUE DE JEAN $$-$$$
39 John St.
(843) 722-8881
www.39ruedejean.com

Here's a little bit of Paris on South Carolina soil. That is, this restaurant is all about French food served in the best tradition of the genre. Located across John Street from the visitor center, this is a great place to begin a dining tour of Charleston. It's known for braised short ribs with espanole sauce and steamed mussels available in 6 different presentations. If you want, a large assortment of French wines is available, but domestic labels are offered too. The full-service bar is a popular stop for locals as well as first-time visitors to our city. A favorite dessert is the crème brûlée. Rue de Jean is open for lunch

or dinner every day from 11:30 a.m. until late night. Their Sunday Brasserie Brunch is served 10 a.m. to 3 p.m.

FAT HEN $$-$$$
3140 Maybank Hwy., Johns Island
(843) 559-9090
www.thefathen.com

Chef and owner Fred Neuville, formerly of Rue de Jean and Coast has created a neighborhood restaurant on Johns Island that is packing them in. Just the right balance of a relaxed atmosphere and his signature French-inspired Lowcountry cuisine draw locals and tourists here from downtown and the Kiawah and Seabrook resorts. Try the scallops wrapped in bacon with pomegranate barbecue sauce and an herb salad or the escargot with garlic butter and grilled bread for an appetizer. Dinner favorites like the coq au vin braised in red wine with bacon lardons and mushrooms and the seared grouper served over butter beans and wild mushrooms more than satisfy. And, of course, to pair with this is an impressive wine list with well- and lesser-known labels. Don't miss the Pluff Mud Pie with chocolate mousse, Oreo cookie crust, and Chantilly crème. They are open daily for dinner starting at 5:30 p.m. and a bar menu starts at 4 p.m. They even have a kids' menu. Sunday brunch is served from 10 a.m. to 2:30 p.m. Limited reservations are accepted for dinner and brunch.

GAULART & MALICLET (FAST AND FRENCH) $-$$
98 Broad St.
(843) 577-9797
www.fastandfrench.org

Tucked neatly into what was once a long, narrow doctor's office, with lovely old molding,

G&M (called Fast and French by locals) is a tiny Parisian-style cafe serving delicious, contemporary French fare. The counter-style service offers cheese plates, salads, and house specials. The owners (French, of course) know what they are doing and are pleasant while doing it. Some favorites are the curried sesame chicken and the Swiss fondue with French bread. They serve breakfast, lunch, and dinner almost every day except Sun. No dinner is served on Mon.

GREEK & MEDITERRANEAN

ATHENS GREEK RESTAURANT $$
1939 Maybank Hwy., James Island
(843) 795-0957
www.athensofcharleston.com
The line moves quickly at Athens, in the Athenian Village, where there is usually a crowd eager to dine. Specialties at this popular Greek place include Greek chicken, spanakopita, lemon chicken soup, Greek salad with feta cheese, and baklava. A full range of spirits is available. Athens is open every day for lunch and dinner. Dashing diners will appreciate their Express Cafe and Pizza Express for a quick bite or takeout, located next door in the same building. A second Pizza Express has been added in the West Ashley area at 1798 Ashley River Rd., Unit D (843-302-8888).

OLD TOWNE RESTAURANT $$
229 King St. (across from Charleston Place)
(843) 723-8170
www.oldtownerestaurant.com
Owners Spiros Fokas and Steve Ferderigos have been serving authentic Greek lunches and dinners here daily for more than 30 years. The menu includes seafood, salads, Greek chicken, and the ever-popular Super Special—a sampler, good for the whole gang. Pictures of classical Greece line the walls, and a grill in the front window offers a tempting display of chicken being roasted on a turning spit.

SERMET'S CORNER $$
276 King St.
(843) 853-7775
After the success of his first eatery west of the Ashley, Sermet's creative artist and chef opened a new location on King Street several years ago to rave reviews and standing-room-only crowds. The cuisine is Mediterranean-influenced, with spicy pastas and fresh green salads, and it's a refreshing option on the King Street luncheon and dinner scene. Look for their lavender honey and black pepper marinated pork tenderloin with creamy ricotta polenta. The desserts are straight from heaven. In season, there's a rhubarb and raspberry pie that is definitely to die for. Sermet's is open daily from 11 a.m. to 3 p.m. for lunch; and it reopens for dinner starting at 4 p.m. A second location is at 115 River Landing Dr., Daniel Island; (843) 471-1777.

IRISH

THE BLUEROSE CAFE $$-$$$
652 St. Andrews Blvd.
(843) 225-2583
www.bluerosecafecharleston.com
This little bit of Ireland may seem out of context, located as it is just across the Ashley from downtown Charleston. But the Bluerose Cafe is a welcome find for all who seek it out. Chef and owner Denis O'Doherty has all the blarney you'd expect of a true son of the Emerald Isle, but he makes true believers of a growing list of happy locals who know his skills in the kitchen are the real thing. The key word here is value. Luncheon

specials are always well under $10 and range from Irish curry chicken salad with golden raisins to grilled prime rib sandwiches. Dinner entrees include a shepherd's pie that's hearty and nourishing, as is the seafood chowder with scallops, shrimp, and salmon. There's also a choice of chops or chicken in a number of presentations, and there's always plenty of soda bread, scones, and authentic Irish jams to satisfy the palate. A choice of imported wines and beer is offered if you like. It's open for breakfast and lunch Mon through Sat. Dinner is served on Thurs, Fri, and Sat from 5 to 9 p.m. Sunday brunch is from 9 a.m. to 2 p.m.

i Health food shoppers have found a proverbial mecca in Earth Fare over in the South Windermere Shopping Center. This large, well-stocked supermarket specializing in natural and organically grown foods also has a handy corner cafe equipped with simple tables and booths. You select your meal from a cafeteria-style line or deli and seat yourself. Bringing home the bacon was never so inviting. You don't even have to be a health nut to dine there.

TOMMY CONDON'S IRISH PUB AND SEAFOOD RESTAURANT $-$$
160 Church St.
(843) 577-3818
www.tommycondons.com

The most authentic Irish pub in Charleston, Tommy Condon's has live Irish music Wed through Sun and serves a variety of imported beers and ales, such as Bass and Newcastle Brown. The menu is a mixture of Irish and Lowcountry items, including shrimp and grits, seafood jambalaya, and

fresh fish of the day. There is a covered deck for outside dining, and patrons are welcome for lunch or dinner any day of the week. The kitchen closes at 10 p.m., but the bar stays open until 2 a.m. (See the Nightlife chapter.)

ITALIAN

BOCCI'S $$-$$$
158 Church St.
(843) 720-2121
www.boccis.com

This cozy Northern Italian family restaurant near the Market keeps them coming back for more calzones, salads, seafood, and pasta topped with a choice of 4 fabulous sauces. Mozzarella lovers go for the hand-pulled cheese. Another favorite is shrimp tortellini. Try the veal saltimbocca, too. There is a front-room view looking onto historic Church Street. Bocci's is open every day for lunch and dinner.

CAPRICCIO RISTORANTE $$
1034 Chuck Dawley Blvd., Mount Pleasant
(843) 881-5550

This affordable and friendly Italian restaurant is actually owned by a Frenchman. That's the beauty of the place—it's for those who love to go out several times a month and customers who love to dine well. All the entrees are around $15, yet the menu reads like an Italian cornucopia. There's a special every day, such as vitello (veal) parmigiana topped with mozzarella pomodoro sauce or rigatoni contadina. Try one of the numerous linguini with Capriccio's special gift for sauces. Mussel lovers say these are the best in town. All the dolces (desserts) are $5.75, and they change daily. There are a number of Italian coffees for after-dinner reflection. This restaurant is for serious lovers of Italian cuisine.

Half portions are available for children for half price. Dinner only is served Mon through Sat. Reservations are preferred.

FULTON FIVE $$$
5 Fulton St.
(843) 853-5555
www.fultonfive.net

Fulton Five is an authentic taste of old Italy tucked away on Fulton Street, just off King Street in the heart of the antiques district. The building looks Old World enough to be European, and the al fresco dining experience is definitely continental in feel. An upstairs dining area adds another perspective on the charms of quaint and narrow Fulton Street. The menu is constantly changing with new and more exciting entrees, but if the following dishes are available, we heartily recommend them. Start with antipasto Spoleto (grilled fresh mozzarella and prosciutto rolled into a romaine leaf with balsamic and tomato vinaigrette). Next, move to the asparagi e ricotta ravioli with mushroom fontina bechamel sauce. Then enjoy the vitello (grilled veal T-bone) with roasted zucchini and squash. For a light, sweet touch, order a grapefruit, orange, or tangerine ice made in-house or tiramisu—the perfect finale. A fine selection of Italian and other wines is always on hand. Fulton Five is open only for dinner Mon through Sat starting at 5:30 p.m. Reservations are suggested.

MERCATO $$
102 North Market St.
(843) 722-8393
www.mercatocharleston.com

A respite in the midst of the bustle of the Market, Mercato transports you to Tuscany, delighting your palette and soothing your soul. The food is beautifully prepared Italian cuisine with a local flare, including such inventive dishes as housemade bavette (linguini) pasta with local shrimp. If you're power shopping at the Market, take a load off your tired feet and enjoy a light bite at the spacious bar. You can choose from an extensive selection of pizza, salads, and antipasti. Or treat yourself to dinner, which features elegant multicourse meals to be savored by candlelight. The primo locale, superb food, live music, and swank (yet fun) setting will leave you exclaiming "bravo," and vowing to return. Mercato is open daily at 5 p.m.

LOWCOUNTRY CUISINE

Lowcountry cuisine is the cooking style found along the coastal areas of South Carolina and Georgia. Charleston, in particular, has embraced this culinary identity incorporating its plentiful seafood, game, produce, and rice culture with a blending of French, English, Caribbean, and African influences. Some of the traditional favorites include Shrimp and Grits, Hoppin' John, Frogmore Stew (Lowcountry Shrimp Boil), and She-Crab Soup.

CAROLINA'S $$$
10 Exchange St.
(843) 724-3800
www.carolinasrestaurant.com

Carolina's is on the site of old Perdita's, a much-respected restaurant of days gone by. There is little in the decor reminiscent of the establishment's roots, as Carolina's is designed for today. There are three main areas: the noisy, see-and-be-seen front dining section, with its showy wine collection (said to be one of the largest in the Southeast); a central bar with tables on two sides; and a more secluded, traditional dining room to the right of the entrance.

The menu is expansive, and the style Low-country with a contemporary approach with seafood, chicken, and beef—grilled in many instances. One favorite is the pan roasted scallops. Their pecan brittle basket with vanilla bean ice cream and fresh fruit berries is ample for two and a perfect ending. Carolina's is open Mon through Fri for lunch and every day for dinner, and the dress, while generally casual, edges toward the snazzy side. Complimentary valet parking is a nice touch. Reservations are suggested. (See the Nightlife chapter.)

82 QUEEN $$$
82 Queen St.
(843) 723-7591, (800) 849-0082
www.82queen.com
This multi-award-winning restaurant has several personalities—one of which is sure to please. Exploring the 11 dining rooms at 82 Queen is an adventure in itself. The grounds include three 18th-century town houses, 2 inside bars (1 full-service and 1 just for shots), an outside raw bar that is a very popular hangout for the after-work crowd, a partly glassed-in romantic gazebo, and outdoor tables for dining. Lowcountry seafood, beef, lamb, and fowl are specialties of their updated traditional Southern cuisine. Farm-fresh herbs and vegetables are locally grown for their kitchen. The wine list includes more than 140 selections. Lunch and dinner are served daily. Sunday brunch is especially nice in this pleasant atmosphere. Reservations are encouraged. (See the Nightlife chapter.)

✳FIG $$$
232 Meeting St.
(843) 805-5900
www.eatatfig.com

Locals fondly remember an affordable Italian restaurant at the corner of Meeting and Hasell Streets that is no more. But in its place came FIG, a new and delightful offering spearheaded by Michael Lata, formerly of Anson. He brings an equally pleasing menu to FIG, inspired by his frequent travels in France, where fine dining is a way of life. Local farmers supply the freshest ingredients at peak flavor, and the results are reflected in every meal served. Vegetarians love the fresh plate of today's best produce specially prepared by the chef for maximum enjoyment. The ever-changing menu frequently includes a tomato and onion tart with creamy goat cheese or sautéed white shrimp and radicchio as starters. Look for crispy Caw Caw Creek suckling pig confit—if you like—have sauteed scamp grouper with braised fennel. Seasonal desserts like spiced apple raisin crumble make a rewarding finale. Wines—domestic and imported—are plentiful and served by the glass or bottle. They're open Mon through Sat for dinner only starting at 5:30 p.m.

HIGH COTTON $$$–$$$$
199 East Bay St.
(843) 724-3815
www.high-cotton.net
In the mix of Charleston's array of fine eateries along the East Bay corridor just north of the Exchange Building is High Cotton. This is another one of the Maverick Southern Kitchens' restaurants (which also brings us Slightly North of Broad across the street and Old Village Post House over in Mount Pleasant). They call this one "an unabashedly masculine and American saloon," but don't look for anything Wild West about it. Instead, there's dark mahogany woodwork, exposed brick walls, lots of alligator skin upholstery, and a hearty

menu of meats, game, lobster, and fresh fish. Local dishes may include South Carolina squab, rabbit loin, venison, and spit-roasted quail. Fresh seafood is also available—for which out-of-town visitors from inland locations all seem to call. The spirits served and the service rendered are up to Maverick group's high standards. Dinner hours are 5:30 p.m. until late night seven days. Lunch is served Sat from 11:30 a.m. to 2:30 p.m. Their jazz Sunday brunch is popular, too. Call for reservations.

i Check the menu or specials board at Lowcountry eateries for Beaufort Stew (sometimes called Frogmore Stew), a hearty one-dish supper that's a staple meal on the islands. It's smoked sausage, fresh ears of corn, and shrimp all boiled together with special spices. This fare is often served at Lowcountry oyster roasts as an alternative menu item.

✳HOMINY GRILL $$
207 Rutledge Ave.
(843) 937-0930
www.hominygrill.com
On Rutledge Avenue, within a stroll from the huge MUSC hospital and medical office complex, there's a small but worthwhile cafe that's anything but institutional. This is a favorite with the medfolk, as you would imagine, so the best time to find a table is off the peak meal rush hours—although breakfast, lunch, and dinner are all offered. The cuisine is contemporary Southern, with several attractively served specials listed daily on the chalkboard menu. Look for some Lowcountry favorites like classic shrimp creole over jasmine rice. Or, there's a sesame-crusted catfish with sautéed okra, baked cheese grits, and Geechee peanut sauce. Desserts

are terrific, and the buttermilk pie and chocolate pudding are special treats. Hominy Grill serves breakfast from 7:30 until 11:30 a.m., when the all-day menu picks up through 9 p.m. Their popular weekend brunch goes from 9 a.m. to 3 p.m.

JASMINE PORCH $$$–$$$$
1 Sanctuary Beach Dr., Kiawah Island
(843) 768-6253, (877) 683-1234
www.thesanctuary.com
The Sanctuary at Kiawah has one dining option that revisits a much-loved tradition for those who know Kiawah from years ago. That's a dining room known as Jasmine Porch—a reincarnation of the first dining room from Kiawah's former Inn. Here the cuisine is Lowcountry fare—kicked up a notch or two. The emphasis here is on the purest and finest ingredients, so when you order shrimp and grits, the shrimp is the freshest caught available, and the grits are stone-ground and cooked to perfection. Same is true for the she-crab bisque and the oysters on the half-shell. Same goes for the Huguenot torte and the pecan pie. Breakfast, lunch, and dinner are served daily, and spirits are on call. Sunday brunch is a special treat with chilled champagne mimosas and live music setting the stage for the sumptuous fare. It doesn't hurt that Jasmine Porch with its outdoor terrace overlooks The Sanctuary's spectacular pool area and the Atlantic Ocean. Nearby is the Loggerhead Grille, offering additional outdoor dining when the weather permits.

✳MAGNOLIAS UPTOWN/
DOWN SOUTH $$$
185 East Bay St.
(843) 577-7771
www.magnolias-blossom-cypress.com

Magnolias tops the list of hot restaurants on the Peninsula. In fact, *Travel + Leisure* called it "the place in downtown Charleston." This is new American-Lowcountry cuisine, and the chef's specialties include spicy shrimp and sausage with tasso gravy over creamy white grits, and tomato bisque dotted with generous lumps of fresh crabmeat. The expansive menu will remind you of the restaurant's California, Tex-Mex, and Cajun inspirations, but the atmosphere is strictly refined New South. Enjoy eating in the beautiful dining rooms at Magnolias, but also try your hand with Magnolias' recipes at home:Executive chef Donald Barickman's *Magnolias Southern Cuisine* is a hot seller cookbook. Lunch and dinner are served daily. Reservations are definitely encouraged.

OLD VILLAGE POST HOUSE $$-$$$
101 Pitt St., Mount Pleasant
(843) 388-8935, (800) 549-POST
www.oldvillageposthouse.com
This is one of the dining options presented by Maverick Southern Kitchens, Inc. This one is combined with a 6-room inn nestled in the heart of Mount Pleasant's quaint Old Village. (See the Accomodations chapter.) The beautifully restored 1888 structure now houses 2 dining rooms and a charming tavern available to inn guests or a la carte visitors looking for fine food at affordable prices. For starters, you can expect to find Lowcountry favorites on the menu like shrimp & grits, but check out the lump crab and avocado with grape tomatoes, orange segments, and citrus vinaigrette. The main dishes making a hit with patrons include crispy fried flounder with saute of asparagus, green beans, and roma tomato. Along with the honey mustard glazed grilled salmon, you can find steaks and lamb on the creative and varied bill of fare. It's open for dinner nightly from 5:30 p.m., and serves a popular brunch on Sun from 10 a.m.to 2 p.m.

POOGAN'S PORCH $$-$$$
72 Queen St.
(843) 577-2337
www.poogansporch.com
Poogan's Porch is in a charming old Charleston house where lunch and dinner can be enjoyed fireside or outside beneath the stars on the porch or patio. Expect casual family dining (including a children's menu) with such Lowcountry favorites as Ms. Bertha's she-crab soup, shrimp creole, okra gumbo, seafood specials, and even—on the wilder side—an occasional alligator dish. Lunch is served weekdays, and dinner 7 days a week; reservations are recommended for dinner. Saturday and Sunday brunch is from 9 a.m. to 3 p.m.

✳ROSEBANK FARMS CAFE $$-$$$
1886 Andell Bluff Blvd., Seabrook Island
(843) 768-1807
www.rosebankfarmscafe.com
Here's a delightful place to get typical Lowcountry cuisine (in other words, "Suh-thun cookin'") done with a modern twist. Rosebank Farms Cafe is in the marina atmosphere of Bohicket Creek. This spot is especially popular during fishing tournaments at Seabrook. Along with choice steaks, local seafood, pastas, and fresh vegetables, try the honey and buttermilk fried chicken. The blue plate lunch specials for $10 are a great deal. And if you saved any room, their triple chocolate oatmeal brownie is to die for. A children's menu is available too. Rosebank is open for lunch daily and reopens for dinner every night.

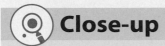

Close-up

The Taste of Charleston: Buy the Book

One of the best ways to a city's (dare we say?) stomach is through the dog-eared pages of its local Junior League cookbook. Perhaps the granddaddy of all tomes dealing with a city's bounty for the table is Charleston's 32-times reprinted, $1 million fund-raising, five-decades-old, classic-of-all-classics Junior League cookbooks. Its official name is *Charleston Receipts* (in the South, recipes are traditionally referred to as "receipts"), and this venerable publication of The Junior League of Charleston, Inc., is clearly a legend in its own time.

As the oldest Junior League cookbook still in print, the publication remains essentially unchanged since its first printing back in 1950—which says a great deal about its popularity and success throughout the years. This classic compilation of Southern gentility and gastronomical goodness was gleaned from cherished old family recipes collected by 21 Sustaining Members seeking to raise funds for a community speech-and-hearing center—the first of its kind in the state. Many of the recipes were family secrets passed down by word of mouth from generation to generation and never before seen in print.

Originally, the cookbook retailed for $2.50 and featured 350 pages with 750 recipes plus quaint sketches of the city by local artists. Interspersed among the recipes were colorful Gullah verses harking back to the days when African-American servants did most of the cooking in proper Charleston households. These days, if you order one by mail, it'll cost you $19.95 plus $7.50 shipping and handling. But it's still a bargain at twice the price. Visit **www.jlcharleston.org,** or write **The Junior League of Charleston, Inc.,** 51 Folly Rd., Charleston, SC 29407.

✳**SLIGHTLY NORTH OF BROAD** $$–$$$

192 East Bay St.

(843) 723-3424

www.slightlynorthofbroad.net

In one of the many 19th-century cotton warehouses that line East Bay Street, there's this trendy option for S.N.O.B. types. Cute name notwithstanding, the folks here are very serious about good food. It's what they call a "maverick Southern kitchen" with multi-cultural overtones. The jumbo lump crab cakes with yellow squash, okra, corn and shrimp gravy are divine. This restaurant is a favorite of those who want to lunch with friends (Mon through Fri) or have a special evening on the town (any day of the week). Reservations are encouraged.

NOUVELLE AMERICAN

Nouvelle American is a modern style of cooking based on nouvelle cuisine that originated in France in the 1970s. It emphasizes a lighter, healthier cuisine over the richer, heavier French haute cuisine that preceded it. Nouvelle American stresses light sauces and purees, and quickly-cooked fresh vegetables using regional, seasonal produce, seafood, and meats in smaller portions with an artful, elegant presentation.

✳ANSON $$$
12 Anson St.
(843) 577-0551
www.ansonrestaurant.com

This elegant restaurant on Anson Street is between the Market and the trendy Anson-borough neighborhood. Anson is as well appointed as it is deserving of its reputation for fine food and good service. The nouvelle American menu includes a decadent whole crispy flounder with apricot shallot sauce that should not be missed. If you're among those who enjoy steak tartare, Anson's consistently gets rave reviews. Other temptations include outstanding first-course shrimp and grits with bacon, roasted tomatoes, and Anson's grits. When it's time for dessert, look for their dense, moist house-made chocolate cake. Dinner is served 7 nights a week; reservations are recommended.

✳CHARLESTON GRILL $$$-$$$$
224 King St. (in Charleston Place)
(843) 577-4522
www.charlestongrill.com

This is the grande dame restaurant in Orient Express' Charleston Place. In this recently renovated and traditionally decorated eatery, quality is the byword. Service is exuberant, for those who demand close attention, and the wine list can compete with any in the South. It isn't exactly stuffy, but the atmosphere is definitely upscale. The food is simply superb. Its nightly specials are always as billed, but the regular menu is abundant in attractive choices. Try the Black River caviar or tuna sashimi for starters. And the grilled dry aged lamb chops with lemon rosemary jus makes for a delectable entree. Desserts are announced nightly for those with a taste for excess. Live jazz begins at 7 p.m. (8 p.m. on weekends) and adds a cool

balm to the well-orchestrated scene. Dinner is served nightly, and the bar opens at 5 p.m. Reservations are welcomed.

CIRCA 1886 $$$-$$$$
149 Wentworth St.
(843) 853-7828
www.circa1886.com

When the giant landmark Victorian town-house on Wentworth Street opened as a high-end B&B, the whole concept for the genre in Charleston expanded upwardly—in more ways than one. Not only would the envelope for luxury accommodations be expanded, an on-site restaurant of similar caliber would be opened for the convenience of the mansion's guests and other discerning diners. Thus, Circa 1886 was born (about a year later), and it seems well worth the wait. Named for the date of the Went-worth Mansion's construction, this small and intimate dining venue in what was once the carriage house offers seasonal cuisine that conceivably might have been served to the home's owner at that time. Executive Chef Marc Collins rotates the menu seasonally—presenting his unique and modern take on old Charleston recipes. Look for the juniper brined pork tenderloin with fig glazed garlic and chestnut sauce. Another find is their seared Carolina bass in grilled oyster mushroom and foie gras broth. Desserts sure to please include sweet potato crème brûlée with blackstrap molasses marshmallow or chocolate cake with grand marnier chocolate mousse.

An intimate bar and attentive but unobtrusive service add to the ambience here—and Circa 1886 provides a quiet evening of fine dining clearly intended to be a cut above the rest of the downtown restaurant crowd. An impressive wine list with more than 280 labels is available. Dinner is served Mon through Sat from 5:30 to 9:30 p.m. Reservations are suggested.

CYPRESS LOWCOUNTRY GRILLE $$$$
167 East Bay St.
(843) 727-0111
www.magnolias-blossom-cypress.com

Many Charleston visitors have tried Magnolia's on East Bay Street and raved about it. Here's another restaurant from the same owners and chefs with a slightly different twist. Cypress is contemporary American cuisine with Asian overtones, and the result is delightful. Wine lovers will appreciate the 21-foot-tall "wine wall" with choices for the most discriminating palate. The 4,500 bottles kept on hand make a stunning background for a memorable evening. The 1834 building that houses Cypress retains a Charleston feel, while the decor is smart and trendy by any standard. The menu is large; for instance, you choose from 12 different appetizers. The beef and spiced cucumber spring rolls are one popular option. Among the dozen or so main dishes, smoked salmon Wellington with sautéed asparagus, gruyère potato fondue, and mustard butter is divine. The desserts are equally attractive. Try the Tahitian vanilla bean crème brûlée with a milk chocolate bonbon. The chocolate banana torte is memorable, as well. Cypress is open for dinner daily starting at 5:30 p.m. Reservations are preferred.

✳LANGDON'S $$$
788 Shellmore Blvd., Ste. 105, Mount Pleasant
(843) 388-9200
www.langdonsrestaurant.com

A popular choice with Mount Pleasant residents is this small restaurant and wine bar in what locals call the Bi-Lo Shopping Center. The decor is upscale, or "urban chic," if you please. The crowd is young and hip, thus so is the menu. For starters, try the creamy wild mushroom soup with lump crabmeat. Or, you might ask for the arugula salad topped with goat cheese, pear slices, and bacon vinaigrette. When it comes to entrees, look for the local grouper over country ham and sweet pea risotto. The hoisen-honey glazed kurabuto pork rib chop with collards and smoked bacon and leek "mac and cheese" is another favorite. The dessert menu changes seasonally, but you can usually find the berry crisp with fresh blueberries and orange liqueur a la mode. The global wine list is ample with more than 100 varieties offered. How 'bout that for a shopping center location? This surprisingly refreshing dining adventure is open Mon through Sat for lunch and dinner. Dinner reservations are strongly recommended—especially Wed through Sat.

MCCRADY'S $$$–$$$$
2 Unity Alley
(843) 577-0025
www.mccradysrestaurant.com

McCrady's experienced a new incarnation several years ago that retains much of the old tavern's charm but adds new space and sophistication. The dark wood and exposed brick interiors hark back to the days when George Washington supposedly supped here, and the huge fireplaces add their own charm. But the service and—most of all—the cuisine are the reasons to go there. Here, fine dining is a major event. McCrady's serves appetizers like crispy sweetbreads with sherry sabayon. There's a charred octopus too. For entrees, try the grouper with chanterelles, corn, and Bull's Bay shrimp. But delicious variations of duck, chicken, beef, pork, and lamb are always on the menu. If you're still able, try a dessert like the South Carolina peach cobbler. The sommelier's wine list is extensive and impressive. It's open daily for dinner. (See the Nightlife chapter.)

THE OCEAN ROOM $$$$$
1 Sanctuary Beach Dr., Kiawah Island
(843) 768-6253, (877) 683-1234
www.thesanctuary.com

The signature dining venue at The Sanctuary, Kiawah's luxury hotel and spa complex, is the Ocean Room. Up a dramatic staircase from the lobby is a handsome bar that introduces the Ocean Room's dining adventure, where expansive views overlooking the Atlantic give the place its name. Elegant decor and excellent service are expected here—the cuisine is New American, and presentation is one of the points of focus. Chef de cuisine Nathan Thurston brings his special touch to the ever-changing menu, which includes some favorites like the baby beet and goat cheese salad tossed in walnut vinaigrette, or the beef carpaccio with summer truffle, heart of palm, citrus, and arugula. Favorite entrees include the roasted rack of lamb and the strip loin of Angus beef. Of course, the sommelier directs guests through an extensive wine list to recommend the perfect accompanying vintage. The pastry chef presents a tantalizing array of fantastic desserts for the Ocean Room's finale. Reservations are definitely recommended. (For more on The Sanctuary, see the Accommodations chapter.)

✳PENINSULA GRILL $$$–$$$$
Planters Inn, 112 North Market St.
(843) 723-0700
www.peninsulagrill.com

The restaurant in the Planters Inn is the Peninsula Grill, an elegantly simple and altogether comfortable dining experience that has "extraordinary" written all over it. For instance, half the menu is devoted to the Champagne Bar, which offers an Old World selection of champagnes by the glass and a list of mixed cocktails that reads like a page from Noel Coward's Private Lives. The Champagne Bar menu includes a full selection of oysters, lobster (fresh from Maine), and other seafood specialties. Try the benne crusted rack of New Zealand lamb. The steaks, chops, and accompanying side dishes are equally fine, and you're tended to by a courteous and capable staff. As for wine, there's an extensive list—mostly from France and California. Several labels are available by the glass. Peninsula Grill is open Mon through Sun for dinner only starting at 5:30 p.m. Reservations are suggested. (See the Nightlife chapter.)

i The footsore traveler who's already enjoyed a full dose of Charleston's charm may be in the mood for a brief respite for some tea and sympathy. The Charleston Tea Company, at 24-B Ann St., across from the visitor center, has just the right medicine—a glass of refreshing mint tea (locally grown right here on Wadmalaw Island) or a cup of coffee and soups or sandwiches or other light fare. There's also cold beer and wine if the mood strikes. In any case, you'll be sustained for further adventures in the Holy City.

SEA ISLAND GRILL $$–$$$
The Boardwalk Inn, Wild Dunes Resort,
5757 Palm Blvd., Isle of Palms
(843) 886-2200
www.wilddunes.com

The premier restaurant at the upscale Wild Dunes Resort is called the Sea Island Grill, formerly the Grill. As the name implies, the cuisine features the freshest Lowcountry seafood creatively presented up by Chef Enzo Steffenelli, who has served up his magic at some of the best seafood restaurants in downtown Charleston during his impressive career. In addition to the wide selection of seafood dishes, entrees include creative presentations of steaks, chops, and poultry. Try the Crab crusted grouper served with a shellfish and bacon polenta cake, and baby spinach with a grainy mustard-ginger coulis. If you are up to it, finish off with the Ultimate Chocolate Cake for two, a thick slice of a rich, multi-layered chocolate cake made with bittersweet chocolate mousse and raspberry marmalade. The Sea Island Grill is open for dinner daily. Call ahead for reservations and the required gate pass for entrance into Wild Dunes.

PIZZA

ANDOLINI'S PIZZA $-$$
414 West Coleman Blvd., Mount Pleasant
(843) 849-7437
www.andolinis.com
Fine dining is one thing, but sometimes nothing beats a good pizza. Especially when the kids are involved or when appetites of the young-at-heart come to the fore—a good pizza is a joy forever. Here in Mount Pleasant is one of the best pizza parlors around. Andolini's Pizza uses marinated hand-tossed dough, homemade sauces, and the best cheeses in its array of pizzas, calzones, and salads. It's open for lunch and dinner Mon through Sun. Check out their website for more area locations.

MELLOW MUSHROOM $-$$
309 King St.
(843) 723-7374
www.mellowmushroom.com
Some visitors to Charleston may be familiar with the earlier version of this specialty pizza den that was a big draw in Atlanta when it first opened in the 1970s. Our version is new to the King Street crowd and the College of Charleston kids who weren't around for the "groovy" version in Hot 'lanta. In addition to the specialty pizzas, like their Mega–Veggie with a garden's worth of fresh non-meat ingredients, their dough is made with spring water. Calzones, hoagies, and salads are on the bill as well. The location is ideal for students, but MM attracts out-of-towners, too. It's especially popular with late-nighters and lunchtimers from King Street's business district. They're open daily for lunch and dinner, and the bar stays open until 11 p.m. Additional locations are at 3110 SR 17 N. in Mount Pleasant (843-881-4743) and at 19 Magnolia Rd. in West Ashley.

SEAFOOD

A. W. SHUCK'S SEAFOOD & OYSTER BAR $$
70 State St.
(843) 723-1151
www.a-w-shucks.com
More than a decade has passed since Shuck's first opened its doors, and a lot has changed in the Market area since then—at Shuck's in particular. What was originally a cozy, popular bar packed with locals has become a bigger, fancier eating establishment where the bar is no longer the major draw. Shuck's features both indoor and outdoor dining. Oyster connoisseurs will be interested to know the mollusks are sold raw or steamed

at market price. Beef, fowl, shrimp, mahi mahi, scallops, flounder, and children's plates are all on the menu. A. W. Shuck's is open daily for lunch and dinner. Locals and visitors alike enjoy the abundance of early artwork by local painter John Doyle throughout the restaurant.

✳ATLANTICVILLE
RESTAURANT & CAFE $$$
2063 Middle St., Sullivan's Island
(843) 883-9452
www.atlanticville.net
Not far from the cluster of businesses, restaurants, and bars across from the island's play-ground-like park is this small and casual option for New American cuisine. Locals and tourists alike go for the fried oysters with house made sausage or the calamari appetizer in Asian spices. Along with the seafood, Atlanticville offers a selection of beef, pork, and fowl. On Tuesdays, the menu is delightfully and authentically Thai, already a local legend. There's a covered deck for outdoor dining and an extensive wine and beer list. It's open daily for dinner only starting at 5:30 p.m. Sunday brunch is from 10 a.m. to 2 p.m. Reservations are a good idea.

THE BOATHOUSE AT
BREACH INLET $$–$$$
101 Palm Blvd., Isle of Palms
(843) 886-8000
www.boathouserestaurants.com
Right on the stretch of water known as Breach Inlet, with spectacular sunset views, is this unique restaurant. The decor is nautical but nice, and the menu includes pastas, grilled fresh fish, and house specialties such as coastal crab cakes with green Tabasco sauce and fried red onions, and the fresh catch of the day. The sides are as interesting

as the entrees. Look for stone-ground grits, bleu cheese coleslaw, and collard greens. Parking is free and dinner is served 7 days a week. Sunday brunch is from 11 a.m. until 2 p.m.

CHARLESTON CRAB HOUSE $$
145 Wappoo Creek Dr., James Island
(843) 795-1963
www.charlestoncrabhouse.com
On the Intracoastal Waterway, the Charleston Crab House is open for lunch and dinner every day. The restaurant specializes in their crab pot, steamed garlic crabs (cooked until they are red, then placed before you for what locals call a "crab crack"). There is a raw bar, and outside tables for dining are close to the water. You can arrive by boat and moor at the restaurant dock. No reservations are necessary. There's a "fiddler crab" (kid's) menu, and Mom and Dad may enjoy frozen tropical drinks. (See listing in the James and Johns Islands section of the Nightlife chapter.) Additional locations are at 1101 Stockade Lane, US 17 N, Mount Pleasant (843-884-1617), and 41 South Market St., Charleston (843-853-2900).

COAST $$–$$$
39-D John St.
(843) 722-8838
www.coastbarandgrill.com
Tucked away on Hutson Alley behind Rue de Jean (on John Street) is this seafood restaurant making big waves with locals as well as out-of-towners. When the question arises, "Where will you find good seafood?" this is always a great answer. The menu lists dozens of options—all prepared in different as well as traditional ways. Their coastal dishes from around the world can take the adventuresome diner on an exciting journey

to Thailand, Peru, Chile, Baja, and the rocky coast of Maine in addition to our own Low-country waters. A full raw bar is part of the scene, but you can order your seafood wood-grilled, steamed, smoked, or fried. Dessert is not to be missed here. Open daily for dinner starting at 5:30 p.m.

i A sweating glass of sparkling iced tea is a Southern tradition, and most restaurants will gladly refill your glass gratis. Be sure to let them know, however, if you are specifically looking for our good old-fashioned sweet tea.

FISH $$–$$$
442 King St.
(843) 722-3474
www.fishrestaurant.net

As the name implies, this is a small restaurant on upper King Street that's mostly about (but not exclusively dedicated to) seafood. You can count on the fact that none of the seafood brought to table will be more than 36 hours from its native waters. The fun decor is part of the charm. You enter through a courtyard past a fountain and discover an environment that's creative and unusual without being too cute. The menu changes seasonally, but look for the sweet chili calamari in sesame tempura batter or the Capers Island steamed clams with kaffir lime broth. If you're game for it, one of their specialties is the pan seared South Carolina Red Porgy. Another favorite is the Mandarin chicken. You might like to try the bouilla-baisse, a traditional steam pot in lemongrass broth, suitable for two seafood lovers. The dessert they're all talking about is the stuffed chocolate french toast minis. Fish is open for lunch Mon through Fri. Dinner is served Mon through Thurs, 5:30 to 9 p.m., or until 10 p.m. Fri and Sat.

FLEET LANDING RESTAURANT $$–$$$
186 Concord St.
(843) 722-8100
www.fleetlanding.net

Curiously, there are not a lot of waterfront dining establishments on Peninsula Charleston. Fleet Landing addresses that problem. They are not only on the waterfront, their building juts out over the marsh and water on a reinforced pier offering up a wonderful view of Charleston Harbor and all its shipping and boating activity. This 6,000 square foot concrete structure built in 1942 served as a debarkation point for US Navy sailors, thus the name "Fleet Landing." Today the chic maritime decor and classic yet contemporary Southern seafood menu make a perfect combination for a fun dining experience. Dine inside or hit the deck. Some of the regular menu items include pan-fried South Carolina lump crab cakes, pimento cheese encrusted ribeye, and fried oysters with Southern Comfort BBQ sauce. Seasonal items may include tempura fried soft shell crab, bacon-wrapped shad roe over creamy grits, and Johns Island tomatoes. They have a nice selection of regular and specialty beers, creative cocktails, and interesting martinis. Fleet Landing is open daily for lunch and dinner and brunch on weekends. Some parking is available in their lot in front or nearby metered parking or a parking garage on Concord Street.

GILLIGAN'S STEAMER AND
RAW BAR $$
14 N. Market St.
(843) 853-2244
www.gilligans.net

Gilligan's Steamer and Raw Bar has a great family atmosphere and delicious fresh steamed seafood. There are steaks and chicken as well, and the cooks will fry the seafood if you like. This is a place where you can order oysters by the bucket in season. Two veggies, a choice of salad or slaw, and hush puppies round out each meal. Crayons are available so the kids can draw while they wait. Their seasonally all-you-can-eat oyster clusters by the trayfull are a hit with locals. Gilligan's is open for lunch and dinner every day. Check out their website for more area locations.

HANK'S SEAFOOD RESTAURANT $$$
10 Hayne St.
(843) 723-3474
www.hanksseafoodrestaurant.com
Old-time Charleston Insiders remember a place called Henry's, which was part and parcel of this city's colorful "renaissance era" in the 1920s and '30s. It was a seafood joint down in the Market (which was a whole lot rougher in those days), and among other distinctions, old Henry's served liquor throughout Prohibition with (apparently) no interference from the city fathers. Hearty *"receipts"* for seafood soups and dishes laden with cream and flavor were always offered at Henry's, and generations of Charlestonians were raised on it. Hank's is today's reincarnation of that tradition, with a lot of sophistication added to the mix. An old warehouse has been carefully outfitted with a quasi-period-looking fish-house decor without being too cute about it. And several of the old Henry's dishes have been reproduced or improved upon for patrons with modern palates who now flock there from all over the world. This is where she-crab soup is done right (lovingly flavored with crab roe and sherry), and

oysters are still served on the half-shell atop beds of crushed ice. Look for some of the old Henry's casseroles, if you like, or try the specialties (like sea scallops or seared tuna). There are several fried seafood platters that feature a variety of old Lowcountry receipts, as well. Spirits are still high and served at Hank's willingly. Reservations are taken from 5 until 10:30 p.m. Sun through Thurs and until 11:30 p.m. on Fri and Sat.

HYMAN'S SEAFOOD COMPANY $$
215 Meeting St.
(843) 723-6000
www.hymanseafood.com
A casual, always-crowded seafood dining experience for lunch or dinner, Hyman's offers a large selection of fresh-caught fish and a wide variety of shellfish. A raw bar and lounge are upstairs. Hyman's regularly fries in vegetable oil for those who want traditionally fried seafood. But you can order your fish broiled or blackened. Try the lowcountry gumbo, for a hearty starter. The she-crab soup is award-winning. Open every day, the restaurant serves meals all day long from 11 a.m. to 11 p.m. We suggest parking in the Charleston Place garage.

LOCKLEAR'S FINE SEAFOOD $$
320 Coleman Blvd., Mount Pleasant
(843) 884-3346
www.locklears.com
Locklear's has been one of the most popular seafood restaurants in Mount Pleasant for years. But it's known for the chicken salad plate and she-crab soup as well. It's also considered a bargain. Now there is a Folly Beach location, too (101 East Arctic Ave., 843-588-6412). Call ahead for take-out lunch, and remember to consider the Heart Choice health-conscious items on the menu.

Locklear's is open 7 days a week for lunch and dinner. This is a popular spot for Sunday brunch starting at 10 a.m. Reservations are accepted.

MARINA VARIETY STORE & RESTAURANT $$
City Marina, 17 Lockwood Dr.
(843) 723-6325
www.varietystorerestaurant.com

Enjoy good food as well as a magnificent view of the Ashley River at what regulars call the Variety Store. Offering breakfast, lunch, and dinner in a very casual setting, the restaurant serves basic, good food. For instance, you can order eggs, bacon, and toast for breakfast after church and come back for a tuna salad sandwich and cup of vegetable soup after the noon regatta. If you want to return that night, a dinner of fresh fish with red rice and a salad is a distinct possibility. Spirits are available, and children are welcome. Take-out is a popular option for City Marina guests and locals. Open daily, except there's no dinner service on Sun.

NOISY OYSTER $$–$$$
24 North Market St.
(843) 723-0044
www.noisyoysterseafood.com

Locally owned and operated for more than a decade, this restaurant offers fresh seafood and a casual atmosphere. Noisy Oyster always has a number of daily specials with fresh shrimp, scallops, and fish. Look for the oysters Rockefeller or the shrimp okra gumbo. Dining is possible inside and out, and spirits are available. Lunch and dinner are served daily. (See the Nightlife chapter.) Additional locations are at 7842 Rivers Ave., North Charleston (843-824-1000), and 9800 Dorchester Rd., Summerville (843-821-1213).

RED'S ICE HOUSE $$
98 Church St., Mount Pleasant
(843) 388-0003
www.redsicehouse.com

Another casual spot where diners get a view of Shem Creek, Red's Ice House is another landmark along the popular restaurant row on both sides of the creek. You'll enjoy oysters, scallops, fish, and shrimp, as well as landlubber fare such as hamburgers and chicken. But make no mistake—right off the boat shrimp and fish are the main draw here.

Red's is right on the water, where shrimp boats dock and boaters cruise, to see and be seen. Red's colorful atmosphere makes this a happenin' place for young singles, especially on weekend nights. Wednesday features "Yappy Hour" where you and your pooch can mix and mingle. Red's is open daily from 11:30 a.m. to 10 p.m., or 11 p.m. on Fri and Sat, and the bar closes at midnight. Their new Bohicket Marina location (1882 Andell Bluff Rd., 843-518-5515) has a spectacular dockside setting too.

SHEM CREEK BAR & GRILL $$
508 Mill St., Mount Pleasant
(843) 884-8102
www.shemcreekbarandgrill.com

To experience dining out the way the locals enjoy it, go to Shem Creek Bar and Grill (just Shem Creek to the regulars) and you'll find yourself surrounded by loyal Lowcountry patrons. (See the Nightlife chapter under East Cooper.) The menu has something for everyone, from burgers and steaks to lobster and grilled seafood specials, and Sloppy John's Oyster Bar is always a temptation. During the warmer months, Shem Creek is the hangout for the boating set, many of whom arrive by power craft. There is casual dining inside and out, with views of the creek from most seats. It's open daily for lunch and dinner and has brunch on Sun. The owners also operate the Banana Cabana on the Isle of Palms.

STATION 22 $$–$$$
2205 Middle St., Sullivan's Island
(843) 883-3355
www.station22restaurant.com
Casual, but not quite flip-flops and a T-shirt, Station 22 offers variety on its menu and island history on its walls, which showcase dozens of photographs of turn-of-the-20th century Sullivan's Island. Find appetizers like the fried green tomatoes with pimento cream cheese and a puree of fire-roasted peppers or the cornbread fried oysters with Thai sriracha and tartar sauce. For an entree, try the black bean ravioli with scallops and shrimp in a garlic cream sauce and fresh tomato salsa or the char-grilled salmon filet over sauteed spinach with mushrooms. Save room for their signature coconut cake. Open every day from 5:30 p.m. for dinner and Sunday brunch from 10 a.m. to 2 p.m. Parking is available in front and next to the restaurant or their private lot directly across the street.

WATER'S EDGE $$$
1407 Shrimp Boat Lane, Mount Pleasant
(843) 884-4074
www.waters-edge-restaurant.com
Water's Edge is an upscale seafood and beef restaurant on Shem Creek. Specialties include local seafood, Maine lobster, and paella. You'll also find one of the most comprehensive wine and champagne lists in Mount Pleasant. Patrons park themselves, if possible, at a table next to the window for a view of the shrimp boats. Or come by your own boat and dock at the cabana bar. Water's Edge is open for lunch and dinner

every day and serves a nice Sunday brunch as well.

THE WRECK OF RICHARD AND CHARLENE $$
106 Haddrell St., Mount Pleasant
(843) 884-0052
www.wreckrc.com
Tucked between Magwood and Wando seafood companies in the Old Village of Mount Pleasant, two flags (there's no official sign or designation) will help find the Wreck. The restaurant is very unpretentious, and you can arrive by your own boat if you don't mind crawling around on the docks to disembark. You may dine either on the deck or the screened-in porch dining area (the porch is sealed up and heated in the winter months). Try the shrimp and grits or the lightly fried scallops. Portions come in either Richard's size (large) or Charlene's size (not as large, but plenty), so order according to your appetite. Beer and wine are available except on Sun. The Wreck is open every day for dinner beginning at 5:30 p.m.

STEAKHOUSES

GRILL 225 $$$–$$$$
225 East Bay St.
(843) 266-4222, (877) 440-2250
www.grill225.com
When the Market Pavilion Hotel opened near the Market on East Bay Street, they promised a restaurant of distinction, and clearly, it was a promise they kept. Fashioned in the style of the great steak houses of yore, Grill 225 prides itself on garnering the freshest and highest-quality beef, veal, lamb, and seafood available. The fare is deliberately simple in its creation, proportion, flavor, and presentation—so the exceptional quality of each ingredient can (and does) carry the day. For

starters, try their tuna tower, and then tackle their generous cut of prime beef or double-cut lamb chops. From the sea come jumbo lump crab cakes and, of course, lobster of almost any size you specify. If you're willing, the dessert menu tempts with banana bread pudding or flaming baked Carolina. Reservations are recommended, and they can be made on-line. Dinner is served daily from 5:30 p.m. Lunch is from 11:30 a.m. to 3 p.m. Mon through Sat. Sunday brunch is from 11 a.m. to 2:30 p.m.

OAK STEAKHOUSE $$$–$$$$
17 Broad St.
(843) 722-4220
www.oaksteakhouserestaurant.com
What locals remember as the little luncheon eatery called BJ's took on a whole new identity when restaurant entrepreneur Brett McKee (formerly of Brett's, Union Hall, and Brett's at the Wickliffe House) decided to create for Broad Street a New York–style steakhouse par excellence. He started by taking the 1840s-era building (originally a bank) through a $3 million renovation and expansion, which took 7 months to complete. When done, the stage was set for high drama, and Brett stepped up to the plate with his usual panache. Today, this is an upscale source for steaks, chops, Italian specialties, veal, and seafood—all served with flair. They use only prime Angus beef, and you may order from a number of specially prepared sauces to complement your selection. Among the favorite starters is the tuna tartare, a sashimi-grade yellowfin tuna in spicy ginger soy sauce with chopped scallions, shaved cucumbers, and a fried wonton. A popular steak for the hearty (read: enormous) appetite is the marinated 36-ounce bone-in rib eye. For those not in a beef state of mind, there's grilled Scottish salmon, Italian pastas, and fresh local seafood. You might want to go for the sesame encrusted yellowfin tuna with avocado slices, cucumber mango slaw and wasabi and ginger soy glaze. The wine selection is served up from a vault that in an earlier life held Confederate bonds (before the "Recent Unpleasantness"). There's even live music in the air as a gentle serenade for diners. Valet parking is offered along busy Broad Street, which is a welcome gesture of true hospitality. Reservations are definitely called for, as space is limited. They're open daily from 5 to 11 p.m. (10 p.m. on Sun).

NIGHTLIFE

When the sun goes down, not all the people in Greater Charleston pack it in. In fact, locals and visitors who seek nighttime entertainment are met with an abundance of choices.

If you are interested in listening to live contemporary music, dancing, or just hitting the bar scene, start with the spots we've described below—you won't be bored. If you like beer and want to sample it straight from the folks who create it, try one of the brewpubs. Many of the nightspots are actually lounges at restaurants where dining is the primary focus, and many of these places are described in greater detail in the Restaurants chapter. We also have a category called Dinner Cruises for those who want to spend an evening on the waters of Charleston Harbor cruising and dining with live music and dancing as after-dinner options.

While Charleston is affectionately called the "Holy City" in reference to its many lovely churches, it also has a reputation for entertaining where socializing has a long and rich tradition. If you plan on enjoying a few beers or cocktails as part of the fun, be aware of the legal restrictions in the Charleston area, and know that area police departments actively enforce these laws. The minimum drinking age is 21 in South Carolina, and open containers are not allowed on the streets or in moving vehicles. A charge of driving under the influence may be levied against anyone whose blood alcohol content is measured at .08 percent or higher. In the city of Charleston, last call for liquor is usually 1:30 a.m., and closing is mandatory at 2 a.m.

OVERVIEW

The coffeehouse phenomenon has taken a firm hold in this area, and aside from larger establishments like Starbucks there are at least a half-dozen non-chain houses to explore around the Peninsula. There are a number of conventional movie theaters showing first-run films here in the Lowcountry. There's even a movie house on James Island, Terrace Theatre, which shows first-run films in a setting where you can enjoy light fare, wine, and beer while you watch the flick. We've listed theater names and phone numbers and suggest you call for titles after checking the local paper's movie listings.

For information about other entertainment options and cultural happenings, we suggest consulting the Arts and Annual Events chapters.

DOWNTOWN CHARLESTON

BLIND TIGER PUB
36 and 38 Broad St.
(843) 577-0088
If you are looking for British pub atmosphere, escape into this friendly environment with

its dark English mahogany walls and cast-iron stools. Order Bass Ale or Guinness Stout, or try a Black and Tan (Bass on bottom, Guinness on top). Fear not: The beer is chilled appropriately for Charleston, not served lukewarm as in England. A nice selection of appetizers is available until 10 p.m. There is live music some nights and a crowd that just keeps coming back. The back courtyard is a nice option when weather permits.

*CAROLINA'S
10 Exchange St.
(843) 724-3800
www.carolinasrestaurant.com

The bar at Carolina's restaurant is an upscale alternative and a very popular meeting spot for professionals. Seating is available at the bar proper and in the surrounding areas. Try one of Carolina's specialty cocktails for an extra treat. Bar customers often feel comfortable staying on for dinner. Carolina's has an additional private dining room. Both areas are nice places to meet after work or after other events for a nightcap.

CLUB HABANA
177 Meeting St.
(843) 853-5900
www.tinderboxcharleston.com

Located in the swanky, upscale space directly above the Tinder Box (where all manner of tobacco products are sold), this is a late-night destination for a cigar and an after-dinner drink any day of the week. The intimate bar serves cordials, ports, wine, martinis, and specialty coffees. Mini Beef Wellingtons among their appetizer list seem the perfect complement to the experience. The cozy spot has both male and female aficionados, so the company is always varied and interesting. The plush couches and tasteful decor encourage patrons to puff away and sip a fine brandy in perfect comfort. Through a brilliant feat of air-conditioning engineering, the atmosphere is actually breathable. Happy hour is Mon through Fri from 4:30 to 7 p.m.

82 QUEEN
82 Queen St.
(843) 723-7591, (800) 849-0082
www.82queen.com

A long-standing, favorite hangout for the local Broad Street business set and others, the bar at 82 Queen is narrow (but comfortable enough) and a good place to see friends. You'll find a fine mix of people there knowing and not knowing each other's names. Patrons especially like the back bar if the weather is nice. They enjoy hanging out in the courtyard while waiters zip by with tempting appetizers, and outdoor diners enjoy their fare beneath the stars.

THE GRIFFON
18 Vendue Range
(843) 723-1700
www.griffoncharleston.com

A popular hangout for young professionals is The Griffon, a cozy English pub with an easy, friendly atmosphere. Especially busy at lunchtime, workers from the financial and legal offices on East Bay and Broad Streets stop here for simple but hearty sandwiches and maybe a cool brew. Others check in for happy hour, and some stay for dinner. It's open each evening and attracts a nice mix of locals and tourists out and about on East Bay.

HENRY'S BAR & RESTAURANT
54 North Market St.
(843) 723-4363

Henry's used to be known for its Old Charleston meals and clubby side bar. Today, under different ownership, it has updated trappings and a new reputation for light food and live music nightly. The ambience is contemporary New Orleans, and the second-floor lounge is open Fri and Sat nights. This is a happening place for the Market Street crowd.

KAMINSKY'S MOST EXCELLENT CAFE
78 North Market St.
(843) 853-8270
www.kaminskys.com
Kaminsky's Cafe tempts the minute you enter the door with their case full of "most excellent" desserts. In addition to specialty coffees, wine, beer, and liquors are on the menu. Kaminsky's serves from noon until late night.

i Late-night revelers who need a rule of thumb to remember Charleston's bar-closing hours, try this: All bars in the Market area close at 2 a.m. If you feel the need to party even later than that, you'll have to go elsewhere.

*MCCRADY'S
2 Unity Alley
(843) 577-0025
www.mccradysrestaurant.com
Neatly tucked down Unity Alley, off the hustle and bustle of East Bay Street, is this small but attractive haven for a quiet drink. It lays claim to the fact that George Washington tipped a few here back in 1791. Today, this beautifully turned-out restaurant and upscale bar is a favorite with downtown business types and professionals because of its cozy atmosphere. Its extensive wine list and premium bar serve happy-hour specials to please the after-work crowd. And its

popular dining room close by makes a natural progression from an after-work respite to an evening on the town.

*MILLS HOUSE HOTEL
115 Meeting St.
(843) 577-2400
www.millshouse.com
Easily the best location in Charleston if you're looking to be at the center of things, the Mills House Hotel is home to 2 nightspots that deserve your consideration. The handsome First Shot Lounge (in honor of the first shot fired at Fort Sumter in the Civil War) just off the Barbados Room Restaurant is a classic Southern setting that oozes charm. There's a grand piano, and often someone is on hand to play your favorite Gershwin tune. The Best Friend Lounge (named for the nation's first steam locomotive originating in Charleston) is a separate, more intimate bar with quiet entertainment Tues through Sat.

MUSIC FARM
32 Ann St.
(843) 577-6989
www.musicfarm.com
Now in its second decade on the Peninsula, one of the most popular nightspots for contemporary music enthusiasts is the Music Farm—affectionately referred to by regulars as the Farm. The beat goes on at weekly gigs when live bands—yes, favorite city sons Hootie and the Blowfish were once among them—perform here. The Farm's website has more information about upcoming entertainment and ticket prices. The college crowd is thick, but also expect to see 30-somethings, 40-somethings, and older-somethings elbowing their way toward the bar. The Farm is across the street from the

visitor center, and parking is available on the street as well as in the nearby garage.

NOISY OYSTER
24 North Market St.
(843) 723-0044
www.noisyoysterseafood.com
Located on bustling Market Street, this friendly little bar offers libations that seem to taste better in the salty sea air of the nearby Cooper River. The restaurant always has a number of seafood specials sure to please. Lunch and dinner are served daily. Additional locations are at 7842 Rivers Ave., North Charleston (843-824-1000), and 9800 Dorchester Rd., Summerville (843-821-1213).

✳PENINSULA GRILL
112 North Market St.
(843) 723-0700
www.peninsulagrill.com
The Peninsula Grill at the Planters Inn offers a very beautiful, romantic, upscale bar tucked inside the restaurant. In warm weather, we recommend a drink here before and after dining outdoors in the gaslit courtyard. This bar always attracts a well-dressed, attractive crowd and is a classy oasis amid the carnival atmosphere of the Market at night. The delightful Champagne Bar carries an extensive list of labels, and several are sold by the glass. The bar opens daily starting at 4 p.m.

ROOF TOP RESTAURANT & BAR
23 Vendue Range
(843) 414-2341
www.vendueinn.com
On the roof of the Vendue Inn in downtown Charleston is this rare find on the Peninsula—a place (for cocktails) with a rooftop view and refreshing sea breezes. (See the Vendue Inn in the Accomodations chapter.)

With two separate levels, the Roof Top Bar was much anticipated by locals. This place is a lovely location for starting a summer evening in Charleston catching the sunset over the rooftops of Charleston. The service is friendly, and you can enjoy live entertainment most nights.

SOUTH END BREWERY AND SMOKEHOUSE
161 East Bay St.
(843) 853-4677
www.southendbrewery.com
Here's a restaurant with its own microbrewery. Ice-cold hand-crafted brews, made on the premises, are served with baby-back ribs, oven-baked pizzas, and specials off the wood-burning grill. The glass elevator takes you up to a third-floor cigar lounge and billiard and game room with spectacular views over the city. South End has live entertainment on weekends and serves both lunch and dinner 7 days a week.

TOMMY CONDON'S IRISH PUB AND SEAFOOD RESTAURANT
160 Church St.
(843) 577-3818
www.tommycondons.com
Every day is St. Patty's Day at Charleston's only authentic Irish pub owned by an Irish family. In fact, families are indeed welcome here. Tommy Condon's has traditional Irish singalongs Wed through Sun and serves Irish spirits as well. The layout of the facility, with its big horseshoe bar, makes for a good party flow, and people mix and mingle all around.

WET WILLIE'S
209 East Bay St.
(843) 853-5650
www.wetwillies.com

Across the street from the Custom House is this watering hole that's popular with the young professionals working up and down East Bay Street. Tourists are lured in as well,because it's right on the street and very inviting by day or night with its big, wide open doors. Thursday, Friday, and Saturday offers dancing with a DJ on site. You'll also find pool, pinball, and foosball. Wet Willie's will ask you to support global cooling by drinking one of their famous frozen daiquiris.

East Cooper

Mount Pleasant

Although Mount Pleasant is still a family-oriented community, there are plenty of exciting destinations for grownups when the sun goes down. The tremendous growth of the Mount Pleasant area and the subsequent boom in population have created a whole new market for after-hours entertainment. That's especially true now that all bars in Charleston are mandated to close at 2 a.m. The days when this quiet East Cooper neighborhood was strictly a bedroom community for downtown Charleston are over. Some of Mount Pleasant's nightspots howl until late night. Mind you, this is no passport to drive irresponsibly or misbehave, and the Mount Pleasant fuzz are out and about at all hours to prove it.

CHARLESTON HARBOR
RESORT & MARINA
20 Patriots Point Rd.
(843) 856-0028, (888) 856-0028
www.charlestonharborresort.com
This hotel in Mount Pleasant on the Point, which extends into Charleston Harbor, is a delightful venue for sunset watching and a taste of coastal nightlife. (See the

Accommodations chapter.) Every Fri during the summer months, hotel employees construct added outdoor bars and light bonfires in the sand for "Rockin on the Point" and hundreds of people come to enjoy the music, spirits, and invigorating night air. Charleston Harbor Resort & Marina brings in entertainment from near and far. Jazz, rock, beach music—it's all here at one time or another. They start pouring signature drinks at 6 p.m. and continue until long after sunset. Light dining options may include beachside barbecue and a seasonal seafood raw bar. Located just over the Cooper River Bridge, this is a popular destination for Peninsula folk and East Cooper residents alike.

SHEM CREEK BAR & GRILL
508 Mill St.
(843) 884-8102
www.shemcreekbarandgrill.com
High on the list of casual nighttime destinations, Shem Creek is one of the most popular watering holes in the area. It certainly has some great things going for it—the dockside bar overlooking the marsh, the raw bar inside, and the salty characters who make it their home away from home. The mood is usually upbeat, and the munchies are delicious.

VICKERY'S BAR & GRILL
1313 Shrimp Boat Lane
(843) 884-4440
www.vickerysbarandgrill.com
Vickery's is a popular spot for a drink with friends. The restaurant does a booming daytime business with its Cuban-American cuisine, and there's a festive Latin flavor in the bar at night. There's a large outdoor seating area for imbibing or dining. Vickery's is in

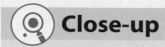

Close-up

All that Jazz ...

If anything about the City of Charleston is known and recognized the world over, it has to be the 1920s dance craze that swept the country and set the tone for America in the Jazz Age. Relatively few people, on the other hand, know the origins of the dance or the story of how it captured the imagination of an American generation bursting with pent-up energy after the so-called war to end all wars (World War I). The popular dance known as **"The Charleston"** is said to have begun on the street beside Charleston's Fort Sumter Hotel (near the Battery) with the energetic dance steps of the **Jenkins Orphanage Band.** In 1892, the Rev. Daniel Jenkins founded an orphanage in the city for homeless black children. To fund his charity, he organized the kids into a band that played on street corners for pennies donated from passersby. These young musicians were a delight to locals and visiting tourists alike. Eventually several bands and choirs evolved that were invited to perform in Florida, the northern states, and eventually Canada and Europe. The Jenkins Orphanage Band and its jaunty jazz tune called the "Charleston" spawned the careers of several great jazz musicians who eventually played in the world-class bands of jazz greats like Count Basie, Louis Armstrong, and Duke Ellington.

the lively mix of restaurants and nightspots located on scenic Shem Creek.

Sullivan's Island & Isle of Palms

Although the islands east of the Cooper River are considered family beaches, there are several notable watering holes nestled behind the dunes. A word of warning: Don't let the casual setting lull you into ignoring the open container laws. In other words, don't stroll outside with an unsealed alcoholic beverage. Police officers take it seriously.

BANANA CABANA
1130 Ocean Blvd., Isle of Palms
(843) 886-4361
www.thebananacabana.com
The Banana Cabana is open 7 nights a week and offers a volleyball net and putting green as well as lots of cool, refreshing libations, and munchies. Locals and visitors seem to

delight in visiting this place after a day at the beach. Sometimes the volleyball court is where you'll find macho men and their female challengers fresh from the beach boasting their sports prowess and their perfect tans.

DUNLEAVY'S
2213-A Middle St., Sullivan's Island
(843) 883-9646
A welcome watering hole for the island, Dunleavy's is an Irish pub with indoor and outdoor dining. The outdoor picnic tables are replete with dog bowls for patrons on a leash. The bar regularly attracts the beach crowd, and it's very family-oriented at the dinner hour. On weekends it features live music (and some Tuesdays feature bluegrass). Bill Dunleavy is usually on hand and makes one and all feel welcome.

STATION 22
2205 Middle St., Sullivan's Island
(843) 883-3355

A handsome, comfortable bar, with walls adorned with wonderful old pictures from the early days on the island, Station 22 has been a local favorite since it opened some years back. You can experience a quiet evening here as well as those occasional nights when the jukebox (said to be one of the best in town) is cranked loud. Revelers have been known to even cut a rug here. A charming train encircles the bar proper, and bartenders blow the whistle when the time is right. Mount Pleasant

West Ashley

Nighttime activity west of the Ashley River is often on or near the water, in settings that are attractive but casual. Most nightspots are part of restaurants, and some with docks cater to the boating crowd.

CALIFORNIA DREAMING RESTAURANT AND BAR
1 Ashley Pointe Dr.
(843) 766-1644
www.californiadreamings.com

This is the fortlike restaurant whose lights beckon from across the Ashley at night. After sundown, the scene is busy, lively, and fun. The bar is a great place to have a drink with a friend or a group of friends. You can see the lights of the Ashley and City Marinas, and it's adjacent to Ripley Light Marina, so the view is breathtaking. Because diners come here by droves, the bar is also a natural place to wait for a table. There's even a small floating dock for boat tie-ups.

GENE'S HAUFBRAU
817 Savannah Hwy.
(843) 225-4363
www.geneshaufbrau.com

This West Ashley spot claims to be Charleston's oldest bar. Nothing luxurious, the new place is a comfortable neighborhood bar, friendly and spacious, with pool, shuffleboard, darts, good pub food, and more than 150 beers and 12 draft labels from which to choose. This bar is popular with the after-work crowd who toil across the Ashley River Bridge. And it's still close enough to The Citadel to draw the thirsty (and legal) cadets who can smell a beer at 40 paces.

TRIANGLE CHAR & BAR
828 Savannah Hwy.
(843) 377-1300
www.trianglecharandbar.com

Stop by the Triangle Bar after work or a long day seeing the sights and enjoy the lively crowd and half price drink specials. "Triangle Kisses" are another draw with house bubbly "kissed" with schnapps in apple, mango, peach, or pear. Happy hour is Mon through Fri 4 to 7 p.m. Starters and sandwiches are available in the bar too, or entrees are served on the restaurant side if your appetite calls for more.

James & Johns Islands

CHARLESTON CRAB HOUSE
145 Wappoo Creek Dr., James Island
(843) 795-1963
www.charlestoncrabhouse.com

This popular spot on the Intracoastal Waterway near the Wappoo Cut Bridge has dockside tables and space for mooring boats. There is live entertainment on weekends after Memorial Day, and it always seems to be packed during the summer months. The deck is a lot of fun for drinks, appetizers, and watching those giant yachts go by. Two more locations are at 1101 Stockade Lane, US 17 N., Mount Pleasant (843-884-1617) and 41 South Market St., Charleston (843-853-2900).

COFFEEHOUSES

EAST BAY MEETING HOUSE BAR & CAFE
160 East Bay St.
(843) 723-3446
www.eastbaymeetinghouse.com
Located in the heart of the French Quarter District on East Bay Street, the East Bay Meeting House brings a touch a European elegance to Charleston's charm. Their intimate bar serves gourmet coffees along with a full selection of wines, cocktails, and signature martinis. You may want to linger a while to try one of their soups, appetizers, hot paninis, or desserts from the After Dark menu. The Meeting House is open 7 days a week from 7 a.m. to 2 a.m.

METTO COFFEE & TEA
354 Coleman Blvd., Mount Pleasant
(843) 216-8832
Here's a trendy coffeehouse that's actually a cross between a place to grab some tasty hot java or tea and a drive-through dry cleaner. Instead of freshly laundered shirts, they dispense coffee, pannini sandwiches, salads, pastries, and desserts—to go. It's a favorite with morning commuters, who can buy a newspaper while waiting in line for their coffee and/or lunch. It's open until 7 p.m. (5 p.m. on Sun). The fare here is far more creative than fast food and almost as convenient.

MUDDY WATERS COFFEE BAR
1739 Maybank Hwy., James Island
(843) 795-0848
www.muddywaterscoffee.com
Owned by a couple of Seattle natives, this independent coffeehouse brews Counter Culture Coffee, which purchases coffees from growers dedicated to sustainable coffee farming from around the world. This means they have taken "freshly brewed" to a new level. A variety of pastries are on-hand to accompany your coffee as well as wine and dessert for the later hours—all set in a cozy atmosphere of leather sofas, small tables, and chairs with local artists' works showcased on the walls. A second location is at 1331 Ashley River Rd., Charleston (West Ashley; 843-225-3683).

COMEDY CLUBS

THE HAVE NOTS!
280 Meeting St., 2nd Floor
(843) 853-6687
www.thehavenots.com
A very popular improv comedy troupe known as The Have Nots! has found a new home at Theatre 99 on the second floor of 280 Meeting, above The Bicycle Shoppe. This three-member troupe has built a strong following in Charleston by finding the funny bone of local audiences and those out-of-towners who came for Piccolo Spoleto, alike. Somehow, they always manage to take the ordinary and turn it into the absurd from point-blank audience suggestions. Having their own space gives them an option of using creative lighting as a prop, which seems to be a trick all their own. Audiences range from teens to tourists of the senior persuasion. Everybody seems to have a great

time. They sometimes tour, so call ahead to be sure they're playing at their home venue. Other comedy programming is offered every Wed, Fri, and Sat. Admission ranges from $5 to $12.50.

DINNER CRUISES

SPIRITLINE DINNER CRUISE
40 Patriots Point Rd., Mount Pleasant
(843) 722-2628
www.spiritlinecruises.com
Dining and dancing aboard this 96-foot luxury tour boat while cruising historic Charleston Harbor make for one of those quintessential Charleston experiences. The Spirit of Carolina serves a three-course meal of she-crab soup, house salad, and a choice of five entrees such as beef tenderloin, chicken, or seafood per prior request. All menu items are served with a nod toward the Lowcountry tradition of cooking. The boat makes its rounds up and down the waterways at sundown and is always a lot of fun. Live music and dancing are part of the weekday bill of fare. Entertainment is provided by a live band who can perform jazz, blues, shag, and country music as per your request. Spirit of Carolina is part of the Fort Sumter Tours group and conveniently departs from the docks at Patriots Point Naval and Maritime Museum, where there's parking at the clearly marked boarding dock for a fee. The boarding begins at 6:30 p.m., and the cruise departs at 7 p.m. and returns at 10 p.m. Rates and schedules change seasonally, but tickets are in the $48 range for adults (Sun through Thurs) and $53 range on Fri and Sat. (See the Cruise and Boat Tours section of the Tours chapter.)

MOVIE THEATERS

Mount Pleasant

CINEBARRE
963 Houston Northcutt Blvd.
(843) 884-7885
www.cinebarre.com
If you are looking for dinner and a movie, here's the place—and all under one roof. As soon as you enter the lobby, you'll see the difference as you step into a lounge and bar offering a dozen or so domestic and imported draft and bottled beers. Wines by the bottle or the glass as well as daiquiri and margarita pitchers are options here too. Casual food like sandwiches, burgers, and pizzas are delivered to your movie seat (with a small table) as efficiently and quietly as can be done. Showing a mix of first-run films along with mainstream and art-house movies on 11 screens, this is an adult movie-lovers haven. No children under 6 are allowed and children ages 6 to 17 must be accompanied by an adult, cutting down on the disruptive atmosphere of some other cinemas.

James Island

TERRACE THEATER
1956 Maybank Hwy.
(843) 762-9494
www.terracetheater.com
In the Terrace Oaks shopping center, this first-run, widescreen movie house features current hits and classic films in an upscale and comfortable atmosphere. Its cafe and lounge features gourmet snacks, coffee, and microbrews on tap. Desserts, wine, and champagne are also available to accommodate every taste. Call the information line (see above) to hear what's on the current bill and to get matinee and nightly showtimes.

CONCERT INFORMATION & VENUES

Greater Charleston's appetite for entertainment and artistic diversions is satisfied by a wide range of performance venues today. From the rafter-filling rock concerts attracting thousands to the most intimate recitals at the College of Charleston, we have a concert hall or a major facility that can handle the crowd.

Ticketmaster is one of the high-tech ways to get tickets to almost any concert or special event in the Lowcountry. This company, with nationwide ticket distribution, adds a surcharge for the convenience of buying tickets through them. You can get tickets by phone or at local kiosks in venues, such as Publix and Piggly Wiggly grocery stores, which work like bank machines (handling charge cards). But the added cost is worth it for some. Most of the events have their own sites as well for purchasing tickets online. Others prefer to shop for their tickets to Spoleto and other hot concerts the old-fashioned way, by standing in line at the Gaillard Auditorium ticket window. You can access Ticketmaster by visiting www.ticketmaster.com. The Gaillard's box office is generally open from 10 a.m. to 6 p.m. Mon through Fri year-round. Before and during Spoleto, the hours are extended. (For more on Spoleto Festival USA and other performing arts events, see the chapters on The Arts and Annual Events.)

GAILLARD MUNICIPAL AUDITORIUM
77 Calhoun St.
(843) 577-7400
www.charleston-sc.gov
Built in 1968, Charleston's 2,734-seat Gaillard Auditorium is the premier venue in the city for major arts events. It was named in honor of longtime Charleston Mayor J. Palmer Gaillard Jr., and it always houses the major opera productions of Spoleto Festival USA (see the chapters Annual Events and The Arts). The Charleston Symphony Orchestra performs here, and Gaillard hosts productions of the Charleston Concert Association and touring off-Broadway shows. At Christmastime, Charleston's children are awed by the Charleston Ballet Theatre's glittering presentation of *The Nutcracker*. The auditorium is easy to find: It occupies the block bounded by Anson, George, Alexander, and Calhoun Streets. A city parking garage is next door. The Gaillard's box office hours are 10 a.m. to 6 p.m. Mon through Fri.

NORTH CHARLESTON COLISEUM
5001 Coliseum Dr., North Charleston
(843) 529-5000
www.coliseumpac.com
Opened in 1993, the North Charleston Coliseum is the largest and most diverse indoor entertainment facility in South Carolina. Various seating configurations are possible, but generally speaking, the coliseum's capacity is 14,000 seats. Because of this, Greater Charleston is now a viable audience for some of the biggest traveling shows and sports attractions in America. The Coliseum has attracted the likes of Rod Stewart, James Taylor, the Ringling Brothers and Barnum and Bailey Circus, Reba McEntire, the Eagles, World Cup figure skating, NHL hockey, and NCAA basketball, to name just a few. It is also the permanent home of the South Carolina Stingrays minor league hockey club, members of the East Coast Hockey League. (See the Spectator Sports chapter.) To get to the Coliseum, take the Montague Avenue exit off I-26 and follow the signs, or take the Montague Avenue exit off I-526 (Mark Clark

Expressway). Ample parking is on-site, but be prepared to pay the price. Tickets for all Coliseum events may be purchased at the box office from 10 a.m. to 5 p.m. Mon through Fri.

NORTH CHARLESTON PERFORMING ARTS CENTER

5001 Coliseum Dr., North Charleston
(843) 202-2787
www.coliseumpac.com

With the advent of the 2,300-seat Performing Arts Center at the Charleston Area Convention Center complex, the Lowcountry won a place on the "road" itinerary for almost everyone who's anyone (or who's going to be) in the music industry. Finally, greater Charleston qualified as a viable destination for major shows and for artists who only want to visit venues that seat audiences of 2,000 or so. When it opened in August 1999 with Harry Connick Jr. and his "Big Band" of 16 hot New Orleans musicians, the $18 million facility was off to a roaring start. Since then, touring road companies of major Broadway shows, big name artists like George Winston and Melissa Manchester, and events that were inappropriate for the 14,000-seat North Charleston Coliseum have found a home.

The on-site ticket office is open from 10 a.m. to 5 p.m. Mon through Fri.

THE SOTTILE THEATRE

44 George St.
(843) 953-5623
www.sottile.cofc.edu

The Sottile Theatre began life back in the 1920s as a venue for live vaudeville acts and the latest movies from Hollywood. Back then, Charleston had a number of downtown movie houses, and this was among the most elaborate. Old-timers who remember it from its movie house days were gratified to see the ceiling restored to its former dazzle—as "pretend" stars twinkle in the darkness as the houselights go down. It fell on hard times and was vacant for many years until, in 1976, the College of Charleston bought the building for college and community use. A decade later, renovations began and continued for a full year. Today, the beautifully restored and technically updated Sottile seats 785 patrons and hosts a variety of performing arts. It is a venue for Spoleto Festival USA, Charleston Ballet Theatre, Charleston Symphony, Charleston Men's Chorus, and many other performing arts organizations.

SHOPPING

For a city that's famous for all that's old and historic, Charleston offers shoppers today easier-than-ever access to things that are new and exciting. From fashions to home furnishings, from bestsellers to sporting goods, the Lowcountry has it all. The older shopping haunts have been updated and expanded, plus whole new shopping destinations have sprung up in high-growth areas where the expanding population has called for them.

No matter how you look at it, the shopping opportunities here in the Lowcountry are almost unlimited. Communities that were geographically isolated only a dozen years ago are now within an easy commute to a diverse and interesting commercial/shopping adventure. The future looks bright, and more shoppers are drawn to the area every day.

The variety ranges in size from specialty shop enclaves in downtown nooks and crannies to major shopping centers and the seemingly endless random strip malls. To provide a useful index for your shopping needs, we've categorized these shopping adventures by location and merchandise.

We'll start with the major shopping areas of downtown Charleston. Some of these famous old streets have been shopping meccas for 200 years. Other streets have only recently become decidedly commercial. Much of downtown's historic district houses a mix of shops and homes and every other aspect of daily life—with a certain deference made to keeping the historic fabric of the city intact.

Next, we'll survey the brightest and best shopping opportunities in the surrounding areas, as we've done with our chapters on accommodations, restaurants, nightlife, and neighborhoods. Within each geographic designation, however, we've categorized stores by the type of merchandise that's dominant there. Included are the most exclusive boutiques and the just-as-welcome discount stores catering to the dollar-conscious consumer. In each case, we've tried to identify businesses with items of particular interest for our visitors and those frequented by a local clientele.

OVERVIEW

In general, we've omitted descriptions of the major chain retailers with which you are already familiar. Some of the best of these are the high-end shops featured in The Shops at Charleston Place. Please note that bookstore browsers will find the familiar chain stores such as Barnes & Noble Booksellers at locations in West Ashley, Mount Pleasant (Towne Centre), and North Charleston. Books-A-Million also has a North Charleston and West Ashley location, and Waldenbooks can be found in Charleston Place. Some of the smaller independents are described in more detail under "Bookstores" in each designated shopping area.

Finally, we'll offer newcomers a brief rundown of the major shopping malls here in the Lowcountry. We hope our guide is a tempting sample of the variety and quality of shopping options in this area. We do encourage you, however, to venture off the beaten path from time to time—new and hidden surprises are everywhere!

DOWNTOWN CHARLESTON

King Street

Let's start with King Street, one of the leading Charleston shopping districts. This is the essence of downtown shopping, and it has been for a couple hundred years. While the street actually begins high on the Peninsula and ends as a narrow throughway past an extraordinary collection of pre-Revolutionary private homes, the real business and shopping district begins at about Mary Street and continues with greater intensity until it crosses Broad Street.

Listed below, by category of merchandise, are some of the more unique shops you'll find on or near King Street.

Bookstores
BOOKS, HERBS AND SPICES
63 Spring St.
(843) 722-4747
www.booksherbsspices.com
This is primarily a health-food store, but for those willing to venture a bit further off King Street, there's a large section of books about foods, herbal remedies, and other health-oriented matters. While you're shopping, treat yourself to something tasty from the kitchen or the blender. There's also a refrigerator case

that's always filled with fresh vegetarian sandwiches and exotic juices promising health benefits. Look for it near the corner of Spring and Coming Streets.

BLUE BICYCLE BOOKS
420 King St.
(843) 722-2666
www.bluebicyclebooks.com
This upper King Street bookshop buys, sells, and trades books. While popular reading material is the main thrust of the store, rare books, collectibles, Lowcountry memorabilia, and souvenirs are also for sale. Local author book-signings are popular events here. Mind you, this store is a fooler. Its tiny storefront belies the seemingly endless series of rooms housing a vast selection of reading matter for every taste. It's even open until 7:30 p.m. Mon through Sat and till 6 p.m. on Sun.

COLLEGE OF CHARLESTON
**   BOOKSTORE**
160 Calhoun St.
(843) 953-5518
www.cofc.edu/bookstore
The College of Charleston's bookstore in the Lightsey Center, actually on Calhoun Street just off King, is typical of university bookstores, but it also carries a nice section representing local authors and local interest books as well as faculty publications. It's also fun to poke around in the college textbook sections just to see what's happening these days. Time flies.

✳PRESERVATION SOCIETY OF
**   CHARLESTON BOOK & GIFT SHOP**
147 King St.
(843) 723-4381
www.preservationsociety.org

The Preservation Society of Charleston Bookstore has what may be the most com-prehensive area collection of books about Charleston, the Lowcountry, and all things Southern. Many Charleston and Lowcoun-try authors are represented here. You also can shop for art books, academic works, entertaining literature, and even some recorded material. (See the Attractions chapter for more on The Preservation Society of Charleston.)

UNIVERSITY BOOKS OF CHARLESTON
360 King St.
(843) 853-8700
www.ubc-cofc.com

This bookstore is not officially affiliated with the College of Charleston, but is a popular source for college students and a place to browse for interesting academic titles. Along with textbooks and reference materials, University Books sells school logo items—everything from T-shirts to bumper stickers for your favorite college team.

Children's Clothing
KIDS ON KING
195½ King St.
(843) 720-8647
www.kidsonking.com

Travel the world by shopping at Kids on King where the children's clothing comes from the most prestigious international fashion destinations. The owners have carefully selected unique styles from New York and around the world to bring to their Charleston store. Some of the brands include Alessia, Biscotti, truluv, Peruvian Trading, Hartstrings, Anavini, deux par deux, Glorimont, Haute Baby, and Elephantito shoes. They cater to infants, girls, boys, and pre-teen girls. Unusual gifts and collectibles can be found here too for all those childhood special occasions.

WORTHWHILE
268 King St.
(843) 723-4418
www.shopworthwhile.com

This boutique sells 100 percent cotton clothing and accessories for infants, children, and adults. (See the Women's Clothing section under King Street in this chapter.) Shop here for earth-friendly, contemporary clothes that feel comfortable in the Charleston heat. In addition to their clothing lines, they have decorative accessories with a touch of whimsy for the home, bed and bath linens for cozy nesting, and personal care products for a sensual delight.

Flowers
TIGER LILY FLORIST
131 Spring St.
(843) 723-2808, (800) 844-8199
www.tigerlilyflorist.com

Oftentimes, visitors to the Lowcountry are especially impressed with the floral displays that grace private parties, special events, and hotel lobbies throughout the city. When asked who did the arrangement, the answer is frequently, "Tiger Lily." This creative and popular florist is located at the corner of Spring Street and Ashley Avenue (a short drive from upper King Street). It's in what was once an art deco–styled auto dealership from the 1930s. The creativity the company brought to rehabbing this distinctive building can be found in its floral arrangements, which range from the most elaborate affair to the single rose on the pillow of a honeymoon bed. One nice touch to Tiger Lily's marketing is the website, which shows shoppers an array of creative displays recently produced by the shop's designers. Clients can choose or modify their orders from a visual starting point, which is very helpful. Tiger Lily also carries accessories and furnishings for outdoor gardens and patios where flowers and design are the main focus.

Gifts
**PRESERVATION SOCIETY OF
  CHARLESTON BOOK & GIFT SHOP**
147 King St.
(843) 722-4630
www.preservationsociety.org
Along with all that's printed on Charleston and the Lowcountry, this terrific store offers local crafts, art prints, even recordings of Lowcountry lore told in the local Gullah dialect. Here, too, are the architectural drawings of Jim Polzois, whose studies of the city's architectural vernacular are beautifully done. They're simply the best available. (See previous listing under Bookstores.)

THE SILVER PUFFIN
329 King St.
(843) 723-7900 (888) 723-7900
www.silverpuffin.com
This King Street gift shop has a large selection of cards, mirrors, pottery, jewelry, prints, and glassware. International gourmet foods and quality children's toys are other draws here. Some of the charming merchandise is domestic, some imported. The owners ship anywhere, so tourists can buy without having to carry things around during their Charleston adventures.

THE SMOKING LAMP
401-B King St.
(843) 577-7339, (800) 745-7465
www.smokinglamp.com

Forget the no smoking signs. Right across from Marion Square, this always-fragrant tobacco shop features a complete selection of fine pipes, cigars, tobacco, cigarettes, and smoking accessories. Beer and wine is offered here too.

VIEUXTEMPS
180 King St.
(843) 723-7309
www.vieuxtemps.net
When it's time to shop for a wedding or anniversary gift, this should be your first stop. Vieuxtemps's deserves a gold star for its complete selection of crystal and fine china. It carries Waterford, Herend, Mottahedeh, William Yeoward, and Towle, as well as a wonderful collection of accent pieces and decorating accessories. Co-owner Pamela Tidwell's hand sculpted porcelain botanicals are a major draw. This is where many Charleston brides register their china and sterling patterns.

Home Accents & Decor
LE CREUSET
241 King St.
(843) 723-4191
www.lecreuset.com
Most folks don't know that the famous French enameled cast-iron cookware known as Le Creuset has a manufacturing plant right here in the Lowcountry. It's in Yemassee, South Carolina, about an hour's drive from Charleston, and the good news is the factory outlet on King Street. The ordinarily pricey cookware is considerably discounted here—a boon to gourmets who happen across this downtown store. You're likely to pick up some wine and champagne accessories, too, along with some nifty cooking gadgets.

MAINE COTTAGE
525 King St.
(843) 722-7188
www.mainecottage.com
Maine Cottage features the hot new trend for painted furniture for use as a vibrant accent for the contemporary apartment or home. Whether you're looking for a large piece or something zany and small, this is a must-see for young homemakers or the young-at-heart with a zest for color in their domestic decor.

YVES DELORME
The Shops at Charleston Place,
246 King St.
(843) 853-4331
www.yvesdelorme.com
This is the store for fine French linens—everything for the bed, bath, and table. All the merchandise is natural fiber—either linen or Egyptian cotton. Palais Royal also carries goose-down duvets and pillows that veritably evoke pastel mornings on the Left Bank. To complete the scene, the shop carries a variety of hand-painted porcelain and other table graces. If you love Paris, there's a little bit of it here.

Jewelry
✳CROGHAN'S JEWEL BOX
308 King St.
(843) 723-3594
www.croghansjewelbox.com
This is a shop that some will remember as a tiny space unobtrusively tucked away behind a small awning on King Street but filled with quality merchandise. It's tiny no more. After more than 80 years as a Charleston shopping institution, this family-owned jewelry store finally has the space to show its worth. Now expanded into the space next door, Croghan's carries exquisite jewelry and wonderful gifts for all the important occasions. The rings are to die for, and there seems to be no end to the trays of earrings, shelves of silver and crystal, and other delights. A Croghan's package delivered to your door or under the tree—sometimes the smaller, the better—is cause for real excitement. (See the Antiques chapter.)

DAZZLES
202 King St.
(843) 722-5997
www.dazzlesjewelry.com
This family of jewelry stores is best known for its 14-karat-gold slide bracelets that have the look, style, and feel of an heirloom. Dazzles has a large selection to choose from, or you may design one of your very own. Gold slide bracelets can be set with diamonds and precious stones in various shapes and motifs. Dazzles also has a large selection of jewelry from internationally known designers such as Hidalgo, Alwand Vahan, Monte Carol, Konstantino, and Lalique. Two other locations are at 86 Queen St. (843-722-5950) and at The Shops at Charleston Place, 226 King St. (843-722-5951 or 800-722-5951).

i Along King Street at about Wentworth Street, you'll note a section of roadway paved in bricks bearing the names of individuals and businesses. In the early 1980s, the construction of Charleston Place required a complete rebuilding of the immediate area's infrastructure. City leaders initiated a fund-raising campaign to cosmetically revitalize the area, and the bricks of the street commemorate those who donated to the cause.

JOINT VENTURE ESTATE JEWELERS
185 King St.
(843) 722-6730
www.jventure.com
Joint Venture is unusual in that it focuses on jewelry on consignment. The inventory at any time can include heirloom and contemporary jewelry as well as watches, and the staff is happy to appraise, restore, or repair your possessions. (See the Antiques chapter.)

Men's Clothing
BEN SILVER COLLECTION
149 King St.
(843) 577-4556, (800) 221-4671
www.bensilver.com
Here is a must-see, whether you're shopping for men's or women's clothing. Ben Silver maintains shops only in Charleston and London, so here's your one chance on this side of the Atlantic. Along with ultra-fine British and American clothes and furnishings, you'll discover exclusive blazer buttons for virtually every college or university in the United States and abroad. In fact, Ben Silver carries button sets for more than 600 fraternal organizations and military schools. It's a classy place for a nifty gift idea.

✳BERLIN'S CLOTHIERS
114 King St.
(843) 722-1665, (877) 722-1665
www.berlinsclothing.com
Since 1883, Berlin's has been a Charleston institution. Four generations of young Charleston gentlemen have purchased their first good suit from Berlin's. You can find all the classics here, from wing-tip shoes to navy blazers, knit shirts to madras shorts. Look for European designer names, too, among the classics, such as Brioni, Canali, Hickey-Freeman, Hart Schaffner & Marx, and

more. Berlin's offers custom sizing, a complete formal wear department, and a big-and-tall section. Patrons love the convenient parking across the street for their own shopping or shopping for something nice for the lady in their life from Berlin's for Women next door. (See listing under Women's Clothing.)

GRADY ERVIN & CO.
313 King St.
(843) 722-1776
www.gradyervin.com
The sign reads CLASSIC CLOTHIERS TO GENTLEMEN and that pretty much sums it up for this shop. This smart store is among King Street's collection of fine men's shops, and it's a real contender. You'll find a complete selection of traditional blazers, yachting wear, sports clothes, and accessories. Expect quality, style, and gracious Old World service.

M. DUMAS & SONS
294 King St.
(843) 723-8603
www.mdumasandsons.com
Charleston men and boys have been buying their outdoor sports clothes at M. Dumas since 1919. This store is all about practicality mixed with style and boasts one of the most complete inventories—hunting jackets, camouflage hats, flannel shirts, corduroy pants, shoes, and even snakeskin boots—in town. Dumas was doing the "hunting look" before doing the hunting look was cool.

MARGARITAVILLE
282 King St.
(843) 577-4145
www.margaritaville.com
Parrotheads will recognize the name instantly. This store is Jimmy Buffett's own 2,000-square-foot retail outlet on

Charleston's King Street, selling men's and women's super-casual clothing, Buffett's compact discs, and assorted Jimmy Buffett memorabilia. JB loves Charleston, and this is one of 12 retail stores—some of the others being in Key West, New Orleans, Orlando, and Jamaica. Here is a haven for chilled-out college kids and good fun for the laid-back crowd.

319 MEN
316 King St.
(843) 577-8807

This shop is a favorite among discriminating shoppers whose tastes edge toward Italian designs. The owners of 319 Men claim to carry the most recognizable designer labels in town, and they probably do. You can always count on personalized service and a pleasant shopping experience.

Natural Beauty
SPA ADAGIO
387 King St.
(843) 577-2444
www.spaadagio.com

This is one of those places you can go for those special pamperings that bring back harmony to your life. The Spa Adagio therapists know just the song your sore muscles need to hear (through massage). Their soft aromas sing to your senses, and their relaxing sounds soothe your soul. You'll find Spa Adagio in the lower level of the Francis Marion Hotel. (See the Accommodations chapter.)

STELLA NOVA
292 King St. (esthetique, makeup studio and salon)
(843) 722-9797
www.stella-nova.com

Stella Nova sells Aveda pure plant products and services for the hair, skin, and body. In their 3,000 square-foot location at 292 King St. (call 843-853-6161 for the salon only), they offer a large inventory of specially selected fragrances, make-up, bath, hair, and men's products from around the world. Check out the natural solutions to stress, ranging from aromatherapy to basic, old-fashioned pampering. Call (843) 723-0909 for day spa appointments at their 78 Society St. location. Visit the website for additional locations.

Shoes
BOB ELLIS
332 King St.
(843) 722-2515
www.bobellisshoes.com

Experience the shoe store phenomenon that is Bob Ellis. People from all over the country make the pilgrimage to Charleston to do just that. Suffice it to say that the downtown tradition's three telephone lines into the women's section say something about the store's popularity. High fashion, a huge selection, and friendly, highly qualified sales folk create the magic. The store carries women's sizes 3.5 to 12 AAAA, AAA, AA, and B. In men's, you'll find sizes 6.5 to 15 and widths from A to EEE. If you love shoes (and fine matching bags), don't miss Bob Ellis.

RANGONI OF FLORENCE SHOES
270 King St.
(843) 577-9554
www.rangonishoes.com

Many think the level of personal service here is simply the best in town. Rangoni's fine collection of Italian-designed shoes for men and women is superb in both quality and style. For women, the store carries (even in hard-to-find sizes) the elegant Rangoni Amalfi shoes, along with the more fashion-forward Icon. For just the right accessory to complement those stylish new shoes, choose from one of the largest selections of handbags in town. Men's lines of foot-wear include Hugo Boss, Sperry Topsider, Moreschi, Auri, Tommy Bahama, and Sandro Moscoloni, among others.

Sports

THE EXTRA MILE
336 King St.
(843) 853-9987
www.theextramileinc.com
This is a service-oriented, specialty sports shop with products preferred by competitive runners and swimmers. The store is owned and operated athletes who are competitive runners and triathletes, so they know a thing or two about running needs. The Extra Mile sells Nike, New Balance, Asics, Saucony, Zoot, Sugoi, New Balance, Adidas, and other name brands.

HALF MOON OUTFITTERS
280 King St.
(843) 853-0990
www.halfmoonoutfitters.com
When friends were gearing up to travel through South America one Christmas sea-son, where did they head first? That's right— Half Moon. They were after brands such as Patagonia, Columbia, Chaco, Adidas, Smith Eyewear, and Dansko. Half Moon carries other lines in its wide assortment of supplies for outdoor sports and adventure-seeking activity. Two more locations are at 425 Cole-man Blvd., Mount Pleasant (843-881-9472) and 94 Folly Rd. (843-556-6279).

SPORTSMAN SHOP
359 King St.
(843) 722-0072
Shop here for sporting equipment of all types, plus clothing and accessories. For years, the simply named Sportsman Shop has served the needs of area school teams as well as the serious and weekend athletes of Charleston.

Women's Clothing

ANNE'S
312 King St.
(843) 577-3262
www.annesdowntown.com
Anne's has developed a loyal following among petites in the community because of the wonderful selection, all the way down to size three. There are happy customers in all the other sizes as well, because Anne's car-ries name brand merchandise and gives per-sonalized service. Many a bride has dressed herself and her wedding party in beautiful gowns from Anne's. Shop here for contem-porary clothing appropriate for business and casual occasions as well as evening attire. There is free customer parking in the city lot behind the store.

✳BERLIN'S FOR WOMEN
114 King St.
(843) 723-5591
www.berlinsclothing.com
At the corner of King and Broad is family-owned Berlin's, one of Charleston's oldest and nicest clothing stores. Established in 1883, Berlin's built a reputation as a fashion landmark specializing in sportswear, lifestyle, and special occasion dressing. It carries one of the largest selections of evening and spe-cial occasion dresses in the Southeast and attracts customers from all over. Some of its

designer lines include Nicole Miller, Tahari, Vera Wang, and Yansi Fugel. A beautifully renovated store, excellent service, and free parking across the street make it a pleasure to shop here.

✳BITS OF LACE
302 King St.
(843) 577-0999, (800) 842-3990
www.bitsoflace.com

For sexy, pretty lingerie, visit Bits of Lace. Please note: These are undergarments that should be treated with care. In fact, many are silk and should be washed only by hand. Most items are simple, top-of-the-line articles of clothing that definitely give the impression that someone cares.

CHRISTIAN MICHI
220 King St.
(843) 723-0575
www.christianmichi.com

At the corner of King and Market Streets, Christian Michi offers collections for women by fashion designers such as Carmen Marc Valvo, Piazza Sempione, Chan Luu, Hoss, Twin Set, Sachi & Babi, and Juliska. The shop also sells assorted home furnishings like imported crystal and Diptyque candles. Check out the handmade 22-karat gold jewelry.

ELLINGTON
473 King St.
(843) 722-7999

Classic style with a new arrangement is Ellington's claim to fame. Located on upper King Street, the retailers say they are to clothing and furniture what jazz is to music. Some of the chic lines of women's clothing available are Babette, Planet, Margaret O'Leary, Crea, and Emelle. Look for great accessories

to accentuate your outfit with their belts and purses. Things for the home include lamps (new and old), bedding, and some American and European antiques (from couches to accent tables). Ellington ships anywhere.

THE FINICKY FILLY
303 King St.
(843) 534-0203
www.shopfinickyfilly.com

The shop of exquisite women's fashions is a delight for the discerning shopper on King Street. In addition to private-label jackets and accessories, look here for Italian fashions and leathers, Parisian couture, and cashmere items. The hand-embellished silks are the inspiration for many a formal ensemble worn here and in other fashionable places. Some of the names you'll find are Etro, Lela Rose, Tory Burch, Nanette Lepore, and Kate Spade. An in-store fashion consultant is available for private appointments.

LUNA
334 King St.
(843) 853-5862
www.shopluna.com

Like its sister store in Charlotte, North Carolina, this King Street shop features clothing, jewelry, accessories, shoes, candles, Mexican pottery, and home furnishings. Eclectic style, lots of color, and sheer exuberance are the keynotes here.

NANCY'S
342 King St.
(843) 722-1272
www.nancysofcharleston.com

Nancy's is another interesting, upscale boutique on King Street that's a must-see for ladies with a strong sense of style. Look here for a unique collection of contemporary apparel. Of special note are the one-of-a-kind metal bracelets imported from Europe exclusively for Nancy's. Belts of leather, chain, and even rhinestones are among the accents found here. The look is chic but timeless—appropriate for the young and the merely young at heart.

THE OOPS CO.
326 King St.
(843) 722-7768
www.theoopsco.com

The shop is every catalog shopper's dream come true. It exclusively features the clothing overruns and irregulars from your favorite name-brand mail-order catalogs. The prices here are about half the regular fare when you order from the book, and the merchandise is plentiful for folks of all ages and sizes. It also carries a nice collection of South Carolina logo items, such as polos, T-shirts, caps, belts, key fobs, and pet accessories. This may be the "find" of your whole shopping day. There is a second location at 696 Coleman Blvd., Mount Pleasant (843-881-6935).

RTW
186 King St.
(843) 577-9748
www.rtwcharleston.com

For interesting clothes that are always on the cutting edge of fashion, visit RTW. Look for designers such as Sylvia Heisel, Peter Cohen, and Jason Wu, and others who present trunk shows here with some frequency. RTW is diagonally across King Street from George C. Birlant & Company. (See the Antiques chapter.)

WORTHWHILE
268 King St.
(843) 723-4418
www.shopworthwhile.com

Selling unique casual and contemporary clothing made from only natural fibers, Worthwhile is, well, a worthwhile boutique on Charleston's trendy King Street. Look for brand names such as FLAX, Morgan, and Krista Larson, and shoes by Collection Privee. (See the previous Children's Clothing listing in the King Street section of this chapter.)

Meeting Street & the City Market

The cross street that, along with Broad Street, defines the "Four Corners of Law" is Meeting Street, another wide avenue of history, prosperity, and faith. Here, after all, is the location of the original church that gave the street its name (see the Historic Churches section of the Attractions chapter). Meeting Street runs virtually the length of the Peninsula and ends at White Point Gardens.

Meeting Street takes you smack-dab into the historic Market, one of the most colorful and popular tourist destinations in the city. The Market's shopping area is flanked by busy, one-way streets (called North and South Market Streets) and East Bay Street.

The Market may be one of the oldest "shopping malls" in the United States. It was built on land that Charles Cotesworth Pinckney, who was a signer of the US Constitution, ceded to the city in the 18th century for use as a public market. Made up of low brick buildings that have survived hurricanes, earthquakes, tornadoes, fires, and even Civil War bombardment, these sheds also were used by vendors selling fish, meat, and vegetables in bygone days.

The Great Hall, stretching from Meeting to Church Streets, recently underwent a $5.5 million renovation and houses a string of new specialty shops, boutiques, and eateries. Here, vendors of all types rent spaces and booths to hawk their wares.

The Market is a must-see for every Charleston visitor, and its magic seems to lie in its eternal spontaneity. It's an ever-changing kaleidoscope of things and smells and sounds and people who all seem to be in a carnival mood. It's different every day, and it's always the same. The Market is a Charleston enigma. Don't miss it.

Bookstores
✳THE SHOPS OF HISTORIC CHARLESTON FOUNDATION
108 Meeting St.
(843) 724-8484
www.historiccharleston.org
This store, as you might expect, stocks books regarding preservation and restoration. From beautiful coffee table books to fascinating reference material, choose from works about everything from gardening to selecting Victorian house colors. The store's selection of gift items also is keyed to the Charleston taste with brasses and china accents and linen tableware. The Historic Charleston reproduction furniture by Baker is shown here as well. (For more, see the Attractions chapter and the Gifts listings in the Meeting Street section of this chapter.)

Candy
GODIVA CHOCOLATIER, INC.
The Shops at Charleston Place,
142 Market St.
(843) 722-6045
www.godiva.com
Tucked seductively inside Charleston Place's trendy shopping arcade, this is where you'll find those famous Godiva chocolates loved the world over by serious chocoholics. Go all out, and take home a whole box, or taste just the individual confections that catch your eye. Be prepared for the not-too-subtle aromatherapy when you walk in the door. It's very beguiling.

LUCAS BELGIAN CHOCOLATE INC.
73 State St.
(843) 722-0461
www.lucasbelgianchocolate.com
You can't miss the cheerful pink awning just block south of South Market Street next to Häagen-Dazs Ice Cream Shoppe. This was one of the first truly fine chocolatiers to open in the Market area, and its longevity is fair testimony to the quality of its chocolate and presentation skills. Not only is just about every chocolate confection offered, but your purchases are also beautifully wrapped, and the service is charming.

MARKET STREET SWEETS
100 North Market St.
(843) 722-1397
www.riverstreetsweets.com
As if the distractions of the Market aren't enough, here's a candy store that hands out free samples. Woe to the poor dieter who happens to pass by here. Market Street Sweets opened in this location in 1984 selling gourmet Southern candies. The devil has had his way with sweet-tooth sufferers here ever since. The shop is most famous for its pralines but also turns out beautiful bear claws, chocolates, and other homemade specialties. This is a first stop for many Charleston visitors who have passed this way before. Market Street Sweets ships anywhere, so no one is really immune.

Gifts
ALPHA DOG OMEGA CAT
40 Archdale St.
(843) 723-1579
www.alphadogomegacat.com

In Majestic Square on the corner of Market and Archdale Streets, this shop is strictly for the dogs (and cats). Gifts range from gourmet pet biscuits, designer collars, and leashes to jewelry, toys, and clothes. We're talking indulgence here, and this shop is serious about it all. Only a pet lover would really understand.

CHARLESTON LUGGAGE & LEATHER
61 South Market St.
(843) 577-4773
www.charlestonleather.com

Down in the Market where all the action can be quite distracting, there's a very nice resource for leather goods of all kinds. The shop carries a number of brand names, including Fossil, Rolfs, Dopp, and Scully for leather items. This collection of duffles, totes, and travel gear can take you to your next destination in style.

THE CHARLESTON MUSEUM GIFT SHOP
360 Meeting St.
(843) 722-2996
www.charlestonmuseum.org

Here in America's oldest municipal museum, there's a gift area that's both comprehensive and tasteful. The emphasis is on items (such as books, jewelry, models, textiles, and educational toys) that have some connection to Charleston and the Lowcountry. It's an ideal place to pick up a souvenir from your vacation while visiting the must-see museum. (See the Other Sites and Museums section of the Attractions chapter as well as the Kidstuff chapter.)

✳GIBBES MUSEUM OF ART SHOP
135 Meeting St.
(843) 722-2706
www.gibbesmuseum.org

The shop at the Gibbes is just inside the front doors of the museum and is open to the public with no admission charge. This is one of the Lowcountry's best stops for art books, jewelry, stationery, small reproductions, and art prints of all kinds. Many locals go in early Nov for the best selection of fine Christmas cards in the city. (For more on the Gibbes Museum of Art, see the Attractions, The Arts, and Kidstuff chapters.)

KITES FLY'N HI
40 North Market St., Rainbow Market
(843) 577-3529
www.kitesflynhi.com

Something about flying a kite brings out the best in people. That's the philosophy behind this colorful little shop in Rainbow Market that is all about kites—of every kind and size. Look here for diamonds, deltas, boxes, and dragons plus wind socks and flags of fantastic design. The shop even has stunt kites for advanced fliers. Put the products to use here on the Lowcountry beaches or take them home to your own sky.

MARKET LEATHER OF CHARLESTON
40 North Market St., #11, Rainbow Market
(843) 722-1156
www.marketleather.com

Here's a shop in the Rainbow Market that's all about leather accessories for men and women. You'll find several lines of imported ladies' handbags, belts, and work-totes for the home or office. For men, there's a wide selection of billfolds, duffles, and utility kits. Look for leather backpacks, passport covers, attachés, briefcases, garment bags, wallets, and computer briefs, plus handsome cases for cell phones. This is a gold mine of gift ideas when holidays and birthdays come around.

NOAH'S NOOK
188 Meeting St., Ste. 111
(843) 722-8002

For those travelers who like to find a year-round Christmas shop and buy that special ornament for the tree that's sure to recall their Charleston vacation, here's a shop that nicely fills the bill. This store, tucked away in the Market between Meeting and Church Streets, is a division of Light Be and features exclusive lines of hand-painted, locally made ornaments with a Charleston theme. Collectible lines include Byers' Choice, Annalee, Seraphim Angels, and Fontanini, among many others. Even on the hottest days of summer, there's a little bit of the North Pole here.

O'HARA & FLYNN, LTD.
225 Meeting St.
(843) 534-1916
www.oharaflynn.com

Here's a direct importer of fine wines and gourmet cheeses plus fresh pâtés, smoked salmon, and saucissons for the discerning connoisseur. With a downtown location near Charleston Place and Theatre 99, it's handy for tourists and locals who know their tastes and want the best. There are even in-shop tastings at the wine bar every Wednesday evening from 5 to 7 p.m.

✳THE SHOPS OF HISTORIC CHARLESTON FOUNDATION
108 Meeting St.
(843) 724-8484
www.historiccharleston.org

A stop at The Shops of Historic Charleston Foundation is often for visitor orientation and resource offerings on preservation and restoration, but this also is easily one of the best gift boutiques in town. Miniatures, reproductions in brass and china, books, textiles, furniture, and even some crafts abound here. Quality reigns, even in gifts for the children. (See the Attractions chapter and the Bookstores listing for Meeting Street earlier in this chapter.)

TOY SOLDIERS OF CHARLESTON
40 North Market St.
(843) 722-0228
www.toysoldiersofcharleston.com

Collectors look for these things wherever they go, and in Charleston this is where they are. We're talking about Toy Soldiers of Charleston. This store in the Rainbow Market carries more than 1,500 of the popular military miniatures representing nearly every major conflict since the American Revolution. It even carries color guards from The Citadel, vintage 1860 as well as today. You'll find 54 mm soldiers by Conte, Wm. Britain, Soldat, Mundiart, and Forward March.

Home Accents & Decor
THE SHOPS OF HISTORIC CHARLESTON FOUNDATION
108 Meeting St.
(843) 724-8484
www.historiccharleston.org

The Shops for the Historic Charleston Foundation is the showroom for home furnishings, accessories, and giftware authorized by the foundation. All items for sale have an accompanying product card explaining the item's historical significance to Charleston's history and the Charlestonian lifestyle. The shop features Baker Furniture's Historic Charleston collection of 18th- and 19th century reproductions of furniture from famous Charleston homes. It also carries dinnerware patterns and brass accessories, fabrics, and wallpaper, as well as rugs, books, and jewelry. Because of its nonprofit status, no sales tax is charged.

Jewelry
NICE ICE FINE JEWELERS
145 Market St.
(843) 577-7029
Cross Market Street from Charleston Place to find Nice Ice. Check out the many cases of costume designs along with displays of the real stuff. Expect to be a bit surprised by the good prices. Some of the most unusual pieces seen around town have been created by Nice Ice. Look here for Slane & Slane, Nanis, Jude Frances, Judith Ripka, Rudolph Friedman, and Charriol.

Women's Clothing
EVERYTHING BUT WATER
195 Meeting St., The Shops at Charleston Place
(843) 722-5884
www.everythingbutwater.com
If you are looking for a bathing suit, try Everything But Water in Charleston Place. The store carries contemporary swimwear and accessories by such designers as Trina Turk, Gottex, La Blanca, Michael Kors, and Juicy Couture in sizes 4 through 26.

East Bay Street

This was once a street of bustling cotton warehouses in the mid-19th century, where silks and satins from exotic lands were bought and sold by the rice and indigo merchants who labored here. The old warehouses that survived the rigors of war and economic stagnation were "rediscovered" in the late 1970s, when a new epoch for the street began. Below Broad Street, East Bay can claim the famous Rainbow Row of town houses and the High Battery along Charleston Harbor. Above Broad you'll find a concentration of galleries, nightclubs, restaurants, and bookstores along East Bay between Market and Broad Streets. Beyond this area, other clusters of shops have emerged worth noticing. Here are some of the shopping venues you won't want to miss.

Gifts
HARBOR SPECIALTIES
190 East Bay St.
(843) 722-3722
www.harborspecialtiescharleston.com
People who love boating and the sea are naturally drawn to Charleston. Therefore, it follows that a store would specifically cater to their nautical fancy with merchandise (clothes and gifts, mostly) centered on the maritime theme. Harbor Specialties carries Sperry, Tervis Tumblers, boat models, canvas bags, and clothing for male and female seafarers. Best of all, same-day monogramming is available on almost any item you buy, which makes this store a hit with birthday gift givers and holiday shoppers.

INDIGO
4 Vendue Range
(843) 723-2983
www.indigohome.com
If you gravitate toward the eclectic, you'll love Indigo. The inventory ranges from antique luggage to Mexican folk art to Brazilian textiles. In this shop, you'll find village baskets nestled near Shaker boxes next to Edwardian bamboo and old Italian marble. You'll never fail to find something wonderful here.

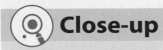 **Close-up**

Lowcountry Tradition: Sweetgrass Baskets

The art form practiced here in the Lowcountry has been recognized and celebrated virtually all over the world. Examples of this rare craft are found in the art museums of New York and Rome and among the Smithsonian collections in Washington, D.C., yet the work is evident all along the sidewalks of Charleston's Four Corners of Law at Meeting and Broad Streets. You'll easily find it downtown in the Market and in makeshift stalls along Lowcountry highways—especially US 17 N.

We're talking about the weaving of **sweetgrass baskets,** a traditional African-American art practiced here in the Lowcountry since the early 18th century. These baskets are handmade of long bunches of sweetgrass, pine needles, and bulrush that are bound together with fiber strips from native palmetto trees. The bunches are coiled and formed to create a variety of baskets—all shapes and sizes, each one unique. The baskets are both functional and beautiful. Creating these baskets requires skilled craftsmanship and long hours of hard work. A simple, average basket may require 12 hours or more to make, while larger, more complicated versions may take up to two or three months. The craft of weaving sweetgrass baskets has been a part of the Lowcountry since the earliest days of slavery. The skills are largely passed on from generation to generation. Traditionally, the men harvest the fiber and other plant material from the local marshes and swamps, and the women weave the baskets.

While the bulrush, pine needles, and palmetto strips are indigenous to and traditionally obtainable throughout the Lowcountry, coastal land development has begun to threaten the artisans' supply. Today, some weavers have to travel as far as Florida and along the Savannah River in Georgia to find natural stands of sweetgrass growing in roadside marshes. Because of this threat to one of the Lowcountry's most endearing traditions, Historic Charleston Foundation sponsored a test project on James Island to cultivate the growing of sweetgrass as a crop. It is hoped the sweetgrass basket tradition will continue to be an integral part of the Charleston experience. Each sweetgrass basket is utilitarian and beautiful, rich in the natural tones of the varied grasses and elegant in its ethnic simplicity. The baskets are true objects of art, and so they're not cheap. We feel the investment (usually $50 or $60 for a standard basket) is very worthwhile. Be sure to discover the wonderful sweetgrass baskets of the Lowcountry for yourself.

Home Accents & Decor

✳**CHARLESTON COOKS!**

194 East Bay St.

(843) 722-1212

www.charlestoncooks.com

For gourmet cooks and those who just love cooking, Charleston Cooks! is a little bit of heaven right here on East Bay Street. The concept is part kitchen store, part cooking school—where Lowcountry visitors can take one-time-only classes in how to prepare those Southern dishes that are so tasty. Executive Chef Frank Lee from the Maverick Southern Kitchens group heads up a program of daily classes that feature guest chefs from restaurants all over the city and beyond. The model kitchen where classes take place holds 40 students, with a video overview allowing close-up observation of the magic at hand.

Next door is the retail side of the operation, with a complete array of fine cooking utensils, cutlery, pots and pans, small appliances, and many cookbooks (some locally inspired). You'll even find some delicious prepared Southern accent foods like relishes, jams, and sauces. Shoppers don't necessarily have to be enrolled in the cooking classes to take away some culinary souvenirs. But to enroll in the classes, call the number above, or visit the website.

MORRIS SOKOL FURNITURE
510 King St.
(843) 722-3874
www.morrissokol.com
Since 1921 Morris Sokol Furniture has furnished homes in Charleston and across the Southeast. Located in the Upper King Street Design District which has emerged around their long-standing 37,000 square-foot showroom, this store offers a large selection of traditional, contemporary or tropically inspired furniture and accessories. Some of the lines carried here are American Drew, Brown Jordan, Century, Charleston Forge, Kingsley Bate, Lane, Lexington, and Tropitone. They also have Sealy and Sterns & Foster bedding. Whether you are looking for a housefull or just one accent piece the sales staff is quite helpful, and they have designers on hand to help create and implement your vision. Free parking is around the corner on Reid Street across from the store.

Jewelry
✳GEISS AND SONS JEWELERS
116 East Bay St.
(843) 577-4497
www.geissjewelers.com

Geiss is on the first floor of a charming little 18th-century brick building on East Bay just south of Broad. Their selections include Roberto Coin, Kwiat, A. Link, and Hans D. Kreiger designer jewelry. They were awarded Couture Jeweler status, one of only 170 jewelry stores nationwide to receive this recognition. While the shop sells custom-designed diamond and colored stone rings, it is also known for its inventory of watches by Rolex and Schoeffel. Watch and jewelry repair, and jewelry redesign are special services here.

Natural Beauty
EARTHLING DAY SPA
245 East Bay St.
(843) 722-4737
www.earthlingdayspa.com
Earthling Day Spa is a great source for skin and body products and books and tapes on health and well-being. Earthling also offers the unique Pilates method of conditioning. With Pilates, clients work out with trained professionals who guide them through a therapeutic body-conditioning regimen of stretching, strengthening, alignment, and toning exercises. There are other gifts for the mind and spirit, such as aromatherapy candles, spa treatments, therapeutic massage, and a nice selection of natural cosmetics.

Broad Street

This is the major Charleston thoroughfare that crosses King, Meeting, and Church Streets, ending at East Bay with the impressive facade of the Exchange Building (see the Attractions and Kidstuff chapters). It is the one made famous by the adage "Below Broad Street," which indicates the mother lode of pricey Charleston real estate south of this line. Historic Broad Street has always been a center of business and political activity since colonial days, but recently the street is primarily commercial between East Bay and King—home to many banks, law offices, and real estate firms. Nowadays, you'll also find a few high-end art galleries and restaurants in the mix, plus a few creative retail venues.

Gifts
THE BOUTIQUE
47 Broad St.
(843) 722-1441
Without a doubt, the Lowcountry's most gorgeous nightgowns, bathrobes, slips, and the like come from The Boutique. It is also a source for the authentic Charleston bonnet donned by many a Charleston baby. This store, located at the corner of Church and Broad, is where the "hat man" is painted on a wall. The shop also sells fine costume jewelry, linens, and other quality gift items, including the Lilly Pulitzer collection.

CABBAGE ROW SHOPPE
13 Broad St.
(843) 722-1528 (888) 722-1528
www.cabbagerowshoppe.com
Needle artists in the know say this is a great place to find cross-stitch and needlepoint supplies. Look for antique samplers and charts, kits, and handpainted canvases of Old Charleston and the South. Brand names include DMC, Medicis, and Paternayan—to name a few. Look here for fine linen, needlework stands, and reference books.

✳THE RSVP STATIONERY SHOPPE
141 Broad St.
(843) 577-9740
For over 30 years this shop has been considered the premier place for fine stationery and invitations. Their move from King Street

to Broad a few years back allowed the new owners to expand their merchandise in an attractive location a little off the beaten path. They carry the exclusive Black Label line, candles, gourmet food, cocktail linens, and frames. They have what you need to entertain with panache.

THE WINE SHOP
3 Lockwood Dr.
(843) 577-3881
www.thewineshopofcharleston.com
Sometimes, there's nothing like having a nice bottle of wine to enjoy in your hotel, yacht, or B&B room at night after a day of shopping or sightseeing in Charleston. This shop, next to the City Marina, is the place to find just the right vintage. It carries a wide selection of wines and champagnes for all budgets as well as cheese, glassware, and wine accessories. It's a good resource for finding a nice gift bottle for a friend or house sitter keeping the pets back home.

Women's Clothing
BELLE COUTURE BRIDAL
100 Church St.
(843) 881-3449
www.bellecouturebridal.com
It should come as no surprise that Charleston has become one of the most popular destination wedding sites in the country. And who wouldn't want to tie the knot in this charming and romantic city? Local and brides from away have some dreamy choices at Belle Couture Bridal for their perfect wedding gown. A few of the designer names are Christos, Melissa Sweet, and Priscilla of Boston. For your bridesmaids they carry Lela Rose, Cynthia Rowley, and Thread. In-house alterations and personal attention from the staff make for a relaxing, yet exciting

shopping experience for that special day. Belle Couture Bridal is open Thurs through Sat and is located just below Broad Street on Church.

EAST COOPER

Children's Clothing

DOODLEBUGS OF DANIEL ISLAND
885A Island Park Dr., Daniel Island
(843) 216-3180
In addition to wonderful toys and gifts, Doodlebugs sells adorable children's clothes and accessories. They carry girls' sizes from 0 to 10 and boys' from 0 to 4T. Check out the hair accessories too. This is the place to find special baby shower gifts and birthday surprises.

GWYNN'S OF MOUNT PLEASANT
916 Houston Northcutt Blvd., Village Pointe Shopping Center, Mount Pleasant
(843) 884-9518
www.gwynns.com
The department for children at Gwynn's is special indeed. For infants through teenagers, Gwynn's offers top-line brands, attractive accessories, and shoes. It's another of those Charleston traditions: outfitting the little one at Gwynn's.

RADICAL RAGS
210 Coleman Blvd., The Common, Mount Pleasant
(843) 884-4814
Radical Rags in the Common sells cute, traditional clothing for girls size 7 to 16, along with some preteen outfits. Boys' sizes range from 8 to 20. The staff is friendly and helpful, and the selection is terrific.

RAGAMUFFIN SHOP
210 Coleman Blvd., The Common, Mount Pleasant
(843) 884-4814
Also in the Common, Ragamuffin Shop shares staff and floor space with Radical Rags. Its specialty is clothing for infants up to size 6X in girls and 7 in boys.

SOUTHERN BELLES
280 West Coleman Blvd., Mount Pleasant
(843) 881-1741
www.southernbellesonline.com
This shop is near Wonder Works in Northcutt Plaza and carries traditional clothing for preemies through preteens. Expect lots of smocked outfits, coordinated sibling attire, and crib shoes. It also has toys, picture frames, signature gift items, and scrapbook supplies.

Gardening

ABIDE-A-WHILE NURSERY & GARDEN CENTER
1460 US 17 N. Bypass, Mount Pleasant
(843) 884-9738
www.abideawhilegardencenter.com
Here in Charleston, where gardens are so beloved, there has to be a nursery where people go to get perennials, seeds, shrubbery, trees, and ornamentals. One of the best is Abide-A-While. Its selection is enormous, the quality is good, and you can always count on getting knowledgeable gardening advice.

MRS. CAPPER'S PLANTS N' THINGS
1608 Palmetto Grande Dr., Towne Centre, Mount Pleasant
(843) 971-1002
A long-standing tradition for Charleston area gardeners is a visit to Mrs. Capper's for fine

hand-crafted home and garden decor—especially when the spring blossoms arrive. The hanging baskets of geraniums and petunias are colorful, healthy, abundant, and irresistible. It also carries a vast array of lush, green interior and tropical plants, and there's a good selection of pottery and decorative garden accents to transform a home into a virtual Eden. Treat yourself or brighten someone else's day.

Gifts

CAROLINA GIFTS & SEASHELLS
1405 Ben Sawyer Blvd., #100, Mount Pleasant
(843) 884-0320
www.gatewaytothebeach.com
Coming or going to the beach on Sullivan's Island or Isle of Palms, stop in Carolina Gifts & Seashells for your beachy souvenirs. In addition to shells from our own coast and around the world, they have starfish, sand dollars, sharks teeth, and other collectible specimen shells. A nice selection of nautical gifts, lamps, candles, books, and prints may be just what you need to remind you of those lazy days in the sun and sand. Charleston items such as benne cookies, saltwater taffy, and T-shirts may provide the perfect gift for someone back home.

THE SCRATCH PAD
409 Mill St., Mount Pleasant
(843) 884-3433
Here is the stop every newcomer should make to buy those smart change-of-address notices to tell friends and family back home that you've arrived in Charleston. Located in Mount Pleasant near Shem Creek and the Common, this store carries the area's best selection of stationery, invitations, note cards, and small gift items that make

Lowcountry entertaining very special. This is the place to order wedding invitations and announcements, too. Choose from brand names like Crane's and William Arthur. The store carries cocktail napkins in every color scheme available to match any party's decor and ensure your event is truly in theme. The paper tableware for children's parties is especially fun. Birthday shoppers find a variety of cards as well as other fine gifts like picture frames and address books. Even visitors to Shem Creek's seafood restaurants enjoy browsing here before or after a meal.

WONDER WORKS
624-D Long Point Rd., Mount Pleasant
(843) 849-6757
www.wonderworkscharleston.com
This is a toy store with an educational theme for kids and adults. Departments include geography, nature, arts and crafts, and a special section with developmental toys for infants and toddlers. There are many of the most famous names in educational toys, such as Brio and Playmobil, and Wonder Works is the largest seller of telescopes in the southeastern United States. A second location is in Charleston at 975 Savannah Hwy. (843-573-9300 or 888-849-5540).

Home Accents & Decor

AUBERGINE HOME COLLECTION OUTLET STORE
1131 Queensborough Blvd., Mount Pleasant
(843) 884-8100
www.auberginehome.com
Aubergine Home Collection is a factory outlet specializing in bed linens, pillows, fabrics by the yard, and even distinctive bathroom shower curtains. The choices range from traditional to contemporary—all offered at a

discount of 50 to 75 percent off retail. Aubergine carries samples, discontinued lines, and trade-show display items, all of which give shoppers a nice pricing advantage. The staff encourages shoppers to bring paint chips, fabric swatches, and carpet samples to mix and match colors for the best designer look. A second location is at 465 Freshfields Dr., Johns Island (843-768-5554).

CELADON HOME FURNISHING & ACCESSORIES
1015 Johnnie Dodds Blvd., Mount Pleasant
(843) 884-7005
www.celadonathome.com
Celadon Home Furnishing & Accessories is one of those stores where you could almost outfit a home from cellar to dome. Its large inventory of affordable sofas, chairs, tables, and accessories is outdone only by the number of options available by order. Choose from more than 700 fabrics, and your upholstered sofa or chair can be delivered in about two to four weeks.

EAST COOPER HABITAT FOR HUMANITY RESTORE
469B Long Point Rd., Mount Pleasant
(843) 849-8002
www.eastcooperhabitat.org

CHARLESTON HABITAT FOR HUMANITY RESTORE
731 Meeting St.
(843) 579-0777
www.charlestonhabitat.org

SEA ISLAND HABITAT FOR HUMANITY RESTORE
3304 Maybank Hwy., Johns Island
(843) 559-4009
www.seaislandhabitat.org

Looking to make a change in your home decor without spending a lot? The Habitat stores have a wonderful selection of ever-changing items donated by many resort home owners in the Charleston area and others moving, downsizing, or redecorating. Some great finds can be discovered here, or maybe you'll want to make a donation too. Either way you can feel good about supporting their funding for their home buidling projects. Stop in often at any of their three locations.

GDC
695 Coleman Blvd., Mount Pleasant
(843) 849-0711
www.gdchome.com
More than a yard goods outlet, GDC is a one-stop option for the home, carrying rugs, gifts, lamps, mirrors, furniture, framed art, accessories, and fabrics. The store offers complimentary design assistance from a well-trained staff of friendly sales folk. Two more locations are at 1290 Sam Rittenberg Blvd., Charleston (843-571-5142) and 420 Freshfields Dr., Freshfields Village, Johns Island (843-768-4246).

KITCHENS BY DESIGN
234 Mathis Ferry Rd., Mount Pleasant
(843) 849-6890
www.kitchensbydesign-sc.com
Since 1980, this unique shop has offered creative design services for new and renovated kitchens and baths. The showroom displays and sells fine kitchen furnishings, gourmet cookware, and tools.

Jewelry

SKATELL'S MANUFACTURING JEWELERS

1036 Johnnie Dodds Blvd., Mount Pleasant

(843) 849-8488

www.skatells.com

The outstanding thing about Skatell's is that customers come here to have jewelry made to their own specifications. Skatell's is a direct importer of diamonds, and it tries to pass the savings on to the buyer. Another location is at 1798 Ashley River Rd., Charleston (843-763-8925).

Men's Clothing

HADDRELL'S POINT

885 Ben Sawyer Blvd.

(843) 881-3644

Serious anglers know Haddrell's Point like they know the back creeks of the Lowcountry. Anything and everything associated with the sport of fishing is here to be found: clothes, shoes, boots, reels, lures, and any other kind of tackle. Any 10-year-old kid worth his or her spinning rod would be thrilled with a gift certificate from here. (See the Hunting & Fishing chapter for information on where to put your new equipment to use.) A second location is at 47 S. Windemere Blvd., Charleston (843-573-3474).

Natural Beauty

STELLA NOVA

1320 Theatre Dr., Towne Centre, Mount Pleasant

(843) 884-3838

www.stella-nova.com

Stella Nova's location in Towne Centre makes a pleasant stop before or after a movie. It stocks Ahava, Kusco-Murphy, Terax, and T. Le Clerc makeup, among many other lines, as well as Aveda pure plant products and services for the hair, skin, and body. Services include haircuts, styling, pedicures, facials, and scalp treatments. Ask about the day spa programs. Visit the website for a list of locations.

STUDIO 921

860 Lowcountry Blvd., Mount Pleasant

(843) 881-3332

www. studio921online.com

This full-service hair and skin care shop offers massage by a certified therapist and specialists in hair color and skin care. They offer manicures, pedicures, facials, body treatments, waxing, and airbrush tans to round out the pampering. For women who know their skin-and hair-care products by name, this option carries Pureology, Matrix, and Redken, among others.

Shoes

THE SHOE FAIRY

1405 Ben Sawyer Blvd., Mount Pleasant

(843) 856-8381

www.shoptheshoefairy.com

One Mount Pleasant's hottest new locations for terrific shoes, The Shoe Fairy is just behind CVS at the corner of Rifle Range Road and Ben Sawyer Boulevard. This locally owned boutique has customers hotfooting it in to see their collection of fashionable women's shoes and accessories. Some of the popular lines here are Sofft, Everybody, Bekka Vita, and Nicole. The reasonably priced footware is available in sizes 5 to 11 from narrow to regular widths. Shoe and jewelry trunk show receptions are regular events at the store.

Women's Clothing

COPPER PENNY
280 West Coleman Blvd., Northcutt Plaza, Mount Pleasant
(843) 881-3497
www.shopcopperpenny.com
This boutique sells stylish clothes for contemporary women. In Northcutt Plaza near Wonder Works, this shop is a good source for unique, casual yet sophisticated clothing that works from day into evening. Bridal, special occasions attire, gifts, and distinctive accessories fill out the inventory, and its popular shoe department has spawned two retail stores called Copper Penny Shooz located at 317 King St. and 1240 Belk Dr. in Towne Centre. Two more locations are at 1228 Belk Dr., Towne Centre, Mount Pleasant (843-881-9889) and 311 King St., Charleston (843-723-2999 or 888-281-8329).

FROM HERE TO MATERNITY
1055 Johnnie Dodds Blvd., Crickentree Village, Mount Pleasant
(843) 884-8250
www.fromheretomaternitysc.com
For those anticipating a visit from the stork, here's a Mount Pleasant option that's more than a maternity store. It carries designer labels to take mothers-to-be from the beach to the most formal black-tie event. Look here for names like Belly Bandit, Michael Stars, Citizens of Humanity, Olian, and Maternite. The staff is experienced at fitting patrons who may be new to the excitement of buying quality maternity wear. The shop is prepared to serve you even after the baby arrives. To outfit the nursery, look here for custom-designed iron cribs and baby bedding, unique toys, and accessories. The Baby Room specializes in newborn-size clothing

to toddlers' wear. Shop from designers like Kissy Kissy and Aden + Anais to welcome your baby to this wonderful world.

GWYNN'S OF MOUNT PLEASANT
916 Houston Northcutt Blvd., Village Pointe Shopping Center, Mount Pleasant
(843) 884-9518
www.gwynns.com
Locals have shopped at Gwynn's in several locations through the years, and they have always been pleased. A nice thing about this store is the wide range of departments under one roof. Women's clothing is a specialty, and the shoe and accessory departments carry top-of-the-line merchandise. Sales consultants are most helpful and will coordinate outfits to your specifications.

WEST ASHLEY

Bookstores

BOOK EXCHANGE
1131 Savannah Hwy.
(843) 556-5051
The Book Exchange sells new and used paperback and hardback books as well as collectible comics. Reader-friendly, this is where the serious mystery novel addicts go for a fix, and where the neighborhood kids swap comic books.

BOOKS-A-MILLION
832 Orleans Rd.
(843) 556-9232
www.booksamillion.com
Books-A-Million is one of Charleston's largest chain bookstores. With its small coffee shop section and expansive inventory, Books-A-Million has a lot to offer. For instance, it stocks nature-related gift items, calendars, and toys. The magazine section covers a

big back wall, and the children's section has a video area to entertain the young ones while parents shop. Books-A-Million offers several discounts, and you can buy a one-year club membership for $20 to maximize your savings. A second location is at 2150 Northwoods Blvd., North Charleston (843-764-2377).

INDIGO BOOKS
472 Freshfields Dr., Johns Island
(843) 768-2255
www.freshfieldsvillage.com/shop
A great hit with the Kiawah and Seabrook crowd, this small but well-stocked bookstore is the place to pick up a great summer vacation read. The shopkeepers do a great job of keeping a wide variety of books on hand, and they special order anything you cannot find post haste. Their section of Southern authors is especially interesting, and the inventory of Lowcountry titles is as good as the major chains. Even wintertime islanders find Indigo a good place to shop for holiday gifts to send grandkids up North.

✳RAVENOUS READER
792 Folly Rd., James Island
(843) 795-2700
This is a favorite bookstore on James Island, and thanks to the James Island Connector, it's now very convenient to those coming from town as well as those traveling Folly Road. The Ravenous Reader has a cafe for leisurely reading with a cup of coffee. This neighborhood bookstore has great books and a friendly staff who'll answer your questions and order just about anything you want.

Gardening

✳HYAMS LANDSCAPING AND GARDEN CENTER
870 Folly Rd.
(843) 795-4570
Here's a favorite of Charleston gardeners. The selection of room-filling house plants is spectacular, but you'll also find bedding plants, seeds and bulbs, fountains, birdbaths, hanging planters, and more. There's always someone nearby with helpful answers to your gardening questions.

Gifts

CAROLINA GIRLS
1890 Sam Rittenberg Blvd., Ste. 119
(843) 763-3006
www.shopcarolinagirls.com
This "girly girl" shop inspires any woman to flash back to her happiest college days. The store features everything a Southern belle could want (but never need), such as cozies trimmed in pink feather boas, pocketbooks made out of rhinestone jeans, and beach shoes with a variety of toppers so you can mix and match. Of course, there's fancy jewelry and purses, as well as cute stationery, napkins, and party favors. Men may not feel at home here, but they're guaranteed to hit the target by purchasing any gift inside. Even Northern girls will toss their heads like Katie Scarlett O'Hara when their friends eye their "quaint" souvenirs from their trip down South. Two more locations are at 130 Harvester Lane, Freshfield's Village, Johns Island (843-768-9858) and 608-F Long Point Rd., Mount Pleasant (843-388-9858).

CHARLESTON COLLECTIONS
625 Skylark Dr.
(843) 556-8911
This shop sells an incredible assortment of things Charlestonian. Look for Charleston wind chimes, Charleston art prints and originals, Charleston seashell lamp kits, Charleston cookbooks, Charleston note cards, and even Charleston jewelry. Get the drift? The clerks are prepared to ship goods anywhere, so this is a great stop for souvenirs to send home.

Home Accents & Decor

CHARLESTON LIGHTING AND INTERIORS
1640 Sam Rittenberg Blvd.
(843) 766-3055
www.charlestonlightingandinteriors .com
Locals and newcomers looking to brighten their homes with distinctive chandeliers, lamps, ceiling fans, and interesting accents in occasional furniture are discovering this shop west of the Ashley. Collections include both period and high-tech pieces that work well in traditional as well as contemporary settings but still have that Charleston touch of class. Look for names like Quoizel (Tiffany), Savoy House, Hinkley, Schonbeck, Minka, and Tech Lighting, to name a few. Two more locations are at 1109 Johnnie Dodds Blvd., Mount Pleasant (843-352-0188) and 850 Bacons Bridge Rd., Summerville (843-285-2884 or 866-959-2887).

IN GOOD TASTE
1901 Ashley River Rd.
(843) 763-5597
www.ingoodtastecharleston.com
This is a store for the serious gourmet, with all kinds of kitchen items, live herbs, wines, cheeses, coffees, teas, and gift baskets. It often sponsors wine tastings and fun cooking classes that have proven very popular with a devoted clientele. Look for In Good Taste near the Charleston Crab Shack restaurant.

Jewelry

POLLY'S
2048 Sam Rittenberg Blvd.
(843) 763-0017
www.pollysjewelry.com
Just across from Citadel Mall on Sam Rittenberg Boulevard, you will find Polly's, a large, locally owned jewelry store. Polly's specializes in diamonds, gold jewelry, and watches. There is ample free parking, and the staff is most helpful. The North Charleston and Mount Pleasant stores are a similar source for diamonds, gold, and watches. Customers can have jewelry designed or repaired on the premises. Two more locations are at 1492 US 17 N., Mount Pleasant (843-884-2447) and 8150 Rivers Ave., North Charleston (843-797-8543).

Men's Clothing

STEIN MART
975 Savannah Hwy., St. Andrews Shopping Center
(843) 763-2444
www.steinmart.com
The men's (and boys') section of this high-end discount store is quite extensive. You can find a good selection of suits and sport coats in short, regular, and long sizes. Expect to see designer labels as well as fine Italian cuts among the lot. Shirts, ties, sport clothes of all kinds, and underwear complete the selection. A second location is at 600 Long Point Rd., Mount Pleasant (843-971-5466).

Natural Beauty

URBAN NIRVANA
8 Windermere Blvd.
(843) 720-8000
www.urbannirvana.com
Here's a day spa with locations convenient for downtowners and visitors to the resort islands, as well. Relax and indulge yourself with massage therapy, skin care, body wraps, hydrotherapy, Swiss and Vichy showers—the works. There are complete men's and women's locker rooms plus a relaxation lounge open daily. A second location is at 636-D Long Point Rd., Mount Pleasant (843-881-1160).

Toys

THE LEARNING CENTER
2049 Savannah Hwy., Ste. 10
(843) 556-1200, (800) 397-1200
www.the-learning-center.com
The Learning Center offers educational books and toys. Located in the West Island Shopping Center near West Marine, the shop is staffed by knowledgeable employees who are prepared to help parents, teachers, and interested friends and relatives find appropriate learning tools for kids with an appetite to learn as well as play.

Women's Clothing

THE RESORT SHOP
526 Freshfields Dr., Kiawah Island
(834) 768-4466
www.theresortshop.com
Visitors to the resorts at Kiawah and Seabrook won't want to miss a stop at The Resort Shop at Freshfields Village. Shoppers can take home some stylish attire to keep that vacation feeling alive. They have the popular and classic Vineyard Vines line.

The shop also carries Eileen Fisher, Vince, Anthony Alexander, Velvet, and more. Their jewelry collection from Chan Luu and accessories like scarves by Tolani and bags by Shiraleah complete the look.

PINK BOULEVARD
639 Freshfields Dr., Johns Island
(843) 768-4600
www.pink-boulevard.com
When famed Palm Beach fashion designer Lilly Pulitzer first introduced her gaily flowered prints, the casual look of beach clothes made a sea change for the better. Even though that seems like eons ago—as fashions change—the vivid Lilly Pulitzer look has never gone out of style. Every new generation seems to rediscover this distinctive, sports-minded brightness and make it their own.

STEIN MART
975 Savannah Hwy., St. Andrews
Shopping Center
(843) 763-2444
www.steinmart.com
It claims to be the only "upscale, off-price specialty store in America," and it may be true. Stein Mart has frontline women's fashion apparel in its Boutique section and accessories that are considerably discounted. There are hats, shoes, purses, jewelry, hair accessories, and hosiery, too. The store also carries a large selection of gifts, linens, and special things for the home. A second location is at 600 Long Point Rd., Mount Pleasant (843-971-5466).

SHOPPING CENTERS & MALLS

CITADEL MALL
2070 Sam Rittenberg Blvd. (US 17 and
SR 7 at I-526)
(843) 766-8321
www.shopcitadel-mall.com

When Citadel Mall opened in the early 1980s, it was the merchandising hit of the decade. Major anchors are Dillard's, Sears, JCPenney, Belk, and Target. The whole mall has undergone a complete refurbishing, with updated and relandscaped bench areas for footsore shoppers, a children's play area, and a multinational food court for catching a quick bite before launching into further shopping expeditions. There are more than 100 shops to satisfy every shopper's needs. The location, at the intersection of I-526 and US 17, makes Citadel Mall convenient for almost anyone in the Lowcountry. Call the Customer Service Center for information as to business hours and special events.

SOUTH WINDERMERE SHOPPING CENTER
22 Windermere Blvd. (at Folly Road)
(843) 766-0261
With shops that front on Folly Road and others on a second row behind, South Windermere is a popular shopping center in the West Ashley area. There is also a shopping strip that borders the center itself, and those stores have addresses on Windermere Boulevard as well. The major anchor is Staples, but there are other worthwhile stops in the complex. There's Robinson's Bicycle Shop, founded in 1888 and still very popular with bike enthusiasts. The Open House is a gift shop with elegant paper goods ranging from Crane stationery to whimsical gift wrap. Sohn & McClure Jewelers is a jewelry store and gift shop that always has enticing window displays. Earth Fare is a popular outlet (set up like a chain grocery store) for all-natural, organically grown food. Shoppers at Earth Fare can also order from a counter and dine in a convenient on-site cafe.

ST. ANDREWS SHOPPING CENTER
975 Savannah Hwy.
(843) 556-9442
Generations of Charleston kids have identified St. Andrews Shopping Center by the Coburg Cow revolving on a sign at the edge of its parking lot on Savannah Highway. The life-size plastic bovine lights up at night and signals to travel-weary kids that they are almost home (or at the shopping center). The St. Andrew Center recently underwent a major facelift making it a more attractive shopping destination. The major anchors here are Harris Teeter grocery store and Stein Mart, the upscale, off-price department store that features items for the home and clothes for men, women, and children (see previous listing). Other tenants include an old-fashioned barber shop called Mooney's, Tuesday Morning, Wonder Works, Wild Birds Unlimited, and Jason's Deli. St. Andrews Is the handy location of a Weight Watchers as well.

TANGER OUTLET CENTER
4840 Tanger Outlet Blvd. (off International Blvd.), North Charleston
(843) 529-3095
www.tangeroutlet.com
After much anticipation, Tanger Outlets opened a center near the Charleston Area Convention Center in North Charleston's Centre Pointe development in 2006. This $45 million, 325,000-square-foot, shopper-friendly mall has over 80 brand-name and outlet stores, including Gap Outlet, Tommy Hilfiger, Reebok Outlet, Banana Republic Factory Store, Black & Decker, Eddie Bauer Outlet, Fossil, Jones New York, Nine West, Liz Claiborne Outlet, Harry & David, and Sunglass Hut. There is a food court, ATM, and pay phones, making it easy to spend the day

here. An added convenience is the availability of wheelchair and strollers for rent.

TOWNE CENTRE
**1600 Palmetto Grande Dr., US 17 N.,
Mount Pleasant
(843) 216-9900
www.mtpleasanttownecentre.com**
This is the Lowcountry's first major offering to shoppers of the newest trend in retailing—the replication of a traditional downtown shopping district in a suburban setting. The fantastic growth of Mount Pleasant and the whole East Cooper area provoked Towne Centre, a whole "new town" that has the best of the old and all the convenience of the new. The look of Towne Centre is based on Charleston's famous King Street—with traditional-looking storefronts (more than 65 of them so far) and attractive sidewalk settings. The difference is—ample free parking with lush landscaping added to avoid the "vast sea of asphalt" look offered by the shopping malls of yore.

Towne Centre was a $40 million, 47-tenant project when it opened in the summer of 1999. Since then, new stores and entertainment options have been climbing aboard at a steady rate. Among the pioneers in this venture were the major anchors of Belk, Old Navy, Barnes & Noble, plus Bed Bath & Beyond. Soon, a 16-screen, 3,100-seat movie theater called Palmetto Grande joined the crowd. Other stores now include Banana Republic, Game Stop, Chico's, Hallmark Creations, Copper Penny, Men's Wearhouse, J. Jill, Gap, and Pier 1 Imports. Even Victoria's Secret moved to Towne Centre to be part of the action. Towne Centre is located on US 17 in Mount Pleasant. The location is convenient to nearly everyone because of the nearby Isle of Palms Connector (SR 517) and the proximity to I-526, which almost completely encircles the Lowcountry.

ANTIQUES

For the insider who wants to buy, sell, study, or just window shop for antiques, Charleston is a mother lode. Because it was first an English city, the Charlestonian sense of taste in antiques is decidedly British. Fittingly, Charleston's many antiques shops and galleries, many of which are clustered along King Street, tend to reflect that English bias.

The affluent, British-educated, 18th-century Charlestonians proudly decorated their homes with the latest in English good taste as an obvious symbol of their cultural status and social position. If they couldn't import their heart's desire for finery and furniture, they imported tradesmen who could re-create it for them on this side of the Atlantic. Eventually, Charleston produced a new generation of silversmiths and cabinetmakers who earned their own reputations for fine craftsmanship. Indeed, early furniture from Charleston is among the best of the pre-1830 furniture crafted in this country. But it's safe to say that long after Britain ceased being a political factor in the colonies, Americans still looked to Mother England for direction in taste. In fact, this artistic and cultural co-dependency has lingered in Charleston for more than 200 years.

Today, Charleston no longer relies on furnishings from local homes and the misfortunes of its old families to fill today's antiques shops and galleries. Local dealers and buyers attend auctions and estate sales up and down the Eastern seaboard, and some make regular buying trips to Europe. Ships carrying 40-foot containers filled with early- to mid-19th century English antiques arrive regularly in Charleston Harbor. Much of the merchandise is sold in local shops, while some of it goes to discerning dealers all over America. Still, Charleston enjoys the lion's share of the top-quality merchandise, largely because of the demand. Many of Charleston's old homes were built to showcase such furnishings, and each new owner cherishes the opportunity to refurbish his or her home appropriately.

OVERVIEW

From St. Michael's Alley and King Street to the shops in Mount Pleasant and along Savannah Highway, there are dozens of opportunities to shop for some of the best antiques sold in America.

One particular section along King Street, between Beaufain and Queen Streets, is sometimes referred to as the **Antiques District,** where you'll find a high concentration of quality shops and fascinating merchandise. But shoppers who really want to "do" the antiques market in Charleston will have to expand their search well beyond King Street these days. Quality shops are found tucked away in nearly all the commercial areas, plus small areas of West Ashley,

Mount Pleasant, and James Island. Seeing them all is getting to be something of a crusade. Lookers are almost always welcome, but if you're a serious collector or a dealer, be sure to talk to the proprietor and make your wishes known. Often, there are back rooms or upstairs galleries available only to those interested enough to ask.

At the corner of King and Queen Streets is a good place to start. Walking north from there, you'll find some of the best antiques stores the city has to offer. Most shops are open Mon through Sat, but hours of operation can be as eclectic as the selections at many of these shops, so if in doubt, call ahead. We've alphabetized the following store and merchandise descriptions for easy reference.

*ACQUISITIONS
273 East Bay St.
(843) 577-8004
www.acquisitionsinteriors.com

This shop offers full interior design services and specializes in English pine originals and beautifully made reproductions of English mahogany and antique painted furniture. It is a great resource for accent pieces as well. These designers are very popular with the Kiawah and Seabrook Island crowd, and one look at their handsome displays tells you why.

ALEXANDRA AD
156 King St.
(843) 722-4897

Walk through the King Street doorway to discover this exclusive shop of 18th- and 19th-century European furniture, decorative wares, fine linens, pillows, china, and oil paintings—many reflecting the French

Provençal ambience now gaining popularity in Charleston.

ANTIQUES MARKET
634 Coleman Blvd., Mount Pleasant
(843) 849-8850

Only 10 minutes from downtown Charleston, you'll find this mall with antiques and collectibles that are fun and decorative. This market hosts more than 100 booths under one roof, with furnishings, sterling silver, antique button jewelry, and other interesting treasures for the finding. Less serious, perhaps, than some of the King Street antiques stores, this is a great place for browsing through the keepsakes and surprises. Parking is free and convenient just off Coleman Boulevard.

A'RIGA IV
204 King St.
(843) 577-3075

Open since 1976, this shop carries a wide assortment of interesting early ceramics, decorative arts, and period accessories. There are no reproductions here at all. Look for an eclectic assortment of 17th- through 19th-century furniture. A'riga IV is best known, however, for its fascinating assortment of antique medical and scientific instruments. This is a special treat for the many docs and nurses who come to Charleston for medical conventions.

*CAROLINA GALLERIES
106-A Church St.
(843) 720-8622
www.carolinagalleries.com

This shop deals in pre-1945 American art, antique prints, sporting, and Southern genre art. It has an extensive assortment of art from Charleston's "renaissance period" of the 1920s and 1930s, including works by Alfred

Hutty, Elizabeth O'Neill Verner, and Alice Ravenel Huger Smith. Purchases can be framed at their exclusive frame maker, Carolina Fine Art Framing at 76-C Spring St. and can be shipped anywhere.

CROGHAN'S JEWEL BOX
308 King St.
(843) 723-3594
www.croghansjewelbox.com
Croghan's is another Charleston institution. Many a sterling wedding gift or baby cup has come from here. Croghan's specializes in antique jewels and elegant jewelry, children's jewelry, rings, estate silver, hollowware, and unusual gifts. Here is where you can find those wonderful Charleston (or plantation) rice spoons—traditionally found on every well-set Charleston table. (See the Shopping chapter.)

DAVID SKINNER ANTIQUES & PERIOD LIGHTING
177 King St.
(843) 853-3104
This wonderful resource of fine antiques and period lighting moved to King Street in 2009 from its former location on President Street. Owner David Skinner has a large selection of American, English, and French furniture as well as Jamaican, West Indian, and Cuban pieces. The lighting may include chandeliers, sconces, torcheres, and table and floor lamps. Decorative accessories, paintings, mirrors, and garden accoutrements round out the many finds to browse here. The showroom is open Mon through Sat from 10 a.m. to 5 p.m. or by appointment.

THE DESIGN GALLERY
28 Hasell St.
(843) 722-6099

What long-time Charleston antiques shoppers remember as Poppe House (on King Street) has its newest incarnation here at the corner of East Bay and Hasell Streets in trendy Ansonborough. Two different and gifted dealers/designers have joined forces in this expanded retail expression of their individual talents. Merrill Benfield Interior Design is headquartered here, and the shop houses his fine collection of 18th- and 19th-century antiques for sale. Joining him is Grace Snead and her unusual assortment of fine period paintings.

✳GEORGE C. BIRLANT & COMPANY
191 King St.
(843) 722-3842, (888) 247-5268
www.birlant.com
This is one of Charleston's oldest and largest antiques stores, having been around since 1929. The owners are direct importers of 18th and 19th-century English furniture and faithful English-made reproductions. They also specialize in antique silver, china, crystal, and brass. Birlant is the exclusive source for replicas of a Charleston Battery Bench like those found in White Point Gardens. They actually own the original cast-iron molds.

GOLDEN & ASSOCIATES ANTIQUES
206 King St.
(843) 723-8886
www.goldenassociatesantiques.com
Clearly, this is one of King Street's largest displays of imported and locally acquired pieces. The vast array of American and European merchandise includes, but is not limited to, furniture, mirrors, chandeliers, sconces, fireplace accessories, and garden items from the 18th and 19th centuries. There are 19th-century Caribbean pieces here too.

GOLDEN & SKINNER ANTIQUES
200 King St.
(843) 670-9182

Andy Golden of Golden & Associates Antiques joined with David and Julie Skinner of David Skinner Antiques & Period Lighting (see previous listings) to form Golden & Skinner Antiques taking advantage of a prime, well-lit location in the heart of King Street's antique district. Both owners have locations nearby but use this location to display even more of their vast collections of art and antiques. The selection changes often so shoppers know to stop in frequently to see what's new.

HUNGRYNECK ANTIQUE MALL
401 Johnnie Dodds Blvd., US 17 Bypass,
Mount Pleasant
(843) 849-1744
www.hungryneck.com

Here is one of the largest antique malls in Mount Pleasant, with more than 60 dealers sharing 15,000 square feet under one roof. They buy and sell antiques and collectibles of all kinds. Look for sterling silver, mahogany and oak furniture, Victorian pieces in wicker, and ornamental iron. We've seen wicker, dolls, architectural pieces, antique stained glass, and even linens here. It's always a changing scene, and there's plenty of parking in front of the mall.

JACK PATLA CO.
181 King St.
(843) 723-2314
www.jackpatlagallery.com

Established back in 1951, this name has long been associated with fine 18th- and 19th-century antiques and English garden ornaments in the classic Charleston tradition. The ownership changed in 1997, but the tradition goes on, and the reputation for reliability still applies. Even the same management is on hand. Look for the extensive collection of antique brass fireplace fenders, English-made lead garden ornaments, and wooden boxes of all kinds. Shipping is never a problem.

JOHN GIBSON ANTIQUES
183 King St.
(843) 722-0909

Because genuine 18th-century pieces are getting increasingly difficult to find (not to mention more costly), this shop can make up remarkably convincing pieces by combining different old but incomplete antiques. Many handsome pieces of furniture have resulted from this practice, but be advised that their value (like the price) has been compromised. This crowded, fascinating shop features mostly 19th-century furniture along with some fine old reproductions. Estate appraisal, interior design, restoration, and gold-leafing services are offered.

JOINT VENTURE ESTATE
JEWELERS
185 King St.
(843) 722-6730, (800) 722-6730
www.jventure.com

This is the area's largest estate and pre-owned fine jewelry consignment shop. The inventory ranges from the most elaborate Victorian ornaments to a very modern, contemporary look. Variety is the strong suit here—with more than 1,200 consignors offering jewelry, flatware, and hollowware for every taste and pocketbook. Specialties found here are platinum, diamonds, sapphires, emeralds, rubies, pearls, and a large assortment of vintage watches. Repairs, restorations, and appraisals are done on-site.

ANTIQUES

KHOURY ORIENTAL RUGS
71 Wentworth St., St. 102
(843) 720-7370
www.khouryorientalrugs.com
This retailer, just off King Street, handles the finest in hand-knotted Oriental rugs. The selection is considerable, with something for every discerning shopper. Here you'll find old and antique Persian rugs, Indian tea-stained rugs, kilims, and Oushak, as well as needlepoints from China and assorted tapestries. Free shipping is available for out-of-town buyers.

LIVINGSTON ANTIQUES
2137 Savannah Hwy.
(843) 556-3502
www.livingstonantiques.com
Livingston is a direct importer of fine English and European antiques whose displays can be seen in this 30,000-square-foot warehouse. Look here for an eclectic mix of merchandise, from larger pieces such as chests and cabinets to handsome old wood boxes and clocks, plus collectible majolica, Imari, Canton, and Staffordshire. Livingston's is open Tues through Sat.

MOORE HOUSE ANTIQUES
105 Broad St.
(843) 722-8065
www.moorehouseantiques.com
Here is a delight for fanciers of Chinese export porcelain. There's always a fine assortment of Canton, Rose Medallion, Fitzhugh, and others from the early 19th century. Look for the shop's 18th- and 19th-century American furniture, including rare Charleston-made pieces. This merchandise is beautifully documented, and safe shipping to anywhere is never a problem. Owner Bryan Riddle has

been serving Charleston Antique District shoppers for many years.

PAGE'S THIEVES MARKET
1460 Ben Sawyer Blvd., Mount Pleasant
(843) 884-9672
www.pagesthievesmarket.net
Since 1959, folks heading for the beach at Sullivan's Island via the Ben Sawyer Causeway have been rubbernecking as they pass Page's Thieves Market in the old barn off to the right. This colorful and eccentric display of antiques, used furniture, knickknacks, and collectibles is always an adventure to explore—rain or shine. You'll never know what you'll find here; this is for the free-spirited shopper with time to hunt for that illusive gem of a buy. Many a rustic beach house, starter home, or college apartment was furnished from this place. They even have new bedding.

QUEEN CHARLOTTE ANTIQUES, LTD.
61 Queen St.
(843) 722-9121
A relative newcomer to the Queen Street antiques scene is this shop, a sister to the original store open for a number of years in Charlotte, North Carolina. Its specialty is 18th- and 19th-century English and French fine antiques and decorative accessories. The shop also carries garden ornaments that are either old or reproductions of old garden decorations (recreated in new, more durable materials). The philosophy here is to provide merchandise for the Charleston market that has the formal elegance of 18th-century England combined with the livability and casual charm of the French countryside. A nice collection of coffee table books illustrating that delightful mix makes this shop a pleasure to visit.

133

✳ROUMILLAT'S ANTIQUES
2241 Savannah Hwy.
(843) 766-8899
www.antiquesandauctions.com
This is something of a departure from the veddy, veddy serious antiques tradition of King Street in Charleston, but it's an awful lot of fun. Roumillat's has a vast array of used furniture and antiques that can surprise you. Some people find real gems in the rough. Roumillat's says the selection includes American and English antiques, Victorian, Edwardian, and plain old-fashioned stuff. Call ahead for directions to its West Ashley warehouse and the twice-monthly auction dates (usually on the first and third Sat at 10 a.m.), then go and enjoy.

THE SILVER VAULT OF CHARLESTON
195 King St.
(843) 722-0631, (843) 571-4342
www.silvervaultcharleston.com
The Silver Vault specializes in the purchase and sale of American, Continental, British, and French silver as well as jewelry and decorative arts pieces. This shop is also a hard-to-find resource for silver-plating, repairs, and full restorations of all metals, including brass and pewter. This is the companion shop of the Brass & Silver Workshop at 758 Saint Andrews Blvd. The owners, Alfred and Charlotte Crabtree, have more than 30 years' experience in silver repair and restorations.

SOUTHERN ACCENT DESIGNER
   SHOWCASE MARKET
630 Coleman Blvd., Mount Pleasant
(843) 856-9131
www.sadsm.com

Over in Mount Pleasant, you'll find the area's only high-end designer showcase market selling to consumers and professionals alike. Along with antiques selected by more than 60 vendors, you'll find a nice selection of fine art, Oriental rugs, accessories, and other decorative items galore. Located in Moultrie Plaza, there's plenty of parking.

✳TERRACE OAKS ANTIQUE MALL
2037 Maybank Hwy., James Island
(843) 795-9689
www.terraceoaksantiques.com
Terrace Oaks is a fun place to browse for unexpected finds, and locals have been doing just that since 1988. It houses 90+ booths and 11,000 square feet of American, European, and primitive furniture, along with a variety of other related goodies, including porcelain, collectibles, estate jewelry, and sterling. Shipping is available, and there's ample free parking.

ZINN RUG GALLERIES
767 Coleman Blvd., #4, Mount Pleasant
(843) 856-5066
www.zinnruggallery.com
Zinn is a direct importer of exquisite antique and semi-antique Oriental, Caucasian, and Turkish rugs, kilims, and kilim accessories. It features a large selection of Aubussons and needlepoint as well. Also look for suzanis and Ottoman furniture.

ATTRACTIONS

However varied the attractions of the Lowcountry and Greater Charleston may be, this is a place where people are drawn to, captured by, and never completely released from the clutches of history. In fact, it's fair to say we focus more on history—a deeper, richer, more romantic history (and more of it)—than any other colonial city in America. At least, that's the traditional and prevailing Charlestonian attitude.

Whether you're a newcomer to the Lowcountry (and soon to be an Insider yourself) or just a visitor to this gentle land, it's easy to be overwhelmed by the amount of history offered here and the seriousness with which Charlestonians deal with it in their daily lives.

Tourism and Charleston have a long working (if sometimes strained) relationship. Charleston and tourist management, on the other hand, are relatively recent and wary acquaintances. In other words, the sheer volume of visitors (especially during the past decade) has begun to seriously impact the fragile charm Charlestonians have stubbornly held onto for the past 200 years.

The quaint, genteel, quiet residential flavor of the 18th-century peninsular city (even with its 19th- and 20th-century scars) is by definition threatened by the economic, cultural, and environmental consequences of 4+ million tourists visiting annually. This collision of mores and economics has resulted in a very carefully planned and closely monitored tourism experience for today's Charleston visitor. We, as the city's guests (whether for a week or a lifetime), are very much the fortunate winners in this tug-of-war between then and now.

Because we truly care, and because it helps to preserve our city's unique cultural identity, Charleston's historic attractions are, for the greatest part, well organized, highly accessible, and intelligently interpreted. In short, there are delightful experiences in Charleston for visitors of all ages and all areas of interest.

OVERVIEW

In this chapter, we will begin by steering you to visitor centers and information outposts. Then we'll take you on a written tour of the Lowcountry's brightest and best attractions, beginning with the house museums, followed by plantations and gardens, forts, historic churches, and other museums. There is a lot to see and do here, and we hope

this guide will help you plan well and miss nothing of interest to you. Unless otherwise noted, all addresses are in Charleston.

Price Code

The following price code table is provided to give you an idea of the price of admission to those establishments that charge an admission fee. Please note that prices, means of payment, and hours change often and may vary seasonally, so call ahead for details. If no price code is designated, there is no charge to enter, but there may be other fees.

$....................**Less than $6**
$$ ....**$6 to $10**
$$$ .... **$10 to $20**
$$$$ .... **More than $20**

VISITOR INFORMATION

CHARLESTON VISITOR RECEPTION AND TRANSPORTATION CENTER
375 Meeting St.
(843) 853-8000, (800) 868-8118
www.charlestoncvb.com

Because parking in the old historic district is nearly always a problem, visitors are encouraged to make their first destination the Charleston Visitor Reception and Transportation Center. Its location on upper (meaning the northern end of) Meeting Street offers visitors a welcome opportunity to leave their cars behind and see Charleston's large historic district (mostly on the southern end of the Peninsula) by any of several alternative transportation options. This is the major, general information resource site in Charleston proper, and when we make a general reference to "the visitor center" in our guide, the Visitor Reception and Transportation Center is the place to which we refer.

Once you've taken in the city's overview of itself, it's time to go out and see the real thing. It's always best to start with a professional tour of some kind. If you're new to Charleston, this will be your only first impression, so why not make it an informed one with a guided tour?

Guided walking tours usually begin in the morning and last from 1 to 2 hours. They start from various central locations in the historic district—at most of the large hotels and bed-and-breakfast inns. The cost is about $20 per person. You may also choose to ride in a comfortable, air-conditioned minibus. These guided, motorized tours take about an hour, and prices range from $20 to $25. Or you might want to take one of Charleston's famous carriage tours and see the city at a clip-clop pace. (See the chapter on Tours for complete information on tour options and prices.)

Inexpensive and convenient motorized shuttle buses called DASH (Downtown Area Shuttle System) cost $1.75 per ride, leave the old depot behind the center at 15- or 20-minute intervals, and carry passengers to the old City Market in the heart of downtown. Some routes are even free. So, it's very possible to "do" the city and leave your car at the visitor center lot or garage. The visitor center is open daily from 8:30 a.m. to 5 p.m.

THE SHOPS OF HISTORIC CHARLESTON FOUNDATION
108 Meeting St.
(843) 724-8484
www.historiccharleston.org

Those who find themselves downtown in the vicinity of 108 Meeting St. (across from the Mills House) have another option for starting their historic Charleston odyssey. The Shops of Historic Charleston Foundation is its official name, but it's the Historic Charleston Foundation's version of visitor orientation. You'll find a well-planned cultural and architectural overview and free and friendly tourist advice.

The shop carries a fine array of merchandise, including many items from the foundation's Reproduction Collections. You'll find a comprehensive selection of books and reference materials relating to preservation, restoration, and Charleston's 18th- and 19th-century cultural life. You can also buy tickets for the foundation's signature house museum, the Nathaniel Russell House, and Middleton Place Foundation's Edmondston-Alston House. (See the House Museums section of this chapter.) The Shops of Historic Charleston Foundation is open Mon through Sat from 10 a.m. to 6 p.m., Sun hours are from noon to 5 p.m. Admission is free.

PRESERVATION SOCIETY OF CHARLESTON
147 King St.
(843) 722-4630
www.preservationsociety.org
Another friendly informational oasis for the sore-footed traveler (especially handy for those touring the many antiques venues scattered along King Street) is the Preservation Society of Charleston.

Its Book & Gift Shop offers a fine collection of books, reference materials, and gift items pertaining to Charleston and the Lowcountry. The accommodating staff of volunteers offers free tourist information as well.

Every fall, starting in mid-Sept and running through Oct, the Preservation Society's tours of private homes and gardens are very popular. This is a lovely time of year to see the city. Tickets are priced at $45 a tour and often sell out early, but you might check here at the book shop at the last minute and still be able to join one of these self-guided, neighborhood walking tours. (See the Annual Events chapter for more on the tours.)

The 147 King St. location serves as headquarters and resource center for the organization (founded in 1920) originally known as the Society for the Preservation of Old Dwelling Houses, one of America's premier preservation organizations. The Preservation Society Book & Gift Shop is open from 10 a.m. to 5 p.m. Mon through Sat. (See the Shopping chapter.)

HOUSE MUSEUMS

Peninsular Charleston contains thousands—yes, *thousands*—of historic buildings considered "architecturally significant." Overwhelming as that may seem, it's even more amazing to realize the vast majority of those buildings are private homes. Of these homes, literally hundreds could legitimately qualify as house museums not only for their exterior architectural sophistication, but also for their sumptuous interiors. In fact, preserving these homes and their remarkable collections of art, china, fine furniture, and fabrics has become an integral part of today's Charleston lifestyle.

While most of these historic homes remain in private hands and are rarely opened to public tours, seven Charleston house museums offer visitors unique adventures behind normally closed doors.

Most of the following house museums are open year-round and operated by various nonprofit preservation organizations in the city. Others are privately owned and run as businesses. In either case, Charleston's house museums afford a fascinating glimpse into the style of the city's interiors during a number of heydays in the development of American decorative arts.

From 18th-century Georgian to late-19th-century Victorian, Charleston's house museums are presented here in the chronological order of their construction dates.

As a quick reference for those who don't happen to keep the eight basic architectural styles of historic Charleston constantly top-of-mind, the following definitions (courtesy of the Historic Charleston Foundation and the National Trust for Historic Preservation) are offered:

- **Colonial** refers to the period from 1690 to 1740. Look for a very low foundation, beaded clapboard siding, a high-pitched gable roof (sometimes with flared eaves), hipped dormers, and raised panel shutters. A good Charlestonian example is the John Lining House, 106 Broad St. at King Street.

- **Georgian** refers to the architectural style popular in England during the reign of Anne and the four Georges. Here in America, the style is generally assigned to the years 1700 to 1790. Look for a hipped roof, box chimneys, triangular pediments (often with oval lights), columns, a raised basement, and a belt course between floors. An excellent Charleston example is the Miles Brewton House, 27 King St.

- **Federal** is the American architectural style seen chiefly between the years 1790 and 1820. In England, the style is called Adam, in reference to the English-Irish architect Robert Adam. Look for geometric rooms, ironwork balconies, a low-pitched roof, decorative bands around interior rooms, exterior trim, spiral stairs, and elliptical fan lights. The Nathaniel Russell House, 51 Meeting St., is a fine Charleston example.

- **Classical** Revival is the architectural return to the lines and look of ancient Greece (and later, Rome). It was popular in America from about 1820 to 1875. Look for large, heavy columns and capitals, temple pediments, triglyph and guttae, and all the other details in classic

Greek architectural order. In Charleston, a great example is Beth Elohim Synagogue, 90 Hasell St.

- **Gothic Revival** refers to the period between 1850 and 1885, when many American building designs borrowed from the upreaching lines of western European architecture between the 12th and 16th centuries. Look for pointed arches, buttresses, stone tracery, and finials. At 136 Church St., the French Huguenot Church exemplifies this style.

- **Italianate** is shown in the popular building style seen here between 1830 and 1900. Look for paired brackets and round head arches, balustrades, a low-pitched roof, and the loggia (or veranda). A classic Charleston example is the Col. John Algernon Sydney Ashe House, 26 South Battery.

- **Victorian** refers, of course, to England's Queen Victoria, who reigned from 1836 to 1901. In American architecture, however, it was a popular style between the years 1860 and 1915. Look for a multi-gabled roof, elaborate wood bracket work (sometimes called gingerbread), turrets, and roof decorations. A rare Charleston example is the Sottile House, on the College of Charleston campus at Green Street.

- **Art Deco** is exemplified in the highly stylized look that many American buildings took during the years between the world wars, roughly 1920 to 1940. Look for decorative panels, narrow windows, flat roofs, and multicolored bands. Charleston's most outstanding example is the beautifully restored Riviera Theater, 225–227 King St.

CALHOUN MANSION (1876) $$$
16 Meeting St.
(843) 722-8205
www.calhounmansion.net

This house museum is one of Charleston's few great Victorian-era palaces. Architecturally, it represents a brilliant expression of the Italianate style, which became extremely popular in America during the last half of the 19th century. This style is a rarity in Charleston's rich display of domestic architecture, possibly because when it was built, in 1876, the city's economy was still devastated by the loss of the Civil War. During the postwar period known as Reconstruction, very little mansion building was going on in Charleston. But the builder, George Walton Williams, a wholesale grocer and banker, was financially undaunted by the war. Unlike most wealthy Southerners, he had invested heavily in England and in the North before the war. When Mr. Williams's huge, new Charleston home was completed, newspapers in New York, Atlanta, and Charleston, immodestly described it as "the handsomest and most-complete home in the South, if not the country."

Indeed, it is still the largest privately owned home in Charleston with its 35 rooms, 24,000 square feet of living space, 23 fireplaces, 3-tiered piazza, Italian water gardens with fountains, and a cupola soaring 90 feet in the air overlooking Charleston Harbor. The Calhoun name comes from the fact that the builder's son-in-law, Patrick Calhoun—grandson of John C. Calhoun, "The Great Nullifier"—lived here until 1929, when he lost the house and his fortune in the stock market crash of that year. Subsequent owners failed to find a viable use for this venerable old mansion. It slowly slid into decline until it was finally condemned by the City of Charleston in the 1970s. A young local attorney bought it and spent a considerable fortune and much of the next 25 years restoring its structural and artistic integrity.

Today, it houses a new owner's extensive personal collection of English and American furniture of the 18th and 19th centuries—with an emphasis on Southern decorative arts. In addition, his fine collection of impressionist art, Chinese ceramics, and other objets d'art look amazingly at home in this huge Victorian-era forum originally designed to create an impressive display. The Calhoun Mansion has been featured in many national magazines and used as a set for the very memorable television miniseries *North and South*. Guided tours of the main 2 floors take place on the hour and half hour starting at 11 a.m., seasonally Tues through Fri and by appointment. A new Grand Tour tours the entire mansion including the cupola and costs $50 per person. Admission is charged, but children under age 6 are free. Toddlers must be carried by a supervising adult; no strollers allowed. In-house photography is prohibited.

THOMAS ELFE HOUSE (1760) $$
54 Queen St.
(843) 722-9161
www.thomaselfehouse.com

This delightfully miniature single house is one of Charleston's wonderful little treasures that, for the past several years, has been open to the public on a limited basis. Built well before the American Revolution, it was a modest craftsman's home like many others throughout the city. The particular craftsman who owned this one, however, was most extraordinary.

Thomas Elfe arrived in Charleston from England in about 1747, bringing along a unique skill for woodworking. Here in

Charleston, he became one of the most prolific and acclaimed cabinetmakers of the colonial era. His work appears in many other house museums and private homes throughout the city, as well as in other fine museums all over the country.

During the period of 1768 to 1775, his own records show that Elfe created more than 1,500 pieces of cabinetwork. He worked primarily in mahogany, with distinctive fretwork, unique leg design, and inner drawer construction being telltale signs of Elfe's craftsmanship.

Restored in 1970, the house interiors show many finishing touches that are attributed to its first, now-famous owner. All four rooms display exquisitely proportioned fireplace walls of cypress paneling. There are china cabinets and deftly scaled closets artfully worked into each chimney alcove. The slightly lowered dados give the effect of higher ceilings and greater space.

The fact that its first owner was a major contributor to the art and lifestyle of colonial Charleston makes it interesting today. Any serious student of fine, Charleston-made, 18th-century furniture or an antiques buff with a nose for history will want to see this house. It is a showplace for 18th- and early-19th-century furnishings. The tour schedule is Mon through Fri from 10 a.m. until noon. Occasionally, the house is open afternoons and weekends, so call ahead to check.

✳HEYWARD-WASHINGTON HOUSE (1772) $$
87 Church St.
(843) 722-2996
www.charlestonmuseum.org
This handsome, early Charleston "dwelling house" is now known by two names because of two prominent Americans associated with

it—one an owner, the other a distinguished guest.

It was built in 1772 by Daniel Heyward, a wealthy rice planter and the father of Thomas Heyward Jr., a South Carolina signer of the Declaration of Independence. It is documented that the younger Heyward lived in the house until 1794.

In 1791 President George Washington made a grand tour of the new nation and included Charleston on his itinerary. In anticipation of this distinguished visitor, the city rented Heyward's house for Washington's accommodations, and Heyward was thus displaced to his country house for the duration. In Washington's diary, he recorded his visit to the property, saying, "The lodgings provided for me in this place were very good, being the furnished house of a gentleman at present residing in the country; but occupied by a person placed there on purpose to accommodate me."

Today the house is furnished with a magnificent collection of period antiques, especially some fine Charleston–made furniture of the 18th century. Look for the famous Holmes bookcase that still bears the scars of an incoming British mortar from the days of the American Revolution. This is the only 18th-century house museum in the city with original outbuildings (kitchen, carriage house, and necessary) still a part of the courtyard. You'll also find a small formal garden, in keeping with the period of the house.

Heyward-Washington House was saved from destruction in the early 1920s by the Preservation Society of Charleston. It is now a National Historic Landmark owned and operated by the Charleston Museum. It's open daily, Mon through Sat from 10 a.m. to 5 p.m. and Sun from 1 to 5 p.m. No entry is allowed after 4:30 p.m. Note that the

Charleston Museum offers discounted combination ticket prices for this house and the Joseph Manigault House.

✳JOSEPH MANIGAULT HOUSE (1803) $$
350 Meeting St.
(843) 723-2996
www.charlestonmuseum.org

At the beginning of the 19th century, Charleston architecture was still very much dominated by what was fashionable in Mother England. This house, designed and built in 1803 by Charleston gentleman-architect Gabriel Manigault for his brother Joseph, was certainly no exception. Today it remains one of America's most beautiful examples of the graceful Adam style.

Both Manigault brothers were wealthy rice planters with sophisticated tastes. Gabriel had studied in Geneva and London, where the Adam influence was at its height, and he maintained an extensive architectural library of his own.

The house is distinguished by one of the most graceful staircases in the city and displays an outstanding collection of Charleston, American, English, and French furniture of the period. Don't miss the charming gate temple in the rear garden. During the 1920s, when the Manigault House was very nearly torn down in the name of progress, Gabriel Manigault's classical gate temple was used as the restroom for an oil company's service station, then on the garden site. Later, during World War II, the house served as a USO canteen for servicemen passing through Charleston's busy Navy Yard en route to battle stations overseas.

Today it is a National Historic Landmark owned and operated by the Charleston Museum. Hours are 10 a.m. to 5 p.m. Mon

through Sat and 1 to 5 p.m. on Sun. The last tour begins at 4:30 p.m.

✳NATHANIEL RUSSELL HOUSE (1808) $$
51 Meeting St.
(843) 724-8481
www.historiccharleston.org

Prominent shipping merchant Nathaniel Russell decided to build his great "mansion-house" on Meeting Street, practically within sight of the busy wharves that produced his wealth. When his house was completed in 1808, Russell was 71, and he had reportedly spent $80,000 on the project—an enormous sum at that time.

Like the Manigault house, Russell's new home was inspired by the work of English architect Robert Adam, whose delicate style was influenced by the airy classical designs only recently uncovered (literally) in the Italian excavations of Pompeii and Herculaneum.

Today's visitor is immediately dazzled by the dramatic, free-flying, elliptical stairway floating up through 3 floors without any visible means of support. Finely proportioned, geometric rooms are furnished with another outstanding collection of Charleston, English, and French pieces, including rare china, silver, and paintings.

Unlike most other Charleston house museums, the Russell House has never been through a sad period of decline and disrepair. First as a fine town house, then as the home of a South Carolina governor, and later as a school for girls and even a convent, 51 Meeting St. has always been a respected and cared-for landmark. Today it is owned and operated by Historic Charleston Foundation, an organization that has done much to preserve and illuminate the city's architectural heritage.

The house is open for tours Mon through Sat from 10 a.m. to 5 p.m. and Sun from 2 to 5 p.m. The last tour begins at 4:30 p.m. The house is closed on Thanksgiving, Christmas Eve, and Christmas Day. A combination ticket for this and the Aiken-Rhett house at 48 Elizabeth St. is available. Call (843) 724-8481 for tickets and group tour information.

EDMONDSTON-ALSTON HOUSE
(1825,1838) $$
21 East Battery
(843) 722-7171
www.middletonplace.org
In 1825, Charles Edmondston, another wealthy merchant and wharf owner, built this handsome dwelling where he could enjoy an uninterrupted view over the expanse of Charleston Harbor. In 1828 the house was bought by Col. William Alston, a rice planter. His son, Charles, redecorated the house in the 1830s, favoring the fashionable Greek Revival style.

Incredibly, today's visitor can still find many family documents, portraits, silver pieces, and fine furnishings—including Charles Alston's almost-intact library—in place. Much of it dates back to the 1830s. The house is notable for its unusual Regency woodwork, as well as its uncompromising views of the harbor. The intimacy and authentic details of the house may leave guests feeling as if the Alstons only recently left the property, perhaps on a visit to the country.

The Edmondston-Alston House is owned by Middleton Place Foundation. Tours are offered from 10 a.m. to 4:30 p.m. Tues through Sat and 1:30 to 4:30 p.m. Sun and 1 to 4:30 p.m. Mon. Admission is

charged, but it's free for children age 7 and younger.

AIKEN-RHETT HOUSE
(1818, 1833, 1857) $$
48 Elizabeth St.
(843) 723-1159
www.historiccharleston.org
Unlike any other house museum in Charleston, the Aiken-Rhett house is a time capsule of Charleston's history and taste. It was the home of Gov. William Aiken from 1833 through 1887, and it owes most of its eerie charm to him.

The structure was built in 1818 by John Robinson as a typical Charleston single house, much like many others built in the city at the time. However, under the later ownership of South Carolina railroad magnate Aiken (who was governor at the time of the Civil War), the house was drastically altered and enlarged. In 1833 it was remodeled to conform to the bold Greek Revival style popular then. Again in 1857, alterations were made, this time in the heavily ornamented Rococo Revival style that was gaining popularity in antebellum Charleston. Rococo Revival, which was popular in 18th-century France, is noted for curvilinear lines, as in shells, foliage, and scrolls.

Here again, an uncanny amount of furnishings and other objects belonging to Governor and Mrs. Aiken can still be found, including portraits, statuary, library volumes, and elaborate chandeliers the couple brought back from Paris in the 1830s. The difference here is that much of the house is unrestored. It is instead preserved, largely as it was presented to the Charleston Museum in 1975 by descendants of the Aiken family.

As a result, the visitor can almost feel the presence of Jefferson Davis, president of the Confederacy, who was a guest in the house in 1863. You can easily picture Confederate general P. G. T. Beauregard using the house as his headquarters during the almost relentless Union bombardment of Charleston in 1864. The haunting, life-size portrait of Mrs. Aiken dressed in her finery belies the emotional and economic hardship she suffered after the war when the governor was arrested and briefly imprisoned for treason.

Another miracle of the Aiken-Rhett house is the remarkably well-preserved slave quarters and outbuildings (including stables and a privy) to the rear of the house. A high masonry wall surrounding the stable yard and slave quarters somehow managed to keep out the forces of time and change. They're shown as they are, unromanticized, making an eloquent statement about slavery and the sociology of the 19th-century South. If woodworking detail is any measure of worth and respect, the horses at the Aiken-Rhett house were more important than the slaves who worked as house servants. The horse stalls have Gothic arches and turned pillars; no such adornment graces the utilitarian slave quarters.

The fragile textures of time and the changing fortunes of war very much show in this remarkable house museum. Surely this is its most romantic and tragic charm. Now owned and operated by the Historic Charleston Foundation, the Aiken-Rhett House is a must-see. The 45-minute audio house tours are given from 10 a.m. to 5 p.m. Mon through Sat. Last tour starts at 4:15 p.m. On Sunday, tours begin at 2 p.m. A combined ticket that includes admission to the Nathaniel Russell house is available.

PLANTATIONS & GARDENS

Here's a suggested route you may want to take: Starting on the Peninsula, take US 17 S. Once across the Ashley River Bridge, you'll drive through some of Charleston's post–World War II urban sprawl. You may choose to start your plantation tour at the very beginning—at Charles Towne Landing State Historic Site, South Carolina's unique state park at the site of the colony's original settlement. There, you'll explore a reconstruction of an early settler's cabin and see the "experimental garden" where test crops of various kinds held the settler's best hope for survival in this brave new world.

Next, you may want to take the same architectural quantum leap Charlestonians did—from that early, crude settler's cabin to the classical grandeur of Drayton Hall (begun in 1738), which was built along the Ashley River's west bank only a generation later.

At Middleton Place (developed ca. 1740) and Magnolia Plantation (started in the 1680s, then expanded about 1840), you can explore the vast gardens so important to these early planter families. Magnolia's informal design (typical of 19th-century gardens) makes an interesting contrast to Middleton's strict geometric patterns (so popular in 18th-century France).

In the spring, you'll want to include Cypress Gardens, originally part of Dean Hall plantation on the Cooper River. Follow SR 61 from Middleton Place to SR 165, join US 17-A through Summerville to Moncks Corner, and follow the signs. There, in a 163-acre black-water cypress swamp, is an incredible azalea garden started in the 1920s and now owned and operated by the City of Charleston Department of Parks. You'll find charming little bateaux (flat-bottomed boats) to use, and there are 3 miles of walking paths through the vibrant spring colors reflected in the mirrorlike waters.

Back through Charleston and 6 miles north along US 17 is Boone Hall, the picturesque, 738-acre plantation used extensively in the ABC TV miniseries *North and South*, filmed in and around Charleston. Boone Hall's best features include the famous avenue of live oaks and the original "slave street" of nine brick slave cabins (ca. 1743).

You won't be able to visit all these plantations in a single day. If you must select only a sampling of Greater Charleston's plantation culture, the following in-depth review of these sites should help you choose.

You won't regret the investment of time and travel it takes to digest these plantations and gardens. They're so much a part of the city, so vital to its development, that to see just one side of Charleston life and not the other might seriously handicap your understanding of the area as a whole.

CHARLES TOWNE LANDING STATE HISTORIC SITE $$
1500 Old Towne Rd. (between I-26 and SR 171)
(843) 852-4200
www.southcarolinaparks.com

Surely this is one of the most unusual state parks in South Carolina, if not America. Charles Towne Landing State Historic Site was created as part of South Carolina's 300th anniversary celebration in 1970 on the plantation belonging to Dr. and Mrs. Joseph I. Waring. Today, the property isn't presented to the public as a plantation per se. Rather, the vast acreage is devoted to re-creating and interpreting the first English settlement in the Carolinas, which existed on this plantation site back in 1670.

Once inside the gate, visitors travel down a long alley bordered by ancient live oaks and swamp. Eventually you come to a parking lot and a complex of modern buildings that serve as a starting point for your adventure.

A new visitor center opened in 2006 as part of a major ongoing renovation of the whole park. It includes extensive interactive exhibits describing how settlers, slaves, traders, and Native Americans came together at this location to begin the first European Colony in the Carolinas. Charles Towne Landing is a working archaeological site where visitors can interact with historians literally unearthing the early story of South Carolina's first English settlement and the Native American history that preceded it. Visitors can also tour the Legare-Waring plantation house and observe many fascinating artifacts found at the site.

Along the river, you may explore a full-scale replica of a typical 17th-century trading vessel called the *Adventure,* docked at the landing in Old Towne Creek. Picture it as a common work vehicle of the early plantation system, plying the waters loaded with fur pelts, indigo shipments, and rice to sell on the wharves in Charleston. These boats also carried people and supplies to the widely scattered plantations upriver.

The redesign of the Animal Forest boasts a 20-acre natural habitat zoo with wolves, pumas, bears, bison, snakes, and alligators—all part of the Lowcountry landscape when settlers first arrived in the 1670s.

The Settlers' Life Area, with its replica colonial buildings, is a handsome example of what early colonists saw every day. You'll see candle making, open-fire cooking, woodworking, and, depending on the season and the weather, even the colony's first printing press in action. Special exhibits and demonstrations can be found here on holidays.

Charles Towne Landing is open all year except Christmas Eve and Christmas day. The hours are 9 a.m. to 5 p.m daily. Picnic tables, a snack bar, and a gift shop are all on-site. The park is largely accessible to visitors with disabilities. Visitors age 6 and older are charged an admission fee. Wheelchairs and strollers are available free of charge.

DRAYTON HALL $$$
3380 Ashley River Rd.
(843) 769-2600
www.draytonhall.org

Not a tour of a reconstructed working plantation or the collected decorative arts from a bygone era, Drayton Hall offers an adventure in architecture. Yes, architecture and a great deal more.

If for no other reason, Drayton Hall should be seen and experienced as the sole survivor of the ugly 1865 rampage by Union troops, who looted and burned nearly every other plantation house along the Ashley River. But there is more to Drayton Hall, as it also stands as a survivor of many other changes, influences, forces, and times.

It was built between 1738 and 1742 as the country seat (primary home) of John Drayton (1716–1779), whose family had emigrated to Charles Towne from Barbados and settled nearby at Magnolia Plantation a generation earlier. The house is considered one of the oldest and finest examples of Georgian-Palladian architecture in America. Its recessed, 2-story portico may have been inspired by Italy's Villa Pisani, designed in 1552 by Andrea Palladio. The portico is one of the architectural signatures of Palladianism, and Drayton Hall's portico may be one of the earliest built in America.

The story of how this very sophisticated English Palladian villa came to be built along the west bank of the Ashley, and how it survived the ravages of time, wars, earthquakes, and hurricanes, is a fascinating saga.

Maybe the greatest curiosity of all is how the old Drayton house survived the enormous forces of changing architectural taste. Oddly, the house was never modernized. Drayton Hall has never seen plumbing or central heat; it never had gas installed for lighting or heating purposes. Its only link with modern electricity is the one meager line that brings life to its sadly necessary modern security system.

Quite simply, Drayton Hall is an architectural time capsule. The structure remains almost untouched as an eloquent statement about 18th-century thinking, craftsmanship, technology, and design. It's one of the few sites left in colonial America so pure, unaltered, and uncompromising.

Visitors will find the Drayton Hall story— how it all came to pass—interpreted by a small group of professional guides. These storytellers lead you through 250 years of time, family genealogy, architectural history, and a smattering of the economic and social realities of the plantation system.

A word or two about "interpretation" might be helpful here. Because each guide at Drayton Hall develops his or her own perspective of the house, every tour will be slightly different. That is, each guide bears the responsibility of interpreting and synthesizing the tremendous amount of research data collected about the property. You hear the guide's words, not a written script. Thus, return visits will only deepen your understanding of the house, its people, and its times. The bare fact that you're touring virtually unfurnished rooms is hardly noticeable, since each room is chock-full of interesting information and rich architectural detail.

Drayton Hall comes to life because imagination is a wonderful artist. Imagination can paint in the faded colors of Drayton Hall's early days, when the settlement of Charles Towne was barely 70 years old. It can flesh out the heady, pre-Revolutionary days when the Ashley River plantation system was at its zenith. Now, through imagination, the visitor can even see Drayton Hall in the grim, dark days following the Civil War, when vagrants and vandals used it at will. Imagination can find the returning prosperity and almost hear the laughter of the Drayton parties and other family occasions held here as recently as the 1960s. All it takes is an informed interpreter and your attentive ear.

Research is an ongoing process at Drayton Hall. The staff has recorded oral histories of the Drayton family as well as the African-Americans so closely associated with the house and its survival. Preserved but unrestored, Drayton Hall and its faded hues and subtle shading, its frayed places and telling stains are all pure Charleston. The house serves to illuminate the whole Ashley River plantation system in a rare and strangely haunting light.

A map is provided to visitors for a self-guided nature walk through the Drayton property. You can walk through various natural environments, including marsh, riverfront, and forest areas. Minimal signage along the trail offers interpretation of each environment. Archaeological as well as historic sites can be seen and understood as to their relevance to the 18th- and 19th-century Drayton Hall lifestyle. Major portions of the nature trails are wheelchair-accessible.

An ongoing project at Drayton Hall is an education program for students in kindergarten through grade 12. Several curriculum-coordinated programs feature student tours, plantation games, archaeology studies, and preservation workshops for both teachers and students.

This historic site is now owned by the National Trust for Historic Preservation. Admission prices include a professionally guided tour of the historic house and a self-guided tour of the grounds, including the African-American cemetery and their interactive Connections program. Tours are offered on the hour from 10 a.m. to 3:30 p.m. Nov through Feb and 9 a.m. to 4:30 p.m. Mar through Oct. A written tour in English, French, or German can be purchased. Group rates, AAA and military discounts, wheelchair access, and prearranged student programs are available. Admission is always free to members of the National Trust and Friends of Drayton Hall who show their membership cards. (See the Annual Events chapter for information on the Annual Spirituals Concert at Drayton Hall.)

i **Looking to add a splash of color to your spring visit to Charleston? Wade into the vast sea of fuchsia, pale pink, and white azalea blossoms during the annual spring bloom at Magnolia Plantation and Gardens. It's truly an overload for the senses.**

MAGNOLIA PLANTATION AND GARDENS $$$–$$$$
3550 Ashley River Rd.
(843) 571-1266, (800) 367-3517
www.magnoliaplantation.com
This is where Thomas Drayton Jr., father of Drayton Hall's John Drayton, settled when he came to Charles Towne in 1679. Early on, the home that Drayton, a successful English

planter from the island of Barbados, built for himself and his family was destroyed by fire. The house built to replace it was subsequently burned by Union troops in 1865. The present structure is said to have been a Drayton family hunting lodge that was moved down the Ashley River in 1873 and placed atop the foundations of the old plantation house. Magnolia Plantation is the original (and continuing) home of the Drayton family, now owned and managed by a ninth-generation descendant. It is famous for its expansive, informal, English-style gardens, which are the legacy of the Reverend John Grimke-Drayton, the plantation's owner during the Civil War, whose parish was nearby at Saint Andrews. In 1843, Grimke-Drayton imported numerous specimens of *Camellia japonica,* and in 1848, *Azalea indica.* Due to a bout with tuberculosis in the late 1840s, he left his parish for a time and devoted himself entirely to his garden.

By 1870, despite the tragedy of the war and the burning of the main house, the gardens at Magnolia Plantation had grown in size and reputation. That year, the property was first opened to the public. Paddle-wheeled steamboats from Charleston made regularly scheduled excursions to Magnolia, where tourists relaxed, took picnics, and strolled along the blossom-laden paths. But for all its lacy bridges arching gracefully over mirrorlike cypress ponds, one little-known, smaller area is well worth finding.

Look for the garden called Flowerdale. This is where it all began. Here is Magnolia's earliest garden area (planted in the late 1680s), and it was possibly the inspiration for Grimke-Drayton's larger, more ambitious plan a century and a half later. Surely the reverend sat here in the 1850s, pondering the moral issues facing his plantation world as the political storm clouds gathered over the South. Perhaps it was amid the beauty of Flowerdale that Grimke-Drayton first thought of expanding the garden plan to create an oasis of beauty so large and lasting it might someday sustain his family home.

Today, the gardens boast 250 varieties of azaleas and 900 varieties of camellias. These, plus many other flowers added through the years, keep Magnolia Gardens in colorful bloom all year long. Its most spectacular season, however, is spring, when the dazzling, vibrant azalea colors seem to vibrate on the landscape as far as the eye can see.

Visitors can get an overview of the property in a 12-minute video on the plantation's history shown at regular intervals in the orientation theater. Magnolia Plantation offers additional activities for nature lovers. Canoes can be rented to glide through the eerie beauty of its 125-acre waterfowl refuge. There are walking and bicycle trails, plus a wildlife observation tower that's very popular with bird-watchers. There's an herb garden, a horticultural maze, newly-opened antebellum slave cabins, a typical Ashley River rice barge, and even a petting zoo for children (as well as adults). You'll find picnic areas, a snack shop, and a gift shop there, too. (See the Kidstuff chapter.)

The property is open daily from 8 a.m. to 5:30 p.m. (8:30 a.m. to 5 p.m. Nov through Feb). Group rates are available. A basic admission is charged, with additional fees added for the Plantation House, Nature Train/Boat, Slavery to Freedom tour, and Audubon Swamp. Note that children under 6 cannot tour the house.

AUDUBON SWAMP GARDEN AT MAGNOLIA GARDENS $$
SR 61
(843) 571-1266
www.magnoliaplantation.com

In the 1980s, Magnolia Plantation and Gardens added a new element—the Audubon Swamp Garden. This separate attraction encompasses a 60-acre, black-water cypress and tupelo swamp. The visitor has the opportunity to see an otherwise inaccessible natural area via boardwalks, dikes, and bridges that provide an intimate view of the horticultural beauty and wildlife, including a few alligators.

The swamp garden gets its name from the great 19th-century American naturalist and wildlife artist John James Audubon, who visited Magnolia in search of waterbird specimens during his many lengthy stays in Charleston. This attraction, a 1 hour self-guided walking tour, is operated apart from the rest of Magnolia Plantation and may be seen without purchase of Magnolia's general admission.

✳MIDDLETON PLACE $$$$
4300 Ashley River Rd.
(843) 556-6020, (800) 782-3608
www.middletonplace.org

Middleton is one of the Lowcountry's most famous plantations and another National Historic Landmark along the rich and fascinating Ashley River. This was the home of Henry Middleton, president of the First Continental Congress, and his son Arthur, a signer of the Declaration of Independence.

The sheer size and scope of Middleton's gardens tell a great deal about the man and his grand vision. When he began his garden plan in 1741 (the framework for it remains unchanged today), the French influence for adopting a formal, geometric design was still very much in vogue. This was the Age of Reason, during which philosophy held that the essence of true beauty lay in humankind's conquest over nature. Thus, all great gardens of the time imposed order and geometric form over the otherwise natural, unruly landscape.

Legend says it took 100 slaves almost a decade to complete the sweeping terraces, walks, and artificial lakes—vistas that are still pleasing to the eye today. But the gardens at Middleton Place are only part of the plantation story interpreted here. Unlike some of the plantations closer and more convenient to Charleston, Middleton Place was a world unto itself. The 12-acre greensward, with its grazing sheep and strutting peacocks, creates an unforgettable image for the first-time visitor. This bucolic, pastoral scene belies the frenzy of activity and the vast labor force needed to maintain this busy world.

Now open on the Middleton Place grounds is Eliza's House, an actual freedman's dwelling. It is furnished as it might have been found in the 1870s, when African-Americans who stayed on the plantation after emancipation lived there. Middleton Place Foundation conducts ongoing research into the lives of the slaves, freedmen, and tradespeople who were so important to the Middleton Place scene. The lively plantation stableyards, with active displays of day-to-day life, provide another glimpse into that busy world. Chances are you'll find a blacksmith, a potter, weavers, and carpenters all busy at work and eager to explain and demonstrate their skills.

The main house, built sometime before 1741, was—like Magnolia's—burned in 1865 by Union troops. It is said the soldiers drank wine and dined in splendor at Middleton Place house, then set fire to it as they left.

The south flanker building (added about 1755) was least damaged by the fire, and it was essentially rebuilt in the early years of the 20th century in its present form. Inside, you'll find Middleton family memorabilia displayed, along with a remarkable collection of important family portraits that include works by Benjamin West and Thomas Sully.

Not to be missed is the view of the Ashley River from the high terraces of the gardens. The green grass ripples down the hillside to the graceful butterfly lakes below. Off to one side, the old rice mill counterbalances the picture-perfect composition of the landscape.

The Restaurant at Middleton Place serves authentic Lowcountry cuisine, and a daily lunch is available to visitors from 11 a.m. to 3 p.m. At night, from 6 to 9 p.m. Fri and Sat and until 8 p.m. Tues through Thurs, and Sun, the restaurant serves a delightful candlelight dinner, and there's no admission charge for entry to the property after 5:30 p.m. with dinner reservations. (See the Middleton Place website for details on dining there.)

In addition to the sensitive and skillful interpretation of the plantation's glorious past, there's an unexpected contemporary side to its present-day life. Just past the rice mill, a path leads into the forest and up a hill to the Inn at Middleton Place, a 55-room riverside oasis for discerning overnight travelers. The inn was designed by Charleston architect W. G. Clark, and it seems to have been born "of" the forest rather than "in" it. With vine-covered stucco and unblinking modern glass walls, each suite looks out over a green, woodland setting or the quiet waters of the Ashley River. A visit to the inn is well worth the short stroll from yesterday into the present. (See the Accomodations

chapter for more.) The Inn at Middleton Place has won numerous architectural awards, plus a spread in *Architectural Digest Travels.*

Middleton Place is open daily. Hours are 9 a.m. to 5 p.m. for the gardens and stableyards. House tours begin at 10 a.m., except on Mondays, when they begin at noon. House tour admission adds $10 per person to Middleton Place rates. An optional carriage ride through the property adds to the admission charge for adults and children. Group rates are available; special events with food service may be arranged on the property. (See the Annual Events chapter for special events at Middleton.)

i To make it even easier to see the three Ashley River Road plantations, Drayton Hall, Magnolia Plantation & Gardens, and Middleton Place, located just minutes apart on SR 61, now have a daily shuttle service from downtown Charleston every morning at 8:45 a.m. Charleston Chauffeur Company's 14-seat air-conditioned van picks up passengers at the bus shed at the visitor center at 375 Meeting St. The continuous loop runs all morning through the three sites and begins return service to Charleston at 2:45 p.m. Tickets are $20 round-trip and reservations are recommended at (843) 737-0654.

CYPRESS GARDENS $$
3030 Cypress Gardens Rd., Moncks Corner (off US 52—8 miles south of Moncks Corner)
(843) 553-0515
www.cypressgardens.info
For those with time and the inclination to go even farther afield, there's yet another

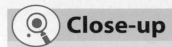 **Close-up**

Ashley River Road: Back Road to the Plantation Life

Before Hurricane Hugo struck the Lowcountry in September 1989—destroying an estimated 7 million board feet of prime, standing lumber—the **Ashley River Road** (SR 61 from Church Creek to Bacons Bridge Road) was oak-lined, moss-laden, sun-dappled, and almost unbearably beautiful. Certainly, that's how many Lowcountry old-timers remember it.

Most of the huge oak trees were hundreds of years old and stood so close to the road they became a hazard to speeding cars. So, for several years, every serious accident (and there were many) became a new excuse to remove more trees and more of the road's ambience. Then came the slow but relentless encroachment of commercial businesses and the addition of more and bigger real estate developments, each taking an even higher toll on the once scenic highway.

In the late 1990s, however, preservationists woke up to the fact that old SR 61 was a unique natural resource—of Lowcountry history and beauty—and it was quickly vanishing in the name of progress and development. Turning back these forces, once under way, turned out to be nearly impossible. But through years of planning and negotiation, a new plan has emerged that hopes to preserve as much of the old road's ambience as possible. Ashley River Road was designated a National Scenic Byway in 2000 and a South Carolina State Scenic Byway in 1998.

The stretch between Drayton Hall and Middleton Place still has the densest tree canopy. The live oaks reach up and over the road, creating a sun-filtered canopy through which you'll feel you're driving into the past.

Remember, the Ashley River itself is always on your right—sometimes just through the trees. Bear in mind, too, that the old road (originally a trail for Native Americans) was only a back road to the Ashley's colonial plantations. It was slow, rutted, and prac-

treat in store. Discover the beauty and wonder of Cypress Gardens—a true Southern cypress swamp and a 162-acre water forest of uncommon natural beauty.

This park, once part of Dean Hall Plantation, is now owned and operated by Berkeley County. You'll find meandering footpaths for hikers, but the traditional way to see Cypress Gardens is by bateau—a flat-bottomed boat poled or paddled by expert young boaters who are always on hand to do the work for a small price. You have the option of rowing yourself if you like, but the serenity of the black waters mirroring springtime azaleas, dogwoods, daffodils, and wisteria deserves

your undivided attention. Scenes from the movies *The Patriot* and *The Notebook* were filmed here.

In a separate building, Cypress Gardens' 24,000-gallon "swamparium" features fish and turtles native to the Lowcountry and has a display of venomous and nonvenomous snakes. There's also a butterfly house, a large greenhouse with flowering plants, birds, a pond, and live butterflies to explore.

Cypress Gardens is open daily except Thanksgiving, Christmas Eve, Christmas, and New Year's. Call ahead for seasonal hours and special admission prices. Hours are usually 9 a.m. to 5 p.m. No admittance is allowed after tically impossible to navigate in wet weather. Most social and business traffic to and from the far-flung plantations went by water. Thus, the great houses were actually built facing the river, the avenue to all agricultural wealth. Still, European settlers are recorded using the back road as early as 1707.

If you look carefully, you'll notice some unexplained low ridges along the roadside. Chances are, these are old rice dikes indicating where the land was flooded and the fields cultivated for rice.

In other places through the forest you'll see larger, unnatural-looking mounds— especially noticeable in the wintertime. These are the outcroppings from old, abandoned phosphate mines. After the Civil War, during the late 1870s, phosphate (an early fertilizer product) was discovered in the ground along the west bank of the Ashley. For a brief but reckless period, this entire landscape was crudely strip-mined. As ecologically careless and harmful as these practices were, the phosphate era provided desperately needed income for a few of the old planter families that had somehow managed to hold onto their properties through the war and Reconstruction.

If the phosphate mining years were not the Ashley River's finest hour, at least they helped rescue what little was left of the plantations after the cataclysmic year of 1865. In Feb of that year, as the war was winding down, Union troops advanced toward Charleston on the Ashley River Road, looting and burning as they came. Of all the great houses once standing along the high, west bank of the river, only Drayton Hall survived.

Once, there were scores of plantations along the Ashley. They had wonderful, lyrical names: MacBeth and Runnymede, Millbrook and Schieveling. Today, three of the old properties are open to the public. These are Drayton Hall, Magnolia, and Middleton Place. (See entries in text.) Each is unique and remarkable in a different way, and each offers special insight into the Ashley River's fascinating plantation story.

4 p.m. Admission is free for children younger than 6.

FORTS

Among the most visited attractions in the Lowcountry are the area's famous forts— standing today in mute testimony to the great strategic role Charleston Harbor played during the conflicts of the past 300 years.

Of course, the most famous of these fortresses is legendary Fort Sumter, where the Civil War began. But Greater Charleston has a number of other forts and former military fortifications that offer fascinating stories, both for the serious historian and for us regular Insiders too. There's Fort Moultrie on Sullivan's Island, Fort Johnson on James Island (now site of the South Carolina Wildlife and Marine Resources Center), and Battery Wagner on Morris Island.

We'll sketch brief histories of these sites—just enough to send you off to see the real thing with a taste of the very real drama and sacrifice associated with these places.

✳FORT SUMTER NATIONAL MONUMENT $$$

Charleston Harbor
(843) 883-3123, (800) 789-3678
www.nps.gov/fosu
www.fortsumtertours.com

Almost every Charlestonian knows the story by heart: The year was 1861. South Carolina had seceded from the Union. And yet, just a few miles east, there at the mouth of Charleston Harbor, Union forces were still stationed at Fort Sumter. The Confederacy officially demanded that Fort Sumter be vacated, but the North adamantly refused. At 4:30 a.m. on the morning of April 12, a mortar shell burst over the fort, fired from nearby Fort Johnson. The Civil War had begun.

At first—largely as a matter of honor—the Union forces defended Fort Sumter. But after 34 hours, they surrendered. It was practically a bloodless battle—no one was killed, and only a few men were wounded.

Amazingly, the Confederates held the fort for the next 27 months, against what was the heaviest bombardment the world had ever seen. Over the course of almost 2 years, no fewer than 46,000 shells (about 3,500 tons of metal) were fired at the island fort. In the end, the Confederate troops abandoned Fort Sumter, but they never surrendered. It was February 17, 1865. By April, the war and the cause would be lost.

Today, Fort Sumter is a national monument administered by the National Park Service of the US Department of the Interior. It is still accessible only by boat, and the only public tour of this tiny man-made island and world-famous fort is offered through Fort Sumter Tours, Inc.

You can board the Fort Sumter tour boat at the National Park Service's new facility at the foot of Calhoun Street on the Cooper River. The impressive $15 million interpretive center took 3 years to build and adds a dramatic new dimension to the Fort Sumter experience. Here, visitors are immersed in the Fort Sumter story with interactive displays and graphics, while Park Service rangers are on hand to answer questions. Among the sights found here, you'll find the actual 33-star Garrison Flag that flew over the fort that historic first night of the Civil War. The trip out to Fort Sumter takes about two hours and 15 minutes (including one hour at the fort). The boat ride affords delightful views of Charleston's waterfront and includes a narrated history of Charleston Harbor given en route. The specially built sightseeing boats are clean, safe, and have on-board restrooms.

Once you're at Fort Sumter itself, you can walk freely about the ruins. There's another interpretive museum area on-site with National Park Service rangers there to answer any questions you may have.

You'll need to check in for your tour at least 25 minutes early for ticketing and boarding. Departure times vary according to the season and the weather, so call the number listed for departure information. During the busy summer season, there are usually three tours a day. Children younger than 6 are admitted free, but a boarding pass is required for them. Wheelchair access is available. Group rates are available, but advance reservations for groups are encouraged. (Visit www.spiritlinecruises.com or see the Tours and Kidstuff chapters for additional information.)

FORT MOULTRIE
1214 West Middle St., Sullivan's Island
(843) 883-3123
www.nps.gov/fosu

From the earliest days of European settlement along the Eastern seaboard, coastal fortifications were set up to guard the newly found, potentially vulnerable harbors. In this unique restoration, operated today by the National Park Service, visitors to Fort Moultrie can see two centuries of coastal defenses as they evolved.

In its 171-year history (1776 to 1947), Fort Moultrie defended Charleston Harbor twice. The first time was during the Revolutionary War, when 30 cannons from the original fort drove off a British fleet mounting 200 guns in a ferocious, nine-hour battle. This time, Charleston was saved from British occupation, and the fort was justifiably named in honor of its commander, William Moultrie.

The second time the fort defended the city was during the Civil War. For nearly 2 years, the Charleston forts (and the city itself) were bombarded from both land and sea. The walls of Forts Sumter and Moultrie crumbled under the relentless shelling, but somehow the forts were able to hold back the Union attacks.

Today, the fort has been restored to portray the major periods of its history. Five different sections of the fort and two outlying areas each feature typical weapons representing a different historical period. Visitors move steadily back in time from the World War II Harbor Entrance Control Post to the original, palmetto log fort of 1776.

Fort Moultrie is open from 9 a.m. to 5 p.m. year-round. It is closed on Thanksgiving, Christmas, and New Year's Day. Groups should make reservations for guided tours. Pets are not allowed. Admission is free.

From Charleston, take US 17 N. (Business) through Mount Pleasant to Sullivan's Island and turn right on Middle Street. The fort is about 1.5 miles from the intersection.

FORT JOHNSON WILDLIFE AND MARINE RESOURCES CENTER
217 Fort Johnson Rd., James Island
(843) 953-9300
www.dnr.sc.gov/marine

Fort Johnson is another Charleston area fortress steeped in history and adaptively reused for modern needs. Since the early 1970s, the waterfront James Island site has been the home of the South Carolina Wildlife and Marine Resources Division, which researches and promotes the state's marine industries.

But savvy military buffs know Fort Johnson in another role. Like Fort Moultrie, this site has military significance that dates back several hundred years.

No trace now exists of the original Fort Johnson that was constructed on the site in about 1708. It was named for Sir Nathaniel Johnson, proprietary governor of the Carolinas at the time. A second fort was constructed in 1759, and small portions of that structure remain as tabby ruins there today. (Tabby is an early building material made from crushed oyster shell and lime.)

Records show the fort was occupied in 1775 by three companies of South Carolina militia under the leadership of Lt. Col. Motte. During the American Revolution, the fort remained in colonial hands until 1780, when the British forces advancing on Charleston reported finding it abandoned. A third fort was built in 1793, but a hurricane destroyed it in 1800. Some work on Fort Johnson was done during the War of 1812, but the following year another storm destroyed that progress. Shortly afterward, Fort Johnson was dropped from official reports of US fortifications.

During early 1861, South Carolina state troops erected mortar batteries and an earthwork of three guns on the old fortress site. Unbeknownst to most Americans, the actual signal shot that opened the bombardment of Fort Sumter and marked the beginning of the Civil War was fired from the east mortar battery of Fort Johnson on April 12, 1861. Fort Sumter was fired upon, not vice versa.

During the Civil War, building activity increased until Fort Johnson became an entrenched camp, mounting 26 guns and mortars. However, apart from routine artillery firing from the site, the only major action at the fort occurred on July 3, 1864, when its Confederate defenders repulsed two Union regiments totaling about 1,000 men. The Union forces sustained 26 casualties and lost 140 men as captives. The Confederate loss was one killed and three wounded. On the night of February 17, 1865, Fort Johnson was evacuated during the general Confederate withdrawal from Charleston Harbor.

After the Civil War, Fort Johnson became a quarantine station operated by the state and the city of Charleston. It continued to be used in that capacity until the 1950s. Today's inhabitants at the site (the Marine Resources folks) do not prohibit exploration, so you might find this history-drenched spot worth a visit. There is no charge to visit.

BATTERY WAGNER, MORRIS ISLAND
Of all the forts and battlegrounds that dot the Lowcountry landscape and pay quiet tribute to the area's military history, perhaps the most muted one is Battery Wagner on Morris Island. The story is a brief one in the long struggle of the Civil War, but it is a

significant one that is especially poignant today. In 1989, the story of Battery Wagner was portrayed in the acclaimed film *Glory*, which starred Matthew Broderick, Denzel Washington, and Morgan Freeman.

Time and tides have long since removed all traces of Battery Wagner. Today, Morris Island is vacant and uninhabited. It is hoped that one day Morris Island will become a National Historic Landmark and interpreted for visitors as the battleground and graveyard it is. Although a monument at Battery Wagner is planned, the site remains remarkably overlooked by the public for now. But whatever its future may hold, the story of Morris Island will always include the story of Battery Wagner and the 54th Massachusetts Regiment.

Because Charleston was the "cradle of Secession," it was a primary target for the Union's high command. On June 16, 1862, the Union forces' first attempt to capture the city failed at the Battle of Secessionville on James Island. Union commanders decided to mount a two-pronged attack using both land and naval forces. There were two possible lines of approach to the city: through Sullivan's Island, which was heavily defended, or through Morris Island, which was more lightly guarded. On Morris Island, the main defense was Battery Wagner, a quickly built fortification with thick sand walls and more than a dozen cannons.

Choosing the Morris Island approach, Union forces landed on July 10, 1863, and opened fire the following day with little success. A week later, they tried again. Even after a 10-hour artillery bombardment, Battery Wagner stood firm.

At dusk on July 18, the Union infantry advanced up the beach toward heavily defended Battery Wagner. Spearheading the attack was the 54th Massachusetts Regiment under the leadership of Col. Robert G. Shaw, the 25-year-old son of a wealthy Boston abolitionist. The regiment under Shaw's command was made up entirely of free blacks from the North. It was one of the 167 black units that fought against the Confederacy in the Civil War.

The bloody, hand-to-hand struggle at Battery Wagner saw 272 men from the 54th (more than 40 percent of the unit) fall dead, and 1,500 Union forces were lost, including Col. Shaw. The valor and courage displayed in the battle proved once and for all to Northern and Southern leaders that black soldiers could and would fight. The story of the 54th was widely publicized at the time, and as a result, the Union Army began to enlist blacks in growing numbers. By 1865, a total of 178,895 black soldiers had enlisted, which constituted 12 percent of the North's fighting forces.

The fight for Battery Wagner continued for 10 more weeks until the Confederates finally abandoned the work on September 6. The 54th continued to serve along the southeast coast for the remainder of the war. It was mustered out of service in Mount Pleasant on August 20, 1865.

HISTORIC CHURCHES

In a city that was a major contributor to the American ethic of religious freedom, there's a deep reverence for church architecture. The "Holy City," as it likes to be called, has dozens of beautiful 18th- and 19th-century churches that bear witness to this history and the 21st-century pride that goes with it.

Several churches are notable because of their early dates of construction, while others impress with their architectural grandeur. Some are survivors of cataclysmic events; a few speak volumes about their ethnic and sociological origins. Here are some churches whose history enriches Charleston and its citizenry, but remember, they are only a few of many. Unless otherwise noted, all are in the downtown vicinity and are still active houses of worship. They are listed in alphabetical order.

CATHEDRAL OF ST. JOHN THE BAPTIST (1890–1907)
120 Broad St.
www.charlestoncatholiccathedral.org

The first Cathedral of St. John the Baptist was completed in 1854. It was an outstanding example of Gothic architecture, built of Connecticut sandstone with a 200-foot spire. The building was completely lost in the great fire of 1861. By 1890, work had begun on what is almost an exact duplicate of the 1854 building. It was designed by P. C. Kelly of Brooklyn, New York, and followed closely the plans for the original structure. The exception is the square tower that, for monetary reasons, replaced the tall spire. A new spire and three bells were added atop the tower 103 years later, completing the reconstruction of the old building. The newer building is made of Connecticut brownstone. The nave is tiled, measures 150 by 80 feet, and seats 700 people.

CATHEDRAL OF ST. LUKE AND ST. PAUL (1815)
126 Coming St.
www.stlukeandstpaul.org

The church that is now the Cathedral Church for the Episcopal Diocese of South Carolina was originally known as St. Paul's, Radcliffeborough. It was organized as a mission in 1806. This building, designed by the architects James and John Gordon, was completed in 1815. At the time of its building, the load of the tower proved too heavy for the supporting walls, and the tower was dismantled. A lighter, Gothic Revival–style parapet was added, which is in contrast to the Classical Revival building below. Inside, the original color schemes have been reproduced as part of the intensive restoration of the building following severe damage in Hurricane Hugo.

CIRCULAR CONGREGATIONAL CHURCH (1891–1892)
150 Meeting St.
www.circularchurch.org

This church was originally called the Independent Church of Charles Towne and was established in 1681 by some of the first settlers of Charleston. It was one of the first two congregations created in the settlement (the other being St. Philip's Church; see subsequent listing).

The first building was of white brick and was known by locals as the White Meeting House. It is from this early euphemism that Meeting Street takes its name. That building was outgrown and replaced in 1804 by the first "Circular Church," an impressive structure designed in the Pantheon style by Charleston's famous architect Robert Mills. It is said to have seated 2,000 people, both black and white. The great fire of 1861 swept across the city and took this building with it. The ruins stood mutely until the earthquake of 1886 turned them to rubble.

A third (and the present) building on this site was completed in 1892 and is circular in form but Romanesque in style. The church's graveyard is the city's oldest, with monuments dating from 1695. This is the burial ground of Nathaniel Russell. (See the

Nathaniel Russell House listing under House Museums in this chapter.)

EMANUEL A.M.E. CHURCH (1891)
110 Calhoun St.
www.emanuelamechurch.org

The African Methodist Episcopal Church had its beginnings in 1787 in Philadelphia with the founding of the Free African Society, based on the doctrines of Methodism and the teachings of John Wesley. A similar organization was founded in Charleston in 1791 by the Rev. Morris Brown, a free black preacher affiliated with another Methodist church in the city. This show of independence from the blacks led to a secession from the Methodists and the founding of three black churches in Charleston, known as the Bethel Circuit.

The Emanuel A.M.E. congregation is one of those churches. The original building was in the Hampstead neighborhood in the east side of the city. By 1818, it had 1,000 members. In 1822, Denmark Vesey, a carpenter who bought himself out of slavery, laid plans in the church for a slave insurrection. Word of the rebellion leaked out, and Vesey and some of his followers were executed. The Hampstead church was burned to the ground. By 1834, all black churches in South Carolina were closed by the state legislature.

During the years following the Denmark Vesey incident, some of the congregation returned to white churches, but others continued the traditions of their African church and met underground. The congregation resurfaced in 1865—3,000 strong. Today's building was completed in 1891. The original gas lamps that line the sanctuary have been preserved. With seating for 2,500, the church has the largest seating capacity of Charleston's African-American congregations.

ℹ️ Some downtown churches are open to visitors who respectfully wish to see these historic interiors during weekday daytime hours. The schedules may be erratic because these are active, working religious organizations with busy calendars of church events scheduled for the congregations. However, if the doors are open, the sanctuary is deserted (usually there's a sign posted for visitors), and you know you're disturbing no one, feel welcome to quietly enter and briefly look around.

FIRST BAPTIST CHURCH (1822)
61 Church St.
www.fbcharleston.org

Here is the oldest Baptist church in the South. The congregation originally emigrated from Maine to the Carolinas in 1696. The building was designed by the first American-born architect, Robert Mills, in the popular Greek Revival style. Mills didn't mince words, saying of his creation, "[it is] the best specimen of correct taste in architecture in the city. It is purely Greek in style, simply grand in its proportions, and beautiful in its detail." Wood for the solid mahogany pulpit was brought from the West Indies for the staggering sum (in 1822) of $1,000. First Baptist's fabulous organ dates from 1845 and was made by Erben.

FIRST (SCOTS) PRESBYTERIAN
CHURCH (1814)
53 Meeting St.
www.first-scots.org

The Scots Kirk (or Scots Meeting House) was organized in 1731 by 12 Scottish families who believed in a strict subscription to the Westminster Standards (church laws) and the Presbyterian form of church

government. Their first simple structure on this site was built in 1734. It was replaced in 1814 by the present structure, which is the fifth-oldest church building in Charleston. By unanimous vote of the congregation, the church bell was donated to the Confederacy in 1862 and was only recently replaced by an English bell made in 1814.

Although the church was badly damaged by a fire in 1945, it was lovingly repaired. In the window over the main door appears the seal of the Church of Scotland, the burning bush, with a Latin motto that reads, *Nec Tamen Consumbatur* (*Nevertheless It was not consumed*).

✳FRENCH HUGUENOT CHURCH (1845)
136 Church St.
www.frenchchurch.org

French Huguenots were followers of the 16th-century French reformer John Calvin. After Louis XIV revoked the Edict of Nantes (1685), there was an enormous flight away from France by Protestants, many of whom came to the Carolinas.

The Huguenot Church in Charleston was organized in 1681, and groups of believers arrived in this area between 1680 and 1763. In 1706 the Church Act established the Anglican Church as the official religion in South Carolina, and slowly, most Huguenot churches were absorbed into what became Episcopal congregations. The Huguenot Church in Charleston is the outstanding exception; it is the only remaining independent Huguenot congregation in America.

This church was the city's first to be built (1845) in the Gothic Revival style. It was designed by Edward Brickell White, a noted Charleston architect who is credited with popularizing the Gothic style in America. The church was damaged by shelling during the

Civil War and nearly demolished by the 1886 earthquake. Each time, it was painstakingly restored. The building underwent a major refurbishing in 1997.

The church's famous Tracker organ, restored in 1967 by the Preservation Society of Charleston and the Charleston chapter of the American Organists Guild, is one of the city's true musical treasures. It is one of the last of its kind anywhere in the country.

GRACE EPISCOPAL CHURCH (1848)
98 Wentworth St.
www.gracechurchcharleston.org
Another magnificent example of Gothic-style church architecture in Charleston is Grace Episcopal Church, designed by Edward Brickell White. This building was completed in 1848.

The memorial windows in Grace Church are teaching windows, each containing scenes from the life of Christ as well as laypersons and clergy associated with the church. The largest window, over the rear doorway, took more than a year to complete and contains more than 10,000 pieces of glass. A small window on the Epistle side of the narthex contains an angel with the face of a small girl who drowned on Sullivan's Island.

Grace Church was closed for a year in 1864 because of the terrible bombardment from Morris Island, but it reopened soon after the evacuation of Charleston, during Federal occupation.

KAHAL KADOSH BETH ELOHIM (1840)
90 Hasell St.
www.kkbe.org
This is the oldest synagogue in continuous use in the United States. The present congregation was organized in 1749. It is also the longest surviving Reform synagogue in the world. Beth Elohim is acknowledged as the birthplace of Reform Judaism in the United States, tracing its origins back to 1824. This is a branch of Judaism that places more emphasis on traditional religious and moral values, instead of rigid ceremonial and ritualistic detail. The present 1840 Greek Revival structure was designed by Cyrus L. Warner. The graceful but massive wrought-iron fence that faces onto Hasell Street dates back to the original 1794 synagogue.

ST. JOHN'S LUTHERAN CHURCH (1817)
10 Archdale St.
www.stjohnscharleston.org
This is Charleston's mother church of Lutheranism, with a history spanning more than 250 years. The congregation was organized in 1742 and worshiped in various places until the present structure was completed in 1817. Frederick Wesner was the architect. The steeple is said to have been designed earlier by famous Charleston miniaturist Charles Fraser and was constructed in 1859. The original bell was given to the Confederate cause (bells were often melted down for use in ammo, cannons, ships, firearms, and the like) and was not replaced until 1992.

ST. MARY'S CATHOLIC CHURCH (1838–1839)
89 Hasell St.
www.catholic-doc.org/saintmarys
Called "the Mother Church of the Carolinas and Georgia," St. Mary's was the first Catholic church established in the English colony. Its first pastor came from Ireland in 1788. Originally known as the Roman Catholic Church of Charleston, St. Mary's officially took its present name in 1837. The Greek Revival building on the site today was consecrated

in 1839, replacing an earlier edifice lost in the city's great fire of 1838. Early communicants were mostly Irish immigrants and French refugees from the West Indies. In fact, church records were kept in French until 1822. Today, the crowded churchyard contains gravestones written in Latin, French, and English representing a congregation that spanned 17 nationalities, three continents, and two centuries. Inside, over the main altar, hangs a painting of the Crucifixion painted in 1814 by John S. Gogdell, a noted Charleston artist. The current organ is a Jardine (built in 1874 and restored in 1980) that is often featured in Piccolo Spoleto concerts held in May.

ST. MATTHEW'S LUTHERAN CHURCH (1872)
405 King St.
www.smlccharleston.org
The huge influx of German immigrants to Charleston during the first half of the 19th century caused the city's second-oldest congregation of Lutherans to greatly expand their house of worship. The magnificently Gothic church, with its tall, German-made stained-glass windows, was finished in 1872 with a 297-foot spire that stands taller than any other in the state. It was designed by John H. Devereaux.

In a spectacular 1965 church fire, the spire collapsed into the street below—the very point, in fact, piercing the sidewalk just to the left of the church's front door. That steeple point is still there (encased in concrete) and commemorated by a plaque honoring the congregation's courage and determination to restore the architectural treasure.

✳ST. MICHAEL'S EPISCOPAL CHURCH (1752–1761)
80 Meeting St.
www.stmichaelschurch.net
While St. Philip's can claim to be the oldest congregation in Charleston, St. Michael's lays claim to having the oldest church structure. There is some mystery as to whom the actual architect of St. Michael's might have been, but there's no question that this magnificent edifice is one of the great treasures of the city.

The church has remained essentially unchanged over the centuries, with the exception of a sacristy added in 1883. However, the structure has undergone major repairs several times because of natural and man-made disasters. In the earthquake of 1886, the steeple tower sank 8 inches, and the church cracked in several places. St. Michael's was damaged by a tornado in 1935 and again in 1989 by Hurricane Hugo. During both the American Revolution and the Civil War, the spire was painted black to make it less visible as a target for enemy gunners.

During his visit to Charleston in 1791, President George Washington worshiped at St. Michael's, where he sat in the Governor's Pew—so marked by a small plaque. In later years, the Marquis de Lafayette and Gen. Robert E. Lee sat in that same pew. Buried in St. Michael's churchyard are several distinguished members of the congregation, including Gen. Charles Cotesworth Pinckney, Revolutionary hero, signer of the Constitution, and Federalist presidential candidate; and John Rutledge, signer of the Constitution and member of the US Supreme Court.

✳ST. PHILIP'S EPISCOPAL CHURCH (1835–1838)

146 Church St.

www.stphilipschurchsc.org

St. Philip's is the mother church of the Episcopal Diocese of South Carolina, and for more than 300 years, this church has been a vital force in the life of Charleston. Today, there are more than 1,500 communicants. It is believed the name is derived from the Anglican parish in Barbados, the island from which many early Charleston planters came after immigration from England.

The first St. Philip's was built in 1680–1681 on the site of what is now St. Michael's Episcopal Church at Meeting and Broad Streets. A new edifice was authorized for what was considered to be the "new" gates of the city (the present site on Church Street) in 1710. This building was destroyed by fire in 1835. The present building was designed by Joseph Nyde, who was influenced by the neoclassical arches inside London's St. Martin's-in-the-Fields Church (1721) designed by James Gibbs.

The history of Charleston is traceable just by reading the names of the memorial plaques around the walls of the sanctuary and in the churchyard outside. Buried here are Col. William Rhett, officer of the Crown; Edward Rutledge, signer of the Declaration of Independence; Charles Pinckney, signer of the US Constitution; and the Hon. John C. Calhoun, statesman and vice president of the United States. Here, too, is the grave of DuBose Heyward, author of *Porgy* and collaborator with George Gershwin on the libretto for the folk opera *Porgy and Bess*.

UNITARIAN CHURCH IN CHARLESTON (1780, 1854)

8 Archdale St.

www.charlestonuu.org

The first building on this site was under construction when the American Revolution began. During the British occupation of the city, the church was used as quarters for the British militia, and its newly installed pews were destroyed. The church, of Georgian design, was finally repaired and in use by 1787. For the next 30 years, it formed one corporate body with the Meeting Street Independent Church (now Circular Church; see previous listing), but in 1839, this congregation was rechartered as the Unitarian Church.

Charleston was experiencing a period of great prosperity in the 1850s, and the Unitarians hired the young architect (and church member) Francis D. Lee to remodel the building in the popular Gothic Revival style. He was commissioned to incorporate the old walls and tower into his new design. Lee was inspired by the Henry VII chapel at Westminster Abbey—especially the delicate and lacy fan tracery ceiling there. He duplicated that amazing ceiling in this church, and it is considered to be some of the finest Gothic Revival work extant in America.

MUSEUMS & OTHER SITES

AMERICAN MILITARY MUSEUM $$

360 Concord St.

(843) 577-7000

www.americanmilitarymuseum.org

Located at Fountain Walk (near the S.C. Aquarium) is the American Military Museum, which will be of interest to dedicated reenactment buffs. Here you'll find hundreds of uniforms, patches, and insignia plus legions of military miniatures and toy soldiers. The

7,000 square-foot museum's collection includes items from Iraq, Afghanistan, and Desert Storm, the Vietnam and Korean wars, World Wars I and II, the Spanish-American War, Indian wars, the Civil War, and the American Revolution. Admission is charged but is free to military personnel in uniform and children under 6. Hours are 10 a.m. to 6 p.m., Mon through Sat. Sun hours are from 1 to 5 p.m.

*THE BATTERY

East Bay Street and Murray Boulevard

One can argue that Charleston's White Point Gardens, which most people know as the Battery, shouldn't officially be called an "attraction," like a museum or a fort. On the other hand, it's a darn good bet that no first-time visitor to the city ever left here without making it a point to walk there or at least drive by.

In a city where almost every other building or street holds some significance, few sites have afforded a better view of Charleston's 300-year history than the Battery.

That seaside corner of land at the end of East Bay Street, where it turns and becomes Murray Boulevard, is now a pleasant park with statues and monuments, long-silent cannons, and spreading live oak trees. There's even a Victorian bandstand that looks like it could sport a uniformed Sousa band any Sun afternoon. But the atmosphere on the Battery hasn't always been so serene.

The Battery has been a prominent feature in Charleston since the earliest days of the English settlement. Then, it was known as Oyster Point because it was little more than a marshy beach covered in oyster shells—bleached white in the Carolina sun.

At first, it was mostly a navigational aid for the sailing vessels going into and out of the harbor. The peninsula was still unsettled, and the first colonial effort was farther upstream on the banks of the Ashley River at what is now called Charles Towne Landing. Later, when the settlement was moved to the much more defensible peninsula site, the point was a popular fishing area—too low and too easily flooded to be much of anything else. Charts used during the years 1708 to 1711 show only a watch tower on the site and just a few residences built nearby.

Remember, Charles Towne was still a walled city at that time, the southernmost wall being several blocks north, near what is now the Carolina Yacht Club on East Bay Street. The point was definitely a "suburban" location. The area took a decidedly higher public profile about a decade later, when the pirate Stede Bonnet (pronounced bo-NAY) and some 40 or 50 scalawags like him were hanged there from makeshift gallows. These executions were apparently quite effective in bringing an end to the pirate activity that had plagued the Carolina coast.

The first of several real forts built on the site came along as early as 1737. This and subsequent fortifications were crudely built, however, and none lasted long against the tyranny of the sea. By the time of the American Revolution, White Point was virtually at the city's door and no longer considered a strategic site for defense.

Hurricanes in 1800 and again in 1804 reduced whatever fortification remained there to rubble. Another fort, this version constructed for the War of 1812, apparently gave White Point a popular new name—the Battery. At least, the new name appears on maps beginning about 1833.

The seawall constructed along East Battery (the "high" one) was built after a storm in

1885. Storms and repairs have traded blows at the seawall for many years—in 1893, 1911, 1959, and, of course, with Hugo in 1989.

The area's use as a park dates back to 1837, when the city rearranged certain streets to establish White Point Gardens. It was from this vantage point that Charlestonians watched the battle between Confederate fortifications across the river and the small band of Union troops holed up in Fort Sumter on April 12, 1861. This, of course, was the beginning of the Civil War. Once the war had started, this peaceful little garden was torn up and convulsed into two massive earthwork batteries—part of Charleston's inner line of defense. And while one of these battery sites housed a huge Blakely rifle (one of the two largest weapons in the Confederacy), neither battery ever fired a shot in anger. (Some incoming artillery rounds probably landed here during the extended bombardment of the city from late 1863 until Charleston fell in February 1865.)

The end of the Civil War was the end of the Battery's role in Charleston's military defense, although several subsequent wars have left poignant souvenirs behind for remembrance. Today no fewer than 26 cannons and monuments dot the Battery's landscape, each of which is described on a nearby plaque or informational marker.

Over the years, the Battery has become something of a balm for the Charlestonian soul. In 1977, Warren Ripley wrote a detailed booklet called "The Battery," which is still available through *The Post and Courier* offices. In it, Ripley sums up the reasons the Battery is so special:

"It has watched the elaborate drill of colonial militia and the 'goose step' of Hitler's sailors on parade before WWII. It has suffered through 're-enactments' of historic events it witnessed in the first place, seen parades, air shows, and fireworks displays without number.

"It has observed three centuries of ocean traffic, watched the evolution from sailing ship to steam and nuclear propulsion as warships and cargo slipped in and out of port.

"It has echoed Sunday afternoon band concerts and heard the weekday cries of street vendors hawking wares to the neighborhood homes. It has harked to the whispers of countless lovers and warmed to the daylight shouts of happy, playing children."

For Charlestonians, clearly the Battery is more than a pleasant little park. Far more, indeed.

THE BELLS OF ST. MICHAEL'S
Meeting and Broad Streets

If your timing is lucky, a visit to the very heart of Charleston and its "Four Corners of Law" at the intersection of Broad and Meeting Streets will be delightfully punctuated by the resonant chime of mighty church bells ringing overhead.

Indeed, the bells of St. Michael's Episcopal Church make more than just a pleasant sound. Their ringing is very much a part of Charleston—one of its oldest and most endearing attractions. In fact, their ringing is another of Charleston's object lessons in faithful perseverance, stubborn Southern survival, and the fleeting passage of time.

St. Michael's Episcopal Church, built in 1761, is the oldest church edifice on the Peninsula and the second-oldest congregation in the city. (See previous listing in the Historic Churches section of this chapter.) This is the church where George Washington worshiped on his famous 1791 presidential tour that included a stay in Charleston (see

Heyward-Washington House listing in the House Museums section of this chapter).

The eight bronze bells hanging in St. Michael's spire were originally cast at the Whitechapel Foundry of London in 1764.

Church records say the bells first sounded here in Charleston on September 21 of that same year, having safely made their first journey across the Atlantic Ocean. Amazingly, the bells have made that long journey back to England three times since.

Their first journey "home" was in 1782 during the War of Independence. The bells had rung in defiance of the Crown during Charleston's protest of the Stamp Act in 1765, and British soldiers confiscated them as a punishing prize of war. Once back on English soil, however, the bells were purchased by a private speculator and promptly returned to Charleston and again placed in St. Michael's steeple.

In 1862, during the Civil War, seven of the bells were removed from the steeple and taken to Columbia for what was hoped to be safekeeping. Charleston was such a likely target that many of the city's treasures were sent to Columbia at that time to escape the Union's wrath. Only the large tenor bell was left behind, to ring the alarm for Charlestonians still in the city. In 1865, the year Charleston fell, the bell rang dutifully until it cracked. Meanwhile, Gen. William T. Sherman's Union army selected upstate Columbia as an artillery target, and South Carolina's entire capital city burned in what was one of the most dramatic episodes of the war.

In 1866, St. Michael's vestry arranged to have the seven charred bells from Columbia and the one cracked bell remaining in the church returned to England to be recast once more in their original molds at the Whitechapel Foundry. When they were returned in 1867, church records show that the melodies of "Home Again" and "Auld Lang Syne" rang from St. Michael's steeple.

The last journey of the bells back to England and the Whitechapel Foundry—still in business after all these years—was in 1993. Their recasting, once more in the original molds, was part of St. Michael's $3.8 million restoration and repair project undertaken as a result of damages suffered in Hurricane Hugo.

The bells of St. Michael's rang anew on July 4, 1993, in a special, daylong hand-ringing ceremony done in the English style. Nostalgic Charlestonians from all denominations made special trips past St. Michael's all day to hear the bells celebrate Independence Day and to acknowledge another homecoming for the bells of St. Michael's at the Four Corners of Law.

CHILDREN'S MUSEUM OF THE LOWCOUNTRY $$
25 Ann St.
(843) 853-8962
www.explorecml.org

This long-planned museum, which opened in September 2003, was the realization of a dream stubbornly defended by its founders for several years. They envisioned a hands-on learning place for children ages 3 months to 12 years celebrating their unique Lowcountry surroundings and the vast creative opportunities available to them here. For example, youngsters can explore the ocean and the life of a pirate on their very own CML Pirate Ship. They can also imagine themselves as medieval royalty living in a mighty castle. They can create artistic masterpieces in an "art room" designed for spirited young minds. And throughout the year, programs, day camps, and special classes will support

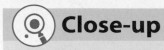

Close-up

Charleston's Museum Mile: A Stroll through History

With the plethora of attractions that historic Charleston has to offer, many tourists wonder where to start. After a stop at the visitor center to collect the brochures of greatest interest, perhaps you are still without a plan. **Charleston's Museum Mile** is a way to begin your journey into history in a simplified and focused manner. The designated 1-mile section of Meeting Street (and nearby side streets) leads to 6 museums, 5 nationally important historic houses, 4 scenic parks, a Revolutionary War powder magazine, numerous historic houses of worship, and 6 historic public buildings—that's right, in only 1 short mile!

A natural beginning is the Charleston Museum across from the visitor center and its museum house nearby, the **Joseph Manigault House**. Other significant houses not to miss are the **Aiken-Rhett, Heyward-Washington, Nathaniel Russell,** and **Edmonston-Alston** houses. These are a special treat for those who appreciate fine architecture and the decorative arts. More architecturally significant edifices to take in are the **South Carolina Historical Society, City Hall,** and the **Charleston County Courthouse.** (See our close-up on "Meet You at 'The Four Corners of Law'" in the History chapter.)

If military history is your hobby, **The Washington Light Infantry, Confederate Museum, Old Slave Mart Museum, Old Exchange and Provost Dungeon, Postal Museum,** and the **Powder Magazine** are sure to delight. The artist in you will appreciate the collection at the **Gibbes Museum of Art,** and the little ones will enjoy a stop at the **Children's Museum of the Lowcountry.** And you'll soon understand why Charleston is called the "Holy City" as you pass by nearly a dozen historic churches, many of which are open to visitors.

If you need a brief respite from all this sightseeing **Wragg Square, Marion Square,** and **Washington Park** offer a lovely, shady setting to contemplate your next move. Most of the sites charge admission as noted in our individual descriptions within this chapter, but some do not. Of course, you pay only at the ones you visit, and you may start at any point along the **Museum Mile.** There are Museum Mile packages for $25 and Museum Mile Weekend in late Sept offers 13 sites for $20. CARTA buses and DASH trolleys provide public transportation for a fee along the route, and a pass allows you to get on and off as needed. Or, you may stroll by foot at your own pace. Museum Mile flags are placed along the way to aid in your explorations. Visit the website www.charlestonsmuseummile.org for more details and take a walk through history.

educational experiences in the arts, sciences, and humanities. The museum is open to Lowcountry children, visitors, and their families from 9 a.m. to 5 p.m. Tues through Sat, and Sun from 1 to 5 p.m.

THE CHARLESTON MUSEUM $$
360 Meeting St.
(843) 722-2996
www.charlestonmuseum.org
Directly across Meeting Street from the Visitor Reception and Transportation Center is one of Charleston's finest jewels: the Charleston Museum. Because it is the first and oldest

museum in America, having been founded in 1773, the museum's collection predates all modern thinking about what should be kept or discarded in preserving the artifacts of a culture.

Instead, the Charleston Museum is heir to the collected memorabilia of real American patriots, early Charlestonian families, and early colonial thinkers, explorers, scientists, and planters. It is their opinion of what mattered then, and what they thought should matter to us today. Although the collection is housed in modern buildings and has the benefit of modern conservation methods and enlightened interpretation, the collection is uniquely eloquent. It speaks of a city that already knew it was great and sought early on to record itself for posterity. That difference alone makes the Charleston Museum a must-see.

The museum's scope is the social and natural history of Charleston and the South Carolina coastal region. Objects from natural science, cultural history, historical archaeology, ornithology, and ethnology are presented to illustrate the importance each had in the history of this area. The Charleston Silver Exhibit contains internationally recognized work by local silversmiths in a beautifully mounted display. Pieces date from colonial times through the late-19th century.

Visitors will see what the museum's many archaeological excavations have revealed about some of the city's best and worst times. Some artifacts date from the early colonial period, while others are from the Civil War years. Some exhibits focus on early Native Americans who lived in this region. Others trace changes in trade and commerce, the expansive rice and cotton plantation systems, and the important contributions made by African-Americans.

Children will be intrigued by the Kidstory exhibit with amazing things to touch, see, and do. They'll see toys from the past, games children played, the clothes they wore, furniture they used, and more. The photographs, ceramics, pewter, and tools reveal a very personal portrait of Charlestonians from the past.

Because the Charlestonian lifestyle is so much a part of the city and its history, the two house museums owned and operated by the Charleston Museum are an important part of its offering. (See previous listings for Heyward-Washington House and Joseph Manigault House in the House Museums section of this chapter.) In these appropriate settings, you'll see some of the museum's remarkable collection of antique furniture and other decorative arts.

The Charleston Museum is open Mon through Sat from 9 a.m. to 5 p.m. and 1 to 5 p.m. on Sun. See the Kidstuff chapter for more on children's programs. Combination tickets, which include admission for the two house museums, are available for two sites or for all three.

OLD EXCHANGE AND PROVOST DUNGEON $$
122 East Bay St.
(843) 727-2165, (888) 763-0448
www.oldexchange.com

A public building has stood on this site at East Bay and Broad Streets since Charles Towne was moved from its original settlement to its present location in 1680. The early settlers built their court of guard here. They imprisoned pirates and Native Americans in the building's lower level and held their town meetings upstairs in the hall.

The British built the present building to create an impressive presence in the bustling colonial port. With its striking Palladian architecture, the Exchange surely did just that. It was completed in 1771 and quickly became the social, political, and economic hub of the growing city.

From its steps, the independent colony of South Carolina was publicly declared in March 1776. During the Revolution, the building was converted to a British prison, where signers of the Declaration of Independence were to be held. In 1788 the convention to ratify the US Constitution met in the building, and President George Washington was lavishly entertained here several times during his Southern tour. From 1815 to 1896, the building served both the Federal and Confederate governments as the Charleston post office. In 1913 Congress deeded the building to the Daughters of the American Revolution of South Carolina.

During an excavation of the dungeon in 1965, part of the original seawall of Charles Towne was discovered. Today, the Old Exchange and Provost Dungeon is leased to the state of South Carolina and open to the public as a museum. The building has two halls that are available to rent for private events. Hours are 9 a.m. to 5 p.m. daily. Admission is free for kids younger than seven. Senior discounts and group rates are available.

✳**GIBBES MUSEUM OF ART**　　　**$$**
135 Meeting St.
(843) 722-2706
www.gibbesmuseum.org
Established in 1905 by the Carolina Art Association, the Gibbes Museum of Art stands one block north of the Four Corners of Law. As locations go, that's fairly close to what Charlestonians traditionally believe to be heaven. And clearly, the Gibbes represents

Charleston's most uplifting experiences in art.

Museum members, residents of the city, and visitors all have access to a distinguished and growing collection along with year-round exhibitions, educational programs, and special events. The building itself stands as a memorial to James Shoolbred Gibbes, a wealthy Charlestonian who bequeathed funds to the city of Charleston and the Carolina Art Association to create a permanent home for the association's collection.

Today that rich and fascinating collection includes American paintings, prints, and drawings from the 18th century to the present. There are landscapes, genre scenes, views of Charleston, and portraits of notable South Carolinians. Faces associated with history (and architectural landmarks all over the Lowcountry) seem to come to life here. You'll find Thomas Middleton painted by Benjamin West and Charles Izard Manigault painted by Thomas Sully. There's John C. Calhoun painted by Rembrandt Peale, plus an outstanding collection of more than 400 exquisite, hand-painted miniature portraits of 18th- and 19th-century Charlestonians.

The Elizabeth Wallace Miniature Rooms offer 10 miniature interiors representing different traditions in American and French architecture, decorative arts, and design. The Gibbes also has an outstanding collection of early Japanese woodblock prints in a special Oriental gallery.

In addition to the regular schedule of exhibitions on loan from international, national, and regional collections, the Gibbes presents major exhibitions in the visual arts during Spoleto Festival USA every May through June. Members and the public are invited to join museum tours, gallery talks, lectures, seminars, and meet-the-artist events, and to see films and videos made for schools and community groups.

One of the most popular aspects of the Gibbes is the museum shop, which offers an excellent selection of art books, posters, note cards, jewelry, and other gift items. Shop early for the best Christmas cards. Museum members receive a 10 percent discount on all purchases. Admission to the shop, which is open during regular museum hours, is free.

The Gibbes provides professional instruction in everything from painting and photography to textile silk screening and jewelry making. Classes and workshops are designed for all ages and levels of experience. Contact the Gibbes at (843) 722-2706, ext. 41 for additional information.

Memberships to the Gibbes Museum of Art are renewable on an annual basis. Dues are tax deductible. You'll find applications for membership at the information desk, or you can call the number above. Guided tours are available by appointment. Ask for the education department to make arrangements. Members are admitted free. Museum hours are Tues through Sat from 10 a.m. to 5 p.m. and 1 to 5 p.m. Sun. The museum is closed on Mondays and national holidays. The Gibbes is fully wheelchair accessible. (For more on the Gibbes, see the Kidstuff chapter.)

CSS H. L. HUNLEY $$$
Warren Lasch Conservation Center, 1250 Supply St., Bldg. 225, North Charleston
(877) 448-6539, (843) 743-4865, ext. 10
www.hunley.org
In 1864, the CSS H. L. Hunley was the first submarine in history to successfully sink an enemy war ship when it launched an attack against the Union ironclad Housatonic off the coast of Charleston. The Hunley

and its eight-man crew never returned to home port, however, and its fate remained unknown until divers located the sub in 1995. It was discovered partially buried in mud not far from the scene of its 1864 triumph. In August 2000, the Hunley made national headlines as it was carefully raised from its watery grave and brought back to Charleston for several years of painstaking conservation and analysis. It rests, for now, at the high-tech Warren Lasch Conservation Center on the former Charleston Navy Base, where scientists are slowly unlocking the mysteries of its disappearance, including how and when the crew died. Tours are available every Sat from 10 a.m. to 5 p.m. and Sun from noon to 5 p.m. Advance reservations are required to view the sub in its tank and see the fascinating exhibits of its contents and ingenious technology. Call or visit the website for available tour times, tickets, and directions.

MAGNOLIA CEMETERY
70 Cunnington Ave.
(843) 722-8638
One of the most telling places in all of Charleston has to be the remarkably distinctive 19th-century cemetery at the north end of the Peninsula, not far off East Bay Street (which becomes Morrison Drive).

Not on any contemporary beaten path, and clearly not a tourist destination, Magnolia Cemetery is the quiet, final resting place of many important Charlestonians and other players in the city's long-running and colorful drama. It is also an intriguing collection of Southern funerary art in an almost unbearably romantic setting.

The site was originally on the grounds of Magnolia Umbria Plantation, which dates back to 1790 and where rice was the principal crop in the first half of the 19th century. By 1850, however, a 181-acre section of that land on the edge of the marsh had been surveyed for a peaceful cemetery, dedicated on November 19, 1850. From that time on (even to the present), many of Charleston's most prominent families chose Magnolia as the place to bury and commemorate their loved ones.

Many of the city's leaders, politicians, judges, and other pioneers in many fields of endeavor are interred beneath the ancient, spreading live oaks of Magnolia. Among them are five Confederate brigadier generals. There is a vast Confederate section, with more than 1,700 graves of the known and unknown. The 84 South Carolinians who fell at the Battle of Gettysburg are included and the *Hunley* crew was interred there after the raising of the submarine in 2000 (see previous listing).

There are literally hundreds of ornate private family plots, many of which bear famous names. You will find the monument of Robert Barnwell Rhett, "Father of Secession," US senator, attorney general of South Carolina, and author. There's also the grave of George Alfred Trenholm, a wealthy cotton broker who served as treasurer of the Confederacy and organized many a blockade run for the cause. Trenholm is thought by many to be the man on whom Margaret Mitchell's Rhett Butler was based. Among the famous artists and writers buried in Magnolia are Charleston's Alice Ravenel Huger Smith and John Bennett.

To find Magnolia, drive north on East Bay (Morrison Drive), and turn right at the traffic light onto Meeting Street (SR 52). Turn right at the first opportunity onto Cunnington Street, and Magnolia's gates (open daily from 8 a.m. to 5 p.m.) are at the end of the street.

PATRIOTS POINT NAVAL AND MARITIME MUSEUM $$$
40 Patriots Point Rd., Mount Pleasant
(843) 884-2727, (866) 831-1720
www.patriotspoint.org

Patriots Point is the name given to a huge maritime museum complex that consists mainly of three in situ ships (permanently situated): a submarine, a destroyer, and an aircraft carrier with 25 vintage aircraft. There's also a replica of a Vietnam Support Base and a Cold War Submarine Memorial. As home of the Congressional Medal of Honor Society, it showcases their official Medal of Honor Museum. For this complex, one of Charleston's major attractions, you'll need comfortable shoes and plenty of time.

Considering all there is to see, Patriots Point Naval and Maritime Museum is a real bargain. Admission is free for children younger than 6. There's a $3 discount for senior citizens and anyone with a military ID. Parking is $5. Plan on spending the better part of your day at Patriots Point; it's open from 9 a.m. to 6:30 p.m. except Christmas Day. Gift shop hours are from 9 a.m. to 5:30 p.m. Below is a detailed rundown of the ships on display.

USS *YORKTOWN* (AIRCRAFT CARRIER)

No one comes or goes through Charleston via US 17 across the Cooper River Bridge without noticing the giant aircraft carrier moored off Mount Pleasant. It dominates—no, commands—a vast stretch of the Cooper's Mount Pleasant shore at the very gates into Charleston Harbor. She is none other than the USS *Yorktown* (CV-10), the famous "Fighting Lady" of World War II and the proud flagship of Patriots Point, the world's largest naval and maritime museum.

Of the three vessels permanently anchored and open to the public, the

Yorktown is the most impressive. Commissioned April 15, 1943, in the darkest days of the war, the ship fought valiantly in some of the worst engagements ever witnessed at sea, inflicting heavy losses against the Japanese at the Truk and Mariana Islands, and supporting the American ground troops in the Philippines, at bloody Iwo Jima, and Okinawa.

Shortly after the ship was commissioned and sent into battle, 20th Century Fox put a film crew onboard to record—on then-rare Technicolor film—the continuing war story of a typical Navy carrier in action. The spectacular footage shot at unnamed, secret locations during then-unnamed battles became the Academy Award–winning documentary film feature of 1944. The film was called *The Fighting Lady,* and it is shown daily at the *Yorktown's* onboard theater at regularly scheduled intervals. Don't miss it. Nothing brings the World War II drama of the *Yorktown* to life like this amazing celluloid time capsule. The terrible explosions and blistering fires, the fierce fighting, and all the brave young faces who served on the *Yorktown* are there to be seen and appreciated by generations then unborn.

But the *Yorktown* story doesn't end there. Not at all. The ship went on to patrol the western Pacific during the cold war and even fought in Vietnam. In fact, the *Yorktown* received the crew of *Apollo 8,* the first manned space flight around the moon, in 1968.

The flight deck, hangar deck, and many of the *Yorktown* crew's living and working quarters are open to visitors today. You'll find actual carrier aircraft and Vietnam-era anti-sub planes on display—25 aircraft in all. And there are other fascinating exhibits on everything from mines to shipbuilding.

Another exhibit is the true-to-scale Vietnam Naval Support Base, showing the living conditions and work areas of a typical support base during the Vietnam War. You'll also find the newly renovated and expanded Medal of Honor Museum, featuring displays representing the different eras of our military history in which the Medal of Honor was awarded. The new interactive displays include a tunnel of murals depicting battles with flashing lights and booming guns. You'll see actual Medals of Honor and some of the artifacts related to their original recipients.

Mercifully, you'll find a snack bar onboard the *Yorktown* and another in the riverside gift shop, so excited youngsters and foot-weary veterans can stop for lunch and a rest.

LAFFEY (DESTROYER)

The heroic destroyer *Laffey* (DD-724) was commissioned on February 8, 1944, and participated in the giant D-Day landings of Allied troops at Normandy four months later. Transferred to the Pacific, she was struck by five Japanese kamikaze suicide planes and hit by three bombs during one hour on April 16, 1945, off Okinawa. The *Laffey's* gallant crew not only kept the ship afloat but also managed to shoot down 11 planes during the attack. After World War II, the *Laffey* served during the Korean War and then in the Atlantic Fleet until she was decommissioned in 1975.

A tour route on the *Laffey* lets you see the bridge, battle stations, living quarters, and various displays of destroyer activities. Note: At press time the *Laffey* was undergoing repairs at another location so check first to see if she has returned to Patriots Point.

CLAMAGORE (SUBMARINE)

The World War II submarine *Clamagore* (SS-43) was commissioned on June 28, 1945, and operated in the Atlantic and Mediterranean throughout its entire career, patrolling tense Cuban waters during 1962. Twice modified, the *Clamagore* survived as one of the US Navy's last diesel-powered subs until it was decommissioned in 1975.

The *Clamagore* tour route covers the control room, berth and mess areas, engine rooms, maneuvering room, and displays of submarine warfare. Note: Spaces are very cramped onboard. Visitors with health problems or claustrophobia are strongly cautioned.

SOUTH CAROLINA AQUARIUM $$$
100 Aquarium Wharf, Calhoun at Concord Streets
(843) 720-1990
www.scaquarium.org
In May 2000, after years of planning, controversy, and nervous anticipation, Charleston's $69 million South Carolina Aquarium opened to rave reviews as a major new attraction in the Lowcountry. This nonprofit, self-supporting institution is dedicated to educating the public about and helping to conserve South Carolina's unique aquatic habitats. Its mission is to display and interpret the state's diverse range of habitats—from rushing mountain streams to the oceanic depths of the Atlantic. It was the first aquarium in the country to open with a complete Education Master Plan in place. Admission is free for South Carolina schoolchildren enrolled in the aquarium's academic programs. Extensive field studies and outreach programs are also in place.

Among the 60 exhibits in the 93,000 square-foot building are more than 6,000 plants and animals, representing more than 500 species. The aquarium is home to otters, birds, turtles, fish, venomous snakes, other reptiles and amphibians, aquatic invertebrates, and insects. The exhibit path leads visitors through five major regions of the Southeast Appalachian Watershed as found in South Carolina—the Mountain Forest, the Piedmont, the Coastal Plain, the Coast, and the Ocean. The aquarium uses a variety of media to enhance the visitor experience. Some are interactive, some are for very young children, some are education "stations" for discovery labs and classrooms. Advance tickets are available by visiting the website or calling (843) 579-8600. Hours vary according to time of year. The aquarium is closed on Thanksgiving and Christmas Day and closes at 1 p.m. on Christmas Eve. Parking is available across Concord Street from the aquarium's entrance.

THE CITADEL MUSEUM
171 Moultrie St.
(843) 953-6846
www.citadel.edu/museum
This museum showcases The Citadel, the Military College of South Carolina. The museum covers the history of the school from 1842 to the present. Various displays represent the military, academic, social, and athletic aspects of cadet life. The museum is on campus, on the third floor of the Daniel Library—the first building on the right inside The Citadel's main gates. Hours are Sun through Fri from 2 to 5 p.m. and Sat from noon to 5 p.m. The museum is closed for college, national, and religious holidays. There is no charge for admission. (See more on The Citadel in the Education chapter.)

KARPELES MANUSCRIPT LIBRARY
   MUSEUM
68 Spring St.
(843) 853-4651
www.karpeles.com

This is one of ten museums in the United States funded by California businessman David Karpeles. They are all nonprofit endeavors to "preserve the original writings of the great authors, scientists, statesmen, sovereigns, philosophers, and leaders from all periods of world history," according to the museum's mission statement.

Scholars, educators, students, and lovers of books and manuscripts are invited to enjoy these collections free of charge. This unusual but fascinating collection is housed in the former St. James United Methodist Church (1856), one of Charleston's best 19th-century replicas of a classical Roman temple. Special exhibits change from time to time, but the permanent collection includes some of the rare, original writings that helped build our country's unique form of government. Among the Karpeles manuscripts is one of the four original drafts of the Bill of Rights and the Emancipation Proclamation amendment to the Constitution.

The museum is open Tues through Sat from 11 a.m. to 4 p.m. For more information on exhibits or special programs, contact the museum. Admission and parking are free.

JOHN RIVERS COMMUNICATIONS MUSEUM
College of Charleston, 58 George St.
(843) 953-5810
www.cofc.edu/~jrmuseum

The College of Charleston's John Rivers Communications Museum offers a unique opportunity to explore the world of broadcasting and communications. John M. Rivers was a Charleston-born banker, businessman, and broadcasting executive who introduced television to the Lowcountry in 1953.

Visitors to the museum can hear early sound recordings from the Kenneth Hanson Collection, learn about the lives of famous inventors such as Marconi and Edison, and trace the advancements in science from the magic lantern to television, from the phonograph to radio.

The museum is open Mon through Fri from noon to 4 p.m., except during College of Charleston holidays. Summer hours may vary, and group tours are conducted by appointment only, so call the museum for scheduling. Admission is free, but donations are appreciated.

POSTAL HISTORY MUSEUM
Meeting and Broad Streets

Unknown to most of the tourists who pass through the intersection of Meeting and Broad Streets (See "Meet You at 'The Four Corners of Law'"), there's a fine and fascinating little gem right there, deftly tucked into one of the corners.

The Postal History Museum is a special room inside the Charleston post office showing visitors some of the interesting tidbits of postal history associated with this coastal colonial town.

For instance, Charleston's first postmaster (on the job before 1694) was actually known as the city's "powder receiver." Not only was he responsible for the mail, he also collected a percentage of gunpowder from every ship that arrived (see subsequent listing for Powder Magazine). He was required to post incoming letters in a public room in his house for 30 days and collected his commission only when the letters were picked up by the recipient. Imagine being in London in 1700, addressing a letter to "John Doe, Charles Towne, Carolina," and it actually getting here.

This little museum is a must for philatelists or anyone else who ever wondered how 18th- and 19th-century mail was handled. It is open during regular US post office hours, and admission is free. It's a great excuse to see Charleston's elaborately detailed 1896 post office building, the oldest continuously operating post office in the Carolinas.

POWDER MAGAZINE $
79 Cumberland St.
(843) 722-9350
www.powdermag.org

Only a couple of blocks from the bustling market area is, quite simply, the oldest public building in the Carolinas. And yet, as Charleston attractions go, the Powder Magazine is relatively unknown to tourists and to some locals as well.

Perhaps the site is overlooked because it's dramatically upstaged by Charleston's sumptuous house museums and romantic streetscapes. And in truth, the utilitarian Powder Magazine actually predates Charleston's legendary aesthetics. It was built for a time when the still-new English settlement was predominantly interested in self-defense and basic survival.

In the early years of the 18th century, Charles Towne was still threatened by Spanish forces, hostile Indians, rowdy packs of buccaneers, and an occasional French attack. It was still a walled city, fortified against surprise attack.

In August 1702, a survey of the armament in Charles Towne reported "2,306 lbs. of gunpowder, 496 shot of all kind, 28 great guns, 47 Grenada guns, 360 cartridges, and 500 lbs. of pewter shot." In his formal request for additional cannons, the royal governor requested "a suitable store of shot and powder . . . [to] make Carolina impregnable." And so, in 1703, the Crown approved and funded such a building, which was completed in 1713 on what is now Cumberland Street.

The Powder Magazine was the domain of the powder receiver, a newly appointed city official entitled to accept a gunpowder tax levied on all merchant ships entering Charleston Harbor during this period.

The building served its originally intended purpose for many decades, but eventually, in an early colonial version of today's base closings, it was deemed unnecessary (or too small) and sold into private hands.

This multi-gabled, tile-roofed, architectural oddity was almost forgotten by historians until the early 1900s. In 1901 it was purchased by The National Society of The Colonial Dames of America in The State of South Carolina. It was maintained and operated as a small museum until 1991, when water damage, roof deterioration, and time had finally taken too high a toll. What the Powder Magazine needed to survive at all was a major stabilization and restoration—something beyond the resources of the owners.

In an agreement whereby the Historic Charleston Foundation did the needed work under a 99-year lease, the Powder Magazine underwent a $400,000 preservation effort, its first ever. This included a temporary roof over the entire structure, allowing the massive walls to dry out before necessary repairs could even begin. Much-needed archaeological and archival research was also done on the site.

The Powder Magazine was opened to the public in the summer of 1997. It is now owned and operated by The National Society of The Colonial Dames of America in The State of South Carolina. Inside, a new, interactive exhibit interprets Charleston's first 50 years—a time when it was still a relatively crude colonial outpost of the British Empire. A nominal admission is charged. Hours are 10 a.m. to 4 p.m. Mon through Sat and 1 to 4 p.m. on Sun.

TOURS

U pon first impression, visitors to Charleston are usually taken with the city's architectural charm. Part of that fascination comes from the unspoken questions that
leap to mind about Charleston's early good times. People want to know more about
how a city of such wealth and architectural sophistication did, in fact, evolve.

The next impulse many visitors have is to seek out some kind of tour to find
answers to some of those questions. Understandably, people want a visual, geographic, or ethnic overview, a point of reference, some kind of perspective. But most
of all, they want to hear the stories about Charleston when everything old was shiny
and new, political independence was still a dream, and the name of Charles Towne was
world famous as the brightest jewel in the British colonial crown.

That's why the telling of Charleston's story has literally become an industry. In fact,
it's so important that to become an officially licensed tour guide here, one must take a
city-sponsored course (and pass very tough written and oral exams). Charlestonians,
you see, care enormously that their story be told well. That's simply because the real
truth is interesting enough to make mere half-truths, downright lies (told by unscru-
pulous tour guides), and corny amateurism wholly unnecessary. It's deceitful, unnecessary, and not at all Charlestonian.

Tours of the city are available in several forms. Most of the walking or riding (be
that in a carriage, car, or van) tours depart from the Charleston Visitor Reception and
Transportation Center on Meeting Street (simply referred to as the "visitor center"
hereafter) or from the City Market area. You may also choose to meet a private guide
at your inn or hotel and depart from there. Ask your hotel clerks or concierges to book
your tour reservations—they have plenty of experience doing so.

OVERVIEW

Whichever tour mode you choose, you'll
have a wonderful adventure. There are many
tours of Charleston offered these days—privately guided, walking, by bus or van, by
carriage, and even by boat. All have merit.
Included in this chapter are some of the
tours currently available that we consider
especially good and interesting. We've listed
categories of tours alphabetically, so we'll
start with a little background information to

help you explore Charleston's rich African-
American heritage.

AFRICAN-AMERICAN HISTORY

As we've mentioned in several places in
this book, no visit to Charleston would be
complete without gaining a better understanding of and appreciation for the strong
African influences on this society, past and
present. The folkways, lifeways, culture, and

achievements of African-Americans have been infused into every fiber of the Charleston experience since the very beginning of the 1670 English settlement.

Among the first settlers in Charles Towne were black and white indentured servants and enslaved Africans. Within a decade, the English settlers had implemented the plantation system (already flourishing in Barbados) to sustain themselves here and create a product for economic exchange. Their labor force came from Africa—particularly the West Coast of Africa—from areas now known as Sierra Leone, Ghana, and Benin.

European and American traders plied the Atlantic waters off these areas, capturing Africans and imprisoning them until they could be boarded onto slave ships. Typically, each African was afforded a mere 4 square feet of living space while chained down in the hold. Under these grim and inhumane conditions, untold numbers of Africans died en route to the New World. From coastal Africa, the ships would sail to the West Indies, where some of the human "cargo" would be sold into slavery. The rest were brought to the South Carolina coast.

Awaiting the slave ships on Sullivan's Island off the coast from Charles Towne were crude structures called "pest houses." Here, the unwilling passengers would be held for a period of at least 40 days to be checked for diseases and infections, during which they would be also groomed for sale. If maladies were suspected or discovered, the captives would be quarantined onboard their ships.

In just the five years between 1803 and 1808, an estimated 40,000 Africans were imported to America. The sheer volume of incoming slaves became a cause for concern among the relatively few white slaveholders, who feared an uprising. In 1808 the importing of additional slaves was banned. However, this ban did little to stem the flow, and slave trade continued as late as 1858.

Once sold, most of the Africans would toil in the fields. Their labor made the early plantation life of coastal South Carolina not only possible but highly profitable. Africans also brought with them vital knowledge of rice and indigo production, cattle tending, boat building, and ironworking. Eventually, their foods, languages, religions, and music all mingled with the European traditions to create the Lowcountry culture called "Gullah" we celebrate today.

Not all Africans living in America were enslaved. From 1690 on, a few free people of color were living in Carolina. They were mostly multiracial and usually lived in the urban areas where they could find work in various trades. There were cobblers, carpenters, wheelwrights, brick masons, and smithies. Some became wealthy and owned slaves themselves.

i For a more extensive look at the hidden historical treasures of the Charleston area, look into one of the day-long excursions planned annually by The South Carolina Historical Society. Every year, the membership is invited to participate in a caravan tour deep into the Lowcountry hinterlands, touring private plantations and fascinating little-known sites. For membership details, you can write the Society at 100 Meeting St., Charleston 29401 or visit www.schistory.org.

With the Emancipation Proclamation and the end of the Civil War, all African-Americans were technically free. However, the opportunistic postwar Reconstruction period and the advent of Jim Crow laws led to constitutional struggles over the 13th, 14th, and 15th Amendments. The much-longed-for freedom of African-Americans in Charleston was shallow, indeed.

Many people of color left their rural homes and sought a better life in urban settings (sometimes moving to large Northern cities), where opportunities for work and education were better. Those who remained behind tended to live in small, rural, self-sustaining villages that were clustered around their beloved churches—mostly free of white control. Visitors to the Lowcountry today can see evidence of this social pattern in communities such as Snowden, in Mount Pleasant, and Maryville, west of the Ashley. During the Civil Rrights movement of the 1960s, Charleston blacks gathered at sites like the old cigar factory at 701 East Bay St. and Moving Star Hall on Johns Island to organize and peacefully gain rights granted to all Americans by the US Constitution.

Because more than one-fourth of the African slaves shipped to the 13 original American colonies before the Revolution came through Charleston, this city's role in African-American history can hardly be overstated. In the years between 1700 and 1775, an estimated 200,000 slaves were put ashore on Sullivan's Island. One expert on slave history has even dubbed Sullivan's Island the "Ellis Island of black Americans" (in the symbolic, if not the literal, sense). Clearly, the Africans brought to South Carolina as slaves did not come as free-willed immigrants (like those arriving at Ellis Island). But Charleston was their point of entry, and, like Ellis Island, this location was the beginning of the American experience for countless African-Americans. Yet, until very recently, this fact

was little known by most contemporary Americans—even South Carolinians.

Realistically, this was not a popular subject for Charleston tour guides in the pre–Civil Rights era. History buffs felt awkward describing the tragedy of 18th- and 19th-century slave trade along with the city's upbeat tourist attractions. In the past, Charleston was criticized in the national media for taking a shortsighted view of its own black history. Today, that history is being explored and celebrated. The annual MOJA Arts Festival in Sept is Charleston's official celebration of its African and Caribbean culture. (See more about MOJA in the chapters on The Arts and Annual Events.) Many popular tourist destinations feature special exhibits and events pertaining to Charleston's African-American history.

As Charleston proceeds deeper into the new millennium, a more enlightened approach to presenting the city's rich African-American heritage is starting to bloom. The African American National Heritage Museum is a multi-site, cooperative educational effort undertaken by the Avery Research Center for African-American History and Culture, the City of Charleston, Historic Charleston Foundation, and the South Carolina African American Heritage Council.

At four primary historic sites, these entities are working together to provide insight into the Greater Charleston African-American experience. At these sites, visitors can start to explore the origins of the culture and the role African-Americans played in shaping Charleston, the South Carolina Lowcountry, and the nation. Historical exhibits, living history demonstrations, site interpretation, and cultural events are offered at the following venues.

✳AIKEN-RHETT HOUSE
48 Elizabeth St.
(843) 723-1159
www.historiccharleston.org

It is rare, indeed, that a property of such prominence and historic importance as this would survive to this day in so authentic a state. But here is a house museum that affords the uncanny opportunity to view an "urban" household of great privilege as it was on the eve of the Civil War.

The central section of the Aiken-Rhett House (see House Museums in the Attractions chapter) was built in 1818 in the Federal style popular at that time. However, when William Aiken Jr. and his wife obtained the property in 1831, they did an extensive remodeling of the first floor in the robust Greek Revival style, which was all the rage at that time. When Mr. Aiken was elected governor of South Carolina, wings were added with a dining room and ballroom for formal entertaining, and even an art gallery eventually came along. But in effect, the decor of the house was arrested in 1857, shortly before the Civil War began. Because of the war's drastic impact on Governor Aiken and his family, the house and the outbuildings that supported it (including the on-site slave quarters) remained remarkably unchanged from that point on. In fact, the house came into the hands of the Charleston Museum in 1975 almost as a sealed time capsule of pre–Civil War taste and technology.

Most notable are the servants' quarters to the rear of the house, which are in sharp contrast to the rest of the property—far more plain and utilitarian than the horse stables and even the privies.

A portable prerecorded tape with appropriate sound effects is available for self-guided tours of the property, and docents are on hand to answer any questions you may have.

The museum house is open from 10 a.m. to 5 p.m. Mon through Sat. Sun hours are from 2 to 5 p.m. The last tour starts at 4:15 p.m. Admission is $10; children 6 to 16, $5; free for those under 6.

AVERY RESEARCH CENTER FOR AFRICAN-AMERICAN HISTORY AND CULTURE
125 Bull St., College of Charleston
(843) 953-7609
www.cofc.edu/avery

In Charleston, the rich culture of South Carolina's African-Americans is recognized for its unique national significance. However, the materials that document this culture have been widely scattered over time, and much has already been lost. The College of Charleston's Avery Research Center for African-American History and Culture was established to document, preserve, and make public the unique historical and cultural heritage of this significant group for this and future generations.

In October 1990, the center was established at 125 Bull St. in Charleston's historic district. Here, at long last, a growing archival collection and on-site museum could share the purpose of gathering together these valuable materials and encouraging scholarship on the subject.

The research center is on the site of the former Avery Normal Institute, the local normal school (for teachers-to-be) and college preparatory school, that served Charleston's black community for nearly 100 years. Avery Normal Institute was organized in October 1865 by black minister F. L. Cardozo of the American Missionary Association for (in his words) "the education of colored children." In

1868 the school moved into the Bull Street building just 5 blocks west of the College of Charleston. There, for nearly a century, the school produced teachers for the community and gifted leaders for South Carolina and the nation.

Today, the center is actively soliciting manuscript collections: the personal and professional papers of individuals and organizations, oral and video histories, photographic records, and other related documents. Donors may be assured their gifts will receive the care needed to store and preserve them properly.

The archival collections are regularly used for exhibits and educational programs for the public. These activities are planned in conjunction with local and national African-American celebrations and holidays. The Avery Research Center reading room is open to the public Mon through Fri 10 a.m. to 5 p.m. and Sat from noon to 5 p.m. Walk-in visitors can enjoy tours of the building and the museum galleries during these same hours. Group tours are available by appointment.

For more information, call the number listed above. Written inquiries should be addressed to Avery Research Center for African-American History and Culture, 66 George St., College of Charleston, SC 29424.

BATTERY WAGNER, MORRIS ISLAND

The first Union regiment of free black soldiers, the now-famous 54th Massachusetts Volunteer Infantry Regiment, fought on Morris Island during the Civil War. The bloody battle was an undeniable confirmation of the bravery, courage, and valor of the black soldiers and their willingness to fight for the North. Although the site is not yet memorialized formally, the island can be viewed briefly during Fort Sumter harbor tours, which leave from Patriots Point in Mount Pleasant or the tour boat facility at Liberty Square near the S.C. Aquarium. What you'll see are just small hills that were originally built as artillery fortifications, a few shanties, and truck farm areas. Call (843) 881-7337 or visit www.fortsumtertours.com for departure times. Fort Sumter Tours are generally from 9:30 a.m. to 5 p.m. Mon through Fri depending on the season. The fare is $16 for adults and teens, $14.50 for seniors, and $10 for children ages 6 to 11. No tours go out to the fort on Thanksgiving, Christmas, or New Year's Day. (See more on Battery Wagner in the Forts section of the Attractions chapter.)

i If you're going to be in Charleston during the spring or early fall, chances are you can find tickets to Charleston's two most-famous house and garden tours of private properties. In the spring, the Historic Charleston Foundation sponsors its annual Festival of Houses and Gardens from mid-Mar through mid-Apr when the city's flowers are at their peak. Late in Sept and well into Oct, the Preservation Society of Charleston sponsors its Fall Tours of Homes and Gardens after the long-anticipated cooler nights have returned to the Lowcountry.

✳BOONE HALL PLANTATION
1235 Long Point Rd., Mount Pleasant
(843) 884-4371
www.boonehallplantation.com

Once one of the largest cotton plantations in the South, Boone Hall dates back to the 1680s. At one time Boone Hall was home to more than 1,000 slaves. Nine of the original slave houses still stand on the plantation's "Slave Street." These structures, now

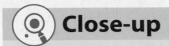 **Close-up**

Gullah: A Language, an Ethic, a Lowcountry Folklore

Part of our country's growing trend toward ethnic self-awareness has been a renewed interest in **Gullah,** the colorful language and accompanying lifestyle that once flourished on the South Carolina sea islands from Georgetown to Daufuskie.

Researchers reported that as late as 1979, 100,000 South Carolinians spoke Gullah. Current estimates count 7,000 to 10,000 people speaking Gullah at home. Without intervention, the Gullah language will soon live only in scholarly textbooks and on fragile academic recordings.

The origins of Gullah date back to a sad chapter in America's past. When slave traders sailed to West Africa and stuffed their ships full of men, women, and children to be sold as slaves to Southern planters, Gullah was conceived. As that black culture meshed with the white, Gullah was born. A thick, lilting mix of African and English dialects, it started as a makeshift second language used among the sea island slaves, and it slowly evolved into the unwritten native tongue of their descendants.

Oddly, slavery and the antebellum South fed energy to the language. Gullah served a very practical transitional purpose, and its use and culture actually developed during those years. After the Civil War, however, the separation between the black and white cultures became highly exaggerated for nearly a century and a half. Cut off from the cultural homogenization that occurred everywhere else in America, life along the sea islands changed very little. Sea islanders still fished the coastline, shrimped the marsh, hunted for game in the woods, and spoke their native tongue unashamedly.

Gullah stubbornly survived in this splendid isolation, until the outside world rediscovered the islands and invested millions of dollars to develop them as resorts. Suddenly, bridges were built that introduced paved roads, indoor plumbing, better education, and access to higher paying mainland jobs. Gullah became thought of as "bad English." Soon it was something to be ashamed of or denied. Then television, the greatest homogenizing influence of all, came along and nearly snuffed the language out altogether.

Finding true Gullah today is like finding gold. It's rare, and it's kept hidden from "outsiders." Still, there are a few islanders determined to keep it alive. There still are those who knit their own fishing nets, who still cook the Gullah receipts (recipes) and serve their families whole meals fresh from the sea. Thankfully, there are still those who take what's left of the sweetgrass from the riverbanks and fashion baskets of great skill and beauty—just like their ancestors did back in Sierra Leone.

frequently used by filmmakers for their stark authenticity, are open to the public on this still-working farm. Boone Hall is open Mon through Sat from 8:30 a.m. to 6:30 p.m. and Sun from 1 to 5 p.m. Mar 22 through Labor Day. After Labor Day until Mar 21, hours are 9 a.m. to 5 p.m. Mon through Sat, Sun 1 to 4 p.m. Admission is $17.50 for adults and teens and $7.50 for children ages 6 to 12. Seniors

60 and over pay $15. (See the Day Trips chapter for more on Boone Hall Plantation.)

CABBAGE ROW
89–91 Church St.

This downtown area was claimed as the inspirational setting for DuBose Heyward's 1925 book *Porgy* and for George and Ira Gershwin's beloved folk opera *Porgy and Bess,* which premiered in 1935. Cabbage Row, the scene of the story, took its name from the vegetables regularly sold from carts and windowsills by the area's black residents. Today, this section houses quaint little shops, but anyone familiar with the opera and its distinctive stage settings will readily see that this place and the alleys around and behind it could easily have been the story's original scene.

Was the story based on truth? Was there ever a crippled vendor named Porgy who won, then lost, the love of a troubled woman named Bess? Many older Charlestonians recall a poor, crippled man who lived here in the early 1920s and used a small goat cart to get around. His name was Samuel Smalls. The other details of the story are hard to pin down, but Charleston certainly had enclaves of black families who struggled against very difficult circumstances, and their sagas of survival and social interdependence were not unlike Porgy's. Charleston obviously experiences the wrath of hurricanes, and in those days, terrible storms struck with little warning. And surely then, as now, the ugly specter of drugs and violence dramatically influenced the lives and loves of these people. We may never actually know if Heyward ever heard of Samuel Smalls, but the connections are intriguing, and the story is timeless.

More avid music lovers and Porgy fans may want to visit Smalls' grave, which is well marked in the churchyard of James Island Presbyterian Church, about a 6-mile drive from the Charleston Peninsula on Folly Road. The grave was unmarked for many years, until an anonymous but concerned Charlestonian took the responsibility of funding a suitable marker for this legendary Charleston icon. To get to the church, take the James Island Connector (SR 30) over the Ashley River, and turn left on Folly Road. The church is at 1632 Fort Johnson Rd., the intersection of Folly and Fort Johnson Roads. Look for the marker to Porgy just outside the fenced churchyard.

THE CHARLESTON MUSEUM
360 Meeting St.
(843) 722-2996
www.charlestonmuseum.org

America's first museum, founded in 1773, has exhibits and art depicting African-American life in the South Carolina Lowcountry. Additional photographs and valued information on African-American history and culture are housed in the museum's archives. Archival research is welcome; call the museum for an appointment. The Charleston Museum is open Mon through Sat from 9 a.m. to 5 p.m. Sun hours are from 1 to 5 p.m. Admission is $10 for adults and teens and $5 for children ages 3 to 12. The doors are closed on Thanksgiving, Christmas, and New Year's Eve. (See the Charleston Museum entry in the Attractions chapter for more information.)

✳DRAYTON HALL
3380 Ashley River Rd.
(843) 769-2600, (888) 349-0588
www.draytonhall.org

This colonial-era plantation house is shown to the public today as an architectural museum. It is considered to be the finest and earliest example of Palladian architecture in America. Built between 1738 and 1742, the structure serves as a monument to 18th-century European and African-American artisans, who displayed highly sophisticated building skills at a remarkably early time.

Now a property of the National Trust for Historic Preservation, Drayton Hall's research and education departments are in the vanguard of the nation's effort to document and acknowledge the contribution of African-Americans to the colonial South. Special events and educational programs at Drayton Hall offer insight into this culture and its modern legacy.

One of our most treasured exponents of African-American heritage is the Lowcountry gospel spiritual. For a little slice of heaven, attend one of the special holiday candle-light concerts performed by local African-American choirs at Drayton Hall during the Christmas season. These concerts, originally sponsored by the Friends of Drayton Hall, are now open to the public and offer a rare opportunity to hear authentic Lowcountry spirituals (with their distinctive double hand clapping) in an original setting. See the Annual Events chapter, or call the number listed for more information.

Drayton Hall is open daily, except Thanksgiving, Christmas Eve, Christmas, and New Year's Day. Admission is $17 for adults, $8 for students ages 12 to 18, and $6 for children ages 6 to 11. Admission to the grounds only is $8. Admission is free to card-holding members of the National Trust for Historic Preservation. (See the Drayton Hall entry in the Attractions chapter.)

ELIZA'S HOUSE AT MIDDLETON PLACE
4300 Ashley River Rd.
(843) 556-6020, (800) 782-3608
www.middletonplace.org

After the Civil War, a number of freed slaves chose to remain living and working on the huge rice plantation that was Middleton Place. They were most likely responsible for constructing in the 1870s the building that was later named "Eliza's House." It was named in memory of Eliza Leach, a South Carolina African American born in 1891 and the last person to live in the building. For 40 years or so, she worked at Middleton Place performing a variety of duties from working in the gardens to greeting visitors. She died in 1986 at age 94, and almost to the end of her life, she lived in the house in much the same way her predecessors did.

The building has been restored and is now shown along with the other former plantation outbuildings that house demonstrations of weaving, spinning, blacksmithing, candle making, carpentry, and pottery making—all tasks of the plantation slaves. Eliza's House was originally built to house two families: Half of the building now depicts typical living quarters; plans are in the works to set up the other half for exhibits of artifacts from Middleton Place slaves.

Eliza's House is open daily from 9 a.m. to 5 p.m. Middleton Place house tours are Tues through Sun from 10 a.m. to 4:30 p.m. and Mon from noon to 4:30 p.m. Admission is $20 for adults to see the plantation gardens and stable yards (including Eliza's House) and $5 for youngsters ages 7 to 15. There is an additional $10 charge (for adults and children alike) for a guided tour of the plantation house and an additional $15 for a carriage tour around the property's woodlands and an abandoned rice field. (See more about Middleton Place in the Attractions chapter.)

Heritage Passport

For the connoisseur intending to become immersed in Charleston's history and culture, there's a way to save nearly 40 percent on regular admission to nine of the most popular attractions. Purchase a **Heritage Passport** (sold only at the visitor center at 375 Meeting St.) and see the Gibbes Museum of Art, Charleston Museum, Heyard-Washington House, Joseph Manigault House, Nathaniel Russell House, Edmondston-Alston House, Aiken-Rhett House, Drayton Hall, and Middleton Place (gardens and stable yards only) at what is a very considerable savings. Ask for details at the visitor center information desk.

MCLEOD PLANTATION
325 Country Club Dr., James Island
(843) 723-1623
www.historiccharleston.org
McLeod Plantation dates back to the late 17th century, when it was one of the first profitable farms to be established along the Ashley River system. Its fine collection of antebellum buildings is considered to be among the best preserved in the American South.

In addition to the main house (ca. 1854), there are barns, stables, a gin house, kitchen, and a dairy plus a street of several slave cabins. According to a census taken in 1860,

there were 74 slaves living in 26 dwellings on the plantation whose work was the cultivation of sea island cotton.

McLeod was occupied by both Confederate and Union forces during the Civil War. The main house served as a field hospital, and it housed officers from the famous 54th and 55th Massachusetts Volunteers. It also became the main office for the Freedman's Bureau serving the James Island area during Reconstruction years.

In 1993 the still privately owned McLeod Plantation was acquired by Historic Charleston Foundation and held in trust while experts assessed how best to use this historic site. The Foundation currently is working with Charleston County Parks and Recreation to preserve and maintain this important historical site.

OLD SLAVE MART MUSEUM
6 Chalmers St.
(843) 958-6467
www.charleston-sc.gov
The one longtime local outlet for black cultural information in Charleston was the Old Slave Mart at 6 Chalmers St. At this site, reproduction slave-made wares and crafts were sold, and actual slave era artifacts were displayed. Unfortunately, the museum failed as a privately owned tourist attraction, and it closed in 1987. A year later, the City of Charleston bought the building, and later reopened it as a museum depicting the slave trading that went on here between 1856 and 1863. Among the self-guided solemn visual materials is a firsthand audio account by former slave, Elijah Green. He was born in 1843 and told his life's story in 1937 to a Works Progress Administration (WPA) writer working to preserve these memories for American history.

The building encloses part of the rear yard of a now-gone tenement building known to have been used for slave auctions. First called "Ryan's Mart" (after city alderman and slave profiteer, Thomas Ryan) and later, the "Mart in Chalmer's Street," this was one of several sites in this neighborhood where African-Americans were sold into slavery. It is South Caroilna's only remaining slave auction house site. Museum hours are Mon through Sat from 9 a.m. to 5 p.m. Admission is $7; free for children younger than 5.

SNEE FARM (CHARLES PINCKNEY NATIONAL HISTORIC SITE)
1254 Longpoint Rd., Mount Pleasant
(843) 881-5516, (843) 883-3123
www.nps.gov/chpi

The interpretation of African-American history at Snee Farm centers on the influence of enslaved people of West African origin on the development of Charles Pinckney's colonial farm. Snee Farm was established in 1988 to highlight the contributions of Pinckney, a famous statesman, politician, and signer of the US Constitution. The contribution of people of African descent is shown through exhibits, park handouts, archaeology displays, and a video program. These contributions were in the form of language, food, agricultural skills, and craftsmanship.

The site has a small gift shop where various publications are sold that help illuminate the African-American story. Sometimes even a maker of sweetgrass baskets is on hand to demonstrate that distinctive local art form. Park hours are from 9 a.m. to 5 p.m. daily but closed Thanksgiving, Christmas, and New Year's Day. There is no admission charge for this site.

ETHNIC TOURS

GULLAH TOURS INC.
43 John St.
(843) 763-7551
www.gullahtours.com

This group offers Charleston folktales told in Gullah, the distinctive language spoken by Lowcountry blacks that's a separate and unique cross between English and various African dialects. Your guide is Alphonso Brown, licensed guide, lecturer, and author of *A Guide to Gullah Charleston*. You will tour many of the important local African-American sites such as the Old Slave Mart, Denmark Vesey's house, and Catfish Row. All tours leave from Gallery Chuma on 43 John St., across from the visitor center. Weekday tours are at 11 a.m. and 1 p.m. Sat tours are at 11 a.m. and 1 and 3 p.m. No tours are given on Sun. Tours are $18 per person.

SITES AND INSIGHTS TOURS
P.O. Box 21346, Charleston, SC 29413
(843) 762-0051, (843) 552-9995
www.sitesandinsightstours.com

Visit little-known black history sites, and gain a knowledge of Charleston's past from an African-American perspective. Hear stories of slavery, free blacks, the Denmark Vesey Slave Uprising, the Stono Rebellion, Catfish Row, and Charleston's colorful sea islands. These are 1- and 2-hour motor tours that depart from the visitor center. Rates are $13 for adults of any age for the 1-hour tour and $10 for children. The 2-hour program is $18 for adults and $13 for children. A 2-hour island tour (of James, Johns, Angel Oak, and Civil War sites) is available upon request. Rates are $23 for adults, $18 for children. Call for schedules.

TOURIFIC TOURS AFRICAN AMERICAN HISTORY
25 8th Ave.
(843) 853-2500

This company, owned by a native Charlestonian and civic leader, offers two privately guided tours of African-American history departing from the visitor center. Tour 1 lasts 1½ hours and takes visitors on a stroll through the streets of Charleston to the boundaries of the original walled city. You'll see typical Charleston "single houses" and antebellum mansions, historic churches, the Dock Street Theater, cobblestone streets, and the famous Four Corners of Law. Tour 2 is by car and takes visitors through the picturesque College of Charleston campus, where free people of color lived prior to the Civil War. Hear about the early contributions of African-Americans to the city's history and see on-site examples of work by Charleston's famous wrought-iron worker Philip Simmons. Learn about slave uprising leader Denmark Vesey, and visit African-American churches. Reservations are required for these tours, and all require a minimum of 2 people to begin. The walking tour is $25 per person. The auto tour is $100 up to 2 people or $125 for 3.

OTHER GUIDED TOURS

Bus & Van Tours

Bus and van tours are very comfortable, if for no other reason than the fact that these tour vehicles are air-conditioned. In the summer months, that certainly counts for a lot. Most of these vehicles have small PA systems, so hearing the driver and tour guide is no problem. Be advised, however, that only certain streets are approved for larger tour vehicles, so you'll miss some of the tiny side streets and alleys that give Charleston so much of its charm. Here are some of the best of the motor tours offered:

ADVENTURE SIGHTSEEING
1090 Ft. Sumter Dr.
(843) 762-0088, (800) 722-5394
www.touringcharleston.com

This company offers a variety of tours of the historic district. You may choose one of the bus or van tours with special features such as The Citadel Dress Parade (Fridays only), a tour through the Old Exchange, or one of Charleston's house museums. There are also Plantaion and Garden tours and a city bus tour with a boat ride to Fort Sumter. Adventure Sightseeing offers free pick-up service from the visitor center or a $2 roundtrip fee from downtown hotels, the City Market, and the City Marina. Reservations are accepted 24 hours daily.

Fares for 2-hour tours are $29 for adults and teens, $17 for children under 12. For Adventure's 90-minute tour, adult fares are $20, $11 for children under 12. The plantation tours are $50 for adults and $25 for children; and the City/ Ft. Sumter tour is $34 for adults and $22 for children. Discounts are available if purchased online. All Adventure tours include a complete history of the city; 2-hour tours include one house museum.

CHARLESTON TOURS INC.
P.O. Box 31716, Charleston, SC 29417
(843) 571-0049
www.charleston-tours.com

These guides say they're "the Southern specialists for city or plantation tours." Tour A is a 90-minute city tour that includes the French Quarter and the Slave Market plus a stop at the Battery. The fare for adults and teens is $21. Tours D and E go out to the plantations

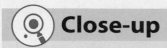 Close-up

The Pest Houses on Sullivan's Island

Today there's just a bronze plaque, and even that plaque is a very recent addition to the history being interpreted for the public at Ft. Moultrie on Sullivan's Island. But it is, at least, a beginning. The plaque commemorates a grim chapter in Charleston's history—the advent of the **"pest houses"** on Sullivan's Island during the city's booming slave trade in the 18th and 19th centuries.

In 1707 the local government was in fear of the diseases carried by slave ships arriving at the colony from West Africa. As a remedy for this, a law was passed requiring all slave ships to dock at Sullivan's Island and unload their human cargo for a period of quarantine—usually 10 days or so. The place for holding these unfortunate people was called a "pest house," in reference to the pestilence hopefully kept inside its primitive walls. After a period of time, during which the "cargo" was inspected for disease, the captives were moved across the harbor and sold at public auction into slavery. An estimated 40 percent of black Americans have ancestors who came through the pest houses of Sullivan's Island.

There are no surviving eyewitness accounts of what actually went on in these long-vanished structures, but in 1759 a Charleston physician, Dr. Alexander Garden (for whom the gardenia plant was named), left this description of the slave ships:

"I have often gone to visit those Vessels on their first Arrival," he writes. "But I have never yet been on board one that did not smell most offensive and noisome, what for Filth, putrid Air, putrid Dysenteries. . . . [I]t is a wonder any [people] escape with Life."

The plaque on Sullivan's Island is a step in the right direction, but it is a far too small (and too late) gesture of acknowledgment for what is clearly an important chapter in American history.

and last about four hours. They include a visit to Magnolia Plantation and Gardens or Middleton Place. Fares are $52 (Magnolia) and $62 (Middleton). Tour C includes the city tour plus refreshments on the piazza of the Palmer Mansion on Charleston's High Battery. Adults and teens go for $30. Tours G and H are billed as an "all-day adventure" that includes the city tour (you do lunch on your own) in the Market area, then continues on to Magnolia or Middleton Place. Fares are $63 (Magnolia) and $73 (Middleton). Ages 4 to 11 are half price for all tours and under 4 are free. Tours run Mon through Sat and depart from the visitor center, with free pick-up service from most downtown locations.

CHARLESTON'S FINEST HISTORIC TOURS
P.O. Box 263, Ridgeville, SC 29472
(843) 577-3311
www.historictoursofcharleston.com
This company offers three daily scheduled tours—all in a luxury touring coach. Tour A begins at 10:30 a.m. and is a city-centered adventure, including seeing and hearing about noteworthy mansions and churches, Civil War forts, the Battery, and Slave Mart (allow 110 minutes). Adult fare is $18; youths

ages 4 to 12, half price. Tour B begins in the afternoon at 12:30 p.m. and lasts 4½ hours. It includes an extended visit to Magnolia Plantation. Adult rates are $48; ages 4 to 12 half price. Tour C is an all-day combination tour for $58 for adults and half price for children 4 to 12. For those with limited time, 90-minute city tours are offered at 11:30 a.m. and 1:30 p.m. leaving from the visitor center; the cost is $16 and again half price for children. Pickup from downtown hotels is free.

"DOIN' THE CHARLESTON" TOURS
P.O. Box 31338, Charleston, SC 29417
(843) 763-1233, (800) 647-4487
www.dointhecharlestontours.com
Here's something of a high-tech motor tour, a new twist on historic interpretation. You travel around Charleston in an air-conditioned minibus with large windows, while historic views of many of the same places you're seeing are displayed via laser disc on a screen inside your motor coach. There's even a musical soundtrack to your guide's live narration. Allow 90 minutes for this tour, which includes a stop at the Battery. Rates for adults and teens are $20, and the price is $14 for children ages 6 to 11. Daily tours leave promptly from the visitor center at 9:30 a.m., noon, 2:30, and 4:30 p.m. (the 4:30 p.m. tour runs during daylight savings time only). Free pickups from downtown lodgings are offered. Call for reservations.

GRAY LINE BUS TOURS
P.O. Box 219, Charleston, SC 29402
(843) 722-4444
www.graylineofcharleston.com
Gray Line offers three tours of Charleston in various configurations—all in minivans with air-conditioning and large windows.

Culinary Tours of Charleston

Believe it or not, there's even a tour of the Carolina Lowcountry's unique culinary history for those seeking insights and instruction on the secrets and traditions of Southern cooking. **Culinary Tours of Charleston** offers walking tours with the inside scoop on many of the foods that have made Charleston famous. You meet chefs, bakers, food growers, and special artisans as you visit restaurants, markets, kitchens, and food shops throughout the city. The **Savor the Flavors of Charleston Tour** is offered Mon through Thurs and Sat from 9:30 a.m. to noon. The Friday afternoon tour runs from 2 to 4:30 p.m. The **Chef's Kitchen Tour** is Fri only from 9:30 a.m. until noon. The cost for each is $42 per person and includes numerous tasting stops along the way. Reservations are required; call (843) 722-TOUR, (800) 918-0701, or visit www.culinarytours ofcharleston.com.

The Historic Charleston Tour 1 (allow 90 minutes) includes a stop at the Battery and points out dozens of historic sites. Adult rates are $20, children younger than 12, $12.

Tour 2 is called Historic Charleston and Restored Home (allow two hours). This tour includes a stop at the Battery and one of Charleston's house museums (which one will vary according to season and availability). Adults and teens are charged $28, children younger than 12, $16.

Tour 3 is a combination Bus and Boat Tour. This is a special pricing of Tour 1 along with a boat tour of Charleston Harbor or Fort Sumter. Adult and teen rates are $32, and children younger than 12 pay $18. Tours depart the visitor center every 30 minutes between 9:30 a.m. and 3 p.m. or 2 p.m. Dec through Feb (on the hour and half hour).

TALK OF THE TOWNE
2166 St. James Dr.
(843) 795-8199
www.talkofthetowne.com
Enjoy panoramic views of the Battery, Rainbow Row, and all the major downtown landmarks from a minibus designed especially for touring Charleston. The 2-hour tours, leaving from the visitor center Mon through Sat, include a 35-minute guided tour of the Nathaniel Russell House or Edmondston-Alston House. Pickup from all major downtown hotels is available. The rate for adults and teens is $29, for children 12 and younger, it's $16. The 75-minute version, leaving from the visitor center at 9:15 and 11:45 a.m. and 3 p.m., is a nonstop, 7-mile ride through Charleston that includes the Battery, Rainbow Row, and the Four Corners of Law. Adult and teen fare is $20; for children ages 12 and younger, it's $12.

TAYLORED TOURS OF CHARLESTON
9158 Markeleys Grove Blvd.,
Summerville
(843) 870-7901
www.toursofcharleston.com
This company offers four historic tours of Charleston for small groups by car or van. Tour 1 is a general history tour (allow 75 minutes) covering more than 110 points of interest including a stop at the Battery overlooking Fort Sumter. Adults and teen

admissions are $28. Tour 2 is a 90-minute trip specializing in specific subjects: the colonial period and the Revolution, the Civil War, black history, and architectural points of interest. Reservations for these tours are required a day in advance, and the cost is $33 per person. Tour 3 offers 90 minutes of general history (same as Tour 1), followed by a guided tour of one of Charleston's house museums (the Nathaniel Russell House, Heyward-Washington House, or the Aiken-Rhett House). Rates for adults and children are $45. Tour 4 is a private plantation tour lasting about 4 hours. It includes a trip up the historic Ashley River Road and a visit to one of two historic Lowcountry plantations (your choice), either Middleton Place or Magnolia Plantation, or over to Mount Pleasant for a visit to Boone Hall Plantation. This tour costs $25 per person plus plantation admission fees. Guests also pay for any additional options they choose at the site. Discounts are available for booking online. Free pickups from downtown hotels are available. All tours depart from the visitor center. Interested parties may ask about day-long tours of Savannah, Georgia, as well.

i Try spending an afternoon at one of the weekly docent-led tours given at the Gibbes Museum of Art at 2:30 p.m. on Fridays. Visitors get an in-depth view of an exhibit and often find they want to stick around and explore some more of the collection on their own. The tours are free with paid admission.

Walking Tours

Walking tours are great if you're up to the exercise. The pace is slow, the interpretation is personal, and the detail you'll see and hear is incredible. These tours—by definition—have the excitement and feel of a treasure hunt, and treasure is always found. Every one of these tours bears the stamp of your particular tour guide, and this seems to make the experience more intimate and fun. On the other hand, you cover a relatively small part of the historic Peninsula and see only a microcosm of all there is to see. Here are some of our favorites:

ARCHITECTURAL WALKING TOURS
173 Meeting St.
(843) 893-2327, (800) 931-7761
www.architecturalwalkingtoursof charleston .com

These are 2-hour tours of Charleston's remarkable architectural heritage. Your guide through 7 local public buildings is Fern Williams Tuten, a local art historian and licensed city guide. The tour of 18th-century buildings begins at 10 a.m.; the tour of 19th century buildings is at 2 p.m. Both tours depart from the Meeting Street Inn, 173 Meeting St. (tours depart 10 minutes earlier from Hawthorne Suites). No tours are offered on Tues or Sun. The charge is $20 a person. Special theme tours and group tours are available with advance notice. These include a house museum along with public buildings.

CHARLESTON STROLLS WALK WITH HISTORY
P.O. Box 1651, Charleston, SC 29402
(843) 766-2080
www.charlestonstrolls.com

This is the walking tour recommended by the *New York Times* and *Southern Living*. It operates Mon through Sat all year long, leaving from outside the Palmetto Cafe in Charleston Place at 9:30 a.m., 9:40 a.m. from

the Days Inn, and from the Mills House Hotel at 10 a.m. A personal guide brings to life Charleston's history from colonial days through the Civil War to the present. You'll stroll cobblestone streets, find hidden gardens, walk in famous footsteps, and much more. Rates are $18 for adults and teens, and $10 for children 7 to 12; under 7 are admitted free. Reservations are accepted, but not required.

*CHARLESTON TEA PARTY WALKING TOUR
(843) 722-1779

This 3-hour tour ends with a tea served in the private garden of your guide after a walk through the oldest section of the historic district. The tour includes colonial and 18th-century architecture, Civil War history with quotations from diaries, church history, Charleston gardens and interiors, plus insight into Charleston's preservation story. Tours begin at the King's Courtyard Inn, 198 King St., and cost $25. The 9:30 a.m. tour is offered daily except Sun. For a private 3-hour tour by van to private historic homes followed by lunch at your guide's own home, call (843) 577-5896. The fee for this special guest experience is $100 each. Reservations are required.

CHARLESTON'S ORIGINAL GHOST HUNT WALKING TOUR
(843) 813-5055
www.charlestonghosthunt.com

Here's another offering for those interested in chasing down Charleston's famous ghost stories. These "adventures" come in a number of guises these days, and this is one of the best. The tour departs from the sidewalk area in front of the United States Custom House on the corner of South Market Street and

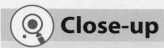 **Close-up**

Gateway Walk

Looking for a way to see Charleston that's a little off the beaten path? **Gateway Walk** is a free self-guided walking tour many find unique, and it's right through the heart of the historic district.

In 1930 Mrs. Clelia Peronneau McGowan, president of The Garden Club of Charleston, came up with the idea for a walkway that would connect the city's churchyards, garden areas, and tucked-away courtyards. She was inspired by a trip to Paris, where she embraced the idea of meandering through serene gardens in the midst of a bustling cityscape. The plan was designed by noted Charleston landscape architect Loutrel Briggs and opened on April 10, 1930, to celebrate the 250th anniversary of the founding of Charleston on its peninsula site.

The walk is designated by unobtrusive plaques and foot-stone markers that lead through historic sites but depart from the sidewalk viewpoint and beckon you into the hidden core of the city blocks between Archdale Street and Philadelphia Alley. Your stroll covers 4 blocks, where you may amble through four churchyards full of fascinating old tombstones with a variety of blooming flora. It continues through the gardens of the Charleston Library Society and Gibbes Museum of Art, with its rose garden that features the Governor Aiken gates, a fountain, and sculpture. Winding your way through several centuries of Charleston history, you'll discover how Gateway Walk was named for the beautiful wrought-iron gates along the way.

An inscription on one of the plaques attributed to Mrs. McGowan reads:

> "Through hand wrought gates,
> alluring paths
> Lead on to pleasant places,
> Where ghosts of long forgotten things
> Have left elusive traces."

The walk underwent its first restoration in 1953 with the continued support of Mr. Briggs. In 1992 the garden club initiated a 3-year restoration designed by T. Hunter McEaddy Associates and spearheads its ongoing maintenance through an endowment established at the Community Foundation. The Gateway Walk is free and open 8:30 a.m. to 5 p.m. Mon through Fri. To print out a map go to www.stjohnscharleston.org/visitors.

East Bay at 7 and 9 p.m. (weather permitting). The tour is appropriate for adults and teens only (no children under 12) and the fare is $13. A late-night tour (at 10:45 p.m.) is offered on weekends. Reservations are required.

CIVIL WAR WALKING TOUR
17 Archdale St.
(843) 270-2417
www.civilwarwalk.com
This walking tour departs from the Mills House Hotel lobby, 115 Meeting St., at 9 a.m. daily. You'll hear the personal accounts and colorful anecdotes of the late Charlestonians

who lived through it all. The tour includes comparisons of photos of Charleston from the 1860s with those of today. Reservations are appreciated. The adult rate is $20. Children under age 12 are free. Group rates are available, and the route is wheelchair accessible.

ED GRIMBALL WALKING TOURS
P.O. Box 458, Edisto Island, SC 29438
(843) 762-0056
www.edgrimballtours.com
Ed Grimball's walking tour of Charleston is a keeper for your memory book. He's a born-and-raised Charlestonian whose family settled on nearby Edisto Island. He knows and loves the city as only a native son can. As a registered tour guide, his entertaining insights and stories run the gamut from architecture and colonial history to the Civil War and the great earthquake of 1886. He's familiar with the stories of the heroes and statesmen, the scoundrels and bizarre characters who've helped make Charleston history what it is—endlessly fascinating. Tours last about 2½ hours and depart from the Pineapple Fountain in downtown's Waterfront Park starting at 9:30 a.m., most Wednesdays, Fridays, and Saturdays. Call for more information or special tour arrangements. The charge is $16 for adults and $8 for children 7 to 12. Reservations are required. He goes rain or shine—even in the heat of summer. Complimentary ice water is provided about an hour after the tour begins (from the middle of May through the end of Aug). Nice touch in our Charleston climate!

GHOST WALK TOUR
1448 Village Rd.
(843) 720-TOUR (8687)
www.ghostwalk.net

This one-and-a-half-hour Ghost Walk tour is an eerie visit through 18th- and 19th-century historic district neighborhoods— this one with tales of ghosts, the plateye, voodoo, graveyards, and "Hags & Haints." Old stories and legends of paranormal experiences are interspersed with the fun and fascinating history of Charleston. These tours begin at 8 p.m. in front of 74-A North Market St. next to the Doubletree Hotel. Adult fare is $15, children ages 4 to 12, $9; reservations are required.

ON THE MARKET TOURS
(853) 853-8687
www.onthemarkettours.com
Tommy Dew is your host (and licensed guide) for this historical tour that covers a timeline of events from the Colonial Period through the War between the States to Charleston's current renaissance. Daily tours begin at the steps of Market Hall, on Meeting Street between South Market and North Market Streets, and end along the waterfront at the Battery. They begin at 11 a.m. and last approximately 1 hour and 45 minutes. Reservations are required. Adult fare is $22; children (12 and under) pay $15.

THE ORIGINAL CHARLESTON WALKS
45 Broad St., 2nd floor
(843) 408-0010
www.charlestonwalks.com
This company specializes in educational and group tours of 20 or more people— perfect for family reunions, small meetings, or groups of history buffs. Choose from the following seven options: the Charleston Walk, Pirates and Buccaneers Walk, the Civil War Walk, Patriots of Charleston Walk, Ghost & Legends Walk, Historic Homes Walk, and Slavery & Freedom Walk. One of these

options is bound to please your crowd. Tours depart Washington Park at the Broad Street gates near the corner of Meeting and Broad Streets and last for around 2 hours. They cover about a mile at a relaxed pace. Call for times, group pricing, and reservations.

THE STORY OF CHARLESTON
(843) 723-1670, (800) 854-1670
www.tourcharleston.com
Reservations are required for this walking tour that claims to show visitors the Holy City "from a Charlestonian's point of view." In addition to architecture and history, this intimate, 90-minute-plus tour profiles some of the city's legendary personalities and recounts the impact of wars and disasters. Tours leave from in front of the circular fountain at Waterfront Park (at the foot of Vendue Range) at 10 a.m. and 5 p.m. Rates are $18 for adults and $12 for children 12 and younger.

The same company, called Tour Charleston, offers the Ghosts of Charleston tour, which is based on the book *The Ghosts of Charleston* by Julian T. Buxton, III. This 70- to 90-minute adventure is a big hit with those interested in the paranormal and departs from the fountain at Waterfront Park at 5, 7:30, and 9:30 p.m. The same pricing applies.

The company's newest offering is the Ghosts of Charleston II, wherein you encounter specters on the edge of town. This tour begins at 7 and 9 p.m. leaving from the fountain at the corner of King and Calhoun Streets at Marion Square.

Carriage Tours

Carriage tours are an enduring Charleston tradition. There's nothing like seeing an 18th- and 19th-century city at an appropriately slow, leisurely, clip-clop pace. You'll ride through neighborhoods above and below Broad Street (ones that are approved for horse-drawn vehicle traffic) while your driver tells the Charleston story. The ambience is wonderful, but again, you're restricted to certain areas of the city for traffic management purposes, and you receive a somewhat limited view of the city's many charms. Here are the carriage tour options now available:

CAROLINA POLO & CARRIAGE COMPANY
181 Church St.
(843) 577-6767, (843) 577-9555
www.cpcc.com
All tour guides on these carriages are city licensed and trained by a company tour director who has been doing carriage tours since 1978. These tours depart from 16 Hayne St., and 181 Church St. (from the lobby of the Doubletree Hotel on the corner of North Market and Church Streets). Adult and teen rates are $20; children ages 4 to 11 pay $12. An advance online reservation offers a $2 discount per person. Private carriage tours are available upon request.

CLASSIC CARRIAGE TOURS INC.
10 Guignard St.
(843) 853-3747
www.classiccarriage.com
One of the South's best-known carriage works, Classic Carriage, specializes in the construction and restoration of 19th- and 20th-century carriages, wagons, and surreys. With Percheron draft horses and experienced, licensed tour guides as drivers, these one-hour tours are popular with visitors and those planning special events in the Charleston area. These carriages are especially popular for traditional Charleston weddings. Reservations are strongly encouraged for the daily tours, which leave from the

corner of Church and Market Streets in the City Market area from 9 a.m. to 5 p.m. daily. Adult and teen rates are $20; rates for children 5 to 11 are $12. If you book your tour in advance by phone or online, there are additional discounts.

OLD SOUTH CARRIAGE CO.
14 Anson St.
(843) 723-9712
www.oldsouthcarriagetours.com
These are the carriage tours narrated by licensed guides wearing red sashes (Confederate uniforms, of sorts). The 60-minute tours depart from 14 Anson St., at the corner of North Market and Anson Streets, every 20 minutes beginning at 9 a.m. daily. Adult fares are $21, and fares for children ages 3 to 11 are $13.

OLDE TOWNE CARRIAGE CO.
20 Anson St.
(843) 722-1315
www.oldetownecarriage.com
These carriage tours by licensed guides leave the company barn at 20 Anson St. near the City Market starting at 9 a.m. Tours are given until dusk and run from 45 minutes to an hour. Fares for those older than 11 are $20, and fares for ages 4 to 11 are $12.

PALMETTO CARRIAGE TOURS
40 North Market St.
(843) 723-8145
www.carriagetour.com
Experienced guides narrate this 1-hour carriage tour that meanders through 25 blocks (2 miles) of antebellum neighborhoods at a clip-clop pace. Tours begin and end at the red barn behind the Rainbow Market, 40 North Market St. Hours are 9 a.m. to dusk

daily. Adult rates are $20, and children ages 4 to 11 are $10.

Cruise & Boat Tours

These tours offer the absolute joy of being on the breezy waters of Charleston Harbor and the wide Cooper River, both of which offer an entirely new perspective on Charleston. It's a perspective that was, after all, the one first seen by pirate scalawags and some of our country's founding fathers. This was the first view for those aboard heavy-laden packet boats and cotton barges as well as those on the first ironclad warships and the crowded slave vessels out of Africa and the Caribbean. Maritime history is clearly one of Charleston's long suits, but we suggest you supplement a boat tour with another type of tour, so you don't miss the urban story. Here are some of our favorite water tours:

BARRIER ISLAND ECOTOURS
50 41st Ave., Isle of Palms
(843) 886-5000
www.nature-tours.com
Here is a chance to become immersed in the ecology and natural history that make the Lowcountry a marine biologist's paradise. Young and old alike will enjoy these adventures on the barrier islands led by personable guides who skillfully teach visitors some of the most fascinating aspects about this environment. Tours depend on weather conditions and availability, but you can choose from the following adventures. Capers Island is an untouched barrier island close to Charleston with diverse wildlife to see and a breathtaking landscape to explore. The 3½ hour tour goes Tues, Thurs, and Sat mornings year round, also Fri mornings Memorial to Labor Day. Fare is $36 for adults, $26 for children under 12. The Blue Crabbing

Expedition (also 3½ hours) teaches guests how to catch, cook, clean, and consume this Lowcountry delicacy. Fare is $38 for adults, $28 for children under 12. The Dolphin Sunset Cruise (2½ hours) is an abbreviated version of the Capers Island wildlife trip and includes a 1 hour walk on the island. Fare is $30 for adults, $22 for children under 12. Call for information on the Creek Fishing Trip for adults and children and the Marine Biology Day Camp for children ages 5 to 12 during summer months. Reservations are recommended. All tours depart from Isle of Palms Marina at the end of 41st Avenue, Isle of Palms.

CHARLESTON HARBOR TOURS
10 Wharfside Dr., Charleston Maritime Center
(843) 722-1112, (800) 979-3370
www.charlestonharbortours.com

These folks say they've been giving water tours of Charleston Harbor since 1908. Their current tour boat, the Carolina Belle, is 85 feet long and carries 300 passengers in comfort. The Harbor of History tour includes 75 points of interest including a ride past Fort Sumter and lasts approximately 90 minutes. Tour hours are 11:30 a.m. and 1:30 and 3:30 p.m. Adult fare is $17; children ages 4 to 11, $12.25. Tickets are sold at the boat, at the visitor center, or on the website.

SCHOONER *PRIDE*
360 Concord St., Aquarium Wharf
(843)-722-1112, (800) 344-4483 (Zerve Ticketing)
www.schoonerpride.com

Ah, here's a fantasy that is delightfully achievable. See Charleston from the water—as countless settlers and 19th-century immigrants saw it—from the decks of a tall ship,

the Schooner *Pride*. She's 84 feet long and US Coast Guard–certified to carry 49 day passengers or 20 overnight guests. The 2-hour cruise of Charleston Harbor costs $31 for adults and children 12 and older and $25 for children under 12. Sunset sails are $39 for adults, and $29 for children under 12.

Experienced sailors and quick learners may help with the ship, or you can simply sit back and enjoy the wind, sea, and unexpected pleasure of almost soundless propulsion. Call for afternoon or evening schedules and reservations. Schooner *Pride* is moored at the Aquarium Wharf directly behind the IMAX on Concord Street. All tours depart from there. Tours are offered spring, summer, and fall.

SPIRITLINE CRUISES
360 Concord St., Ste. 201
(843) 722-2628, (800) 789-3678
www.spiritlinecruises.com

This is the only boat tour from Charleston that actually stops at the Ft. Sumter National Monument, where the Civil War began. Tours leave daily from two locations: The National Park Service Visitor Education Center dock at Liberty Square beside the S.C. Aquarium and Patriots Point in Mount Pleasant. Tour hours vary seasonally, so call for details. Adult rates are $16; seniors are $14.50; rates for children ages 6 to 11, $10.

SpiritLine also has a nonstop Harbor Tour that departs from Liberty Square at Aquarium Wharf and from Patriots Point (only on weekends in Jan and Feb). The tour lasts approximately 1½ hours and cruises past the Battery, Patriots Point Maritime Museum, Castle Pinckney, Fort Sumter, and Fort Johnson. Adults $16; seniors are $14.50; rates for children (age 6 to 11), $10. The dinner cruise is aboard the Spirit of Carolina and departs from Patriots Point at 7 p.m. and returns at 10 p.m. (boarding begins at 6:30 p.m.). A sumptuous 3-course meal is served—prepared to order—with table-side service, spirits, live entertainment, and dancing. Prepaid reservations are required and are made by calling (843) 881-7337. The weekday fare is $48.38 per person; the weekend rate is $53.38, including taxes but not gratuity.

Air Tours

FLYING HIGH OVER CHARLESTON
202 Commons Way, Goose Creek
(843) 569-6148
www.flyinghighovercharleston.com
If getting the "overview" is something you want—literally—there are even a couple of airplane tours available to Charleston area visitors. Jim Ellison is an FAA-licensed commercial pilot with more than 25 years of flying experience in the Charleston area. Package A: Historic Charleston & Sea Island Tour includes historic plantations, harbor and aircraft carrier *Yorktown* views, beautiful beaches and sea islands, The Citadel, Ft. Sumter, Morris Island lighthouse, and 40 miles of ocean coastline vistas in addition to Historic Charleston from the air. This is an hour-plus tour in a photo-friendly airplane. Package B: Taste of Charleston Sightseeing Tour is about 60 minutes in length and slightly more limited in subject matter, but just as exciting. Package C, City of History Tour, is a 50-minute viewing of all of Historic Downtown Charleston plus Patriots Point, Ft. Sumter, and Ft. Moultrie. Package D, City Tour, is a 40-minute tour of the old city, harbor sites, and Mount Pleasant and Sullivan's Island locations. Tours are available seven days a week (weather permitting) and take off from Atlantic Aviation, ¾ mile from Charleston International Airport. The rate for Tour A is $185 for up to 3 passengers; Tour B is $165. Tour C is $145 for up to 3 passengers. Tour D, appropriate for children, goes for $125 for up to 3.

THE ARTS

Some people would tell you the verdict on Charleston and the arts is still out—that after an early, spectacular (even historic) colonial era start, the city fell asleep artistically and has stayed that way since . . . well, the Civil War. Others would have you believe this city, today, is a virtual mecca for experimental and traditional artists of all kinds, if only during Spoleto Festival USA. The truth probably lies somewhere in between. While there have been dormant stretches, there have also been times, such as the 1920s and early '30s, when Charleston experienced artistic stirrings that resulted in truly exciting art.

In literature, there was Charleston's own DuBose Heyward (1885–1940), whose legendary 1925 novel, *Porgy,* inspired a renaissance of artistic effort in and about the city and its people. The story, for those who may not be familiar with it, is based on the life of a poor, crippled black street vendor and his tragic love for an abused, drug-addicted woman. The novelist's playwright wife, Dorothy, co-wrote the successful stage play that opened on Broadway in 1927.

In 1926 none other than George Gershwin—already famous for "Rhapsody in Blue" and bound for immortality as the composer of dozens of American musical standards—was fascinated by the story. He felt *Porgy* was just the vehicle he was looking for to create a new art form: the American folk opera.

Although it took several years to finally put it on the boards, the world-famous work known as *Porgy and Bess* was at last produced by New York's Theatre Guild in 1935. While it was never a staggering financial success (not many things were in 1935), the work was universally and artistically acclaimed. Since then, the opera has played all over the world, including in Milan's prestigious La Scala. But no audience could love it more than an audience in Charleston.

OVERVIEW

But what about today? And what is all this Spoleto hoopla about? Following is an introduction to the big event, along with a couple of other popular festivals. After that, we offer listings and information under self-explanatory headings: Festivals, Organizations and Venues, Theater, Dance, Music, and Galleries. Unless otherwise noted, all addresses are in Charleston.

FESTIVALS

MOJA ARTS FESTIVAL
180 Meeting St., Ste. 200
(843) 724-7305, (843) 724-7295 (Box Office)
www.mojafestival.com
The MOJA Arts Festival in Sept is the city of Charleston's celebration of the Lowcountry's rich and wonderful heritage from the African and Caribbean cultures. This 10-day

performance schedule offers exciting theater, visual arts, dance, music, films, and lectures.

MOJA is a Swahili word meaning "one" and "unity" or "the source" and "the beginning." Hence, the city's celebration of black arts is indeed appropriately named, as Charleston was the port of entry for thousands of slaves during the 18th and 19th centuries. Their contribution to American culture is clearly enormous. The festival is sponsored by the city's Office of Cultural Affairs and is funded in part by the South Carolina Arts Commission and the National Endowment for the Arts. (See the Annual Events chapter for more on MOJA.)

✳ PICCOLO SPOLETO FESTIVAL
180 Meeting St., Ste. 200
(843) 724-7305
www.piccolospoleto.com
Piccolo Spoleto (Italian for "Little Spoleto") is the city of Charleston's way of saying, "Encore! Encore!" It is Charleston's official companion festival (a series of festivals, really) running concurrently with the internationally acclaimed Spoleto Festival USA.

Piccolo's focus, however, is on local and regional talent of every artistic discipline. There are literally hundreds of events offered every year through Piccolo, most of which are relatively low cost or free. Expect to see performances ranging from chamber music and provocative theater to experimental dance and visual arts.

The city's Office of Cultural Affairs handles the project and sees to it, through its Artreach program, that the festival's high spirits and fine performances are exported to artistically neglected sections of the community. This way, the arts can be experienced by everyone, regardless of economic status or educational background. (For more on Piccolo Spoleto, see the Annual Events chapter.)

✳ SPOLETO FESTIVAL USA
Various locations, 14 George St.
(843) 722-2764, (843) 579-3100 (Box Office)
www.spoletousa.org
Not every newcomer to the Lowcountry is familiar with the city's spectacular May showcase for the arts called Spoleto Festival USA. By the same token, no one stays in Charleston very long before hearing "Spoleto this . . ." and "Spoleto that. . . ."

For openers, know that Spoleto (pronounced spo-LAY-toe, like tomato) is the New World counterpart to the summertime arts extravaganza in Spoleto, Italy, called the "Festival of Two Worlds." The latter was founded back in 1958 by Pulitzer Prize–winning composer–librettist–director Gian Carlo Menotti.

Menotti saw the quaint, medieval town of Spoleto's rich architectural heritage, suitable performing facilities, and central European location (about 60 miles north of Rome) as the perfect backdrop for an interdisciplinary arts celebration. There, he created a world-famous showcase and exchange for international talent, both young and old, rich and poor.

By 1977, Menotti was looking for an American home for his festival, and for many of the same reasons he chose Spoleto, Italy, he thought Charleston could neatly fill the bill here in America. With support and encouragement from Charleston Mayor Joseph P. Riley Jr., other important members of the local community, and the then-well-funded National Endowment for the Arts, Spoleto Festival USA premiered as a two-week explosion of opera, jazz, theater, visual arts, and dance, including classical ballet. It explored new ways to look at traditional works as well as the cutting-edge and the avant garde. Tickets to Spoleto events are sold in packages as well as for individual events. They aren't inexpensive, but much of Spoleto's infectious enthusiasm is palpable on the city streets—that is, free, and available to everyone.

Almost anyone would agree that Charleston takes on a special glow during the festival. Maybe the illumination comes from the corps of international critics who review performances daily in a special section of *The Post and Courier* or from the crowded restaurants and traffic-clogged streets. Perhaps it's the joyful noises that seem to be floating on the air all over town, the street performers, the sudden profusion of sidewalk art galleries, and the excitement of a population swollen with young, animated, talented people. But for whatever reasons, Spoleto is a time of great fun and good art. Don't miss it.

i The Spoleto finale concert at Middleton Place is a great site for an all-day picnic. Go early, and spread out a blanket to reserve your spot on the open greensward before the orchestra shell. Eat, drink, and toss the Frisbee all afternoon. Stroll the magnificent gardens. Then settle down for a great evening of festival music followed by spectacular fireworks under the stars.

When the festival is over, and alas, they pack up the sets and costumes and truck them off to distant parts, take heart. The arts in Charleston—and by that we mean a number of quality offerings—don't completely cease.

They just slow down a bit after those hectic weeks of intense saturation. We try to think of it this way: The spirit of Spoleto fosters the development of greater and more appreciative audiences for arts activities in and around Charleston throughout the year. (See the Annual Events chapter for more on Spoleto.)

ORGANIZATIONS & VENUES

CITY OF CHARLESTON OFFICE OF CULTURAL AFFAIRS
180 Meeting St., Ste. 200
(843) 724-7305
www.charleston-sc.gov

The city of Charleston devotes this office to advocating, providing services for, and helping fund the various arts organizations that contribute to promoting the city. They provide assistance and grants to arts groups and maintain a full year-round calendar of arts events. The Office of Cultural Affairs also maintains the revolving exhibits of the City Gallery in the Dock Street Theatre and the Waterfront Park. It produces the MOJA Arts Festival each fall and Piccolo Spoleto in the spring.

NORTH CHARLESTON COLISEUM
5001 Coliseum Dr., North Charleston
(843) 529-5000
www.coliseumpac.com

This beautiful venue has already helped put the Lowcountry on the map for many nationally known performing arts groups. Opened in 1993, the much-anticipated North Charleston Coliseum is the largest and most diverse indoor entertainment facility in South Carolina. Various seating configurations are possible, but, generally speaking, the Coliseum's capacity is 14,000 seats. Because of this, Greater Charleston is now a viable audience for some of the biggest traveling shows and sports attractions in America. The Coliseum has attracted the likes of Rod Stewart, Neil Diamond, the Ringling Brothers and Barnum and Bailey Circus, James Taylor, Metallica, World Cup figure skating, NHL hockey, and NCAA basketball, to name just a few. The Coliseum is also the permanent home of the South Carolina Stingrays hockey club. (See the Spectator Sports chapter.) Tickets for all Coliseum events may be purchased at the Coliseum box office at (843) 529-5000, ext. 5113. To get to the Coliseum, take the Montague Avenue exit off I-26, and follow the signs, or take the Montague Avenue exit off I-526 (Mark Clark Expressway).

NORTH CHARLESTON CULTURAL ARTS PROGRAM
Sterett Hall (P.O. Box 190016, North Charleston, SC 29419-9016)
(843) 740-5854
www.northcharleston.org
The Cultural Arts Program for North Charleston was created in 1979 to plan for and support artistic and cultural activities throughout the community. It provides programs and services intended to enhance the quality of life for citizens and assists in the cultural and economic development of the area. The Cultural Arts Program is located in the North Charleston Cultural & Civic Complex, formerly Sterett Hall, on the former Charleston Navy Base, and many of its performances are held in the Park Circle Auditorium.

The program's other offerings include the North Charleston City Gallery in the Charleston Area Convention Center Complex at 5001 Coliseum Dr. Gallery hours are daily from 9 a.m. to 5 p.m. The Dinner Theatre series in the Embassy Ballroom at the Convention Center Complex is another popular

feature. By far the largest project undertaken through the program is the annual North Charleston Arts Festival, held every May. Most events and parking are free (some tickets cost up to $20) at this 9-day extravaganza mounted in the North Charleston Coliseum. The festival is a kaleidoscope of color and images with original artwork, photography, arts, and crafts plus live entertainment and food concessions.

THEATER

In the 18th century, when Charles Towne was the capital of the colonial province and a thriving port of entry, there were reports in England that it was "the gayest, politest, and richest place in America," so naturally it follows that Charles Towne was one of the first American towns to patronize the cultural arts—including the world of drama.

According to Eola Willis and her copious 1933 study of the city's early theatrical life, *The Charleston Stage in the XVIII Century*, drama was alive and well here as early as the 1730s. The city's first newspaper, the *Charleston Gazette*, described at some length the theatrical season of 1734. That year on Jan 18, the *Gazette* carried the following notice: "On Friday the 24th instant, in the Court-Room will be attempted a Tragedy called 'The Orphan, or the Unhappy Marriage.' Tickets will be delivered out on Tuesday next at Mr. Shepheard's at 40s each."

Apparently, the season's opening performance was a hit, because on February 8, the *Gazette* published its first review, in which the prologue to *The Orphan* was reprinted in its entirety. Quickly following on February 18, *The Opera of Flora* or *Hob in the Well* opened with the dance of the two Pierrots and the pantomime of Harlequin and Scaramouch. This was another first for Charleston theater—the first time a musical play had been performed on American shores. Apparently, the theatrical life of Charleston was off and running by 1734 and shines just as brilliantly today.

＊DOCK STREET THEATRE
135 Church St.
(843) 720-3968, Box Office: (843) 965-4032
www.charlestonstage.com

Much ado is made about Charleston's many firsts, not the least of which is the story about the Dock Street Theatre being the first and oldest theater in America.

Let's split hairs here just for accuracy's sake. It has been academically determined that the first theater in America was erected in Williamsburg, Virginia, in the second decade of the 18th century. The second was built in New York in 1732. The third was in Charles Towne in 1736, while poor old Philadelphia didn't have a playhouse until 1749.

In the early 18th century, certain buildings were called theaters, though they were no more than "long rooms"—rooms big enough to hold an audience. These places lacked a traditional stage and other theatrical facilities. The 1734 production of *The Orphan*, for instance, was actually performed in a courtroom—just such a place.

Charleston's first (technical) theater was on the site of the old Planters Hotel on Church Street, which was then the only major route running the entire length of the city. It ended at White Point, which is now known as the Battery. (See more on the Battery in the Attractions chapter.) Thus, Church Street was the thoroughfare for all the traffic to and from the bustling and noisy docks. It made good sense to build a theater near this main traffic route, so in 1736, the first

building was constructed on the south side of Queen (then called Dock) Street, just a little west of heavily traveled Church Street. Records show it was less than 100 yards from the Huguenot church and St. Philip's Episcopal Church. It was said to have had a stage, pit boxes, and a gallery. Some ill fate likely soon befell this building, because no mention of it is found after 1737.

Eventually, a second theater was constructed nearby, and an early hotel was built on the rear portion of the old theater lot. The year was 1800. It was called the Planters Hotel because it was popular lodging for Lowcountry planters and their families, who would traditionally leave their plantations at certain times of the year. It was customary to be in town for the winter social season and for Race Week, an exponent of Charleston's torrid 19th-century love affair with horse racing. In 1835, the Planters Hotel was remodeled and expanded.

The old Planters Hotel is the structure that was still standing but in ruins when, in the 1930s, the New Deal's Works Progress Administration, giving work to unemployed architects and craftspeople during the Depression, rebuilt it as the theater we know today. Technically, it is the oldest building still standing that was part of a colonial theatrical enterprise. But the charming stage proscenium and the handsome paneled boxes we encounter today in the Dock Street were not around for the prologue to *The Orphan*—not in 1734, anyway. It would be more than 200 years later, on November 26, 1937, that Charleston's own DuBose Heyward, already famous for *Porgy*, would write a special dedication to reopen a new facility. The reconstructed theater was called the Dock Street in honor of those early Charleston productions on the site.

None of the above, of course, takes anything away from Dock Street Theatre's enormous popularity and charm or the tremendously important role it plays in the theatrical life of the city today.

The reconstruction of the Dock Street auditorium recaptures the spirit of early Georgian theaters. It seats 463 people, with a pit and a parquet of 13 boxes. The walls are paneled with natural local black cypress, rubbed soft and mellow. The wood was treated with an old formula of iron filings dissolved in vinegar and then waxed to bring out the grain. The lighting fixtures carry out the feeling of candle brackets, and the cove ceiling has exceptional acoustic properties, as did many theaters of the time. Over the stage hangs a carved wood bas-relief of the Royal Arms of England (obligatory in all Georgian theaters), duplicated from an original that still hangs above the altar in Goose Creek's chapel of ease, built in 1711.

The Dock Street's stage has a proscenium opening of 34 feet (somewhat larger than the original would have had) and features an apron forestage with "proscenium doors" on either side. This is typical of Georgian theaters. Today's Dock Street stage floor is flat, whereas the original was most likely tilted. The rebuilt Dock Street was never intended to be a museum piece or an exact reconstruction. It is, however, a modern theater capable of handling a wide variety of productions, and an integral part of Charleston's rich cultural life.

After dutiful service for some 70 years, the venerable theatre was due for a facelift. The Dock Street Theatre closed in 2007 for three years, re-opening for the third time in 2010 after a $19 million renovation. This major renovation brought 21st-century state-of-the-art improvements to the theater to include new lighting and sound, seating, temperature control, and upfitting for seismic security and handicapped accessibility.

Acting Companies

Whether you're a confirmed theater patron, an experienced actor, or just a thespian wannabe, there's a Lowcountry theater company that will interest you. Some of these companies are long-standing members of the Greater Charleston arts community; others are embryonic or just getting off the ground. A new website for the League of Charleston Theatres, www.theatrecharleston.com, provides current information on most of the theater groups in the area or you may call (843) 813-8578 for more information.

The College of Charleston's multi-award-winning theater department is flourishing, with four groups currently taking bows. The work is first-rate, and these quality productions stand out as some of the best bargains in town. All college productions are mounted in various venues in the Simons Center for the Arts at 54 St. Philip St. and the Chapel Theatre at 172 Calhoun St. on campus. Thumbnail sketches of some of our local theater groups follow.

ART FORMS & THEATRE CONCEPTS
P.O. Box 20130, Charleston, SC 29413
(843) 723-5399, (843) 724-7295 (Box Office)
www.aftcinc.com
This exciting African-American theater group has more than a decade of successful productions behind it, including August Wilson's *Joe Turner's Come and Gone* and *Seven Guitars* and the Fats Waller musical *Ain't Misbehavin'.* The members are always busy preparing for their next MOJA production or Piccolo Spoleto performance. The director is actor,

director, playwright Art Gilliard. Call for more details.

CENTER STAGE SIMONS CENTER FOR THE ARTS
54 St. Philip St.
(843) 953-6306
www.cofc.edu/theatre
Center Stage is the College of Charleston student organization that, together with the school's Theatre Department, produces a varied season from Oct through Apr in the Simons Center's flexible and highly creative "black box" Theatre 220. Productions are staged and directed by faculty and guest directors. Admission is free for College of Charleston students and $10 for the general public. For more information, call the number listed above.

CHARLESTON STAGE COMPANY
P.O. Box 356, Charleston, SC 29402
(843) 577-7183
www.charlestonstage.com
This group presents a full season of family-oriented plays and children's theater from Sept through Apr in the the historic Dock Street Theatre. It also offers various educational programs that explore stage management, scene study, projection, and creative dramatics for beginners and advanced students. Volunteers are encouraged to contact the theater to become involved. For ticket information, call (843) 577-7183.

FLOWERTOWN PLAYERS
133 South Main St., Summerville
(843) 875-9251
www.flowertownplayers.org
This is a community theater in Summerville whose educational and literary objectives are to stimulate interest in the arts, music, literature, and drama in people of all ages. It has a regular season of productions and its own home facility, The James F. Dean Theatre, in downtown Summerville. Volunteers are welcome. Call the theater for more information.

THE FOOTLIGHT PLAYERS
20 Queen St.
(843) 722-7521, (843) 722-4487 (Box Office)
www.footlightplayers.net
This group enjoys strong support from Charleston's theater community for its long-standing record of exposing local audiences to interesting, instructive, and cultural plays that are in keeping with Charleston's traditional mores. Since the early 1940s, the Footlight Players have performed in a converted cotton warehouse (ca. 1840) on Queen Street, easily one of the city's most charming theatrical venues. Production director is Richard Heffner. Volunteers are welcome. Call for additional information.

MAIN STAGE
Simons Center for the Arts,
54 St. Philip St.
(843) 953-6306
www.cofc.edu/theatre
Main Stage is a series of several plays produced each semester that are exclusively directed and designed by faculty from the college's department of theater. Productions—often of classical or traditional works such as Shakespeare's *Macbeth* and Ibsen's *Ghosts*—are at the College of Charleston's Emmett Robinson Theater. For production information, call (843) 953-6306, or the box office at (843) 943-5604.

PURE THEATRE
P.O. Box 448, Charleston, SC 29402
(843) 723-4444, (866) 811-4111
(OvationTix)
www.puretheatre.org

PURE Theatre has quickly garnered notice in Charleston's theatre community for its commitment to quality and excellence in its productions. It is a small professional theatre focused on producing new plays by contemporary playwrights as well as new interpretations of established works. PURE Theatre's mission is to create theatre experiences that "enliven thought, ignite dialogue, and expand consciousness," and they have received audience and critical acclaim and awards for their efforts. Their venue is the Charleston Ballet Theatre at 477 King St. in downtown Charleston. Call the numbers above or visit the website for the upcoming performance schedule.

ROBERT IVEY BALLET PRODUCTIONS
1910 Savannah Hwy.
(843) 556-1343
www.robertiveyballet.com

Although Robert Ivey Ballet is primarily a dance company with a full-time studio, this production operation offers popular musicals on a fairly regular basis. For theater productions, open auditions are held, usually in the fall. Their performance venue is the Sottile Theatre at 44 George St., just off King. Call for more information on ballet, modern, and jazz dance instruction at the Charleston Dance Studio.

SHAKESPEARE PROJECT AT THE
   COLLEGE OF CHARLESTON
College of Charleston, Simons Center for the Arts, 172 Calhoun St.
(843) 953-5604
www.cofc.edu/theatre

This college-sponsored Shakespeare group sponsors performances by student and community-based actors. The plays are presented in Sept at the Chapel Theatre, and shortened versions are performed in local schools and other venues. There's general seating, with adult tickets costing $15, student seating, $10.

THE VILLAGE PLAYHOUSE
730 Coleman Blvd. Mount Pleasant
(843) 856-1579
www.villageplayhouse.com

In a very short time, The Village Playhouse has grown into a vital performing arts organization, offering more than 150 nights of theater to the East Cooper community each season. The company brings a diverse selection of drama, comedy, and musicals, both classics and new works, to area residents and visitors. Ticket prices range from $20 to $30 for these popular productions. Call or visit the website for more details on upcoming performances.

DANCE

Dance Companies

*CHARLESTON BALLET THEATRE
477 King St.
(843) 723-7334
www.charlestonballet.org

This energetic group presents professional dance concerts in Charleston and throughout the Southeast. Performances include such classics as *The Nutcracker, Sleeping Beauty,* and *Swan Lake,* as well as contemporary works. Call Don or Patricia Cantwell, artistic directors, for more information. The group's resident facility, near the visitor center, includes a 300-seat theater space, public parking, and spacious studios. Charleston

Ballet offers an annual series. For box office information, call the number above.

Dance Schools

In a town that gave its name to a famous dance step that put flappers of the '20s on the world map, it should be no surprise that Charleston is still the scene for a variety of dancing and dance instruction. Below we have listed some good schools, but we encourage new residents to also check with your local area's recreation department and/ or continuing education programs.

BALLET ACADEMY OF CHARLESTON
1662 Savannah Hwy.
(843) 769-6932
www.ballet-academy.org
Ballet Academy of Charleston is under the direction of Corina Fimian, who now directs the school founded by Mara Meir, former ballerina with Ballet de Paris and prima ballerina of the Israeli Opera. This is a fee-based school offering scheduled semesters of classical ballet training for children ages 4 to 17, with separate adult classes. Trial classes for children are offered. No recital performances are held. Instead, parents view their children's progress through regularly scheduled, end-of-year open classes and periodic conferences with the director.

CHARLESTON BALLET STUDIO
477 King St.
(843) 723-7334
www.charlestonballet.org
This school is affiliated with the professional dance company Charleston Ballet Theatre. Classes and workshops are offered for ages 3 through adult, and performances—a serious goal for serious students—are held at the Gaillard Municipal Auditorium, Sottile

Theater, and the North Charleston Performing Arts Center as well as their own CBT Black Box Theatre.

CHARLESTON DANCE STUDIO, ROBERT IVEY BALLET
1910 Savannah Hwy.
(843) 556-1343
www.robertiveyballet.com
Robert Ivey, a professional dancer and artist-in-residence at the College of Charleston's School of the Arts, directs this dance company and school. His professional instructors teach classes in ballet, jazz, and dance exercise. The school has a nurturing attitude toward children, and their families and friends appreciate the seasonal performances that let the students show off their talents. His groups also perform frequently at College of Charleston events and have represented the city and the United States in international competitions.

MUSIC

CHARLESTON COMMUNITY BAND
P.O. Box 30274, Charleston, SC 29417
(843) 849-6121
www.charlestoncommunityband.com
Started in 1977, this all-volunteer concert band of around 75 members performs 15 free concerts a year throughout the greater Charleston area. Some of their regular performances are Memorial Day, Carolina Day, July 4th, The Citadel graduation, Christmas tree lighting in Marion Square, and Towne Centre in Mount Pleasant. This group of brass, woodwind, and percussion players provides a wonderful opportunity for talented local adults to continue their musical pursuits after finishing high school. Call the number listed above to speak with Conductor Todd Jenkins for more information.

i Opera lovers take note: The Charleston County Public Library at 68 Calhoun St. sponsors high-definition simulcasts of the Metropolitan Opera season. Shown in the library's auditorium, the productions are held on Saturdays and are free. Visit www.ccpl.org for dates and times.

*CHARLESTON CONCERT ASSOCIATION
131 King St.
(843) 727-1216
www.charlestonconcerts.org

The Charleston Concert Association (CCA) is Charleston's oldest nonprofit presenting arts organization. Founded in 1936 as a sister organization with the Charleston Symphony Orchestra (CSO), CCA's original mission was to bring internationally acclaimed musicians to Charleston as a complement to CSO. Back in 1931, the symphony's aim was to create an avenue for local musicians to develop their skills.

Today, the CCA's mission is to provide local access to classical artists of international caliber throughout the year (whereas Spoleto Festival USA is a more concentrated exposure of only 2 weeks). In recent years, the CCA has expanded its vision to include all of the performing arts, including theater and film as well as dance. Among the CCA's recent presentations were the highly acclaimed Opera Verdi Europa, Orpheus Chamber Orchestra, Les Ballets de Monte-Carlo, the Warsaw Philharmonic, Vienna Boys Choir, and the Duke Ellington Orchestra. Tickets are sold by subscription to the series, and individual prices range from $16 to $68. Call the number above for subscription rates and concert season details. Area Publix supermarkets are ticket outlets as well.

CHARLESTON SYMPHONY ORCHESTRA
145 King St., Ste. 311
(843) 723-7528
www.charlestonsymphony.com

Charleston has a long, rich, and varied musical history. Records indicate several different orchestras were organized in the city during the years from 1819 to 1919. Today's organization, known as the Charleston Symphony Orchestra, has been in existence for more than 75 years.

In December 1936, Miss Maud Winthrup Gibbon and Mrs. Martha Laurens Patterson founded what is known today as the Charleston Symphony Orchestra, and they presented a concert in Hibernian Hall on Meeting Street. The orchestra provided music for the official grand opening of the newly-restored Dock Street Theatre in 1936, and the Dock Street in turn became the orchestra's official home for its first 3 years. Through the 1940s and 1950s, Memminger Auditorium was home for the group, as it brought in such famous artists as Robert Merrill, Jan Pierce, Blanche Theirbom, and Eleanor Steber. The orchestra played under the batons of conductors J. Albert Frecht, Tony Hadgi, Don Mills, and, from 1962 to 1982, Lucien DeGroote.

In the late 1970s, the orchestra emerged as a fully professional organization with the employment of a core of full-time, conservatory-trained, first-chair players. The orchestra achieved "metropolitan" status in the American Symphony Orchestra League and adopted Gaillard Auditorium as its official home. In 1984 David Stahl became music director and conductor. Under his leadership, the CSO has become one of the leading arts organizations in the Southeast. A resident orchestra of about 46 professional musicians now performs a demanding concert schedule on stage and throughout the community, including special events and school programs throughout the state from Sept through May.

The orchestra has several major concert series—Masterworks, Charleston Pops, Dock Street Theatre Concerts, and Young People's Concerts. In addition, the CSO performs other special concerts that cover a broad range of musical tastes.

Individual ticket sales are handled through the Gaillard Auditorium box office at 77 Calhoun St., or by calling (843) 723-7528, ext. 110, or the website, or at any Publix supermarket. Ticket prices vary according to the series, but they range from $20 to $60 for individual concerts.

**CHARLESTON SYMPHONY ORCHESTRA
   LEAGUE**
145 King St., Ste. 311
(843) 722-0020
www.csolinc.org
Although it's mostly known in the community as sponsor of the annual Symphony Gala and the Symphony Designer Showhouse, the 400-member Charleston Symphony Orchestra League serves its namesake group in many ways. (See the Annual Events chapter for more on the Designer Showhouse.)

Through fund-raising events, the league provides major financial support to the orchestra. It annually awards scholarships to orchestra musicians for advanced study and to school-age musicians who are members of the Charleston County Youth Orchestra. Members volunteer many hours of service in the CSO office promoting the orchestra and aiding in the sale of season tickets, and they also serve as concert ushers. The league welcomes anyone wishing to join and support the CSO.

i The easiest ways to get the best tickets to major arts events in Charleston are to become a patron of that arts organization, participate in their annual fund-raising drive, or buy series tickets whenever possible.

CSO CHORUS
145 King St., Ste. 311
(843) 723-7528
www.cso-chorus.org
First organized in 1978 as the CSO Singers Guild, to be the choral complement of the Charleston Symphony Orchestra, this group is now called the CSO Chorus. The group performs with the CSO in major works several times a year. In addition to the large concert group of nearly 125 singers, there are 2 smaller performance groups that appear throughout the season. The Chamber Singers, under the direction of Robert Taylor, perform 20th-century music. Participation in CSO Chorus groups is by regularly scheduled audition. Call Dr. Taylor at (843) 953-8231.

EAST COOPER CONCERT SERIES
P.O. Box 279, Mount Pleasant, SC 29464
(843) 881-9350, (843) 884-9090
www.ecmow.org
This annual 7-concert series, scheduled from Sept through May at Christ Episcopal Church, benefits Meals on Wheels. Admission to all concert events is a monetary donation. Performers include various ensembles from the Charleston Symphony Orchestra, visiting concert choirs, and individual artists. The church is at 2304 US 17 N. in Mount Pleasant. Contact Marne Rummler for scheduling and more details at the number above.

INTERNATIONAL PIANO SERIES
College of Charleston, 44 George St. (Sottile Theatre)
(843) 953-6575
www.cofc.edu/music
Since 1989, the School of the Arts at the College of Charleston has had an annual International Piano Series that's also open to the general public. The series was designed to introduce students and the Charleston community to an array of fine, established performers from around the world. This is a major inspiration to music students on campus who have come from as far away as Spain, Korea, China, and Costa Rica to study in the college's piano performance program. All concerts are at 8 p.m. in the Sottile Theatre on George Street just off King, and admission is $20 at the door. Call the number above for a performance schedule and a calendar of School of the Arts events.

MONDAY NIGHT CONCERT SERIES
College of Charleston, Simons Center for the Arts, 54 St. Philip St. (Recital Hall)
(843) 953-8228
www.cofc.edu/music
This is one of those little gems that few people know about, and yet it's one of the best arts events going on in the city. These regularly scheduled Monday night concerts are usually presented in the Simons Center Recital Hall and feature faculty and adjunct faculty talent, and advanced students from the music department. The programs vary from jazz to Renaissance music, from organ concerts to choral works from the College's Concert Choir (at the Cathedral of St. Luke and St. Paul, 126 Coming St.). The overall quality of the concerts is always quite wonderful, and the admission price of $10 (free for College of Charleston students) can't be

beat. Call the School of the Arts for more information and specific concert schedules.

GALLERIES

With so much history and architecture to brag about, Charleston may not be terribly famous for its art. But the fact is the city has produced a number of fine artists over the years. The charming illustrations Elizabeth O'Neill Verner created from the 1920s to 1940s were certainly not the first artistic views of the city to catch the public's eye, but they were (and still are) among the most popular. Other great talents include Charles Fraser and Samuel Morse (the inventor of the telegraph), who were portraitists working here. Some of the works of those artists are on display at the Gibbes Museum of Art. (See the Other Museums section of the Attractions chapter.)

Today, downtown Charleston hosts an amazing array of fine art galleries that expand the view and viewpoint far beyond the city Elizabeth O'Neill Verner loved to draw. Generally, when you're browsing in any of the downtown galleries, you're within easy walking distance of another . . . and another . . . and another. All are free to enter.

The serious shopper with an appetite to see more than just a few galleries may want to park the car and use Charleston's DASH shuttle system between stops. If you decide to give it a try, take the Meeting–King Street route. (For more on DASH, see the Getting Here, Getting Around chapter.)

THE AUDUBON GALLERY
190 King St.
(843) 853-1100
www.audubonart.com
This is one of Charleston's best galleries for the natural history and sporting art

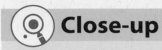 **Close-up**

Philip Simmons & the Wrought-Iron Connection

The lacy wrought-iron gates, grills, and balconies seen throughout Charleston punctuate the city's eloquent architectural statement. Many of them are original 18th-century works still in situ—proud survivors of a nearly lost art. But Charleston's **wrought-iron artwork,** thanks to a man named **Philip Simmons,** is still being practiced and (perhaps more important) being taught to young artisans. Born in 1912 in the city's Mazyck-Wraggborough neighborhood (see the Neighborhoods chapter), the young Philip Simmons learned the ironworking trade from his father, who learned it from his father, and so on, back through time. Indeed, Philip Simmons is an example of Charleston's rich heritage in the arts passed on through the African-American community since the days of slavery. His works have long been recognized for their fine sense of scale, balance, and craftsmanship. Mr. Simmons was a recipient of the American Folklife Award, the highest honor bestowed on folk artists in America. He is in South Carolina's Hall of Fame, and his work has been exhibited in major museums and galleries throughout the United States. Today, more than 300 documented works by Philip Simmons—gates, fences, railings, and window guards—are scattered throughout Charleston. They meld handsomely with the surviving antique works and add a meaningful continuum to the city's architectural and aesthetic history.

enthusiast! You'll find old and new limited-edition nature prints, Audubon prints, 19th-century city views, engravings, and antique plates. It also offers museum-quality framing and conservation services. Hours are 10 a.m. to 5 p.m. Mon through Sat.

BIRDS I VIEW GALLERY
119-A Church St.
(843) 723-1276, (843) 766-2108
www.anneworshamrichardson.com
Anne Worsham Richardson is a South Carolina artist and naturalist recognized across America for her wildlife paintings—especially her birds. Richardson has received many honors over the years, including induction into the South Carolina Hall of Fame at Myrtle Beach. Gallery hours are Mon through Sat from 10 a.m. to 5 p.m.

✳**CAROLINA ANTIQUE MAPS**
  AND PRINTS, LLC
91 Church St.
(843) 722-4773
www.carolinaantiqueprints.com
This shop exclusively carries those handsome and fascinating antique maps, prints, and botanicals that make such a striking addition to an office, library, or study. Some of these maps originate from the 16th to the 19th century and depict various locations, both local and international. Of added interest is the shop's location—in Cabbage Row, which Dubose Heyward, along with George Gershwin, immortalized as "Catfish Row" in the folk opera *Porgy and Bess.* Hours are Tues through Sat, 11 a.m. to 5 p.m. or by special appointment.

✳CAROLINA GALLERIES
106-A Church St.
(843) 720-8622
www.carolinagalleries.com
This gallery specializes in pre-1945 American art (including a fine selection from Charleston's own renaissance period) and what's called sporting art. Carolina Prints has been putting artists and collectors together since 1963. You'll find a wonderful selection of works by Alfred Hutty, Alice Smith, Anna Heyward Taylor, and Elizabeth O'Neill Verner, plus antique prints, original paintings, and sculpture. The gallery carries Audubon prints and architectural drawings too. The staff is qualified to act as framing consultants. Hours are Mon through Sat from 11 a.m. to 6 p.m., or by appointment.

✳CHARLESTON ARTIST GUILD
  GALLERY
160 East Bay St.
(843) 722-2425
www.charlestonartistguild.com
With over 70 artists' work on display, the Charleston Artist Guild Gallery has something to appeal to all artistic tastes from traditional to contemporary. The ever-changing work on display includes original paintings in oil, pastel, and watercolor; photography; and fiber art. The Charleston Artist Guild was founded in 1953 and is dedicated to serving the arts community of Charleston. They conduct workshops for the practicing artist, offer lectures for the burgeoning collector, and provide other opportunities for arts education. The Guild holds an annual Signature Show and annual Holiday Show which are juried exhibitions open to artists across the state. They also work with the City of Charleston Office of Cultural Affairs in sponsoring the Piccolo Spoleto Juried Exhibition,

a display of over 100 pieces of artwork seen by thousands of residents and visitors during the Spoleto Festival. (See Annual Events for more on the Piccolo and Spoleto Festivals.) Their Spring and Fall Sidewalk Art Shows are the longest-running art events of their kind in Charleston. Prices for original art are really good here, and even better—a portion of the proceeds goes to their community outreach programs and funding for art scholarships for talented high school students.

CHARLESTON CRAFTS INC.
161 Church St.
(843) 723-2938
www.charlestoncrafts.org
This gallery, across the street from Tommy Condon's Restaurant, showcases the works of South Carolina's finest craft artists. Exhibits include works in clay, fiber, wood, jewelry, metals, glass, photography, paper, traditional crafts, basketry, leather, toys, and even soap making, with exhibitors chosen by a jury of other artists and gallery owners. Charleston Crafts offers a wide variety of gifts—from traditional to contemporary, from utilitarian to decorative, from affordable to exclusive. Demonstrations and featured craft artists change every week. Hours are from Mon through Sun from 10 a.m. to 6 p.m.

CHARLESTON FRAME WORKS
  AND GALLERY
738 St. Andrews Blvd.
(843) 556-9373
Across the Ashley River about a mile down St. Andrews Boulevard, this gallery is making a name for itself as a source for affordable artwork. Prematted and framed prints and posters are featured here. There is a custom framing department that's well stocked and creative. Hours are Mon through Fri from 10 a.m. to 5:30 p.m. and Sat by appointment.

✳CHARLESTON RENAISSANCE GALLERY

103 Church St.
(843) 723-0025
www.fineartsouth.com

This charming gallery is at the intersection of St. Michael's Alley and Church Street. Restructured to present a mix of old and new works, it appeals to visitors from all over the world as well as local Charlestonians. It features 19th-century Southern masterworks and the art of the Charleston renaissance period (1920s and 1930s). Among the gallery's contemporary works are paintings by William Halsey, Jonathan Green, and Linda Fantuzzo. For a complete list of artists represented, visit their website. Gallery hours are Mon through Sat, 10 a.m. to 5 p.m.

CITY GALLERY AT WATERFRONT PARK

34 Prioleau St.
(843) 958-6484
www.charleston-sc.gov

The City Gallery at Waterfront Park is a wonderful venue for local, regional, national, and international talent with an emphasis on contemporary and innovative visual art. The city's mission here is to broaden the Charleston art outlook through a series of six to eight rotating exhibits each year. The glass-walled second and third stories of the building next to the Waterfront Park offer stunning views of the harbor to boot. The hours are Tues through Fri, 11 a.m. to 6 p.m.; Sat and Sun, noon to 5 p.m.

COLEMAN FINE ART

79 Church St.
(843) 853-7000
www.colemanfineart.com

This is the needle in the haystack for anyone looking for an art restoration specialist. Services include cleaning and revarnishing damaged or dirty oil paintings, plus museum and custom framing for art of all kinds. It carries children's books illustrated by Mary Whyte plus other original works and some limited-edition prints as well. Commissions are accepted for portraits. Hours are Mon 10 a.m. to 4 p.m. and Tues through Sat 10 a.m. to 6 p.m. or by appointment.

CONE 10 STUDIOS

1080-B Morrison Dr.
(843) 853-3345
www.cone10studios.com

Those with a penchant for pottery, sculpture, jewelry, handmade paper, and more, will enjoy this studio featuring potters and artists from across the country. This is a working studio, as well, so even the uninitiated can enjoy watching the creative process or take part in lessons in wheelthrowing and clay sculpture. They also offer studio memberships for experienced potters. Located in the newly coined "NoMo" (North of Morrison Drive) area of Charleston, hours are Mon through Sat, 10 a.m. to 5 p.m.; Sun, 1 to 5 p.m. or by appointment.

✳CORRIGAN GALLERY, LLC

62 Queen St.
(843) 722-9878
www.corrigangallery.com

The Corrigan Gallery opened in 2005, presenting what artist/owner Lese Corrigan describes as "art with a future and backed by intellectual process." Located in the heart of the historic district, the gallery combines the charm of the old city of Charleston with a look to the future. Paintings, drawings, fine art prints, photography, and sculpture in a range of prices be purchased here. Some of the artists represented include Manning

Williams, Candice Flewharty, Kevin Bruce Parent, John Moore, Mary Walker, Kristi Ryba, Lynne Riding, Sue Simons Wallace, Daryl Knox, Richard Hagerty, and Lese Corrigan. The gallery is open Mon through Sat from 10 a.m. to 5 p.m. and also by appointment.

ELLA WALTON RICHARDSON FINE ART GALLERY
58 Broad St.
(843) 722-3660
www.ellarichardson.com
Located in an architecturally impressive building on Broad Street, this gallery seems especially blessed in its convenient downtown location. Artistically, however, the gallery is far reaching in its wonderful representation of contemporary American, Dutch, Korean, and Russian artists specializing in classical realist and impressionistic art. Wildlife sculpture, jewelry, and photography join the selection of paintings by nearly a dozen artists with impressive regional and national credentials. Hours are Mon through Sat, 10 a.m. to 5 p.m., or by appointment.

EVA CARTER GALLERY
6696 Bears Bluff Rd.
(843) 557-0006
www.evacartergallery.com
Relocated to her idyllic Wadmalaw Island setting from her former gallery downtown on East Bay, is now Eva Carter's own River Studio displaying her bold abstract-expressionist paintings. Her sophistication in the arrangement of line, color, space, and texture creates emotional intensity in her unique work. One of Charleston's better-known artists, Eva Carter's work is a must-see for contemporary art lovers. Her work is also shown around the country at galleries in Santa Fe, NM; Laguna Beach, CA; and Highlands, NC. Eva's studio

also features abstract works of the late William Halsey and mixed media textile collages by Karen Olah. Hours are by appointment only.

GALLERY CHUMA
43 John St.
(843) 722-7568
www.gallerychuma.com
There is always a colorful and changing collection at this showcase for African and African-American art. Just across from the Charleston Visitor Reception and Transportation Center, the exhibition room features original works from local, national, and international artists. New exhibits are mounted every 2 months. The gallery's prints and custom framing department has more than 1,500 limited-edition prints and posters.

Gallery Chuma also offers a number of educational programs for schools, local community groups, and visitors. These include gallery tours, lectures, poetry readings, meet-the-artist events, classes, workshops, multimedia presentations, and more. African-American heritage tours to areas of historic importance in and around Charleston are offered in conjunction with licensed tour guides. (See the Tours chapter.) Hours are 10 a.m. to 6 p.m. Mon through Sat.

Downstairs, Gallery Chuma features the large-format, stunning imagery of Jonathan Green, famous Gullah artist now of Naples, Florida.

GAYE SANDERS FISHER GALLERY
124 Church St.
(843) 958-0010
www.gayesandersfisher.com
This is the showcase for Gaye Sanders Fisher's imaginative originals in oil and watercolor. The Carolina Lowcountry, its unique

architecture, nature, and color have been Fisher's subjects for over 30 years. She also accepts commissions for a painting of your favorite house. Her work is included in many private and corporate collections throughout the country. Gallery hours are Mon through Sat from 10 a.m. to 5 p.m. and Sun from 1 to 5 p.m.

GORDON WHEELER GALLERY
180 East Bay St.
(843) 722-2546
www.gordonwheeler.net
The gallery of local artist Gordon Wheeler offers original acrylic paintings of Charleston and other Lowcountry scenes. He's mostly known for his commission work, but the shop has limited edition prints and some very popular golf art. Gallery hours are 10 a.m. to 6 p.m. Mon through Sat; 11 a.m. to 5 p.m. Sun.

HALSEY INSTITUTE OF CONTEMPORARY ART, COLLEGE OF CHARLESTON SCHOOL OF THE ARTS
161 Calhoun St.
(843) 953-4422
www.halsey.cofc.edu
The Halsey Gallery, located in the new Marion and Wayland H. Cato, Jr. Center for the Arts, is administered by the School of the Arts at the College of Charleston. It exists to advocate, exhibit, and interpret visual art with an emphasis on contemporary art. In addition to housing seven major exhibitions each year, the gallery serves as an extension of the undergraduate art curricula and sponsors interpretive programs such as accompanying lectures and seminars. While the primary audiences served include the college's students, faculty, and staff, the gallery is open to the public, and participation in its programs is encouraged. Gallery hours vary according to the building's use for performances and school-related functions, but are generally 11 a.m. to 4 p.m. Call for more specific details.

THE HAMLET FINE ART GALLERY
7 Broad St.
(843) 722-1944
www.hamletgallery.com
Only three doors from the Old Exchange building, this is one of the galleries associated with Charleston's famous French Quarter and the many fine art dealers located there. Look here for light, bold watercolors and oils of Charleston scenes and landscapes by more than a dozen new and established artists. Owner Stephanie Shuler Hamlet's mixed media abstracts are intensely colored and vibrant. Hours are Mon through Wed from 11 a.m. to 5 p.m. and Thurs through Sat until 6 p.m.

HORTON HAYES FINE ART
30 State St.
(843) 958-0014
www.hortonhayes.com
Here you'll find fascinating marshscapes and Lowcountry images of shrimpers, crabbers, clammers, and oyster harvesters done in oils, pastels, watercolor, and acrylics. Architectural depictions and still-life paintings are other popular subjects displayed here. The works of Mark Horton are also featured. Gallery hours are Mon through Sat, 10 a.m. to 5:30 p.m. and Sun 12:30 to 5 p.m.

JOHN CARROLL DOYLE ART GALLERY
125 Church St.
(843) 577-7344
www.johncdoyle.com
Visitors to the Market area who stop in at A. W. Shucks for lunch or for oysters and beer

are totally surrounded by the unique work of popular Charleston artist John Doyle. His bold colors and striking figures are filled with life, drama, and his very special treatment of light. Doyle is nationally known for his energetic painting of blues musicians, blue marlins, and blue hydrangeas. John Doyle fine art prints of his work are for sale here too. His gallery also features the work of fellow native Charleston artist Margaret Petterson whose Lowcountry scenes blend old and new, traditional and contemporary. You're invited to visit with the artist as she paints in her studio within the gallery. Gallery hours are Mon through Sat from 10 a.m. to 5 p.m.

LOWCOUNTRY ARTISTS LTD.
148 East Bay St.
(843) 577-9295
www.lowcountryartists.com
A number of local artists operate this gallery on East Bay Street's busy gallery row. The quaint shop has a fine selection of original watercolors, woodcuts, pottery, oils, and prints. The specialty here is Charleston and Lowcountry scenes. You'll also find collages, hand-painted tiles, colored-pencil drawings, linocuts, mono-prints, etchings, and other graphics. Portrait, fine art, and commercial art commissions are welcomed. Every month, one of the participating artists has a show of new works. Hours are Mon through Sat from 11 a.m. to 6 p.m., Sun 1 to 5 p.m., or by appointment.

MARTIN GALLERY
18 Broad St.
(843) 723-7378
www.martingallerycharleston.com
Located in the Grand Salon of the People's Building, here's a showcase for contemporary works by nationally acclaimed artists working in oils and acrylics—including works of Italian master painter Imero Gobbato; bronzes by wildlife sculptor Leo Osborne, marble, bronze, terracotta sculpture by Claire McCardle, and photography by Michael Kahn. Hours are Mon through Sat 10 a.m. to 6 p.m., Sun 11 a.m. to 5 p.m., and by appointment.

MCCALLUM-HALSEY GALLERY AND STUDIOS
20 Fulton St.
(843) 723-5977
www.halseyfoundation.org
Work by longtime Charleston favorites, the late Corrie McCallum and her late husband, William Halsey, is shown at their Fulton Street studio (second right turn off King Street past Charleston Place). The works are primarily in oils but often incorporate interesting textiles (sometimes even objects). Graphics and sculptures are included. William Halsey, by the way, is the artist for whom the College of Charleston named its exhibition gallery in the Marion and Wayland Cato, Jr. Center for the Arts. Hours are by appointment only for the discerning collector.

NINA LIU AND FRIENDS
24 State St.
(843) 722-2724
Nina calls this "a gallery of contemporary art objects." We call it fun. This quaint gallery is quite possibly the heartbeat of Charleston's French Quarter art scene. Her gallery makes bold and changing statements with very distinctive collections of glass, porcelain, jewelry, decorative ceramics, and fiber art. Solo shows by nationally known artists are featured periodically, and you'll find paintings, photography, and sculpture as well. Her gallery/salon, which attracts an international

clientele of shoppers and art patrons, is in a 19th-century town house on State Street. Hours are Mon through Sat from 10 a.m. to 5 p.m. and Sun noon to 5 p.m. or by appointment.

PINK HOUSE GALLERY
17 Chalmers St.
(843) 723-3608
http://pinkhousegallery.tripod.com
In one of the city's most picturesque buildings (first used in 1694 as a tavern), this quaint gallery features architecturals, wildlife, and florals. Look here for original works by Alice Stewart Grimsley, Nancy Wycoff Rushing, Audrey Price, Bruce Krucke, and Alexandria H. Bennington. Ravenel Gaillard's remarkable Lowcountry plantation scenes are featured here, as well. Works are shown on all three floors, and special exhibits are held in the courtyard just off the cobblestone street. Hours are Mon through Sat, 10 a.m. to 5 p.m.

SMITH KILLIAN FINE ART
9 Queen St.
(843) 853-0708
www.smithkillian.com
Treat your eyes to the bold colors and contemporary realism in Smith Killian Fine Art. Lowcountry artist Betty Anglin Smith keeps it all in the family showcasing her work and that of her triplet children, painters Shannon Smith and Jennifer Smith Rogers, and photographer Tripp Smith—all quite popular in their own right. Other works in oil are shown by Kim English, Don Stone, and Susan Romaine. Expect to find subjects ranging from local to European landscapes to still life to architectural works. Bronze sculptures by

Darrell Davis and black and white photography by Leigh Limehouse complete the list of dynamic offerings here. Gallery hours are Mon through Sat 10 a.m. to 5 p.m., Sun, noon to 5 p.m., and by appointment.

SPENCER ART GALLERIES
55 & 57 Broad St.
(843) 722-6854, (843) 723-4482
www.spencerartgallery.com
Spencer Art Galleries I & II in 2 side-by-side galleries on Broad Street show work by more than 35 local, regional, national, and international artists. You'll find a broad range of contemporary fine art—everything from paintings, prints, and photography to sculpture. The friendly atmosphere offers a relaxed setting to view the art, and meet and chat with some of the featured artists. Collectors enjoy the opportunity to purchase from a range of prices among their master, mid-career, and emerging artists. The galleries' hours are Mon through Sat 10 a.m. to 5 p.m. or by appointment by calling (843) 886-6617.

STUDIO 151 FINE ARTS
151 East Bay St.
(843) 577-6909
www.studio151finearts.com
One of Charleston's newest fine art galleries, Studio 151 Fine Arts represents a group of 12 artists to include some well-known names such as Darryl Knox, Detta Cutting Zimmerman, Dixie Dugan, and Carole Carberry. The broad range of works encompass traditional realism, impressionism, collage, wildlife subjects, and abstracts. Each artist executes these styles through their individual focus of pastels, watercolors, oils, monotypes or mixed media—a veritable feast for the eyes. Hours are Mon through Sat 10 a.m. to 5 p.m.

THE SYLVAN GALLERY
171 King St.
(843) 722-2172
www.thesylvangallery.com
Located in the heart of the antique and art district of historic Charleston, The Sylvan Gallery focuses on 20th- and 21st-century traditional art. Their award-winning artists are nationally and internationally recognized. Some names here are Rhett Thurman, Scott Burdick, Ted Ellis, Karol Mack, and Guido Petruzzi. Among the notable sculptors are Glenna Goodacre, Richard Loffler, and Frank DiVita. Owners Joe and Janie Sylvan together have more than 30 years of gallery experience making this a warm and inviting gallery stop. Hours are Mon through Sat from 10 a.m. to 5 p.m. or by appointment.

UTOPIA
27 Broad St.
(843) 853-9510
www.utopiacharleston.com
This small fashion boutique/art gallery on Charleston's very traditional Broad Street seems like a non sequitur, but it's a welcome and refreshing break. It also displays alternative and avant-garde fashions and art, which is attracting a dedicated following. Hours are Mon through Sat from 11 a.m. to 7 p.m., and Sun noon to 5 p.m.

WELLS GALLERY
125 Meeting St.
(843) 853-3233
www.wellsgallery.com
The Wells Gallery presents a diverse palette of original work from artists who enjoy regional, national, and international success. Works range from contemporary realism to abstract expressionism, from landscape to figure, from full color to somber neutrals as well as hand blown glass. Regular gallery artists include Mark Bailey, John Geci, Evan Harrington, Wendy Whitson, Gary Gowans, Russell Gordon, George Pate, Sue Stewart, Karen Larson Turner, and David Goldhagen. Gallery hours are 10 a.m. to 5 p.m., Mon through Sat. There is a second location at 1 Sanctuary Beach Dr. on Kiawah Island (843-576-1290) with later hours.

ANNUAL EVENTS

Tradition is of utmost importance to Lowcountry residents, and successful annual events always fall into that category. Events in the Trident area run the gamut from the Lowcountry Oyster Festival—where salty oyster juice stains and face-painting masterpieces serve as souvenirs—to the sophisticated and comprehensive arts festival that is Spoleto Festival USA. Charlestonians and visitors alike turn out in big numbers for all the events listed in this chapter, so we strongly suggest you make your reservations early.

For information about any of the activities, we recommend contacting the Visitor Information Center of the Charleston Metro Chamber of Commerce (part of the area's convention and visitors bureau) at (843) 853-8000 or (800) 868-8118, or visit the website at www.charlestoncvb.com. The City of Charleston Office of Cultural Affairs, 180 Meeting St., Ste. 200, (843) 724-7305, www.charleston-sc.gov, and the automated ticketing service Ticketmaster, at (843) 554-6060, www.ticketmaster.com, are other good sources for information. The following listings will serve as good starting points in your efforts to dive into the traditions of the Trident. Unless otherwise noted, all events take place in Charleston proper.

JANUARY

✳THE CITADEL DRESS PARADE
The Citadel, 171 Moultrie St.
(843) 953-5000
www.citadel.edu

Almost every Friday during the school year, the nearly 2,000-member Corps of Cadets at The Citadel marches in retreat parade or review on Summerall Field to close out each week. In addition to the family and friends turnout, the Dress Parades are a long-standing local and visitor favorite due to the impressive precision of the Corps. Spectators are welcomed (for free)—just be sure to take your seat before 3:45 p.m. when the action commences. Call or visit the website for a schedule.

MAKE YOUR OWN HISTORY
Charleston Area Convention and Visitors Bureau, P.O. Box 975, Charleston, SC 29402
(843) 853-8000
www.beatourist.net

If you are a Tri-County local and haven't quite gotten around to seeing all the wonderful attractions in your own town, this is your big chance. Purchase this pass with local ID, and play tourist during the month of Jan. For $20 per person and $50 for a family of 4, this pass entitles Charleston-area residents to free admission to more than 30 of the area's best attractions. Some of the most popular house museums such as the Aiken-Rhett House and the Edmonston-Alston House are on the list. Plantations include Magnolia Plantation, Charles Pinckney National Historic Site, Middleton Place, and Drayton Hall. Patriots Point Maritime and Naval Museum, Charles Towne Landing State Historic Site, Fort Moultrie, several county parks, and the Gibbes Museum of Art are a few more on the diverse menu of attractions that may be just a little less crowded in Jan and well worth checking out. (See the Attractions chapter for more on these special sites.) Dining discounts are offered too at over 20 area restaurants. Passes may be ordered online or picked up at the official visitor centers in Charleston, Mount Pleasant, North Charleston, or Kiawah Island.

LOWCOUNTRY OYSTER FESTIVAL
Boone Hall Plantation, 1235 Long Point Rd., Mount Pleasant
(843) 577-4030, (843) 452-6088
www.boonehallplantation.com
www.charlestonrestaurant association.com
The very first Lowcountry Oyster Festival gathered a small but hardy crowd back in 1982. That was then. And now? Well, now we would marvel if snow scared off the thousands who loyally appear. This festival, organized by the Greater Charleston Restaurant Association, is built around the mighty oyster but is geared to the whole family's appetite for fun. The gates of beautiful Boone Hall Plantation in Mount Pleasant open at 10:30 a.m., and ticket holders are welcomed until the gates close at 5 p.m. An oyster-eating contest as well as other competitions and games are held, all in the name of fun and for the support of local children's charities. Barbecue and chili fill the void for non-oyster eaters, and if the winter temps aren't enough, there are plenty of chilled

beverages—beer being the most popular— to keep things cool. Held the Sunday prior to Super Bowl Sunday in Jan. Festival admission is $10 in advance and $12 at the gate. Children under 10 are free with an adult.

FEBRUARY

LOWCOUNTRY BLUES BASH
Various locations, P.O. Box 13525, Charleston, SC 29422
(843) 762-9125
www.bluesbash.com
In the past, as many as 50 acts have participated in the Lowcountry Blues Bash. Musicians such as Dave Peabody and Rob Mason, the Love Dogs, Big Boy Henry, Lil' Brian & the Zydeco Travelers, Carl Weathersby, and Shrimp City Slim have played to enthusiastic crowds at more than two dozen venues throughout the area. The event proudly showcases some of the area's older blues musicians along with ones up-and-coming on the scene. Cover charges range from free to $15 per performance. The 12-day event is held in early Feb. Festival promoter, musician, and radio personality Gary Erwin runs the show, and you can call him for more information about the Bash and other blues happenings around town at (843) 762-9125 from 10 a.m. to 6 p.m. Mon through Sat. A Lowcountry Blues Bash brochure is available by sending a self-addressed, stamped envelope to the above address.

✳SOUTHEASTERN WILDLIFE EXPOSITION
Various downtown locations
(843) 723-1748
www.sewe.com
This exposition is said to be the largest celebration of wildlife art anywhere. Incredible displays of paintings, prints, sculpture,

carvings, photography, collectibles, and crafts are all inspired by the boundless wonders of nature. More than 40,000 ticket-holding guests crisscross between the dozen or so exhibition sites on the Peninsula during the three-day event. Most are also interested in the expo's conservation motif. Hence, the booths, student contests, and the like are devoted to the green theme. Tickets for the 2011 event, held on Presidents' Day weekend, were $20 a day or $40 for a 3-day pass (children 10 and under are free with a paying adult). VIP packages start at $150 and include an insiders' look at the Expo. VIPs get opportunities to preview and purchase original artwork, attend special receptions and parties, and enter exhibits through separate entrances and move to the front of lengthy lines. For more information on the next annual exposition or advance ticket purchases, write the SEWE at P.O. Box 20635, Charleston, SC 29413.

MARCH

CHARLESTON WINE + FOOD FESTIVAL
P.O. Box 22823, Charleston, SC 29413
(843) 727-9998
www.charlestonwineandfood.com
One of Charleston's newest and most anticipated events, the Charleston Wine + Food Festival delights foodies with the opportunity to indulge in the unique flavors of Lowcountry cuisine in early Mar. Patrons will choose from a wide variety of epicurean events presented by the country's best chefs, authors, and wine experts. The festival kicks off with a "Salute to Charleston Chefs" on Thurs and ends with a "BBQ, Blues and Brew" finale on Sun afternoon. Friday morning features the opening ceremonies at Marion Square, which are open to the public. Marion Square is also the site of the Culinary Village's Grand Tasting Tent, which features food, wine, and interactive events from more than 90 vendors. Other special events at local restaurants and various venues include seminars, excursions, and dining like "Food Plus Wine with a View," "Brewmasters Beer School," and "6 Chefs, 1 Lowcountry Ingredient Challenge." For a complete listing of the events and ticket prices, visit the website or call the number above for a brochure. Many events sell out quicky so reserve your tickets early and get ready for a weekend of culinary treats.

✳HISTORIC CHARLESTON FOUNDATION'S FESTIVAL OF HOUSES AND GARDENS
Various downtown locations
(843) 723-1623, (843) 722-3405 (festival info)
www.historiccharleston.org
Those who want to move beyond a passive, coffee-table-book enjoyment of Charleston's private homes and gardens wait for this event each year. It's a mouthful, but what the foundation undertakes and offers is also expansive. For a month's time in Mar and Apr, more than 600 volunteers make it possible to tour more than 150 private houses and gardens. Every day the itinerary changes, with the focus on historically and architecturally distinct dwellings and gardens. To broaden the experience further, the foundation also hosts oyster roasts at Drayton Hall Plantation, and there is a series of garden-only tours. Tickets start at $45 and are available from the The Shops of Historic Charleston Foundation at 108 Meeting St. or by calling the number above after Nov 1. Proceeds support Historic Charleston Foundation's many preservation programs.

CHARLESTON SYMPHONY ORCHESTRA LEAGUE ASID DESIGNER SHOWHOUSE

Location varies, 14 George St.
(843) 723-0020
www.csolinc.org

Each year, a private historic dwelling is placed in the capable hands of volunteers from the Charleston Symphony Orchestra League to be presented in all its dazzling glory to the public in a one-house tour. The annual showhouse event, which opens in mid-Mar and continues for a month, is sponsored by the orchestra league, and each room is decorated by an ASID designer. It provides a great opportunity to tour an attractive home, shop the in-house boutique, and have lunch at the same residence in the tearoom. Sometimes the boutique might be in a garage or carriage house; the tearoom might be set up in the garden. It all depends on the layout of the chosen home. Tickets are $15 in advance or $20 at the door, and proceeds benefit our outstanding orchestra. Hence, it's a win–win situation and another opportunity to experience the inside of Charleston.

KIDS FAIR

Gaillard Municipal Auditorium,
77 Calhoun St.
(843) 571-6565, ext. 304
www.charleston-sc.gov

Since 1988, the Charleston Jewish Community Center has sponsored this indoor fair for children ages 3 to 12 at the Gaillard Auditorium. We like the safety precaution of not allowing any adult to enter if not accompanied by a child, and we appreciate the wide range of age-appropriate entertainment—from face painting, arts and crafts, and school group performances, to health-issue booths, all free of charge. The hours are 10 a.m. to 5 p.m. on a Sun in Mar. In a nice change of pace, parents are admitted free with children, whose tickets are $1. Parking is free, too.

✳CHARLESTON INTERNATIONAL ANTIQUES SHOW

40 East Bay St.
(843) 722-3405
www.historiccharleston.org

Benefiting from the rich historical, architectural, and cultural heritage of Charleston, the Charleston International Antiques Show has quickly established itself as a premier event for collectors and browsers alike since its inception in 2004. Benefiting the Historic Charleston Foundation, the weekend kicks off the Foundation's Annual Festival of Houses and Gardens ever-popular tours (see previous listing) with world-class exhibitors showcasing a full spectrum of period furnishings, decorative pieces, and fine art from the late-17th to the early-20th century. American, Asian, and European antiques are presented by some of the most recognized names from around the country. In addition to the exhibits next to the foundation's headquarters on East Bay Street, special events such as a preview party, young advocates' soiree, and guided group tours as well as luncheon lectures provide even more opportunities to learn and to enjoy the display. The show runs from Fri through Sun in mid-Mar. Daily passes are $15. The special events range from $75 for the luncheon lectures to $200 for the preview party. Call the number above for more details.

✳THE CHARLESTON ART & ANTIQUES FORUM

P.O. Box 22322, Charleston, SC 29413
(800) 926-2520
www.charlestonantiquesforum.org

Another not-to-be-missed event on Charleston's spring cultural scene is the premier lecture series, The Charleston Art & Antiques Forum, held during "Antiques Week" in mid-Mar. Wendell Garrett, editor at large of *The Magazine Antiques*, deemed it "the best fine and decorative arts program in the country today." Nationally recognized scholars cover architecture, furniture, paintings, silver, and ceramics as they relate to the annual theme such as "Made in America—Century by Century." Benefiting arts education and preservation initiatives, the Forum presents outstanding lectures in small-scale sessions, informal chats with the speakers, elegant receptions, and a plantation picnic. Tour options include opportunities to visit some of Charleston's landmark properties. A Connoisseur Package is priced at $525 with additional fees for the optional tours. Single tickets are available if the packages have not sold out and start at $25. Tickets may be purchased online.

✳THE GARDEN CLUB OF CHARLESTON'S ANNUAL HOUSE AND GARDEN TOURS
Various downtown locations
(843) 534-5164
www.thegardenclubofcharleston.com
Some of Charleston's finest historic district homes and gardens are showcased on The Garden Club of Charleston's tours on a Fri and Sat afternoon in the latter part of Mar. The members have organized this tour for more than 75 years and continue to delight tourists and locals alike with the selection of private homes, breathtaking gardens, and their own flower arrangements that enhance the homes' interiors. Tickets are in the $40 range for each day or $75 for both days and can be purchased by visiting the website listed or by writing to P.O. Box 20652, Charleston, SC 29413. If not sold out, they also may be purchased the day of the tour at the visitor center or Market Hall at the corner of Market and Meeting Streets.

APRIL

COOPER RIVER BRIDGE RUN AND WALK
P.O. Box 22089, Charleston, SC 29413
(843) 856-1949
www.bridgerun.com
The Bridge Run, as the natives call it, is a social event as much as it is a run. Men, women, and children begin training for the run months before the race date, and some even attend clinics scattered around the area as part of their preparation. Bumper stickers dare us with slogans like "Gone Runnin," and banners fly around the city for weeks ahead of time—we can't say we just forgot. Still, a 10-kilometer (6.2-mile) run or walk is a bit much for some of us, if not too great a challenge for the 50,000 or so participants who pound the pavement each year (usually in early Apr). The race begins in Mount Pleasant, continues across the Cooper River on the new Arthur Ravenel Jr. Bridge, and finishes downtown. The early entry fee for the run/walk is $30. All entrants receive a T-shirt and other goodies. A 1-mile Kid's Race takes place at Hampton Park (see our Parks & Recreation chapter) for an early entry fee of $8. For more information and an application, write to the Cooper River Bridge Run, P.O. Box 22089, Charleston, SC 29413 or register online. (For more information, see the Spectator Sports chapter.)

FLOWERTOWN FESTIVAL
140 South Cedar St., Summerville
(843) 871-9622
www.summervilleymca.org/flowertown

Summerville, a 20-mile drive from Charleston, is the setting for this wonderful small-town festival each spring (see more on Summerville in the Day Trips chapter). If the winter has been kind, the city—affectionately called Flowertown—will be ablaze with color on the first weekend in Apr, and the events are nonstop. Sponsored by the Summerville Family YMCA, the festival is a 3-day affair that includes arts and crafts displays with more than 200 vendors, a youth festival, sports tournaments, the Taste of Summerville food festival, and much more. There is no admission fee, but there are charges from individual vendors for food and activities.

LOWCOUNTRY CAJUN FESTIVAL
James Island County Park,
871 Riverland Dr.
(843) 795-4386
www.ccprc.com
Crawfish-crazed connoisseurs, take heart. There's a chance for you to get your fill this side of New Orleans at the annual Lowcountry Cajun Festival. Set in early Apr, it's a stompin' good time at the James Island County Park, where more than 5 tons of crawfish, eating contests, crawfish races, and a genuine Louisiana Cajun band make up the mix for family fun. Sponsored by the Charleston County Park and Recreation Commission, tickets for the festival are $10 for adults and free for children 12 and under with a paying adult.

FAMILY CIRCLE CUP
Daniel Island Tennis Centre
161 Seven Farms Dr., Daniel Island
(843) 856-7900, (800) 677-2293
www.familycirclecup.com

Take in some tennis at the $9 million Daniel Island Tennis Centre, the home of the Family Circle Cup. This tournament relocated in 2001 to Charleston after a longtime run in Hilton Head, South Carolina. The 9-day Women's Tennis Association Tier I event attracts many of the top seeds in women's tennis. Some of the past competitors were Serena Williams, Conchita Martinez, Monica Seles, Arantxa Sanchez-Vicario, Jennifer Capriati, Lindsay Davenport, and Mary Pierce. Held in mid-Apr, the Family Circle Cup is another highlight in Charleston's spring events lineup. Ticket prices range from $10 for qualifying matches up to $55 for the finals. Call the number or visit the website above for more information. (See the Spectator Sports chapter for more on the Family Circle Cup.)

FOLLY BEACH SEA & SAND FESTIVAL
21 Center St., Folly Beach
(843) 513-1836
www.cityoffollybeach.com
What could be better than enjoying the beach before the crowds descend for the season? The Sea & Sand Festival at Folly Beach lets fun-loving beachgoers do just that by celebrating all things "beachy" one Sat in mid-Apr. The city closes down the beachfront street for leisurely strolling and browsing during this event, so break out the shorts and flip-flops. The festival is full of vendors serving up local seafood delicacies, an arts and crafts show, a martial arts demonstration, and live music. An auction, children's games, and a hula hoop contest add to the entertainment, and the sandcastle competition gets more creative and spectacular every year. Admission is free. Call the number above for more information.

EAST COAST CANOE & KAYAK FESTIVAL
**James Island County Park,
871 Riverland Dr.
(843) 795-4386
www.ccprc.com**

Since 1991, the Charleston County Park and Recreation Commission has sponsored the popular East Coast Canoe & Kayak Festival at James Island County Park. The event is a full weekend of canoeing and kayaking history, technique, and hands-on experience appropriate for the beginner as well as the experienced paddler. In addition to on-water classes and boat demonstrations, lectures, workshops, and ACA instructor courses are held. There is an interpretative canoe and kayak exhibition, along with over 40 commercial exhibits by equipment designers and manufacturers. Try out new boats, paddles, and accessories at the festival site, or shop the used boat sale to pick up used gear at bargain prices. And for the early riser, sunrise paddling trips are led by local paddling clubs and outfitters. Family activities and a kids' camp round out the weekend of fun. Festival attendees are encouraged to stay on-site at the 640-acre park which features a 16-acre freshwater lake, tidal creek access, tent and RV camping, and miles of nature and bike trails. (See the Parks & Recreation chapter for more on this park and other Charleston County Parks.) Package fees range from $15 per day up to $105 for the full weekend of events.

✳CHARLESTON FARMERS MARKET
**Marion Square (between King and
Meeting at Calhoun)
(843) 724-7305
www.charleston-sc.gov**

Held every Sat from Apr through Dec at Marion Square (King, Meeting, and Calhoun Streets), the Charleston Farmers Market gives you a chance to pick out fresh fruit and veggies from our best local growers. Other vendors offer light fare such as crepes, omelets, bakery goods, and barbecue for sustenance during a leisurely stroll. Each week brings a variety of special activities, and the food and family fun are offered from 8 a.m. until 2 p.m. (or often later during Spoleto and other special event weekends). Music, arts and crafts, and "Ask a Master Gardener" are just a few of the attractions. On the December Saturdays be sure to gather loads of fresh greenery and goodies to "deck the halls." We know lots of folks who are regulars at the Farmers Market—hooked on that fresh-harvested produce and free fun.

BLESSING OF THE FLEET AND SEAFOOD FESTIVAL
**Mount Pleasant Memorial Waterfront
Park, 99 Harry Hallman Jr. Blvd.
(843) 884-8517
www.townofmountpleasant.com**

The town of Mount Pleasant and the shrimping industry pull out their finest when they invite the public to celebrate the Blessing of the Fleet. Along with prayers for a successful shrimping season and a parade of shrimp boats, organizers offer a wide range of entertainment and culinary delights. From shrimp-eating and shagging contests to a crafts show and face painting, the formula is for fun, and the setting—beautiful. With its gorgeous view of Charleston, Memorial Waterfront Park can't be beat. The festival is held the last Sun in Apr. Drawing more than 10,000 people each year, the Blessing of the Fleet is Mount Pleasant's largest tourism event. The festival is sponsored by the town of Mount Pleasant and the Blessing of the Fleet Committee. Admission is free, but food from a variety of East Cooper restaurants ranges from about $2 to $5.

LOWCOUNTRY SENIOR GAMES
Lowcountry Senior Center,
2110 Maybank Hwy.
(843) 795-6517

Attention all 50 and older athletes: These senior games feature competitions in more than 25 recreational events, so display your competitive nature. No matter what your interests, there is something for you in this 5-day event in late Apr. The events include bowling, golf, croquet, swimming, basketball, tennis, track and field, and softball, held at various locations such as The Citadel. In addition to the competitive events, other opportunities for friendship and fun include the opening social with live big band music, and a Senior Expo. And who knows—qualifying here may lead to the chance to compete at the state and national senior sports classics. Registration, which includes events and the banquet, is $25, with additional fees for golf, softball, and bowling. Registration forms are available at area recreation departments or by using the address or phone number listed.

"WINGS OVER CHARLESTON" AIR EXPO
Charleston Air Force Base, North Charleston
(843) 963-3976
www.charlestonairexpo.com

Gates open at 9 a.m. for the crowds of more than 100,000 people who turn out each year for this free air show. Launched from the Charleston Air Force Base, the aerial demonstrations of the Charleston Air Expo may feature the US Army Golden Knights parachutists, as well as US Air Force F-22 Raptor and F-18 Hornet demos, and the Thunderbirds, whose daring maneuvers will leave you in awe. Static displays allow access to look in cockpits and cargo areas—a real hit with the kids. Crowd control and parking are well organized, and food and souvenir concessions are on site. For more details on the Wings over Charleston Air Expo, visit the website or call the number above. Note: Sometimes, due to increased airlift operations in support of our troops overseas, this event may be cancelled or relocated.

MAY

DINING WITH FRIENDS LOWCOUNTRY AIDS SERVICES
3547 Meeting Street Rd.
(843) 747-2273, (877) 874-0230
www.aids-services.com

Hundreds of volunteers host private dinner parties for friends in their homes in a joint fund-raising effort supporting Lowcountry AIDS Services one Sat in May. (For more information on the services provided by LAS, see the Health Care chapter.) The kinds of parties run the spectrum from barbecue to black tie. Guests make a tax-deductible donation and enjoy a pleasant evening with old and new friends topped off with a Champagne and Dessert Grand Finale at 9 p.m. at the Charleston Maritime Center.

NORTH CHARLESTON ARTS FESTIVAL
Performing Arts Center of the Charleston Area Convention Center Complex, 5001 Coliseum Dr., North Charleston
(843) 740-5854
www.northcharleston.org

Bring the family and spend some time at the North Charleston Arts Festival. The indoor/outdoor entertainment at this weeklong festival encompasses everything from juried adult and youth art exhibits, a photography competition, and a local arts and crafts show and sale, to puppet and magic shows, live theater, and dance performances. Just listening to the variety of musical entertainment (including reggae, school choral groups, classical music, and contemporary gospel) is reason enough to check it out. Event hours begin at 9 a.m. and run into the evening hours daily. Some events are free, and others are ticketed events in the $5 to $20 range. The festival wraps up with a grand finale with performances, children's events, and fireworks at the Riverfront Park. Ample parking is available for free.

SPOLETO FESTIVAL USA
Various locations
(843) 722-2764, (843) 579-3100 (Box office)
www.spoletousa.org
Since 1977, Spoleto Festival USA has continued as a bright star on Charleston's arts calendar. One resident put it well when she said that anticipating Spoleto each year is "like looking forward to another Christmas, without having to dread the discarded gift paper mess." Already accustomed to an unusually strong year-round arts agenda, the city becomes blissfully hyperactive during Spoleto with world-class theater, music, dance, opera, and visual and literary presentations. It begins on Memorial Day weekend and lasts 17 days or so.

Highlights of the 2010 festival included the operas, "Flora" and "Proserpina," and performances by Les Ballets Trockadero de Monte Carlo and Ireland's Gate Theatre, as well as the ever-popular chamber music series and Westminster Choir.

Tickets for individual Spoleto events range from about $15 to $75. For an up-to-date schedule, contact the event box office at 14 George St., Charleston, SC 29401. (See The Arts chapter for more on Spoleto.)

PICCOLO SPOLETO FESTIVAL
Various locations
(843) 724-7305
www.piccolospoleto.com
We are particularly proud of Piccolo Spoleto, the city of Charleston's creative companion to Spoleto Festival USA. Piccolo events—including jazz cruises, a children's festival, a juried art exhibit, cabaret, and "brown bag and ballet"—are held in unusual places (anywhere from boats to parks to churches) and showcase local as well as national talent. The calendar is booked, and the ticket prices are very reasonable, ranging from free events to others that are almost always less than $25. For a more comprehensive schedule of events, write the City of Charleston Office of Cultural Affairs, 180 Meeting St., Ste. 200, Charleston, SC 29401 or visit the website. (For more on Piccolo Spoleto, see The Arts chapter.)

i In the Lowcountry, it doesn't get much more paparazzi-friendly than the black-tie opening night of Spoleto Festival USA's major opera presentation at Gaillard Municipal Auditorium. Don the good threads and check it out, along with the gala reception that follows, if you're lucky enough to score a ticket.

*GRACE EPISCOPAL CHURCH TEA ROOM

98 Wentworth St.
(843) 723-4575
www.gracechurchcharleston.org

Another of Charleston's special spring tearooms is the one put on by the volunteers of Grace Episcopal Church, near the College of Charleston. Lowcountry specialties are the fare here, and who can pass up an opportunity to sample a few of these: crab and okra soup, ham biscuits, and shrimp remoulade with an assortment of freshly baked desserts. Prices run from $2 to $5 an item, and you may find yourself returning several times during the 2 weeks the tearoom is open. The dates correspond with the Spoleto Festival, the last week of May and first week of June. Lunch is served Mon through Sat from 11:30 a.m. to 2 p.m., and takeout is available for your own Spoleto picnic. Proceeds benefit church outreach programs.

GREEK FESTIVAL

Greek Orthodox Church of The Holy Trinity, 30 Race St.
(843) 577-2063
www.greekfest.us

Another in Charleston's delectable ethnic festivals is the Greek Fest held in mid- May at the Greek Orthodox Church. Greek food, dancing, jewelry, crafts, and cooking demonstrations are some of the highlights of the weekend-long family fun. Dine in or take out the gyros, Greek chicken dinners, spanakopita, and pastries. Check out the bazaar, and take in a tour of the beautiful church. You're bound to be speaking a little Greek by the time you leave. Hours are 11 a.m. to 10 p.m. Fri and Sat, noon to 5 p.m. on Sun. Admission is $3 at the gate for ages 12 and older, $1 for seniors and students.

JUNE

CAROLINA DAY

1214 Middle St., Sullivan's Island
(843) 723-3225, (843) 883-3123
www.nps.gov/fosu

Sullivan's Island in the summer is cause for celebration in itself. Add to the natural charm of the venue an event like Carolina Day, and you're in for some serious fun. No admission is charged for this annual reenactment program at Fort Moultrie, and it is a wonderful opportunity to learn about the history of the patriots' Revolutionary War victory over the British Navy on June 28, 1776. Other Carolina Day events include a special church service and the ringing of church bells in Charleston, Mount Pleasant, Sullivan's Island, Isle of Palms, and North Charleston. An open house at the South Carolina Historical Society and a South Carolina Art Tour at the Gibbes Museum of Art (see the section on Other Museums in the Attractions chapter) are both free of charge. A procession takes place in the afternoon. It is composed of historical and lineal groups that make up the Palmetto Society of Charleston, the group that sponsors Carolina Day. The parade moves from Washington Park downtown to White Point Gardens at the Battery, where a wreath-laying ceremony and band concert wrap up the procession. The program runs from 9 a.m. to 8 p.m. (See the Kidstuff and Attractions chapters for more information on Fort Moultrie.)

JULY

PATRIOTS POINT 4TH OF JULY BLAST

Patriots Point Naval and Maritime Museum, 40 Patriots Point Rd., Mount Pleasant
(843) 884-2727
www.patriotspoint.org

With one of the biggest Fourth of July fireworks displays in the Palmetto State, the festivities at Patriots Point Naval and Maritime Museum on Charleston Harbor are a blast. It all begins at 4:30 p.m. with free admission to the ships of the museum, including the aircraft carrier USS *Yorktown*. Food and arts and crafts vendors add to the fun atmosphere, and the kids will enjoy a jump castle, climbing rock wall, and more in the Kids Zone. Popular area bands perform live before and after the fireworks for dancing the night away. The fireworks light up the sky usually just after 9:30 p.m. More than 10,000 people have celebrated our nation's birthday here in earlier years, so allow time for traffic and parking. (For more on Patriots Point Naval and Maritime Museum, see our Attractions chapter.)

AUGUST

KEY WEST BOATS FISHING FOR MIRACLES KING MACKEREL TOURNAMENT
P.O. Box 21199, Charleston, SC 29413
(843) 554-0177
www.fishingformiracles.org
This king mackerel fishing tournament, held in mid-Aug, is one of the largest saltwater fishing tournaments in South Carolina. Based out of Ripley Light Yacht Club, the tournament awards cash prizes (and we're talking more than $115,000 in total prize money) for the biggest catch as well as other categories. The tournament proceeds benefit the Medical University of South Carolina Children's Hospital (see the Health Care chapter) and the Coastal Conservation Association of South Carolina. The entry fee is $300 before Aug 1 and $350 thereafter. (For more on this and other fishing tourneys in the area, see the Hunting & Fishing chapter.)

SEPTEMBER

SCOTTISH GAMES AND HIGHLAND GATHERING
Boone Hall Plantation, 1235 Long Point Rd., Mount Pleasant
(843) 529-1020
www.charlestonscots.org
The tartan-clad clans gather, and traditions abound when the Scottish Games and Highland Gathering, sponsored by the Scottish Society of Charleston, is held at Boone Hall Plantation. All ages are incorporated into the festivities, which range from highland and country dancing and bagpipe music to tossing the caber. Those interested in finding out more about their Scottish roots enjoy talking to clan members at various booths, and everyone has a chance to sample Scottish culinary delights such as meat pies, scones, and shortbread. Boone Hall Plantation is a lovely setting, for all of this, and Sept is usually a very temperate month in the Lowcountry. Advance tickets for the 9 a.m. to 5 p.m. gathering are $15 for adults and teens and $4 for children ages 6 to 12. Gate prices are $20 and $5, respectively. Parking is $5 per car, which includes a program. For more information, contact the Scottish Society at P.O. Box 31951, Charleston, SC 29417–1951.

*PRESERVATION SOCIETY OF CHARLESTON'S FALL TOURS OF HOMES AND GARDENS
Various downtown locations
(843) 722-4630
www.preservationsociety.org
Beginning in Sept and running through Oct, the tours, sponsored by the Preservation Society of Charleston, are a splendid opportunity to experience the interiors of homes and churches in Charleston at night. Tourists

and locals alike enjoy the romantic walk along several city blocks between dwellings and appreciate the commentary on the architecture, history, and folklore of each property by the volunteer guides. Tours run from 7 to 10 p.m. on Thurs and Fri nights. The Sat and Sun afternoon tours run from 2 to 5 p.m. Tickets are $45 per tour or $120 for the weekend package of three, which features different locations in the historic district each week. You can find out more about the tours by writing the Preservation Society at P.O. Box 521, Charleston, SC 29402. (See the Attractions chapter for more information about the Society.)

MOJA ARTS FESTIVAL
Office of Cultural Affairs, 180 Meeting St., Ste. 200
(843) 724-7305
www.mojafestival.com

Running for 10 days in Sept and Oct, MOJA—a Swahili word for "source" or "beginning"—celebrates the long and fascinating African-American and Caribbean traditions and contributions to western cultures. Charleston becomes a stage for lectures, theater, and dance performances, art exhibits, concerts, and general festivities. Activities for the young and old provide the opportunity for sharing good times and harmony among people. Expect broad strokes of color, graceful movement, and beauty and revelry in abundance. Check *The Post and Courier* for special features and a listing of specific events with admission prices (many events are free), or call the above number for more information. (See the Tours and The Arts chapters for more about MOJA and Charleston's African-American tradition.)

OCTOBER

LATIN AMERICAN FESTIVAL
Wannamaker County Park,
8888 University Blvd., North Charleston
(843) 795-4386
www.ccprc.com

Celebrate the sights, sounds, and tastes of the Latino world at the Latin American Festival on a Saturday afternoon in early Oct. In between nachos, salsa, and chicken tamales, delight in the red-hot beat of hot Latin music. The Parade of Nations and folk dances add to the colorful display of the beautiful ethnic costumes. Admission is $10 for adults; children 12 and under are free. Food, beverages, and merchandise are purchased with tickets in $1 increments.

TASTE OF CHARLESTON
Boone Hall Plantation, 1235 Long Point Rd., Mount Pleasant
(843) 577-4030, (843) 452-6088
www.charlestonrestaurant association.com

If you have ever dreamed of sampling just a bite here and a bite there from the great restaurants all around town, this event is your dream come true. The Taste of Charleston is an all day affair at Boone Hall Plantation, where more than 50 restaurants, all members of the Greater Charleston Restaurant Association, sell their specialties in sample proportions at bite-size prices. The fare may include shrimp and grits, beef kabobs, Greek chicken, seafood dishes, and a variety of desserts. Plan to nibble your way around the plantation grounds, then watch the Waiters Wine Race (make a bet on who'll spill) and ice-carving competition. Adults love the beer- and wine-tasting booths, and children delight in the pony rides and face painting. The event is usually scheduled for a Sun in

Oct, and admission is $12 in advance or $15 at the gate. Food tickets are incremental and cost $1 at the event. Children 10 and under are admitted free with an adult.

KOMEN CHARLESTON RACE FOR THE CURE
9300 Medical Plaza Dr., Ste. F, North Charleston, SC 29406
(843) 556-3343
www.komenlowcountry.org

Since starting out in 1994 with 900 participants in the Charleston area, the Race for the Cure has quickly grown in popularity among runners of all ages to become the largest 5K race in South Carolina. The event is held by the Susan G. Komen Breast Cancer Foundation, which sponsors the 5K Race for the Cure around the country. It is a breast cancer awareness race, in which participants are invited to wear the name of loved ones who have battled cancer. The race takes place at the Family Circle Cup Tennis Centre on Daniel Island (see the Neighborhoods chapter for more on Daniel Island), and early registration fees are $25 for the 5K run/walk and the 1-mile family fun run/walk. Children under 5 are free but must be registered. Late registration is $30. Proceeds benefit both local and national grants awarded for breast cancer prevention and research.

MOUNT PLEASANT CHILDREN'S DAY FESTIVAL
Park West Recreation Complex, Mount Pleasant
(843) 884-8517
www.townofmountpleasant.com

On an October Sunday afternoon, the town of Mount Pleasant holds the Children's Day Festival to honor the children of the community and provide them with live entertainment, games, food, and fun. The event is organized by the Mount Pleasant Recreation Department and East Cooper schools, all of which set up game and food booths at the Park West Recreation Complex. Games are free, with prizes awarded, and food sales benefit the school PTAs and PTSOs. Past years' entertainment lineup delighted more than 10,000 children and families. The Rhinestone Roper, Mandrake the Magician, Becky Becker's Box of Puppets, the Gravity Brothers Comedy Juggling Duo, the Citadel Cheerleading Squad, and the band, Lunch Money, have all performed here. If that's not enough to make the little ones' eyes light up, there's laser tag, jump castles, a climbing wall, a giant slide, and mechanical animal rides. A Halloween costume contest also puts the children in the spotlight. Parking and admission are free.

THAT BIG BOOK SALE
Gaillard Municipal Auditorium, 77 Calhoun St.
(843) 805-6978
www.ccpl.org

Organized by the Friends of the Library's volunteers to raise money for Charleston County libraries, this used-book sale just gets bigger and better. Since 1983, the event, held at the Gaillard Exhibition Hall, has included categories such as fiction, non-fiction, history, cooking, and travel, just to name a few. The books all are donated by the public—paperbacks sell for $1; hardbacks are $3. A "better book" section has individually priced books. Children's hardcover books are $1 and paperbacks are 50 cents. Peruse the selection of more than 70,000 books, tapes, DVDs, and CDs during the three-day event, which has no admission fee. Event hours are Fri from 9 a.m. to 7 p.m., Sat from 9 a.m. to 5 p.m., and Sun from 10 a.m. to 3 p.m.

NOVEMBER

THE JUNIOR LEAGUE OF CHARLESTON "WHALE OF A SALE"
Gaillard Exhibition Hall, 77 Calhoun St.
(843) 763-5284
www.jlcharleston.org
This is the rummage sale to end all rummage sales. If you don't believe it, ask the dozens who camp out the night before in the parking lot to be the first ones through the door. Everything from large appliances, furniture, and computers to toys, sports equipment, clothing, and "you name it" is donated by the Junior League's membership, and there is new merchandise from area merchants. Of course, it's all available at rock-bottom prices. This event is a treasure hunter's paradise, so come prepared to search for loads of bargains. The doors open at 8 a.m. and close at 1 p.m., usually on the second Sat in Nov.

✳PLANTATION DAYS AT MIDDLETON PLACE
4300 Ashley River Rd.
(843) 556-6020, (800) 782-3608
www.middletonplace.org
No wonder so many brides ache to marry close by the spectacular butterfly lakes of Middleton Place: The grounds are the essence of romanticism and classic beauty (for more on Middleton Place, see our Attractions chapter). Perhaps it's a fantasy about living in a magnificent setting like Middleton with the mythical prince until death do you part. Back here in reality, consider getting a feel for plantation life at Middleton Place's Plantation Days. On one weekend in Oct and one in Nov, visitors can observe craft workers in action as they showcase the tasks necessary for existence on an 18th- or 19th-century plantation. It's not hard to imagine the harvest season in full swing as you watch demonstrations of actual quilting, dyeing, candle making, leather tanning, and cider making. Sweetgrass baskets, like those sold downtown at the City Market (see the Close-up in the Shopping chapter), are fashioned before your eyes as you immerse yourself in a different era. Regular gate admission to see the stable yards and gardens during Plantation Days is $25 for adults and children or $20 in advance online. An additional $10 is charged to see the house.

CHARLESTON FINE ART ANNUAL
Charleston Fine Art Dealers' Association,
P.O. Box 942, Charleston, SC 29402
(843) 722-9868
www.cfada.com
Immerse yourself in the visual arts when the Charleston Fine Art Dealers' Association holds its annual event weekend in early Nov. There are 12 of Charleston's finest galleries that sponsor receptions, painting demonstrations, a high school art competition, and special exhibit openings with extended hours over the 2 days. The plein air painting demonstrations by CFADA gallery artists take place under the live oaks in Washington Park on Sat morning. Completed paintings are sold that evening at an auction event, with proceeds benefiting local schools' art programs. What better remembrance of your experience could you take home than an original work by one of Charleston's leading artists? Most events are free. The art auction held at the Renaissance Charleston Hotel on Sat evening is a $50 per person ticket.

THE BATTLE OF SECESSIONVILLE
Boone Hall Plantation, 1235 Long Point Rd., Mount Pleasant
(843) 884-4371
www.boonehallplantation.com

Sponsored by the Confederate Heritage Trust, the Battle of Secessionville is re-enacted right before your eyes with all the splendor and tragedy of the Civil War. Some of the activities to witness on this mid-November weekend include cavalry and artillery performances, battle aftermath reenactments, uniform demonstrations, and tours of the Boone Hall Plantation house and slave village. (For more on Boone Hall, see the Lowcountry Day Trips and Tours chapters.) Camps open at 9 a.m., and the battle commences at 2 p.m. Admission prices are $17.50 for adults, $15 for seniors 65+, and $7.50 for children ages 6 to 12. (To learn more about the Battle of Secessionville, see "Battery Wagner" in the Forts section of the Attractions chapter.)

HOLIDAY FESTIVAL OF LIGHTS
**James Island County Park,
871 Riverland Dr.
(843) 795-4386
www.holidayfestivaloflights.com**
Young and old delight in the more than 200 magical lighting displays set up in the James Island County Park from mid-Nov through New Year's. Set your own pace as you take the 3-mile driving tour, winding through the park and enjoying the spectacle. The lights burn from 5:30 to 10 p.m. Sun through Thurs and until 11 p.m. on Fri and Sat. Admission is $10 a car and $25 for 16-passenger vans. A Holiday Festival of Lights Fun Run and Walk the day before opening gives participants a preview of the 2,000,000 glittering lights. The 5K Fun Run or the 2-mile walk is a $10 advance entry fee for ages 3 and up. Start a new family tradition of viewing the dazzling display every year.

DECEMBER
✳ANNUAL SPIRITUALS CONCERT AT DRAYTON HALL
**3380 Ashley River Rd.
(843) 769-2605
www.draytonhall.org**
African-American spirituals, rooted in the work songs of West Africa and developed during the days of slavery, are incredibly moving. A cappella voices and rhythmic double-clapping are characteristic of the songs. The opportunity to hear them performed is rare. This early-December event begins with an informal candlelight house tour and refreshments on Sat evening at 5:30 p.m. followed by the hour-long concert around 7 p.m. Two matinee performances are offered on Sat and Sun at 3 p.m. To order tickets at $35 per person ($30 for Friends of Drayton Hall), write Drayton Hall at 3380 Ashley River Rd., Charleston, SC 29414 or call the number above. Seating is limited in Drayton Hall, so advance reservations are required. (For more on Drayton Hall, see the Attractions chapter.)

FAMILY YULETIDE
**4300 Ashley River Rd., Middleton Place
(843) 556-6020, (800) 782-3608
www.middletonplace.org**
There's a fire for chestnut roasting, Jack Frost could very well be nipping at your nose, and you can bet that yuletide carols are going to be sung by a choir. It's all part of Family Yuletide at Middleton Place, which is usually held on the second Sat in Dec. There will be holiday storytelling by the bonfire, and crafters will be working by torchlight in their shops to get the venerable plantation ready for Christmas. The children can make angels out of corn husks, and a live nativity scene is planned. Reservations are recommended for

Christmas in Charleston

If you're thinking of spending the holidays in history, look into the **"Christmas in Charleston"** festival. Plan to celebrate during November and December with a variety of special events such as Christmas carriage rides, gallery art walks, holiday shopping excursions, and tree lightings complete with visits from Santa. The music of the season can be experienced through children's choir performances and plantation concerts, and the tastes can be enjoyed at Victorian teas, oyster roasts, and progressive dinners in historic Charleston. Homes, churches, storefronts, boats, and parks are all decked out for the holidays, and Christmas walking tours as well as holiday tours of homes and gardens provide an up-close view of the finery. For a complete schedule of events, call the CACVB at (800) 853-8000, or visit www.christmasincharleston.com.

participants and spectators in Charleston. Usually the first Saturday evening in Dec, festively decorated boats of all descriptions leave from Mount Pleasant around 5 p.m. (depending on weather, current, or other conditions) crossing the Cooper River and Charleston Harbor to the Ashley River. These boats and skippers often get quite creative, and prizes are awarded for the top displays. Many viewers go first to the City of Charleston's Christmas Tree Lighting Ceremony in Marion Square at 4:30 p.m. and then get to a location along the Cooper River from the Aquarium to Waterfront Park to the Battery to watch this fun, nautical parade.

HAPPY NEW YEAR, CHARLESTON!
Various downtown locations
(843) 724-7305
www.charleston-sc.gov
Happy New Year, Charleston! marks the passage of one year into the next with a broad selection of arts and cultural performances in the downtown historic district. The slant is a family-oriented, affordable, non-alcoholic, entertaining way to ring in the New Year. The 30- to 45-minute offerings include ballet, theater, improvisational comedy, puppetry, and an array of music from choral, chamber, and ethnic, to folk and big band. Much of King Street is blocked off for pedestrian-only traffic, allowing a festive atmosphere at every turn with roving musicians and actors, jugglers, face painters, and dancing. All the events are within walking distance. Children's programming begins at 4 p.m.; the major events begin at 7 and last until 10:30 p.m. with free admission.

this family event. Admission is about $10 per adult and $5 for children ages 3 to 12.

HOLIDAY PARADE OF BOATS
Various downtown locations
(843) 724-7305
www.charleston-sc.gov
For more than 30 years the Holiday Parade of Boats has been a popular spectacle for

KIDSTUFF

For starters, know that Greater Charleston is a fabulous vacation destination. Over four million people come to the Lowcountry every year, and a majority of those visitors arrive in the form of families.

A quick glance through the Attractions chapter might give you the impression that Charleston primarily serves up nothing but history—forts, house museums, plantations, and historic sites. While this wouldn't seem to be very kid-friendly, we've found that, almost without exception, Charleston's major annual events and attractions have been designed (at least partially) with children in mind.

And don't forget that children love to learn. Greater Charleston is a living, breathing, three-dimensional, full-color, interactive classroom for learning about America (which is really learning about ourselves). Here's the best part: It's a classroom with a beautiful ocean nearby, and that means beaches! Are we talkin' fun, or what?

Let's take stock. What have we got here? Interesting (new and old) places to go with really neat stuff to see; places where people used to live and work (and play) hundreds of years ago; ships of all types and all sizes that you can actually climb around on; and beaches close by with plenty of sand and sunburn to go around. We've got ball parks, game parks, and parks where you can swim. There are places to camp, rivers to explore, even new foods to taste. Ever eat a crawfish? We've got farms where you can pick your own strawberries and blueberries when the season is right. We've got something for every kid out there.

This chapter is dedicated to fun activities that children and parents can do together. Let's get started.

Price Code

The following price code table is provided to give you an idea of the price of admission to those establishments that charge an admission fee. Please note that prices, means of payment, and hours change often and may vary seasonally, so call ahead for details. If no price code is designated, there is no charge to enter, but there may be other fees.

$	Less than $5
$$	$5 to $10
$$$	$10 to $20
$$$$	More than $20

OUTDOOR EXPLORATIONS

As you will note in our Parks & Recreation chapter, there are many public parks in the area. We have found that some are particularly appealing to children, and we describe those in more detail below. Whatever outdoor plans you make, be sure to bring plenty of sunscreen during the warm months and bug repellent for those pesky no-see-ums (gnats) present most of the year.

BOONE HALL FARMS
US 17 N., Mount Pleasant
(843) 884-4371, (843) 856-5366
www.boonehallfarms.com

During the spring and summer months, area farms offer you-pick-it produce, and one of our favorite spots is Boone Hall Farms, the working farm of Boone Hall Plantation in Mount Pleasant. Children carry buckets out into the fields and delight in gathering and eating seasonal berries right off the vine. Strawberries (as well as other seasonal produce such as tomatoes, pumpkins, and peaches) are carried home by the pound and can stimulate some creative pie and ice-cream making later. This can be a pleasant morning or afternoon that teaches kids that food doesn't just come from the grocery store or drive-through. The fields are open 9 a.m. to 8 p.m. Mon through Sat and 10 a.m. to 7 p.m. on Sun in season; call the number listed for directions and produce selections. Also check out the wonderful Boone Hall Farms Market at 2521 US 17 N., where produce and more are available. (See the Tours and Day Trips chapters for more on Boone Hall Plantation.)

*CHARLES TOWNE LANDING STATE HISTORIC SITE $$
1500 Old Towne Rd., between I-26 and SR 171
(843) 852-4200
www.southcarolinaparks.com

This state park is many things to many people, and it really is a terrific introduction to a hands-on history lesson. Founded in 1970, Charles Towne Landing State Historic Site is 663 acres of walking, bicycling, and in-line skating paths; an animal forest; an area dedicated to the depiction of the lives of settlers; and more. Children can expect to see native animals such as wolves, alligators, pumas, otters, bison, and maybe even a bear or two in a natural habitat setting. Children enjoy the craft-making demonstrations and appreciate the period clothing worn by the park staff. Recent archaeological digs are centered on uncovering information about the original settlement of Charles Towne prior to its relocation across the Ashley River on the peninsular site. These excavations are bound to stir some excitement among visitors of all ages.

We recommend strolling or biking through the park passing by the original house and down to Old Towne Creek, where a reproduction of a 17th-century trading vessel named *Adventure* is ready for exploring.

Wonderful special events throughout the year as well as summer and holiday day camps attract a steady flow of young people. The park is open daily (except Christmas Eve and Christmas) all year. Hours are 9 a.m. to 5 p.m. Children younger than 5 get in free. (See the History, Attractions, and Parks & Recreation chapters for more information.)

DANIEL ISLAND WATERFRONT PARK & TRAILS
River Landing Dr., Daniel Island
(843) 724-7327
www.charlestonparksconservancy.org

Among the many green spaces on Daniel Island, this is a favorite one because of its access to the scenic beauty of the Wando River. Walking, biking, and boardwalk trails provide access to the gorgeous vistas. There is a children's park with ample playground equipment. There are benches and picnic tables under the moss-draped live oaks for Mom and Dad to relax while keeping a close eye on the kids' climbing, swinging, and romping. There is no admission charge.

Mysterious Charleston

Take the kids to help solve the mystery of the *H. L. Hunley*— the world's first submarine to sink an enemy ship in combat. After attacking and sinking the USS *Housatonic* 4 miles off Sullivan's Island in February 1864, the Confederate sub disappeared with its brave crew. For 136 years it remained on the ocean's floor until its raising in August 2000. Archaeology and conservation are under way at the **Warren Lasch Conservation Center** on Charleston's old Naval Base, but visitors are allowed every Sat from 10 a.m. to 5 p.m. and Sun from noon to 5 p.m. Advance tickets are $12 plus a service charge (a limited number are available on a walk-up basis), and proceeds support the conservation work. They may be purchased by calling (877) 448-6539, or visiting www.hunley.org.

(Learn more about Daniel Island in our Neighborhoods chapter.)

FORT SUMTER NATIONAL MONUMENT $$$
Charleston Harbor
(843) 722-2628, (800) 789-3678, (843) 883-3123 (National Park Service)
www.fortsumtertours.com
What could be a more awe-inspiring setting and thrilling experience for a young person than arrival by tour boat at Fort Sumter, the fort where the Civil War began? In the middle of Charleston Harbor, Fort Sumter looks much like it did over a century ago and affords an incredible view of the city and surrounding islands. We recommend careful supervision of children, as the fort is surrounded by water, and there are many precarious climbs. The gift shop has an array of interesting items (a kit of historically accurate paper dolls or replica buttons, for example) and Civil War books, and it is air-conditioned—a major plus after a hot day scouring the fort. National Park Service rangers are on-site to answer questions, and there is a museum.

Tour boats depart from the National Park Service dock and visitor education facility at Liberty Square next to the South Carolina Aquarium in downtown Charleston and also Patriots Point in Mount Pleasant. Call for schedules and ticket prices; the fort is open year-round. (For more on Fort Sumter, see the Forts section of the Attractions chapter and the Tours chapter.)

HAMPTON PARK
30 Mary Murray Dr.
(843) 724-7327
www.charlestonparksconservancy.org
As children, we came to Hampton Park to play around the 60 inner-city acres, so it's a particular treat to experience the park these days with the next generation. Children delight at the same simple pleasures we remember: feeding ducks and geese in the pond, smelling the gorgeous roses, and just frolicking in the wide-open spaces. The parcourse exercise trail is a favorite of older children and adults. The Piccolo Spoleto finale, a city-sponsored Easter Egg hunt, and in-line skating night during warm weather are great reasons to plan a Hampton Park visit. The park is free, but keep in mind the midtown location and possible safety con-

cerns if you're venturing to Hampton Park at night.

✳JAMES ISLAND COUNTY PARK $-$$
871 Riverland Dr.
(843) 795-7275
www.ccprc.com
This beautiful, 643-acre park offers biking, keowees (junior-size kayaks), skating, fishing or crabbing, a climbing wall, a super playground, and much more. Splash Zone, however, is the James Island park's great water attraction. With two 200-foot tube slides, a 500-foot lazy river is enlivened by a spray-filled, waterfall-peppered "adventure channel." There's a leisure pool perfect for kiddies and a Caribbean play structure with interactive elements. Splash Zone is simply awesome. Showers, concessions, lockers, and restrooms are available. The annual Holiday Festival of Lights will dazzle young and old alike with more than 100 lighting displays on view mid-Nov through New Year's. (See Annual Events for more on this festival.) Park hours vary, so call for details. Gate admission is $1 per person (2 years and under are free), but Splash Zone will run you an additional fee. (For more, see the Parks & Recreation and Boating & Water Sports chapters.)

MAGNOLIA PLANTATION
AND GARDENS $$$-$$$$
3550 Ashley River Rd.
(843) 571-1266, (800) 367-3517
www.magnoliaplantation.com
While the horticultural maze and antebellum cabin (an original, dating back to around 1840) are first stops for the little ones, the petting zoo with African pygmy goats, deer, and other friendly animals is the real calling card for toddlers and elementary school kids

visiting Magnolia. They can buy handfuls of grain to feed the gentle creatures but should expect an occasional nibble on the posterior from a pushy goat or two. The topiary gardens, trimmed to resemble animals, and Barbados Tropical Garden (with plants native to Barbados—homeland of the original settling family—and points south) are also fun to see. Older children can rent canoes or bikes (or you can bring your own), and everyone enjoys the 45-minute, 4-mile tram ride through the property. Leashed pets are welcome too.

Magnolia is open 365 days a year from 8 a.m. to 5:30 p.m. (Winter hours may vary slightly). A basic admission price is charged, with additional fees for the Plantation House, Nature Train/Boat, Slavery to Freedom tours, and Audubon Swamp. Kids under 6 are admitted free. (See the Attractions chapter for more on Magnolia Plantation and Gardens.)

MIDDLETON PLACE $$$-$$$$
4300 Ashley River Rd.
(843) 556-6020, (800) 782-3608
www.middletonplace.org
In addition to being lots of fun for the kids, the incredible beauty of the gardens and forest trails of Middleton Place tends to leave parents lingering, trying to drag out the good times a little bit longer. A shady picnic area near the greensward is a delightful place to enjoy the vistas. And here's the chance for everyone to milk a cow, card wool, or grind corn. Middleton is a working plantation. Free-range farm animals mill about, and craftspeople are hard at work so that visitors can observe or even take part in the reenactment of history.

Plantation Days are a fun, educational series of Saturdays in Nov when demonstrations of plantation harvesting, candle dipping, syrup making, shepherding, and more take place (see the Annual Events chapter). Gates are open daily from 9 a.m. until 5 p.m. Middleton Place is open year-round. Children younger than 7 are admitted free. An additional $10 is charged for the house tour, and a carriage tour is offered for an additional fee. (For more on Middleton Place, see the Plantations and Gardens section of the Attractions chapter.)

PALMETTO ISLANDS COUNTY PARK $-$$
444 Needlerush Pkwy., Mount Pleasant
(843) 884-0832
www.ccprc.com

This nature-oriented park is on more than 900 acres of typical Lowcountry terrain and features a mile-long wilderness trail along a boardwalk through the marsh. Little children enjoy playing at the Big Toy, a play area with lots of wooden equipment such as towers, slides, and swings; their older siblings enjoy the tunnel, slide, and view associated with the observation tower. Pedal boats and canoes are for rent, and many visitors enjoy exploring on bicycles—rent one or bring your own.

Splash Island is the hot attraction here for warm-weather patrons. A 200-foot slide, a 16-foot otter slide (no otters, just a fun name), sprays, waterfalls, geysers, and a delightful sand play area await. In addition to the park admission of $1 per person, there are fees for Splash Island with a small break for Charleston County residents. Hours vary by season, so call or visit the website for specifics. (See the Parks & Recreation and Boating & Water Sports chapters for more information on this park.)

Plan to bring swimsuits, but leave the coolers at home for your day at Splash Island or Splash Zone at Palmetto Islands or James Island County Park. Proper swimming attire is required, and no outside food or beverages are allowed.

SULLIVAN'S ISLAND PARK
1610 Middle St. (Station 21 and Middle Street), Sullivan's Island
(843) 883-3198

Involved parents and other residents of Sullivan's Island have worked hard to make this park the little gem that it is. With two sections of play equipment, lots of wooden things to crawl in and on, and sliding-friendly apparatuses, children are fairly contained and easily occupied. There is even a fence around one area for additional safety for younger children. The man-made mound, left over from World War II, was built as a mortar battery to store ammunition. It is referred to by locals as "The Hill" and is the place to go if your kids are into sliding. Dress appropriately, bring a big piece of cardboard and your steady nerves, then climb to the top and slide down . . . over and over and over again. At least, that's the way it works with kids. While this is the same good, clean fun we had here as children, be forewarned that there is danger in the shape of a huge pit in the mound's center that is not particularly well marked. Keep children away from the edges, and also avoid letting the kids make solo treks into the bamboo groves or other isolated areas. Although Sullivan's is an island of good neighborhoods, there is safety in numbers where children are concerned. There is no admission charge. (See the Parks & Recreation chapter for more on Sullivan's Island Park.)

✴WATERFRONT PARK
1 Vendue, Cumberland Street to North Adgers Wharf
(843) 724-7327
www.charlestonparksconservancy.org

Just off East Bay Street in downtown Charleston, the lovely Waterfront Park is another nice picnic and cool-your-heels spot. Sea breezes keep the tables under the covered pier area perfect for just these pursuits. Children have fun splashing around in the pineapple-shaped fountain or getting soaked in the circular spray fountain. We've seen pictures of half a kindergarten class in one of the large swings that line the pier, a 400-foot extension into Charleston Harbor. No admission is charged. (See the Parks & Recreation chapter.)

WHITE POINT GARDENS AT THE BATTERY
2 Murray Dr., South tip of East Bay and King Streets
(843) 724-7327
www.charlestonparksconservancy.org

Frisbee throwers and cannon climbers love White Point Gardens. Children can run free beneath the canopy of trees and pretend to lift the immensely heavy and immovable cannonballs. Lots of photo ops here! There is usually a pleasant breeze off the water (the harbor circles around the point), and this open space is a much-loved haven of respite in the city. We used to search through the oyster-shell fill along the walks to find ancient shark teeth or other treasures. Don't expect any more luck than we had decades ago, but do plan to enjoy the leisurely pace of an old-fashioned park. Of course, no admission is charged. (For more info, see the Parks & Recreation, History, and Attractions chapters.)

KID-FRIENDLY BEACHES

Though there are many great beach destinations in a coastal area like this one, one of our favorite swimming areas for children is on Folly Beach at the Folly Beach County Park, (843) 588-2426. Unlike some other area beaches, this one has its own parking, lifeguards, and facilities. Take a right off Folly Road onto Center Street, and follow it to its end. Young surfers will want to head for the midsection of the island, where waves are best. Admission is $7 a car.

Kiawah, most of which is a private resort community, does offer public access at Beach-walker Park, (843) 768-2395, on the west end. Lifeguards, parking, restrooms, and equipment rentals are available from Apr through Oct. Turn just before the gates to Kiawah to find the park. The ocean frontage is somewhat off-the-beaten-path, thus allowing for 11 miles of unspoiled sand and surf. A $7 fee is required per car.

We can cautiously recommend the beaches on Sullivan's Island and the Isle of Palms, but urge parents to keep several general cautions in mind before you send the children skipping to the surf. Note that strong, tricky currents are prevalent at each end of Sullivan's Island as well as the south end of the Isle of Palms. Convenient parking can be tough to find on both islands, but the Isle of Palms County Park, (843) 886-3863, located mid-island, offers lots of parking and lifeguards on duty during the summer months for a $7 per car entrance fee. Walk-ins and bicycles are admitted at the three beach parks at no charge. Showers and picnic areas are other nice amenities at each of these beach parks. (The Parks & Recreation chapter offers more information on all of these parks.)

CULTURAL FUN

CHARLESTON BALLET THEATRE SCHOOL
477 King St.
(843) 723-7334
www.charlestonballet.org

If your youngsters fancy standing on their tippytoes, put that talent to good use by enrolling them in the Charleston Ballet Theatre's official school. Classes in creative movement, ballet, and jazz dance for ages 3 and older are offered. While the school's graduates dance with major companies throughout the country, students without professional ambition are welcome. The downtown school and its parent theater company are located in a King Street facility downtown just a block from the Charleston Visitor Reception and Transportation Center. A James Island location at 1748 Maybank Hwy. and a Mount Pleasant location at 598 Belle Station/Long Point Rd. serve these communities. Call the number above for class offerings and fees. Regular ballet performances and Piccolo Spoleto tickets are in the $20 range for adults and $10 for children. Season tickets for 5 performances offer discounts for children younger than 18 and seniors. The annual *Nutcracker* ballet, performed by many of the ballet school students during the Christmas season, is a long-standing favorite. (See The Arts chapter for more on the Charleston Ballet Theatre.)

*THE CHARLESTON MUSEUM $$
360 Meeting St.
(843) 722-2996
www.charlestonmuseum.org

In addition to being the oldest history, art, and science museum in the country (founded in 1773), the Charleston Museum is one of the best resources for children in the city. We love to try to keep pace with the kids as they scamper through the modern complex (the facility is well designed and very kid-older-than-4 friendly). There are interesting programs throughout the year—such as "Mad Science Saturdays," "Charleston Critters," and "Historic Crafts"—that usually last one afternoon session and are included in admission. We've found that starting off on a rainy day in the Kidstory room, with its "touch-me" exhibits, is the best way for little ones to unwind and connect with the museum. The museum is across the street from the visitor center. It is open 9 a.m. to 5 p.m. Mon through Sat and 1 to 5 p.m. on Sun but closed on major holidays. Free parking is available in a small lot behind the museum off John Street. (For more information, see the Attractions chapter.)

CHARLESTON STAGE COMPANY THEATRE SCHOOL
Dock Street Theatre, 135 Church St.
(843) 856-3822
www.charlestonstage.com

"All the world's a stage" . . . and maybe your youngster would like a chance to learn more about it. Charleston Stage is a prime creative outlet for that dramatist in the family. The Theatre School offers a variety of acting and theatre education opportunities for children in grades K–12. The program introduces theatrical skills in classes designed to enhance acting skills, bolster self-confidence, and encourage self-expression. Advanced students may participate in KidStage, the performing troupe for middle school students, and TheatreWings, the apprentice program for high school students. The Theatre School students are encouraged also to audition for roles in the Charleston Stage's Main-Stage and Family Series productions each season. Classes are offered year-round in 2-week summer sessions to weekly afternoon classes throughout the school year at the rehearsal studios at The Plaza at East Cooper in Mount Pleasant.

CHILDREN'S MUSEUM OF THE LOWCOUNTRY $$
25 Ann St.
(843) 853-8962
www.explorecml.org

The newest museum on the scene with a focus on kids is the Children's Museum of the Lowcountry. Located near the visitor center in the Camden Tower Sheds, this popular concept is to inspire a love of learning in children through interactive, interdisciplinary, hands-on environments and experiences in the arts, sciences, and humanities. The fun exhibits include climbing a tower in the Castle, sliding into the art room, painting on a mural wall, playing with water in Water-Wise, racing golf balls, and searching for buried treasure about the CML Pirate Ship. This immersion environment for children and their families leads to creative thinking, problem-solving skills, and confidence. Who knows what a visit here may spark? Children under age 1 are admitted free. Hours are Tues through Sat 9 a.m. to 5 p.m. and Sun 1 to 5 p.m.

GIBBES MUSEUM OF ART $$
135 Meeting St.
(843) 722-2706
www.gibbesmuseum.org

The Gibbes is a source of pride for many Charlestonians. Not only are the collections impressive, but the facility itself and the enthusiasm of the membership also spark creativity in the young and old alike. Studio art classes at the Gibbes are very popular with Charleston children. From drawing to working with clay to watercolor art or photography, the offerings appeal to many levels of artistic interest and skill. Classes cost between $40 and $180. A variety of special events and activities are held for children throughout the year, so call for a calendar with all the details. With exhibits ranging from the contemporary to the abstract, a simple visit to the museum any time can be a visual thrill. Hours are 10 a.m. to 5 p.m. Tues through Sat and 1 to 5 p.m. on Sun. The museum is closed on Monday. Annual family memberships are $100, and they include a 10 percent discount on museum shop purchases and classes. (For more on the Gibbes, see the chapters on The Arts and Attractions.)

OLD EXCHANGE AND PROVOST DUNGEON $$
122 East Bay St. (at Broad Street)
(843) 727-2165, (888) 763-0448
www.oldexchange.com

Make history really come to life for your child. The period-costumed docents at the Old Exchange and Provost Dungeon tell the stories of the extraordinary events of Old Charles Towne at this site, including the imprisonment of the notorious pirate, Stede Bonnet, seizure and storage of British tea, ratification of the US Constitution, and George Washington's visit. Animatronic storytellers in the Provost Dungeon entertain all ages with wonderful tales of pirates and patriots held captive within these eerie confines. Remnants of the 1698 fortification wall surrounding Charles Towne are here too. The Old Exchange is open daily from 9 a.m. to 5 p.m. Children 6 and under are admitted free. (For more about the Old Exchange and Provost Dungeon, see the Attractions chapter.)

ℹ️ For even more ideas about things to do with kids while in Charleston, visit the Charleston Area Convention and Vistors Bureau website dedicated to family fun. It's www .charlestonfamilyfun.com and has categories for attractions, tours, beaches, recreation, and dining—many arranged by areas of town. It even has money-saving coupons from lots of the area sights and restaurants to get you started on your way to a memorable family vacation.

INDOOR FUN & GAMES

CAROLINA ICE PALACE $$
7665 Northwoods Blvd., North Charleston
(843) 572-2717
www.carolinaicepalace.com
Charleston's coolest place for family fun is the Carolina Ice Palace with 2 NHL-size ice rinks for recreational skating, instruction, hockey teams and leagues, and birthday parties. Open 7 days a week for you to perfect that double axle, the Ice Palace has hours designated for public skating, after-school skating, and Family Night specials. Other on-site attractions are the video arcade, virtual reality center, and giant pro shop for skate rental and sharpening. Burgers and pizza can take care of the hungries, and an alcohol-free lounge with satellite TV provides a little relaxation while watching your future Olympic star. A 17,000 square-foot outdoor skate park features ramps, rails, quarter pipes, and spires for skateboarders, in-line skaters, and bikers. Call the number listed for a seasonal

schedule of times and fees. Of course, birthday parties are a popular option here for ages 3 to 18. Skating and hockey classes, conducted by professional instructors, are available on a group or individual basis.

CHARLESTON COUNTY LIBRARY STORYTIMES
68 Calhoun St.
(843) 805-6930
www.ccpl.org
"Tell me a story, please." Charleston County Libraries have the answer. They offer a series of storytimes for young children ages 12 months to 5 years old. "Wee Reads" is a 20 minute weekly morning program for ages 12 to 24 months. "Time for Twos" is another weekly morning program lasting 30 minutes for ages 24 to 36 months. All toddlers must be accompanied by a parent or caregiver. There is a preschool storytime for ages 3 to 5 that includes 30 minutes of interactive storytelling, sometimes with videos and crafts. Family Storytime welcomes all ages. Call the number above or your branch library to register. (See the Education chapter for a list of branch libraries.)

FRANKIE'S FUN PARK $–$$$$
5000 Ashley Phosphate Rd., North Charleston
(843) 767-1376
www.frankiesfunpark.com
This is Charleston's answer to the kiddies' cry for an amusement park. Children can spend money on a variety of activities—from bumper boats and a batting cage to go-karts and fun slides. A rock-climbing wall offers another challenge. Three miniature golf courses and a lighted, 90-position driving range offer a slower-paced experience. There is no general admission, but park activities

cost between $2 and $10 each. (A $25 fee allows 2 hours of unlimited fun with 6 activities.) A family with two kids can expect to spend $20 to $30 at Frankie's if Mom and Dad don't participate; it'll likely be $40 or more if everyone joins in. There are picnic tables, a snack bar, and clean restrooms. Frankie's is open daily but hours vary seasonally. It's closed on Thanksgiving, Christmas Eve, Christmas, and New Year's Day.

✳SOUTH CAROLINA AQUARIUM $$$
100 Aquarium Wharf (near Calhoun and Concord Streets)
(843) 720-1990
www.scaquarium.org
The South Carolina Aquarium, which opened in May 2000, is located at the edge of historic Charleston harbor. Two-thirds of the building projects over the water, and multiple decks complete the views of the Cooper River, both the bustling activity of the shipping industry and the serene natural landscape. The aquarium interprets South Carolina's diverse variety of habitats from mountain streams to the depths of the Atlantic Ocean. The 93,000 square-foot facility displays more than 60 exhibits representing over 500 species with 6,000 living organisms. Otters, birds, turtles, fish, reptiles, aquatic invertebrates, and insects are all a part of the habitats here. Visitors will experience five major regions of the Southeast Watershed of South Carolina: the Mountain Forest, the Piedmont, the Coastal Plain, the Coast, and the Ocean. Their education master plan, developed with local teachers, naturalists, and community leaders, encompasses interactive displays, special toddler exhibits, an education center, a discovery lab, and several education stations. Group sleepovers are a slumber party extraordinaire. Call (843) 577-FISH to book

this adventure. Open daily, hours are generally 9 a.m. to 5 p.m. The aquarium is closed Thanksgiving and Christmas Day and a half day on Christmas Eve. (See the Attractions chapter for more on the South Carolina Aquarium.)

i If you need a stroller when in town, just call at least 24-hours ahead to Tots Around Town, (843) 442-3118, to rent one.

DAY CAMPS

Many community centers, schools, and churches operate day camps around the Trident. Extended-day programs are available for many working parents and run from the end of the school day until 6 or 6:30 p.m. at most schools and centers. Like camps, some offer enrichment courses such as karate, piano, foreign language study, drama, and arts and crafts.

CHARLESTON COUNTY AFTER SCHOOL
Charleston County Community Education Program
75 Calhoun St.
(843) 937-6421, (843) 762-2172
www.charlestoncoce.org
Working parents of school-age children will be glad to take advantage of the extended-day programs available in many of the local public elementary and middle schools. These programs provide a safe, supervised, and educational environment at your child's own school. This affordable after-school alternative offers organized activities, snacks, and time to complete homework assignments, and many have a selection of enrichment courses. The average cost is $55 a week, but it varies by school and activity. The following community school directors' offices can

provide additional information: Downtown, (843) 579-4828; Mount Pleasant, (843) 881-8273; North Charleston, (843) 529-3926 or (843) 818-1499; James Island, (843) 762-2793; Johns Island, (843) 559-6208; West Ashley, (843) 573-1212; McClellanville, (843) 887-5027 or (843) 887-4229; Hollywood, (843) 889-6852.

SUMMER CAMPS

It has an all-too-familiar ring: "Mom, Dad, I'm bored."

Once school is out, you better have a plan to keep the kids occupied and happy on those never-ending, lazy summer days. Fortunately, several of the recreation departments, county parks, private schools, arts organizations, churches, and scout groups around the Trident area offer a plethora of summer day-camp adventures. Lots of fun stuff is organized to pique your child's interest in something new or improve skills in a favorite pastime. A brief sampling of some of the day camps with a mix of activities are listed below, plus a few sports- and arts-oriented camps. Prices may vary slightly.

i Three hundred thousand and counting: That's the number of kids who have enjoyed a unique overnight camping experience aboard the aircraft carrier USS *Yorktown* at Patriots Point in Mount Pleasant. Campers (in groups of at least 10 plus a chaperone) sleep in the bunks once occupied by the crew, dine in the ship's galley, and hop in the cockpit of a real fighter jet. Fun-filled excursions are an option, too. Call (800) 248-3508, or visit www.patriots point.org for more information.

THE CITADEL BASKETBALL CAMP
McAlister Field House, The Citadel,
17 Moultrie St.
(843) 953-5070, (843) 953-5904
www.citadelsports.com
Citadel head basketball coach Chuck Driesell serves as camp director of this popular basketball program for boys and girls ages 5 to 15. The staff includes Citadel basketball coaches, area high school coaches, and collegiate players. The younger Bulldog campers (ages 5 to 8) play on scaled-down facilities, and instruction takes place in McAlister Field House, where the big Bulldogs play their college games, and also at the Park West Gym in Mount Pleasant. The 1-week sessions run from 9 a.m. to 4 p.m. on Mon through Fri. Fees are $200 for the week. The Citadel also offers baseball, soccer, football, track & field, volleyball, and wrestling camps. Contact the school's athletic department for more information. (For more on The Citadel's academic offerings, see the Education chapter.)

CITY OF CHARLESTON JUNIOR TENNIS
SUMMER CAMP
Maybank Tennis Center,
1880 Houghton Dr.
(843) 406-8814
www.charleston-sc.gov
The city's Junior Tennis Summer Camp has an excellent program for your budding tennis enthusiast. The camp is for beginners to advanced intermediate students ages 4 to 18. It meets from 9 a.m. to noon (ages 4 to 12), and 3:30 to 6 p.m. (ages 10 to 18) Mon through Fri. Daily instruction includes working on fundamental strokes, video analysis, and personal attention. Games and prizes add to the positive, fun environment. Fees are $90 per week. (See the Tennis section

of the Parks & Recreation chapter for more information.) The City of Charleston offers many more summer camps with a range of activities from athletics to crafts. Visit the website for more details.

SUMMER PROGRAMS AT ASHLEY HALL
Ashley Hall, 172 Rutledge Ave.
(843) 965-8452, (843) 722-4088
www.ashleyhall.org

Ashley Hall's campus provides a perfect in-town setting for summer programs designed to entertain, educate, and challenge your children (girls only except the co-ed Early Childhood Summer Program for ages 3 to 6). (See the Education chapter for more on Ashley Hall.) Day camps, athletics, enrichment adventures, academic skills, and computer workshops let you sign 'em up for a variety of sessions throughout those long summer months. The day camps keep campers on the go with tennis, swimming, gymnastics, group games, and arts and crafts. Athletic challenges sap some of that boundless energy with basketball, volleyball, dance, soccer, scuba, swimming, and tae kwon do.

The enrichment adventures allow students to explore and develop new interests in areas such as guitar and piano lessons, jewelry making, fiction writing, and French. Computer skills and study and reading skills workshops are some of the academic offerings. Contact the school for a complete brochure outlining sessions and fees.

CREATIVE SPARK
757 Long Point Rd., Mount Pleasant
(843) 881-3780
www.creativespark.org

Let your child's creativity and imagination be sparked. Creative Spark Center for the Arts presents a wonderful variety of summer camps in the performing and visual arts to do just that. Art, an improvisational drama workshop, and musical theater camps, along with creative writing, dance, and private music instruction, are among the choices for ages 3½ and older. Call the above number for a complete brochure with details on sessions and fees. Birthday parties with an art, music, or dance theme are fun options here. A cake, favors, activities, supervision, and cleanup are provided for up to 12 for $250 on Saturdays.

EAST COOPER GYMNASTICS
633 Marina Dr., Mount Pleasant
(843) 849-6668
www.eastcoopergymnastics.com

Half-day and full-day camps are offered in June and July for ages 3 to 5 and ages 6 to 12. The goal of each camp is to provide a fun and relaxed atmosphere where each child can build strength, flexibility, and coordination. Instruction covers vault, bars, beam, tumbling, and TumbleTrak. Campers also have play time in the tumble jungle—an indoor, soft playground. Call for schedules and fees.

STONO RIVER RIDING ACADEMY SUMMER RIDING CAMP
2962 Hut Rd. (at 3000 River Rd.), Johns Island
(843) 559-0773, (877) 777-8951
www.stonoriverridingacademy.com

Learn about the splendor of the horse! Stono River Riding Academy is the new equestrian facility at the former Stono River Stable. It provides professional instruction under the direction of Michelle Folden who has an extensive background in training and competing on the national level. The emphasis here is on safety and fun. One-week sessions are offered throughout the summer months for ages 6 to 16. The classes last from 9 a.m. to 1 p.m. daily and cover grooming and tacking up, riding lessons, and horse care. The last hour changes each day from bareback riding to games on horseback to trail rides and more. Classes are limited to 12 students per day and the 1-week fee is $295. (See the Parks & Recreation chapter for more on Stono River Stable.)

SUMMER ART CAMP
Gibbes Museum of Art, 135 Meeting St.
(843) 722-2706, ext. 41
www.gibbesmuseum.org

Hands-on art and imaginary travels await your 4- to 7-year-old at the Summer Art Camp at the Gibbes School of Art. Each of the 3 one-week sessions encourages creativity, helps develop fine motor skills, and builds confidence. Classes like "In the Forest" and "Art Story" are sure to get those little hands busy.

The Summer Art Camp for ages 8 to 12 focuses on art-inspired adventures through different eras and cultures. Past offerings have included "Painting My Image," where students learn to draw faces by painting portraits inspired by works in the Gibbes collection and "Uncovering Plantations" using the visual arts and history to investigate a local landmark plantation. The Summer Art Camps meet Mon through Fri from 9 a.m. to noon. Tuition is $175 per week for Gibbes members, $200 a week for nonmembers. (See the Attractions chapter for more about the Gibbes Museum of Art.)

SUMMER FUN ON THE ISLAND DAY CAMP
James Island Recreation Complex, 1088 Quail Dr.
(843) 795-5678
www.charleston-sc.gov

Sponsored by the City of Charleston Department of Recreation, Summer Fun on the Island is a camp for youths between the ages of 6 and 12 years old. Mon through Fri from 7 a.m. to 6 p.m., campers are engaged in arts and crafts, swimming, storytelling, movies, music, aerobics, and sports divided by age groups. Once a week, campers venture out on field trips to great spots such as James Island and Folly Beach County Parks, Middleton Place, Riverbanks Zoo, and Splash Zone. Four sessions are offered from June to July, with fees for city residents set at $150 per 2-week session. Nonresidents of the city pay $175 per 2-week session.

DAY TRIPS

ere are some day trip adventures into the very heart of the Lowcountry—great excuses to go afield in search of unusual fun and a deeper understanding of what makes this area unique.

The first is a day-long journey into a land of winding rivers offering a fascinating look at some of South Carolina's early rice plantation history. The second will allow you to spend an afternoon discovering a real Lowcountry gem, Summerville, and all the strange twists of fate that have led to its various incarnations: railroad boomtown, international health resort haven, and azalea paradise (a title the community still proudly boasts). The third is a morning walk on the Lowcountry's wild side—along Marrington Watchable Wildlife Trail near the town of Goose Creek in Berkeley County. A fourth day trip is a must for families with school-age children—Old Santee Canal State Park up in Moncks Corner. Children and parents alike enjoy the interactive adventures at the park, where the Lowcountry's days of canal building and horse-drawn barges are revisited.

IT WAS (ONCE) ALL ABOUT RICE . . .

In the 18th- and early-19th centuries, this Lowcountry land and its waters spawned a rich, romantic, fragile culture largely based on a single cash crop—rice. Any real understanding of the Lowcountry and its ethic includes an appreciation for rice and the major role it played in the development of the area.

To that end, on our first day trip we will visit the sleepy fishing village of McClellanville—once a cool summer home for old rice plantation families, more recently the brave survivor of 1989's devastating Hurricane Hugo.

We'll pay a call on two important 18th-century rice plantations presented to the public in totally different, but equally valid, ways. And we'll explore old Georgetown, formerly the "Rice Capital of the Carolinas."

On the way, we'll encounter charming little chapels of ease that served the faithful plantation dwellers so far flung and isolated in South Carolina's earlier days.

Finally, we'll wander the quiet paths of Brookgreen Gardens, a unique and unexpected museum of 19th- and 20th-century American sculpture, built on rice plantation lands once granted to Lowcountry colonists by King George II of England.

Start at the foot of Charleston's new Arthur Ravenel Jr. Bridge on US 17 N. Watch for the signs to Georgetown and US 17-701. Continue along the US 17 Bypass for about 8 miles through commercial development. Then look to your right for a small, tin-roofed chapel with an octagonal cupola. Pull into the churchyard through the open gate.

CHRIST EPISCOPAL CHURCH
2304 US 17 N., Mount Pleasant
(843) 884-9090
www.christch.org
Here's your first chance to encounter one of the Lowcountry's most charming undiscovered treasures, one of the little-known but much-loved chapels of ease. Millions of tourists visit the area and never even know these little testimonies to the Lowcountry's bygone plantation era still exist. Amazingly, they do exist, in various forms and in varied states of repair and use. First, however, a little background information is required.

The colony of Carolina was founded with the Anglican Church as its established religious force. Early on, Anglican congregations received financial assistance from the British government to construct houses of worship. These first Anglican churches also tended to benefit from the generosity of wealthy planters in their congregations. As a result, these churches were built with greater architectural sophistication than the early buildings of other religious organizations, and it's mostly these better-built, early Anglican structures that survive today as mute witnesses to the strength of religion in the early colonies and the isolation of plantation life.

Christ Church Parish was one of 10 parishes established by the Church Act of 1706. The following year, a wooden building was in place on this site, serving a slowly growing· number of communicants. After fire destroyed the wooden building in 1725, a brick structure was completed in 1726.

In 1782, British soldiers burned the church to the walls during the Revolution, and it wasn't restored until about 1800. In 1865, during the Civil War, fire all but destroyed the church again, and although it was once more rebuilt, regular services were discontinued by 1874. Finally, in 1925, both the structure and the congregation were restored by caring descendants of early Christ Church Parish families. Despite its long, hard struggle for survival, Christ Church is a viable, active congregation today. Sunday services offer Holy Eucharist at 8 and 10:30 a.m.

Chances are, your initial excursions into the Lowcountry's plantation past (including many of the sites documented in the Attractions chapter) led you along the Ashley River, not the Cooper. If so, you missed the opportunity to visit some of the vast plantations that once flourished along the Cooper River. First, we'll stop at Snee Farm, country home of one of America's founding fathers, Charles Pinckney (1757–1824), then, we'll visit one of America's most photographed plantations, Boone Hall.

To find Snee Farm and Boone Hall Plantation, cross the 4-lane highway opposite Christ Church to Long Point Road, and look for the sign. Less than a mile up Long Point Road on your left is the entrance to Snee Farm.

✳SNEE FARM (CHARLES PINCKNEY NATIONAL HISTORIC SITE)
1254 Long Point Rd., Mount Pleasant
(843) 881-5516, (843) 883-3123
www.nps.gov/chpi
Only 28 acres remain of what was once the expansive Snee Farm, colonial plantation home of Charles Pinckney, a major molder of the US Constitution. But those relatively few acres are fast becoming a home base for thousands of African-Americans who come to the Lowcountry seeking more information about their heritage and the important role Charleston plays in that story.

Let's begin with Charles Pinckney, the man. He began his public career at age 22, when he was admitted to the South Carolina Bar and the South Carolina General Assembly. Pinckney served as one of four South Carolina delegates at the Constitutional Convention in Philadelphia. He served as governor of South Carolina, was ambassador to Spain from 1801 to 1805, and held seats in both the state and national legislature. He retired from public life in 1821 and died 3 years later.

Originally, Snee Farm was part of a 500-acre royal grant awarded in 1698 to Richard Butler. By 1754, the farm comprised 715 acres and was purchased that year by Pinckney's father. The property was the family's "country seat" and an integral part of Charles Pinckney's life. Like many other Charleston aristocrats, Pinckney relied on slave labor (mostly imported from West Africa) to raise the "Carolina gold" (rice) that grew on Snee Farm.

Today, the contributions of those people of African descent are being unearthed by National Park Service archaeologists. Historians working behind the scenes are following the threads of African contributions to the Lowcountry culture in the fields of language, diet, agriculture, mechanics, and craftsmanship. The Pinckney site is a rich resource for this information.

The present house on the site, built in the 1820s, is an excellent and charming example of the type of coastal cottage once common here in the Lowcountry. Guests will find interesting interpretive exhibits in and around the house. There's an informative 20-minute video telling of Charles Pinckney, Snee Farm, George Washington's colonial era visit to the property and the United States as a young, emerging nation. Park hours are from 9 a.m. to 5 p.m. Admission is absolutely free, a real bargain.

Turn left back onto Long Point Road, and less than a mile down the way is Boone Hall's entrance.

BOONE HALL PLANTATION
**1235 Long Point Rd., Mount Pleasant
(843) 884-4371
www.boonehallplantation.com**

Today's Boone Hall Plantation is a 738-acre estate dating back to the 1680s, when the Lords Proprietor made this sizable land grant to an early English settler, Maj. John Boone.

During the 18th and 19th centuries, Boone Hall was a thriving cotton plantation covering more than 17,000 acres. Brick was also a plantation product and was used in the construction of the original mansion, cotton gin house, slave cabins, and circular smokehouse. Later, Boone Hall was famous for its large groves of pecan trees, many of which are still productive today.

Boone Hall is a favorite of photographers and filmmakers because of its magnificent avenue of live oaks and the nine original, unrestored slave cabins (ca. 1743) that once housed the plantation's skilled craftspeople and house servants. The original Boone Hall mansion was lost in a tragic fire. The present structure dates from the mid-1930s. Extensive location filming was done here for the ABC-TV miniseries *North and South*.

Admission is $17.50 for adults and teens, $15 for seniors 65+, and $7.50 for children ages 6 to 12. The property is open every day except Thanksgiving and Christmas. Hours are Mon through Sat from 9 a.m. to 5 p.m. and Sun from 1 to 4 p.m. From Mar 22 through Labor Day, hours extend to 8:30 a.m. to 6:30 p.m. on weekdays and 1 to 5 p.m. on

Sunday. (For more on Boone Hall, see the Tours chapter.)

Return to US 17, and turn left. (Note that this is a 4-lane highway, and use extreme caution while crossing the 2 oncoming lanes before turning left.) Follow US 17 and note the signs designating the Francis Marion National Forest on both sides of the highway.

FRANCIS MARION NATIONAL FOREST
US 17 N., Mount Pleasant
(843) 336-3248, (843) 887-3257
www.fs.fed.us/r8/fms

This quarter-million-acre tract includes sections of both Charleston and Berkeley Counties. Once the battleground where the legendary Gen. Francis Marion—The Swamp Fox—engaged Col. Banastre Tarleton's British troops during the American Revolution, this vast park is now a wildlife reserve and a microcosm of the Lowcountry's natural habitat.

Here, as in no other place, the power and destructive range of 1989's Hurricane Hugo is dramatically apparent. The tall, mature forest was completely devastated by the storm, yet nature's recovery process is equally fascinating. Today, what is most obvious to passing visitors is not the storm's aftermath but the lush thicket of natural regrowth that has appeared since the 1989 storm.

The Francis Marion National Forest offers a·wide variety of recreational activities, including picnicking and camping sites, boat ramps, fishing ponds, rifle ranges, and hiking, horse, and motorcycle trails. For more information, contact the Witherbee District Ranger in Moncks Corner or the Wambaw District Ranger in McClellanville at the numbers listed. (For more on camping options in Francis Marion National Forest, see the Parks & Recreation chapter.)

Continue on US 17. At about mile marker 33, look for the sign on the right marking the intersection of SR 45. Turn right to discover McClellanville.

McClellanville

This sleepy old fishing village, nestled among the live oaks along Jeremy Creek, was once the summer haven for 19th-century rice planters living along the Santee River. More recently, however, McClellanville is best known as one of the small towns where residents bravely and miraculously survived Hurricane Hugo in 1989.

Eons before the town was known as McClellanville, it was one of the small villages occupied by the Sewee Indians. Archaeology shows it's one of the few sites in South Carolina that have been continuously occupied by humans for thousands of years.

The beginnings of the existing village date back to the mid-1800s, when rice planters on the Santee River built retreats here, away from the disease-ridden backwater plantations. A devastating hurricane in 1822 had completely wiped out a village of planter homes on nearby Cedar Island, and the new site was thought to be safer from storms. After the Civil War, economics forced some of the area planters to completely abandon their large plantations and move into the little summer village on a permanent basis.

McClellanville wasn't actually "McClellanville" for many years, until it became necessary to christen it something for postal and other municipal purposes. Several names were discussed, including "Jeremy" or "Jerryville," after the creek of the same name. Even "Romain" was considered, after nearby Cape Romain. But the village was finally named McClellanville for one of its early citizens, A. J. McClellan.

In the 1920s, it became one of the first places in the state where shrimpers from the west coast of Florida would come to trawl the rich coastal waters. Eventually, the town developed into one of the major shrimping ports in the state. The old buildings in McClellanville reflect the architectural development of the town from a summer retreat for plantation families to a thriving, incorporated municipality. You'll find residential, commercial, religious, and educational properties dating from the 1860s to the 1930s.

Of the hundreds of thousands of stories spawned by the forces of Hurricane Hugo on September 21, 1989, the story of McClellanville is among the most memorable.

A small plaque has been placed on a wall near the cafeteria door in McClellanville's Lincoln High School. It's a little more than 6 feet above the floor, and it shows how high the water rose that night. But no 8-by-10-inch plaque can measure the level of fear experienced by the 400 or so people who had gathered at the school for shelter against the storm.

In the pitch-black night, as the storm center pushed violently over peninsular Charleston some 35 miles to the south, the accompanying tidal surge rushed in on McClellanville with horrendous force and speed. The school was a designated storm shelter, and what was almost the entire population of the town had just settled in for what they hoped would be only a moderately uncomfortable night. There was excitement, to be sure. And dread. And worry. But the primary concern was getting the children and older people settled in as comfortably as possible. To that end, people were scattered throughout the building in

various hallways and classrooms. Suddenly, they heard a strange, rushing noise above the already fierce storm. The cold, black water of Hugo's tidal surge rushed in from everywhere, pinning the exit doors shut and turning the school into a nightmarish death trap.

Some people scrambled onto the bleachers in the gymnasium as the waters quickly climbed after them. Others crowded up onto the school's stage and literally held their children over their heads as the water surged in up to their chests. They sang and prayed, cried and comforted each other throughout the seemingly endless night. Finally, the water began to recede. What the stunned survivors found outside by dawn's earliest light was unrecognizable.

Amazingly, no one drowned in the McClellanville calamity at Lincoln High School. One life was lost, later (a heart attack victim), but it could easily have been a disaster costing hundreds of lives. Today, McClellanville is remarkably recovered. If you drive into the village via Pinckney Street, note the "new" Wappetaw Presbyterian Church (ca. 1830) on the right. Turn right on Oak Street and drive about 2 blocks to St. James Santee Episcopal Church. There, the congregation dates back to 1706. This charmingly pure, shingled Gothic structure was built in 1890. Don't leave town before you drive up to the docks for a view of the McClellanville shrimping fleet harbored along the Intracoastal Waterway.

Return to US 17 via Pinckney Street and turn right. About 5 miles up the road, a sign marks the intersection of S. Santee Road (marked SR 857). Turn left and follow it about 2 miles to the entrance of Hampton Plantation.

✳HAMPTON PLANTATION
1950 Rutledge Rd., McClellanville
(843) 546-9361
www.southcarolinaparks.com

The origins of Hampton Plantation (ca. 1750) can be traced back to the earliest European settlement of the Santee delta. The Horry family, who built and developed the property, were descendants of French Huguenots who had immigrated to Carolina in search of religious freedom and economic advancement.

The Horrys are thought to have acquired the land on which Hampton now stands during the period between 1700 and 1730. The actual date of construction for Hampton's main house is not known, but according to early records, Col. Daniel Horry built it around 1750.

The Horry land holdings on Wambaw Creek comprised some 5,000 acres, and they all were worked by slaves like most other Lowcountry plantations at the time. Rice was grown on the swamplands along the water, and these fields were connected by a complicated system of canals and ditches. The fields were flooded and drained as the demands of the rice-growing season required.

Indigo—used in the dyeing of wool—was another Hampton cash crop. For a time, there was a profitable demand for indigo because England used it in vast quantities for the dyeing of British naval uniforms. In fact, the Daniel Horry who supposedly built Hampton Plantation married the daughter of the famous South Carolina woman Eliza Lucas Pinckney who is credited with growing the first successful indigo crop in the Lowcountry.

During the American Revolution, while most of the prominent men were off engaging the British enemy at various locations, a colony of wives and children sought refuge at Hampton—relatively isolated from the military action. The dozen or so ladies sheltered there represented something of a Who's Who of South Carolina colonial history. Women with names such as Drayton, Middleton, Rutledge, Izard, and Huger were in attendance at various times.

Hampton's famous portico played an interesting role in the plantation's long story. It may have been built specifically to impress one of Hampton's distinguished early visitors. In 1791, President George Washington made a grand tour through the still very young United States of America. On May 5, according to Washington's own diary, he "breakfasted and dined at Mrs. Horry's about 16 miles from Georgetown." The traditional story is that as the president was brought up the steps of the glorious new portico at Hampton, Mrs. Horry and her mother, along with the youngest Horry daughter, greeted Washington wearing "sashes and bandeaux" hand-painted with likenesses of the president.

Another story is that Washington was asked whether a young oak tree growing directly in front of the house should be removed to improve the view. The president is supposed to have suggested the tree be spared, and so it was. At any rate, what remains of a giant old live oak can still be seen today directly in front of the house.

Circumstances found the actual welfare of Hampton Plantation left largely up to the Horry women during the busy years between the Revolution and the beginning of the Civil War. As ownership passed down (and the married name became Rutledge), Hampton faded as a viable agricultural operation.

In 1865, when he was just 22, the young master of Hampton, Henry Middleton Rutledge, joined the 25th Regiment of North Carolina. Eventually, he was elected to lead his unit through the war. Before the war was over, his regiment had suffered 200 killed in action, 280 dead from disease, and 470 wounded, with 140 of those wounded more than once.

Of course, life at Hampton was drastically altered following the war. The family struggled to cope with the financial requirements of maintaining the house, but the altered economic climate made life very difficult. Rice was no longer profitable, and Hampton was too far from the struggling markets to try to raise cotton, corn, or tobacco in any volume. Hampton, during those years, must have presented quite a strange juxtaposition: the proud, classical portico once surrounded by a formal lawn now planted in string beans and crowded with chickens.

By 1923, both Col. Henry Rutledge and his wife, Margaret Hamilton Seabrook, were dead. Hampton sat empty and neglected for a number of years until 1937, when the colonel's youngest son, Archibald Rutledge, retired to his family's ancestral home.

Archibald Rutledge was a man of letters; he'd published his first book of poetry in 1907. His prowess with poetry and prose always reflected his love and nostalgia for life on the Santee. By 1934, in recognition of his burgeoning literary reputation, Archibald Rutledge was named poet laureate of South Carolina. In 1941 he published his most popular work, *Home by the River*, in which he described his efforts to restore Hampton Plantation to its former glory. Over the course of more than 30 years, hundreds of visitors were eventually received at Hampton, drawn to the plantation and its owner by the popular works of Archibald Rutledge. By 1971, in failing health, Rutledge sold the house and 75 acres to the state of South Carolina. He died in 1973 and was buried in the family cemetery on Hampton's grounds.

When Hampton Plantation became a state park in 1971, the house had been unoccupied for several years. Initial inspections quickly indicated that an extensive renovation would be absolutely necessary. While documentary research about the house and its owners went on, another story began to unfold—the evolution of the house itself.

The exposed fabric of the house revealed that most of the interior walls had been covered with modern materials at various times over the course of the previous century. As the newer surfaces were removed, the ancient framework of Hampton became exposed. This afforded researchers an excellent opportunity to display sections of the original house as well as the different patterns of modernization and change that evolved in a Lowcountry plantation house on the Santee delta.

Like Drayton Hall on the Ashley River, Hampton Plantation offers visitors an architectural look at the sophisticated lifestyles pursued by some of the Lowcountry's earliest families.

Admission to Hampton Plantation, the state park with its picnic grounds and screened cabanas, is free, and the grounds are open daily from 9 a.m. to 6 p.m. The house is open Thurs through Sun from Nov to Feb and Tues through Sun Mar through Oct from noon to 4 p.m. Admission to the house is $4 for adults, $2.50 for SC seniors, $3 for youths ages 6 to 15, and free for children younger than 6.

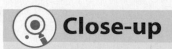

Angel Oak: A Lowcountry Treasure

Don't laugh, but we're about to suggest taking a drive to the countryside of Johns Island for the sole purpose of seeing . . . a tree.

That's right, a tree. It's an oak tree, but it's a very special one, a very old one, and a very famous one.

The tree is called **Angel Oak,** and everything about it is pure Lowcountry. No visitor has really seen the Charleston area without making the trip out to the island to be summarily awed and embraced by the Angel Oak's mighty outstretched arms.

Let's start with some background information.

Live oak trees (*Quercus virginiana*) are native to the Lowcountry and found throughout the area, but they are especially common on the sea islands. During the 18th and 19th centuries, lumber from the live oak forests was highly valued for shipbuilding. In fact, most of the area's ancient live oaks were harvested during those two centuries.

This live oak, however, survived. Angel Oak has been reported to be in excess of 1,400 years old, although the exact age is difficult to calculate. Very old live oaks are prone to heart rot (they become hollow at the center), which makes core sample ringcounting unreliable. This much is documented: Angel Oak is only 65 feet tall, yet its circumference is 25½ feet. The area of shade under this huge canopy is an incredible 17,000 square feet, and the longest outstretched limb reaches out 89 feet and has a circumference of more than 11 feet. Clearly, the Angel Oak is ancient. It knew the Lowcountry long before the English settlers arrived. It was already an old tree when the Kiawah tribe lived on this land and no doubt enjoyed its shade. It knows more than any of us ever will about hurricanes, wars, fires, earthquakes, and time. To see it is to gain worthwhile perspective on the entire Lowcountry environment.

The property where the Angel Oak stands was originally part of a land grant to Abraham Waight in 1717. Waight became a prosperous planter with several plantations in the Lowcountry, including one known as the Point, where the Angel Oak stands. The property passed through generations of the Waight family, acquiring the Angel name when Martha Waight married a Justis Angel in 1810. The Angel family plantation was sold in 1959 to the Mutual Land and Development Corp., but a small parcel of land and the old tree itself were held back and leased to the South Carolina Agricultural Society for $1 a year. The society cared for the tree until 1964, when it became the property of an S. E. Felkel, who eventually fenced in the tree and charged visitors a small fee to view it. The City of Charleston acquired the Angel Oak property in 1991, and it was opened to the public with no admission fee on September 23, 1991.

Generations of Charlestonians have journeyed to the property for picnics, family reunions, weddings, and private parties. Permits are required for large events and the consumption of alcoholic beverages at the site. You won't regret making the effort to visit the old Angel Oak. It's part and parcel of the Lowcountry experience. To get there, take US 17 to Main Road, looking for the signs to Kiawah and Seabrook. After Main Road crosses Maybank Highway to become Bohicket Road, look for Angel Oak Road on your right. Signs mark your route to this magnificent tree of life. For more information, call (843) 559-3496. Admission is still free.

As you leave Hampton and return to SR 857, turn right and go about a mile. This will bring you to a sandy road leading off to the left. This remote, almost abandoned stretch of wilderness eventually brings you to another early chapel of ease—this one built for the spiritual needs of the planters along the Santee delta.

Bear in mind, you're well off the beaten path here. Real Insiders shouldn't be daunted by a lonely, sandy road apparently leading into the pages of history and the beguiling mists of time . . . but we'd better add that if the road is wet and muddy, proceed at your own risk. If you see recent tire tracks, you can be safely encouraged to try it. When you get there, you won't be disappointed.

ST. JAMES SANTEE EPISCOPAL CHURCH
Off SR 857, McClellanville

Finding this incredibly sophisticated, early architectural treasure sitting here alone in the apparent wilderness is your first surprise. Your second jolt may be learning it was built (in about 1768) not as the first but as the fourth church to serve St. James Santee Parish. Let this simple fact dramatically emphasize just how important religion was to these early Carolina settlers.

St. James Parish was a thriving neighborhood of planters who petitioned the church for a "new" chapel that would be more conveniently located near Wambaw Creek. The building eventually provided for them was finished shortly after the completion of St. Michael's Episcopal Church in Charleston at Meeting and Broad Streets. In fact, the impressive design of St. Michael's may have influenced this structure in that both designs employ the use of two bold, classical porticos. Here the porticos are supported by four

gently fluted brick columns complete with brick bases and brick Doric capitals.

If you're lucky, the church will be open, and you can see the high-backed, boxed pews separated by a cross axis of clay tile flooring. If the church isn't open, discreet window peeking is definitely called for.

Amazingly, these beautiful, hand-hewn box pews have never been painted, never in the church's history, although sometime in the 18th century they were rearranged so the chancel might face the east wall. What is now the rear portico has been enclosed as a vestry room, and the simple pulpit on the north wall is a modern replacement, but the general ambience of this little chapel in the wilderness is overwhelmingly authentic.

Sitting here so proudly in this quiet, woodland setting, St. James Santee Church seems to generate its own will to survive. This relic of the Lowcountry's plantation past is so powerful that, although the church's communion silver was stolen during the Civil War, it was quietly returned at a later date.

In the churchyard, barely legible tombstones (best translated by paper rubbings) relate stories of fierce Revolutionary battles and the closely held relationships between the strong early families of the Santee delta.

Turn around, go back to US 17 and turn right, heading northeast toward Georgetown. At about mile 56, there's a sweeping curve in the road that preludes the delta of the South Santee River and its plantation system. Your vista both to the right and the left is not natural marsh but what remains of vast rice fields, once worked by 19th-century slaves when Georgetown was the "Rice Capital of the Carolinas." Just across the high bridge over the North Santee—another branch of the Santee's widespread watershed to the Atlantic—you'll encounter the painted white gates of Hopsewee Plantation on your left.

✳HOPSEWEE PLANTATION
494 Hopsewee Rd., Georgetown (12 miles south of Georgetown)
(843) 546-7891
www.hopsewee.com

Hopsewee Plantation was built in 1740 and was the birthplace of Thomas Lynch Jr., a signer of the Declaration of Independence. This is the only early rice plantation in Georgetown County that is currently open to the public.

Amazingly, only five families have ever owned Hopsewee. Today, it is owned by Mr. and Mrs. Franklin D. Beattie, who graciously open their home and its grounds to the public. Theirs is a remarkably refreshing attitude toward historic preservation in that the Beattie's actually live in Hopsewee, but with a respect for its place in history.

Although the main house at Hopsewee has been modernized for today, it is handsomely furnished with fine antiques and family-owned period furniture that make it very easy to picture life here as it was in Thomas Lynch's day. Be sure to visit the two cookhouses, as so few of them survive today. These are furnished with tools, crockery, and cooking utensils appropriate to their original purpose. It's important to realize that the work in these "dependency" structures—like the backbreaking work done in the rice fields—made the more formal life of the main house possible. Guests are invited to walk along a marked trail past quiet rice fields and the foundations of 18th- and 19th-century slave cabins—mute testimony to the countless African-Americans who worked the plantation in another era.

Hopsewee is on the North Santee River overlooking the river's broad, flat delta. Imagine the beautiful views Lynch was able to see every day as he pondered the dangers and daring consequences of national independence.

Hopsewee is open "by chance or by appointment," as their literature puts it, but the Beattie's have a generous attitude about sharing their historic property. Chances are you'll find Hopsewee open and well worth the investment of your time. Tours of the house are hourly, and there's a nice gift shop to browse through if you need to wait a few minutes until the next tour. The River Oak Cottage serves southern tea and sweets or traditional Southern lunch specialities. Hopsewee is usually open 10 a.m. to 4 p.m. Tues through Fri and Sat, noon to 4 p.m. Feb to Thanksgiving. Admission is $15 for adults and $7.50 for children ages 5 to 17. For carloads entering the grounds but not touring the house, the fee is $5.

Continuing north on US 17 for about 12 more miles past Hopsewee Plantation, you'll cross a high bridge over the Sampit River and pass a large industrial complex, the Georgetown Steel Corporation, on your right. Then, once in Georgetown proper, turn right off US 17, and you'll quickly find yourself downtown.

Georgetown

More than any other South Carolina community of its size, age, and historical importance, Georgetown is respectful of its past. What the visitor sees here today—streets and streets lined by charming 18th- and 19th-century homes—reflects this consciousness quite beautifully.

Several preservation organizations in the community can share credit for this effort. They include the Georgetown County Historical Society, the Georgetown County Historical Commission, and the Historic Georgetown County Foundation. These groups were instrumental in collecting data pertaining to the community, marking and preserving historic homes and sites, and educating new generations about the former rice capital of the Carolinas.

Downtown Georgetown was recently revitalized and now has interesting shops and restaurants backed up against the once-bustling riverfront docks. At the intersection of Front and Scriven Streets, you'll see an interesting old brick building with a clock tower. This is Georgetown's famous Rice Museum—a great first stop in your search to understand the giant rice industry that made Georgetown the thriving agricultural focus of the Lowcountry.

RICE MUSEUM
633 Front St., Georgetown
(843) 546-7423
www.ricemuseum.org
The real story of the rice culture of Georgetown County is one of the most exciting and colorful chapters in the history of South Carolina—maybe even in the whole history of American agriculture. It's all been captured here in the Rice Museum through fascinating maps, pictures, artifacts, exhibits, and intricate dioramas that portray a rice crop from planting through processing and eventual shipment to markets all over the world.

The Rice Museum is in the Old Market Building, which locals call "the town clock." This clock tower has become the architectural symbol of Georgetown, and this is an appropriate place to browse through booklets and tourist information pertaining to Georgetown County.

Next door in the Kaminski Hardware Building, look for the exhibit called "The Brown's Ferry Vessel." This is what remains of an early commercial river vessel that plied the waters of the Carolina coast during the first half of the 18th century. Heretofore, very little has been learned about South Carolina river vessels of this early period. This one, which was carrying a load of bricks when it sank near Brown's Ferry in about 1740, has been excavated from its longtime resting place in a riverbank and laboriously preserved for this display. The remaining sections of its hull and keel shed invaluable light on a dimly lit facet of the Lowcountry's transportation history. There you'll also find a 17-minute video presentation called "Garden of Gold," which beautifully illustrates the area's rice culture.

Museum hours are 10 a.m. to 4:30 p.m., Mon through Sat. Admission is $7 for adults, $5 for seniors 60+, and $3 for students 6 to 21. Admission is free for children 5 and younger. Members of the museum get in free. Admission to the next-door gallery, which features changing exhibits of paintings, crafts, and sculpture relating to Georgetown, is free.

The entrance to another adventure, Brookgreen Gardens, is 18 miles north of Georgetown, still on US 17. Rest assured, it's well worth the long drive.

✴BROOKGREEN GARDENS
US 17, Georgetown
(843) 235-6000, (800) 849-1931
www.brookgreen.com
Brookgreen Gardens plugs nicely into the plantation theme of this day trip in that the property encompasses four 18th- and 19th-century plantations: the Oaks, Springfield, Laurel Hill, and (old) Brookgreen. But since the late 1920s, agriculture has hardly

been the primary harvest here. Instead, Brookgreen now has 350 acres of beautifully landscaped gardens specifically designed to display more than 500 pieces of outdoor sculpture, all created by leading American artists of the 19th and 20th centuries.

Brookgreen Gardens was the brainchild of noted American sculptor Anna Hyatt Huntington, who, with her husband, philanthropist Archer M. Huntington, planned and endowed a museum back in the 1930s. Today the property is managed by a private organization, Brookgreen Gardens, a Society for the Southeastern Flora and Fauna. You may choose to get an initial orientation at the visitors pavilion for an overview of the property, or you may want to wander the seemingly endless paths and encounter the breathtaking sculpture by surprise. There's also a nature area where wild animals native to these plantations are housed and viewable in natural settings. From mid-Mar through the end of Nov, Brookgreen has a tour boat that takes guests four times daily on a brief trip out into the swamp waters and estuaries. A custom vehicle offers overland excursions but is not recommended for children under 6. There is an additional cost of $7 for adults and $4 for children to ride on either of these excursions.

Brookgreen's hours are 9:30 a.m. to 5 p.m. every day except Christmas. There are extended hours during the summer season. Admission is $12 for adults and teens, $10 for seniors, $5 for ages 4 to 12, and free to children 3 and younger. It's also free for members of the Brookgreen Society.

To return to Charleston, follow US 17 S. back to Mount Pleasant, and cross the Cooper River Bridge into the city.

SUMMERVILLE, FLOWERTOWN IN THE PINES

Our second day trip suggestion is perfect for either a crisp spring afternoon or one of those Lowcountry summer scorchers that's so hot you will gain a true appreciation for the natural wonder that is your destination. We're headed to Summerville, the Flowertown in the Pines.

If you're coming from Charleston along SR 61 (the old Ashley River Road), veer to the right on Bacons Bridge Road, which is SR 165. This will lead you into Summerville at S. Main Street (US 17-A). If you're arriving via I-26 from Charleston, take the second Summerville exit onto US 17-A, then follow the signs.

In Summerville, you're 25 miles inland from the Atlantic Ocean on a ridge that's just 75 feet above sea level. The longleaf pine forest all around you helps keep temperatures moderate and the air freshly scented with refreshing pine vapors borne on soft sea breezes.

These are the basic elements that first attracted a few planter families to build summer camps in this pineland spot away from the mosquitoes and deadly swamp fevers that plagued the lower areas. The first few families to establish summer homes in Summerville settled between the end of the Revolutionary War and 1790. By 1828, there were 23 houses in the village. Two years later, a chapel of ease to St. Paul's Episcopal Church was built, indicating a growing desire of some families to maintain full-time residences there. The summer homes were often built high on pilings with large, wrap-around porches to catch the breezes. Today, you still find many of them scattered in the half-mile Old Town area around St. Paul's Episcopal Church.

By 1832, the South Carolina Railroad had come to Summerville, and the new areas of growth (unlike Old Town) had the benefit of better planning. There were regularly spaced streets running parallel to and at right angles with the train tracks. A large, open space was reserved for a town square, and today's town hall overlooks that site. Victorian commercial buildings soon sprang up around the square, and many of them are still standing. With its umbilical railroad connection to Charleston at last in place, the once sleepy village started to grow rapidly, and in 1847, Summerville was incorporated.

A series of fever epidemics struck Charleston during the late 1850s, sending even more new residents to this relatively disease-free locale. As a Charleston newspaper lamented during those difficult years, "The eyes of Charleston sadly turned toward Summerville. . . ." By 1860, the population had grown to 1,088 residents—548 white, 540 black.

The Civil War brought an abrupt end to Summerville's growth and prosperity. Not until the end of the century would the town see another boom. When it did come, however, it would bring the pineland village international fame.

In 1889 a world congress of specialists in respiratory diseases met in Paris and named Summerville, South Carolina, of all places, one of the two best resort areas in the world for the cure of lung and throat disorders. This widely publicized "Tuberculosis Congress" introduced a whole new era for Summerville. Special excursion trains came in from New York and St. Louis, and numerous establishments were built to accommodate the flood of health-minded visitors. The grandest of these lodges was the Pine Forest Inn (unfortunately, no longer standing), where President Theodore Roosevelt, among other luminaries, stayed.

But alas, the fame of Summerville as a health resort waned with the coming of the Depression. However, post–World War II prosperity in the Lowcountry gave the town new reason to succeed.

Summerville has traditionally been known as a center for azalea culture. The lushly landscaped gardens and homes all seem to be extensions of the city's own Azalea Park, which is a focal point on the town's Main Street. Come spring of every year, Summerville still earns the title "Flowertown in the Pines." What follows are listings that give information on places and events you will want to see on your visit to Summerville, including an auto tour of more than a dozen architecturally significant homes.

i Try to be especially patient in Charleston traffic during Apr, May, and June. That's when Charleston's spring flowers are in bloom (bringing thousands of visitors), and Spoleto Festival USA is going full tilt. Traffic can be especially heavy during these months, and the city's narrow streets are easily overwhelmed by the volume.

GREATER SUMMERVILLE CHAMBER OF COMMERCE
402 North Main St.
(843) 873-8535, (866) 875-8535
www.greatersummerville.org
www.visitsummerville.com
Day trippers to Summerville may first want to check in at the city's chamber of commerce, located right on Main Street near Town Square. This green-roofed building serves as a mini welcome center with newcomer information, maps, brochures, and

friendly advice. It is open Mon through Fri from 9 a.m. until 5 p.m., Sat from 10 a.m. to 3 p.m., and Sun 1 to 4 p.m.

SUMMERVILLE-DORCHESTER MUSEUM
100 East Doty Ave.
(843) 875-9666

The Summerville-Dorchester Museum is an easy walk from the chamber offices, and it is another must-see on your visit to Summerville. Officially opened in 1993 for the Flowertown Festival (see the following listing), this museum gives visitors a fascinating look at the city's and the county's past. The inspiration was simple enough—it was intended to be a place where the area's children could learn about their own hometown, and visitors could see some of the area's rich and romantic past. You'll find local fossils, natural history, memorabilia from an earlier Summerville, and photographic displays tracking the city and Dorchester County from the days following the Great Earthquake of 1886 to the present. There is a special emphasis on the area's historic architecture and Summerville's many memorable characters.

The building was formerly a police station and is in the same block as the chamber of commerce, less than a block from Town Square. Admission is free. Museum hours are Mon through Sat 9 a.m. to 2 p.m. except major holidays.

FLOWERTOWN FESTIVAL
Various sites
(843) 871-9622
www.summervilleymca.org/flowertown

If you're lucky enough to be stopping in town sometime around Easter, chances are you'll see vestiges of Summerville's biggest annual bash, the Flowertown Festival. The entire town participates in this gala, planned

for when the town is ablaze with color, and the area's spectacular azaleas, camellias, and dogwoods are all in bloom.

The fun has been going on each spring since 1973 and includes concerts, dancing, a food fair, a health fair, kiddie rides, historic house tours, and craft exhibits of all kinds. In fact, the Flowertown Festival (sponsored by the Summerville Family YMCA) is highly regarded in craft circles up and down the Eastern Seaboard. The quality of crafts traditionally displayed here is exceptional.

Each year, tens of thousands of visitors celebrate spring in the Lowcountry by attending the 3-day event. The atmosphere is like an old-fashioned country fair. For more details, call the number above or write the Summerville Family YMCA, 140 South Cedar St., Summerville, SC 29483. (Also, see the Annual Events chapter for more on the festival.)

If, however, the calendar finds you in Summerville when the flowers are not quite so showy, don't fret. There's more to see in this special little town. The following driving tour will take you through the Old Town section of Summerville, with its winding streets, architecturally significant homes, and gleaming aura of uniqueness.

Summerville's Old Town

The cool, shady streets of this part of Summerville recall the days when this was a hot-weather retreat for wealthy planters. The charming homes and well-kept gardens seem little changed from those days in the mid-1800s.

For a nice driving tour, turn from US 17A—Main Street—onto West Carolina Avenue and begin at St. Paul's Episcopal Church. The church parking lot is a good place to pause and get your bearings.

ST. PAUL'S EPISCOPAL CHURCH
316 West Carolina Ave.
(843) 873-1991
www.stpaulssummerville.org

The history of St. Paul's Episcopal Church dates back to 1828, when the Rev. Philip Gadsden, rector of another Lowcountry chapel of ease, followed the growing number of communicants moving to the thriving village of Summerville.

Services were first held in the leaky old village hall or a parishioner's residence, but in 1829 a decision was made to build a proper house of worship. The first church building, dedicated in 1832, stood just a few feet south of the present structure, but Summerville's rapid growth soon made this simple wooden building inadequate for the growing number of believers. By 1857 a new church (the present structure) was built at a cost of $5,000.

The terrible earthquake that rocked the Lowcountry on the night of August 31, 1886, badly damaged the building, but somehow the sturdy church survived. Inside, you can still note the metal earthquake rods running through the structure for reinforcement.

There was a move in the early-20th century to replace the building with a more modern structure. Fortunately, those plans were never realized. Today St. Paul's rector, vestry, and congregation work to preserve the old church, an architectural focal point for Old Town and Summerville.

Exit the church parking lot left onto Gadsden Street, which will take you back to West Carolina Avenue. Take a right, then an immediate left onto Sumter Avenue, where in a few short blocks you will encounter at least 13 architecturally significant homes or "cottages" dating from the mid- to late-19th century. What follows are brief descriptions

of the homes, arranged in geographical order for a brief but pleasant driving tour past some of the most charming houses of Summerville's Old Town.

GELZER BROTHERS HOUSE (CA. 1852)
413 Sumter Ave.

This home, like several others on this end of Sumter Avenue, was actually built facing a street that's no longer in existence. You're viewing what was originally the rear of this very early Summerville dwelling.

BRAILSFORD-BROWNING HOUSE (CA. 1830)
408 Sumter Ave.

Here is an example of early Summerville architecture in which the house is lifted high off the ground to catch cool breezes. The lower area was once open; the present enclosure was added after 1915. Early records show this house was occupied in 1838 by a Dr. W. M. Brailsford, when it was listed among 29 houses in the growing village of Summerville.

BROWNFIELD HOUSE (CA. 1875)
230 Sumter Ave.

This residence belonged to the Brownfield family, who built on the site of a defunct boarding school for girls known as the Brownfield Academy. In 1893, the school was advertised as "particularly desirable for Northern young ladies with impaired health who would probably be successful in following their studies in this health-giving climate."

BUCKHEIT HOUSE (CA. 1884)
317 Sumter Ave.

Existing documentation indicates that, in 1862, a baker from Charleston named Philip

Buckheit bought this land. Perhaps because of the war, he didn't actually build his house until more than two decades later.

DISHER HOUSE (CA. 1862)
303 Sumter Ave.
Deeds for this property go back to 1862 when Robert W. Disher bought 2 acres of land from A. W. Taylor. Disher's house (and presence) on this site must have been noteworthy, as the adjoining road, now called Charleston Street, was formerly known as Disher Street.

WILLIAM PRIOLEAU HOUSE (1896)
302 Sumter Ave.
Built by Charleston druggist William H. Prioleau, this is one of the many Victorian homes built during the big health resort boom around the turn of the century. The lacy architectural style is called Queen Anne.

KINLOCH HOUSE (CA. 1861)
233 Sumter Ave.
This house was built in 1861, shortly after the shelling of Fort Sumter in Charleston Harbor, on land formerly owned by the Rev. Philip Gadsden, first rector of St. Paul's Episcopal Church.

PURCELL HOUSE (CA. 1820)
224 Sumter Ave.
Records date this home to between 1811 and 1828. The architecture is typical of the very early hunting lodges or summer homes built by nearby planters.

PREFERENCE (CA. 1885)
223 Sumter Ave.
Note the West Indian character of this home. The broad porches and high elevation would have offered friendly shade and cool breezes to residents and guests. Although the exact date of construction is unknown, this handsome Victorian house is thought to have been built for one Mary Webb around 1885. As for the unusual name, it seems that after the Civil War, many summer homes took on the names of the owner's former plantations, most of which were lost or sold after the conflict.

CHARLES BOYLE HOUSE (CA. 1888)
220 Sumter Ave.
This house was built by Summerville attorney Charles Boyle around 1888 on land that at one time straddled the Colleton-Berkeley county line.

SAMUEL PRIOLEAU HOUSE (CA. 1887)
217 Sumter Ave.
This was the home of Dr. Samuel Prioleau, in whose honor the first Summerville infirmary was named. The land was given to the doctor's wife by her mother, Mrs. Benjamin Rhett, who lived next door.

RHETT HOUSE (CA. 1882)
205 Sumter Ave.
Dr. Benjamin Rhett served as a surgeon for the Confederacy and later practiced medicine in Summerville. His Victorian house was built on land that was once owned by the South Carolina Canal and Railroad Co. during Summerville's first boom days in the 1830s.

SAMUEL LORD–ELIZABETH ARDEN HOUSE (CA. 1891)
208 Sumter Ave.
This handsome Victorian house was built for Samuel Lord in 1891 by the same contractor who built the town's celebrated Pine Forest Inn. With its three stories and impressive double piazzas, the ornate house was

purchased in 1938 by Elizabeth Arden, the famous cosmetics magnate, who used it as her winter retreat. It remained in her possession until 1954.

To return to Charleston, stay to the right on Sumter Avenue until it intersects with West Fifth Street at the First Baptist Church. Turn right and follow West Fifth back to Main Street, take a left and follow US 17-A through town until you see signs for I-26 S. That will be your quickest route back to Charleston.

A WALK ON THE WILD SIDE

MARRINGTON WATCHABLE WILDLIFE TRAIL
Charleston Naval Weapons Station, Goose Creek
(843) 764-7951
www.sctrails.net

In a city famous for its bittersweet history and sophisticated architecture, it's easy to follow that same suit when you go afield in search of some Lowcountry day trip adventures. The previous sojourns (to the fishing village of McClellanville and the quaint towns of Georgetown and Summerville) basically offer more of the same with a country flavor. So, for the sake of variety and an adventure into another world, here's a day trip expressly for nature lovers, serious birders, wildlife photographers, and anyone who wants an up-close and personal look at the Lowcountry's true environment—the Carolina wetlands.

Marrington Plantation is on land now owned by the Charleston Naval Weapons Station outside the town of Goose Creek. It was a typical working plantation during colonial times. In the late 1600s, when rice was introduced to this area and became a major cash crop, this was only one of hundreds of rice operations flourishing here. By the 1850s, more than 150,000 Lowcountry acres were under rice cultivation.

Rice fields were man-made. They comprised an elaborate system of dikes and canals used to control different water levels needed for planting, growing, and harvesting the rice. Today, many of those agricultural fields—long since gone feral—have become natural wetlands, teeming with wildlife.

Under the Navy's Natural Resources Program and its local initiative dubbed "Watchable Wildlife," some of Marrington Plantation's former rice fields (not used for any military purposes) were developed in 1995 as a self-guided nature trail for the public. The mile-long trail opened in 1997 and includes more than 1,200 feet of boardwalk that winds its way around several ponds.

Today, these ponds offer a natural habitat for wading birds, migratory waterfowl, alligators, eagles, hawks, wood ducks, snakes, turtles, frogs, and insects. White-tailed deer, river otters, gray squirrels, and other wildlife can sometimes be seen there too.

Even winter visitors are treated to many of the Lowcountry's natural delights. Look for egrets, herons, and ring-necked ducks. But lower temperatures usually drive the alligators and snakes out of view for the Lowcountry's short cold season. (This may or may not come as welcome news to hardcore nature lovers.)

Two observation towers offer a panoramic view of the 1,000-acre plantation, and 27 numbered stations serve as markers along the way—each with a corresponding paragraph in an accompanying brochure that explains the cultural and natural history of each feature.

To find this nifty natural diversion, take I-26 to the Goose Creek/Moncks Corner exit (at Northwoods Mall) and follow US 52 about 2 miles, past a number of auto dealerships and commercial buildings. Turn right on Snake Road (which crosses the Goose Creek Reservoir), and turn right, again, onto Redbank Road (CR 29). You'll pass several signs announcing the Naval Weapons Station, and after 2 miles or so you'll see a large green sign for Marrington Plantation. Follow the dirt road to the parking lot, where you'll see the trail's starting point and some accompanying brochures for interpretation. A tip to the wise: Pack plenty of insect repellent for this outing. Call the number above in advance to check fees and any additional security requirements for admission.

THE STORY OF SANTEE CANAL

OLD SANTEE CANAL PARK
900 Stony Landing Rd., Moncks Corner
(843) 899-5200
www.oldsanteecanalpark.org

Another fun day-trip adventure is to Old Santee Canal Park, just 30 minutes from Charleston. Opened about a decade ago, Old Santee Canal Park interprets the building and operation of America's first man-made inland waterway.

To find this colorful and kid-friendly park, take I-26 north from Charleston to exit 209A (US 52), then follow US 52 about 18 miles past Goose Creek and into Moncks Corner. Two miles down the main road of the town (US 52), look for an Old Santee Canal Park sign on the right. Plan to bring a picnic basket (rain or shine—there's a large, covered picnic area with tables) and spend your day absorbing the tranquil inland beauty.

Santee Canal was America's first summit canal, a type of canal that uses a multi-lock system to raise and lower cargo-laden barges. It was praised as a great engineering and economic development in the 1800s. The canal provided a cost-efficient, dependable way to ship crops between the uplands and the coast. While ideas for such a solution had been tossed about as early as the 1700s, the Revolutionary War intervened, and it was not until 1793 that construction actually began. Seven years and $650,000 later, with the labor of 700 men who worked with shovels and picks, a canal 22 miles long, 35 feet wide, and 5½ feet deep was a reality.

At first, mules and horses walked alongside the canal and pulled the heavy barges or boats with their cargo. Later, crewmen with poles replaced the beasts. In all, there were 16 years of profitable operation before severe droughts in 1817 and 1819 dried up the canal and ended operations for the time being. The rains returned, and 1830 was the canal's busiest year, with 700 cotton-heavy barges passing through the waterway.

Progress in transportation technology within the state spelled disaster for the canal, however, when a railway between Columbia and Charleston was completed in 1840 and took a substantial portion of the canal's business. The final blow came in 1846, when the railroad tracks were laid to Camden. In 1850, the shareholders threw in the towel.

Today, most of the canal is covered by the waters of Lake Moultrie. But where the still waters of Biggin Creek and the nearby swamps intersect with the southernmost section of the canal, the South Carolina Department of Parks, Recreation, and Tourism has created the Old Santee Canal State Park. Included in the park is the plantation house at Stony Landing bluff, built after 1840 by John Dawson. The house—restored and open to the public free of charge—faces Tail Race Canal (flowing from the Santee Cooper lakes, created during the 1940s).

Throughout the 19th century, cement and building blocks were made here, and during the Civil War, gunpowder was manufactured.

After a house tour, a good place to get oriented is the park's 11,000 square foot interpretive center. There are nifty exhibits showing the canal in different phases, a 30-foot simulated oak tree with man-made wildlife inhabitants (we bet you can't tell the difference!), and a cave. Short films about canals and the environment are also up-to date and well done. If it's a pretty day, we suggest a hike on a nature trail—either the swamp walk, the creek walk, or the canal walk —or renting a canoe.

The 195-acre park is open from 9 a.m. to 5 p.m. For more information, call or write Old Santee Canal Park, 900 Stony Landing Rd., Moncks Corner, 29461. Admission is $3 for adults; seniors age 65+ pay $2; children age 6 and younger get in free.

PARKS & RECREATION

The warm climate and natural resources of the Lowcountry make recreation and physical fitness top priorities with locals. This chapter deals specifically with some of the things we do for fitness and fun and offers a sampling of the public places designated for them. Spectator sports, boating and water sports, fishing, hunting, and golf are detailed in separate chapters due to the immense popularity and numerous outlets for these recreational activities.

As you will see reflected in many of the listings in this chapter, the Charleston County Park and Recreation Commission and Charleston County Community Education Program provide wonderful opportunities for recreation. The school programs are set up at public schools after regular hours to serve adults and sometimes children who are interested in noncredit self-enhancement courses. For detailed information, write to Adult and Community Education Programs, Charleston County School District, 75 Calhoun St., Charleston, SC 29403 (the phone is 843-937-6407), or call Charleston County Park and Recreation Commission at (843) 762-2172. Free brochures on recreational opportunities are often available at one of the public libraries.

The following is an overview of specific places, organizations, and businesses that keep the fun flowing through the Lowcountry. The listings will let you know how to go about participating in some of the Trident's most popular recreational activities. We start off with descriptions (arranged geographically) of the public parks and recreation centers where you and your family can fashion your own fun. Then we get more specific, breaking down information on individual recreational pursuits by type of activity (arranged alphabetically).

Price Code

The following price code is provided to give you an idea of the price of admission to those establishments that charge an admission fee. Please note that prices, means of payment, and hours change often and may vary seasonally, so call ahead for details. If no price code is designated, there is no charge to enter but there may be other fees.

$	Less than $6
$$	$6 to $10
$$$	$10 to $20
$$$$	More than $20

PARKS & RECREATION CENTERS

The parks we like best are sizable tracts of land that give young and old alike a chance to enjoy the great outdoors. We make a distinction here between "park" and "playground" because, although the former may include the latter, "park" implies more space and characteristics that appeal to both children and adults. We list several playgrounds under a separate heading later in the chapter. For more information on the public parks, call the City of Charleston Department of Parks and Recreation, (843) 724-7321. Call the same number if you would like to schedule a special event at one of the parks.

Also included here are several community center complexes scattered throughout the Lowcountry. These offer various indoor activities, usually at a bargain price. All listings are arranged geographically, starting with parks and centers in Charleston and East Cooper (including Mount Pleasant, Sullivan's Island, and Isle of Palms). Then we go to West Ashley and James, Folly, and Kiawah Islands. Welcome to a few of our favorite places.

Downtown Charleston

Officially this subject comes under the auspices of the City of Charleston Department of Parks and Recreation. It offers an extensive program of activities, sports, special events, and multigenerational recreation for residents and visitors. Here are the best-known spots.

HAMPTON PARK
30 Mary Murray Dr.
(843) 724-7321
www.charleston-sc.gov
Near the Citadel, Hampton Park is a 60-acre downtown park with a lake (complete with lots of resident ducks for feeding), one of the largest rose gardens in the state, grassy areas, a trail for workouts, and a bandstand (the site of many an afternoon concert). A giant Easter egg hunt and the Piccolo Spoleto finale are held here. Sometimes the park is closed off (usually Tues and Thurs evenings from Apr to Sept and Sat mornings year-round) for walkers, runners, joggers, skaters, and bikers—a great traffic-free treat for city kids and their parents. (For more, see the Kidstuff chapter.)

✳WATERFRONT PARK
Cumberland Street to North Adgers Wharf
(843) 724-7321
www.charleston-sc.gov
Just off East Bay Street, from Cumberland Street to North Adgers Wharf, this is one of the city's most popular and most delightful parks. On site are a 400-foot pier for viewing harbor activity and 2 inviting fountains in which the young and young-at-heart are allowed to play. You'll also enjoy grassy areas and swings. (See the Kidstuff chapter.)

✳WHITE POINT GARDENS
South tip of East Bay and King Streets
(843) 724-7321
www.charleston-sc.gov
At the tip of the Peninsula, boxed in by East Bay Street, Murray Boulevard, King Street, and South Battery, White Point Gardens has a beautiful view of the harbor and some of the homes of the Battery. Children love to climb on the old cannons (and stacked cannonballs) or picnic in the grassy areas. You may even catch a glimpse of a bride and groom exchanging vows here in the old bandstand. It is often crowded on Sun when the weather is nice, but is less so during the week. (For more on the history of White Point Gardens, see the History chapter; see Kidstuff for more on fun activities.)

Mount Pleasant

ALHAMBRA PARK
131 Middle St., Mount Pleasant
(843) 884-2528, (843) 856-2166
www.townofmountpleasant.com
This simple, lovely park across from Alhambra Hall is wide open with free public admission from sunup to sundown. It offers a nice lawn and scenic view of Charleston

Harbor. The selection of playground equipment (swings, slides, climbing toys, and a merry-go-round) keeps the children busy. For picnics, there are several tables under the shade of big oaks.

MOUNT PLEASANT RECREATION DEPARTMENT AT PARK WEST
1251 Park West Blvd., Mount Pleasant
(843) 856-2196
www.mtpleasantrec.com
Located just off US 17 in the Park West development is this 59-acre sports and recreational complex built to serve the new communities in the upper part of Mount Pleasant. The Park West facility has a 6,000-square-foot program building with lots of parking, lighting, and fields for baseball, softball, soccer, football, and other activities sponsored by the Mount Pleasant Recreation Department. (See the following listing on the Richard L. Jones Recreation Complex for more on the programs.) With Mount Pleasant's rapid population growth along US 17 and SR 41, this complex is expected to serve about 30,000 people in the area. The fourth and final phase of construction, completed in spring 2004, added 2 tennis courts, an asphalt walking trail, a 6-lane, 25-meter pool, another baseball field, playground equipment, a dog park, and an additional 1,400-square-foot program building. This is Mount Pleasant's largest and finest recreational offering.

PALMETTO ISLANDS COUNTY PARK $-$$
444 Needlerush Pkwy.
(843) 884-0832
www.ccprc.com
This family-oriented, 943-acre nature facility is in a heavily wooded area, with a 2-acre pond and 1-mile canoe trail. You'll enjoy a well-designed playground, picnic sites, and boat docks. It is a perfect place to jog, walk, or rent a pedal boat, kayak, or a bike. Call or check the website for rental fee information. Splash Island, with its 200-foot water slide, is quite popular in the warm months. Park admission is $1 per person (no charge for children younger than 3), with an annual individual pass available for $15 for Charleston County residents, $25 for nonresidents. Additional fees are charged for entry to Splash Island. Annual family and senior passes are available also. (For more on this park, see the Kidstuff and Boating & Water Sports chapters.)

RICHARD L. JONES RECREATION COMPLEX $
391 Egypt Rd., Mount Pleasant
(843) 884-2528
www.mtpleasantrec.com
Opened in March 1991, this large, modern building provides a facility for scheduled recreation programs, a gymnasium, a 6-lane pool, and an activity room. There is a 1-year membership fee of $2 each for everyone 5 and older. The pool usage fee is $2 a day, but it's free for children younger than 5. Non–Mount Pleasant residents pay $136 for an annual family membership. There are separate fees for T-ball, softball, basketball, baseball, track, soccer, and a supervised skate park. Crafts, painting, dance and theater classes, swimming lessons, and gymnastics camps (half-day and full-day) are some of the activities offered. The unified athletics program includes softball, basketball, and soccer leagues providing the opportunity for children with disabilities to play with children their own age. Call the number above for more information on programs, athletics, and current events.

Sullivan's Island & Isle of Palms

✳ISLE OF PALMS COUNTY PARK $$
1–14th Ave., Isle of Palms
(843) 886-3863
www.ccprc.com
Everyone can hit the beach straight off the Isle of Palms Connector at one of the newer county parks. Enjoy one of the area's nicest beaches, open daily year-round, with the convenience of paved parking, outdoor showers, restrooms, a sand volleyball court, and children's play area. Just in case you forget your beach gear, you'll find chairs and umbrellas available for rent. Hours are generally 10 a.m. to 5 p.m., with extended hours in the warmer months. Admission is free for walk-ins and bicycles, but there is a fee for vehicles. (See the Kid-Friendly Beaches section of the Kidstuff chapter for more information.)

ISLE OF PALMS RECREATION DEPARTMENT
24–28th Ave., Isle of Palms
(843) 886-8294
www.iop.net
This comprehensive facility includes a big playground (complete with separate equipment and areas for different ages), a volleyball court, athletic fields (for soccer, football, and kickball), baseball fields, tennis courts, a frisbee golf course, and basketball courts. An indoor center houses night basketball courts, tumbling equipment, Ping-Pong tables, a cardio room, and more. There are also sheltered tables and grills for picnics.

The department sponsors special programs, such as a summer day camp, youth dances, and a senior citizens group, and organizes events such as kite-flying and sandsculpting contests. Bring your favorite canine friend to the Bark Park on 29th Avenue

behind the recreation center. The park is open from sunup to sundown; the recreation building is open all day (with the kids' programs in the morning) Mon through Fri and afternoons on Sat and Sun.

SULLIVAN'S ISLAND PARK
1610 Middle St., Sullivan's Island
(843) 883-3198
www.sullivansisland-sc.com
Sullivan's Island has a nice park at the Mound (constructed by the military during World War II) on Middle Street between stations 20 and 22 (street names on Sullivan's are based on the old streetcar station stops). There is a bandstand, plus basketball courts, 2 tennis courts, and children's wooden play equipment in a fenced-in tot lot (see the Kidstuff chapter). Although there is no official recreation department on Sullivan's Island, one member of the town council serves as head of recreation.

West Ashley

CAW CAW INTERPRETIVE CENTER $
5200 Savannah Hwy., Ravenel
(843) 889-8898
www.ccprc.com
A bit farther out, but worth the trip (about 15 miles south of Charleston on US 17 S.), is the Caw Caw Interpretive Center in Ravenel, South Carolina. Part of the Charleston County Park system, this 654-acre park is managed specifically for birds and wildlife. There are 7 miles of interpretive trails, a 1,200-foot swamp boardwalk, and a bird and butterfly garden. Loads of educational programs, daily walks, workshops, and demonstrations complete the natural, cultural, and historical experience. Admission is $1 and free for children 2 and under. Pets and bicycles are not permitted. Hours are 9 a.m.

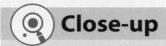

Close-up

A rose . . . is a rose . . . is a rose . . .

Anyone who spends any time at all in Charleston's **Hampton Park** will be dazzled by the ancient trees, the handsome bandstand, lovely duck pond, and refreshing fountain arranged on the pastoral grounds. In fact, the park was originally landscaped by the firm of Frederick Law Olmsted, the brilliant designer of New York's Central Park. It was all part of Charleston's 1902 "would-be" World's Fair, the once glittering South Carolina Interstate and West Indian Exposition—an ill-fated enterprise that drew little attention to the city at the time. Even less of Olmsted's original plan survives today, but Hampton Park remains a pleasant oasis of beauty on the city's west side.

Ringing the park is an exercise path, part of which passes one of the city's most impressive rose gardens, and among the colorful hybrids and showy cabbage roses is a shy, pink beauty that is Charleston's very own.

In 1802 a wealthy Charleston plantation owner and plant enthusiast named John Champneys crossed two roses to produce what he called "Champneys' Pink Cluster." One of the roses he used for his experiment was called "Old Blush," a rose given to him by French-born horticulturalist Philippe Noisette. When the seeds of "Pink Cluster" found their way to Paris and were raised by Noisette's brother, the name evolved into "Blush Noisette"—a whole new class of roses that soon became extremely popular throughout the continent. Today, Noisette roses are grown all over the world.

Of the 80 different Noisettes marketed worldwide, Hampton Park is currently growing nearly 50 as part of a special scientific study. A conference of rose experts recently gathered in Charleston and attracted visitors from as far away as South Africa, Australia, Germany, Bermuda, and France—all here to see Hampton Park's famous Noisette roses. True beauty is timeless, it seems, and apparently knows no bounds.

to 5 p.m. Wed through Sun. The park is closed on Mon and Tues.

CHARLES TOWNE LANDING STATE HISTORIC SITE $$
1500 Old Towne Rd., SR 171
(843) 852-4200
www.southcarolinaparks.com

In West Ashley, this is a wonderful, low-key, recently renovated park for all ages on the site of the original settlement called Charles Towne. There is an animal forest, playground, replica of the ship Adventure,

early settlement village, gift shop, restaurant, and a new visitor center with interactive exhibits. Ask about the annual bike passes and vehicle passes (good at any state park). They are good deals if you are going to be spending lots of time here. (For more on Charles Towne Landing, see the Attractions, History, and Kidstuff chapters.)

WEST ASHLEY PARK
3600 Mary Ader Ave.
(843) 724-7321
www.charleston-sc.gov

The 270-acre West Ashley Park includes four baseball and soccer fields, bicycle and pedestrian trails, picnic areas, a playground, and restrooms. The $4 million facility is, in fact, the largest of all the City of Charleston's parks. The unusual concept of this park is that it will remain largely undeveloped, allowing residents "to get away from the city without leaving the city." The pedestrian trails wind through the woods and along Church Creek, giving visitors a change of pace (and vista) from nearby suburbia. Fishing is a pleasant pastime in the park's large lake surrounding a 10-acre island accessible by footbridge. The playground has a tot lot with a giant slide popular with the little ones. Ask about special recreation programs offered on a seasonal basis, such as canoeing, by calling the number above. The park is open 8 a.m. until dusk.

i After finishing lunch at one of the fine restaurants scattered along East Bay Street, take a stroll through Charleston's Waterfront Park. It's safe, nearby, and perfect for "taking the air," as the old-timers in this area might put it.

James Island

JAMES ISLAND COUNTY PARK $–$$
871 Riverland Dr.
(843) 795-7275
www.ccprc.com
This incredible, 643-acre park offers biking, nature trails, a climbing wall, an elaborate playground, a dog park, pedal boats, kayaks, Hydrobikes, 16 acres of lagoons, a SprayPlay fountain area, a fishing and crabbing dock, and picnic areas. There are 10 vacation cottages, camping sites (see "Camping" later in this chapter), and three picnic shelters that can accommodate 200 or more people each. Hours are generally 8 a.m. to 5 p.m., and later in the warmer months. Admission is $1 per person (no charge for children younger than 3). The ever-popular Splash Zone costs an additional fee, but most agree it is well worth the price to escape to the land of the tropics via slides, waterfalls, and spray effects (see our Kidstuff chapter). Additional fees apply for the climbing wall as well. Annual individual, family, and senior passes are also available.

Folly Beach

FOLLY BEACH COUNTY PARK $$
1100 West Ashley Ave.
(843) 588-2426
www.ccprc.com
At the tip of Folly Beach, this county park is an easy-to-reach, family-oriented beach destination. Enjoy the sand and waves, or bring along binoculars for viewing feathered friends in the marsh or nearby Bird Key. In addition to seasonal beach chair and umbrella rentals, you'll find a snack bar and gift shop. The Pelican Watch Shelter provides natural gas, an oyster-roasting pit, barbecue cookers, and horseshoe equipment.

Owing to recurring winter high tides, erosion is a problem at this beach park. Each year a renourishment program replenishes the sand, but the parking has been cut to 150 spaces. This may make parking here more difficult in the summer months, so it's best to get there early in the day. Admission is $7 per car, $10 per camper, or $25 per bus. Walk-ins and bicycles are free. Hours are generally 10 a.m. to 5 p.m., with extended hours in the warmer months. (See the Kid-Friendly Beaches section of the Kidstuff chapter for more details.)

Kiawah Island

✳BEACHWALKER PARK   **$$**
1 Beachwalker Dr.
(843) 768-2395
www.ccprc.com

This county park is just outside the gates into Kiawah (take a right on Beachwalker Drive). Hours are generally 10 a.m. to 5 p.m., with extended hours in the warmer months. They are open weekends only in Mar, Apr and Oct. Nov through Feb the park is closed. This is 10 miles of pristine beach with white sand. Admission is $7 per car, $10 per camper, or $25 per bus, and all 150 parking spots often fill early. Walk-ins and bicycles are free. There are lifeguards, a picnic area with grills, outdoor showers, and restrooms, and beach chair and umbrella rentals are available. (Also see the Kid-Friendly Beaches section of the Kidstuff chapter.)

RECREATION

What follows is a good representation of the recreational opportunities scattered throughout the Lowcountry. Categories are in alphabetical order, and so are the businesses that are listed with each type of activity.

The following departments are also good clearinghouses for information on specific sports and recreational opportunities throughout the Lowcountry. In Charleston, call the City of Charleston Department of Recreation, (843) 724-7327, or the James Island Recreation Complex, (843) 795-5678. In Mount Pleasant, call the Richard L. Jones Recreation Complex, (843) 884-2528. For Isle of Palms information, call the town's Recreation Department, (843) 886-8294. Sullivan's Island Town Hall, (843) 883-3198, can provide information on options on that island, and the North Charleston Recreation Department, (843) 745-1028, can answer recreation questions in that area.

Aerobics

Individual recreation departments often offer aerobics classes. The parks and recreation departments and facilities listed in the Recreation introduction are good places to look for further information. Also, most full-service fitness centers offer a plethora of aerobics classes. (See the Fitness Centers section in this chapter.)

CHARLESTON COUNTY COMMUNITY EDUCATION PROGRAM
Charleston County School District,
75 Calhoun St.
(843) 937-6421
www.charlestoncoce.org

This program offers moderately priced aerobic classes at locations all over the county. For a schedule and more information pick up a free brochure at one of the public libraries.

Archery

ARCHERY SHOP II
1161 Cainhoy Rd.
(843) 884-8872

Bow-and-arrow enthusiasts will find a fine source of archery equipment and information here. The Archery Shop II employs full-time technicians and offers custom services such as bow tuning and arrow building. It is by far the most popular archery services vendor in the Lowcountry.

Aviation

PALMETTO AIR SERVICE
700 Faison Rd., Mount Pleasant
(843) 884-8914
www.palmettoair.com

For primary flight instruction east of the Cooper River, talk to the instructors at Palmetto Air. Their lessons are $125 per hour for dual instruction and $89 per hour to learn solo in a Cessna 152. In a Cessna 172 dual instruction is $175 per hour, and solo is $139 per hour. They also offer sightseeing flights over Charleston for those of us who are not yet ready to earn our wings.

Baseball

The area's recreation departments organize baseball leagues (T-ball for toddlers through baseball for teens), and there's a batting range for those who want to go it alone. Call the department in your area for information about spring registration, and plan to have on hand your child's birth certificate, social security card, and insurance as well as a registration fee of about $30 for city residents, $55 for nonresidents.

FRANKIE'S FUN PARK
5000 Ashley Phosphate Rd., North Charleston
(843) 767-1376
www.frankiesfunpark.com

You're never too old to swing it! Frankie's has a nine-position baseball batting cage with a variety of pitch-speed options. It costs $2 for 24 pitches or 144 swings for $10. (See the Kidstuff chapter for more about Frankie's.)

Basketball

Public basketball courts are adjacent to most local playgrounds. Here are a few spots for shooting the rock convenient to various parts of the Greater Charleston area. More playgrounds are listed later in this chapter.

Both Moultrie Playground, across from Colonial Lake at 41 Ashley Ave., and Hazel Parker Playground, next to the Carolina Yacht Club at 70 East Bay St., have outdoor courts that are very convenient if you are downtown.

In Mount Pleasant, the Richard L. Jones Recreation Complex on Egypt Road (see previous listing in Parks and Recreation Centers) has an indoor gymnasium and active basketball programs for youth ages 5 to 17, adults, and seniors age 50 and older.

If you are on one of the East Cooper beaches, consider playing at the Isle of Palms Park, 24–28th Ave., which has 2 outdoor lighted courts and 1 indoor court. There are youth and adult basketball leagues organized by the recreation department there as well. Another island option is the lighted court at Sullivan's Island Park, conveniently located on Middle Street in the center of the business district and usually swarming with players eager to shoot some hoops.

If you are in West Ashley, try playing outdoors at St. Andrews Park on Playground Road or the St. Andrews Family Fitness Center on Sam Rittenberg Boulevard for indoor courts. The James Island Recreation Complex has an indoor court that is open for recreational play daily and organizes adult and youth leagues Jan through Mar. For more information, contact the area recreation departments.

St. John's Community School offers coed adult (18 and older) pickup basketball and a men's league for those age 20 and older. The school is at 1518 Main Rd. on Johns Island.

Bicycling

COASTAL CYCLISTS
P.O. Box 32095, Charleston, SC 29417
(843) 209-2578
www.coastalcyclists.org
Coastal Cyclists is an organization of bike riders and racers that meets once a month (usually on the first Monday) at an area restaurant. Members enjoy supper together and have a meeting with a guest speaker. Coastal Cyclists organizes club rides for Class 1 to Class 4 riders covering 20 to 40 miles on average. The group has a racing team that travels to compete around the state. Annual family membership costs $30; single membership is $20 and includes a newsletter on upcoming events. This group is open to riders of all levels.

Cyclists in South Carolina have the same rights on the road as a vehicle driver and are required to obey specific traffic laws: Ride on the right side of the road and in the same direction as traffic, obey all traffic signs and signals, do not ride on freeways (multi-lane divided highways), and form a single line in heavy traffic. Equipment must include a bell audible for 100 feet, and night use requires a front lamp with a white beam visible for 500 feet and a red rear reflector. Don't forget to wear a helmet!

Bowling

Bowling is popular in the Lowcountry, with active leagues playing every night on area lanes right next to the occasional group or office outing. For information about leagues, talk to the management at the following lanes, and beware of those gutter balls!

AMF CHARLESTON LANES $-$$
1963 Savannah Hwy.
(843) 766-0241
www.amf.com/charlestonlanes
Just off the Mark Clark Expressway, west of the Ashley, AMF Lanes has automatic scoring, a pro shop, and a lounge. There are 24 lanes and leagues every evening. Fees are nominal, with an extra fee for shoe rental. This is a choice venue for birthday parties.

ASHLEY LANES $-$$
1568 Sam Rittenberg Blvd.
(843) 766-9061
Ashley Lanes has numerous leagues and a total of 24 lanes. Rates are lower before 6 p.m. and for seniors. Shoe rental is additional. In addition to bowling, you'll find an amusement center with a snack bar and several video games, plus a restaurant, lounge, and nursery.

TWIN RIVER LANES $-$$
613 Johnnie Dodds Blvd., Mount Pleasant
(843) 884-7735
www.twinriverslanes.net
Twin River Lanes is the East Cooper venue for bowling and offers 16 lanes for play. Before 6 p.m. rates are slightly lower. Shoe rental is an added fee. You can rent lanes by the hour. Other fun activities are the arcade, the sports bar and grill, and a pool table and video games.

Camping

There are government-owned, public places for camping in the Charleston area as well as private options, and the best clearinghouse for information on them is the Charleston County Park and Recreation Commission,

(843) 762-2172. We've included our favorites here.

If you've got a youngster who wants to get outdoors, the Boy Scouts are on top of things at their two campsites, Camp Ho Non Wah on Wadmalaw Island and Camp Moultrie on Lake Moultrie. For more information on joining the Boy Scouts of America or if you would like to volunteer to help out, call or write the Coastal Carolina Council of the BSA, 1025 Sam Rittenberg Blvd., Charleston, (843) 763-0305, or visit www.coastalcarolina bsa.org.

The Girl Scout Outdoor Program Facility is a wonderful site in Cordesville (about 38 miles from Charleston) that's listed on the National Register of Historic Places. The summer resident camp is called Camp Low Country and runs June through Aug. The site includes a Junior Olympic–size pool, 20-stall stable, lighted riding ring, screened dining hall, 3 units of platform tents, and 1 cabin unit. For more information about the Outdoor Program Facility or other Girl Scout programs, call (843) 552-9910, (800) 868-9911, or visit www.girlscoutsesc.org.

CAPERS ISLAND HERITAGE PRESERVE
C/O SCDNR
P.O. Box 12559, Charleston, SC 29412
(843) 953-9300
www.dnr.sc.gov

This 2,000-acre barrier island can only be reached by boat but is well worth the effort of securing a ride. South Carolina's only primitive beachfront camping area, Capers has no facilities, and camping here is absolutely in the rough—exactly the way plenty of people want it. It is protected under the Heritage Preserve Program and managed by the South Carolina Department of Natural Resources Marine Resources Division. Contact the Marine Resources Division at Fort Johnson on James Island at the number listed above for a permit.

i For children (and adults) with physical, social, and behavioral disabilities, Anchors Away! is a special program for recreational opportunities designed by the Department of Neurology of the Medical University of South Carolina. Options include Jet Skiing, fishing, waterskiing, canoeing, harbor tours, sailing, swimming, kayaking, and more. For additional information call (843) 792-0721 or visit www .anchorsawayprogram.org.

FRANCIS MARION NATIONAL FOREST
Pinckney Street, near intersection of US 17 and SR 45, McClellanville
(843) 887-3257, (843) 336-3248
www.fs.fed.us/r8/fms

There are 4 sites in the Francis Marion National Forest, a little more than 2 miles past Awendaw. It's hard to beat this place for seclusion and an opportunity to get back to nature. The forest still bears scars from Hurricane Hugo, but it stands testimony to nature's resilience. To get there, take US 17 N. toward Georgetown. Just after the intersection of US 17 and SR 45, about 33 miles from Charleston, turn right onto Pinckney Street and look for the ranger station. All the sites are free except at Buck Hall Campground, where they cost $15 per day for tents, $20 per day for full hookups, on a first come, first served basis. Call (877) 444-6777 for information about availability, or write the Wambaw Ranger District, P.O. Box 788, McClellanville, SC 29458.

JAMES ISLAND COUNTY PARK
871 Riverland Dr.
(843) 795-4386
www.ccprc.com

One lovely spot is the James Island County Park, with 125 camping sites. Campers can spend the night in tents or in recreational vehicles. Most sites are equipped with full water, sewer, and electricity hookups. Call or visit the website for fee information. (Please note that these fees do not include the 12 percent accommodations tax levied here.) Round-trip shuttle service is available to downtown Charleston, Folly Beach County Park, and Folly Beach Fishing Pier for $10 per person.

KOA KAMPGROUND
3157 US 17 North, Mount Pleasant
(843) 849-5177, (800) KOA-5796
www.koa.com

This Mount Pleasant KOA campground offers large pull-through sites with 20-, 30-, and 50-amp hookups. Amenities include restrooms, showers, heated swimming pool, convenience store, laundry, free Wi-Fi and cable TV, firewood, and propane. There is a 30-acre lake fully stocked for fishing and water recreation. The 2.5-mile hiking trail and bike rentals offer other opportunities for enjoying the great outdoors. Deluxe and wilderness tent sites are available for those who really want to get away from it all. Located on US 17 N., this KOA has many nearby attractions including Boone Hall Plantation, Sewee Environmental Education Center, Patriots Point Maritime Museum, and historic Charleston. (See the Attractions, Kidstuff, and Day Trips chapters for more on these and other area points of interest.) Call the number above for rate information.

OAK PLANTATION CAMPGROUND
3540 Savannah Hwy.
(843) 766-5936, (866) 658-2500
www.oakplantationcampground.com

This is an RV campground with modern facilities. Campers park on concrete pads with 30 and 50-amp hookups available. The campground is landscaped with privacy in mind, and campers enjoy fishing for bream and bass in the freshwater lake. There is a playground with swings, a swimming pool, and a small grocery with propane. A dog run and Wi-Fi (for a fee) are new additions. The office is generally open from 7:30 a.m. to 7 p.m., depending on the season, so call for fee information.

Fitness Centers

EAST SHORE ATHLETIC CLUB
910 Johnnie Dodds Blvd., Mount Pleasant
(843) 856-8877
www.eastshoreac.com

East Shore Athletic Club centers are locally owned, state-of-the-art fitness centers. The facilities are sparkling clean and attractive with an antibacterial exercise floor, free weights, a dumbbell section, circuit-training machines, cardiovascular equipment (including steps, bikes, and treadmills), racquetball courts, and a heated pool at the Johnnie Dodds location. A full schedule of classes is available, and personal training as well. Child care for children 3 months and older is an option at some locations. Memberships are discounted for each additional family member. Additional locations in Moncks Corner, Goose Creek, North Charleston, and Hanahan make it awfully convenient to work on keeping in shape. Call for more information and special package rates. Visit the website for a list of locations.

ST. ANDREW'S FAMILY RECREATION CENTER
1642 Sam Rittenberg Blvd.
(843) 763-3850
www.standrewsfitness.com
Affiliated with the St. Andrew's Park and Playground Department, this is a full-service health fitness facility. The whole family (even the little ones, who play in the nursery) can enjoy water aerobics classes, 5 racquetball courts, a squash court, 2 basketball courts, a Junior Olympic pool, Nautilus equipment, free weights, an indoor track, stair machines, treadmills, personal trainers, and more. Annual, monthly, family, and daily passes are available, and prices vary according to factors such as residence and age. Daily passes are available. Special discounts may apply, so call for more information. Hours are 5 a.m. to 10 p.m. Mon through Thurs, 5 a.m. to 9 p.m. Fri, 8 a.m. to 5 p.m. on Sat, and 1 to 6 p.m. Sun.

TOWN AND COUNTRY INN FITNESS CENTER
2008 Savannah Hwy.
(843) 571-1000, (800) 334-6660
www.thetownandcountryinn.com
Although it's in a motel complex, this $1 million 10,000-square-foot fitness center is open to the public for memberships. For an initiation fee and monthly payment, members can use the Calgym exercise equipment, stair machines, stationary bikes, dumbbells, 2 racquetball courts, an indoor, heated lap pool, showers, and sauna. Call for membership information. In early 2011 the fitness center was undergoing an extensive renovation. Although scheduled to reopen

late summer 2011, be sure to call ahead before visiting.

Football

There are many leagues for youth football. For more information about children's teams, contact City of Charleston Youth Sports at (843) 724-3747. Registration is held throughout June through early Aug. Children must be ages 7 through 14 to play, and be sure to bring your child's birth certificate when you sign up. Play starts in mid-Sept and runs through the fall. Also, the Mount Pleasant Recreation Department offers flag football for children ages 7 and 8 during the fall and a full schedule of football from small fry to middle school varsity age groups. Call them at (843) 856-2196 for details.

Frisbee

Charleston is on top of the Frisbee fun. On a pretty day, White Point Gardens (down by the Battery) is usually covered with young people throwing Frisbees. Call the City of Charleston Department of Recreation, (843) 724-7327, for more information.

Gymnastics

It seems most extracurricular community programs and recreational department programs offer gymnastic courses. Another option we can recommend is Charleston Gymnastics Training Center.

CHARLESTON GYMNASTICS TRAINING CENTER
1088 Quail Dr.
(843) 795-4207
www.charleston-gymnastics.com
This is a very serious, well-respected program that is safety-certified. Competitive

teams go to the state, regional, and national level. Preschool, recreation, cheerleading, and competitive team classes are offered throughout the school year. There is an annual $15 registration fee, plus the cost of the specific class. Call the number above for pricing.

Horseback Riding

The equestrian set is quite active in the Greater Charleston area. We've included one stable each in Mount Pleasant, West Ashley, Hollywood (south of Charleston on the way to Edisto Island), and Seabrook, and two on Johns Island.

BRICK CHURCH FARM
1131 Wando Rd., Mount Pleasant
(843) 881-1310

This is a popular riding school, away from city congestion, with caring, competent personnel. Call for directions and information. This is primarily a private show barn that prepares riders for hunter-jumper competitions on the local and southeastern levels. No horse rentals are available here, but boarding for their show programs for hunters and jumpers is $850 a month. Lessons are offered on a limited basis (on your own horse), so call the number listed for more details.

MIDDLETON RIDING AND HUNT STABLES
4280 Ashley River Rd.
(843) 556-8137
www.middletonplace.org

A premier boarding and lesson facility, Middleton has a dressage arena, cross-country course, and lighted ring for evening riding. Stall boarding is $650 per month, and private lessons are offered for $40 per half hour or $45 per hour. The nearby Middleton Inn (see the Accomodations chapter) arranges trail rides for ages 10 and older. Contact Middleton Inn, (843) 556-8137, for these walking trail rides through the Middleton woods and wetlands.

MULLET HALL EQUESTRIAN CENTER
2662 Mullet Hall Rd., Johns Island
(843) 768-5867, (843) 795-4FUN (4386)
www.ccprc.com

Opened in April 2001 by the Charleston County Park and Recreation Commission, this 60-acre equestrian center features fenced warm-up and open-lunge areas, four permanent show rings, and jump sets. The center also has 2 barns with 140 stalls and areas for temporary stalls and for exercising horses. For riders who trailer their horses in, there are 20 miles of riding trails through the 738-acre park site. Passes are required for trail riding. A 1-year pass is $35 for individuals and $60 for families. Ample parking is available for all kinds of vehicles. This facility serves as the host site for a variety of competitive horse shows. Call for more information about upcoming events.

SEABROOK ISLAND EQUESTRIAN CENTER
3772 Seabrook Island Rd., Seabrook Island
(843) 768-7541, (866) 586-6380
www.seabrookresort.com

This center is at Seabrook but is open to the public. Reservations should be made for private lessons, trail rides into the undeveloped portions of the island's woods and marshes, rides on the beach in the summer, and boarding. The walking trail rides for ages 8 and older are $65 per person. The advanced rider may go on a trotting/cantering trail ride for $70 per person; beach rides are $95 per person for advanced riders. Parent-led pony rides are $40 per half hour. Lessons cost $55 per half hour for private training. Boarding fees here are $600 a month or $40 per day. Advanced riders may also call for more information on the monthly adopt-a-horse program.

STONO FERRY STABLES
5304 Stono Ferry Course, Hollywood
(843) 763-0566
www.stonoferry.com
Stono Stables offers lessons, dressage, hunter-jumper training, boarding, and sales. Staff members are involved in polo, and this is a good source for information about that sport as well. Stall boarding runs $575 per month, and lessons for children are $140 per month for 1 lesson per week. These can either be 1-hour group lessons (with a maximum of 5 riders) or half-hour private sessions.

STONO RIVER RIDING ACADEMY
2962 Hut Rd., Johns Island
(843) 559-0773
www.stonoriverridingacademy.com
This new riding school on the site of the former Stono River Stable offers weekly and private lessons with children's summer and holiday camps. The daily trail riding lessons cover miles through the heart of a sea island maritime forest area. There is dressage, show jumping, and a cross-country course at this 300-acre facility. The owners welcome visitors, and children regularly drop by to feed a favorite pony a carrot. Lessons are $55 per hour for a private lesson and $45 for a one-hour group lesson. Stall boarding is available for $550 per month.

Martial Arts

There are numerous martial arts studios in the Charleston area. In addition, some courses are also offered at many of the recreation centers mentioned in the Parks and Recreation Centers section in this chapter.

ARTS FOR FITNESS
3545 Mary Ader Ave.
(843) 556-4391
www.artsforfitness.net
The Arts for Fitness Academy of Taekwon-Do offers classes for men, women, and children ages 5 and older who are interested in tae kwon do, and self-defense, dance and yoga. Classes are taught at the West Ashley studio and on Long Point Road in Mount Pleasant. There is a registration fee, plus additional monthly lesson fees. Four-month and yearly fees are less per month. Call for special packages, and check it out with a free trial class. A second location is at 539 Long Point Rd., Ste. 201 (in GymMasters Gymnastics), Mount Pleasant (843-343-9585).

MASTERS STUDIOS OF SELF DEFENSE
1021 Rifle Range Rd., Mount Pleasant
(843) 881-4866
www.massersstudios.com
With five locations convenient to a good portion of the Greater Charleston area, Masters Studios offers classes for all ages in a variety of self-defense disciplines—shaolin kempo karate, jujitsu, kung fu, and t'ai chi. Group as well as private lessons are available. Call for fee information. Visit the website for a list of locations.

Minigolf

BLACKBEARD'S COVE
FAMILY FUN PARK $$$
3255 US 17 North, Mount Pleasant
(843) 971-1223
www.blackbeardscove.net

Blackbeard's Cove has loads of entertainment including miniature golf on two 18-hole courses and is a great place for a birthday party. Charges vary with age. Special group and off-season rates are available. Hours vary seasonally but are generally noon to 9 p.m. or later in the summer.

Playgrounds

There are 16 playgrounds in the city, some of which are downtown and in West Ashley. The playground and special events coordinator for the Charleston Department of Recreation can be reached at (843) 724-7332. We've described some of our favorites.

HAZEL PARKER PLAYGROUND
70 East Bay St.
(843) 724-7332
www.charleston-sc.gov
Open sunup to sundown, this park has playground equipment as well as athletic fields, a tennis court, and basketball hoops. You can see Charleston Harbor from the grounds, and you are in skipping distance of the Battery.

MARY UTSEY PLAYGROUND
1360 Orange Grove Rd.
(843) 724-7334
www.charleston-sc.gov
West of the Ashley, this playground's shady areas are much appreciated during the hot months in Charleston. It has swings and other standard playground equipment.

MOULTRIE PLAYGROUND
41 Ashley Ave.
(843) 724-7398
www.charleston-sc.gov
Completion of an extensive renovation relocated 4 new tennis courts beside the existing 2 along Broad Street. The new baseball field moved to the old tennis court site and opened in spring 2001. New concrete walkways and bleachers were installed also. The playground has nice equipment for kids including climbing sets, swings, and a sand pit, plus basketball courts. Moultrie Playground is across from Colonial Lake and is a popular destination for families.

Dog Day Afternoon

If your faithful companion is your regular exercise pal, you may want to take note that the city of Charleston has provided some "dog" water fountains in two Peninsula playgrounds to quench Fido's thirst. One is located in **Hazel Parker Playground** on East Bay Street near Rainbow Row, and the other, in **Moultrie Playground** at the corner of Broad Street and Ashley Avenue at Colonial Lake. The fountains come with one lever but two basins, a high one for people and a low one for their four-legged friends. Most canines agree—this is a great way to beat the heat!

ST. ANDREW'S PARKS AND PLAYGROUND
1095 Playground Rd.
(843) 763-4360
www.standrewsparks.com
This recently revamped playground features the basic fun stuff—monkey bars, slides, and swings. This is the headquarters for the St. Andrew's Parks and Playground Commission,

and up-to-date information on sporting events and activities is available here. There are lighted tennis courts, athletic fields for baseball, softball, football, and soccer, basketball courts, and a gymnasium. A picnic shelter is available.

Racquetball

Racquetball enthusiasts can find camaraderie and court time at the fitness centers listed above and at some recreation centers and playground complexes. (See both categories in this chapter for phone numbers.)

Running

Running is a very popular Lowcountry activity, and most every weekend offers a charity benefit run/walk for the serious and not-so-serious runners here. By far the largest race is the Cooper River Bridge Run, drawing an international field of competition of over 30,000 participants.

Along with the Cooper River Bridge Run, other annual races include a 5K and 10K that happen in conjunction with the Flowertown Festival in Summerville. Some of the other popular runs are the North Charleston Arts Festival run, the Holiday Festival of Lights run, the Turkey Day Run, the Reindeer Run, and the South Carolina Race for the Cure. (See our Annual Events chapter for more on these happenings.) Also, Kiawah Island hosts a marathon and a half marathon, and the James Island County Park sponsors a triathlon series during June, July, and Aug. (See the Parks and Recreation Centers section of this chapter for more on this county park.)

CHARLESTON RUNNING CLUB
P.O. Box 30224, Charleston, SC 29417
(843) 856-4206
www.charlestonrunningclub.com

The Charleston Running Club holds meetings the last Tues of every month at different locations around town such as Earth Fare grocery store and Time Out Sport and Ski has about 300 members. The organization publishes a substantial newsletter bimonthly in booklet form (with results from races, stories, book reviews, and a calendar). The club sponsors about a dozen races and a summer track series. It also organizes a schedule of Charleston area group runs at Holy Cow Yoga at South Windemere Shopping Center, MUSC Harper Student Center, and Charleston Bicycle Company & Running Shop on Savannah Highway. Members enjoy a party after the Cooper River Bridge Run and discounts at local athletic stores. Membership costs $20 a year for an individual, $15 for a student, and $25 for a family. Write or visit the website for more information and a membership application.

Skating

People in this area skate indoors and outdoors and even have a club, the Charleston Roll Patrol, to promote their interests. Hampton Park and James Island County Park, where you can also rent in-line skates, are great outdoor skating sites (see the Parks and Recreation Centers section in this chapter).

With the advent of the professional ice hockey team, the South Carolina Stingrays, ice-skating has seen a surge of interest in the Lowcountry. (For more about the Stingrays see our Spectator Sports chapter.) The North Charleston Coliseum and the Carolina Ice Palace (see below) are the venues for this type of skating fun.

Here are some popular indoor rinks for roller-skating and one for ice-skating.

CAROLINA ICE PALACE $$
7665 Northwoods Blvd., North Charleston
(843) 572-2717
www.carolinaicepalace.com

The Carolina Ice Palace has two NHL-sized ice rinks for public skating year-round. This is a fun atmosphere for family entertainment with youth and adult hockey and figure skating. The facility encompasses an arcade, virtual reality center, full service pro shop, party rooms, and a jumbo TV lounge. The Ice Palace is open daily, but hours vary, so call or check the website for more details. Skating fees are in the $6 to $7 range, with $3 for skate rental. (See the Kidstuff chapter for more on the Ice Palace.)

HOT WHEELS SKATING
   CENTER, INC. $-$$
1523 Folly Rd.
(843) 795-7982, (888) 505-7982
www.hotwheelsskating.net

Even the little ones can skate here in clamp-on skates. The management at Hot Wheels is enthusiastic, and this is a very popular place for birthday parties, which are often booked weeks in advance. A snack bar stocks light refreshments. Skating prices range from $3 up to $12 for a family of 5. Call for hours.

STARDUST SKATE CENTER $-$$
2035 Spaulding Dr., North Charleston
(843) 747-0111

A popular skate center, Stardust is large and can accommodate several parties and many individual patrons at the same time. Supervision and safety are emphasized at this family oriented center. The snack bar is extensive, and there are many video games to play. Skating prices vary, ranging from about $6 per person on school nights (and for children under 12 on Sat mornings) up to $7.50 per person on Friday and Saturday between 7:30 and 11:30 p.m. including skate rentals. Skating lessons for children 12 and younger are offered as well.

Soccer

The popularity of soccer in this area has led to new venues for the sport. The Ansonborough Fields, downtown near the Charleston Maritime Center, are providing fields for soccer and football. In the fall of 2001, a new soccer complex opened on James Island off Ft. Johnson Road.

Again, the area recreation departments are the clearinghouses for information on soccer. They can steer adults and children alike to a soccer team in their area. Sign-up includes a modest fee of around $20 to $30 and commitment to weekday practices and weekday and Saturday games or both. Birth certificates are required. Call the recreation departments previously listed for more information on youth and adult leagues.

Softball

In the spring, it seems softball games pop up everywhere in the Lowcountry. To learn more about teams and competition for youth and adults, call the city and town recreation departments listed at the beginning of the Recreation section of this chapter. Also check with churches, as many sponsor their own teams.

Tennis

An empty tennis court on a pretty day is hard to come by in this area. The City of Charleston maintains 60 hard courts, (plus 3 clay courts) 43 of which are lighted and available on a first-come, first-served basis for free (except for a nominal fee at the Charleston and Maybank Tennis Centers). With headquarters at the Charleston Tennis Center, the city organizes leagues, round-robins, socials, and tournaments for tennis enthusiasts of all ages. Lessons can be arranged by calling (843) 769-8258. A new $9 million tennis complex was constructed on Daniel Island instigated by the announcement that the Family Circle Cup would move to Charleston from its long-standing run in Hilton Head. This is fostering the further growth of tennis here.

The very popular local United States Tennis Association league has around 45 men's and ladies' teams competing at nearly every National Tennis Rating Program level of play on public and private club courts around the area. Call the city tennis manager at (843) 769-8258, or one of the tennis centers listed below, for more information about specific locations, court reservations, and joining tennis leagues. The following list will give you some ideas about the options.

Charleston sports enthusiasts have access to some of the best sports, recreation, and fitness activities in the country, and are said to be the most active and competitive recreational folks, per capita, than anywhere else in the country. The Charleston Metro Sports Council is a great resource for all things sporty taking place in Greater Charleston for both locals and visitors. Visit their website at www.sportscouncil.org for information on sporting events; fitness, runs and endurance events; recreational departments; and local clubs or associations. Their A to Z listing makes it easy to find your specific interest.

CHARLESTON TENNIS CENTER $–$$
19 Farmfield Ave.
(843) 769-8258
www.charleston-sc.gov

These city of Charleston courts are conveniently located in West Ashley and are popular with the tennis crowd. Hours are based on demand, but are generally Mon through Thurs 8:30 a.m. to 10 p.m.; Fri from 8:30 a.m. to 7 p.m.; Sat from 9 a.m. to 6 p.m.; and Sun, 10 a.m. to 3 p.m. Junior Tennis Summer Camps are held in July and Aug (see the Summer Camps section of the Kidstuff chapter). Court fees vary, so please call for information.

CREEKSIDE TENNIS AND SWIM
790 Creekside Dr., Mount Pleasant
(843) 884-6111
www.creeksidetennis.com

Creekside Tennis and Swim has 11 lighted courts. Members enjoy use of lockers, a lounge, 2 lighted beach volleyball courts, and a 6-lane swimming pool. The club hosts active adult and junior programs. There are no court fees, but monthly dues are charged. Nonmembers can take lessons. (See the Neighborhoods chapter for more on the Creekside community.)

✳KIAWAH ISLAND RESORT
12 Kiawah Beach Dr., Kiawah Island
(843) 768-2838
www.kiawahresort.com

In recent rankings, Kiawah was rated the No. 1 tennis resort in America by *Tennis* magazine, which bases its top-50 selections on quality of instruction, off-court amenities, and facilities. The resort has two separate tennis complexes open year-round. The West Beach Tennis Club has 14 Har-Tru clay courts, 2 lighted hard courts, and a backboard for practice. The Roy Barth Tennis Center boasts 9 Har-Tru courts (1 lighted), 3 hard courts (1 lighted), and a fully automated practice alley. Members and resort guests pay in the $33 range per hour for court time. Nonmember play is available for a $43 per hour fee. (For more on Kiawah, see the Neighborhoods and Accommodations chapters)

MAYBANK TENNIS CENTER $–$$
1880 Houghton Dr.
(843) 406-8814
www.charleston-sc.gov
Another city-owned tennis facility is the Maybank Tennis Center with a full-time staff on site. You'll find a total of 11 courts here, 8 lighted hard courts and 3 Har-Tru. Annual city resident adult membership is $100 for hard courts and $240 for clay courts. The hours are generally all day and into the evening. Call for more details.

WILD DUNES RESORT
5757 Palm Blvd., Isle of Palms
(843) 886-2113, (888) 778-1876
www.wilddunes.com
Wild Dunes features 17 Har-Tru tennis courts, a ball wall, and a stadium court for tournaments. Five of the courts are lighted. Resort guests and members have priority, but non-members can take part in clinics, lessons, and round-robins. (See the Neighborhoods and Accommodations chapters for more on Wild Dunes Resort.)

Volleyball

Some bars on the beach provide a volleyball net and encourage random competition, which we hear can get pretty fierce among beer buddies. If you are interested in something more predictable and organized, there are teams put together by the Mount Pleasant and Isle of Palms recreation departments. The Isle of Palms Recreation Department, (843) 886-8294, organizes coed adult teams in Jan and Feb. The Mount Pleasant folks

can be reached at (843) 884-2528. There is a charge of about $35 for participation. Teams are also often sponsored by local restaurants and merchants. Inquire at one of the area recreation departments about signing up.

Reach for the Sky

If you've "hit a wall" searching for a new outlet for your exercise regimen, give the **climbing wall** at the James Island County Park a try. The 50-foot-tall, 4,500-square-foot climbing surface or the 10-foot bouldering wall is perfect for working on your technique. The walls are open from noon to 5 p.m. on weekdays and 9 a.m. to 5 p.m. on weekends (or later in the warmer months). An all-day pass is $10 for county residents and $12 for non-county residents. Trained instructors are on hand for assistance and rental of harness and shoes. So, hit the wall, and scale new heights!

CHARLESTON BEACH VOLLEYBALL
    & SOCIAL CLUB
191 Line St.
(843) 343-7802
www.charlestonvolleyball.net
The Charleston Beach Volleyball & Social Club organizes spring, summer, and fall leagues for coed teams at all levels. It welcomes those new to the sport as well as highly competitive players with tournament experience. The action takes place on the sand courts on the beach at Station 22 on Sullivan's Island on Sunday afternoons and

Monday and Tuesday nights. A men's league takes place on Thursday evenings at the Windjammer on the Isle of Palms. Sunday afternoons and Tuesday evenings are also pickup game days for anyone who cannot commit to play on a regular basis. After all that exercise, teamwork, and spiking, enjoy the social side too with food and beverages after the matches. The group even organizes other recreational events like dancing nights and hiking trips. Check out the website for a calendar of events, league schedules, and roster sign-ups.

GOLF

Greater Charleston can take justifiable pride in the variety of golf challenges available to the area's visitors and residents.

If you're a serious tournament player with world-class experience, or if you're just one of those relatively harmless twice-a-year duffers, Charleston has you well covered when it comes to golf. After all, this is the site of America's very first golf course—among the city's many claims to fame. The actual site of the first course, laid out in 1786 and known as "Harleston Green," has long ago been overtaken by subsequent urbanization, but golf is always proudly mentioned when the list of Charleston's "famous firsts" comes up.

Today, Lowcountry golf is a wealth of opportunity. From the world-ranked resort courses to the ever-popular public tracks, from the private courses to the semi-private offerings, it's possible to golf every day for nearly a month and play a different 18-hole course each day.

Clearly, the great drawing card for Lowcountry golf is the weather. Here the winter chill hardly ever discourages the stouthearted player, and the summer's sweltering heat only adds another challenge to the dedicated would-be pro. Indeed, for the vast majority of the year, Charleston area golf courses sing the siren's call to golfers from (literally) all over the world.

We'll start with some of the famous designer names that are associated with Lowcountry golf courses. Then, we'll take you on a brief tour of some of our infamous signature holes, where even the best players are tested to make birdie.

We'll give you a tour of the area's public courses, and then go out to the island resorts where an array of designer courses await the serious golfer determined to be tested by the very best.

BETTER BY DESIGN

Every area course is different in some way. Each has its own charm and individual characteristics, not to mention frustrations. That, in part, may be because most of the world's best golf architects have designed courses here in the Lowcountry. You'll find the work of Pete Dye, Tom Fazio, Arthur Hills, Jack Nicklaus, Gary Player, Arnold Palmer, Robert Trent Jones Sr., and Rees Jones, among them.

Pete Dye's name is one of the biggest in the industry. His most famous courses include Harbour Town on Hilton Head Island and the Stadium Course at PGA West in La Quinta, California. A more recent Dye offering is the Ocean Course at Kiawah Island, which hosted the 1991 Ryder Cup matches, the prestigious World Cup of Golf in 1997 and UBS Warburg Cup 2001, the 2003 World

Golf Championships World Cup, plus the 2007 Senior PGA Championship. The 1997 World Cup was the world's most-watched golf competition when the event was transmitted via satellite to more than 80 countries. Won by the Irish for the first time since 1958, the team's 4-day total of 31-under-par led the field by 5 strokes. Each team player pocketed $200,000 for his effort. A major upcoming event at the Ocean Course is the PGA Championship in 2012.

The Ocean Course rivals Tom Fazio's Lowcountry masterpiece, the Links Course at Wild Dunes Resort, which is ranked among the world's best by Golf magazine. Fazio's golf courses are possibly the best known here in the Lowcountry, because he designed both courses on Wild Dunes (the Links and Harbor Course), and he also laid out Kiawah's popular Osprey Point.

Whereas Pete Dye frequently uses railroad ties (a signature of his work), Arthur Hills prefers to use more of a site's natural elements in his designs. Hills did the newest course at Dunes West, which opened in 1991 and showcased the 1992 Amoco Centel Championship. Hills' other famous golf course designs include Eagle Trace, a TPC course in Coral Springs, Florida, cited in Golf Digest's "100 Best Courses in America."

Another name to note among the Charleston area's most popular golf designers is Willard Byrd, who gave us Patriots Point in Mount Pleasant back in 1981. He's also responsible for the Ocean Winds course on Seabrook Island.

Dr. Michael Hurdzan is another of the "name" designers to provide Charleston-area golfers with a challenge to their skills. His contribution is the 27-hole Golf Club at Wescott Plantation in North Charleston. Dr. Hurdzan's design allows players to enjoy the natural elements on the course and "play in various directions and lengths" around them.

And Arnold Palmer's signature course at RiverTowne Country Club in Mount Pleasant is drawing plenty of accolades with its 5 sets of tees, multi-tiered greens, and spectacular views.

SIGNATURE HOLES

Here's a sampling of the flavor of Lowcountry golf—a few of the area signature holes you'll want to be prepared for.

Patriots Point has its famous No. 17, a par 3, 112-yard island green that catches the uninitiated off-guard. This hole requires the player to take into careful consideration the ever-changing winds off Charleston Harbor.

The No. 6 hole at Fairfield Ocean Ridge is another island hole that can be a spoiler. It's a tough 380-yard, par 4 challenge.

Crowfield Plantation offers its par 5,500 yard No. 7 hole that features treacherous mounds that make players feel as if they've found a bit of old Scotland.

Rees Jones's Charleston National design, which opened in 1990, features the demanding No. 15 hole, a par 3, 183-yarder from the white tees. It plays 210 yards from the blue tees and has an innocent-looking pond on the right that attracts errant balls like a magnet.

On the Links Course at Wild Dunes, No. 9 is said to be the most difficult. It is a long, straight 451-yard par 4 that often plays even longer, because it is usually played into the wind. The green is closely guarded on the left by a hidden pond. This green is also the most unforgiving on the course—it slopes severely from back to front. All things considered, a par on No. 9 is an excellent score.

The signature hole at Kiawah's Turtle Point is No. 11. There's water along the entire right side from the tee past the green. According to Jack Nicklaus, its designer, "You can drive the ball as far as you want, but the farther you drive it, the greater the chance of slicing it into the water. There is a secondary landing area, or an out where those who won't want to chance it can play the shot. Then putt it or chip it or, as the Scots say, 'play a bumble' back into the green."

SCENERY

Pete Dye's Ocean Course on Kiawah and Tom Fazio's Links Course at Wild Dunes both make spectacular use of the Atlantic Ocean in their designs. Fazio's Harbor Course on Wild Dunes uses the Intracoastal Waterway as a backdrop. The Links at Stono Ferry, designed by Ron Garl in 1989, is another opportunity to play along the colorful and busy Intracoastal. But most of the Lowcountry's golf courses take full advantage of the beautiful salt marshes, signature of the area itself, in their layout designs. Gary Player's recently redesigned Cougar Point on Kiawah is probably the best example. A curious alligator has even been known to occasionally wander onto the course.

In fact, the area's multiple charms make the Lowcountry a favorite destination for golf widows and widowers and the assorted family members who often get swept up in a spouse's or parent's pursuit of the sport. The rationalization usually goes something like this: While golfers are challenged to play the many private, semi-private, and public courses throughout the area, the unenlightened can always explore the beautiful Lowcountry plantations, the splendid museums, the beaches, and the interesting shops, thus staying contented and amused.

That brings up another benefit of Charleston area golf: Because there are so many other things to do here, the area courses are relatively uncrowded. That means excellent starting times and an unhurried atmosphere.

Here we provide brief profiles of the area courses, so tee up when it suits you, and play at least 18 relaxing and scenic Lowcountry holes. You'll find descriptions of who designed the courses and when, plus who can play them, how much it costs (during high season), and where to call for more details. Greens fees quoted are in-season rates (unless otherwise noted) and exclude tax.

CHARLESTON AREA GOLF COURSES

CHARLESTON NATIONAL COUNTRY CLUB
1360 National Dr., US 17 N., Mount Pleasant
(843) 884-4653
www.charlestonnationalgolf.com
The idea for Charleston National Country Club was conceived more than 20 years ago, but the once-private golf community was just coming into focus when Hugo struck in 1989. Redesigned and refurbished with input from original designer Rees Jones, the par 72, 18-hole course (now semiprivate) is 7,084 yards long. Charleston National has a beautiful 8,000-square-foot clubhouse with luxury amenities including a pool and tennis center. Charleston National's pro is Terry Bryan. Green fees range from $38 to $58.

CITY OF CHARLESTON GOLF COURSE
2110 Maybank Hwy.
(843) 795-6517
www.charleston-sc.gov/dept
This public course, only 5 minutes from downtown Charleston, has been around

since 1929. Although it lost some 350 mature trees in Hugo's wrath, the course was beautifully replanted and is now in very good shape. The par 72 course is 6,432 yards long from the blue tees; it's 5,200 and par 72 from the forward tees. You'll find small greens, well-tended fairways, and an on-site pro shop with a snack bar. PGA- and LPGA-trained instructors are on hand for lessons, and this is the only public course in South Carolina with a Slazenger club-fitting system available for beginners and experts alike. Individual green fees are $22 (for walkers). The rate goes up to $24 on weekends. Add $15 per person for a golf cart. Charleston residents get a $7 discount on green fees. Call about a week in advance for tee times.

COOSAW CREEK COUNTRY CLUB
4110 Club Course Dr., North Charleston
(843) 767-8988
www.coosawcreek.com
Coosaw Creek, a 645-acre residential community in North Charleston, offers an Arthur Hills course designed in 1993. The par 71 semiprivate course is 6,593 yards long from the middle tees. The bonus here is on accuracy instead of length; good tee shots, as well as a deft short game, are the keys to low scoring. Hills had more natural topography to work with at Coosaw Creek than most Lowcountry layouts offer. You'll find rolling fairways, subtle mounding, and gradual elevation changes. The best opportunity to score low is on the front nine, as the back side brings more of the water and wetlands into play. Mike Benner is the pro on hand. In-season, weekday greens fees are $65, Sat and Sun fees are $70, taxes and cart included.

Prestigious Putt-Putt

The list of designers whose courses carve beautiful curves through the Lowcountry reads like a who's who in the industry. Pete Dye put his signature railroad ties to use at the **Ocean Course on Kiawah Island,** home of the 1991 Ryder Cup and 1997 World Cup of Golf. Arthur Hills designed the course at **Dunes West,** which showcased the 1992 Amoco Centel Championship. Tom Fazio crafted both the **Links and Harbor Course at Wild Dunes.** And Willard Byrd is responsible for **Patriots Point and Seabrook's Ocean Winds.** Throw in Rees Jones (**Charleston National**), Gary Player (**Cougar Point** at Kiawah), and the Golden Bear himself, Jack Nicklaus (**Turtle Point**), and you see that Lowcountry courses have come off the drawing boards of the very best.

CROWFIELD GOLF PLANTATION
300 Hamlet Circle, Goose Creek
(843) 764-4618
www.crowfieldgolf.com
Crowfield Golf Plantation offers championship golfing on a semi-private course designed in 1990 by Tom Jackson and Bob Spence. Their par 72, 18-hole layout is 6,590 yards long. The course is slightly Scottish in that it has a rolling terrain accompanied by acres of fairway and green-side bunkers. Shooting ability is of prime importance here. Undulating greens and imaginative pin placements test the nerves of the most skilled players. Crowfield's pro shop is well stocked, and there's a restaurant and cocktail

lounge on-site. Breakfast, lunch, or dinner may be ordered from the menu. Call pro Rob Brock for lesson details. Tee times are accepted up to 1 week in advance. Mon through Fri green fees are $42.50 before noon and $32.50 after noon; Sat through Sun fees are $52.50 before noon and $42.50 after noon.

DUNES WEST GOLF & RIVER CLUB
3535 Wando Plantation Way, Mount Pleasant
(843) 856-9000
www.duneswestgolfclub.com
Ten miles northeast of Charleston in the fast-growing East Cooper area, Dunes West is part of a 4,700-acre residential community that's been in development since the late 1980s. The highly rated course—set on a high, marshy peninsula bounded by three tidal creeks—was designed by Arthur Hills on the site of the historic Lexington Plantation house.

Like its sister course on Isle of Palms, Dunes West takes full advantage of its natural setting. The par 72 championship course is 6,871 yards long. The opening holes, cut from tall pines, have fairway corridors leading to elevated and bunkered greens. The back nine has a typical Lowcountry flavor with moss-draped oaks lining the fairways and expansive views of the marsh from several of the tees and greens. There's a handsome clubhouse with every modern luxury amenity. The pro is Kevin Zemnickas. The Hills course at Dunes West was the site of the 1992 Amoco Centel Championship, and it is now a semi-private course. High season green fees Mon through Thurs are $78; Fri through Sun, they are $95.

THE GOLF CLUB AT WESCOTT PLANTATION
5000 Wescott Club Dr., North Charleston
(843) 871-2135, (866) 211-GOLF
www.wescottgolf.com
Opened in the fall of 2000 with the full 27 holes up and ready for play early the following year, the Club at Wescott Plantation is North Charleston's worthy answer to the trendy designer courses on the resort islands closer to the coast. Designed by Dr. Michael Hurdzan, who took full advantage of the natural elements on the course, all 27 holes are tree-lined with plenty of definition to each hole. Each hole has 5 tees so golfers can choose tees from 5,018 yards up to 7,100 yards—depending on their ability. The course winds through streams, ponds, wetlands, and key sentinel trees, with holes playing in various directions and lengths from these features. The club also features a full driving range, a completely outfitted pro shop, a full-service restaurant, and meeting/conference spaces. Steve Rudd is the head pro. Weekdays (except holidays), SC resident fees are $40, weekend fees are $47. Nonresident fees are $89. Prices are $31 during twilight hours.

LEGEND OAKS PLANTATION
118 Legend Oaks Way, Summerville
(843) 821-4077, (888) 821-4077
www.legendoaksgolf.com
Located about 30 minutes from Charleston along scenic SR 61 is Legend Oaks Plantation, a traditional-style golf layout on the site of an old rice plantation. A romantic avenue of 250-year-old live oaks leads to the Clubhouse, which is reminiscent of Augusta National. The par 72 course was designed by Scott W. Pool, an associate of Pete Dye, and savvy players say it's akin to Pinehurst No. 2

with its presentation of challenges described as being "straightforward."

Spacious fairways, generous greens, and staggered tees give everyone a chance to enjoy the game, but water comes into play at half the holes, and huge live oaks stand between the golfer and the green. An ability to work the ball is required to score well here. From the blue tees, the course is 6,626 yards—a near-perfect test for the average bogey shooter. Joey Bradley is head pro, and green fees are around $55 on weekdays and $65 on weekends with discounts for Tri-County residents.

THE LINKS AT STONO FERRY
4812 Stono Links Dr., Hollywood
(843) 763-1817, (888) 785-1813
www.stonoferrygolf.com
This 18-hole, par 72 course is on SR 162, off US SR 17 S. near the little town of Hollywood, about 15 miles or a half hour from Charleston. The Links opened in 1989 and was designed by Ron Garl to accompany the exclusive Stono Ferry Plantation development. In 2003 the course was upgraded with all-new greens of championship Bermuda grass—adding luster to the Stono challenge. The course is 6,814 yards long and open to the public 7 days a week. It has three scenic holes on the Intracoastal Waterway, and it is a fair test from the back tees. You'll find a complete pro shop and a driving range, plus a full-service restaurant. Head pro Will Freeman is on hand for tips and lessons. Rental clubs are available. Advance registration is required. Green fees range from $77 to $87. Cart fees are included. Rates may vary in season.

PATRIOTS POINT GOLF LINKS
One Patriots Point Rd. (off US 17
Business), Mount Pleasant
(843) 881-0042
www.patriotspointlinks.com
This 18-hole public course is across the Cooper River Bridge in Mount Pleasant, just off US 17 N., near the towering USS *Yorktown*, anchored in Charleston Harbor. (See the Attractions chapter.) The par 72 layout, open since 1980, has had a $2.1 million upgrade with a new state-of-the-art irrigation system installed. Patriots Point affords spectacular views of the harbor, with oceangoing cargo ships frequently passing by.

The course is 6,955 yards in length, with well-contoured fairways and well-bunkered greens. PGA teaching pro Brandon Ray is on hand for lessons and more information. Amenities include a complete pro shop, a driving range, rental clubs and carts. A grill and snack bar are available, too. Call ahead for tee times. Green fees vary by season but range from $65 to $85.

PINE FOREST COUNTRY CLUB
1000 Congressional Blvd., Summerville
(843) 851-1193
www.pineforestcountryclub.com
The 18 holes at Pine Forest Country Club in Dorchester County wind through the tall Summerville pines with some live oaks, dogwoods, and a lake system thrown in for good measure. Designed by architect Bob Spence in 1992, Pine Forest is noted for their well-kept golf challenges. It is one of the most talked about USGA courses in the Lowcountry. The course is 6,905 yards long from the middle tees, with an equal representation of straightaways, doglegs, and elevation changes. It is nicely balanced, with fun in store for golfers of all abilities. Rental clubs

and carts are available. The head pro is Kenny Cashwell. Call for reservations. Green fees vary by season, but weekdays are about $35. Sat and Sun fees are $60. Carts are included in the prices.

THE PLANTATION COURSE AT EDISTO
21 Fairway Dr., Edisto Beach
(843) 869-1111
www.theplantationcourseatedisto.com
This 18-hole championship layout, designed by Tom Jackson in 1976, was renovated and reopened in October 2006. The 6,175-yard, par 70 course features water holes, dense subtropical vegetation, and (for early risers) frequent visits by native wildlife. The Plantation Course has its share of old bull gators, but local wisdom says they prefer sunning and running to fighting.

The course has dune ridges throughout. Where the Nos. 2 and 3 tees are now situated was once a Confederate stronghold. The overall feel of the course is natural, as it was primarily carved from tidal marsh and jungle-thick Lowcountry vegetation. The No. 1 green provides a spectacular view of the Atlantic.

You'll find a fully stocked pro shop opened in May 2007 with club and cart rentals available. Clinics and private instruction are offered. Tee-time reservations are required. Daily rates are $59 for 18 holes.

RIVERTOWNE COUNTRY CLUB
1700 RiverTowne Country Club Dr.,
Mount Pleasant
(843) 849-2400
www.rivertownecountryclub.com
RiverTowne Country Club, just off SR 41 in Mount Pleasant, is Arnold Palmer's first signature course in the greater Charleston area. Palmer is quoted as saying, "We wanted to create a golfing experience as distinctive and memorable as the city itself." His 7,188-yard championship layout features beautiful tree-lined fairways, spectacular views of the Lowcountry marsh, and 13 holes positioned along the Wando River and Horlbeck Creek. RiverTowne was the site of the LPGA Championship hosted by Annika Sorenstam in 2007 and 2008. Club amenities include GPS-equipped golf carts with full-color graphics of each hole and tournament leader boards. There's also a driving range, chipping and putting greens, and a fully stocked golf shop with apparel, clubs, shoes, and accessories. Head pro is Ray Garbiras. Tee times for the public may be reserved by phone or on the website. Green fees range from $76 to $121.

SHADOWMOSS PLANTATION GOLF AND COUNTRY CLUB
20 Dunvegan Dr. (off SR 61)
(843) 556-8251, (877) 897-1016
www.shadowmossgolf.com
Public play is welcome at this scenic course, designed by Russell Breeden and opened in 1973 along SR 61, the old Ashley River Road. In 1986, the 18-hole par 72 course was extensively renovated, and several water hazards were added to increase the challenge. Other modifications were made after Hurricane Hugo. The course is 6,701 yards long and cuts through pines, oaks, and hickories. A mosaic of ponds and streams comes into play in an area once dotted with early 18th- and 19th-century plantations.

You'll find a well-stocked pro shop, a snack bar, a grill with a lounge, and locker rooms. There's also a putting green as well as a chipping green and driving range. The golf pro at Shadowmoss is J. P. Ringer. Tee times can be arranged through a number of local hotels and inns or by calling Shadowmoss.

Mon through Fri green fees (with cart rental included) are $42, Sat and Sun fees are $52.

COURSES AT LOWCOUNTRY RESORTS

Wild Dunes

Only 15 miles from Charleston is Wild Dunes, which offers a total of 36 holes of Tom Fazio golf among its many upscale amenities.

THE HARBOR COURSE
5757 Palm Blvd., Isle of Palms
(843) 886-2164, (888) 343-7921
www.wilddunes.com
The Harbor Course, which opened in 1985, has four holes set directly along the Intracoastal Waterway. The course is a par 70, with a 6,446-yard layout that really challenges players. Two holes play from one island to another across the Yacht Harbor, where the wind can be a major factor. Frequent players say to beware the challenging 17th hole. The pro is Paul Helle, and instruction is available through the fully stocked pro shop. From Mon through Sun (Mar 25 through May 31), the green fees range from $60 to $110, cart included.

*WILD DUNES LINKS COURSE
5757 Palm Blvd., Isle of Palms
(843) 886-2164, (888) 343-7921
www.wilddunes.com
The Links opened in 1980, with a 6,397-yard par 70 layout from the middle tees. Because two of the finishing holes (a par 4 and a par 5) are right on the Atlantic, you'll want to pray for a nonwindy day. Indeed, wind can make the course different every day, but the scenery compensates for its fickle nature. The course is in great condition from tee to green, with rolling fairways and oak and palm trees in abundance. The Links (and Wild Dunes' other offering, Harbor Course) have a high-tech yardage system for golf guests. Using a golfcart-mounted display screen linked to a GPS system, players can determine the distance to a target with pinpoint accuracy. The pro shop is first rate, with Paul Helle riding herd on the whole golf program. *Golf Magazine* included Wild Dunes Links among its Top 100 courses in the country. The daily green fees are $95 to $165, cart included.

Kiawah Island Resort

Internationally famous Kiawah Island offers no fewer than six separate, distinct golf layouts for the adventurous Lowcountry golfer. Popular Brian Gerard heads Kiawah's golf program. The River Course is exclusively reserved for property owners on the island, but Kiawah golf is so famous and popular there's still great opportunity for the tour elite, low handicappers, and the average player, too. Oak Point, on Johns Island, is the newest acquisition. Four Kiawah courses—Cougar Point, Turtle Point, Osprey Point, and the Ocean Course—are semiprivate and open to homeowners, guests visiting the island, and Lowcountry vacationers who call specifically for reservations at least 24 hours in advance. Call Kiawah's main switchboard, and check with each course individually for tee times. Note that summer green fees are slightly lower.

COUGAR POINT WEST BEACH VILLAGE
12 Kiawah Beach Dr., Kiawah Island
(843) 266-4020, (800) 654-2924
www.kiawahresort.com
Cougar Point, formerly called Marsh Point, reopened in 1996 after a complete year-long makeover by original (1981) course designer

Gary Player. Now, this par 72 course has a 6,875-yard layout from the championship tees. Ric Ferguson is the resident pro, with a topflight shop to boot. There's even a halfway house on the 10th hole. Sometimes, four-footed furry creatures, along with alligators, ospreys, hawks, and a few snakes, have been known to be in the gallery here. Daily green fees in season are $212, cart included.

> **i** When you're playing on one of the Lowcountry's many marshfront golf courses like Cougar Point on Kiawah or the Harbor Course at Wild Dunes, don't be surprised if you find yourself sharing the green with a curious alligator. The unofficial rule is: Let the gator keep the ball; no penalty stroke incurred.

OAK POINT

4394 Hope Plantation Dr., Johns Island
(843) 266-4100, (800) 654-2924
www.kiawahresort.com

Part of Kiawah Island Golf's comprehensive golf package, Oak Point is tucked away within Hope Plantation adjacent to Kiawah and Seabrook Islands. It was designed by Clyde Johnson and built in 1989. The par 72, 6,701-yard-long course is challenging to both the novice golfer and the experienced professional.

Wide areas of windswept fairways stretch along salt marshes and heavily foliaged woodlands. There are numerous vistas of freshwater ponds and winding creeks. Word is that some area golfers prefer this course to Kiawah's Turtle Point, and it's a great choice for 36-hole-a-day players seeking a variety of challenges in the Kiawah-Seabrook area. The pro shop was recently renovated, and pro Scott Ammon provides

instruction for golfers at all levels of play. Hours can vary seasonally; call for tee times and more information. Daily green fees in season are around $141, cart included.

✳THE OCEAN COURSE

1000 Ocean Course Dr., Kiawah Island
(843) 266-4670, (800) 654-2924
www.kiawahresort.com

The Ocean Course was designed by Pete Dye and completed just in time for the Ryder Cup matches in 1991. That year, *Golf Digest* named the Ocean Course "best new resort course of the year." Now the magazine calls it America's Toughest Resort Course, and a $2.5 million overhaul finished in the fall of 2002 means the challenge is even greater. More recently this was the site of the 2007 Senior PGA Championship, and it will host the PGA Championship in 2012. The cliffhanger finish of the 1991 Ryder Cup put the course on the must-play list of pros and amateurs everywhere. Dye's beautiful design gives you a par 72, 7,356-yard challenge from the championship tees.

All 18 holes of the Ocean Course offer panoramic views of the Atlantic Ocean, and 10 holes play directly along the pristine, windswept beach. The clubhouse includes a restaurant, bar, pro shop, and locker rooms. The head pro at the Ocean Course is Stephen Youngner. Daily green fees are $338, cart included.

OSPREY POINT

Vanderhorst Plantation, 1000 Governors Dr., Kiawah Island
(843) 266-4640, (800) 654-2924
www.kiawahresort.com

Tom Fazio designed Osprey Point in 1986. The par 72 course is 6,932 yards from the middle tees and has four large, natural lakes.

At Osprey Point, Fazio used this superb natural canvas to create a golf challenge of amazing playability and variety. In addition to the natural lakes, there are fingers of saltwater marsh and dense forests of live oaks, pines, palmettos, and magnolias. Jim Kelechi is the head pro here, and the club has a restaurant, bar, lounge, and locker rooms. Daily green fees in season are $212, cart included.

TURTLE POINT
East Beach Village, 1 Turtle Point Dr., Kiawah Island
(843) 266-4640, (800) 654-2924
www.kiawahresort.com
Turtle Point, designed by Jack Nicklaus, is an 18-hole, par 72 course that's 7,061 yards long from the middle tees. It opened in 1981. Turtle Point is a low-profile design with fairway and green settings blended into the existing landscape. Nowhere is this more evident than along the spectacular 3-hole stretch woven through rolling sand dunes directly along the Atlantic Ocean. Head pro at Turtle Point is Mark Schaffer. Turtle Point has been the site of the Carolina Amateur and the 1990 PGA Cup Matches. Daily green fees in season are $212, cart included.

Seabrook Island

Golf on Seabrook Island is limited to island residents, friends of club members, and visiting resort guests. There are two distinctly different golf challenges on the island: Crooked Oaks, designed by Robert Trent Jones Sr.; and Ocean Winds, designed by Willard Byrd. Both courses have been executed in beautiful, undisturbed surroundings for challenging championship play. Seabrook's golf courses are the only ones in all of South Carolina that have earned full certification in the Audubon Cooperative Sanctuary Program.

CROOKED OAKS
1002 Landfall Way, Seabrook Island
(843) 768-2529, (866) 650-7918
www.discoverseabrook.com
Crooked Oaks is an 18-hole, 6,780-yard, par 72 course that meanders through the lush maritime forest and around several blackwater lagoons. When Jones designed it back in 1979, he described it as his "hard par-easy bogey" course. After its $2.3 million renovation, most of the greens are elevated or well-bunkered; there are no lucky shots to the bentgrass greens. It has rolling fairways weaving through stately live oaks, Spanish moss, sea marsh, and thick forest. Private and group instruction is offered by PGA pro Brian Thelan. The fully stocked pro shop has sports fashions as well as equipment. Peak season green fees are $160, cart included. Nine-hole rates are available.

OCEAN WINDS
1002 Landfall Way, Seabrook Island
(843) 768-2529, (866) 650-7918
www.discoverseabrook.com
Ocean Winds, designed by Willard Byrd, is slightly older (1973) and is a 6,765-yard, par 72 course from the middle tees. It plays a bit closer to the ocean. As a result, the Atlantic breezes can be a real test for even the best golfer. Ocean Winds golfers enjoy the benefits of a full-service clubhouse facility and a large pro shop, plus clinics and private instruction offered by an excellent teaching staff. Tournament coordination is available from PGA pro Brian Thelan. Daily green fees are $160 and include golf cart. Nine-hole rates are available.

BOATING & WATER SPORTS

Boating is an integral part of the Lowcountry lifestyle. State figures reveal that Charleston County is home to the most boats in South Carolina. The Trident area represents around 14 percent of the South Carolina total. There seems to be no end in sight for the boating frenzy, as newcomers and old salts alike discover and rediscover the pleasures of spending time on the water. From moonlight sails and family picnics on barrier islands to morning hunts in the back creeks and deep-sea fishing adventures, many are the occasions when "by boat" is the only way to go.

You can bring your own, or you can buy, rent, or charter a boat while you are here. Whatever the case, make certain to acquire, in navigational terms, "local knowledge" before you leave shore. We recommend contacting the US Coast Guard about its Auxiliary Public Education Courses. These cover information about navigational rules, aids to navigation, legal requirements, safety equipment, trailering, and coping with emergencies. State law requires that any person younger than 16 operating a boat or personal watercraft with an engine of 15 horsepower or greater without adult supervision must complete the boating safety training. The courses are held several times a year. For a schedule, call (803) 737-8483 or (800) 277-4301.

The local Marine Resources Division is at 217 Fort Johnson Rd. and can be reached at (843) 953-9300. We suggest you request the department's pamphlet on equipment requirements, rules, and regulations. To find out specifically about licensing, boat titles, and registration, call (843) 953-9301.

Those who want to launch their boat in the Lowcountry will be happy to know that there are a number of landings for public use. On weekends they are generally crowded, and early risers will find it easier to park a car and trailer. The parks department has completed a major renovation project to improve the public access to 19 area boat ramps. For more information about the area landings, contact the Charleston County Park and Recreation Commission at (843) 795-2628 or visit www.ccprc.com.

MARINAS

If you are interested in docking your boat at a Lowcountry marina, consider the following options. We offer several choices, scattered throughout the Trident area and listed alphabetically.

＊**BOHICKET MARINA & YACHT CLUB**
1880 Andell Bluff Blvd., Seabrook Island
(843) 768-1280
www.bohicket.com
Next to Kiawah and Seabrook resorts, Bohicket is 12 miles south of Charleston but just 6 miles from the Intracoastal Waterway.

Within minutes, boaters are in the open sea. Bohicket's 200 wet slips and floating docks are on deep water, and dry storage is available. A recent renovation has expanded the dry stack storage and converted many of the wet slips to dockominiums with 60 wet slips reserved for long-and short-term rentals. Shower and bathroom facilities, a laundry, shops, and restaurants make this marina a first-class destination. Boat charters, parasailing, and water tours are offered, and fuel is available at the ship's store.

THE BRISTOL MARINA
145 Lockwood Blvd.
(843)723-6600
www.thebristolmarina.com
One of Charleston's newest marinas, The Bristol is located on the peninsula's Ashley River side just north of the Ashley River bridges. It offers 148 wet slips (for boats less than 70 feet) and 38 drive-on docks (for boats 12–20 feet). Cable, water, and 30 and 50 amp service is at every slip. There are shower and bathroom facilities and a nice gazebo for gatherings before or after your boating. No transient traffic is served here. A short drive from the marina brings you into the historic district for shopping, dining, and cultural events.

✳CHARLESTON HARBOR RESORT & MARINA
24 Patriots Point Rd., Mount Pleasant
(843) 284-7062, (888) 856-0028
www.charlestonharbormarina.com
This full-service marina offers convenient ocean access with its location at the southwestern tip of Patriots Point in Mount Pleasant. (See more about Patriots Point Naval and Maritime Museum under the Museums and Other Sites section in the Attractions

chapter.) The deepwater marina with 459 permanent and transient slips features state-of-the-art design with wide floating docks and protective breakwaters.

Amenities include gasoline and diesel fuel, a laundry, restrooms, and showers, electric and manual courtesy carts, a ship's store, and potable dockside water. Other special services are a shuttle service to downtown Charleston and the Charleston International Airport; rentals of power boats, sailboats, and windsurfers; and inshore and offshore fishing and sailing charters. Adjacent to the Charleston Harbor Resort (see the Accommodations chapter) and the Patriots Point Links (see the Golf chapter), this resort complex provides endless opportunities for entertainment and recreation.

CHARLESTON MARITIME CENTER
10 Wharfside St.
(843) 853-DOCK (3625)
www.charleston-sc.gov
The Charleston Maritime Center has an all-season, deepwater marina with floating docks for 30 wet slips that can accommodate boats up to 180 feet in length. Located on the Peninsula's Cooper River side, this facility is near the city market with loads of shops and restaurants for exploring and a major grocery store, Harris Teeter. The Maritime Center is part of Charleston's waterfront area development that includes the South Carolina Aquarium and Liberty Square complex nearby. (For more on these sites see the Attractions and Kidstuff chapters.) On-site there are showers, a dock shop, pump-out stations, gas and diesel fuel, ice, and 30- and 50-amp power. Transient boaters are a specialty here. US members receive a discount on fees.

☀CITY MARINA
17 Lockwood Dr.
(843) 723-5098
www.charlestoncitymarina.com
This marina is close to all the action around the Peninsula. There are 400 slips and transient dockage, and there is a convenient downtown shuttle service. This marina can accommodate vessels as large as 300 feet at its new megadock. Electric 30-, 50-, and 100-amp power as well as gas and diesel fuel are available. The Marina Variety Store restaurant and Salty Mike's Deck Bar are adjacent for a little land-side dining and recreation. A 5-year expansion and improvement project at the marina added more slips and facilities such as the ship's store, the reception center, the MegaDock, and state-of-the-art control room.

COOPER RIVER MARINA
1010 Juneau Ave., North Charleston
(843) 554-0790
www.ccprc.com
Your fastest tack to Charleston Harbor may be the Cooper River Marina, located 2 miles north of the Cooper River bridges at the former Charleston Naval Base. This deep-water marina is operated by the Charleston County Park and Recreation Commission and has floating, concrete docks with electric hookups and plenty of free parking. Boat yard storage, security, laundry, fax, and Wi-Fi service, restroom facilities with a shower, a marina store, and ice are available. Charleston County residents receive a discount on slip fees.

DANIEL ISLAND MARINA
669 Marina Dr.
(843) 884-1000
www.danielislandmarina.com
This marina has 44 wet storage slips and 375 in dry stack storage. With the development of Daniel Island (see the Neighborhoods chapter), the marina is seeing more traffic, and it now has a ship's store and deli, a shower, and restrooms. Fuel, ice, and live bait are available. No ramp is here, but work racks and a boat washing area are offered.

DOLPHIN COVE MARINA
2079 Austin Ave., North Charleston
(843) 744-2562
www.dolphincovemarina.net
Dolphin Cove is on very deep water on the Ashley between the Ashley River Bridge and the North Bridge. The marina offers 125 wet slips with an additional 350 in dry stack storage. Gas is available here, along with complete on-site engine, hull, and accessory service. Short-term dockage is available, and the facility is equipped with showers, a laundry, a lounge, and a restaurant.

THE HARBORAGE AT ASHLEY MARINA
33 Lockwood Dr.
(843) 722-1996
www.ashleymarina.com
This 230-slip marina, at intracoastal marker 470 on the Ashley River, is on the Peninsula and convenient to all areas of the city. A courtesy shuttle takes transient boaters to downtown's popular attractions. Diesel and gasoline are available at the fuel dock, and there is room for 880 feet of boat docking. In addition to a captain's lounge, ship's store, showers, and a laundry, there is a fax machine, cable tv, and Wi-Fi, and a notary public is on the premises. The marina also deals in new and brokered sailboats, trawlers, sportfish, and motor yachts. Marina managers can supply names and phone numbers of charter boats that leave from

Manatee Watch

Boaters, keep your eyes out for **manatees** in area waters during the summer months. The gentle, huge, seal-like mammals migrate northward from Florida by ocean, estuaries, and creeks, often swimming along the edges of waterways and in shallow water near marsh grass. Be sure to slow to no-wake speeds, and stay in deeper channels where manatees can dive to avoid collisions. If you see a manatee in South Carolina, call the state's Department of Natural Resources at (800) 922-5431 or visit www.dnr.sc.gov/marine /manatee. The department is tracking and recording sightings of this endangered species.

their marina. (See the Hunting & Fishing chapter for more on charters.)

ISLE OF PALMS MARINA
50 41st Ave., Isle of Palms
(843) 886-0209
www.iopmarina.com
This marina, on the Intracoastal Waterway marker 116 at Wild Dunes Resort, is a full-service facility with 50 wet slips, floating docks, a restaurant, bathrooms, showers, a laundry, Wi-Fi, cable tv, and a ship's store with supplies for boating. Isle of Palms Marina also offers inshore- and offshore-chartered trips, ecotours, and Jet Ski and boat rentals. (See the Hunting & Fishing chapter.) Limo service is also available here.

MARINER'S CAY MARINA
3-A Mariner's Cay Dr., Folly Beach
(843) 588-2091
www.marinerscay.net
Mariner's Cay is part of Mariner's Cay Resort and is on the Folly River across from the Folly boat ramp. Just 2 miles from the ocean and 9 miles from the Intracoastal Waterway, this 83-slip marina is one of Charleston's closest facilities to the Atlantic and has slips for sale and for rent. Their services include gas and diesel fuel, ice, and 24-hour security. A laundromat, restrooms with showers, cable TV hookups, and a ship's store complete the amenities.

RIPLEY LIGHT MARINA
56 Ashley Pointe Dr.
(843) 766-2100
www.ripleylight.com
Just west of the Ashley, in the shadow of California Dreaming (see the Restaurants chapter), you'll find Ripley Light. The marina has 200 dry stack units for rent on a monthly basis. This private marina accommodates transients, short-, and long-term dockage. Their 6,500-foot pier is nice for a stroll or to watch the boats returning from a day's fishing. Fuel and ice are available as well.

RIVER'S EDGE MARINA
4354 Bridge View Dr., North Charleston
(843) 554-8901
www.riversedgemarina.com
River's Edge, on the Ashley River in North Charleston, is both a wet and dry storage marina. It has 50 wet slips, 486 inside dry stack spaces, and a Captain's lounge, ship's store, fish cleaning station, picnic, and grill area, plus restrooms and showers.

SEABREEZE MARINA
50 Immigration St.
(843) 853-0932
One of the newer marinas on Charleston's Peninsula is the dry stack storage facility called Seabreeze Marina. Conveniently located near the new Ravenel Bridge on the Cooper River, this site is unobstructed with deepwater access to Charleston Harbor. The experienced marina staff is ready to make your day on the water hassle-free and fun. Call ahead to have your boat launched and fueled, and the cooler packed with your favorite refreshments and snacks from the ship's store. When you return they are ready to wash down the boat inside and out, flush the engine, drain the bilge, and return her to her storage berth. All this service practically guarantees an enjoyable boating experience. A fish cleaning station, maintenance work racks, air-conditioned restrooms and showers, and plenty of floating dock space and parking are other amenities featured here.

i Note that laws governing boating under the influence are strictly enforced on South Carolina waters. Boat operators will be tested for blood-alcohol content in the event of accidents. For more information, call the Boating Safety Division of the South Carolina Department of Natural Resources at (843) 953-9382.

SHEM CREEK MARINA
526 Mill St., Mount Pleasant
(843) 884-3211
www.shemcreekmarina.com
Shem Creek offers 200 dry stacks for boat storage. Convenient for East Cooper residents, Shem Creek is often filled to capacity, and offers some basic amenities like outdoor showers, restrooms, fuel, and ice. A new deck area with umbrella tables and chairs, fans, and misters overlooks the creek. Adjacent to the Shem Creek boat ramp, this marina bills itself as "Mount Pleasant's neighborhood marina."

ST. JOHN'S YACHT HARBOR
2408 Maybank Hwy.
(843) 557-1027
www.stjohnsyachtharbor.com
Near Intracoastal marker 11, is a deepwater marina that's just minutes from the city's municipal golf course. New owners bought the former Buzzard's Roost and Stono marinas to create this facility. There are wet slips along with dockage for transients. A laundry, shower, and gas and diesel fuel are available, and free in-slip pump out. You will find a Captain's retreat, ship's store, outdoor kitchen, and pool and cabanas here.

TOLER'S COVE MARINA
1610 Ben Sawyer Blvd., SR 703 at Intracoastal Waterway, Mount Pleasant
(843) 881-0325
www.tolerscovemarina.com
East of the Cooper, Toler's Cove—surrounded by the Marsh Harbor development—is across the harbor from Charleston and across the Intracoastal Waterway from Sullivan's Island and the Isle of Palms. Toler's Cove can accommodate vessels up to 100 feet in length. The marina has showers and a laundry as well as gas, bait, ice, and other necessities.

BOAT SALES & REPAIRS

If you are in the market for a new boat, shop the retail stores in the Trident area for reliable sales and service. Beware of fly-by-night operations selling boats out of cow pastures, however, as they are sometimes fronts for liquidation operations and may not be there to help mediate with the manufacturer when your new boat springs a leak.

From the city out to North Charleston, here's a sampling of some of the older establishments. These are also good places to start if you find yourself in need of a boat mechanic while visiting the Lowcountry. If you require a boatyard for more extensive repairs and maintenance contact one of the following: Charleston Boatworks at (843) 554-7775, Charleston City Boatyard at (843) 884-3000, Rockville Marine, (843) 559-1124, Detyens Boatyard, (843) 553-0091, or Ross Marine at (843) 559-0379.

CHARLESTON YACHT SALES
3 Lockwood Dr., Ste. 201
(843) 577-5050, (866) 429-0958
www.charlestonyachtsales.com
These knowledgeable yacht brokers handle both sail and powerboats with a large selection to choose from. They also offer service, repairs, appraisals, delivery, and surveys. They're next to the municipal marina and are a longtime fixture (since 1965) on the Peninsula.

LONGSHORE BOATS
2650 Clements Ferry Rd., Wando
(843) 216-4700
www.longshoreboats.com
Located on Daniel Island at the entrance to Daniel Island Marina Village, Longshore Boats is a Mercury and Yamaha Outboards dealer. The staff continues to work on all models with parts, service, and accessories available. Some of the popular lines of new boats are Edgewater, Chaparral, and Robalo.

RENKEN BOAT CENTER, INC.
2476 Savannah Hwy.
(843) 767-0515
www.renkenboatcenter.com
Renken sells a variety of boats including Sea Fox, Mariah, Hurricane, and Mercury, Yamaha, and Suzuki outboards. It also offers parts, service, and accessories. The Renkens have been doing business for more than 20 years in the Lowcountry, and theirs is a trusted name.

i Remember that Charleston Harbor is a busy "highway" for large ships coming in and out of the Port of Charleston daily. Recreational boaters (both power and sail) must stay clear by avoiding the ship channels, where possible, or crossing them quickly at right angles. Always be alert, and watch for ship or tug-boat traffic.

SEA RAY-SCOUT OF CHARLESTON
142 Sportsman's Island Dr.
(843) 747-1889
www.hallmarine.com
This store is the area's exclusive Sea Ray dealer, selling sport boats, cruisers, and yachts as long as 68 feet. Scout, Boston Whaler, Meridian, and Harris Flote Bote are other brand names here, and service and accessories are also offered.

SEEL'S OUTBOARD
1937 US 17 S.
(843) 556-2742
www.seelsoutboard.com
Seel's carries Evinrude, Johnson, and Yamaha motors, and Grady White boats as well as Alumacraft, Sundance, and Sea Hunt. With two locations, on Savannah Highway in West

Ashley and the bypass in Mount Pleasant, Seel's is an established boat dealership that has been in operation since the 1960s. A second location is at 2910 US 17 N., Mount Pleasant (843-849-8788).

ST. BARTS YACHTS
3 Lockwood Dr., Ste. 301
(843) 577-7377
www.st-barts.com

In recent years, Beneteau USA moved its North American corporate headquarters to Charleston, and St. Barts is the local dealer for Beneteau Yachts. Beneteau's factory in Marion, South Carolina, builds sailboats from 30 to 46 feet long as well as custom lengths. St. Barts also represents the CNB and Sabre lines and handles brokerage of all types of sailboats.

SAILING INSTRUCTION

Sailors or aspiring sailors will find plenty of company in the Lowcountry. If you are interested in learning more about the sport or the local regatta schedule, talk to the enthusiasts at the College of Charleston Sailing Association. They are based at the Charleston Harbor Marina and can be reached at (843) 953-8252. (See listing.) Another good source for information as well as sails, rigging, and repairs is UK-Halsey Sailmakers at (843) 722-0823.

The following listings will steer your ship in the right direction when it comes to sailing instruction and service.

COLLEGE OF CHARLESTON SAILING ASSOCIATION
Charleston Harbor Marina, 24 Patriots
Point Rd., Mount Pleasant
(843) 216-8450, (843) 953-8252
www.cofc.edu/sailing

The College of Charleston offers adult noncredit sailing classes that meet at the Charleston Harbor Marina. Equipment is furnished, and no advanced skills are required. Basic and intermediate classes are offered Apr through Aug. The cost is $350 for 15 hours of sailing instruction on J/22 boats and 2 hours of classroom instruction. Call the association for details.

OCEAN SAILING ACADEMY
Charleston Harbor Marina, 24 Patriots
Point Rd., Mount Pleasant
(843) 971-0700
www.osasailing.com

The Ocean Sailing Academy offers US Sailing Certification courses from the Learn to Sail level on up through Open Ocean Passage Making. Instructors even guarantee skippering ability at the conclusion of any of their courses. Completion of just one course will give you the freedom and certification to rent a boat and head out for a day of sailing. Instruction is given on a range of boats, including Colgate 26, J 105, and Beneteau 323 and 473s. Classes may be customized to fit your needs, or you may participate in one of the regularly scheduled courses. The academy operates Charleston's only public charter sailing club. For more information about classes, the sailing club, team-building programs, and prices, call the number above, or visit the website.

CHARTERS

If you are dreaming of gliding across Charleston Harbor at sunset or entertaining your friends on a weekend outing, several area power and sailboat charter companies have all types and sizes of yachts to match your fantasy.

AQUASAFARIS, INC.
Charleston Harbor Marina, 24 Patriots
Point Rd., A-Dock, 2nd Floor Marina
Building, Ste. 1, Mount Pleasant
(843) 886-8133, (800) 524-3444
www.aqua-safaris.com

AquaSafaris is a watersport facility at Charleston Harbor Marina, Isle of Palms, Shem Creek, and Bohicket Marinas (see previous listings). Bareboat rentals of kayaks and 16- to 21-foot skiffs are available by the hour or half-day and full-day. Prices range from $30 per hour up to $455 for the full day. Other adventures here are private sailing charters, including day sails, harbor cruises, sunset sails, or island beach excursions. The fleet of inshore and offshore fishing boats consists of all types—flats boats, sportfishing yachts, island hoppers, and head boats. Charters are arranged for 1 to 100 people by the hour, or half or full day (see our Hunting & Fishing chapter for more details). Group charters are offered for parties and special events, and catering with customized menus is available. AquaSafaris, Inc., also handles charters worldwide. Call for reservations and more details on pricing.

BOHICKET BOAT ADVENTURE
AND TOUR CO.
2789 Cherry Point Rd., Wadmalaw Island
(843) 559-3525
2408 Maybank Hwy.
www.bohicketboat.com

Bohicket Boat provides all kinds of boating fun for visitors and locals alike. They offer powerboat rentals, sailing charters, river and kayaking tours, and sunset cruises. Bohicket Boat even customizes tours geared to your special interest, be it dolphin watching, crabbing, shrimping, shelling, or fishing around the barrier islands in the Lowcountry. Prices range from $60 per hour (2-hour minimum)

for a 16-foot jon boat to $330 per day for a 23-foot deck boat. The custom tours cost $240 to $475 for 2 to 4 hours with up to 6 passengers. Call for a monthly calendar of activities and reservations. (For more information on sportfishing trips, see the Hunting & Fishing chapter.)

Boating News

Old salts (and new ones too) will want to pick up a copy of *Tideline* for the latest scoop on all the area's boating and water sports info. The monthly tabloid, published by *The Post and Courier* is distributed along the Lowcountry waterfront. With stories about regattas, boat shows, boatyards, marinas, fishing, and other maritime pursuits, this is a lively read. The free paper can be found at marinas, boating supply stores, and nautical shops, or call (843) 937-5568 or visit www.tidelinemagazine.com to subscribe.

SCHOONER *PRIDE*
360 Concord St.
(843) 722-1112, (800) 979-3370
www.schoonerpride.com

Sit back, relax, and take a 2-hour harbor or sunset cruise on a three-masted, gaff topsail schooner (class C tall ship). What better way to enjoy the vistas of Charleston's historic waterfront? Reservations are recommended, and the fee is $31 for adults and children 12 and older and $25 for children ages 3 to 11. The sunset sail is $39 for adults and $29 for children, and the moonlight cruise is $45,

$30 for ages 6 to 11. The Schooner *Pride* is also available for private parties of up to 49 people. Call for group rates. The *Pride* departs from the Aquarium Wharf (near the South Carolina Aquarium). (See the Cruise & Boat Tours section of the Tours chapter for more on the *Pride*.)

CANOEING

With the amazing system of waterways in the Lowcountry, there are many great opportunities for canoeing. The Charleston County Park and Recreation Commission, (843) 795-4386, can help with a list of community school courses in paddling. Also, each spring, it cosponsors the East Coast Canoe & Kayak Festival with the Trade Association of Paddlesports (TAPS). The event is held at James Island County Park. The symposium regularly attracts more than 1,000 paddling enthusiasts of all skill levels for a weekend of lectures, on-water demos, and classes. Reflecting the growing national interest in paddling, local support has made this one of the top events of its kind in the country. See the Annual Events chapter for more on this event.

LOWCOUNTRY PADDLERS
P.O. Box 13242, Charleston, SC 29422
(843) 556-5865
www.lowcountrypaddlers.net
Regular meetings are open to anyone interested. Guest speakers talk about their experiences as well as conservation issues and upcoming trips. Meetings are held the third Mon of each month at Providence Baptist Church on Daniel Island. An all-day trip is planned for the third Sat of the month. This family oriented group publishes a monthly newsletter and has about 150 members. The annual membership (which includes

membership in the American Canoe Association) is $45 for an individual or $61 for a family. Call the Charleston County Park and Recreation Commission for contact information about this group.

PALMETTO ISLANDS COUNTY PARK
444 Needlerush Pkwy., Mount Pleasant
(843) 884-0832
www.ccprc.com
This 943-acre nature facility is in a heavily wooded area, with a 2-acre pond and 1-mile canoe trail. It is a perfect place to canoe (rentals are no longer available, but you can bring your own), and a nominal admission fee of $1 a person is charged. (See the Parks & Recreation and Kidstuff chapters for more on this exciting park.)

KAYAKING

Not too many years back, Charlestonians didn't know a whole lot about kayaks. But this is the here-and-now, and kayaking has definitely become a cool and popular sport. The waterways around Charleston make an ideal venue for both the beginning and expert kayaker to take in the scenery and tranquility. To find out more, check into the following groups and venues.

CHARLESTON WATERSPORT
 OUTFITTERS
1225 Ben Sawyer Blvd., Mount Pleasant
(843) 884-9098
www.charlestonwatersport.com
Charleston Watersport carries a complete line of quality watersport equipment and accessories. It handles sales and rentals of the Ocean Kayak, Necky, and Old Town lines of kayaks. The store is conveniently located on the US 17 Bypass in the K-Mart shopping center to serve vacationers on nearby

Sullivan's Island and the Isle of Palms. A full-day kayak rental costs $40, plus $30 for each additional day, and $60 for an entire weekend. In addition to kayaks, Charleston Watersport has a large selection of surfboards (Robert August, Maya, Stewart, Hobie, and Orion), and stand-up paddle (SUP) boards (Waterman, Starboard, Quickblade, and Rusty). The friendly staff can help you choose your on-the-water fun.

COASTAL EXPEDITIONS TOURS
514-B Mill St., Mount Pleasant
(843) 884-7684
www.coastalexpeditions.com
Coastal Expeditions rents kayaks and offers kayak tours all over the Lowcountry from marsh creeks to secluded beaches. Naturalists and instructors certified by the American Canoe Association and British Canoe Union run this operation and take groups of 2 to 40 on nature tours. A quality operation, Coastal Expeditions welcomes beginners and experienced kayakers and also sells new and used equipment. It offers private and group lessons as well. The half-day tours are $58 per person and $88 per person for a full day. Single kayaks rent for $38 for a half-day and $48 for a full day; double kayaks are $48 for a half-day and $58 for a full day. Overnight expeditions for 4 or more people are a fun option too.

JAMES ISLAND COUNTY PARK
871 Riverland Dr.
(843) 795-7275
www.ccprc.com
James Island County Park offers lots of classes and clinics; and day, after-work, and overnight tours are offered in sea kayaking, and canoeing, and stand-up paddleboard (SUP). Canoe lessons range from $15 to $45

for Charleston County residents and $18 to $54 for nonresidents.

Kayak classes and tours range from $35 for county residents and $42 for non-residents for a basic course, up to $70 for residents and $84 for nonresidents for more advanced offerings. SUP classes start at $15 for residents and $18 for non-county residents. Trips are around $30, resident, and $36, non-resident. Contact the park for the quarterly program guide to check out the variety of paddler offerings.

*MIDDLETON OUTDOOR PROGRAM
4290 Ashley River Rd.
(843) 628-2879, (800) 543-4774
www.theinnatmiddletonplace.com
Middleton offers nature-based kayaking on the Ashley River year-round and in the blackwater cypress swamp seasonally from Dec through Apr. Learn to roll and rescue while perfecting your paddle techniques, then follow your guide on a Lowcountry adventure. The basic kayak instruction with guided two-hour tour costs $40 per person. A 2-hour private tour is available on a limited basis for $60 per person for inn guests. Kayak rentals are also available for $20 to $30 per person for 2 hours or $10 for inn guests.

WATER SPORTS

Other water recreation opportunities abound in our area and don't necessarily involve owning or chartering a boat. Local waters offer lots of spots that are waiting to be explored on personal watercraft or investigated by scuba diving. Surfing, windsurfing, and waterskiing provide ways to catch a wave or a breeze or jump a wake while demonstrating your finesse. Or maybe just plunging into a pool for a refreshing swim is your answer to the oft-daunting Lowcountry heat. A list of the folks who can help you get started follows.

PERSONAL WATERCRAFT & OTHER WET TOYS

To jump on your own Jet Ski and zip around the endless waterways, inlets, and creeks in the Lowcountry for the day, contact one of the following for rental or purchase of personal watercraft.

CHAMPION HONDA BMW
4155 Dorchester Rd., North Charleston
(843) 554-4600
www.championhondabmw.com
Champion sells the full line of Honda watercraft and accessories at competitive prices. It is a full-service center open Mon through Fri from 9 a.m. to 6 p.m. and Sat from 10 a.m. to 3 p.m.

CAROLINA WATERSPORTS AT TROPHY LAKES
3050 Marlin Rd., Johns Island
(843) 559-2520
www.carolinawaterskischool.com,
www.trophylakes.com
Trophy Lakes is the place for waterskiing, kneeboard, and wakeboard lessons taught by instructors who are nationally ranked on the pro tours. The lessons are taught on two private lakes on Johns Island and are scheduled by appointment. The rates are $50 for approximately 20 minutes. Water-ski and wakeboard pulls are $35 for 25 to 30 minutes. In their wakeboard park with jumps and rails, 20 minute Jet Ski pulls cost $20. A full-day package of 3 individual lessons is $125. A kids' camp, birthday parties, and rental of the lake for your private event are other options here. Waterskiing competitions are held here as well, so call Carolina

Watersports for a schedule of events. Their www.4wake.com website shows the full range of gear available at their shop. A disc golf course is a new attraction for those who prefer to keep their feet on the ground.

TIDAL WAVE WATERSPORTS
69 41st Ave., Isle of Palms
(843) 886-8456
www.tidalwavewatersports.com
Tidal Wave Watersports' locations have personal watercraft rentals, parasailing, and water-skiing. The Jet Ski rental rates are $60 per half hour for a single or $75 double and $90 an hour for a single or $110 double.

A special safari tour from Wild Dunes (that's the Isle of Palms address) is a very popular, 90-minute guided excursion by WaveRunner. You venture out into the ocean, up to Capers or Bulls Island (with a stop for beachcombing) and return on the Intracoastal Waterway. The 30-mile round trip starts at $115.

Parasailing choices are offered at all locations, with flights costing $60 (at Isle of Palms or Kiawah Island beach or at Charleston Harbor) for the 600-foot pull and $80 for the 800 foot thrill (it's a 1½-hour trip). What a way to check out the beach from a bird's-eye view. Believe it or not, takeoff and landing are dry, and anyone age 2 and older may try it. (The minimum weight requirement is 80 pounds, or you fly with someone else.)

Tidal Wave Watersports also offers waterskiing and wakeboarding at the Isle of Palms location. For 90 minutes it's $300 plus $125 for each additional hour for up to 6 people and includes a boat, captain, and equipment. Another location is on John's Island at 1880 Andell Bluff Blvd. (843-768-3482). Tidal Wave Watersports locations are open seasonally (Mar through Nov) in the warmer

The Lowcountry Splash

Are you ready to take the plunge? The annual **Lowcountry Splash,** a 2.4-mile open-water swim organized by Rehabilitation Centers of Charleston, is attracting more participants who are up to the challenge. The race through Charleston Harbor starts at Hobcaw Yacht Club on the Wando River in Mount Pleasant and continues under the Cooper River Bridge past the USS *Yorktown,* finishing at the Charleston Harbor Resort & Marina's floating docks. The Splash is held in late May or early June so that the water temperature has usually warmed up a bit, and, depending upon the tide and weather, swimmers may experience varying conditions—all part of the event. The cost to enter is $60 ($50 in advance), and more information can be found at www.rcc therapy.com or by calling (843) 884-7880.

months. Call ahead for more information and reservations.

CHARLESTON POWER SPORTS
5870 Dorchester Rd.
(843) 552-7900
www.charlestonpowersports.net
Representing the Sea-Doo line, Charleston Power Sports has the largest selection in the area of personal watercraft and jet-powered boats for sale. They run from 85 to 310 horsepower, with lengths up to 20 feet. These boats are good for touring, skiing, and all-around family fun.

SCUBA DIVING

There are many scuba enthusiasts in this area. Diving the numerous wrecks under Charleston's waters is a real kick. For information about dive trips and activities, our listings give you some good places to start. The College of Charleston also offers a scuba class from time to time. Call (843) 953-5960 to find out about the next scheduled class.

LOWCOUNTRY SCUBA
1237 Ben Sawyer Blvd., Mount Pleasant
(843) 884-1500
www.lowcountryscuba.com
Lowcountry Scuba offers beginning dive classes and certification. The open-water weekend class is $295 (transportation not included) plus $175 for training at a local area lake. Lowcountry Scuba also organizes trips to many locations, including the Caribbean, the Bahamas, and Florida. To dive local waters, call to schedule offshore dive charters.

CHARLESTON SCUBA
335 Savannah Hwy.
(843) 763-DIVE
www.charlestonscuba.com
This conveniently located store is a center for diving enthusiasts. It provides retail sales, gear rentals, on-site repairs, scuba charter trips, and classes—from open-water certification to dive master. Basic classroom and pool sessions are $400 for the 2 classes plus 3 pool sessions. An additional $215 covers four open-water dive sessions that are necessary for certification. Charleston Scuba is adjacent to the Holiday Inn Riverview west of the Ashley.

SURFING

The surfing craze has been reborn among the young crowd, much to the delight of all those baby-boomer surfer dudes. The Lowcountry's most popular spots for wave action are on Folly Beach and the Isle of Palms. The Washout at East Ashley Avenue, a designated surfing area on Folly Beach, attracts all ages in search of the perfect wave. Other good surf can be found near the Folly Pier at East Atlantic Avenue, 10th Street on Folly Beach, and near the pier and the county park on the Isle of Palms. (Keep in mind that it is illegal to surf closer than 200 feet to a pier.) Bert's Break, at Station 22 on Sullivan's Island, is probably the best low tide break in the area. Local surf shops are equipped with surfing and beach-going needs. A couple of options follow.

MCKEVLIN'S SURF SHOP
8 Center St., Folly Beach
(843) 588-2247, (843) 588-2261 (Surf Line)
www.mckevlins.com
Opened back in the '60s, McKevlin's carries a full line of surfboards, clothing, and accessories. Some of its better-known board brands are Bing, Island Inspired, Sharp Eye, Lost, Channel Islands, and Allison. McKevlin's offers rental of surf and body boards and videos seven days a week. Call the Surf Line for the latest on wind and wave conditions, tides, and water temperatures.

OCEAN SURF SHOP
31 Center St., Folly Beach
(843) 588-9175
www.oceansurfshop.com
Ocean Surf Shop sells surfboards and all the accessories you can think of to catch a wave. Just getting started? No problem—this place gives lessons and rents boards, too. Some of their major brands are Aloha, Webber, Surftech, and Luke Short Designs. You'll find fins, nose guards, leashes, car racks, decals, and sports watches to complete the gear. Wetsuits, tees, board shorts, sandals, and sunglasses from Billabong, Reef, Volcom, Ambsn, and Insight outfit you wet or dry. This is the place to get "Edge of America" logo items to prove you've spent a day on the Edge. (See the Neighborhoods chapter for more on Folly Beach.)

SWIMMING

JAMES ISLAND RECREATIONAL COMPLEX
1088 Quail Dr.
(843) 795-5756
www.charleston-sc.gov
Operated by the city's Department of Recreation Aquatics Division, this 25-yard, outdoor pool with lifeguards is open June through Aug. Water fitness classes and swimming lessons are planned for the mornings, and open swimming is the norm in the afternoon. Adult city residents can swim for $2, nonresidents for $4; residents 17 and younger pay $1.50; nonresidents, $3. City residents pay $20 for youth swimming lessons and $25 for adult lessons; parent and tot swims are $15. Nonresidents pay $30 for youth lessons, $35 for adults, and $25 for parent and tot swimming.

PALMETTO ISLANDS COUNTY PARK
444 Needlerush Pkwy., Mount Pleasant
(843) 884-0832
www.ccprc.com
The outdoor water playground at Palmetto Islands County Park is open 10 a.m. to 6 p.m. on weekends in May and mid-Aug through Labor Day, and every day from Memorial Day

The *Spirit of the South*

Work on the ***Spirit of South Carolina*** was recently completed on the Charleston Peninsula at Ansonborough Field, just south of the South Carolina Aquarium. A small crew of boatwrights and volunteers constructed the big timber pilot schooner (138 feet in length) as part of a project initiated by the South Carolina Maritime Heritage Foundation. The tall ship project represents the state's long shipbuilding history and provides educational opportunities for the youth of South Carolina. The crew sails the ship from port to port, with Charleston remaining as its home base. For more information, visit www .scmaritime.org.

until mid-Aug. Charges for county residents are $6.99 for an adult and $5.99 for a child under 42 inches tall; nonresidents pay $7.99. Children younger than 2 can swim for free. Swimming fees are in addition to a $1 per person park admission. (For more on this and other Charleston County parks, see the Kidstuff and Parks & Recreation chapters.)

RICHARD L. JONES RECREATION CENTER POOL
391 Egypt Rd., Mount Pleasant
(843) 884-2528
www.mtpleasantrec.com
There is a 6-lane, indoor swimming pool at the Richard L. Jones complex. Swimming lessons, aquatic exercise classes, lap and recreational swimming are some of the many

options. Membership is open to anyone. Mount Pleasant residents pay only $2 for a one-year membership plus $2 each time they swim. Children 4 and younger swim free. Nonresidents pay $136 for annual memberships plus the $2 swim fee. Swimming lessons range from $28 to $45 for residents and from $35 to $52 for nonresidents. A similar schedule of lessons is also offered at the Park West Complex Pool. Call (843) 856-2196 for more information.

i Practice Plus-One Boating, meaning what you take out on your boating trip be sure to bring back plus one—one piece of litter or debris, every time. If it floats, net it. If it blows out, go back and get it. Act ethically and responsibly to keep our waterways clean for the enjoyment of all.

W. L. STEPHENS AQUATIC CENTER
780 West Oak Forest Dr.
(843) 769-8261
www.charleston-sc.gov
This is a good place to start your exploration of swimming pools in the Greater Charleston area, as the City of Charleston Aquatics Division has an office here. Open year-round, this indoor pool has 6 lanes and is 25 yards long. It is a popular winter birthday-party venue—nothing like a warm swim when there's frost on the windows—and draws its share of regular lap swimmers. There are full showers. The price to use the pool is $2 for adults and $1.50 for children younger than 17. Swimming lessons for residents are $15 for parent–tot, $20 for children, and $25 for adults; nonresidents, $25 for parent–tot, $30 for children, and $35 for adults.

HUNTING & FISHING

Hunting and fishing are major recreational traditions in the Trident area. When the Hon. William Elliott published *Carolina Sports by Land and Water* in 1846, it was called a "description and defense" of these sports in the Lowcountry. Today, the best defense of these outdoor activities is that many who participate in them are also conservation-minded people who help implement and adhere to laws protecting wildlife. Limits, seasons, and a licensing program are part of an overall system that fosters responsible sportsmanship and helps maintain diversity and numbers in fields and streams.

HUNTING

Hunting is one of the most important industries in the state. Deer hunters alone contribute more than $180 million to South Carolina's economy. Overall, there are more than 200,000 licensed hunters here. To ensure the future of the industry, the South Carolina Department of Natural Resources sponsors a number of events to expose youth to hunting. Parent–child and adult–youth hunts for doves, ducks, and turkeys are among the outings they organize. The DNR also works closely with the many active conservation groups to promote youth and adult hunting. For more information on these and other programs, visit www.dnr.sc.gov.

From raccoons to deer, turkeys to ducks, there is both variety and quantity in Lowcountry habitats. Deer hunting has overtaken dove hunting as the most popular type of hunting in South Carolina. The high deer population and the relative ease of accessibility, combined with the long Lowcountry season (usually Aug 15 to Jan 1), are factors in its popularity. There are a lot of public and private lands set up specifically for deer hunting in this area.

The mourning dove continues to be popular quarry for hunters. It's ranked as the No. 1 game bird in South Carolina. Dove shoots are quite common in Sept, late Nov, and late Dec/early Jan and provide social events for many Lowcountry hunters. The sport is strong, but a slight decline in the dove population during the last few years has led to some restrictions, including the elimination of morning hunts during the first three days of the season and a bag limit of 15 doves per hunter per day. Turkey hunting has grown in popularity because of a very successful restoration project that moved turkeys from the Francis Marion National Forest in the 1950s and from the Piedmont and Savannah River Plant areas in the 1970s to other habitats across South Carolina. The season lasts four to six weeks in the spring and is an option in every county in the state.

Small game hunting for squirrel, rabbits, fox, raccoon, opossum, and quail provides more seasonal hunting opportunities. Most quail hunting takes place from late fall to early spring on public shooting reserves. On private lands in the Trident area, the season usually runs from late Nov to early Mar with a limit of 12 birds per hunter per day because of the limited numbers of coveys of quail.

Waterfowl hunting has experienced a big rebound after more than a decade of drought in the Canadian breeding grounds. More abundant moisture on the grounds and more acreage of nesting cover provided by the Conservation Reserve Program have increased the continent's waterfowl population. The past couple of years have seen the Lowcountry's numbers increasing as well. Blue-winged teals and northern shovelers are at all-time population highs, according to the Office of Migratory Bird Management for the US Fish and Wildlife Service. Other species on the rise include greenwings, goldeneye, and buffleheads, in addition to the diving ducks such as canvasbacks and redheads.

BEFORE TAKING TO THE FIELD

So how does the would-be hunter in the Lowcountry get set for those early-morning outings in a duck blind or late afternoons in a deer stand?

The South Carolina Department of Natural Resources publishes a booklet, *South Carolina Rules and Regulations for Hunting, Fishing, and Wildlife Management Areas,* that details hunting areas, regulations, education, limits, and check stations. For your free copy, write to the department at P.O. Box 167, Columbia, SC 29202, or call locally at (843) 953-9307. The booklets can also be found at local sporting goods stores and the sporting goods departments at large retailers (such as Wal-Mart and Kmart), where you also can purchase hunting and fishing licenses. (Licenses are also available by phone 24 hours a day at (866) 714-3611 or on the Internet at www.dnr.sc.gov with an additional $3

processing fee.) Turkey, migratory bird, and waterfowl hunting regulations and seasons are outlined in even more detail in separate brochures available just before the various seasons. Initiated in 1998, a migratory game bird permit is required in South Carolina. To get the free permit, hunters must obtain a migratory bird Harvest Information Program (HIP) permit by answering a few questions on forms available at all license vendors.

The South Carolina DNR Wildlife and Marine Resources Division designates private land in the Trident area as Game Zone 6. In addition to laws restricting hunting by personal invitation on private property, state game wardens also actively enforce regulations on other lands—marked as either Wildlife Management Areas (WMAs) or US Forest Service property—where public hunting is allowed.

Obviously, residents or visitors must be licensed to hunt in the Trident area. Remember that seasons, prices, gender restrictions, and limits change virtually every year. Deer season generally lasts from mid-Aug to Jan 1. Migratory game bird season always comes in the fall. Other hunting season dates are available by calling (843) 953-9307. The annual price for a state resident to hunt in a management area is $30.50, with an additional $6 needed to hunt big game. For nonresidents, it costs $125 for an annual license to hunt small game. A 10-consecutive-day, nonresident, small-game-only license costs $75. Nonresident fees for hunting big game are $100 plus $76 for a management area permit.

For annual waterfowl season, hunters may buy a management area permit (in addition to their state hunting license and a migratory waterfowl permit) to hunt in designated areas (prices are the same as listed in the previous paragraph). Always make sure you know that you are within the scope of state and federal game laws before you head out to hunt.

For information about the South Carolina Department of Natural Resources' free 10-hour hunter education course, contact the department at the address given, and mark the letter: "Attention: Hunter Education." You can call the department at (803) 734-3995 or (800) 277-4301 or locally at (843) 953-9302. The course combines classroom instruction (covering hunting ethics, hunter-landowner relations, and basic conservation and wildlife management principles) and hands-on experience in hunter safety and hunting techniques. Other options include an online course and self-study courses with either a workbook or CD. It is required that all residents and nonresidents born after June 30, 1979, successfully complete the course before a hunting license can be obtained. This course is accepted by other states that require safety certification for licenses, and South Carolina recognizes certification from other states.

ℹ **Hunters often ignore the danger of hearing loss, but prolonged exposure to the sounds of gunfire can lead to gradual, permanent deterioration. Nonelectronic and electronic devices can alleviate the problem and are available at a wide range of prices. The over-the-counter models start as low as $8 or $9, a small price to pay to preserve good hearing.**

FISHING

The Trident area offers some of the best fishing on the East Coast. Charleston County, blessed with some 60 miles of protected coastline, is a fishing enthusiast's paradise. The fresh waters of the Ashley and Cooper Rivers, with their adjacent rice field breaks and salt creeks, bays, and (of course) the ocean, are all open to the public. Fish for largemouth bass, bream, trout, flounder, or spottail bass in these rivers and bluefish in the harbor, or head out to the deep water to match wits with dolphin, wahoo, marlin, sailfish, or tuna.

Berkeley County's Marion and Moultrie Lakes cover 170,000 acres with striped bass, largemouth bass, sunfish, white bass, crappie, and catfish aplenty. Dorchester County includes part of the Edisto River, home to striped bass and American shad—the roe of which, often prepared and served with grits, is a Lowcountry delicacy. Largemouth bass, redbreast, and bluegill bream and catfish also swim the Edisto.

Before You Drop a Line

Residents and out-of-state visitors pay fees to fish or shrimp, with rates varying according to the fishing venue and angler's age. (No license is necessary for dock or pier fishing.) For residents and nonresidents, saltwater fishing licenses (Marine Recreational Fisheries Stamps) are $10. Freshwater licenses are $10 on an annual basis for South Carolina residents. For out-of-state anglers, annual licenses to fish only fresh waters cost $35, and one-week freshwater licenses are $11. Ask the South Carolina Marine Resources Division about combination discounts if you plan to be both hunting and fishing.

In an effort to protect the fish population, South Carolina has also established regulations regarding limits on the sizes and number of fish that may be taken, the use of seines and gill nets, and guidelines concerning crabbing, shrimping, and other fishing activities. Saltwater fishing conservation and ethical angling practices are not only encouraged but enforced. Undersized fish and fish over the quantity limits should be released, helping to ensure future fish populations. Fortunately, the number of saltwater finfish tagged and released in South Carolina waters is increasing each year as more and more anglers take up this practice. Already, it is conserving resources and providing valuable information on the growth and movement of fish for further study and management. Again, for more specific information about seasons, rules, and licenses, refer to the South Carolina Department of Natural Resources' annually issued rules and regulations booklet (see Hunting for details on how to pick up a copy), or contact the Marine Resources Division at (843) 953-9300.

Deep-Sea Fishing

Deep-sea fishing is a popular sport, and charter boats allow visitors and locals alike to enjoy the experience. Locals say that the best offshore fishing is during the months from May through Sept, when water temperatures are warmer, although, weather permitting, you can venture out at other times of the year. Charter trips are on luxury boats—air conditioned and large enough to ride out the ocean swells, yet small enough to put you on a first-name basis with the captain. The average cost for ocean reef charter trips—although prices can vary at the captain's discretion—is $1,100 for a half-day (that's for up to 6 passengers) and $1,800 for a full day (again, for 6 passengers).

Gulf-stream charters are only offered on a full-day basis and run about $1,500 for 10 hours, and $2,000 for 12 hours for 6 passengers. A gratuity is not included, and you'll want to tip the captain and mates whether the fish were biting or not. These guys earn their keep by charting the course, baiting the lines, and doing their best to find the fish. On both charter and "head" boats, which accommodate dozens more people on a "per head" basis at a fraction of a charter's cost, all rods, reels, bait, and tackle will be provided. Visiting anglers may be amazed to see that a little bit of everything is used to catch fish here—from ballyhoo with skirts to live bait to lures without bait. On charter boats, anglers usually bring along food and a drink cooler. On head boats, you can almost always count on a snack bar.

Call at least a month before you visit to book a charter. It is not normally necessary to contact a head boat more than a couple of days before you want to go out. Most captains are going to lead you to the reefs or the Gulf Stream and want you to plan on a long, physically challenging but exhilarating day. Be prepared: If you tend to get seasick, ask your doctor to recommend good over-the-counter preventive medicine. General common sense suggests you get a good night's sleep before your day on the boat, which will usually begin before dawn.

While on the sea, drink lots of nonalcoholic fluids, and don't forget your sunglasses and sunscreen, a long-sleeved shirt, a hat that shades your face, deck shoes with good traction, a couple of towels for drying off periodically, and a camera to prove the size of that mighty one that got away.

Expect to land fish such as king and Spanish mackerel, cobia, sea bass, and even barracuda if you are on the reefs. In the Gulf Stream, you'll likely pull blue or white marlin, wahoo, tuna, dolphin, or sailfish, so break out the recipes. Bottom fishing in the Gulf Stream could lead to good hauls of snapper, grouper, porgy, or amberjack—all good eating.

i **Fishing for more information? Check out the area's source for weather, fishing reports, charters, tournaments, classifieds, recipes, and more. Visit www.charlestonfishing.com for the lowdown on local recreational fishing.**

Inshore Fishing

Perhaps inshore fishing is more to your liking. The ubiquitous winding rivers, creeks, and inlets in the Trident area offer lots of action without the lengthy trip out to the Gulf Stream. The quiet beauty of the setting and the salt marsh air can afford a memorable experience and, we hope, some good eating afterward. Go after flounder, king mackerel, trout, jack crevalle, spottail bass, or redfish.

The cooler months of the year, usually from Sept through Apr, are the best times to wet a line inshore. The clarity of the water is good then, and in shallow water, you may even see the fish and cast directly to them. (The summer months may be slightly less inviting for fishermen because of the heat and prevalence of gnats and mosquitoes.) Anglers use light-tackle rods and reels and saltwater fly rods for snagging most inshore catches.

Charter Boats

The main charter operators in the area are based around five marinas: Charleston Harbor Marina, (843) 284-7062, Isle of Palms Marina, (843) 886-0209, and Toler's Cove, (843) 881- 0325, in East Cooper; Ripley Light Marina, (843) 766-2100, west of the Ashley;

and Bohicket Marina, (843) 768-1280, on Johns Island. Contacting them should provide the latest information on available charters for all kinds of fishing.

The following listings should give you a good head start on some of the head or charter boats available for offshore or inshore fishing. Take note that these salty seagoing veterans don't always like to be tied down to specific price ranges. Be ready to bargain. (For more information, see the Boating & Water Sports chapter.)

AQUASAFARIS, INC.
24 Patriots Point Rd., A-Dock, 2nd Floor Marina Building, Ste. 1, Mount Pleasant (843) 886-8133, (800) 524-3444 www.aqua-safaris.com
AquaSafaris operates an offshore/inshore fishing charter fleet that departs from all the Charleston area marinas. The fleet encompasses boats ranging in size from 19 to 60 feet. Aqua Safaris offers some of the best guides and offshore fishers in the area with the better-known sportfishing yachts. The offshore trips for up to 6 passengers range from $1,200 for a half-day up to $2,300 for a full day depending on the size of the boat. Inshore rates for four people range from $450 to $800 depending on the length of time booked. (See the Boating & Water Sports chapter for more on AquaSafaris.)

BOHICKET BOAT CHARTERS
2789 Cherry Point Rd., Wadmalaw Island (843) 559-3525 www.bohicketboat.com
Bohicket offers inshore, flats, offshore, and Gulf Stream fishing trips out of Bohicket Marina, near Kiawah and Seabrook Islands. Charters include full-, three-quarter-, and half-day trips on 24- to 43-foot passenger

boats. Rates start at $375 for 2 people for 4 hours of flats fishing for redfish and trout. Inshore family fishing for 4 to 6 passengers begins at $360 for 3 hours. Offshore rates are $750 to $880 for half-days, $1,300 to $1,700 for three-quarter days, and $1,300 to $2,000 for full-day trips. Boat rentals from 16-foot jon boats to 23-foot deck boats are also available, along with tackle, trips to find shells, sunset cruises, and other customized journeys. Rates begin at $100 to $225 for half-days and $150 to $330 for a full day. (For more on Bohicket Marina, see the Boating and Water Sports chapter.)

CAPTAIN IVAN'S ISLAND CHARTERS
805 Duck Hawk Retreat
(843) 762-2020
www.captainivan.com
Specializing in live-bait and light-tackle fishing, Captain Ivan's 30-foot, wide-beam boat has custom rods, reels, and tackle and is Coast Guard certified. Half-day trips for up to 4 passengers are $750 with each additional passenger adding $100. Full-day trips for up to 4 are $1,300, adding $100 for each additional person. Gulf Stream trolling or bottom fishing runs $1,800 for up to four with additional passengers adding $100 each. Specialty trips for shark fishing and tournaments are available for booking, too.

CAPT. RICHARD STUHR INSHORE
LIGHT-TACKLE AND FLY FISHING
547 Sanders Farm Lane
(843) 881-3179
www.captstuhr.com
Capt. Richard Stuhr, a native Charlestonian with lifelong experience on the water, offers custom trips into the inland waters of the Lowcountry on his 19-foot Action Craft. His specialties are inshore light-tackle and fly fishing. This Orvis-endorsed guide offers full- and half-day trips for 1 to 2 people (add $50 for each additional person) year-round. Prices range from $350 for half-days to $600 for full days. Capt. Stuhr also offers casting instruction for $100 per hour.

FIN STALKER CHARTERS
6 Hillcreek Blvd.
(843) 509-9972
www.backwaterfishing.com
Lowcountry native Captain Chris Chavis really knows his way around the area's inshore estuaries, tidal creeks, and barrier island waters. He offers full- and half-day charters for light-tackle and fly-fishing year round. The half-day rate is $400 and full-day is $600. All equipment is provided, and trophy photos are available. His Action Craft "flats boat" is ideal for stalking redfish, trout, jack crevalle, tarpon, Spanish mackerel, sharks, and cobia, among other sportfish challenges and accommodates three anglers. His 26-foot center console takes four out for inshore, near shore, and offshore fishing adventures. Rates range from $550 to $1,150. No license is required. Call for more information and reservations.

HARBOR FISHING CHARTERS
640 Pelzer Dr., Mount Pleasant
(843) 452-8844
www.fishcharlestonsc.com
To fish the backwaters of the Lowcountry, including Charleston Harbor and the barrier islands, charter with Reed Simmons, an experienced inshore guide. Using light tackle and live bait, you will pursue red drum, flounder, tarpon, mackerel, ladyfish, and speckled trout on his 17-foot Actioncraft flats boat. Half-day rates start about $350, and a 6-hour trip is about $550 for charters

for up to 3 people. A 2-hour children's trip and sightseeing tours are offered by Captain Reed as well.

ISLE OF PALMS MARINA CHARTERS
41st Ave. at Intracoastal Waterway, Isle of Palms
(843) 886-0209
www.iopmarina.com

Isle of Palms Marina offers a variety of inshore and offshore fishing trips with half-, three-quarter, and full-day options. Inshore flats fishing for 4 hours is $375 for 2 people. For inshore fishing around the jetties, the cost starts at $525 for 6 hours. Offshore fishing on a 9-hour trip for 4 people starts at $1,295. Crabbing trips, shelling, beachcombing, motorboat rentals, as well as sunset and moonlight cruises are also available. (See the Boating & Water Sports chapter for more on Isle of Palms Marina.)

✳SALTWATER CHARTERS
522 Old Bridge Court, Mount Pleasant
(843) 830-0448
www.saltcharters.com

Full-time guide Capt. Peter Brown spends 280 days a year targeting gamefish along South Carolina's coast. And what does he do on his days off? Goes fishing, of course! His private charters are aboard a 17-foot flats skiff, ideal for stalking big fish in very shallow water. He also takes up to 6 people in his 23-foot center console for tarpon and near-shore fishing. Rods and tackle are provided for year-round inshore light-tackle and fly fishing. U.S.C.G. licensed and insured, Peter specializes in sight casting, and (depending on the season) he'll put you on the red drum, black drum, trout, flounder, Spanish mackerel, and jack crevalle. A 4-hour trip is

$400, a 5-hour $450, and a 6-hour runs $500 on the flats boat. Add $100 to each price for the center console.

Fishing Piers & Bridges

Maybe you just want to escape for a couple of hours to see what you can find by dropping a line in the neighborhood waters. After all, scheduling a charter or putting the boat in the water often takes advance planning and a major commitment of time. Or perhaps you have the kids in tow—those attention spans may only be good for an hour or so. The Charleston area provides ample opportunity for this leisurely walk-up pastime. A number of piers and bridges for saltwater fishing are maintained and operated by the Charleston County Park and Recreation Commission and the City of Charleston.

THE BATTERY
East Battery at Murray Blvd.
(843) 724-7321
www.charleston-sc.gov

The seawall at White Point Gardens is a historic spot that has served as a promenade for Charlestonians for a couple of hundred years. This tip of the Peninsula is where the Ashley and Cooper Rivers meet, as Charlestonians are fond of saying, to form the Atlantic Ocean. The confluence of the rivers here can make for some good fishing, too, so drop a line anywhere along the 1-mile waterfront access. The Battery is open year-round and, with any luck, parking is found alongside.

BREACH INLET BRIDGE
SR 703, Sullivan's Island, Isle of Palms
This bridge connecting Sullivan's Island and the Isle of Palms is almost never without

some anglers. Because of the narrow inlet connecting the ocean with the creeks and waterway behind the islands, the currents are very strong, and swimming in the area is prohibited. But these currents can make for some lively fishing, as the fish are funneled through with the changing tides. Free parking is nearby on either side of the bridge, and the bridge's catwalks on both sides are open year-round.

BRITTLEBANK PARK PIER
Lockwood Dr.
(843) 724-7321
www.charleston-sc.gov
Operated by the city of Charleston, this pier with a floating dock extends 200 feet out onto the Ashley River on the west side of the Peninsula. At Lockwood Drive and Fishburne Street next to the Joseph P. Riley Ballpark, the 10-acre park is a venue for many large outdoor concerts and events. Parking is available, but there are no restrooms or other facilities. No fee is charged. It is open sunrise to 11 p.m. daily.

FOLLY BEACH EDWIN S. TAYLOR
FISHING PIER
101 East Arctic Ave., Folly Beach
(843) 588-FISH
www.ccprc.com
Extending more than 1,045 feet into the Atlantic Ocean, this 25-foot-wide pier is noted for the distinctive design of a diamond-shaped platform at its end. The platform itself covers a 7,500-square-foot area, with part of it under a covered shelter. The pier is 23 feet above sea level and affords great fishing, walking, birding, and viewing of Folly Beach and the ocean. Landward, a large facility provides restrooms (unisex restrooms are available, too, for people with

disabilities and parents with small children), a tackle shop, and the Locklear's Beach City Grill. The pier is operated by the county park system and is open daily from 6 a.m. to 11 p.m. Apr through Oct, 7 a.m. to 7 p.m. Mar and Nov, and from 8 a.m. to 5 p.m. Dec through Feb. Parking is $7, and the fishing fees are $5 for an adult Charleston County resident ($8 for king mackerel fishing), $3 for children 12 and younger, and $8 for a nonresident adult ($10 for king mackerel fishing). You can also rent rods and get annual passes here.

JAMES ISLAND COUNTY PARK DOCK
871 Riverland Dr.
(843) 795-4386
www.ccprc.com
On a tidal creek on the Stono River, this floating dock offers tranquil fishing and crabbing with complete facilities and wheelchair access. Crabbing classes, which give pointers on catching and cooking crab, are offered here from time to time. Part of the dock is covered, and picnic tables are nearby. The park has plenty of parking and is open daily May through Aug, from 8 a.m. to 8 p.m.; Sept, Oct, Mar, and Apr from 8 a.m. to sunset.; and Nov through Feb 8 a.m. to 5 p.m. The individual admission price is $1, with no charge for children younger than 3. (See the Kidstuff and Parks & Recreation chapters for more about the recreational opportunities at James Island County Park.)

i **Anglers in privately owned boats need to remember that it is unlawful to fish within 150 feet of commercial fishing piers extending into the Atlantic Ocean.**

PALMETTO ISLANDS COUNTY PARK FISHING DOCK
444 Needlerush Pkwy., Mount Pleasant
(843) 884-0832
www.ccprc.com
Wind down a paved walking trail to this large, floating dock at the Peninsula Center on Horlbeck Creek and Boone Hall Creek. There are also several smaller docks for peaceful fishing and crabbing within the Palmetto Islands County Park, which offers full facilities. Hours are 8 a.m. to 8 p.m. May through Labor Day; 8 a.m. to sunset Mar, Apr, Sept, and Oct; and 8 a.m. to 5 p.m. from Nov through Feb. Park gate admission is $1 per person, with children younger than 3 free. (For more on the Palmetto Islands County Park, see the Kidstuff and Parks & Recreation chapters.)

PITT STREET BRIDGE
End of Pitt Street, Mount Pleasant
(843) 849-2022
www.mtpleasantrec.com
At the end of Pitt Street, on the Intracoastal Waterway overlooking Charleston Harbor, is the old Pitt Street Bridge. The half-mile bridge is the former trolley car causeway, now closed to traffic, which used to connect Mount Pleasant and Sullivan's Island. It's a good place to fish and a great spot for watching waterway boat traffic. The town of Mount Pleasant provides year-round access to the bridge at no fee.

WATERFRONT PARK PIER
Cumberland Street to North Adgers Wharf, Charleston
(843) 724-7321
www.charleston-sc.gov
Waterfront Park is quite a popular spot for tourists and locals because of its setting overlooking Charleston Harbor toward Mount Pleasant and Ft. Sumter. Fishing may be a good excuse to spend the day here, but there are many pleasant distractions like the passing boats and wildlife—don't forget to check your line every now and then. There is no entry fee, but you will have to search for a metered parking spot or enter one of the nearby garages for a charge. The park and pier are open daily year-round from 6 a.m. to midnight. No facilities are available, but an easy stroll down Vendue Range leads to restaurants and shopping on East Bay Street. (See the Kidstuff and Parks & Recreation chapters for more on Waterfront Park.)

Fishing Tournaments

Almost year-round (with the exception of the coldest winter months), a fishing tournament of some description can be found, usually benefiting conservation groups and charities in the Trident area. Some of the bigger ones offer large purses and prizes in the thousands of dollars. Competition can be pretty stiff, but the changing seas and good old-fashioned luck often come into play, and . . . anything can happen. If you are serious about getting into the competitive sportfishing tournament circuit, here are a few of the major ones to check out. For a more complete listing of the year's saltwater fishing tournaments held in South Carolina, pick up the brochure from the South Carolina Department of Natural Resources Marine Resources Division at area bait and tackle shops, or write to SCDNR, P.O. Box 12559, Charleston, SC 29422.

BOHICKET MARINA INVITATIONAL BILLFISH TOURNAMENT
1880 Andell Bluff Blvd., Johns Island
(843) 768-1280

http://govcup.dnr.sc.gov

One of the five tourneys in the Governor's Cup Series, the Bohicket Invitational is one of the major tournaments in the area. Held in mid-May, this one brings in the big boys competing for serious money; first prize for the largest marlin garners $7,500. Placing here can lead to even bigger prizes in the Governor's Cup competition. This tag-and-release tourney also awards $1,000 for the largest wahoo, dolphin, and tuna and the best female and youth angler. Get your crew, sportfishing yacht, and checkbook ready for an entry fee of $2,000 and a sportin' good time. It's called an invitational, but anyone can join in the fun.

CAROLINA LADY ANGLERS "FISHING FOR THE CURE" OPEN TOURNAMENT

P.O. Box 13141, Charleston, SC 29422
(843) 509-5062
www.carolinaladyanglers.org

The Carolina Lady Anglers is the only all-female saltwater fishing group in the area. They are dedicated to promoting sportfishing in the Lowcountry and raising funds for a cure for breast cancer. Proceeds from club events such as the "Fishing for the Cure" tournament are donated to breast cancer education and research. The inshore fishing tournament is held in late May/early June and takes place at the Charleston Maritime Center. The competition is open to all—female, male, and youth anglers—with an entry fee of $30. Eligible species include Spanish mackerel, king mackerel, trout, flounder, sheepshead, and ladyfish. First-, second-, and third-place prizes are awarded as well as Outstanding Female, Outstanding Male, and Outstanding Youth (ages 12 and under). A raffle, buffet supper, and live music add to the fun. (If you are interested in joining this group, attend a meeting on the first Wed of the month at 6 p.m. Call for the location.)

CHARLESTON TRIDENT FISHING TOURNAMENT

861 Riverland Dr.
(843) 762-8023, (843) 795-4FUN
www.ccprc.com

For over 35 years the Charleston County Park and Recreation Commission, area businesses, and individuals have cosponsored this free tournament, which covers the year-long fishing season from Nov 1 through Oct 31. Competitors enter catches on entry blanks after weighing in at official weigh stations. Points are amassed for classes of eligible fish in both saltwater and freshwater divisions. Awards and certificates are given for outstanding saltwater and freshwater anglers, outstanding lady and youth (16 and younger) anglers, outstanding light-tackle and fly rod, ecology, and more. There are also awards for the largest fish caught in various categories. The competition is restricted to the waters of Berkeley, Charleston, and Dorchester Counties, and boats leaving from and returning to the waters between the South Santee and South Edisto Rivers.

FISHING FOR MIRACLES KING MACKEREL TOURNAMENT

P.O. Box 21199, Charleston, SC 29413
(843) 554-0177
www.fishingformiracles.org

Another of the South Carolina King Mackerel Governor's Cup Series tournaments in the area, the Annual Fishing for Miracles event is one of our favorite summertime competitions. Held in mid-Aug, this tournament is one of the largest fishing tournaments in South Carolina. Its proceeds benefit the

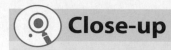 **Close-up**

Lowcountry Lunkers

Several state-record-size gamefish have been landed in Lowcountry waters. Here's a listing of several, with the type of fish, weight (in pounds and ounces), port, year, angler, and angler's hometown noted. This information is provided courtesy of the South Carolina Department of Natural Resources Marine Resources Division.

African Pompano—43-8; Mount Pleasant, 2008; by B. Powell, Charleston.

Albacore Tuna—37-4; Charleston, 1976; by W. Crump, Johns Island.

Bigeye Thresher Shark—406-0; Edisto Island, 1978; by J.H. Mixson, Johns Island.

Blackfin Tuna—40-6; Charleston, 2005, by Mark Hartley, Mount Pleasant.

Bluefish—21-0; Charleston, 1975; by J.A. Curtis, Charleston.

Blue Marlin—881-13; Charleston, 2005; by W.C. Taylor, Spartanburg.

Bonnethead Shark—27-11; Charleston, 2005; by B. Mattison, Raleigh, N.C.

Bull Shark—477-12; Stono Inlet, 1985; by C.R. Faust, Folly Beach.

Croaker—4-9; Charleston, 1979; by C.I. Frasier, Charleston.

Cubera Snapper—118-0; Mount Pleasant, 2007; by B. Williams, Easley.

Dolphin—77-5; Seabrook Island, 2008; by R. Riggs, Wando.

Dusky Shark—466-12; Charleston, 1981; by M. Almond, Charleston.

Florida Pompano—8-12; Charleston, 1975; by C. Mullinax Sr., Charleston.

Gag Grouper—48-8; Charleston, 1997; by R.L. Price, Ladson.

Gray Snapper—11-1; Charleston, 2002; by R.L. Price, Ladson.

Hammerhead Shark—588-3; Charleston, 1989; by B. Bass, Charleston.

Jack Crevalle—40-1; Charleston, 1993; by J. Benich, Mount Pleasant.

Medical University of South Carolina Children's Hospital and the Coastal Conservation Association of South Carolina. There are some terrific prizes (first place could net you as much as $25,000), and it is all based out of the Ripley Light Marina just across the James Island Connector. To get involved, contact the tournament committee by calling or writing. The boat entry fee in 2010 was $300 prior to Aug 1 and $350 after that date. (See the Annual Events chapter for more on this tournament.)

JAMES ISLAND YACHT CLUB KING MACKEREL CLASSIC
P.O. Box 12840, Charleston 29422
(843) 795-6060
www.jiyc.org
Held in late June, this tournament is one of the area's popular competitions (many of

Jolthead Porgy—18-4; Charleston, 1984; by J. Currie, North Charleston.

King Mackerel—62-0; Charleston, 1976; by J. Brownlee III, Charleston.

Ladyfish—5-14; Charleston, 1994; by B. Raver, Charleston.

Little Tunny—29-7; Charleston, 1975; by C. Edwards Jr., Columbia.

Longbill Spearfish—53-0; Mount Pleasant, 1986; by H.L. Johnson Jr., Mount Pleasant.

Sandbar Shark—199-4; Charleston, 1984; by T. McGuiness, Charleston.

Sand Tiger Shark—350-2; Charleston, 1993; by M. Thawley, Summerville.

Sheepshead—16-6; Mount Pleasant, 2008; by J. Widener, Hanahan.

Shortfin Mako Shark—391-15; Charleston, 2002; by P. Ford, Charleston.

Silky Shark—248-0; Charleston, 1981; by R. Keenan, Charleston.

Skipjack Tuna—25-14; Charleston, 1986; by D.L. Stubbs, Charleston.

Southern Flounder (tie)—17-6; South Santee, 1974; by L.C. Floyd, Florence.

Spinner Shark—159-0; Mount Pleasant, 1998; by J. Short, Ellenboro, N.C.

Spot (tie)—1-1; Charleston, 1967; by J. Stehmeyer, Charleston.

Striped Bass—46-13; Combahee River, 1993; by B.W. Chambers, Canadys.

Tautog—5-4; Charleston, 2003; by T. Crull, Charleston.

Vermillion Snapper—6-10; Charleston, 1975; by D.H. Long, Charleston.

White Grunt—5-10; Charleston, 2009; by P. Godbout, Summerville.

White Marlin—108-0; Charleston, 1981; by D.C. Critz Jr., Savannah, Ga.

Yellowfin Tuna—241-12; Charleston, 1979; by T.C. Lewis, Mount Pleasant.

Yellowtail Snapper—10-8; Mount Pleasant, 2003; by T. Snelgrove, Lexington.

which offer less pressure than the billfish ones) with an emphasis on having a good time. Locals and visitors compete for cash and prizes, and the boat early entry fee is $160 or $200 late registration. First-, second-, and third-place prizes are awarded for the heaviest king mackerel, paying around $9,600. Other noncash awards go for the outstanding catch by a James Island Yacht Club member, outstanding female angler, and outstanding youth angler (16 and younger).

SOUTH CAROLINA GOVERNOR'S CUP BILLFISHING SERIES
P.O. Box 12559, Charleston, SC 29422
(843) 953-9365
http://govcup.dnr.sc.gov

The Governor's Cup is an annual, umbrella tournament that encompasses five billfish competitions along coastal South Carolina each spring and summer. Anglers and boats participate by entering two or more member events in the series and either landing or tagging and releasing billfish to accumulate points. More points are given for tagged and released fish, encouraging conservation of marine resources. A perpetual trophy is inscribed with the names of the winners in the categories of Outstanding Billfish, Outstanding Boat, and Outstanding Billfish Conservation. The tournament series runs from May through July and has included area events such as the Charleston Harbor Resort & Marina, the HMY/Viking Megadock (at the Charleston City Marina), and the Bohicket Marina Invitational billfish tournaments (see previous listing). The Governor's Cup is an official program of the South Carolina Department of Natural Resources in cooperation with the South Carolina Department of Parks, Recreation, and Tourism. North Carolina and Georgia have a Governor's Cup, too, and the three states compete in a shootout at the end of the year. For more information, write to the address above.

HUNTING & FISHING OUTFITTERS

The Lowcountry is loaded when it comes to terrific stores that stock all the stuff you'll need to bag your limit or catch a mess of fish for cooking. Here are a handful of our favorite outdoor goods suppliers.

CAROLINA ROD & GUN, INC.
1319 Savannah Hwy.
(843) 571-7972
www.carolinarodandgun.net
Carolina Rod & Gun has a large selection of sporting firearms, knives, and outdoor clothing, boots, and gloves in their 6,000-square-foot store. A full-line Browning dealer, this shop also carries Benelli, Blaser, and Beretta. A full-time gunsmith is also on hand for all gunsmith service and repairs.

Sporting optics from Leupold, Zeiss, Leica, and Schmidt & Bender provide a range of binoculars and scopes. Outdoor clothing by Browning, Mossy Oak, Beretta, Filson, and Boyt/Bob Allen, as well as shoes and boots from LaCrosse, Danner, and Chippewa, completes your hunting gear.

✳THE CHARLESTON ANGLER
654 St. Andrews Blvd.
(843) 571-3899
www.thecharlestonangler.com
The Charleston Angler is out to improve your luck with everything you need for a day of inshore or flats fishing. It specializes in fly fishing and light tackle and carries fly and surf rods and reels from manufacturers such as G.Loomis, Sage, St. Croix, Shimano, Orvis, and Ross Reels. They have live, frozen, and plastic bait and even offer fly-tying and casting lessons if you need a refresher. Men's, women's, and kids' clothing lines include Columbia, Aftco, Mossy Oak, and Guy Harvey. And if you want it personalized with the name of your new boat, they embroider on shirts, shorts, jackets, towels, or ballcaps. If you're just visiting, the helpful staff is happy to make suggestions for your selection of tackle or which guide to book. They are up on the recent conditions and what time of year which fish are running. Give 'em a call and try your luck. Two more locations are at 1113-J Market Center Blvd., Mount Pleasant (843-884-2095) and 2139 N. Main St., Unit F, Summerville (843-871-9362).

HADDRELL'S POINT TACKLE &
HUNTING SUPPLY CENTER

885 Ben Sawyer Blvd., Mount Pleasant
(843) 881-3644, (800) 881-5201
www.haddrellspoint.com

Haddrell's Point offers a complete line of inshore and offshore fishing equipment for the novice to the serious angler. It is one of a few local stores carrying a full line of saltwater and freshwater fly-fishing gear. Daiwa and Shakespeare rods, Star Rods, and US Reels and Ross reels are a few of the brands the center carries, and it is the only Shimano warranty station in South Carolina. The stores handle warranty work for Penn and Quantum reels, too. Haddrell's also sells hunting accessories for turkey, duck, and deer hunters, with clothing from Columbia, Aftco, and Old Harbor. Talk with the friendly, knowledgeable staff for sales assistance, education, and instruction on hunting and fishing pursuits. A second location is at 47 South Windermere Blvd., Charleston (843-573-3474).

SPECTATOR SPORTS

When most people in the Lowcountry think of sports, they think of grabbing their equipment and getting involved directly in a game of tennis, a round of golf, a dip in the swimming pool, and other activities. However, neither visitors nor locals should overlook the excellent professional, amateur, and collegiate spectator sports available for our enjoyment.

There's nothing like taking off for a day at the stadium to watch the great American sport of baseball, and Charleston's own RiverDogs provide an action-packed brand of play. There's also the option of cheering for the big-name professionals who regularly show up at area golf and tennis matches. And who among us doesn't enjoy an autumn afternoon spent cheering on the college football team, even if our own college days are but a dim, gilded memory.

Tennis, sailing regattas, soccer, ice hockey . . . you name it—if it translates into action, it can probably be found somewhere in the Lowcountry. So take some time off from your own sports regimen to sit and watch the following folks in action. You'll probably find yourself screaming "Hey batter, batter, batter!" right along with the best of 'em!

BASEBALL

CHARLESTON RIVERDOGS
360 Fishburne St.
(843) 723-7241, (843) 577-DOGS (Ticket Office)
www.riverdogs.com
The minor league team, reborn the Charleston RiverDogs in 1994, is a Class A South Atlantic League farm team for the New York Yankees. The RiverDogs' season runs Apr through Aug. Locals turn out regularly and appreciate exciting baseball while enjoying the antics of Charlie the RiverDog, the giant costumed mascot who plays to the stands and brings out the kid in everyone. After 57 years at College Park, Charleston baseball moved to a new ballpark. Home, as of 1997, is the 5,900-seat Joseph P. Riley Jr. Park on the banks of the Ashley River. This downtown location is next to Brittlebank Park, Stoney Field, and Lockwood Drive. General admission seats are $5 with a range of prices up to $12 for box seats. Watch for special, reduced-admission games and promotions such as fireworks displays after Friday night games and prize giveaways throughout spring and summer. Plenty of parking is available adjacent to the ballpark for $4.

GOLF

NATIONWIDE TOUR CHAMPIONSHIP
Daniel Island Club, 600 Island Park Dr., Daniel Island
(843) 971-3555
www.danielislandclub.com

For 3 years, October 2009–2011, the Daniel Island Club will host the Nationwide Tour's season-ending event. The competition features the top 60 players on the Nationwide money list competing in a $1 million, 72-hole stroke play, no-cut event. The winner will take home $180,000, and the top 25 on the list after the event will earn their promotion to the PGA Tour for the next season. Typically, two-thirds of the players on the PGA Tour have come through the Nationwide Tour, so this is your chance to watch high-level golf up-close on the Rees Jones–designed Ralston Creek Course on Daniel Island. (For more on Daniel Island see the Neighborhoods chapter.) Call the number above for more information.

i Be in the know: Call the Joseph P. Riley Jr. Park "the Joe." Amid a flurry of modesty, Charleston Mayor Joseph P. Riley Jr. tried to dissuade officials from naming the new ballpark in his honor—to no avail. The official name has been unofficially shortened to "the Joe," and the nickname has stuck.

*PGA CHAMPIONSHIP
Kiawah Resort, 1000 Ocean Course Dr., Kiawah Island
(843) 266-4679, (800) 654-2924
www.kiawahresort.com/golf,
www.pga.com
Kiawah Island's Ocean Course will set the scene for the 94th PGA Championship held August 9–12, 2012. It will become only the 5th golf course to play host to the Ryder Cup (1991), the Senior PGA Championship (2007), and the PGA Championship. The Ocean Course's oceanfront links-style layout designed by Pete Dye will test the skills of the PGA professionals at the final major tournament of 2012. (See the Golf chapter for more on the Ocean Course at Kiawah.) Ticket sales are underway and information can be found by visiting the websites above.

RICE PLANTERS AMATEUR GOLF CHAMPIONSHIP
Snee Farm Country Club, 1200 Club Dr., Mount Pleasant
(843) 884-2600
www.sneefarmcc.com/rpa
Since 1973, Snee Farm Country Club has hosted the Rice Planters Amateur Golf Championship. This tournament attracts top collegiate golfers, seasoned talent from across the United States, and terrific international amateur players. Past champions and competitors have included current pros Tom Lehman, Davis Love, III, Scott Hoch, Stewart Cink, Andy Bean, Hal Sutton, and Allen Doyle. Held in late June, this event is open to the public at no charge. Call Snee Farm for more information.

ICE HOCKEY

SOUTH CAROLINA STINGRAYS
3107 Firestone Rd., North Charleston
(843) 744-2248
www.stingrayshockey.com
The North Charleston Coliseum reverberates with very vocal ice hockey fans who pack in to watch the Stingrays do their thing each season from Oct through Mar (even later if we make the playoffs). The team's loyal fans turn out in the red, white, and blue team colors and average more than 7,400 in attendance for each home game. The Stingrays, affiliated with the NHL's Washington Capitals, are in the Southeast Division of the East Coast Hockey League. In 1997 they ascended to the top of the

heap by winning the ECHL Championship and the Kelly Cup. Again, in 2001 and 2009, they won this title. During intermissions, mascots Cool Ray and Li'l Puck keep the kids entertained. And when the frozen stuff has melted, the children come out to enroll for in-line hockey camps scheduled all summer long. The excitement never fades with the hockey crowd, so call for more schedule and ticket information. Tickets range from $14 to $21. Coliseum car parking costs $5.

INTERCOLLEGIATE SPORTS

With several institutions of higher education in the area, opportunities for checking out college sporting events are abundant. The most popular are, of course, football, baseball, and basketball, but you can also find soccer, track and field, and other events if you are interested.

The College of Charleston's Cougars made it to the Trans-America Athletic Conference championships in previous seasons and in 1997 made some major noise by knocking off regional power Maryland in the NCAA tourney. Charleston Southern also cut the rug at the NCAA's Big Dance in '97. The College of Charleston and The Citadel are members of the Southern Conference. Former College of Charleston Coach John Kresse, with more than 500 Cougar wins to his credit, was inducted into both the NAIA and the South Carolina Athletic Hall of Fame. Added excitement for the College of Charleston's basketball program is evident with the opening in fall 2008 of their new 5,000 seat arena adjacent to the old facility.

In 2001, 2004, and 2010 The Citadel Bulldogs won the Southern Conference Baseball Championship. The College of Charleston captured the 2004, 2005, and 2007 Southern Conference regular-season titles and won

the 2006 championship. This tournament returned to Charleston at Joseph P. Riley Jr. Park in May 2010 and affords collegiate baseball fans an opportunity to see some of the best teams in action. Details can be found at www.soconsports.com.

Citadel football fans gloated as one of their own, alumnus Travis Jervey, played for the 1998 NFC and the 1997 Super Bowl champions, the Green Bay Packers. Another Citadel standout, Nehemiah Broughton joined the Washington Redskins in 2005. So if you'd like to get up close to this college talent and competition while it's happening, get tickets by contacting The Citadel, (843) 953-DOGS (3647), www.citadelsports.com, the College of Charleston, (843) 953-COFC (2632), www.cofcsports.com, and Charleston Southern University, (843) 863-7678, www.csusportstickets.com.

RUNNING

COOPER RIVER BRIDGE RUN AND WALK
716 South Shelmore Blvd., Mount Pleasant
(843) 856-1949
www.bridgerun.com
Just because you don't feel up to walking or running over the new Arthur Ravenel Jr. Bridge, don't give up on the 10-kilometer (6.2-mile) Cooper River Bridge Run. Each Mar or Apr (usually the weekend before Easter), you can be a spectator or a volunteer and get your own thrill from the collective energy of it all. Hit the streets and cheer the participants onward—hundreds of like-minded folks will be right out there with you. For more information, call the number above. (For more on the festivities, see the Annual Events chapter.)

SAILBOAT RACING

With the popularity of the Around Alone (formerly the BOC Challenge), the solo sailor around-the-world yacht race, hosted by Charleston in 1994–95 and 1998–99, sailboat racing events have sprung up in this area. The Charleston Ocean Racing Association, established in 1967, holds 35 to 40 sailing events year-round in Charleston Harbor and offshore waters, promoting sailing and assisting members in obtaining competent crews and desirable berths. Also, a Charleston to Bermuda Race sails its eighth competition from Charleston Harbor in May 2011.

Local regattas are popular events too, particularly in the warmer months. From the Carolina Yacht Club and Charleston Yacht Club regattas to those hosted by the Hobcaw, James Island, and Sea Island clubs, there are races throughout the summer. A schedule is set in Jan and posted in the area yacht clubs. Spectators enjoy watching these races, free of charge, from the Battery or from the grounds of the club hosting the event. Children are welcome and may even start asking about those Charleston Yacht Club Summer Junior Sail Program lessons (see Insiders'Tip in this chapter). Call the sailing department at the College of Charleston (which, by the way, traditionally has a fine sailing team) at (843) 953-8252, or visit www .cofc.edu/sailing for more information about noncredit community sailing classes or sailing association memberships.

CHARLESTON RACE WEEK
Charleston Ocean Racing Association, P.O. Box 22405, Charleston, SC 29413
(843) 722-1030, ext. 18
www.charlestonraceweek.com,
www.charlestonoceanracing.org

The South Carolina Maritime Foundation in association with The Charleston Ocean Racing Association (CORA) presents the annual Charleston Race Week during the month of April. Race Week comprises the Palmetto Cup regatta, an inshore competition for sailboats from 20 to 70 feet, selected one-design regattas, and a harbor race. The Charleston Race Week Cup and overall Race Week winners are determined based on cumulative scoring results. Race Headquarters and the Race Village are located at the Charleston Harbor Resort & Marina in Mount Pleasant. More than 150 boats competed in 2010, and a good time was had by all.

CHARLESTON TO BERMUDA RACE
(843) 722-1030
www.charlestontobermuda.com
Alternating years with the Daytona to Bermuda Race, the Charleston to Bermuda Race,

---

Set Sail!

For more than 25 years, children have learned to sail in the **Charleston Yacht Club Summer Junior Sail Program.** If you have kids ages 8 to 18, this may be just what you're looking for to add a little excitement to their lives. Five 3-week sessions are offered each summer. Beginner sessions are $300 and intermediate are $325. For more information, call (843) 722-4968, visit www.charlestonyachtclub.com, or write to the Summer Youth Sailing Program, Charleston Yacht Club, P.O. Box 20474, Charleston, SC 29413.

also known simply as "C2B," leaves our city in May 2011. The 777-nautical-mile race is hosted on the receiving end by the Royal Bermuda Yacht Club (formed in 1844), and the finish line is off the St. David's Lighthouse in Bermuda. The 30-foot and larger sailboats are entered in either a double-handed class (two crew) or the fully crewed class with a minimum of four. Hundreds of spectators lined the Waterfront Park and the Battery and also watched from more than 100 spectator boats as the sailors set out on this challenge in May 2009.

SOCCER

CHARLESTON BATTERY
Blackbaud Stadium, 1990 Daniel Island Dr.
(843) 971-GOAL (4625)
www.charlestonbattery.com
In 1993 a professional men's soccer league team, the Charleston Battery, was formed, joining the United Systems of Independent Soccer Leagues. After placing at the top of the Atlantic Division in '94 and '95, the team advanced to the USISL finals in 1996 and won the league championship in a thriller: a 3-2 match decided in a shootout. In 1997 the Battery changed to the new Division II A-League (one notch below Major League Soccer), and in 2000 they won the Atlantic Division Championship. In 2003 the Battery claimed the A-League crown. The team was a 2006 USL semifinalist and won the USL-2 championship in 2010. You can catch all the action at the $4.5 million soccer-specific Blackbaud Stadium on Daniel Island (just off I-526 between the Cooper and Wando

rivers). The facility provides fun for the whole family with an expansive kids' "Fun Zone" and the Three Lions Pub. The games run Apr through Aug. Charleston Battery tickets range from $10 bleacher seats to $18 club seats. Kids younger than 4 are admitted free. Parking is $5 per car.

TENNIS

✳FAMILY CIRCLE CUP
161 Seven Farms Dr., Daniel Island
(843) 856-7900, (800) 677-2293
www.familycirclecup.com
Spectator tennis took a major leap forward in the Charleston area with the announcement of a relocation of the Family Circle Cup to our city in 2001 after a long-time run in Hilton Head, South Carolina. As many as 100,000 tennis fans have attended the nine-day Women's Tennis Association Tier I event. A $9 million tennis complex for the tournament was built within the new Town Centre Park in the planned community of Daniel Island. (See the Neighborhoods chapter for more on Daniel Island.) It served up an inaugural venue for this competition that attracts many of the top seeds in women's tennis. Some of the past competitors were Justine Henin-Hardenne, Conchita Martinez, Monica Seles, Arantxa Sanchez-Vicario, Mary Pierce, Serena Williams, Lindsay Davenport, and Jennifer Capriati. Held in early Apr, the Family Circle Cup is a hot ticket in Charleston's busy spring tourism events. Ticket prices range from $15 for qualifying matches up to $55 for the finals. Call the number above, or check the website for more information.

Appendix

LIVING HERE

In this section we feature specific information for residents or those planning to relocate here. Topics include real estate, education, health care, and much more.

RELOCATION

If you're among those thinking seriously about moving to the Lowcountry and making Charleston your permanent or part-time home, we have a news flash for you: This idea is not entirely original. It has occurred to others, with some frequency. Starting with the influx of military retirees who fell in love with the area during their World War II Navy days spent here, the concept of retiring to Charleston has only grown more popular with each passing year. And why not? The Lowcountry really has it all—sun, sea, golf, history, culture, plus educational and entertainment opportunities galore. Young people are similarly attracted to the area. Employment opportunities, especially for professionals, are getting more plentiful as the population surges upward. Therefore, a Relocation chapter is in order—as a helpful service to the next generation of insiders who will soon be calling Charleston and its environs "home."

The Neighborhoods chapter will give you an overview of some areas where newcomers are currently finding homes. We've included a spectrum of price alternatives. And we've listed, below, a few of the major real estate companies ready and willing to help newcomers start their relocation process. Some newcomers choose to rent apartments, condos, or even homes while they acclimate to the area and select a neighborhood that's best for them. There's information for apartment dwellers, also. We've thrown in some practical information, too, such as where to get your new driver's license, how to register to vote, what are the utility hookup contacts, and even some recycling information for our new neighbors who, we hope, will be ecology-minded citizens here in the Lowcountry.

REAL ESTATE COMPANIES

If you are new to the area and have turned to the **Charleston Metro Chamber of Commerce** (4500 Leeds Ave., Ste. 100, North Charleston, SC 29405; 843-577-2510; www.charlestonchamber.net), for any of its excellent visitor information, you might want to ask for its free list of area member real estate agencies too. This will give you a handy overview of the residential realtors as well as the commercial and industrial specialists who are currently chamber members and working here in the Lowcountry.

One of the best resources for specific real estate information in Greater Charleston is the **Charleston Trident Association of Realtors** (5300 International Blvd., Ste. C-105, North Charleston, SC 29418; 843-760-9400; www.charlestonrealtors.com). At last count, there were 4,200 member Realtors working throughout Charleston, Dorchester, and Berkeley Counties. The association can easily recommend a professional to help you find the home that's right for you.

Naturally, choosing a real estate company is a very personal matter. Because it is such an important decision, be sure to find an agent who truly understands your priorities. Sometimes that's easier said than done.

An agent who specializes in investment properties may not understand why you want to see only pre-Revolutionary houses, or why an otherwise acceptable house won't do because your grandmother's furniture won't fit in the dining room. By the same token, an agent with a reputation for handling plantations and historic properties may not grasp the needs of a first-time buyer or the advantages of one school system over another. You can find agents who are such specialists if you ask the right questions. Be sure to be specific about your needs.

In general, the agents in the Greater Charleston area are well versed in the needs of a broad-spectrum market. And with computerized multiple-listing services, almost all agents can show you any house or property you might be interested in seeing. As with any business relationship, some frank discussions early on about your price range and what you're looking for can help avoid wasting your time and patience. Just remember that open communication with your real estate agent is the first key to finding the right home. Again, more information on the feel and price ranges in various Charleston-area neighborhoods can be found in the Neighborhoods chapter.

DOWNTOWN CHARLESTON PROPERTIES

Residential real estate in downtown Charleston is a very specialized market. You're looking at properties with historic and aesthetic values that often override the considerations of ordinary shelter. And then there's that awesome specter of restoration to consider—whether it's something already accomplished at someone's great expense, or it's something you feel you want to tackle yourself. These variables affect property values enormously. There are special tax strategies and things such as "facade easements" to learn about, which can actually make owning a home in the historic district a little more affordable. Pricing is also affected by something called "comparables"—that's the price recently paid for a comparable house in the same neighborhood. That can change monthly or even (gasp!) weekly.

Sound complicated? It is, so It's best to get some help from people who deal with this on a daily basis. Here are some of the companies with plenty of experience selling residential real estate in downtown Charleston.

i Look for the Reader's Digest–size catalog of listings called *The Real Estate Book,* which is a free pickup in shops and restaurants throughout the Lowcountry.

ARTHUR RAVENEL JR. CO.
635 East Bay St.
(843) 723-7847
www.ravenelrealestate.com
Ravenel is a small, family-owned company that has been in business since 1945. Its experienced agents can help you with purchases of historic downtown properties, waterfront properties, and commercial real estate. They also handle property management.

CARRIAGE PROPERTIES
19 Exchange St.
(843) 266-8000, (877) 266-8005
www.carriageprop.com

Early in 2002, six veteran sales associates from a top-producing downtown Charleston real estate company decided to form their own company. These agents—all major players in the fast-paced and highly competitive marketplace for historic homes in the Holy City—set up shop at a newly renovated downtown building and soon took on agents to help handle their growing business. The company specializes in high-end luxury homes and condominiums in the Charleston area, particularly on the historic Peninsula.

DANIEL RAVENEL REAL ESTATE CO.
33 Broad St.
(843) 723-7150, (800) 382-2279
www.danielravenel.com
This is a full-service independent agency with deep roots in the community. An affiliation with Sotheby's International Realty expands their offerings to a larger audience. With offices in downtown Charleston, the agency provides customized residential, commercial, and waterfront real estate services throughout the Lowcountry, from the Battery to the beaches.

DISHER, HAMRICK & MYERS
25 Cumberland St.
(843) 577-4115, (800) 577-4118
www.charlestonrealestate.net
This company's agents primarily focus on historic properties in downtown Charleston. It is one of the leading brokerage firms in the historic district. Many of the agents are downtown residents who have been through the restoration process themselves, giving them a perspective that clients find invaluable. They have also opened a Seabrook Island office at 1101 Landfall Way to serve this resort community.

HISTORIC CHARLESTON PROPERTIES
17 State St.
(843) 853-3000, (800) 965-6111
www.historicrealestate.com
Begun in 1997, this real estate company came on fast and strong in the Charleston market, earning $18 million in sales their first year. The company now focuses on upscale residential properties and discreet, personalized service.

LANE & SMYTHE REAL ESTATE, LLC.
9 Broad St.
(843) 577-2900, (877) 451-4801
www.laneandsmythe.com
This firm, founded in 1999, is proudly owned and operated by Lois Lane and Ruthie Smythe, who are skilled at presenting a total point of view, including the female perspective, on relocating to the Charleston area.

PATE PROPERTIES, INC.
11-A Isabella St.
(843) 577-3193
www.pateproperties.com
This closely held company, with more than 30 years' experience in the market, has a fantastic track record for handling downtown residential real estate, small investment properties, and property management. The owner is one of the city's few buyer representatives, sanctioned by the National Association of Realtors.

POSTON & CO. REAL ESTATE, INC.
304 Meeting St.
(843) 853-5300
www.postonco.com
Marketing mostly residential real estate in the upscale residential neighborhoods of downtown Charleston, West Ashley, James Island, Mount Pleasant, and Daniel Island, this firm has been in business for over two

decades. It focuses on residential sales and relocation services, including the marketing and sale of existing homes, new construction, and residential lots. It also offers property management services.

TRICOUNTY REAL ESTATE COMPANIES

In addition to the independent real estate companies that specialize in historic properties or beach homes, the giant franchise networks are established here. These companies are eager to meet your real estate needs and offer comprehensive, one-stop real estate service—whether you're moving across the country or across town. Look for names such as Century 21, Carolina One, Coldwell Banker, RE/MAX, and the Agent Owned Realty Co.

In fact, we're seeing an ongoing trend among some of the older, larger, independent real estate companies toward joining these nationwide franchise networks. The idea here is that there's strength in numbers—that teamwork and standardization lead to better efficiency and greater success.

THE BEACH COMPANY
211 King St., Ste. 300
(843) 722-2615
www.thebeachcompany.com
Founded in 1945, this is the largest full-service real estate company in Charleston. In addition to residential sales and property management, agents handle acquisition, development, construction services, and commercial brokerage.

CAROLINA ONE REAL ESTATE
Relocation Services, 4390 Belle Oaks Dr., Ste. 100, North Charleston
(843) 202-2030, (800) 476-1929
www.carolinaone.com
This company takes an aggressive stance in the local real estate market with a wide-reaching array of regional offices throughout the greater Charleston area. It also serves newcomers with a full-time staff in the Relocation Services office. The relocation staff can help with school applications, tax forms, tuition fees, wheelchair accessibility, and even career assistance. The relocation agent then refers you to a handpicked agent in one of the local offices. For a listing of their offices, check out their website.

RE/MAX PROFESSIONAL REALTY
9209 University Blvd.
(843) 767-7777
www.remaxprorealty.com
This agency partnered with a well-known independent local realty company for several years when they were establishing their beachhead in the Lowcountry market. Today, they serve the entire Tri-County area.

APARTMENT RENTALS

There are many apartment and townhouse complexes in Greater Charleston, the majority of which are in West Ashley, Mount Pleasant, North Charleston, and the Ladson, Summerville, and Hanahan areas. Amenities vary wildly, with some including furnishings, balconies, fireplaces, ceiling fans, carpeting, or window treatments. Some apartment complexes have clubhouses, pools, and sports facilities; others have playgrounds or, especially downtown, reserved parking. Monthly rents range from $450 to $1,250 (more for luxury town houses and properties on the historic Peninsula), but the average hovers in the $750 to $800 range.

Lease agreements are usually for 6 or 12 months, although short-term leases, some with military-transfer clauses, are available.

RELOCATION

Security deposits also vary but are half to a full month's rent. Many places allow pets, but some complexes have size limits, and most require a deposit or a fee.

Apartment seekers will find these free real estate publications helpful: *Apartment Finder* and *Charleston Apartment Guide*. Look for these publications wherever newspapers are sold and at restaurants, sports facilities, and all information centers. Or you may want to write or call for a current issue and do some apartment shopping before you arrive.

ℹ️ By far the major clearinghouse for Lowcountry real estate information is the *Saturday Real Estate* tabloid and the Sunday Home and Garden section of *The Post and Courier*. Here, the properties are listed by specific region, and all listings are comprehensive and coded for descriptive details.

Apartment Directories

APARTMENT FINDER
4500 Leeds Ave., Ste. 112
(843) 745-1315
www.apartmentfinder.com

This digest-sized format booklet of apartment options is published four times a year. It is colorful and includes Greater Charleston neighborhoods from downtown through North Charleston to Hanahan, Ladson, Goose Creek, and Summerville. West Ashley, James and Johns Island, and East Cooper neighborhoods are included as well. Detailed maps help readers get acclimated to the various residential areas and transportation routes, and a handy comparison chart reduces the advertising hype to bare facts and figures for finding the bottom line. This is perhaps the most comprehensive apartment guide currently published in the Low-Country.

Distribution of this free publication is widespread. You can almost always find a kiosk or rack of them outside any area grocery store or post office. Some convenience stores have them next to where the newspapers are sold. Of course, the Charleston visitor center on Meeting Street always has an ample supply.

CHARLESTON APARTMENT GUIDE
461 Jessen Lane, Ste. G, Wando
(843) 388-0085
www.apartmentguide.com

This revamped pocket-sized booklet is published monthly. It is well organized, with full-color photos, maps, and an easy-to-use color code for area neighborhoods from downtown to Moncks Corner. Sometimes hard to find, it is worth tracking down because of its comprehensiveness. One good bet is to look just outside area grocery stores and wherever newspapers are sold. Also, the Charleston Metro Chamber of Commerce always has copies on hand.

MOTOR VEHICLE INFORMATION

New South Carolina residents may use a valid out-of-state driver's license for up to 90 days. Military personnel may use their home state license as long as it is valid. Licensed newcomers must take a vision test and bring their birth certificates or other proof of citizenship, proof of South Carolina residency, liability insurance information, and proof of Social Security number. New drivers must meet the same requirements and take the road, written, and vision tests. A quick review of the rules of the road booklet available in the South Carolina Department of Public Safety Division of Motor Vehicles offices or online may be beneficial prior to taking the written test. Drivers should apply at the SCDMV offices listed below.

New residents have 45 days to purchase South Carolina license tags for their vehicles. Before getting a tag, property taxes on the vehicle must be paid at your local county tax office. Then, new residents may apply by filling out Form 400 at any of the SCDMV locations below. General information on driver's licenses and tags/registration and their fees is available at (800) 442-1368 or www.scdmvonline.com.

- 3790 Leeds Ave., North Charleston
- 135 Wimberly Dr., Ladson
- 438 North SR 52, Moncks Corner
- 1189 Sweetgrass Basket Parkway, Ste. 500, Mount Pleasant
- Express Office (No Road Tests or Tags/ Registration): 1119 Wappoo Rd., Unit G

VOTER REGISTRATION

To register to vote, a new resident must be a US citizen, 18 years old by the date of the election, mentally competent, and not under conviction of a felony or, if previously convicted, have served the entire sentence, including probation or parole. Proof of residency is required. Registration must take place at least 30 days prior to an election to vote in that election. Newcomers may register at the local county voter registration office, driver's license offices, or by mail. Visit www.charlestoncounty.org, www.berkeleycountysc.gov, or www.dorchestervotes.org for more information, or call the following numbers:

- Charleston County: (843) 744-8683
- Berkeley County: (843) 719-4056, Moncks Corner line; (843) 723-3800, ext. 4056, Charleston line; (843) 567-3142, ext. 4056, St. Stephen line

- Dorchester County: (843) 563-0132, St. George line; (843) 832-0071, Summerville line

UTILITIES

For natural gas, electricity, water, and telephone services in Greater Charleston, call one of the following:

Natural Gas & Electricity

SOUTH CAROLINA ELECTRIC AND GAS (SCE&G)
(843) 554-7234, (800) 251-7234
www.scana.com/sce&g

BERKELEY ELECTRIC COOPERATIVE
(843) 572-5454
www.becsc.com

SANTEE COOPER (SOUTH CAROLINA PUBLIC SERVICE AUTHORITY)
(843) 347-3399
www.santeecooper.com

Water

CHARLESTON WATER SYSTEMS— WATER & SEWER
(843) 727-6800
www.charlestonwater.com

BERKELEY COUNTY WATER AND SANITATION AUTHORITY
(843) 572-4400
www.bcwsa.com

DORCHESTER COUNTY WATER AUTHORITY
(843) 875-0140
www.dcwaonline.com

DORCHESTER COUNTY WATER & SEWER DEPARTMENT
(843) 832-0075 (Summerville line),
(843) 563-0075 (St. George line)
www.dorchestercounty.net

MOUNT PLEASANT WATERWORKS
(843) 884-9626
www.mountpleasantwaterworks.com
Many other municipalities have their own water and sewer commissions such as Isle of Palms, Kiawah Island, Folly Beach, Summerville, Goose Creek, Moncks Corner, and North Charleston. If you are relocating to one of these areas, consult the telephone directory for their individual numbers.

Telephone

AT&T provides telephone services for the majority of the area. For residential services, call (800) 288-2020; for business services, call (866) 620-6000. You may also visit the website at www.att.com.

i It's easy to suffer from serious sticker shock when you talk about real estate in downtown Charleston. If that seems to be your problem, simply look farther afield. Prices are far more reasonable once you're off that hallowed peninsular ground.

RECYCLING

Curbside recycling in blue bins is offered in most of the urban areas of Charleston County on an every other week basis. Drop-off sites are located throughout the county. Materials currently recycled include plastic containers (nos. 1 through 7), steel food cans, aluminum and aerosol cans, and glass jars and bottles. Newspapers, magazines, office paper, and mail are recyclable as well, and corrugated cardboard can be brought to the drop sites. (Visit www.charlestoncounty.org for a complete listing of sites and what they accept.) For more information about recycling in Charleston County, call (843) 720-7111, in Berkeley County, (843) 572-4400, and in Dorchester County, (843) 832-0070.

NEIGHBORHOODS

There was a time when living in Charleston meant hanging your hat somewhere on the Peninsula. Somewhere in between the world wars, all that started to change. Mind you, Charleston is and always will be largely defined by the geographic boundaries of the Peninsula and the charming old houses that exist in the prestigious neighborhood referred to as Below (meaning south of) Broad (Street). Living in one of those grand old houses will always be part of the quintessential Charleston lifestyle. Earthquakes, storms, fires, and wars have worked their woes and done their best to alter that reality, but an address Below Broad will always be a prestigious one in Charleston.

Meanwhile, it's also true that thousands upon thousands of other certified Charlestonians are thriving in other neighborhoods—living full, complete, happy, and productive lives.

We'll start this description of Charleston's neighborhoods with some of the spectacular statistics surrounding real estate Below Broad. This includes the soaring values that have been asked and paid there since Charleston encountered tourism and the nation's growing fascination with historic preservation.

OVERVIEW

For better or worse, there's apparently a steady national market for Below Broad property and the prestige of owning it. Even with the housing market slow down, several dozen Below Broad properties sold for over $1 million. An out-of-town buyer paid $7.37 million as the record price (so far) for residential property on the Charleston Peninsula.

Despite this kind of transaction, properties Below Broad are selling in the $625,000 to $3.5 million price range. Thanks to the efforts of preservation-minded groups, institutions, and individuals, there are several other historic neighborhoods on the Peninsula where residential properties are a little more affordable.

According to the Charleston Trident Association of Realtors (Multiple Listing Service), the average selling price of a single-family residential house on the Peninsula through the third quarter of 2010 (including new and previously owned homes) averaged $1,039,016.

Naturally, real estate prices fluctuate greatly in different areas. And in a market as attractive as Greater Charleston, some homes and condominiums sell quickly and never make it to the Multiple Listing Service. But wherever real estate sales are a matter of public record, we've based our information on neighborhood home values on real numbers. Of course, this chapter is only a sampling of what is available, and the prices mentioned are approximate indicators of the current values. Ask a real estate professional for more complete guidance.

Although the historic area south of Broad Street is considered the quintessential Charlestonian neighborhood, several other locales north of Broad (between Broad and Calhoun Streets are now looked at very favorably, too. The French Quarter—so-named for the French Huguenots who once lived and worked there—includes the area around Philadelphia Alley, State, Queen, and Chalmers Streets and is a mixture of commercial and residential buildings with inns, offices, restaurants, bars, and shops. Even the theatrical entity known as the Footlight Players (see the chapter on The Arts) coexists with busy families in this bustling cosmopolitan atmosphere. Because the French Quarter is a small neighborhood of only a few square blocks, we're only talking about 40 town houses or so. Behind their relatively common facades, they vary in size, configuration, and building date. However, a late-18th-century to mid-19th-century, 2-bedroom, 2-bath home might average $715,000.

Ansonborough is one of Charleston's more famous examples of institutionally inspired restoration. In the early 1970s many architecturally significant homes in this neighborhood were in grievous disrepair. The Historic Charleston Foundation initiated a program that effectively and expediently changed the economic course of the entire area. A decade later, Ansonborough was one of the city's more sought-after neighborhoods, and it still is today. The advent of the South Carolina Aquarium, Liberty Square, the Ft. Sumter tour boat facility, and the other associated redevelopment along the western bank of the Cooper River just across East Bay Street from Ansonborough has added even more attractiveness to this downtown neighborhood. A typical 1830s house in Ansonborough with 3 bedrooms and 2 to 3 baths can sell in the $700,000 to $2 million range.

Mazyck-Wraggborough includes the blocks between Calhoun Street and the Charleston Museum. Here you'll find an interesting mix of restored houses, beautiful churches, and light industry. Major historic anchors in this neighborhood include the Aiken-Rhett House, operated by the Historic Charleston Foundation, the Charleston Museum, and its neighboring house museum, the Joseph Manigault House. (See the House Museums section of the Attractions chapter.) In this neighborhood, a 3-bedroom, 3.5-bath house would sell for about $625,000.

The area around the Medical University of South Carolina, the College of Charleston, Colonial Lake, and all points in between is Harleston Village. Here you'll find an eclectic mix of bed-and-breakfast inns, condos, town houses, stately 18th- and 19th-century properties, and even a couple of high-rise apartment buildings. Some 2-bedroom rental houses are in the $1,500- to $1,950-per-month range. One-bedroom condos sell for about $275,000. An average selling price for a 3-bedroom, 2.5-bath home is about $800,000.

Radcliffeborough is the area north of Calhoun Street, from the medical complexes east to Mazyck-Wraggborough. Ashley Hall, an independent school for girls, is situated here on a 4-acre campus that includes the recently restored historic (ca. 1816) McBee House. There are several other fully restored mansions nearby plus rental properties, and many fixer-uppers can still be found in this area. There are also several new construction projects under way here. There are 2-bedroom apartment rentals in Radcliffeborough average $1,400 per month. A 3-bedroom,

2.5-bath home is in the range of $600,000 to $700,000.

EAST COOPER

Many neighborhoods east of the Cooper River—which include those in Mount Pleasant, Sullivan's Island, and the Isle of Palms—are experiencing unprecedented growth. According to 2000 census figures, Mount Pleasant was the second-fastest growing city in the state, with 58.1 percent growth in the last decade. Although slowed down a bit, in the first three quarters of 2010, more than 580 homes were sold here. The main corridor of growth seems to be along US 17 N. to SR 41 and beyond.

All this projected growth will undoubtedly have a major impact on the real estate market east of the Cooper. However, recent figures from the Charleston Trident Association of Realtors (MLS) for the median East Cooper residence (south of SR 41) show a very respectable $354,000.

Another major growth area is the southern end of the Isle of Palms. The IOP Connector, linking the island to the Mark Clark Expressway and I-26, has fueled a flurry of new construction at both the southern tip of the Isle of Palms and at Wild Dunes Resort. In 2010 the average Wild Dunes residence was in the $900,000 range.

For newcomers who want a short list of lifestyle options, East Cooper offers a wide variety. There's the charm and quaintness of the Old Village in Mount Pleasant. There are a number of older, established neighborhoods where families flourish—some of Mount Pleasant's best are listed below. East Cooper's newer neighborhoods tend to offer several levels of home ownership to more easily accommodate first-time buyers as well as the upwardly mobile movers and shakers.

And, of course, East Cooper's beach communities are always popular with laid-back folk and the second-home crowd.

Established Neighborhoods

Creekside

Just off US 17 N., Creekside is an established community and home to the Creekside Tennis & Swim Club. Residents have access to this facility with its courts and swimming pool. Winding streets and moderately upscale homes are handsomely individual. Many have a nice view of Shem Creek. An average 4-bedroom, 2.5-bathroom home in Creekside would be priced in the $570,000 to $800,000 bracket.

The Groves

Between Coleman Boulevard and US 17 N. is the Groves. This neighborhood is one of few established Mount Pleasant neighborhoods convenient to downtown Charleston. It consists of mostly 1- or 1.5-story brick homes built in the 1950s and 1960s. In this family neighborhood with a nice park for the children, you'll also enjoy the quiet streets for bike rides and leisurely strolls. A 3-bedroom, 2.5-bath ranch in the Groves might sell for about $340,000.

Hobcaw

Off Mathis Ferry Road is Hobcaw, a large, established subdivision. Hobcaw has homes in many price ranges and is popular with longtime residents as well as young couples with children. Public records show recent sales ranging from $310,000 to $1 million, with the average 3-bedroom, 2.5-bath home selling for $590,000. Proximity to the Hobcaw Yacht Club, with its outdoor swimming pool and other recreational facilities, is an appealing feature. Some houses are on the water, and these, of course, tend to be the priciest.

Old Village

This Mount Pleasant neighborhood is one of the most appealing in the Trident area. Many of the restored antebellum homes are situated on large lots, while others are clustered along the tree-lined streets to form a village setting. One harborfront home here sold for $2.5 million recently—the highest price paid in the Old Village in several years. Many houses were built in the last 25 years, some even in this decade. Though certainly a real estate target for young affluent professionals, the Old Village has retained much of the unpretentious, casual charm it was known for 100 years ago. An average home in the Old Village is in the $800,000 range.

Snee Farm

Just south of where Long Point Road intersects US 17 is Snee Farm, a large, established community with a country club. The golf course, tennis facilities, and the clubhouse are in great demand, and homes range in style from ranch to Georgian Colonial. Old oaks and gum trees soften the skyline and enhance a very attractive neighborhood. Here a 3-bedroom, 2.5-bath home sells for about $310,000.

New Neighborhoods

A quick glance at the map will tell you the East Cooper area, especially Mount Pleasant, is ripe for growth. Charleston's annexation of Daniel Island is a prime example; the corridor along SR 41 is another. Look to these areas for some of the Lowcountry's best new communities.

Daniel Island

If you've harbored a dream to sail into new territory, Daniel Island may give you that chance. Annexed as part of the city of Charleston but located east of the Cooper River, you're just minutes from downtown or North Charleston via I-526. Daniel Island and its 20 miles of virgin waterfront on the Cooper and Wando Rivers are being developed into a town with public parks, residential neighborhoods, a town center with a waterfront park, and a corporate complex with two million square feet of office space. Ultimately, between 4,000 and 7,000 homesites are planned there. Residents are proud of the Blackbaud Stadium, home of the Charleston Battery, a professional soccer team, and the tennis facility that is home to the Family Circle Cup (see the Spectator Sports chapter). One of Daniel Island's newer assets is the private high school, Bishop England, which moved from downtown. It now sprawls on a 40-acre campus (see the Education chapter). Another newer educational facility, this one a public school, is the 74,000-square-foot elementary school Hanahan Elementary, which houses over 900 students.

> **i** Many of Charleston's downtown neighborhoods have very active membership associations that serve both social and economic (and sometimes even political) purposes. They have parties, sponsor tours, and work to govern future development. They also represent the neighborhood when resolving issues such as parking variances and utility construction.

Many new families are living on Daniel Island now. Homes in one phase of a new condominium project are selling in the

$375,000 range. More upscale, custom-built homes with 4-bedroom, 3-bath floor plans sell for $500,000 and more. It's reasonable to expect this rapid development to continue throughout the next decade and a half.

Dunes West

A catalyst for the building boom off SR 41 is Dunes West. This golf course community also offers swimming and tennis in a beautiful woodland and waterway setting. Many of these homeowners enjoy terrific views of the golf course and surrounding waterways. The upscale, 2,011-acre private development was well under way by the mid-1980s, and complete build-out is scheduled for sometime after the year 2011. The variety of housing options in Dunes West is an unfinished story; major tracts of the vast acreage are still on the drawing board. For now the price of a 4-bedroom, 2.5-bath home near the golf course is in the vicinity of $575,000.

I'on

One of the newer planned communities on Mathis Ferry Road, I'on is known for its family-friendly feel, with wide sidewalks, parks, lakes, and trees. The homes are designed with a nod to traditional Lowcountry architecture—reminiscent of downtown Charleston neighborhoods and Mount Pleasant's Old Village. The new I'on Club houses upscale amenities for residents which include tennis and pool facilities, a community dock and a boat ramp on Hobcaw Creek. Homes there range from $570,000 to $2.8 million.

Long Point

North of the Snee Farm Country Club community, just off US 17, is Long Point. Beautiful views of the marsh are among this neighborhood's best features. These upscale, newly constructed homes are nestled amid mature gum and pine trees. Nearby are tennis and basketball courts, a soccer field, and Palmetto Islands County Park. (See the Parks & Recreation chapter.) Prices here range from $360,000 to $575,000.

Park West

This amalgam of 17 distinctive neighborhoods located along US 17, 5 minutes north of Mount Pleasant's Towne Centre, has been created by some of the nation's leading builders. Park West has bike and jogging trails, forested habitats, sports complexes, retail shops, and professional offices. Charles Pinckney Elementary and Thomas C. Cario Middle School are within the community. Top-ranked Wando High School relocated here in 2004. A wide variety of prebuilt and custom homes in Park West range from $250,000 to over $2 million.

Seaside Farms

Only minutes from Sullivan's Island and Isle of Palms, the community of Seaside Farms is a popular option in Mount Pleasant with homes ranging in price from $300,000 to $800,000. Located near shopping, dining, and the convenience of I-526, residents of Seaside Farms can be near the beach and still commute to work almost anywhere in the Lowcountry. While family-size homes of 3 bedrooms, 2 baths dominate this community, the latest trend in building is toward upscale condos—some with marsh and waterfront views.

East Cooper Beaches

Sullivan's Island, Isle of Palms, Wild Dunes, and Dewees Island all have beautiful ocean or Intracoastal Waterway vistas. These upscale communities are among the Lowcountry's most popular. Land and real estate values are priced accordingly.

Dewees Island

Billed as "Charleston's Only Private Island," Dewees is being developed carefully as an environmentally protected enclave. Modern homes are nestled discreetly among the island's vegetation, and a limited number of others are planned. Dewees's developers are hoping to preserve the natural integrity of this barrier island while they create a quiet, isolated upscale community. Bear in mind you must be willing to make your way to Dewees by boat—no bridge is available and none is planned. Most of the real estate activity on the island is new construction. Homesites in this unique community range from $375,000 to $1.1 million, and the few resale homes there have ranged in price from $500,000 to $2 million.

i The only way to get to Dewees Island is by private boat or a 20-minute ferry ride from the Isle of Palms. Once you're there, the only way to get around other than on foot is by electric vehicle. And get this: More than 65 percent of the island has been officially designated "development free" forever.

Isle of Palms

This beach community has an inviting, sandy beach and access to the creeks along the back of the island. In most cases, renovation after 1989's Hurricane Hugo has enhanced the real estate values here. Bigger and better houses, built high on stilts, will hopefully avoid future water damage. There are still many wonderful old beach houses, however,

that have defied a century's worth of storms and tourism's relentless intervention.

The commute to peninsular Charleston from Isle of Palms is about a half hour. Large beachfront homes (as in 6 bedrooms and 4 baths) can soar as high as $3 million. Condos sell for $300,000 and higher. The average 5-bedroom, 3-bath home fetches about $1.3 million.

Sullivan's Island

There are no official subdivisions on Sullivan's Island, a laid-back beach community that's about a 20-minute commute from downtown Charleston. Rather, the location of property is described by its proximity to the water or local landmarks ("front beach" or "near Fort Moultrie," for example). This was the 19th-century summer community for many Below Broad families of that time as well as today. The heightened real estate values of this historic island have encouraged more full-time residents. The current values range from $1.2 million for a 3-bedroom, 2-bath house to $2.9 million for a 4-bedroom, 4.5-bath home on the beach front. The median price is in the $1.6 million range.

Wild Dunes

Just 15 miles from Charleston proper, Wild Dunes is a separate community at the north end of the Isle of Palms. This luxury resort has conference facilities, vacation rentals, villa accommodations, and homesites for sale. Homes here can go as high as $3.3 million for a 6-bedroom, 4.5-bath house, or as low as $550,000 for a more modest 3-bedroom, 2-bath place. (See the Boating & Water Sports chapter for information on Wild Dunes Yacht Harbor facilities.)

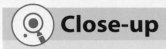

Close-up

Condo Living

Needless to say, the number of charming, old historic homes in Charleston is limited. Only so many were originally built, and fewer have survived the calamities of war, fire, storm, and earthquake—not to mention the ravages of neglect and time. This scarcity has driven real estate prices up and, some say, out of sight for most home buyers. Thus, the popularity of **condominium living** has seen a recent rise in Charleston's urban neighborhoods. From rehabilitated schools and updated commercial buildings to the new, upscale construction now seen along the downtown waterfront, condo living is all the rage. The Greater Charleston area is a very popular choice for a second home—one that might someday serve the owners as a retirement nest for part or most of the year. Even older apartment complexes in many suburban areas are being converted into condos as more and more people move to the Lowcountry for its unique lifestyle. So, if buying a historic home is beyond your means, or you're thinking more along the lines of regular Charleston visits or just a carefree retirement, the condo option might be right for you. The choices are getting more plentiful, it seems, every year. Charleston's neighborhoods are nothing if not ever-changing and constantly evolving as fascinating places to live.

NORTH CHARLESTON

Although the city of North Charleston is largely outside the scope of this book, we'd be remiss if we didn't say there are many viable neighborhoods here that are both family oriented and affordable. According to the Charleston Trident Association of Realtors (Multiple Listing Service), the median selling price of a North Charleston home was $136,000 through the third quarter of 2010.

There's a notion (often an unfair one) among some Charlestonians that North Charleston is a good place to work but not a good place to live. It is mostly a city of main corridors where people clip through at the speed limit noticing all the business and industry but not the residential neighborhoods. The city is determined to remedy this perception with the encouragement of upscale neighborhoods such as Coosaw Creek, Whitehall, and Yeamans Hall. Newer

options seem to appear on the city planner's drawing board with increasing regularity.

WEST ASHLEY

Since 1960, the population in the West Ashley area has doubled. That fact alone speaks volumes about the neighborhoods in this part of the Lowcountry. The growth was accelerated by a major City of Charleston annexation in 1979. Many of these new residents have chosen apartments and subdivisions built since 1980.

West Ashley seems to thrive on the myriad small stores and businesses that line the major traffic arteries (SRs 171, 61, and 7, plus US 17 S.). Tucked behind these throughways are many neighborhoods that house families of every ilk and category. The Trident Association of Realtors (MLS) average price for a West Ashley home through the third quarter of 2010 was $235,439. Some of the better-known neighborhoods in this section of Charleston follow.

Established Neighborhoods

Byrnes Down

Barely a mile from the Ashley River Bridge along US 17 is one of Charleston's first major subdivisions, Byrnes Down. It was built after World War II and named after James Byrnes, a South Carolina-born US secretary of state. These small brick homes are popular with many first-home buyers who enjoy the advantage of being so close to the city. A recent average sales price for one of these trendy starter places was $258,000.

The Crescent

Folly Road and the Intracoastal Waterway border the Crescent. Described once as "the country, only 5 minutes from town," this highly desirable old neighborhood, built in the 1950s and 1960s, consists of established homes and yards with wonderful old trees. Generations of children have fed the resident ducks that inhabit the twin lakes, and all age groups take advantage of the quiet streets for walks and bike rides. A 4-bedroom, 3.5-bath home sells in the $1.1 million range.

Parkshore I, II, III, IV

The Parkshore family of subdivisions is bordered by SR 7 and the Ashley River. These are newer executive homes with large lots and some availability remaining. Many have marsh views, and some have docks. Residents love the access to a community center within the Parkshore complex with its pool, park, and tennis courts. Most of these houses are 3- and 4-bedroom places with 2.5 to 3.5 baths. These homes recently ranged in price

from $300,000 to $570,000, with an average home going for about $425,000.

Shadowmoss

Shadowmoss is a mid-priced, country club community. It started in the 1970s and has been growing ever since. Many different builders have contributed to the development's housing mix, so there's something for every budget here. Shadowmoss was designed around an 18-hole golf course and pool complex (see the Golf chapter). Residents enjoy community clubs and events and can make use of the on-site facilities. Real estate values range from $155,000 to $570,000, but an average 3-bedroom, 2-bath home might bring $245,000.

JAMES, JOHNS, & FOLLY ISLANDS, KIAWAH, & SEABROOK

The islands west of the Ashley River, connected by a series of bridges, are a diverse and intriguing group. When the James Island Expressway (SR 30) opened in 1993, it made these islands prime targets for developers.

Already densely populated, James Island has spectacular views of the Charleston Harbor and Peninsula and has many neighborhoods housing people who work throughout the Trident area. Much of Johns Island is still rural. Bohicket Road, the main highway through the island, has been widened in part near the resorts of Kiawah and Seabrook. New neighborhoods along this road are only a matter of time. Low-key Folly Beach is a casual, year-round island community with an eclectic mix of new construction and rustic old beach houses from Folly's days of yore. Real estate offerings include front beach, marsh and river, along with inland houses and lots. The average home price for a James Island home in the third quarter of 2010, according to the Charleston Trident Realtors, was $282,558. On Folly Beach, the average was $532,787. Johns Island homes ranged from $184,000 all the way up to $14 million for a Kiawah ocean front resort home (the highest sale price for a home in Charleston County to-date).

i New players on the real estate stage who fall in love with the proverbial historic fixer-upper can find solace in the Resource Center at the Preservation Society of Charleston. Therein lies a wealth of information on preservation and restoration techniques scripted by those who've performed that role in the recent past. This can be a major help in saving you time or money (or both).

James Island

Country Club of Charleston

Across the Wappoo Bridge off Folly Road is Country Club of Charleston (sometimes called Country Club I). This older, established community with beautiful homes and well-kept lawns is one of the area's most desirable addresses. The private club, pool, and golf course are obvious assets, and the proximity to the Peninsula is another plus. Homes on the waterway are priced in the $2.75 million range for 4 bedrooms and 3.5-baths. Properties off the water sell in the $1.1 million range for 4 bedrooms and 2 baths.

Parrot Creek

There is much to see in Parrot Creek. These newer houses and lots are large and beautifully landscaped—some fronting on deep water or marsh. Composed of mostly 2-story homes on 0.5-acre lots, Parrot Creek offers architectural variety and desirable extras such as wide porches to catch those prevailing breezes. A 3-bedroom, 3.5-bath home recently sold for $432,000. The average sale price is about $450,000.

Riverland Terrace

Riverland Terrace, off Maybank Highway, is an established neighborhood with origins dating back to the 1920s. Today, you'll find a conglomeration of sizes, styles, and prices. There are interesting rehab possibilities as well as extraordinary turnkey dwellings throughout. Young people have been drawn to this area in recent years because of its tranquility and, in some instances, its affordability. The few houses on the waterway command the highest prices, while smaller houses in the middle of the neighborhood can be had for less. A 3-bedroom, 2-bath home might sell for as low as $215,000; a 4-bedroom, 2-bath house might be as high as $470,000. The average price for a home that's not on the waterway would be about $360,000.

Headquarters Island Plantation

Across the Stono River from James Island are Johns Island and Headquarters Island Plantation. Incredibly, this spacious development on the vast open marsh is only 4.5 miles from downtown Charleston. This upscale, planned community is close to restaurants, shopping, and championship golf, but has the feel and openness of a far more distant setting. Property values for a 4-bedroom, 3.5-bath home reach $710,000 with some waterfront properties even higher. The low end of the price spectrum is about $300,000 for some 3-bedroom, 3-bath town homes.

Folly Island

Real estate on this small resort island has exploded in price over the past several years. Articles describe the island as "the edge of America" with tongue only slightly in cheek. Like Key West in the 1970s, Folly is attracting a chic and mixed crowd who choose digs that range from dilapidated rental properties to impressive, dramatic, and upscale homes. Most properties fall somewhere in between. Many artists and dedicated surfers can still be found on Folly, but the buying trend is moving toward the beach-loving executive types. In 2008, a beachfront home sold for $2.1 million. Folly has several new condominium developments. There, average prices can be around $445,000.

Sunset Point

Near the west end of Folly, Sunset Point is an attractive newer subdivision. It is divided into six sections—some are a block from the beach; others front the marsh and deep water of Folly River. Prices here have been in the $650,000 to $850,000 range.

Kiawah & Seabrook

These famous resort islands need no introduction here. (See the Area Overview and Golf chapters.) The residents of these islands are among the wealthiest in Charleston County according to the latest figures from the Center for Business Research. Real estate on these barrier islands is blazing to new heights.

Kiawah

With 10 miles of beach and 10,000 acres of forest, marshes, creeks, and rivers, Kiawah is a world-class destination where you'll find some of the nation's most interesting resort architecture. Although the houses blend unobtrusively into the environment, they are by no means uniform. Palatial residences with creative use of glass and materials make the most of spectacular views from ocean to lagoon, and there is a consistency in landscaping throughout. In 2010, the average Kiawah home was $1.2 million, a dramatic increase over 1998's $116,644.

A variety of wildlife abounds, and the athletic facilities and social activities also lure homeowners. At your disposal are more than 18 miles of paved bike paths, a 20-station fitness trail, golf, tennis, swimming, and a 21-acre park and pool complex. Kiawah also has an active vacation rental program, which contributes to the real estate's value.

Seabrook

Bordered by the North Edisto, Bohicket, and Kiawah Rivers and the Atlantic Ocean, Seabrook Island is awash in spectacular water views. Kiawah's smaller next-door neighbor has more than 3 miles of beach and 2,200 private residential acres. The demographic makeup is similar to Kiawah, with Seabrook being another upscale island community with a wide assortment of real estate options and amenities. More residential than the other resort communities in the area, Seabrook incorporated as a town in 1987. There is a complete sports and recreation program, including a well-maintained equestrian center with aesthetically pleasing trail and beach rides. A recent $31 million capital project deconstructed their original club amenity facilities and built beautiful new ones, making Seabrook even more attractive to homeowners. The average home price on Seabrook increased from $247,052 in 1998 to $851,020 in 2010. Seabrook, like Kiawah, also has a range of prices, from $200,000 up to $3.5 million.

RETIREMENT

With its mild climate and natural beauty, the Trident area is an attractive retirement destination. The mature market represents over 30 percent of the adult population here, and that number is growing every year. There are numerous residential communities, geared to different levels of independence, and a growing array of services in the business sector that are tailored to the needs of those enjoying their golden years. Many stores such as Rite-Aid, Kerr Drug, Harris Teeter, Publix, Lowe's, Belk, SteinMart, Ross, and Waccamaw Home Superstore even run regular discounts for shoppers 60 or older. A 1 percent sales tax discount is given to seniors age 85 and over.

The Charleston County Public Library system maintains a community Information database that provides detailed listings of organizations and resources, many geared toward senior citizens. It is updated on a continual basis and can be accessed by contacting any of the 15 county libraries. A listing of the county libraries can be found in the blue pages of the phone book or within the Education chapter. For more information about this useful resource, contact the Main Library at 68 Calhoun St., (843) 805-6930.

RESOURCES

ADVANTAGE/SENIOR SERVICES
Roper Hospital, first floor,
316 Calhoun St.
(843) 724-2489
www.rsfh.com

A senior services department at Roper St. Francis Healthcare is set up to deal with age-specific health issues. The Advantage program is a membership program for South Carolina residents 55 years and older that provides discounts on selected hospital services. Monthly meetings are held for an Alzheimers' support group, Mall Walkers, and an AARP chapter with locations in Roper Downtown, Roper North, and Bon Secours-St. Francis hospitals. (For more on these hospitals, see the Health Care chapter.) Other community programs are offered throughout the year on topics such as Parkinson's disease. Additional benefits include a no-cost discount prescription card, eyewear discounts, and insurance assistance. Social activities include fitness classes and travel opportunities. Advantage Gold membership costs $15 per year. Advantage Silver offers less benefits but keeps South Carolina residents informed and is free.

The Senior Resource Center is a clearinghouse of information about resources for seniors not only at Roper St. Francis Healthcare but also throughout the Greater Charleston area. Visitors will find a library full of senior-related topics. Internet access is available to provide more information. A dedicated phone line covers topics such as fitness programs, retirement planning, support groups, household safety, and continuing education.

CENTER FOR CREATIVE RETIREMENT
**Lightsey Center, College of Charleston,
9 Liberty St.
(843) 953-5488
www.cofc.edu**

There is ample opportunity for seniors to join umbrella service organizations such as the Center for Creative Retirement at the College of Charleston, which is an affiliate of the Elder-hostel Institute Network. Classes are held at the St. Joseph's Family Center, 1695 Wallenberg Blvd. in the West Ashley area, during fall, winter, and spring. Noncredit courses comprise educational seminars, tours, lectures, and discussion groups. Some past topics have included "Revolutionary Changes in Publishing," "India/Pakistan Relations," "Latest Trends in Medication," "History of Huguenots in Charleston," and "Legal Concerns of the Elder Population." The annual membership fee is $50.

CHARLESTON AREA SENIOR CITIZENS SERVICES INC.
**259 Meeting St.
(843) 722-4127**

This nonprofit agency serves older adults in the Tri-County area. Its information and assistance line operates from 8 a.m. to 4 p.m. Mon through Fri. The senior center offers a noon meal, programs, activities, and health education. For the homebound, home-delivered meals and transportation on the Peninsula are provided. The agency's major focuses, which are making a difference in our community, are sponsorship of the Foster Grandparent Program and a job-training program with subsidized employment for people

55 and older. The agency also operates a 77-unit housing complex for seniors.

CHARLESTON COUNTY COMMUNITY EDUCATION
**Charleston County School District,
75 Calhoun St.
(843) 937-6407
www.charlestoncoce.org**

For those who are ready to plunge into creative stimulation, an interesting option is the moderately priced Adult and Community Education Programs, sponsored jointly by the Charleston County School District and the Charleston County Park and Recreation Commission. Categories of classes encompass arts and crafts, business and vocational concerns, computers, culinary arts, fitness and health, language arts, sports, and special interests. The 10 community schools across Charleston County are the sites of the classroom instruction. Offerings run the gamut from 1-night, free sessions to 6-week classes with fees of up to $150. Charleston County residents age 60 and older may request a Gold Card by calling (843) 937-6414 which allows a 20 percent discount off of class fees. Pick up information on the quarterly programs from the county school district offices on Calhoun Street or at Charleston County libraries. Please note that the district does not mail out class schedules.

THE CITADEL
**171 Moultrie St.
(843) 953-5188
www.citadel.edu/cgps**

COLLEGE OF CHARLESTON
**66 George St.
(843) 953-5620
www.cofc.edu**

South Carolina resident seniors 60 or older who are eager for an intellectual challenge can take any of the wide array of courses offered (on a space-available basis) at these two outstanding Charleston colleges. The cost is just $25 a semester at the College of Charleston and only a $15 registration fee plus a one-time application fee of $30 at The Citadel. Another academic resource is the Senior Scholars Program for ages 55 plus, sponsored by The Citadel. For a $35-per-term fee, non-degree-seeking seniors become members and select lectures presented by Citadel faculty and staff and community leaders. Members are issued student ID cards allowing use of parking facilities, Daniel Library, computer labs, recreational facilities, and the college bookstore. Fall, spring, and summer term programs have covered such topics as "Fort Moultrie," "The History-Shaping Women of Charleston," "Maritime Piloting in South Carolina," and "Energy Efficiency at Home." Social activities are offered as well. These include lectures, tours, picnics, and dancing classes. Anyone who is retired or semi-retired can enroll by calling (843) 953-5089.

LOWCOUNTRY SENIOR CENTER
865 Riverland Dr.
(843) 762-9555
www.rsfh.com/seniorcenter
After more than 5 years of fundraising and planning, the new 10,500-square-foot Lowcountry Senior Center opened in the spring of 2002. The concept behind the center was to build a place for active seniors who want more out of life than "sitting in front of the tube all day." The center, managed by Roper St. Francis Healthcare, serves adults age 50 and older with a wide variety of programs and coordinated activities focused on wellness, education, fitness, recreation, and volunteer services. It also serves as a resource for senior-oriented information and houses a computer lab, fitness and arts and crafts rooms, and a main room for social activities like dancing, movies, and wine tastings. The Lowcountry Senior Center is located near the entrance to the James Island County Park on Riverland Drive and offers ample free parking. One-year memberships are $50 for Charleston County residents and $60 for nonresidents. Gold memberships including use of the fitness room are $85 for county residents and $95 for nonresidents.

SHEPHERD'S CENTER OF EAST COOPER
Meets at Mount Pleasant Presbyterian Church, 306 Church, Mount Pleasant
(803) 318-8654
The Shepherd's Center of East Cooper holds weekly meetings on Tuesday from 9 a.m. to noon for a diverse program of lectures, workshops, and fellowship. Diverse topics covered have included "Noted S.C. Statesman, Ben Tillman,""A Visit to China,""The Myth of Aging . . . Care for Life," and "Memoirs Done Write." Bridge, movies, and garden and plantation tours are offered as afternoon activities. The registration fees are $20 per session, plus a $10 annual membership. Shepherd's Center is an interfaith senior center with older adults organizing the programs for their peers.

RETIREMENT HOUSING

Charleston offers retirement housing options ranging from resort living to private-patio or high-rise apartments to supervised care. The choice is yours, depending on the physical wants and needs of those involved, as well as budget. Note that we do not include the resort areas (Kiawah, Seabrook, and Wild Dunes) in this chapter. The resorts are upscale choices that are popular with many retirement-age residents, but they do not offer any provisions for assisted living. See the Accommodations, Neighborhoods, and Relocation chapters for more specific information about resort properties and amenities. The following living arrangements for seniors in the Trident area are a sampling of what is available.

Retirement Apartments

CANTERBURY HOUSE
175 and 165 Market Street
(843) 723-5553

Those interested in relocating into an apartment building for seniors will find the Canterbury House an appealing option. The Episcopal Church–sponsored complex added a new building in 2000 of 46, 1-bedroom apartments to the original 1 of 204 apartments. The location on the Peninsula is within easy walking distance of shopping on King and Market Streets. The independent-living facility offers efficiencies, 1-bedroom efficiencies, and 1-bedroom apartments for seniors 62 years old and older whose income does not exceed certain specified levels for individuals or couples. Location and convenient parking make it handy for visitors and volunteers such as local musicians and children's choirs, who participate in special programs for residents. There is usually a lengthy waiting list for these apartments, so get your name on the list early if the Canterbury House is the place for you.

Retirement & Life-Care Communities

BISHOP GADSDEN EPISCOPAL RETIREMENT COMMUNITY
1 Bishop Gadsden Way
(843) 762-3300, (800) 373-2384
www.bishopgadsden.org

Affiliated with the Episcopal Church, Bishop Gadsden is on a 70-acre site on James Island. Members enjoy the benefits of group living in a lovely setting and are often entertained and enlightened with lectures or presentations by volunteers from Episcopal churches and others in the community. An assisted-living option is also available. A 1999 expansion added 215 apartments and individual homes to the existing facility, and further expansion plans are in the works. A full range of amenities includes a wellness center, pool, casual and formal dining, beauty parlor, banks, a chapel, and convenience stores on the premises. Services such as skilled nursing and dementia care make Bishop Gadsden the only nonprofit, church-sponsored life-care community in the state.

THE ELMS OF CHARLESTON
9102 Woodcreek Court, North Charleston
(843) 572-8170
www.theelmsofcharleston.org

The Elms is a beautifully landscaped, controlled-access, 55+ community of custom-built patio homes, duplexes, town houses, and condominiums. Next to Charleston Southern University and Trident Regional Medical Center, the amenities at the Elms are extensive and include tennis and croquet courts and an 8,000-square-foot clubhouse with a fitness center, swimming pool, exercise area, spa, and library. The Wannamaker County Park with walking trails borders the property. Shopping, dining, golf, and other cultural opportunities are minutes away. Management maintains the yard and home exteriors. Assisted living and long-term care are in nearby facilities.

FRANKE AT SEASIDE
1885 Rifle Range Rd., Mount Pleasant
(843) 856-4700, (800) 940-7435
www.lutheranhomessc.com,
www.frankeatseaside.org
This residential-care facility, operated by Lutheran Homes of South Carolina, is located in Mount Pleasant, just 1 mile from the beach at the Isle of Palms. It offers private and companion rooms with some assistance available. A full-time staff of licensed practical nurses and certified nursing assistants provides quality medical attention. There are 158 one- and two-bedroom apartments in multiple buildings as well as 75 patio homes for independent living options. Residents enjoy a wellness program, meals, housekeeping, and transportation. Emotional support is offered through family support groups, volunteer interaction, and a chapel program. A new 44-bed skilled nursing center was recently added to the community, and plans are under way for additional independent living cottages, patio homes, and apartments. The Burges Center is a 24,000-square-foot resident's club and wellness center.

THE PALMS OF MOUNT PLEASANT
937 Bowman Rd., Mount Pleasant
(843) 884-6949, (877) 203-6207
www.thepalmsofmtpleasant.com
Several options are available at The Palms, including apartments, lakefront villas, and assisted-living quarters. A 2008 $3.5 million facelift of the former Cooper Hall upgraded the full range of choices available here.

Assisted-living options include studio and 1- or 2-bedroom apartments with kitchens and private bathrooms. Housekeeping services, respite care, medication management, 3 meals a day plus snacks, and a full slate of recreational activities are offered with transportation into town. Those in retirement living may choose from standard or deluxe 1- or 2-bedroom apartments with amenities such as an indoor swimming pool, piano cocktail lounge, hair salon, laundry facility, fitness center, and billiard rooms. There is a licensed nurse on call at all hours, and residents can order from the dining room menu.

i For active and retired businesspeople who want to lend a helping hand to young entrepreneurs and their start-up businesses, there's the Service Corps of Retired Executives (SCORE). These counselors offer indepth, one-on-one consulting to help their clients plan, market, manage, and package their ideas. They can be reached at (843) 727-4778, or visit www.score285.org.

PRESBYTERIAN COMMUNITY IN SUMMERVILLE
201 West 9th North St., Summerville
(843) 873-2550, (866) 315-4725
www.preshomesc.org
The independent living options at this Presbyterian Community called The Village at Summerville include 59 outside cottages, 20 efficiency apartments, and 17 two-bedroom apartments. There are also 120 residential rooms with private baths, and residents are served 3 meals a day. Assisted living is an option here. On-site are a beauty shop, barber services, and entertainment such as

field trips to the Spoleto Festival, Monday night movies, ceramics, painting, and exercise classes. Bible classes and chapel are conducted, and transportation to the doctor or shopping facilities is furnished. Licensed nurses run a 90-bed infirmary. Opened in 1958, this community gives priority to South Carolina resident Presbyterians.

SANDPIPER VILLAGE
1224 Village Creek Lane, Mount Pleasant
(843) 884-5735, (888) 830-5105
www.sandpipervillage.com
Sandpiper Village is an 11-acre campus-like community with independent living in 1- and 2-bedroom cottage-style homes. These attractive residences have front and rear entrances with convenient access to the Community Center. The Sandpiper Courtyard apartments offer assisted living. Meals, housekeeping, transportation to doctor appointments, and emergency call buttons are included. Home health care, rehab, and skilled nursing facilities are available as well. Daily activities and social events, bingo, bridge, arts and crafts, church services, a beauty and barbershop, swimming pool, and a library are available. Small pets are allowed.

i One publication focusing on the interests and needs of Tri-County seniors is *Lowcountry Sun*. The free pickup is distributed all over town and covers senior events, health and wellness, gardening, finances, travel, entertainment, and timely information "for the young and active after 50."

SWEETGRASS VILLAGE SENIOR LIVING COMMUNITY
601 Mathis Ferry Rd., Mount Pleasant
(843) 881-9809
www.sweetgrassvillagealf.com
Opened in 2000, this center offers 4 floor plans in room or suite choices. Varying levels of care are available from short-term and traditional assisted living. The 69-unit facility offers licensed nursing care on-site 24 hours a day. Independent living is available here as well. Amenities include activity/exercise rooms, lounges, a library, outdoor patios, a housekeeping/linen service, and a beauty and barbershop. A full-time social director is on staff. Small pets are welcome. A nearby facility for Alzheimer's and memory care patients called Sweetgrass Court is affiliated with Sweetgrass Village Senior Living.

HEALTH CARE

Everyone is concerned about health care these days, and here in the Lowcountry we're very fortunate to have exceptional health care facilities offering high-quality professional services. Local hospitals provide comprehensive services ranging from state-of-the-art neonatal care to heart and liver transplants. Thanks to Roper St. Francis Healthcare's Life-link ground and air mobile intensive care units and the Medical University of South Carolina's Meducare Air, a helicopter transport service that extends across a 150-mile radius, patients can be placed in the hands of professionals by the fastest route possible.

WALK-IN MEDICAL CENTERS

Visitors to Greater Charleston, and sometimes even locals, need a handy reference to the neighborhood medical clinics for those minor but often vacation-spoiling emergencies that can slow down the busy traveler. The following list contains some of the clinics that will see patients on short notice. Most clinics are open every day for extended hours, and no appointment is necessary.

Charleston

ACCESS HEALTHCARE, LLC
235 Calhoun St.
(843) 853-8870

PEDS PLUS AT ST. FRANCIS HOSPITAL
2095 Henry Tecklenburg Dr.
(843) 402-2275

Mount Pleasant

DOCTOR'S CARE
631 Johnnie Dodds Blvd.
(843) 881-0815

MEDCARE EXPRESS
1031 SR 41
(843) 971-3627

NASON MEDICAL CENTER
1101 Bowman Rd.
(843) 284-4911

ROPER ST. FRANCIS MOUNT PLEASANT URGENT CARE
570 Long Point Rd., Ste. 150
(843) 856-6970

North Charleston

DOCTOR'S CARE
8091 Rivers Ave.
(843) 572-7000

MEDCARE EXPRESS
8720 Dorchester Rd.
(843) 552-3629

West Ashley

DOCTOR'S CARE
1851 Sam Rittenberg Blvd.
(843) 556-5585

DOCTOR'S CARE
3424 Shelby Ray Court
(843) 402-6834

James & Johns Islands

DOCTOR'S CARE
743 Folly Rd., James Island
(843) 762-2360

JAMES ISLAND MEDICAL CARE
347 Folly Rd., James Island
(843) 762-1440

ROPER ST. FRANCIS KIAWAH SEABROOK MEDICAL AND URGENT CARE
345 Freshfields Dr., Building J, Ste. 101, Johns Island
(843) 768-4800

Dorchester County

DOCTOR'S CARE
10160 Dorchester Rd., Summerville
(843) 871-7900

410 N. Main St., Summerville
(843) 871-3277

HOSPITALS & HEALTH CARE FACILITIES

Downtown Charleston

KINDRED HOSPITAL
326 Calhoun St., 3rd Floor
(843) 876-8340
www.khcharleston.com
Kindred Hospital of Charleston is a private, long-term acute care hospital specializing in providing care for patients with complex medical needs. Patients are referred to Kindred Hospital for ongoing acute medical care, because the severity of their medical condition precludes them from acceptance into a rehabilitation facility, subacute facility, or a skilled nursing unit. There are 59 beds for catastrophically ill, medically complex patients.

Kindred Hospital of Charleston is part of Kindred Healthcare, Inc., a national health care services company based in Louisville, Kentucky, that operates hospitals, nursing centers, institutional pharmacies, and contract rehabilitation services. The company's mission is "taking care of people who cannot take care of themselves."

MEDICAL UNIVERSITY OF SOUTH CAROLINA MEDICAL CENTER
171 Ashley Ave.
(843) 792-2300
www.muschealth.com
The MUSC Medical Center, a state-of-the-art teaching hospital, is the heartbeat of the Medical University of South Carolina. (See the Education chapter.) This acute care center, along with MUSC's outpatient clinic, serves not only patients from the Greater Charleston area, but also those attracted to it from all over the state and the nation. In addition to more than 50 certificate, baccalaureate, master's, and doctoral programs in virtually all areas of the health sciences, MUSC offers continuing education programs that help South Carolina's health professionals stay current with the latest medical treatments and procedures.

Under the umbrella of MUSC are several specialty facilities, including the Albert Florens Storm Eye Institute, MUSC Children's Hospital, MUSC Digestive Disease Center, MUSC Heart and Vascular Center, Hollings Cancer Center, Musculoskeletal Institute, MUSC Institute of Psychiatry, Women's Health Center, and MUSC Transplant Center. A new facility houses the Heart and Vascular

Physician Referral Services

Bon Secours–St. Francis/ Roper Hospital
(843) 402-2273, (800) 863-2273

Charleston County Medical Society
(843) 577-3613

East Cooper Regional Medical Center
(843) 884-7031, (800) 311-4803

Medical University of South Carolina
(843) 792-1414

Trident HealthFinders
(843) 797-3463, (866) 874-3368

Center and the Digestive Disease Center. *Child Magazine* recently named the Children's Hospital one of the top 25 children's hospitals in the country. For more information on services, classes, physician appointments, or health information library topics, call the MUSC Health Connection number at (843) 792-1414 or (800) 424-MUSC. General visiting hours are from 9 a.m. to 9 p.m. daily.

i A local resource for more extensive listings of area health and social services is the Community Information Database compiled and continuously updated by the Reference Department of the Charleston County Library. It is an excellent source and may be found in Charleston County libraries or online at www.ccpl.org under "Local Resources."

RALPH H. JOHNSON VA MEDICAL CENTER
109 Bee St.
(843) 577-5011, (888) 878-6884
www.charleston.va.gov
This Department of Veterans Affairs medical center has 124 beds and nearly 1,000 employees. The center provides acute medical, surgical, and psychiatric inpatient care plus primary and specialized outpatient care to veterans in a 15-county area of South Carolina. The VA Medical Center is affiliated with 50 different educational institutions but primarily works with MUSC, the main source of the center's paid resident staff. In fall 1996, the VA/MUSC Strom Thurmond Biomedical Research Center opened, providing a 42,000-square-foot location for the VA center's research staff. The hospital's 44 clinics work in a variety of health disciplines ranging from audiology to vascular surgery. Call the main switchboard at the number listed for additional information. Visiting hours are generally from 11 a.m. to 8:30 p.m. daily.

ROPER HOSPITAL
316 Calhoun St.
(843) 724-2000
www.rsfh.com
With 453 beds and more than 2,000 employees, Roper Hospital is one of the Lowcountry's oldest and largest health care facilities. In 1998 Roper merged with Bon Secours-St. Francis Xavier Hospital to form CareAlliance Health Services, which has evolved into the new Roper St. Francis Healthcare. The hospital recently opened a $77.4 million 7-story, 245,000-square-foot tower to replace its oldest hospital rooms. Included in its services are several special units: Roper Heart and Vascular Center, a complete cardiac care facility that addresses education, prevention,

diagnosis, and treatment, including surgery and rehabilitation; Roper Cancer Center, offering compassionate care, state-of-the-art diagnostic and treatment services, and special resources for cancer patients and their families; and Roper's NeuroScience Center, providing the area's only acute stroke unit and specializing in neurological treatment, including epilepsy monitoring and surgery with advanced microscopy, ultrasound, and laser technology.

Women's, Infants', and Children's Services at Roper include a resource center, family-centered maternity care, lifestyle services, diagnostic breast and osteoporosis services, plastic and reconstructive surgery, and Peds Plus after-hours urgent care for infants, children, and adolescents.

The Roper St. Francis Rehabilitation Hospital is a 52-bed facility that focuses on rehabilitation and functional recovery. According to hospital statistics, patients who have been treated here consistently achieve higher levels of functional independence than the national norms. In addition to this inpatient facility, there are outpatient rehabilitation services, such as physical therapy, occupational therapy, and speech therapy available in Goose Creek and Walterboro. The direct line for the Rehabilitation Hospital is (843) 724-2482.

Roper has diagnostic centers offering convenient access to lab, X-ray, and EKG services throughout the Trident area. To find the one nearest you, call (843) 402-2273. The centers are generally open from 7:30 a.m. until 5 p.m. Mon through Fri. Roper's downtown emergency room, (843) 724-2010, is open 24 hours a day with full-service emergency care. As a Heart and Stroke Emergency Network location, it also provides specialized heart care with its Chest Pain

Observation Unit, which is next door to the ER. The patient information desk can be reached at (843) 724-2111. General visiting hours are 9 a.m. to 9 p.m.

East Cooper

EAST COOPER REGIONAL MEDICAL CENTER
2000 Hospital Dr., Mount Pleasant
(843) 881-0100
www.eastcoopermedctr.com
This hospital serves the communities east of the Cooper River but also draws patients from throughout the Lowcountry. East Cooper Regional Medical Center has 130 beds and about 560 employees. The hospital moved to a larger, 250,000-square-foot facility in 2010, doubling the size of the previous center on Johnnie Dodds Boulevard in operation since 1986 . The hospital (formerly called East Cooper Community Hospital) provides inpatient acute care and 24-hour emergency room services. Additional special services include outpatient diagnostics, ICU/CCU, MRI, home health care, spinal care, ambulatory surgery, imaging, and OB/GYN. Call the main switchboard for patient information and room assignments. Visiting hours are from 9 a.m. to 9 p.m. daily.

MOUNT PLEASANT HOSPITAL
3500 US 17, Mount Pleasant
(843) 606-7000
www.rsfh.com
Opened in 2010, this $180 million facility is Roper St. Francis Healthcare's answer to the population growth (up 58 percent in the 2000 census) in Mount Pleasant, one of the fastest growing cities in South Carolina. The 85-bed hospital encompasses 219,000 square feet and is located on 78 acres, 38

of which are protected woodlands and wetlands, creating a natural and potentially healing environment. The hospital offers inpatient and outpatient surgery, a 24-hour emergency room, an intensive care unit, medical-surgical units, and home-like labor and delivery suites. Imaging services, a laboratory, and a pharmacy are on-site as well as a medical office building housing doctors of a variety of specialties. A helipad is also available for ease of transportation.

North Charleston

CONCENTRA MEDICAL CENTER
8780 Rivers Ave., North Charleston
(843) 572-0810
www.tridenthealthsystem.com
A part of the Trident Health System, these facilities offer a freestanding, comprehensive occupational medicine program serving more than 300 employers in Berkeley, Dorchester, and Charleston Counties since 1980. Services include post-offer physical examinations (when a prospective employee has been offered a job by a business pending the outcome of a physical exam), work injury treatment, drug and alcohol testing, and occupational injury and illness prevention programs. The physicians and staff are dedicated exclusively to the practice of occupational medicine. A second location is at 4115 Dorchester Rd. (843-554-6737).

HEALTHSOUTH REHABILITATION HOSPITAL—CHARLESTON
9181 Medcom St.
(843) 820-7777
www.healthsouthcharleston.com
Alabama-based HealthSouth opened HealthSouth Rehabilitation Hospital in Charleston in 1994. The full-service, 46-bed acute

rehabilitation hospital spans patient care from injury or illness to maximum independence and function. Additional services include outpatient rehabilitation services, diagnostic imaging, outpatient surgery, and industrial rehabilitation. The center's stated mission is "getting people back . . . to work . . . to play . . . to living." It is the only freestanding rehabilitation hospital in the Lowcountry and is accredited by the Joint Commission on the Accreditation of Healthcare Organizations (JCAHO).

INTREPID USA
9241 University Blvd., Ste. A, North Charleston
(843) 766-2929
www.intrepidusa.com
Intrepid USA provides home care for both recovering, chronically ill, or disabled persons throughout Charleston, Berkeley, Dorchester, and Colleton Counties. Services include skilled nursing care, personal care, infusion therapy, medical social services, physical therapy, speech pathology, occupational therapy, respiratory therapy, home medical equipment, and hospice. Nationally, Intrepid USA has more than 100 offices in 24 states.

NAVAL HEALTH CLINIC CHARLESTON
Naval Weapons Station
(843) 743-7000
www.med.navy.mil/sites/chas
This new joint ambulatory care clinic is located in a state-of-the-art, 188,000 square-foot building. This facility is a $41.5 million joint Department of Defense and Veterans Administration health clinic that moved in the fall of 2010 from its old location at 3600 Rivers Ave. It serves active duty military and

their families, retired military and veterans with the latest in outpatient care, pharmaceutical services, and preventive medicine.

ROPER ST. FRANCIS MEDICAL CENTER NORTHWOODS
2233 Northwoods Blvd.
(843) 824-8733
www.rsfh.com
Near Northwoods Mall, this facility offers full-service emergency care 24 hours a day. It also provides lab and X-ray and other diagnostic services.

TRIDENT MEDICAL CENTER
9330 Medical Plaza Dr., (I-26 and SR 78)
(843) 797-7000, (877) 300-6062
www.tridenthealthsystem.com
The Trident Health System has 11 centers serving the health care needs of the Lowcountry by offering heart, cancer, women's health, sports medicine, skilled nursing, industrial medicine, surgery, home health care, and senior services. The Trident Medical Center is the largest facility in the Trident Health System, with a 296-bed, acute care hospital employing more than 2,000 workers. The center provides diagnostic and outpatient and inpatient surgical services, and the hospital provides 24-hour emergency services. Other specialties include ICU/CCU heart care, cardiac rehabilitation, OB/GYN, pediatrics, sports/industrial medicine, physical rehabilitation, and a cancer center. Trident Medical Center recently completed a $60 million expansion and renovation, adding 64,000 square feet to its facility and a 400-space parking deck. For patient information, call (843) 847-4000, then dial 4 plus the room number.

TRIDENT SENIOR HEALTH CENTER
9302 Medical Plaza Dr., Ste. C
(843) 797-0416
www.tridenthealthsystem.com
Under the umbrella of the Trident Health System (see listing under Trident Medical Center), the Senior Health Center provides health care that meets the needs of residents age 65 and older. The center, which accepts Medicare assignments, is near Northwoods Mall. Staffed by Board-certified primary care physicians with advanced training in geriatric medicine, the center also includes nurses, a geriatrician, and other health care professionals who are experienced in the special needs of the senior population. Primary medical care is provided for chronic illnesses such as heart disease, diabetes, and Alzheimer's. Trident Senior Health Center also takes a partnership role in wellness, with monthly health education programs, health screenings, and a senior health library. Additional assistance is offered with insurance or billing questions as well as other social service needs.

TRIDENT SURGERY CENTER
9313 Medical Plaza Dr., Ste. 102,
(843) 797-8992

TRIDENT EYE SURGERY CENTER
9297-B Medical Plaza Dr.
(843) 824-5024
www.tridenthealthsystem.com
The Trident Surgery Center and Trident Eye Surgery Center specialize in same-day surgery, performing about 500 procedures a month. The centers feature state-of-the-art medical equipment, 4 operating rooms, and 10 private recovery rooms. Affiliated with the Trident Health System, the Trident Surgery Center is the only surgery center in the Lowcountry accredited by the Accreditation Association for Ambulatory Health Care.

West Ashley & James Island

BON SECOURS–ST. FRANCIS HOSPITAL
2095 Henry Tecklenburg Dr.
(843) 402-1000, (843) 402-2273
(Healthline)
www.rsfh.com

Bon Secours–St. Francis Hospital is the oldest Catholic hospital in South Carolina and the only one in Charleston. Its long history in this community goes back to 1882, when five sisters of Charity of Our Lady of Mercy opened a small, wood-framed building called the St. Francis Xavier Infirmary. A 1998 merger with Roper CareAlliance made Bon Secours–St. Francis Xavier Hospital part of CareAlliance Health Services, now called Roper St. Francis Health-care. Then and now, the emphasis has been on a devotion to caring for the whole person—physically, spiritually, and emotionally.

The hospital relocated in December 1996 from its previous downtown address to a new facility west of the Ashley River. The new hospital focuses on several signature services including spine and sports medicine, women's, infants', and children's health services, digestive disorders and urological care, heart and stroke emergency network, diabetes management, ambulatory surgery, and emergency services. The patient information and location number is (843) 402-1118, and Home Health Care services can be contacted at (843) 402-7000. (For information on Bon Secours' Senior Services, see the Retirement chapter.)

ROPER ST. FRANCIS HOME HEALTH CARE
1483 Tobias Gadson Blvd., Ste. 208
(843) 402-7000, (800) 353-7421
www.rsfh.com

Roper St. Francis Home Health Care has three components: Home Health, Home Infusion, and Telemonitoring. Home Health provides home care by nurses, aides, medical social workers, and therapists. Services include skilled nursing, personal care, wound care, physical, speech, and occupational therapy, and a centralized intake department. Home Infusion IV therapies are located at 7 Amy Elsey Dr. and can be reached at (843) 763-2600. The telemonitoring program places a monitor in the home that transmits health data to the home health agency for review. The number for this service is (843) 402-7000.

ROPER HOSPITAL AMBULATORY SURGERY & PAIN MANAGEMENT— JAMES ISLAND
347 Folly Rd.
(843) 789-1550
www.rsfh.com

Opened in 2010, this James Island center performs more than 3,000 outpatient surgeries each year. Affiliated with the Roper St. Francis Healthcare system, the Surgery Center provides general surgical services for adults and children.

OTHER NEARBY HEALTH CARE FACILITIES

MONCKS CORNER MEDICAL CENTER
401 North Live Oak Dr., US 17A,
Moncks Corner
(843) 761-8721, (843) 577-9319
(Charleston)
www.tridenthealthsystem.com

This Trident Health System outpatient diagnostic and rehabilitation facility serves the residents of Berkeley County. The center sponsors a number of community wellness programs in addition to providing laboratory testing, physical rehabilitation, radiology,

Emergency & Health Care Numbers

Al-Anon/Alateen
(843) 762-6999

Alcohol & Drug Abuse
Helpline
(843) 722-0100

Alcoholics Anonymous
(843) 723-9633

Alzheimer's Assoc.,
Palmetto Chapter
(843) 571-2641

American Cancer
Society
(843) 744-1922

American Heart/
American Stroke
Association
Lowcountry Regional
Office
(843) 853-1597

American Lung
Association of South
Carolina, Coast Branch
(843) 556-8451

American Medical
Association
(312) 464-5000

American Red Cross,
Carolina Lowcountry
Chapter
(843) 764-2323

American Social
Health Association
STI Hotline
(800) 227-8922

Berkeley County
Health Department
(843) 723-0766
(Charleston line)

Berkeley County
Rescue Squad
(843) 723-3800

Charleston County
Health Department
(843) 579-4500

Charleston County
Vol. Rescue Squad
(843) 225-7728

Child Abuse Hotline
(800) 422-4453

Coastal Crisis
Chaplaincy
(843) 724-1212

Compassionate
Friends
(877) 969-0010

Dorchester County
Health Department
(843) 832-0041

Elderlink, Inc. Trident
Area Agency on Aging
(843) 554-2275

Family Services
(843) 744-1348

CDC Info
(800) 232-4636

Carolina Center for
Hospice and End of
Life Care
(800) 662-8859

United Way's 211 for
South Carolina
(843) 744-HELP

Lowcountry Children's
Center
(843) 723-3600

March of Dimes Birth
Defects Foundation
Lowcountry Division
(843) 571-1776

Mental Health
America
(800) 969-6642

MUSC Health
Connection
(843) 792-1414

Muscular Dystrophy
Association
(843) 556-3654

Multiple Sclerosis
Society
(800) 922-7591

Narcotics Anonymous
(843) 852-3001

Federal Substance
Abuse and Mental
Health Administration
(800) 789-2647

National Suicide
Prevention Lifeline
(800) 273-TALK

People Against Rape
(843) 745-0144

Poison Control
Hotline
(800) 922-1117

St. Francis Diabetes
Treatment Center
(843) 402-1099

Runaway Hotline
(800) 621-4000

Teenline
(843) 747-TEEN

and mammography services. Physician services are available by appointment at this location as well.

ROPER ST. FRANCIS MEDICAL CENTER BERKELEY
**730 Stoney Landing Rd., Moncks Corner
(843) 899-7700, (800) 846-7707
www.rsfh.com**
Roper St. Francis Medical Center Berkeley has Berkeley County's only 24-hour emergency services department. The center also offers access to primary care and specialty physicians as well as diagnostic services, including laboratory testing, X-rays, mammography, CT scans, physical therapy, cardiopulmonary testing, endoscopy, and bronchoscopy.

Helpful Links

Here's a short list of health-oriented websites for your exploration:

- www.aha.org
- www.ama-assn.org
- www.cdc.gov
- www.charlestonphysicians.com
- www.familydoctor.org
- www.healthfinder.gov
- www.tuw.org/211.asp
- www.nlm.nih.gov (Medline)
- www.webmd.com

SUMMERVILLE MEDICAL CENTER
**295 Midland Pkwy., Summerville
(843) 832-5000
www.tridenthealthsystem.com**

The Summerville Center is a 94-bed, full-service facility with 24-hour emergency, general, medical, and surgical services, a heart center, intensive care and skilled nursing units, sports medicine and rehabilitation, women's services, and a sleep lab. It sponsors numerous wellness programs for the community in addition to providing medical imaging and X-rays, and diagnostic and physical rehabilitation services. The emergency room phone is (843) 832-5160. Summerville Medical Center is a part of the Trident Health System.

MENTAL HEALTH CENTERS

BERKELEY COMMUNITY MENTAL HEALTH CENTER
**403 Stoney Landing Rd., Moncks Corner
(843) 761-8282, (888) 202-1381
(Charleston/Summerville)
www.bcmhc.org**
This mental health center serves children, adolescents, and adults in Berkeley County with outpatient psychiatric services. The staff of 53 plus includes psychiatrists, nurses, and counselors. Day treatment programs, short- and long-term therapy, and specialized clinics on such topics as attention deficit hyperactivity disorder (ADHD) and family preservation are offered. Their outpatient program is CARF accredited (Commission on Accreditation of Rehabilitation Facilities). Private insurance coverage is accepted with prior approval, as well as Medicaid, Medicare, and the Civilian Health and Medical Program of the Uniformed Services. A sliding fee scale may be applied based on ability to pay. Transportation service is available for Berkeley County residents.

CHARLESTON/DORCHESTER COMMUNITY MENTAL HEALTH CENTERS
2100 Charlie Hall Blvd.
(843) 852-4100, (843) 414-2351,
(emergency/intake)
www.cdcmhc.org

With children and adolescent programs serving Charleston and Dorchester County residents, the Community Mental Health Center offers a comprehensive program of general mental health services for adults, adolescents, and children. The staff provides assessment and ongoing treatment, and the facility is affiliated with the South Carolina Department of Mental Health. A crisis stabilization center is operated to provide an alternative to hospital admission with early crisis intervention. The center accepts Medicare, Medicaid, and private insurance. A sliding fee scale is offered, based on ability to pay. Other locations are at 2090 Executive Hall Rd., Ste. 170 (843-852-3633), 5 Charleston Center (843-958-3428) and 106 Springview Lane, Summerville (843-873-5063 or 800-768-2936).

MUSC INSTITUTE OF PSYCHIATRY
67 President St.
(843) 792-9888, (800) 922-5250
www.muschealth.com

The Institute of Psychiatry at the Medical University of South Carolina serves not only as a center for professional education and psychiatric research, but also as a provider of state-of-the-art care for a full range of psychiatric problems. Nationally-recognized psychiatrists, psychiatric nurses, social workers, psychologists, and researchers work together to offer personalized treatment to individuals and families. The programs are designed to help people of all ages meet the impact of behavioral, emotional, and substance abuse problems. The Institute of Psychiatry's services include Adult Services, the Center for Drug and Alcohol Programs, Geriatric Services (including an Alzheimer's Care Program), Youth Services, and Health and Wellness Services. Some of their programs include the Eating Disorders Program, Crime Victims Research and Treatment Center, Weight Management Center, Tic and Tourette Disorders Services, and Attention Deficit Disorders Services. To receive a brochure on any of the services or to make an appointment, call the number previously listed.

PALMETTO LOWCOUNTRY BEHAVIORAL HEALTH
2777 Speissegger Dr.
(843) 747-5830, (877) 947-3223
www.palmettobehavioralhealth.com

Palmetto Lowcountry Behavioral Health offers 24-hour help, assessment, and referral for treatment of depression, anxiety, drug and alcohol abuse, and other emotional problems. Formerly Charter Charleston Behavioral Health System, Palmetto Lowcountry provides inpatient treatment in their 102-bed facility, outpatient, and partial services for children, adolescents, and adults at the above location.

ALTERNATIVE HEALTH CARE

Growing in popularity here in the Lowcountry and almost everywhere else are alternative health care practices such as chiropractic services, acupuncture, yoga, and holistic and homeopathic therapies. Here are some resources for those seeking new avenues toward well-being.

CHARLESTON NECK AND BACK CENTER

1835 Savage Rd.
(843) 763-2225
www.neckandbackcenter.com

Charleston Neck and Back Center has three licensed chiropractors at each of their locations specializing in pain control, rehabilitation, family care, and spinal injury care, plus full diagnostic and outpatient care. Two more locations are at 1123 Queensborough Rd., Mount Pleasant (843-881-7797) and 2102 Otranto Rd., North Charleston (843-569-2225).

CHARLESTON THERAPEUTIC MASSAGE

310 Broad St., Ste. 8
(843) 723-7005
www.charleston-massage.com

Licensed and certified massage therapists work here specializing in relaxation, aromatherapy, medical, hot stone, sports and deep tissue massage, as well as cranio sacral therapy and holistic integrated bodywork. Charleston Therapeutic Massage offers corporate on-site chair massage at your location, too.

HEALTHSOURCE OF MOUNT PLEASANT

309 Coleman Blvd., Mount Pleasant
(843) 884-8444
www.healthsourcemtpleasant.com

This center, with one licensed chiropractor, specializes in conservative chiropractic treatment of lower back pain, headaches, pinched nerves, scoliosis, and other difficult disorders of the back and neck. Sports and work injuries as well as auto accident injuries are treated here.

HOLY COW YOGA & HOLISTIC CENTER

10 Windermere Blvd.
(843) 769-2269
www.holycowyoga.com

Located in South Windermere Center (see the Shopping chapter) across from Earth Fare health foods supermarket, Holy Cow offers a variety of yoga classes in a multidisciplinary Hatha style, with over 30 classes every week. There are also offer workshops, seminars, and special guest speakers monthly to promote yoga knowledge, health and wellness, and spirituality. A staff of massage therapists specializes in neuromuscular and Swedish deep tissue, full body, and deep relaxation massage, hot stone therapy, and Reiki.

ISLAND CHIROPRACTIC CENTRE

3546 Maybank Hwy., Johns Island
(843) 559-9111
www.charlestonchiropractic.com

Island Chiropractic is run by a certified sports physician with postdoctoral certification in X-ray interpretation, pain management, impairment ratings, CPR, and first aid. The staff has been treating area patients at this location since 1987.

ISLAND THERAPY GROUP

2201 Middle St., Sullivan's Island
(843) 883-9497

A staff of licensed certified massage therapists provide services including Swedish deep tissue and sports massage, craniosacral and neuromuscular therapy, and reflexology.

MARTI CHITWOOD, RD, CCN

349 Folly Rd., Ste. 1-C
(843) 406-8945
www.martichitwood.com

With a background in dietary therapy and healthful nutrition, Marti Chitwood RD, CNN and her staff are a good resource of holistic nutritional advice. Their approach considers the whole person, including lifestyle, emotions, attitudes, beliefs, and symptoms.

RE-SOUL ACUPUNCTURE & CHINESE HERBAL MEDICINE
118 E. Elliott St.
(843) 566-2855
www.re-soul.com

Amy Jo Gengler, LAc, offers drug-free health care as a licensed acupuncturist practicing this ancient Chinese treatment. Many receive effective relief from conditions such as back and neck pain, post-injury recovery, and PMS relief. She also provides treatment for improving digestion, and sleep, stress management, and increasing energy at her convenient downtown location.

OTHER SERVICES

CENTER FOR WOMEN
129 Cannon St.
(843) 763-7333
www.c4women.org

The Center for Women is a nonprofit organization dedicated to improving the lives of women in the Lowcountry through personal and professional success. Services include information and referral resources and peer counseling for individual problem-solving strategies. Among the numerous support groups offered are Depression and Anxiety, Separation and Divorce, Career Transitions, and Post Partum Depression. The Thursday Brown Bag Lunch Series is quite popular and has covered topics such as "Get Organized," "Building a Budget You Can Live With," and "Overcoming the Super Woman Syndrome" Most services and programs are held at the Center for Women and are free. Call the number above, or visit the website for the latest innovative programs and events.

HOSPICE OF CHARLESTON INC.
3870 Leeds Ave., Ste. 101, North Charleston
(843) 529-3100, (843) 266-3497, Bereavement Center
www.hospiceofcharleston.org

Licensed as both a hospice and home health agency, Hospice of Charleston has served the residents of Charleston, Dorchester, and Berkeley Counties since 1981. Now affiliated with Gentiva Health Services, Inc., it provides medical, emotional, and spiritual care to terminally ill people and their families, with a staff of both full-time professionals and trained volunteers. In 2006 Hospice opened Hospice Center, a new 20-bed inpatient facility on Wando Park Boulevard in Mount Pleasant. Their Mourning to Morning Bereavement Center offers a variety of grief support programs including grief recovery workshops that are cosponsored with area hospitals and meet once a week for 6 weeks. Twice a year Shannon's Hope Camp (at Camp St. Christopher on Seabrook Island) is held for bereaved children, ages 6 through 15. The camp involves the children in fun activities such as music, drawing, and arts and crafts designed to help them work out their grief. Each November, Hospice of Charleston sponsors the Candlelight Memorial Ceremony at Colonial Lake in downtown Charleston. For a $15 donation to Hospice, luminarias are lit surrounding the edge of the lake in memory of lost loved ones. A short program and music add to the remembrance ceremony. For more information on Hospice of Charleston programs, call the listed number.

LOWCOUNTRY AIDS SERVICES
3547 Meeting Street Rd.
(843) 747-2273, (877) 874-0230
www.aids-services.com
Founded in 1985, Palmetto AIDS Life Support Services of South Carolina (PALSS) evolved into a statewide, community-based service agency now called Lowcountry AIDS Services (LAS). Lowcountry AIDS provides case management, counseling, and direct volunteer support to men, women, and children with HIV or AIDS in 3 counties—Charleston, Berkeley, and Dorchester. In addition to the practical and emotional support, this nonprofit social service agency works to educate and acts as an advocacy, resource, and referral agency for HIV/AIDS-infected people and their families. LAS is supported by the Community Foundation, Trident United Way, and private donations. (For information on LAS's Dining with Friends celebration, look under May in the Annual Events chapter.)

ODYSSEY HEALTHCARE OF CHARLESTON
5965 Core Ave., Ste. 603, North Charleston
(843) 554-4048, (877) 637-9432, 24 hours
www.odyssey-healthcare.com
Serving Charleston, Berkeley, Dorchester, Colleton, and Beaufort counties (plus 11 other counties), Odyssey HealthCare provides interdisciplinary care for the terminally ill in their own homes as well as nursing homes, long-term care, assisted living facilities, or hospitals. Providers are licensed to serve by the state and are Medicare-certified and accredited by the Joint Commission on Accreditation of Healthcare Organizations. Periodic educational and support programs are offered. Annual memorial services are held to provide rituals for grieving persons.

PALMETTO CHAPTER, THE ALZHEIMER'S ASSOCIATION
2090 Executive Hall Rd., Ste. 130
(843) 571-2641, (800) 860-1444
www.alz.org/sc
Palmetto is a voluntary health, nonprofit organization dedicated to providing services and support to persons and families affected by Alzheimer's disease. The Palmetto Chapter serves Charleston, Berkeley, Dorchester, Colleton, Hampton, Jasper, Beaufort, Horry, Georgetown, and Williamsburg counties. It offers educational seminars, workshops, and literature. Other services include support groups, a help line, and referral information. It is also an advocacy group and publishes a newsletter for its membership.

EDUCATION

A s in most communities its size, the academic options in Greater Charleston are greatly varied. Newcomers to the area with school-age children need to know specific details about the public and private schooling options and make their educational decisions accordingly. Sometimes this information is closely guarded (especially when the news isn't particularly good), but be diligent in your quest for detail. Finding good schools and good teachers is obviously extremely important.

If you're new to the city, one of your first sources of information about schools in your residential area should be your realtor. Ask about the area schools' comparative test scores, student teacher ratios, college placement percentages, and athletic options. Don't hesitate to ask about any recorded incidents of violence. Another resource with reliable information is your county school district office. Addresses and phone numbers for offices in Charleston, Dorchester, and Berkeley Counties are listed in this chapter.

PUBLIC SCHOOLS

Records from the first general public school system in the Lowcountry date back to 1856. Today, separate public school systems are in place in Charleston, Berkeley, and Dorchester Counties. More than 93,000 students are enrolled in pre-kindergarten through 12th grade at more than 139 schools in 4 school districts—Berkeley County, Charleston County, Dorchester II, and Dorchester IV.

The school year runs 180 days from late-Aug until the end of May or early June. All children entering first grade must present a birth certificate and must be 6 years old by Sept 1. Those entering South Carolina schools for the first time must show two forms of proof of residency and a current vaccination certificate. School bus service is available for students who live more than 1 mile from their assigned school.

Among the area's educational options are 16 schools serving children with special needs, 22 magnet schools for academically gifted students, and a special South Carolina–mandated program in each district for children with high test scores and strong academic potential.

CHARLESTON COUNTY SCHOOL DISTRICT
75 Calhoun St.
(843) 937-6300
www.ccsdschools.com
The Charleston County School District operates 80 schools in a 1,000-square-mile area along the South Carolina coast. About 43,000 students attend these schools. The county school system, governed by a 9-member board of trustees, is divided

into 8 constituent school districts, each one administered by an area superintendent. These 8 districts, in turn, have elected school boards of various sizes that are responsible for establishing the attendance zones for local schools. The district employs 3,300 teachers and maintains an average pupil–teacher ratio of 19 to 1.

The district has been a trailblazer for the magnet school concept, and has now expanded to 22 locations divided among K–12 schools. These special schools serve a student population that is academically or artistically gifted. Located on the Peninsula, in West Ashley, and in North Charleston, they draw students from surrounding neighborhoods as well as areas spread throughout the district. Magnet school educational programs provide an alternative curriculum that integrates resources from the community, higher education, the arts, business, and technology. Call (843) 937-6305 for qualification information, as magnet schools can differ in entrance requirements.

SAIL—Students Actively Interested in Learning—is a state-mandated program in place in the Charleston County public school system. Offerings are innovative and challenging, designed to stimulate the academically talented students who are accepted into the program. Creative, critical problem-solving skills make up the focus of the curriculum content through programs such as the Academic Bowl and Odyssey of the Mind competitions, Advanced Placement courses, and a mentor program for grades 8 through 10. For more information on SAIL, call the supervisor at (843) 937-6471.

Special needs programs for students with emotional, mental, or physical disabilities are available through the school district

as well. The contact number to learn more is (843) 937-6567.

All told, Charleston County administers 37 elementary schools, 11 middle schools, 8 high schools, 22 magnet schools, 7 charter schools, and 16 specialized programs. Relying on the phone book for numbers to reach specific offices for the different constituent school districts can be confusing, so we have compiled a list of important contacts in various Charleston County areas for easy reference:

- **Districts 1 and 2,** McClellanville and East Cooper: (843) 849-2878
- **Districts 3 and 9,** James Island, Johns Island: (843) 762-2780
- **District 4,** North Charleston: (843) 745-7150
- **District 10,** West Ashley: (843) 763-1500
- **District 20,** Charleston: (843) 937-6598
- **District 23,** Hollywood, Edisto, Ravenel: (843) 889-2291

BERKELEY COUNTY SCHOOL DISTRICT
229 East Main St., Moncks Corner
(843) 899-8600, (843) 723-4627
(in Charleston)
www.berkeley.k12.sc.us
Berkeley County School District is the third largest in the state, with 40 schools serving over 28,000 students. The northern end of Berkeley County is rural and sparsely populated, while the area from Moncks Corner to Hanahan is suburban.

The curriculum is designed to meet the educational needs of all students, regardless of their academic achievement level. Accelerated students benefit from classes tailored to their advanced abilities. Call (843) 899-8640 or (843) 723-4627, ext. 8640, for information on Berkeley County School District's gifted programs. Students receive a steady diet of core courses designed to prepare them for the challenges posed by college and postgraduate jobs.

Remedial education is available for students requiring special attention. Special needs programs are targeted to children with disabilities ranging from those who are visually impaired to the educable mentally retarded. All Berkeley County schools offer support personnel and services to students, including guidance counselors, psychologists, and speech therapists.

The breakdown shows Berkeley County administering 4 primary, 13 elementary, 2 elementary/middle, 12 intermediate and middle schools, 8 high schools, and 1 alternative school program.

DORCHESTER COUNTY SCHOOL
DISTRICT 2
102 Green Wave Blvd., Summerville
(843) 873-2901
www.dorchester2.k12.sc.us
District 2 in Dorchester County has been designated one of the fastest-growing public school districts in the state. A study conducted for the school district by The Citadel indicated that 95 percent of the residential growth in Dorchester County occurred in District 2, the Greater Summerville area. In addition, 98 percent of this growth took place in the eastern or Oakbrook section of Summerville, where school enrollment bears this out by jumping from 10,106 in 1979–1980 to 21,201 in 2009–2010.

District 2 operates 21 schools, specializing in extracurricular activities for students in kindergarten through grade 12. Students graduating from Summerville High School have consistently scored above the state norms on the Scholastic Aptitude Test.

GATE (Gifted and Talented Education) is Dorchester 2's state-mandated program for those students who qualify for special enrichment and academic challenges. Call (843) 821-3960 for more information on the qualifications needed to participate. Alternative programs for young people in District 2 high schools offer special counseling and basic skills aimed at lowering the dropout rate. These specialized programs are conducted at an off-campus site—during regular school hours.

Based on high achievement in standardized testing, District 2 has several schools that earned "deregulation status" from the state for updating school curricula, allowing greater innovation in teaching methods, and meeting the increasingly complex needs of young people. There are 11 elementary schools, 6 middle schools, and 3 high schools in Dorchester District 2. The Givhans Alternative Program and Rollings School of the Arts complete the list of schools in this district.

DORCHESTER COUNTY SCHOOL
DISTRICT 4
500 Ridge St., St. George
(843) 563-4535
www.dorchester4.k12.sc.us
Dorchester District 4 serves the outer region of Dorchester County and, with only about 2,300 students, is one of the smallest districts in the state. The district has a pupil–teacher ratio of one instructor for every 18.5 students. Setting high standards for its faculty, the district provides incentives for the professional growth and advancement of its teachers and administrators through in-service training programs and membership in the Salkehatchie Consortium, which

provides graduate courses at no cost to teachers.

The district's curriculum is designed for students looking to enter the workforce after high school as well as students heading for college. District 4 maintains 2 elementary schools, 2 middle schools, and 1 high school.

HOME SCHOOLING

Parents who wish to teach their children at home can do so and should contact the school system in their county for specific guidelines and assistance. Standards are strict, so the number of home schooled students fluctuates. Call (843) 937-6590 to find out more about home schooling in Charleston County. In Berkeley County, call (843) 899-8618 or (843) 723-4627, ext. 8618; in Dorchester County, call (843) 873-2901.

PRIVATE SCHOOLS

There is an excellent selection of over 100 independent schools in the area, ranging from parochial to all-girl. Some offer financial aid, and most sponsor open houses on campus for visitors. A good source for more information on private educational options in the Lowcountry is the Tri-County Admissions Council, which publishes an informational brochure complete with locator map, phone numbers, and important facts about member schools. A copy of this publication is available from local Realtors or the Charleston Metro Chamber of Commerce. Write for a copy to P.O. Box 39612, Charleston, SC 29407 or visit the website www.chastac.org. For contacts at nonmember schools, check the telephone directory. The following list of private schools is a sampling of what is available in the Greater Charleston area.

ADDLESTONE HEBREW ACADEMY
1639 Raoul Wallenberg Blvd.
(843) 571-1105
www.addlestone.org
Addlestone accepts children from 18 months through grade 8 and provides secular as well as religious training. Conversational Hebrew classes are offered along with a full curriculum in the elementary grades.

ARCHIBALD RUTLEDGE ACADEMY
1011 Old Cemetery Rd., McClellanville
(843) 887-3323
www.archibaldrutledgeacademy.com
The Archibald Rutledge Academy, named for the South Carolina poet laureate, offers full college preparatory and general curricula for students in K4 through grade 12. The school's small classes and updated facilities, as well as an emphasis on surrounding ecological and cultural resources, are important features.

ASHLEY HALL
172 Rutledge Ave.
(843) 722-2854
www.ashleyhall.org
Founded in 1909, Ashley Hall is a college preparatory day school dedicated to educating girls from age 2 through grade 12. It remains the only all-girl independent school in the state. A full 100 percent of the school's graduates are accepted by colleges and universities across the nation. The school's early childhood program also admits boys ages 2 to 4.

BISHOP ENGLAND HIGH SCHOOL
363 Seven Farms Dr.
(843) 849-9599
www.behs.com

EDUCATION

Bishop England High School is a Roman Catholic coeducational secondary school operated under the auspices of the Diocese of Charleston. Grouping by academic ability is a unique feature of the school, whereby students of similar abilities are placed together for concentrated instruction. In summer 1998 the school relocated from its downtown campus to a state-of-the-art high school on a 40-acre site on Daniel Island. (See the Neighborhoods chapter for more on Daniel Island.)

CATHOLIC SCHOOLS
1662 Ingram Rd.
(843) 402-9115
www.catholic-doc.org
A full academic curriculum with all basic disciplines is offered at all 8 Lowcountry Catholic elementary, middle, and high schools, in addition to the study of religion and Christian values. The schools are Blessed Sacrament, Christ Our King-Stella Maris, Divine Redeemer, Nativity School, St. John's Catholic School and the Charleston Catholic School, Summerville Catholic School, and Bishop England (see previous listing). For more information, contact the Catholic schools office at the address listed above.

CHARLES TOWNE MONTESSORI
SCHOOL
56 Leinbach Dr.
(843) 571-1140
www.charlestownemontessori.org
Situated on a 12-acre wooded campus in West Ashley, Charles Towne Montessori accepts children from 3 months through grade 6. The school offers a learning environment in keeping with Montessori principles, encouraging creative expression in all aspects of a child's development. There

is a studio program for the arts as well as an after-school sports program.

CHARLESTON COLLEGIATE SCHOOL
2024 Academy Dr., Johns Island
(843) 559-5506
www.charlestoncollegiate.org
Charleston Collegiate School, on a 30-acre site in the middle of Johns Island, offers a college preparatory curriculum stressing the fundamentals in all academic disciplines. The school accepts qualified students age 4 through grade 12.

CHARLESTON DAY SCHOOL
15 Archdale St.
(843) 722-7791, ext. 2
www.charlestondayschool.org
Charleston Day School is a coed day school enrolling about 185 students in grades 1 through 8. Graduates go on to local secondary schools and a variety of preparatory schools around the country.

FIRST BAPTIST CHURCH SCHOOL
48 Meeting St.
(843) 722-6646
www.fbschool.org
First Baptist Church School, established in 1949, offers a college preparatory education in a Christian setting for children age 3 through grade 12. The academic curriculum is enriched by Bible study and extracurricular activities.

JAMES ISLAND CHRISTIAN SCHOOL
15 Crosscreek Dr.
(843) 795-1762
www.jics.org
James Island Christian is a ministry of James Island Christian Church. It offers an interdenominational, comprehensive curriculum

for students in K4 through grade 12. The school's standards exceed the requirements for entrance into most colleges.

MASON PREPARATORY SCHOOL
56 Halsey Blvd.
(843) 803-6015
www.masonprep.org
The mission of Mason Preparatory School is to provide a solid academic foundation to students in grades 1 through 8. In addition to a well-rounded curriculum, a wide variety of after-school activities is offered.

NORTHSIDE CHRISTIAN SCHOOL
7800 Northside Dr., North Charleston
(843) 797-2690
www.northsideministries.com
Northside is a Christian school offering a complete educational program for students age 3 through grade 12. In addition to general, college preparatory, and advanced placement instruction, a fifth-quarter summer program is available.

NORTHWOOD ACADEMY
2263 Otranto Rd., North Charleston
(843) 764-2285
www.northwoodacademy.com
Northwood Academy has small classes emphasizing the basics in both college preparatory and honors level courses for students in K4 through 12. The school offers Biblical integration in their curriculum, chorus, drama, and athletic programs.

PINEWOOD PREPARATORY SCHOOL
1114 Old Orangeburg Rd., Summerville
(843) 873-1643
www.pinewoodprep.com
This coeducational, college preparatory day school enrolls 700 students in preschool through grade 12. It offers a full developmental preschool starting at age 3, a kindergarten program, and a challenging academic program for all students. A full athletic program and extracurricular activities, such as art and music studies, student literary productions, and special interest clubs, are available.

PORTER-GAUD SCHOOL
300 Albemarle Rd.
(843) 402-4775
www.portergaud.edu
Episcopal-affiliated Porter-Gaud is a coeducational, college preparatory school with students in grades 1 through 12. All of its graduates go on to 4-year colleges. In addition to its strong academic program, participation in a wide variety of sports and extracurricular activities is encouraged at all grade levels of this school on a West Ashley campus.

ST. JOHN'S CHRISTIAN ACADEMY
204 W. Main St., Moncks Corner
(843) 761-8539
www.sjcacavaliers.com
St. John's (formerly known as Lord Berkeley Academy) is a coeducational, college preparatory day school for students age 3 through grade 12. In addition to academics, St. John's offers extracurricular activities such as athletics and service clubs.

ST. PAUL'S ACADEMY
5139 Gibson Rd., Hollywood
(843) 889-2702
www.stpaulscountryday.org
St. Paul's Academy provides academic instruction in a nondenominational Christian atmosphere. Students age 2 through grade

8 attend classes on a 10-acre consolidated campus.

TRIDENT ACADEMY

1455 Wakendaw Rd., Mount Pleasant
(843) 884-3494
www.tridentacademy.com
Trident Academy serves children age 5 through grade 12 who have been diagnosed with learning disabilities. The basic philosophy at Trident is to teach students to compensate for their differences in learning, allowing them to mainstream as quickly as possible.

COLLEGES & UNIVERSITIES

Higher education has been a priority in the Lowcountry since the founding of the College of Charleston in 1770. Today there are many academic institutions of advanced learning with expansive, formal campuses and wide-ranging course offerings. In addition, there are junior colleges, business colleges, and branches of out-of-state colleges and universities in the Trident area. Major institutions with strong ties to Greater Charleston are described below.

CHARLESTON SCHOOL OF LAW

P.O. Box 535, Charleston, SC 29402
(843) 329-1000
www.charlestonlaw.edu
Tracing its origins back to 1825 when the Forensic Club was founded by a group of Charleston attorneys, the Charleston School of Law is carrying on the tradition in the present day. The Forensic Club offered lectures on law essentially starting the earliest law education in the South. The new school offers full- and part-time courses of study to college graduates interested in pursuing a career in the legal profession. Completion of the requirements for eligibility for a Juris Doctor degree may be reached in 3 years of full-time course work or 4 years for part-time. One goal for the school, in addition to preparation for successful SC Bar passage, is to encourage the practice of law for providing public service and to coordinate legal outreach programs. All students are required to participate in pro bono and externship work in the community. Approximately 500 students attend the Charleston School of Law, one of two law schools in the state.

CHARLESTON SOUTHERN UNIVERSITY

9200 University Blvd., Charleston
(843) 863-7000
www.csuniv.edu
When it was founded in 1964, Charleston Southern was called Baptist College—the only church-affiliated college in the area. Now elevated to university status and ranked as the second-largest church-affiliated university in the state, it offers 33 undergraduate degrees as well as master's degrees in business administration, education, nursing, and criminal justice. The student body has grown from an enrollment of 528 to more than 3,000. Sponsored by the South Carolina Baptist Convention, Charleston Southern University remains committed to its mission of "promoting academic excellence in a Christian environment."

THE CITADEL

171 Moultrie St.
(843) 953-5000
www.citadel.edu
Consistently ranked by *U.S. News and World Report* as one of the South's best colleges, The Citadel is a state-supported military college with an enrollment of more than 2,000 cadets. The 150-year, all-male tradition of

the school was challenged in court, and the college accepted its first female cadets in fall 1996, with more entering every year.

With a formal campus and regimented activities, The Citadel combines academic requirements with military training in the areas of discipline, responsiveness, and leadership. Students select from 19 baccalaureate degree programs and must complete eight semesters of Air Force, Army, Navy, or Marine ROTC training, but they are not required to accept military commissions. Some undergraduate and a wide selection of graduate courses—including those leading to master's degrees in business administration, arts, science, and education—are offered through The Citadel Graduate College.

The Citadel Archives contain some very impressive collections: In 1966 Gen. Mark W. Clark, president emeritus of The Citadel, donated his personal, military, and official papers covering his career as commander of the Fifth Army in World War II, the Austrian Occupation, and the Korean War. Other notable collections include the Civil War letters of Gen. Ellison Capers (Citadel class of 1857) and the papers of Pulitzer Prize–winning historian Bruce Catton.

COLLEGE OF CHARLESTON
66 George St.
(843) 805-5507
www.cofc.edu
Recognized as the first municipal college in the United States and the oldest institution of higher learning in South Carolina, the College of Charleston (founded in 1770) offers a broad range of undergraduate majors. This thriving academic institution provides a liberal arts education to 11,500 undergraduate and graduate students. The graduate studies program is called the Graduate School of the College of Charleston and offers degrees in such areas as education, marine biology, and public administration. The student–faculty ratio is 16 to 1, and 85 percent of the faculty members hold doctorates or the highest degree in their field. The college was named one of the best institutions for undergraduate education according to *The Princeton Review*'s 2008 edition of *The Best 368 Colleges*.

Three original buildings made up the College of Charleston for nearly 200 years. Now more than 100 buildings—from historic structures to high-tech classrooms—constitute the campus in the heart of historic downtown Charleston. Within this setting, the college showcases beautiful landscaping with botanical displays for every season.

MEDICAL UNIVERSITY OF SOUTH CAROLINA
171 Ashley Ave.
(843) 792-2300
www.musc.edu
The oldest medical school in the South, MUSC was founded in 1824 and now is at the center of the largest medical complex in the state. The MUSC campus consists of 89 buildings covering 76 acres in downtown Charleston. The university includes 6 colleges—medicine, nursing, health-related professions, pharmacy, dental medicine, and graduate studies. Student enrollment is 2,400, with a teaching staff of more than 1,000 full-time. The university coordinates statewide training of more than 800 interns and residents. Patient care is provided within the Medical University of South Carolina Medical Center (see the Health Care chapter), and faculty research is encouraged through facilities, funds, and administrative support provided by MUSC. MUSC is joining Johns

Hopkins, Duke, the University of Kentucky, Case Western Reserve, Washington University, and University of Maryland to increase public awareness of its academic and clinical opportunities for medical students.

TRIDENT TECHNICAL COLLEGE
7000 Rivers Ave., North Charleston

i **It's another one of those perfectly Southern traditions the Low-country is famous for: At graduation exercises each spring at Ashley Hall, college-bound girls descend the spiral staircase at McBee House (ca. 1816) in long white dresses with armloads of red roses.**

(843) 574-6111, (877) 349-7184
www.tridenttech.edu
Trident Technical College is part of the state system and offers 2-year programs for a variety of technical degrees. Trident Technical College also offers continuing education courses and customized training for business, industry, and government, helping to promote economic development in Charleston, Berkeley, and Dorchester Counties.

Merging with Palmer College (a private business college in downtown Charleston) in 1973, adding its Berkeley campus near Moncks Corner and a job training site in Hollywood, SC, and expanding its main campus in North Charleston gave Trident Tech a four-campus network. Among the newest additions are the Complex for Industrial and Economic Development and the Culinary Institute of Charleston adjacent to the main campus, the Veterinary Technology Building on the Berkeley campus, and the St. Paul's Parish (Hollywood) site in southern Charleston County.

The four campuses together serve around 12,000 undergraduate students, and 20,000 take continuing education classes each year. More than 150 associate degree, diploma, and certificate programs are offered. The curriculum includes programs in aeronautical studies; humanities and social sciences; business technology; health sciences; nursing; law-related services; hospitality, tourism, and culinary arts; community, family, and child services; science and mathematics; and industrial and engineering technology. Classes are offered days, evenings, and weekends.

CHARLESTON COUNTY LIBRARY SYSTEM

Twelve years in the making (from the public bond referendum for expansion of the library system to construction of the new main library), the new downtown location of the Charleston County Public Library opened in the spring of 1998. The library building, relocated on Calhoun Street, is almost two and a half times larger than its previous site on King Street. The old 200,000-volume library now has more than 300,000 books, with a capacity for 570,000. The handsome edifice is a 3-level structure with ground-level covered parking offering the first hour free with library validation. The first floor contains cataloging, circulation desks, fiction, large print, and young adult books and audiovisual materials. Expanded children's services include a youth services librarian and a children's story room. Conference rooms and a larger auditorium are available for public use.

The top floor houses the reference desk and materials, periodicals, nonfiction books, and the South Carolina Room. Banks of computers are available for research and general word processing by library patrons. Check it out, along with any of the other branch locations:

MAIN LIBRARY
68 Calhoun St.
(843) 805-6930
www.ccpl.org

COOPER RIVER MEMORIAL LIBRARY
3503 Rivers Ave., North Charleston
(843) 744-2489

DORCHESTER ROAD REGIONAL LIBRARY
6325 Dorchester Rd., North Charleston
(843) 552-6466

EDGAR ALLAN POE LIBRARY
1921 I'on Ave., Sullivan's Island
(843) 883-3914

EDISTO ISLAND LIBRARY
Thomas Hall, Trinity Episcopal Church
1589 SR 174, Edisto Island
(843) 869-2355

FOLLY BEACH LIBRARY
55 Center St., Folly Beach
(843) 588-2001

i For those Charleston County residents who are permanently or temporarily homebound, the Charleston County Library offers Books by Mail (also audio books, music CDs, videos, and DVDs) for free. Those interested must apply by calling (843) 805-6878 or by visiting the website at www.ccpl.org.

HOLLYWOOD/ST. PAUL'S LIBRARY
5151 Town Council Dr., Hollywood
(843) 889-3300

JAMES ISLAND LIBRARY
1248 Camp Rd.
(843) 795-6679

JOHN L. DART LIBRARY
1067 King St.
(843) 722-7550

JOHNS ISLAND REGIONAL LIBRARY
3531 Manybank Hwy.
(843) 559-1945

MCCLELLANVILLE LIBRARY
222 Baker St., McClellanville
(843) 887-3699

MOUNT PLEASANT REGIONAL LIBRARY
1133 Mathis Ferry Rd., Mount Pleasant
(843) 849-6161

OTRANTO ROAD REGIONAL LIBRARY
2261 Otranto Rd., North Charleston
(843) 572-4094

ST. ANDREWS PARISH REGIONAL LIBRARY
1735 North Woodmere Dr.
(843) 766-2546

VILLAGE LIBRARY
430 Whilden St., Mount Pleasant
(843) 884-9741

WEST ASHLEY LIBRARY
45 Windermere Blvd.
(843) 766-6635

BOOKMOBILE
(843) 805-6881

CHILD CARE

Because many Charleston-area families are of the single- or two-career, working-parent varieties, there is a real need in the Lowcountry for full-time child-care facilities—reputable establishments that provide quality care for children from the early morning until after regular work hours.

The options that are out there for full-day, extended-hour centers are easy to obtain. The phone book and the local social services office are two good places to start. In this chapter, we provide some helpful hints to assist you in your search for this type of care provider, but we have concentrated on alternative care options and harder-to-find services and support groups.

WHERE TO START

South Carolina licenses day-care centers only if they maintain standards in areas such as cleanliness, acceptable child-to-caregiver ratios, and adequate space-per-child allotments. There are three levels of regulation for child care facilities in the state.

- **Level 1: Regulated.** Meets basic requirements of the Department of Social Services, Division of Child Day Care Licensing and Regulatory Services, including fingerprinting and background check on all caregivers.
- **Level 2: ABC Enhanced.** Means that child care providers voluntarily meet higher educational requirements and are monitored (unannounced) yearly.
- **Level 3: NAEYC Accreditation.** Equates to even higher standards and accreditation through the National Association for the Education of Young Children.

Call the local office of the South Carolina Department of Social Services at (843) 953-9780 or (800) 260-0211 to request more detailed information about this process. A visit to http://childcare.sc.gov listings gives the licensed or registered child care providers by county. We encourage parents to investigate some of the options, listen for word-of-mouth tips, and read the classified section of the daily newspaper, the *Post and Courier*, for additional possibilities. Another helpful source of information is the Trident United Way's Child Care Resource & Referral program. Started in 2001, the free program provides education and guidance for finding quality child care, answers questions, and offers referrals based on a family's individual needs. Call (843) 747-9900 or (877) 227-3454, or visit www.tuw.org to access the information.

Before you make a decision about where to take your child, make sure the operation's license is up-to-date and the implemented programs fit your preference in terms of structure or freedom. Nose around the playground and check out the general atmosphere, but remember that this is real life, and kids will be kids. You could stumble upon a bad day for everyone at a good day-care or early childhood center. But overall, you should expect a day-care center to take care of your child in a way similar to a babysitter and expect an early childhood center to teach your child according to his or her age of development. Choose a center that allows drop-ins from parents, then, do so regularly to ensure the center meets your standards.

i If you are a visitor to the Charleston area or a local parent, Lowcountry Kidsitters Inc. offers a babysitting referral service. Contact the Kidsitters at (843) 881-1862 or www .lowcountrykidsitters.com for details on scheduling a responsible sitter to watch the kids in your hotel room or your home on your next evening out.

There seem to be more centers in West Ashley and in other parts of Greater Charleston than on the Peninsula, and we hear parents complaining about that fact all the time. Mount Pleasant residents have convenient access to several good child care facilities. Often there are waiting lists at these establishments, so it would be a good idea to think ahead and get your name on a few. We recommend you schedule visits during the center's working hours, so you will have a chance to observe the children, the care providers, and the facilities on a normal day.

The following listings will give you a rundown on some child care resources that can help guide you in your search for the most compatible solution for you and your child's needs. We have created a category with alternatives to traditional day-care centers, such as AuPairCare and Mother's Morning Out. While these are not total child care solutions, they are wonderful options. Samplings of some parent support groups and children's classes are included as well. Omitted are private, business-affiliated child care operations run strictly for the children of employees, as they are closed to the public.

MOTHER'S MORNING OUT

Local Area Churches

Depending upon the age of the children, Mother's Morning Out programs are offered throughout Lowcountry churches two or three mornings a week. They usually take newborns through preschool and kindergarten ages. You do not necessarily have to be a member of the church to enroll your child, but church members are given first priority.

AN INTERNATIONAL OPTION

If you are able to provide lodging and would enjoy a cultural exchange experience to enhance your child's learning environment, you might consider contacting an au pair placement service. AuPairCare, at (800) 428-7247 or www.aupaircare.com, can help put you in touch with a live-in caregiver. This service arranges for English-speaking au pairs from over 40 countries between ages 18 and 26 to come to the United States for a year. Host families supply lodging, meals, and a salary in return for 45 hours of child care a week.

Unlike employees, au pairs usually end up becoming much like family members, sharing meals and social occasions. A local community counselor is on hand to help the year go smoothly for both the au pair and the family. The folks we know who have used au pairs say it is a fun way to help solve the child care problem and broaden their children's vision of world boundaries.

Get the Lowdown on Lowcountry Child Care

The *Lowcountry Parent* is the Charleston area's parenting magazine full of good tips and information on education, family-oriented businesses, health and fitness, plus a calendar of family fun events. Pick up a free copy monthly and learn about preschools, camps, time management, birthday party planning, and other parent-helpful topics. You'll find the *Lowcountry Parent* at branch libraries, schools, health care offices, and local businesses, or call (843) 958-7394, or visit www.lowcountryparent.com.

RESOURCES & SUPPORT GROUPS

The Charleston County Library maintains a Community Information Database that lists more than 800 different organizations under subject categories such as education, child care, counseling, community service and civic organizations, hospital and medical associations, parenting, recreation, and support groups. The directory is available for reference at the Charleston County Library and online at http://ccpl.org.

FAMILY SERVICES INC.
4925 Lacross Rd., Ste. 215, North Charleston
(843) 735-7802, (800) 232-6489, ext. 7802
www.fsisc.org

Family Services, founded in 1888, is a private, nonprofit organization offering a full range of services designed to meet the needs of Trident-area families in the home, workplace, and community. The counseling staff is composed of social workers, marriage and family therapists, educational specialists, and budget and debt management counselors. Education and assistance are offered through seminars and workshops focusing on stress management, parenting, divorce adjustment, and self-esteem. Family Services groups have addressed anger management, helping children cope with divorce, and family violence intervention. For more information on sessions, fees, and the complete range of services, call one of the listed numbers.

HOTLINE—2-1-1
P.O. Box 63305, Charleston, SC 29419
(843) 747-3007 (office),
(843) 744-HELP, (800) 922-2283, (843) 747-TEEN, (866) 873-TEEN
www.tuw.org/211
Run by Trident United Way, the 2-1-1 Hotline provides a caring ear with information and referral services 24 hours a day to anyone in crisis or facing a problem. A Teen line is available for middle and high school students for discussing problems and concerns with others their own age. Educational programs and support groups are offered on a confidential and free basis. The 2-1-1 Hotline compiles a frequently updated volume, the Tri-County Resource Directory, with cross-referenced listings of community organizations to assist families, which is available at the Charleston County Library, or you may request a copy by calling the office number.

LIFE MANAGEMENT CENTER
628 St. Andrew's Blvd., Summerville
(843) 852-5705
www.lifemanagement.org
The Life Management Center helps people with learning differences and attention deficit disorder (ADD/ADHD), as well as their families. Its services include individualized academic instruction, coaching, and time management and organizational strategies. Seminars, consultations, support groups, and referral services round out this valuable resource aimed at creating success for children and adults. A second location is at 1114 Orangeburg Rd.

MAYOR'S OFFICE FOR CHILDREN, YOUTH, AND FAMILIES
50 Broad St.
(843) 965-4190
www.charleston-sc.gov
This group serves as a clearinghouse for information about resources available to children, youth, and their families in the Trident area. The commission meets quarterly Sept through June. The office provides information about area organizations involved in day-care, youth services, mentoring programs, infant and child health, parenting, and support groups.

MOUNT PLEASANT & CHARLESTON AREA MOMS CLUBS
Various locations
(843) 278-8157
www.momsclub.org
The MOMS Clubs of Mount Pleasant and Charleston were started as chapters of the national support group for mothers who stay at home with their children or work part time. The group's broad range of activities includes special programs for mothers, play

LIVING HERE

Mom Knows Best

Another helpful publication to keep handy (maybe in the car) is *Moms in the Know.* This guidebook for families in Charleston has sections such as "One's on the Way" (announcements, fitness, maternity clothes), "Doctor, Doctor" (family medicine, dentists), "Home Sweet Home" (housekeepers, contractors, realtors), "Not Just the Bear Necessities" (clothing, gifts, haircuts), "School Days" (child care, schools), "Out and About" (camps and community events), "Time Out! For Moms" (baby sitting, salons/spa, homebased businesses), and much more. It is a free pickup at retail locations and public libraries, or visit www.momsintheknow.com.

---

groups for children, and get-togethers for the whole family. Recent guest speakers presented talks on subjects such as college savings plans and children's dental care. The Mount Pleasant Dunes West (anyone living in a community with a main entrance off of SR 41) MOMS Club meets the first and third Thurs of each month at the Dunes West Golf Club (3003 Dunes West Blvd.; momsclub-mtpn@yahoo.com). The Park West group (anyone living north of SR 41) meets the third Fri of the month (momsclub-mtppw@yahoo.com). The Mount Pleasant South club is for those living south of US 17 (momsclubmp@hotmail.com). There are Moms Clubs in the Summerville and Goose Creek areas as well. The Charleston Club does not hold regular meetings, but call the number listed to learn about activities. There is an annual fee of $25. You may visit the first time for free to check it out. Children are always welcome at the meetings.

PARENTING CLASSES

BIG BROTHER/BIG SISTER CLASS

Bon Secours–St. Francis Hospital,
2095 Henry Tecklenburg Dr.
(843) 402-2273
www.rsfh.com

This sibling class is a fun way to help children prepare for their new role as big brother or sister. Games, a short film, refreshments, and a trip to see the babies in the nursery are all part of this class. It meets one Thurs evening or one Sat morning at St. Francis each month (also less often at Roper Hospital at 316 Calhoun St.), and parents should schedule attendance during the last month of pregnancy. The class is free and is designed for children ages 3 and older. Call the number above to register. Roper St. Francis Healthcare also offers classes on childbirth preparation, breastfeeding, and infant CPR. For more details visit their website.

MEDIA

As a result of relaxed federal ownership rules, the shift toward consolidation in media has swept across the nation's print and broadcast industries, and the Charleston market has been no exception. Local, privately owned Evening Post Publishing Co., publisher of Charleston's daily newspaper, *The Post and Courier,* has expanded its holdings across the media spectrum. The company owns 11 television stations in Texas, Montana, Colorado, Arizona, Louisiana, California, and Kentucky, and 10 newspapers in South Carolina, three in North Carolina, one in Texas, and internationally, one in London.

This national trend is evident in the local radio and television businesses also. Covington, Kentucky–based Jacor Communications Inc., and New York–based Wicks Broadcast Group purchased radio stations in the Charleston market. More switches took place when Clear Channel Communications of San Antonio, Texas, bought up Jacor's four stations while adding an AM talk radio format station. Most of the stations consistently rank highly in the Arbitron ratings. Citadel Broadcasting Corp., based out of New York, gobbled up the Wicks Group's stations in a move to grow its eastern expansion. This purchase of combined listenership is said to reach about 40 percent of the Charleston market.

Overall, the radio market is young and trendy in its tastes, and the local stations respond accordingly. There are numerous choices on the dial in the Charleston area, and formats change frequently as a result of the fierce competition among the national broadcast groups and the independent stations. One constant, however, is a large following for Christian, "family" radio in the Lowcountry.

OVERVIEW

Sinclair Broadcast Group of Baltimore, Maryland, has boosted its television holdings in midsize markets with aggressive expansions. Locally, the group purchased two stations, WTAT-TV (Fox Network) and WMMP-TV (MyTvNetwork). Sinclair, one of the country's biggest broadcasting companies, owns or provides programming to 58 TV stations in 35 markets. Recent purchases have increased the company's reach to about 22 percent of US television households.

The Greater Charleston area ranks 100th among the nation's television markets. There are affiliates for all three major television networks, plus Fox Broadcasting and the Public Broadcasting System. The larger cable television providers are Comcast Cablevision, serving the Greater Charleston area, Johns Island, Folly Beach, Kiawah/Seabrook, and Wild Dunes, (843) 554-4100; and Time Warner, (843) 871-7000, in the Summerville and Georgetown areas. Be sure to check in your specific area, since new cable, Internet, and mobile communications providers are springing up across the Lowcountry.

NEWSPAPERS

Daily

THE POST AND COURIER
134 Columbus St.
(843) 577-7111
www.postandcourier.com

As the oldest daily newspaper in the South, *The Post and Courier* is published by Evening Post Publishing. Today's newspaper is actually the combination of two of the town's longtime daily papers. *The News and Courier*, founded in 1803, and *The Evening Post*, founded in 1894, merged as *The Post and Courier* on October 1, 1991.

Tabloid sections are published highlighting business news on Mondays (Business Review) and entertainment on Thursdays (Charleston Scene). Weekly neighborhood sections are published every Thurs and provide local news to the communities making up the Trident area. Daily paid circulation is 88,939; the number for Sunday is 95,289. Similar to newspapers across the country, their online readership is growing daily.

Through the years, the staff has won numerous *Associated Press* awards and has been recognized for excellence by the Society for Professional Journalists. Editorially conservative, *The Post and Courier* gives the liberal point of view a nod on its op-ed page. However, the best airing of liberal opinion in the Lowcountry market will be found on the broadcast television stations.

Weekly

AIRLIFT DISPATCH (USAF)
102 East Hill Blvd., Ste. 223, Charleston AFB
(843) 963-5608
www.charlestonmilitary.com

With 7,500 copies printed each week, this exclusive Charleston Air Force Base newspaper is published 50 weeks per year (excluding the two Fridays after Christmas). The paper covers base and military news. The *Dispatch* is distributed to on-base private residences and to 60 pick-up points throughout the base.

BERKELEY INDEPENDENT
323-B East Main St., Moncks Corner
(843) 761-6397
www. berkeleyind.com

The *Berkeley Independent* is a community-based weekly appearing on Wednesdays. Circulation is 8,000, which is the largest paid distribution of any weekly in South Carolina. The Independent covers the economic, recreational, school, and entertainment news in Moncks Corner and surrounding, fast-growing Berkeley County.

CATALYST (MUSC NEWSPAPER)
135 Cannon St.
(843) 792-4107
www.musc.edu/catalyst

Published weekly, with 5,400 free copies distributed every Thursday evening, this tabloid is the Medical University of South Carolina's faculty and staff newspaper. Text and editorial content are produced by MUSC's public relations department. This publication reaches the highest concentration of degree-holding professionals in South Carolina. Dealing with issues of the medical community (including grants, awards, educational news, nursing, and medical breakthroughs), the *Catalyst* is highly respected among members of the medical profession.

CHARLESTON MERCURY
134 Columbus St.
(843) 937-5547
www.charlestonmercury.com

The *Charleston Mercury* was launched in March 2000 by way of the Internet and soon made its way into newsprint, mailing 18,000 copies every other week to households downtown, West Ashley, James Island, East Cooper, and Kiawah. This community newspaper with a "cosmopolitan attitude" presents a different perspective on news, analysis, and opinion. The *Mercury* covers a wide variety of information from correspondents' reports from Europe, South America, Africa, and beyond to the local hunting and fishing scene from a conservation viewpoint. Also included are the fine arts, family profiles (both historical and present-day), gardening, the buzz about town, travel, wine, and fine dining. The overall mission is to honor the region's rich cultural heritage and the individuals and organizations that nurture it, making the *Mercury* an entertaining and stimulating read.

CHARLESTON CHRONICLE
1111 King St.
(843) 723-2785

This African-American-oriented weekly is published on Wednesday. Paid circulation is 6,000. Covering the Greater Charleston area, the *Chronicle* deals with issues related to African-Americans, including news on schools, religion, business, and politics.

THE DANIEL ISLAND NEWS
225 Seven Farms Dr., Ste. 108, Daniel Island
(843) 856-1999
www.thedanielislandnews.com

Covering the community of Daniel Island (see the Neighborhoods chapter) since 2003, *The Daniel Island News* is published on Thursdays and distributed free throughout the island. This independently owned and operated weekly is available for pick-up at businesses on the island as well as Mount Pleasant, downtown Charleston, and Hanahan. The distribution is 8,000.

THE GAZETTE
104 E. Doty Ave., Summerville
(843) 572-0511
www.ourgazette.com

The Gazette covers news of Goose Creek and Berkeley County and is published Thursdays. The free distribution is 13,000 copies. *The Gazette* focuses on business and industry news due to the industrial growth in the county over the last several years. Local features also cover school and church news.

HANAHAN GOOSE CREEK NORTH CHARLESTON NEWS
1231 Yeaman's Hall Rd., North Charleston
(843) 744-8000

This community-oriented weekly covers news of Hanahan, Goose Creek, North Charleston, and part of Berkeley County. It is published on Wednesdays. Circulation is 12,000. Church, school, and local news is covered.

JAMES ISLAND JOURNAL
134 Columbus St.
(843) 577-7111
www.jamesislandjournal.com

The *James Island Journal* carries community news for James Island and Folly Beach. It is published every Thurs as a part of *The Post and Courier*. Paid circulation and rack sales are 7,299.

MOULTRIE NEWS
134 Columbus St.
(843) 571-7111
www.moultrienews.com
This is a free weekly carrying community news for Mount Pleasant, Sullivan's Island, Daniel Island, and Isle of Palms. The focus is on the happenings in this fast-growing, East Cooper community. Published on Wednesdays, its total market coverage is 28,225.

SUMMERVILLE JOURNAL SCENE
104 East Doty Ave., Summerville
(843) 873-9424
www. journalscene.com
This community paper is published on Wed and Fri with comprehensive coverage of the Summerville area and Dorchester County. National wire reports are interspersed with local news and features. The total distribution is 27,000.

Tabloids

The tabloid press in Greater Charleston is on the upswing, with several special-interest newspapers holding sway against the long-time survivors in this highly competitive advertising market.

CAROLINA ARTS
P.O. Drawer 427, Bonneau, SC 29431
(843) 825-3408
www.carolinaarts.com
Published by Shoestring Publishing Co., this is a free monthly publication distributed throughout the Carolinas as a voice for the local arts scene. The writers take on difficult and controversial subjects (such as arts funding) and do extensive background research. Reviews of local arts offerings and gallery profiles are standard fare, and you'll find a comprehensive calendar of each state's arts exhibitions, shows, and special events. The publication was formerly known as *Charleston Arts,* which appeared in the Lowcountry from 1987 to 1994, and as *South Carolina Arts,* from 1995 to 1996.

CHARLESTON CITY PAPER
1049 B Morrison Dr.
(843) 577-5304
www.charlestoncitypaper.com
This alternative, weekly entertainment and review tabloid is a voice for Charleston's way-cool crowd. It is the successor to *Upwith,* which the Jones Street Publishers took over in 1997. The owners renamed the tab and have picked up the following of the college and young adult set. Look for reviews of the local club scene, movies, dining, and commentary on the area arts in general. *City Paper* circulation is 40,000, and copies are found in area restaurants and cafes, clothing stores, and college campus locations.

CHARLESTON NAVY SHORELINE
Naval Weapons Station Charleston, 2316 Red Bank Rd., Bldg. 84, Goose Creek
(843) 764-4094
www. charlestonmilitary.com
Published every other Fri, this tab is the official publication of the Charleston Naval Weapons Station. Started in June 2000, it covers the Navy news for the government and civilian employees in Charleston. Its 5,000 circulation is distributed free on base and to all base housing.

CHARLESTON REGIONAL BUSINESS JOURNAL
389 Johnnie Dodds Blvd., Ste. 200, Mount Pleasant
(843) 849-3100
www.charlestonbusiness.com
Tapping into the success of business journal tabloids around the country, Charleston Regional Business Journal, now published by SCBiz News, was launched in 1995 by Setcom, Inc. After a year of providing in-depth business news coverage on a monthly basis, the publication doubled its frequency to twice a month In 1997. It is distributed free to area businesses with five or more employees, or it may be purchased by subscription. The circulation is 10,000.

ISLAND LIFE
P.O. Box 447, John's Island, SC 29457
(843) 768-4404
http://islandlife.homestead.com
This monthly tabloid is delivered to seven sea islands in the Lowcountry: Edisto, Folly Beach, James Island, Johns Island, Kiawah, Seabrook, and Wadmalaw. It's also distributed in the downtown Charleston area, parts of Mount Pleasant and Beaufort, SC, and wherever books and newspapers are sold. Total circulation is 8,000 copies. Editorial content includes community news, entertainment, natural history, and political articles.

SKIRT!
7 Radcliffe St., Ste. 302
(843) 958-0028
www.charleston.skirt.com
This trendy monthly tabloid, launched in 1994, is dedicated to, but is not always exclusively about, women. It presents what's happening as viewed from the female perspective. Top-notch writers and smart, contemporary graphics make this idea really work. News, features, and regular columnists deal with local and national trends, political issues, creative arts, motherhood, and relationships—all delivered with a little cheek. In fact, Skirt! has dubbed itself "the monthly newspaper with an attitude." Total circulation is 30,000, and the tab is a free pickup available throughout the Lowcountry.

VIDA LATINA
The Mundial Group, 111 West 28th St., Ste. 2A, New York, NY 10001
(770) 698-9992, (877) 571-9824
www.vidalatina.cc
This all-Spanish language newspaper serves the rapidly growing population of Hispanics in South Carolina, Georgia, and North Carolina. It covers local as well as international news stories of special interest to its Spanish-speaking readership. The free publication distributes 15,000 papers every month to Lowcountry locations that cater to Hispanic patrons, primarily Mexican stores and restaurants.

MAGAZINES

CHARLESTON GATEWAY
P.O. Box 80626, Charleston, SC 29416
(843) 626-8911
www.charlestongateway.com
Charleston Gateway, founded in 1955, annually distributes 600,000 free copies to area hotels, motels, restaurants, galleries, and information centers. Issued every three months, this pocket-size publication is a handy guide to sightseeing, dining, shopping, and cooking. It contains a three-month calendar of events, a map of the Greater Charleston area, and a Peninsula street map.

CHARLESTON MAGAZINE
782 Johnnie Dodds Blvd., Ste. C, Mount Pleasant
(843) 971-9811
www.charlestonmag.com
Charleston Magazine provides Charleston residents and visitors a lively, informative, entertaining, and sophisticated resource about the Peninsula and outlying districts on a monthly basis. Colorful features are offered on homes, gardens and architecture, dining, health and fitness, arts and entertainment, travel and style. Profiles of the region's most provocative and influential personalities, essays, and opinion columns tackle some of the tougher issues and concerns facing Lowcountry residents. Also in the family of magazines published by Gulfstream Communications are *Charleston Home* and *Charleston Weddings.Charleston Magazine* has a circulation of 37,200 and is available on newsstands or by subscription.

WHERE CHARLESTON
www.wheretraveler.com
Where Charleston is the local edition of the Where tour and travel publications currently in many markets around the country. Color-coded pages make it easy to find children's activities, golf course listings, a calendar of events, dining, tours, lodging, and maps. It is spiced up with short editorial features on local folklore, historical spots, nature trips, and other points of interest. The publication can be picked up in hotels, motels, restaurants, retail outlets, and visitor centers.

TELEVISION

Three major cable providers serve the Greater Charleston area, so network channel numbers vary in different towns. Comcast Cable (www.comcast.com, 843-554-4100) serves Charleston, Johns Island, Folly Beach, Kiawah, Seabrook, Wadmalaw, Wild Dunes, Awendaw, Edisto Beach, and the Hollywood-Ravenel area. Time Warner (www.timewarnercable.com, 843-871-7000) serves Summerville and Georgetown. Home Cable TV (www.hometelco.com, 843-761-4778) serves Berkeley County. The following is a list of local affiliates, with the channel numbers where each can be found in different area locales.

- **WCBD, Channel 2 (NBC)**—Comcast (Channel 3); Time Warner (2); Home Cable TV (3)
- **WCIV, Channel 4 (ABC)**—Comcast (8); Time Warner (4); Home Cable TV (8)
- **WCSC, Channel 5 (CBS)**—Comcast (9); Time Warner (5); Home Cable TV (9)
- **WITV, Channel 7 (PBS)**—Comcast (11); Time Warner (7 in Summerville, 16 in Georgetown); Home Cable TV (11)
- **WTAT, Channel 24 (FOX)**—Comcast (6); Time Warner (6); Home Cable TV (12)

RADIO

Here is a fairly comprehensive list of the current radio station options arranged by format. Remember, radio stations are after the listener's attention, which is a moving target. Formats practically change with the weather. Your best bet is to use your radio dial and go exploring.

Country
WIWF 96.9 FM
WEZL 103.5 FM
WJKB 950 AM

News/Talk
WSCC 94.3 FM
WTMA 1250 AM

Oldies

WQSC 1340 AM
WIOP 95.9 FM

Public Radio

WSCI 89.3 FM

Urban

WWWZ 93.3 FM
WXST 99.7 FM
WMGL 107.5 FM

Rock

WKZQ 96.1 FM
WCOO 105.5 FM
WYBB 98.1 FM
WRFQ 104.5 FM

Sports

WTMZ 910 AM
WQNT 1450 AM
WSPO 99.3 FM

Adult Contemporary

WAVF 101.7 FM
WXLY 102.5 FM

Christian, Gospel, Family

WALC 100.5 FM
WYFH 90.7 FM
WKCL 91.5 FM
WJNI 106.3 FM
WTUA 106.1 FM
WQIZ 810 AM
WXTC 1390 AM
WZJY 1480 AM

Hispanic

WAZS 980 AM

Contemporary Hit Radio (CHR)

WIHB 92.5 FM
WSSX 95.1 FM

INDEX

Getaway ideas for the local traveler

Need a day away to relax, refresh, renew?
Just get in your car and go!

To order call 800-243-0495 or visit www.GlobePequot.com

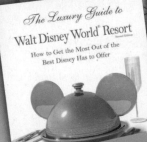

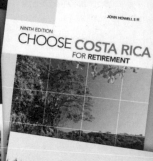

INSIDERS'GUIDE®

The acclaimed travel series that has sold more than 2 million copies!

Discover: Your Travel Destination.
Your Home. Your Home-to-Be.

Albuquerque

Anchorage & Southcentral Alaska

Atlanta

Austin

Baltimore

Baton Rouge

Boulder & Rocky Mountain National Park

Branson & the Ozark Mountains

California's Wine Country

Cape Cod & the Islands

Charleston

Charlotte

Chicago

Cincinnati

Civil War Sites in the Eastern Theater

Civil War Sites in the South

Colorado's Mountains

Dallas & Fort Worth

Denver

El Paso

Florida Keys & Key West

Gettysburg

Glacier National Park

Great Smoky Mountains

Greater Fort Lauderdale

Greater Tampa Bay Area

Hampton Roads

Houston

Hudson River Valley

Indianapolis

Jacksonville

Kansas City

Long Island

Louisville

Madison

Maine Coast

Memphis

Myrtle Beach & the Grand Strand

Nashville

New Orleans

New York City

North Carolina's Mountains

North Carolina's Outer Banks

North Carolina's Piedmont Triad

Oklahoma City

Orange County, CA

Oregon Coast

Palm Beach County

Palm Springs

Philadelphia & Pennsylvania Dutch Country

Phoenix

Portland, Maine

Portland, Oregon

Raleigh, Durham & Chapel Hill

Richmond, VA

Reno and Lake Tahoe

St. Louis

San Antonio

Santa Fe

Savannah & Hilton Head

Seattle

Shreveport

South Dakota's Black Hills Badlands

Southwest Florida

Tucson

Tulsa

Twin Cities

Washington, D.C.

Williamsburg & Virginia's Historic Triangle

Yellowstone & Grand Teton

Yosemite

**To order call 800-243-0495
or visit www.Insiders.com**